DISCARD

COLONEL HENRY THEODORE TITUS

★ COLONEL ★
HENRY THEODORE
TITUS

ANTEBELLUM
SOLDIER of FORTUNE
and FLORIDA PIONEER

Antonio Rafael de la Cova

The University of South Carolina Press

© 2016 University of South Carolina

Published by the University of South Carolina Press
Columbia, South Carolina 29208

www.sc.edu/uscpress

Manufactured in the United States of America

25 24 23 22 21 20 19 18 17 16   10 9 8 7 6 5 4 3 2 1

Library of Congress Cataloging-in-Publication Data
can be found at http://catalog.loc.gov/.

ISBN: 978-1-61117-656-8 (cloth)
ISBN: 978-1-61117-657-5 (ebook)

This book was printed on a recycled paper
with 30 percentpostconsumer waste content.

To Carlina, my virgin love

But avoid foolish questions, and genealogies, and contentions, and strivings about the law; for they are unprofitable and vain.

Epistle of Paul to Titus, 3:9,
King James Version

★ CONTENTS ★

ILLUSTRATIONS

MAPS

following page x

FIGURES

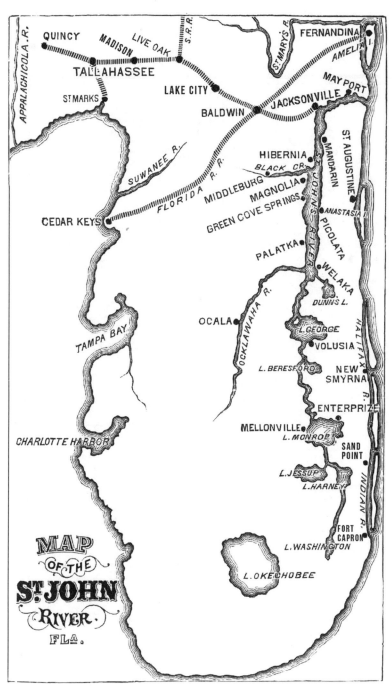

Map of the St. Johns River, Fla. Ledyard Bill, *A Winter in Florida* (1870)

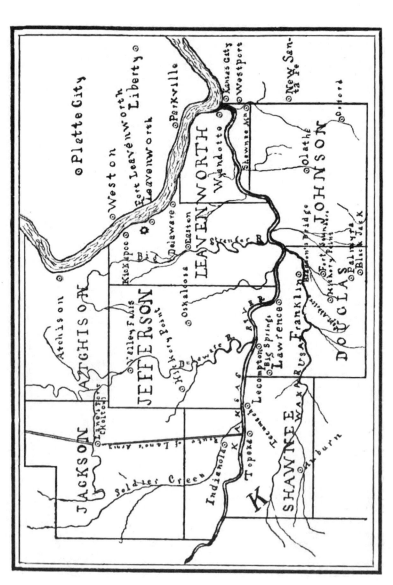

Map of the early Kansas wars.
From William E. Connelley, *John Brown* (1900)

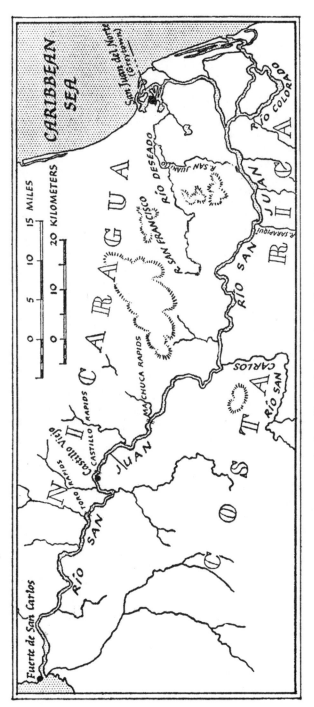

San Juan River. Map by Jessica E. Tompkins

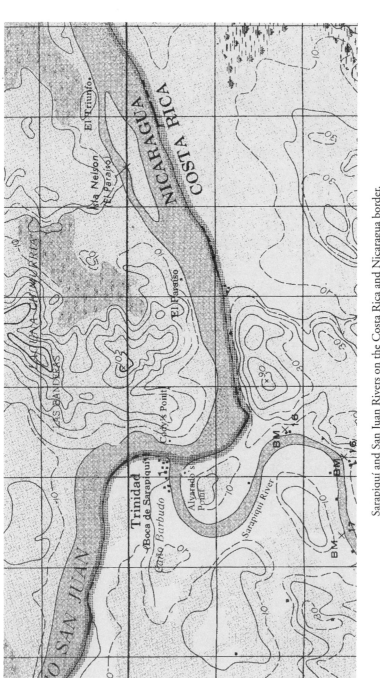

Sarapiquí and San Juan Rivers on the Costa Rica and Nicaragua border.
Courtesy of www.mapasdecostarica.info

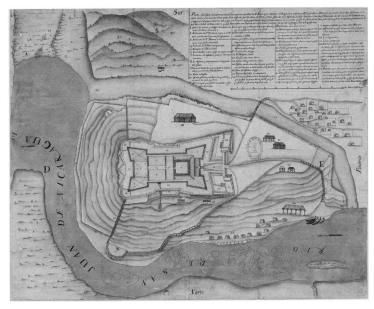

Nuestra Señora de la Inmaculada Concepción fortress, El Castillo, Nicaragua.
Courtesy of El Archivo General Militar de Madrid

William B. Hartley's map of Arizona, 1865. Courtesy of the Library of Congress

Introduction

During the dozen years between the Mexican War and the Civil War (1848–60), thousands of youthful American adventurers pursuing fame, fortune, and glory joined the military filibuster expeditions that invaded Cuba and Nicaragua. A multitude of others migrated west desiring preemptive land or went prospecting for gold and silver in the western mountains. It was a generation whose general needs and aspirations were destined to redefine the character of the American nation. Henry Theodore Titus (1822–81), brash, boisterous, hefty, and short-tempered, personified these men seeking those multiple opportunities. A lifelong Whig Party adherent, he fit well into the strange anomaly of native northerners, such as Gen. John Quitman, governor of Mississippi, and John Calhoun, the surveyor general of Kansas and Nebraska who presided over the Lecompton Constitutional Convention, who passionately defended slavery after relocating to the South. Titus was a colorful figure, and his exploits were quite amazing.[1]

Titus inherited his pioneering spirit and stubborn, independent character from his pilgrim ancestors who after arriving in the Massachusetts Bay Colony port of Boston in 1635, were eventually banished from the community. His father had the same personal traits in addition to taking reckless risks with life and property, which became his son's hallmark. Henry Titus's business enterprises included operating a sawmill, a grocery store, a cannery, and a combination restaurant/billiard hall/saloon; and being a land speculator, a slave overseer, a planing mill salesman, a miner, a hotel keeper, a farmer, and a hunter of Florida sea turtles and their colossal eggs. At the age of thirty he wed into "one of the best and most influential families" of Florida and proved to be an exemplary family man. His thirty-year matrimony produced eight children who survived into adulthood, some of whom became notable citizens and another a wayward son.

There is no documentary evidence that Titus had formal soldierly training, and he probably briefly belonged to a local state militia unit as a teenage rite of passage. He participated in the doomed Narciso López filibuster military expeditions to Cuba as an adjutant lieutenant in 1850 and as colonel of the stranded Jacksonville contingent in 1851. Titus invested thousands of dollars in this last failed endeavor, which he afterward was able largely to recoup. Five years later he upheld the cause of slavery in Bleeding Kansas, and the abolitionist press gave him a preeminent role in the sacking of Lawrence and the torching of its Free State Hotel barracks. As a result, according to the *New York Times,* Titus became "one of the few 'marked men,' whom the Sharp-shooters of Kansas have devoted to destruction if they ever get him within range of their rifles." Gov. Wilson Shannon appointed him as colonel of the proslavery Second Regiment, Southern Division, Kansas Territorial Militia. His Lecompton blockhouse, a Border Ruffian stronghold dubbed Fort Titus, was destroyed by a free-state artillery attack and conflagration. It was regarded as "one of the boldest strokes of the Kansas war." Titus, wounded and captured, surrendered his pearl-handled sword, which today is on display in the Kansas Museum of History at Topeka. The abolitionist John Brown, who had recently massacred five men at Pottawatomie Creek, was part of a kangaroo court that sentenced Titus to death. Shannon's quick intervention gained his freedom under a prisoner swap. A month later the superseding governor John White Geary commissioned Titus as special aide-de-camp with the rank of colonel. Titus is depicted standing in military uniform as the central figure on a colorful mural at the Freedom's Frontier National Historic Area in Lawrence, Kansas. A reenactment of the Battle of Fort Titus, which can be viewed on YouTube, was done in 2012 at the Constitution Hall State Historic Site in Lecompton, under the direction of administrator Tim Rues. I am grateful to Tim for his research assistance during the last fifteen years and for reading chapter 2, "Bleeding in Kansas, 1856."[2] I am also thankful to Jessica E. Tompkins for her help with archival documentation and the Henry Titus web page development. I likewise owe Daymé Sánchez a debt of gratitude for her assistance.

Titus was never dissuaded by presidential proclamations against filibuster movements. He accepted an invitation to lead an expedition of 250 men in 1857 to assist William Walker in Nicaragua, where he participated in the San Juan River campaign and the final battle of Rivas. After returning to Kansas later that year, Titus was instrumental in a failed county electoral fraud to install a proslavery territorial constitution. He did not join the Confederate army during the Civil War but served briefly instead as an assistant quartermaster in the Florida Militia and profited largely from supplying the Confederacy with foodstuffs. After the war the Titus family gravitated between Florida and the North until finally settling in 1868 at Sand Point, Florida, on the Indian River, across from the present-day Kennedy Space Center. Titus built a sawmill, a general store, and the Titus House hotel and saloon and changed the name of the town to Titusville in May 1872. The following year the Reconstruction governor of Florida commissioned him as a notary public, and in 1875 another Republican governor appointed him as justice of the peace for Volusia County. In 1880, after donating land for a courthouse and a church, the colonel helped make Titusville the county seat of Brevard County. A lifetime of intemperance, early chronic inflammatory rheumatism, gout, and neuritis diminished his health and prompted his death in 1881. Northern newspaper obituaries recalled his "remarkably adventurous career" of filibustering, scuffles in Kansas, wild life in the West, and having "founded the flourishing town that bears his name."[3]

Unfortunately few Titus manuscripts have survived, and fewer than a dozen of his letters were published in newspapers. He was sporadically interviewed by reporters during his lifetime. The bulk of the material for this biography is from hundreds of contemporary newspaper accounts, memoirs, private correspondence, property records, and archival material. The national press steadfastly followed Titus during most of his adult life, especially in the 1850s. It is sometimes difficult to discern truth from fiction regarding Titus in nineteenth-century newspaper accounts. The abolitionist and northern press distorted and ridiculed his endeavors. They delighted in reporting his misfortunes and spreading false rumors that he had been hung for horse stealing or tortured to death by Indians in Arizona. In contrast, the southern press glorified his exploits and justified or ignored his blunders. William Walker's memoirs denounce him as a traitor for deserting the filibuster camp. Titus added to the mix with his braggadocios in letters to the editor replete with exaggerations and lies.

Titus was the archenemy of the abolitionists and the bête noire of the northern press, especially the *New York Tribune,* which had the largest national circulation. He was depicted as a terrorist with denunciations akin to those used by current writers to condemn Osama Bin Laden. The colonel was portrayed with a multitude of negative labels, including bad egg, black-hearted villain, bloody, blustering blatherskite, brigand leader, brutal blackguard, brute, bushwhacker, coarse-grained bully, conceited, cowardly old bully, dangerous character, depredator, desperado, drunken coward, fool, grand horse thief, great humbug, highwayman, hound, house burner, incompetent, notorious proslavery fire-eater, of objectionable character, obnoxious, poltroon, reckless, redoubtable, reprobate, robber and land pirate, selfish, swaggering braggart, thief, vagrant, vain, vermin, vile ruffian, wicked, and wretch. The Kansas *Herald of Freedom* wrongly prophesied that Titus would perish in a violent affray or on the gallows. In contrast, his friends and admirers called him a brave soldier, courageous, doughty, gallant, jovial, meritorious citizen, patriot, talented gentleman, valiant, warrior, and a hero "overflowing with love for the South."[4]

Titus displayed many of these traits in varying measure while trying to enhance his personal fortune and ambitions. He briefly joined the Masonic fraternity and used its grand hailing sign of distress to avoid being hung by abolitionists in Bleeding Kansas. Titus considered himself a cavalier but was more akin to Dugald Dalgetty, who was described as "a strange mixture of shrewdness and idealism, of practicality and pedantry, of aggression and caution, of cosmopolitan experience and simple Scottish prejudice, that he provokes our disgust, excites our amusement, and finally earns our respect." Titus nearly prompted an international incident between the United States and Great Britain when he was arrested in Nicaragua for threatening to shoot a British naval officer and cursing the Queen of England. He enjoyed boasting, "I am the man *The New York Tribune* says has killed more men and murdered more women and children, and sacked more towns, than any Border Ruffian in Kansas." Titus took pride in identifying himself as a "soldier of fortune" and exhibited his mangled hands as badges of courage in battle. His daughter Mary Evelina "Minnie" Titus (1862–1949) in her eighteen-page memoirs in 1945 stated that her father had "an adventure loving nature and danger and excitement seemed to be his element." He had "such a commanding personality that men either hated or loved him. Many hated him without a cause."[5]

During an era when the average American adult male was five feet, seven inches tall, weighed 146 pounds, and had a life expectancy of forty-five years, Titus stood well over six feet, tipped the scales at 250 pounds, and died at the age of fifty-nine. In 1856 a *Tribune* reporter described him as "decidedly the handsomest man in Kansas." Titus used his towering figure and loud, abusive, "vile and foul" language to intimidate his opponents or otherwise resorted to violence. In the 1850s he was charged in St. Augustine and Kansas City with assault and battery with intent to kill, he knocked down a hotel keeper in Kansas who refused to reveal his vote, and he was at the center of bar brawls in luxury hotels in New York and St. Louis. In 1860 Titus was jailed in the Tombs in Manhattan for being unruly and defying a police order while trying "to organize the desperate classes for a riot." In 1866 he was acquitted in Jacksonville of assaulting a former Union soldier in a hotel saloon over a political argument, and the following year he was arrested for attacking a revenue officer with a harpoon. Titus survived his principal enemies by two decades, including the abolitionist warriors James A. Harvey, James Henry Lane, and John Brown; Costa Rican president Juan Rafael Mora; and the filibuster leader William Walker. The last three were executed by 1860, Lane committed suicide six years later, and Harvey died of heart disease the year after he burned the Titus homestead in Kansas.[6]

My interest in Titus began in the 1990s while I was writing my Ph.D. dissertation, which dealt in part with the Narciso López filibuster expeditions to Cuba. In 1996, while I was teaching history at Jacksonville University, I discovered that Titus had owned a sawmill in the city and had lived on the San Pablo plantation. I then expanded my research to libraries, archives, and county record centers in Florida cities where Titus left his imprint, including Titusville, St. Augustine, Baldwin, Fort Pierce, Gainesville, Lake City, and Madison. I gave academic presentations on the various aspects of his life at the "Florida before and during the Civil War" session of the Florida Conference of Historians in 1997; the Bleeding Kansas series at the Kansas State Historical Society in 1998; the "NineteenthCentury Florida Town Founders" session of the Florida Historical Society in 2003; and the "International Symposium on Filibustering and Manifest Destiny in the Americas" at the University of Costa Rica in Guanacaste in 2007.

I completed my research for this book with additional filibuster investigations in the Military Archive at Madrid in 2012 and the following year visited the archives at Tucson and Phoenix, Arizona. I located Titus's abandoned silver mines in the Patagonia Mountains in Arizona, ten miles from the Mexican border, and the spot of his nearby former hacienda where his brother Ellett died during an Apache raid. I afterward rummaged in courthouse archives and historical societies in three south-central counties of New York State and in Wilkes-Barre, Pennsylvania, where Titus spent his youth and his mother was killed in a railroad accident at the historic Ashley Planes. I discovered that the St. Stephen's Episcopal Church graveyard in Wilkes-Barre, where his parents were interred, is now a paved alley and that their final resting place is a mystery.[7]

I also traveled the Titus filibuster route on the San Juan River bordering Costa Rica and Nicaragua, where he engaged in combat at Fort Sarapiquí and El Castillo fortress. The former was located on the northern bank of the Sarapiquí River where it flows into the San Juan River. On the southern shore of the Sarapiquí, across from where the fort stood, a monument was erected in 1998 by the Museo Histórico Cultural Juan Santamaría dedicated "in recognition to the glory and bravery of the Costa Ricans who heroically defended the national sovereignty in this place." The grounds are today the property of La Trinidad Cabins, an eco-tourism resort owned by Mayron Urbina. He explained that during the Contra War of the 1980s, his family and all those living on both banks of the Sarapiquí, as well as the Nicaraguans on the opposite shore of the San Juan River, fled the region.

On the former spot of Fort Sarapiquí, the Costa Rican Civil Guard dug trenches and established a military outpost. It was abandoned in 1990 after the Sandinistas lost the presidential election, peace was restored to the region, and thousands of land mines were extracted. Members of the Urbina family were the only ones who returned to the jungle location inhabited by howler monkeys and built their home and six rustic cabins that rented for ten dollars per night. When I went there, accompanied by my wife, Carlina, Jessica E. Tompkins, and the Costa Rican historians Raúl Aguilar Piedra and Werner Korte, Mayron provided an oral history of the area. He gave me as a memento a spent shell of a U.S. military flare from the Contra War that he had recently found on his land. It was impossible to visit the Nicaraguan side, formerly called Cody's Point, where Titus and his men were entrenched during the attack on Fort Sarapiquí, as it is a restricted military border post. We were able to discern the layout of its landscape and hills from across the river and take photographs. Returning to San José, at the Costa Rica National Archive I completed extensive research, which I had started in 2007.

The last segment of our sojourn included the Nuestra Señora de la Inmaculada Concepción fortress, completed by Spain in 1675 and dubbed El Castillo, on the San Juan River in Nicaragua. The only available route from Costa Rica was on a twenty-eight-passenger boat, powered by a Suzuki 225 outboard engine, from Los Chiles via the Frío River for ten miles to San Carlos on Lake Nicaragua. From there another water taxi took us thirty-five miles east on the San Juan River to El Castillo village. Some twenty-five hundred people presently live there on a one-mile coastal strip with stilt houses over the riverbank. There are no motor vehicles, and all necessities are imported by boat. The main, narrow thoroughfare parallel to the river is five hundred yards long and flanked by small stores and a few cheap eco-tourism lodgings. The residents generally labor at farming, cattle ranching, dairy production, and African palm oil extraction, much as they did two centuries ago. Carlina, Jessica E. Tompkins, and I climbed across the three hills ranging parallel to the castle, retracing the 1857 Titus filibuster trail. We then had a guided tour of the Spanish fortress that Titus placed under siege for three days and visited its adjacent one-room museum. It contains the rusted remains of two filibuster rifles, three bayonets, and two broken small cannons that were retrieved from the river.

Filibusters are villains in Central American historical memory. They continue to be a source of excoriation, especially in Nicaragua and Costa Rica. The Nicaraguan Marxist Sandinista government used the Walker affair as political propaganda against twentieth-century U.S. policy in the region. The filibuster war became a Costa Rican symbol of national identity. It produced the national hero Juan Santamaría, and the Santa Rosa Hacienda in Guanacaste, where Walker's men were defeated and driven from the country, is a national shrine.[8]

In contrast, filibusters are depicted as heroes in Cuban historiography. The Narciso López expeditions sought to overthrow Spanish colonialism on the island. The López flag and coat of arms became the national emblems of a free republic half a century later. In 1955 the Cuban government donated a bust of the Cuban independence leader José Martí to the youth ambassadors of Jefferson County, Kentucky, who visited the island that year, and its plaque reads as follows: "As a tribute to the valiant Kentuckians who fought for the liberation of Cuba in 1850." The recently refurbished monument stands on the grounds of the Shively City Hall. There are monuments to López in Cuba, a street in Havana bears his name, and his image and that of the Cárdenas invasion appear on postage stamps.[9]

Titus posthumously received the honorable recognition he always sought after braving with fortitude and courage the hardships of pioneer life in Florida for more than a decade. A large portrait of him in military uniform and slouch hat prominently hangs in the Titusville City Hall. The Florida Board of Parks and Historic Memorials erected a public marker in 1961 describing the Titus House hotel as "one of the best in Florida." Titusville became the gateway to the Kennedy Space Center in the 1960s and is known as "Space City, USA." NASA built the fifty-two-story Vehicle Assembly Building on the Indian River bank opposite Titusville, making the city shoreline a favorite spot for thousands of tourists viewing space rocket launches. The guided Historic Titusville Walking Tour has eight signs, including one for the Titus House with a photo of its founder, who is inaccurately described as a Civil War blockade runner.

Titus was first mentioned in historiography in a 485-word entry in the *Kansas Cyclopedia of State History* in 1912. There he was erroneously identified as being born in Kentucky and arriving in Kansas in 1856 with the Buford Expedition instead of with his family and slaves a day earlier. Numerous biographies of the abolitionist John Brown have referred to Titus as a notorious proslavery leader. Some Florida history books mention him in passing as the founder of Titusville. In 1926 Ohioan George B. Christian wrote about meeting Titus during a short stay at his hotel fifty years earlier. He described Titus as being in early life "a soldier of fortune" with an "adventurous career." Christian, however, mistakenly indicated that "General Titus had been adjutant-general of Pennsylvania, hence his title" and that Titus was wounded as a result of "a revolver duel at short range" with William Walker in New York. These inaccuracies, due to faulty memory after a half century, were afterward repeated by other writers.[10]

A thirteen-page Titus biography appeared in 1950 as a chapter in the book *Florida's Golden Sands* by Alfred and Kathryn Hanna. It contains a number of factual errors, including that it took Titus thirty-eight days to sail from New Orleans to Nicaragua and that he afterward departed for San Francisco instead of New York. Titus is also wrongly portrayed as the captain of the blockade-running British schooner *Charm,* captured on February 23, 1863, on the Indian River twenty miles north of the Jupiter lighthouse, at the Narrows near Sebastian Creek. The authors based their assertion on the single mention of a "Captain Titus, from Nassau, New Providence" in the Civil War *Official Records of the Navy.* However, U.S. Admiralty Records regarding the seizure and disposal of the *Charm* do not provide the first name of the *Charm* master, who was not detained because he was a British citizen. Likewise the log books of the gunboat *Sagamore* and the bark *Gem of the Sea,* which effected the confiscation, do not mention Captain Titus. The U.S. Navy Register of Persons Captured on Blockade Runners does not list Titus, nor is he mentioned in the State Department's Domestic Letters of 1863 dealing with blockade runners. The *New York Times* and other northern newspapers reported the capture of the *Charm* but omitted identifying its captain. They had previously for years closely followed the trail of the notorious Kansas proslavery militia colonel and filibuster leader and would have been thrilled to announce his capture and imprisonment as a blockade runner. In fact Henry Titus was three hundred miles away in Lake City, Florida, where three days later he sold nearly six thousand dollars in foodstuffs to the Confederacy.[11]

The myth that Henry Titus was a blockade runner was repeated in 1967 by Marjory Stoneman Douglas in *Florida: The Long Frontier* and continued replication in subsequent publications. Douglas, whose grandparents were abolitionists, spitefully referred to Titus as "that crippled old reprobate" who "swaggered even in a wheelchair among his admiring tourists." A 1999 history of North Brevard County erroneously has Titus going to Kansas in 1854, being captured in Nicaragua as an adjutant general of Pennsylvania, serving as a Confederate blockade runner, and being postmaster of Sand Point.[12]

An early fictitious account of how Titusville got its name was published by Anna Pearl Leonard Newman in 1953. She was told by fifty-six-year-old Clark Rice, the grandson of Elisha Higgerson Rice, that his grandfather arrived at Sand Point about the same time that Titus did and that they "wanted to give the place a name, so they agreed that the winner at a game of dominoes should have the name. Riceville, if Rice won and Titusville if Titus won. The result we know, for Titusville it is." However, Elisha Higgerson Rice, born in Alabama in 1841, had followed his parents to Victoria County, Texas, before 1860. During the Civil War he was a private in the Alabama Twenty-second Infantry Regiment. In June 1870 Rice was living in Lauderdale County, Alabama, with his three sons, the youngest born in Texas in 1867. He was enumerated in the 1880 Florida census at the village of Concord, Gadsden County, more than 285 miles from Titusville. His last child was born in Florida in December 1879 and all the others in Texas. The census records disprove that Elisha Higgerson Rice was an early settler at Sand Point. His family appeared in the 1885 Florida state census residing two houses away from the Tituses long after the colonel had passed away. Clark Rice was born in Florida in September 1897, and his father was born in Texas in March 1863. The apocryphal Rice version of the Titusville name continues to be repeated by writers.[13]

The three-volume *The East Coast of Florida: A History,* published in 1962, made the first reference to Titus being the postmaster at Sand Point and says that "he had the post office station changed to Titusville." The Record of Appointment of Postmasters and the Postmaster General Journals at the U.S. National Archives and Records Administration indicates that a postmaster was first commissioned to Titusville in May 1872 and that Titus never held the position, which was a presidential appointment. A year earlier Dr. John Milton Hawks wrote that Titus proposed changing the name of Sand Point to Indian River City. In 1967 the Titusville Centennial *Countdown in History: Historical Booklet and Program* quoted Dr. George Washington Holmes as saying that when he visited Titusville in the winter of 1874–75, its "name had just been changed from Sand Point. Much of the mail still was addressed to Sand Point. Col. Titus himself was postmaster and had had the name changed to Titusville." The memoirs of Minnie Titus do not mention her father being postmaster, but subsequent writers kept perpetuating this mistake.[14]

A 1994 history of Brevard County erroneously has Titus briefly attending the U.S. Military Academy at West Point, being a cowhand in Texas, owning no slaves, being "taken prisoner by Federal troops in Kansas," and serving as the Titusville postmaster. A decade later Leo J. Titus Jr. published the 658-page genealogy *Titus: A North American Family History,* in which four pages are dedicated to Henry Theodore Titus. Most of it was borrowed from Minnie's memoirs and from a 1980 80-page compilation of newspaper articles and commentaries entitled "The Titus Trail" by the late Harry Wayne Titus, who had no direct relation to the colonel in census records. Copies of both of these documents are in the Henry Titus File in the Brevard County Public Library. In 2006 the journalist James D. Snyder published *A Light in the Wilderness: The Story of Jupiter Inlet Lighthouse & The Southeast Florida Frontier,* in which the only sources cited to identify Titus as a blockade runner are the testimonies of two Florida psychics. He incorrectly wrote that Titus "appropriated" the title of colonel, that he went to Kansas in 1854, and that he was the postmaster at Titusville.[15]

During the last four decades Titus has been remembered in Brevard County, Florida, newspapers and magazines with sensationalist headlines. In 1973 an article titled "Henry Titus: Hero or Hoax?" claimed that "not even the historians seem to be sure." A year later "Henry Titus: Scurrilous Pioneer" called him a "proponent of slavery, accomplice of draft dodgers, blockade runner, autocrat and public servant." In 1978 "Old Henry T. Was Quite a Character" incorrectly described Titus as "a military leader in Nicaragua and a Confederate blockade-runner" who "never owned a slave." Three years later "Henry Titus: The Revolutionary Rheumatic Who Settled Brevard County" mistakenly claimed that "he was born in the Oklahoma Territory in 1815," had a "turbulent soldier-trader-filibuster career," and that "during the Civil War, records indicate the colonel found it beneficial to serve both sides." In 1986 "Man for Whom Titusville Is Named Had Scandalous and Colorful Past" emphasized his role in Bleeding Kansas and his redemption as a civic leader. While Titus at times hardly inspires empathy, his life and times provide an insight into the ambivalent legacy of proslavery thought and action in the nineteenth-century Atlantic world. This biography, whose research material appears on my Web site at http://www.latinamericanstudies.org/titus.htm, deconstructs the written accounts and separates fact from fiction regarding this nineteenth-century renowned adventurer, entrepreneur, slavery advocate, soldier of fortune, rugged pioneer, and dedicated civic leader.[16]

★ *Chapter One* ★

The Road to Cuba Filibustering
1849–1855

Robert Titus, a thirty-five-year-old English agriculturalist from St. Catherine's Parish, Stansted Abbey, Hartfordshire, boarded the ship *Hopewell* in London on April 3, 1635, with his twenty-one-year-old wife Hannah and their sons John, age eight, and Edmond, five, along with sixty-four other passengers. Titus was going to settle a land grant he received in what is presently Brookline, Massachusetts, near Muddy River. After two or three years there, the family moved to a six-acre farm in Weymouth, Massachusetts, where four other offspring were born. They worshiped at the Church of Weymouth and followed the congregation in 1643 to the shore of the Blackstone River, where they founded Rehoboth, Massachusetts. The following year Titus received one of the fifty-eight land lots drawn "for a division of the woodland between the plain and the town." He then signed a compact of mutual assistance with the other pioneers.[1]

Titus was highly esteemed in his community. At a general town meeting in 1645 he was appointed as collector of revenue, and he was later assigned with seven other men to inspect and judge the sufficiency of the fences on their colony. However, Titus had a stubborn, independent character that soon led to conflicts with other townspeople. The Titus family was banished from the colony on June 6, 1654, for letting Abner Ordway and family, deemed "persons of evil fame," reside in their home. The Tituses were the first expulsions listed in the Plymouth Colony record.[2]

Robert's grandson John Titus (1677–1761), born in Newtown, Cape Cod, Massachusetts, moved with his wife Rebecca to Hopewell, Mercer County, New Jersey, nine miles northwest of Trenton, in the early eighteenth century. They bought land on a bluff overlooking the Delaware River that they dubbed Titusville, adjacent to present-day Washington Crossing State Park, commemorating where George Washington made his historic river landing during the American Revolution. The couple had nine children, the second of whom, Andrew (1723–1800), married Hannah Borrowes and had a son, John (1752–1827). John wed Sarah Mershon of nearby Lawrenceville. Their firstborn, Theodore Titus, described as "the finest-looking man of his time," at the age of twenty-six married Catherine Ellett Howell in June 1820. She was the twenty-one-year-old daughter of Ellett Howell, a sixty-four-year-old Trenton merchant and former second lieutenant of a company of light infantry militia during the Revolutionary War. Their first of eight children, Henry Theodore Titus, was born on February 13, 1822, at the family estate on the road two and one-half miles northwest of Trenton. It was a four-hundred-acre farm with a hillside stream that powered a gristmill and a brewery operated by forty slaves. The soil was "fertile and the landscape varied and beautiful" with a 150-foot elevation that offered "a fine view of the City of Trenton, South Trenton and Morrisville, and a beautiful and extensive prospect of the country on both sides of the Delaware river." In 1824 Theodore Titus sold his land, manumitted his slaves, and moved to Auburn, New York.[3]

Five years later the New York legislature authorized the construction of the Chemung Canal to connect Seneca Lake and the Erie Canal with the Chemung River, a branch of the Susquehanna River extending through Pennsylvania and Maryland. The twenty-three-mile canal and its sixteen-mile feeder would require fifty-three wooden locks. Theodore Titus saw it as an opportunity to speculate in land and subcontract as a sawyer for its development. In 1829 he moved with his family to Havana, New York, near the head of Seneca Lake. Today it is the village of Montour Falls in Schuyler County. Titus became an agent for Amasa Dana, who had recently purchased the lands of David Ayers, which comprised 150 Havana lots. Titus advertised in the *Havana Observer* that all persons indebted to Ayers, or "Persons desirous of purchasing lots in said village, will call upon the said Titus, who is duly authorized to sell."[4]

On April 30, 1830, Theodore Titus purchased from Harmon Pumpelly nine lots in Havana for $1,545.47. The next day he and his wife sold a $40.00 lot to Elijah H. Goodwin, the future Chemung Canal superintendent, director of the Chemung Canal Bank, and state legislator. The 1830 federal census indicates that the Titus family had three boys and four girls. Eight-year-old Henry received his primary education from the pioneer schoolteacher Thomas Nichols Jr., a Revolutionary War veteran, who infused patriotism in his students with tales of battlefield glory and contempt toward the British.

On July 4 the Titus family joined a large celebrant crowd around the Elmira courthouse that gathered to witness the nearby groundbreaking ceremony for the construction of the Chemung Canal. Young Henry was impressed with the festivity in which whiskey flowed freely during "25 regular and 28 volunteer toasts" and artillery boomed in celebration. The canal, mostly dug with pick and shovel, would have a prism "42 feet across at the surface, 26 feet across at the base, and 4 feet deep."[5]

The Chemung Canal, its locks, the transportation vessels, and the laborers' dwellings were all built with nearby choice stands of pine, white oak, maple, and beech. Theodore Titus established a lumber business at Havana, a trade that he and his son pursued for the rest of their lives. The patriarch also owned and operated a "mammoth distillery" that serviced the canal workers, mostly recent Irish immigrants. Henry Titus spent his early years assisting his father at the sawmill and the distillery alongside the working poor, who were characterized by intemperance and swearing, traits that the youth permanently adopted. The canal construction prompted an increase in land value. On November 9, 1830, the Tituses transacted lot 68 in Havana to the thirty-year-old lumber dealer Calvin Cooley Jr. for $130. Four months later the couple sold lot 38 to the thirty-eight-year-old lumberman and New York Militia lieutenant colonel Jonathan Paul Couch for $150. Cooley and Couch were constituent members of the local Presbyterian church.[6]

By early 1832 the Titus family had moved ten miles south of Havana to Catlin as the canal work progressed along the eastern boundary of Tioga County. Catlin had a sawmill, a gristmill, a tavern, a cemetery, and a log schoolhouse that ten-year-old Henry Titus probably attended. The Tituses then sold Havana village lot 53 to the Scottish investor James Talcott Gifford for one hundred dollars on March 8. The Chemung Canal progress decreased that summer due to bad weather and after many workers deserted upon not being paid by subcontractors. In August, Theodore Titus traveled to New York City, where his name appeared on the "List of Letters Remaining in the Post Office." Later that month he was among more than one hundred republican electors from Tioga, Tompkins, and Steuben Counties who called for a town meeting in Havana on August 22 to denounce the Jacksonian Democratic "*misrule* of the present national and state administrations." Henry apparently accompanied his father during his travels and to political meetings at an early age, as he later became involved in similar Whig activities. By 1833 the Tituses had drifted another fifteen miles southwest to the village of Painted Post, at the confluence of the Chemung and Cohocton Rivers, in Steuben County. It was located at the summit level of the Chemung feeder canal, its guard-lock, dam, and log chute. On February 22 the patriarch sold one quarter of an acre of land in Havana to Elijah H. Goodwin for four hundred dollars. He then traveled to New York City late that summer and afterward relocated with his family another ten miles farther southwest to Addison in Steuben County. On September 9 Mr. and Mrs. Titus sold lot 97 in Havana for seven hundred dollars to the lumber manufacturer Gen. Ransom Rathbone. The Chemung Canal became fully operational in November 1833 and then closed for the winter the following month until reopening in late April.[7]

Canal maintenance and distilling whiskey kept Theodore Titus busy for the next few years. While seeking work opportunities, he was one of seventy-five delegates at a convention held at the courthouse in Bath, Steuben County, on December 17, 1834, calling for the construction of a railroad between New York City and Lake Erie through the southern counties of their state. Titus envisioned his sawmill providing railroad ties for the enterprise. Committees were appointed to prepare resolutions and a memorial to the state legislature. The economic crisis called the Panic of 1837 temporarily derailed the plans of the New York and Erie Railroad and also affected the Titus family finances. The Tituses then moved by stagecoach, canal boat, and river steamer to Philadelphia, where fifteen-year-old Henry enrolled in public school. He became prominent "not from proficiency in his studies or development of intellect," as he was not noted for either, but because "he was large for his years and possessed of great physical beauty." The patriarch soon returned to Havana, where on November 22, 1837, he bargained village lot 50 to the state assemblyman Elijah H. Goodwin for one hundred dollars. Goodwin had been instrumental a year earlier in the incorporation of the village. While the price of the lots had steadily risen during the previous seven years, they had by now bottomed out. Titus made less than one hundred dollars profit from the sale of all his landed property.[8]

Ten days later Theodore Titus petitioned Steuben County court judge John Cooper Jr. so "that his estate might be assigned for the benefit of his creditors and that his person might be hereafter exempt from arrest or imprisonment by reason of debts arising from contracts previously made." Titus afterward published an advertisement in the *Albany Argus* calling on his creditors to appear before Judge Cooper on March 3, 1838, relating to "voluntary assignments by an insolvent, for the purpose of exonerating his person from imprisonment." A week later the patriarch was back in Havana executing the indenture of the last property he sold in the village. In April he was in New York City looking for other business opportunities. His oldest son, Henry, in all likelihood accompanied him during these travels.[9]

Theodore Titus made a partnership agreement on November 2, 1838, with John Rice of Allentown, Pennsylvania, for sixty-six hundred acres of land on Hickory Ridge, near the Lehigh River and White Haven, in Luzerne County, purchased from Henry Colt for seventy-five hundred dollars in "joint promissory notes." Rice advanced two thousand dollars to erect on the premises "a saw mill, a dwelling house, a tenant house, and a stable" and clear ten acres of land for a lumber "manufacturing and agricultural business." Titus would be the only partner residing on the property and receiving a five-hundred-dollar salary for the first year. The 1840 federal census indicates that the family lived in Wilkes-Barre, Pennsylvania, and that Henry had five younger sisters and a brother. Two other brothers had died in infancy. In August 1840 the patriarch and eighteen-year-old Henry, who worked with him at the sawmill, were part of a local group of citizens invited to travel on the completed first section of the Lehigh and Susquehanna Rail Road. The line spanned twenty-one miles and connected the North Branch division of the Pennsylvania Canal at Wilkes-Barre with the Lehigh River at White Haven. Theodore Titus was appointed to a committee of twenty-two persons assigned to draft a preamble and resolutions expressive of the event. They reported that "This Rail Road will be the great thoroughfare to market for the Agricultural, Commercial, and Mineral wealth of those counties north of the Lehigh river, that seek an outlet to New York, or Philadelphia."[10]

During the first week of July 1843, fifteen-year-old Ellett Titus accompanied his mother to visit the patriarch at his sawmill. They traveled for four hours on the bright-red cars of the Lehigh and Susquehanna Rail Road from Wilkes-Barre to White Haven. While heading home on Saturday, the 8th, the family rode a train ten miles from White Haven to the head of the Ashley Planes at Solomon's Gap, an elevation of 1,681 feet on Penobscot Mountain. The newly built Ashley Planes were three tiers of a steep incline rail line leading down to the village of Ashley in the Wyoming Valley. The three planes were from top to bottom 4,361, 3,775, and 4,894 feet long, with 1,320 feet between the planes with two parallel tracks, making a total distance of more than 2.5 miles. Upon finding that public conveyance on the planes was unavailable that day, Theodore Titus put his family in a truck car that he used for transporting his lumber. The Tituses passed the first incline at a 9.3 percent grade with the aid of a common brake. When they reached the top of the second plane, which descended at an 8.6 percent grade, the patriarch was advised to fasten onto the car the wooden brake blocks that were applied to the wheels by means of a hand lever. This was a mandatory safeguard of the railroad company for all cars passing the planes. In a hurry to get home before dark and being confident of his control over the car, the headstrong Theodore rejected the advice and began the steep drop without the additional brakes. The freight car rapidly gained uncontrollable speed and smashed into another one stopped in the middle plane, scattering its cargo. The forty-three-year-old Mrs. Titus was thrown nearly fifty feet and was a "mangled mass" when her head fatally struck a rock. Her husband was found some ten feet away from the wreck "bruised, lacerated, senseless." Ellett landed some thirty feet distant "with a skull fracture, and other dangerous wounds." Father and son were so gravely injured that their recovery was initially considered doubtful. Three weeks later the *Philadelphia North American* wrote that they were "out of danger" and "rapidly recovering." The dreadful accident was reported in more than a dozen eastern newspapers.[11]

Henry Titus blamed his father's recklessness for the death of his beloved mother. He angrily left home and returned to Philadelphia, where in 1845 a relative who was a distinguished lawyer helped him obtain employment as a postal inspector. The youth was one of the most "dashing and fashionable boarders at Jones' Hotel in Chestnut Street, drove a splendid pair of fast trotters, and was the admiration of all the ladies." Titus did not keep permanent lodging, because his name frequently appeared on the "List of Letters Remaining in the Philadelphia Post Office" in the *Public Ledger* newspaper. He later boasted that he had "traveled some" as "Secret Agent of the Post Office Department." In 1846 Titus did not join either of the two Pennsylvania volunteer regiments raised to fight in the Mexican War. Instead he was employed the following year as a clerk on the steamer *Germantown,* plying the Ohio and Mississippi Rivers between Cincinnati and St. Louis. After the vessel was destroyed by fire in September 1849, Titus remained in Louisville, Kentucky. His father had married a Virginia woman, and they were living in Manhattan's Lower West Side, where he worked as a "wood sawyer."[12]

That fall Titus got involved in the Cuba filibuster expeditions of 1849–51 to overthrow the Spanish colonial regime. The plot was headed by forty-five-year-old Venezuelan-born Narciso López, a disgruntled former Spanish army general wed to a Cuban aristocrat; his Cuban aide-de-camp Ambrosio José Gonzales, a lawyer and college professor; and other Cuban separatists. They were following the Texas independence model by obtaining American volunteers, weapons, and funds to gain independence from an abusive and corrupt colonial regime. López, who fled from Cuba in 1848 after the initial plot was discovered, expected his former military subordinates to mutiny on the island and the populace to join them. The conspirator John L. O'Sullivan, editor of the *Democratic Review,* who coined the phrase "Manifest Destiny," claimed that López had contacts in Cuba "with more than one Colonels of regiments, and with various other officers."[13]

The filibusters worked covertly under code names and barely kept records because they were violating the Neutrality Act of 1818. They were supported by expansionist Democrats and proslavery Whigs who advocated Manifest Destiny and coveted Cuba as a southern state. Northern Whigs and abolitionists derided filibusters as mercenaries of a slaveocracy conspiracy. López, Gonzales, and Titus were Freemasons, and fraternal bonds attracted supporters to the movement. Titus and other recruits were offered pay equal to that of U.S. Army officers and soldiers and either a one-thousand-dollar bond redeemable by the future Republic of Cuba or a land bounty on the island. An initial attempt to invade Cuba in the summer of 1849 was frustrated when the U.S. Navy blockaded Round Island, Mississippi, for six weeks and dispersed 450 expeditionaries gathered there. It did not discourage López and his followers from renewing their efforts.[14]

A gathering point for Cuban separatists was Willard's Hotel in Washington, D.C. Titus registered there on November 21, 1849, and five days later O'Sullivan checked in. A few days before Christmas, Ambrosio Gonzales met in the capital with twenty-eight-year-old Theodore O'Hara, twenty-seven-year-old John Thomas Pickett, and thirty-year-old Thomas Theodore Hawkins. These Kentuckians vowed to raise volunteers and funds from their state and agreed to meet the Cubans in Louisville later to finalize plans. Titus may have encountered these recruiters as passengers on his Ohio River steamer or at a Louisville hotel and impressed them with his resolve, towering size, and hefty physique. He was described as having "dark brown eyes and hair; standing well over six feet in height and weighing 250 pounds."[15]

O'Hara, a lawyer and Democratic newspaper editor in Frankfort, Kentucky, had been a captain in the U.S. Army during the Mexican War. Pickett had entered the U.S. Military Academy at West Point in 1841 but had too "wild and erratic a disposition to remain long enough to graduate." He had studied law at Transylvania University in Lexington, Kentucky, and along with O'Hara belonged to Young America. Pickett was U.S. consul at Turks Island and resigned his post to join the filibusters. Hawkins, a Freemason from a prominent family in Newport, Kentucky, had been an adjutant of the First Regiment Kentucky and a second lieutenant in the Sixteenth Regiment U.S. Infantry in the Mexican War. Other Kentucky Mexican War officers covertly recruited for the invasion among veterans and Freemasons in Louisville, Frankfort, Shelbyville, Covington, and the northern Campbell and Scott Counties.[16]

López and Gonzales departed Washington, D.C., in late February 1850 for Louisville, where on the 27th they registered at the Louisville Hotel. The next day, when they met with O'Hara, Pickett, and Hawkins, López "exhibited correspondence with some of the leading citizens of Cuba, urging him to come to their assistance as soon as possible—alone, if need be." The landing was planned for "where a large number of the people were already organized and armed" in readiness to join the invaders. This would be "the signal for a general rising of the people." The Kentuckians were promised military commissions and agreed to raise a skeleton regiment that would fill up with local volunteers on the island. Titus was offered the rank of adjutant lieutenant of the Kentucky Regiment.[17]

López and Gonzales departed down the Mississippi River in March for New Orleans, where they met with prominent supporters, including Mississippi governor John Anthony Quitman, a Mexican War hero called the "Father of Mississippi Masonry"; Louisiana Legion Militia general Jean Baptiste Donatien Augustin; and Laurent Sigur, publisher of the *New Orleans Delta.* Quitman agreed to lead a reinforcement expedition after Cubans revolted as the Texans had done. The Louisiana and Mississippi state arsenals provided most of the filibuster weapons, and revolutionary bonds were sold at ten cents on the dollar. The conspirators acquired the 165-foot, 306-ton steamer *Creole* for sixteen thousand dollars.[18]

Two additional filibuster skeleton regiments were mustered in the Crescent City by Mexican War veterans: the Louisiana Regiment, led by Chatham Roberdeau Wheat, who was six feet, four inches tall and weighed more than 250 pounds; and the Mississippi Regiment, under McDonough J. Bunch, from Memphis. The latter was the principal clerk of the U.S. House of Representatives during 1845–46, and his father, Samuel Bunch, was a Creek War veteran and Whig representative from East Tennessee during 1833–37. McDonough J. Bunch fought at the Battle of Buena Vista and afterward joined Gen. Winfield Scott on the march to Mexico City. Wheat, who befriended Titus and later figured prominently with him filibustering in Nicaragua, was a twenty-four-year-old native of Alexandria, Virginia, who had graduated from the University of Nashville in 1845. He enlisted in the Mexican War for one year as a second lieutenant in the Tennessee Mounted Volunteers and was promoted to captain. Wheat reenlisted with the same rank a year later in the Second Dragoons and served on Maj. Gen. Winfield Scott's

Body Guard. After the war he settled in New Orleans in 1848, practiced law, and dabbled in Whig politics. Wheat wrote to his father, the Episcopalian clergyman John Thomas Wheat, that he joined the Cuban expedition "not only from universal feelings of philanthropy, but for the patriotic purpose of aggrandizing the South" after being inspired by his Masonic brethren and "several prominent Southern statesmen." He told the attorney Thomas R. Wolfe that his major ambition was to be a major general before the age of twenty-four, like the Marquis de Lafayette.[19]

A filibuster contingent of 120 men from southwestern Ohio, led by Maj. William Hardy, left Cincinnati for New Orleans on the steamer *Martha Washington* on the evening of April 4. Hardy, a twenty-five-year-old, "tall and athletic" Democrat activist, had been a sergeant in Company B, Second Regiment Kentucky during the Mexican War and was wounded in the face during the siege of Veracruz. Across the river at Covington some fifty Kentucky filibusters boarded the steamer. The vessel stopped at Louisville the next day and took on Titus and about forty local volunteers and others from nearby Shelby and Scott Counties. Colonel O'Hara and a "little squad" from Frankfort boarded the steamer *Saladin,* which departed at dusk on the 6th from the Louisville suburb of Portland. That day the *Louisville Courier* announced that "180 adventurers" were going "to New Orleans en route for California—or are on another secret expedition." The *Martha Washington* arrived at 3:00 A.M. on April 11 at Freeport, Louisiana, three miles north of New Orleans, where the expeditionaries disembarked and sought lodgings. Titus went to the exclusive St. Charles Hotel, which served as filibuster headquarters, and signed the register as "H. T. Titus" from Philadelphia.[20]

O'Hara and other Kentuckians reached New Orleans the next day in the *Saladin.* Pickett was there to greet them and accompanied the officers to check in at the St. Charles Hotel, where they met with Titus and Gonzales. Most of the Kentuckians relocated to cheaper lodgings. On April 13 López gathered with Titus and other officers and ordered final expedition preparations. The next morning the *New Orleans Picayune* reported that "some sort of an expedition is about to start against Cuba," headed by López. Four Cubans who joined the expedition arrived at the St. Charles Hotel a few days later. Arrangements were made for the three volunteer regiments to leave New Orleans on the three-mast bark *Georgiana,* the brigantine *Susan Loud,* and the paddle-wheeled steamer *Creole.* They would rendezvous at Contoy Island, off the coast of Yucatán, before going to Cárdenas, Cuba. The filibusters were "the subject of several newspaper notices, and the Cuba expedition was the barroom conversation all over the city." The adroit Spanish consul in New Orleans had been reporting the filibuster movements to the Spanish minister at Washington and the captain general in Havana. The colonial government was "exercising the greatest vigilance of the apprehended outbreak of the revolutionists" from one extreme of the island to the other.[21]

Two weeks later, on April 25, Titus and O'Hara met on the Lafayette wharf at 5:00 p.m. with Capt. John "Jack" Allen and some thirty Kentuckians, who started boarding the bark *Georgiana.* Allen was a thirty-nine-year-old veteran of the battle of San Jacinto in the Texas revolution and the battle of Buena Vista, Mexico, on February 22, 1847, where he fought on foot as a second lieutenant of Company G, First Regiment, Kentucky Mounted Volunteers. Most of the Kentucky Regiment soon joined them, and the vessel cleared port at 9:00 p.m. The expeditionaries received three parting cheers from a large crowd, and it was enthusiastically returned by Titus and others on the bark. The next morning the *Georgiana* was boarded by a customs officer six miles from the mouth of the Mississippi River and cleared for sailing. The vessel advanced farther downstream and rendezvoused at 2:00 p.m. with a fishing smack piloted by Laurent Sigur. Titus assisted in retrieving from it ten boxes containing 250 Louisiana Arsenal brown muskets with bayonets and some 10,000 ball cartridges, which were put in the captain's cabin. The *Georgiana* was pulled out to sea by a tugboat on the morning of the 27th and quickly unfurled its sails for Yucatán. Four days later the brigantine *Susan Loud* left New Orleans with 170 Louisiana Regiment volunteers.[22]

A correspondent of the *New York Herald* reported from New Orleans on May 4 that the Kentucky and Louisiana Regiments had already sailed for the rendezvous point. He wrote that two other regiments from Tennessee and Mississippi would leave in a few days and that a distinguished Mexican War officer, "at present the Executive of an adjoining State, will follow with the *corps de reserve,* and take command of the entire forces of the new Republic." According to Chatham Wheat, Governor Quitman would depart between June 1 and 15 with the second contingent after resigning as governor of Mississippi. Three days later the *Creole* left New Orleans with some 170 men of the Mississippi Regiment and 20 stragglers from Kentucky and Louisiana. The steamer stopped farther downstream to receive crated weapons, boots, and compounds.[23]

A week later, on May 14, the three expeditionary vessels were anchored under the lee of Contoy Island, five miles northeast of the Yucatán Peninsula. Titus and some other filibusters drilled on the beach, while others took the *Creole* to Mujeres Island for provisions and water. The next day López gathered the regimental officers on the steamer and issued them written commissions. The new officers, in turn, appointed their subalterns. Titus officially received the rank of adjutant lieutenant from Colonel O'Hara, who organized the Kentucky Regiment into six companies. The commissions were formalized outside United States territory to avoid violating the Neutrality Act. On May 16, when some dissenters demanded to leave, General López ordered that those who "did not wish to go to Cuba could now have permission to return to the United States in the *Georgiana*." Thirty-eight defectors remained on Contoy Island when the *Creole* left for Cuba at 1:00 A.M. the next day. Titus helped inscribe the muster roll, indicating that the Liberation Army consisted of 610 men, including 230 in the Kentucky Regiment. The 170 volunteers of the Louisiana Regiment were divided into ten equal companies, each led by a captain and two lieutenants. The Mississippi Regiment had a similar number, but most were not from that state. The expeditionaries were described as "mostly young men. . . .Three-fourths of them have served with distinction in Mexico," and included in the group was a grandson of Davy Crockett.[24]

Titus was regarded as "a fine officer" by an expeditionary and helped distribute the arms and uniforms on the *Creole* in international waters to avoid American jurisdiction. He received one of the best weapons, a 54-caliber Mississippi rifle, fifty of which were assigned to the Kentucky Regiment because it had the best leadership and organization. The older flint muskets went to the Louisianans, and the Jennings breechloading 54-caliber rifles were given to the Mississippians. Each volunteer was issued a red flannel shirt and "a black cloth cap, with a Lone Star cockade." The captains received white pants, the lieutenants black, and the troops were given trousers of various shades and stripes. Almost everyone had a revolver or a Bowie knife and received sixty rounds of ammunition. That evening López outlined his plan to Titus and the other officers. He abandoned the projected landing in the Vuelta Abajo region of southwestern Pinar del Río, opting for a nocturnal surprise attack on the unfortified northern coastal town of Cárdenas. They would then proceed thirty miles west to Matanzas by railroad and attack the rear of the fortress facing the sea. The general expected his skeleton regiments to expand with volunteers by then, in addition to raising three new ones, and amount to some five thousand troops. After the arrival of Quitman's reinforcements, López envisioned having thirty thousand troops surrounding Havana.[25]

The *Creole* entered the fifteen-mile-long Cárdenas Harbor on May 19 after nearly two days of sailing some four hundred miles at ten knots. The town had a population of 4,524, including 885 slaves, with a considerable number of American resident merchants and planters in nearby estates. The

mile-wide waterfront had warehouses and sixteen docks open to international commerce. The military force in the town and vicinity was between
sixty and one hundred men of the León and Nápoles regiments in addition
to a native squadron of mounted Royal Lancers. The *Creole* grounded at low
tide at 3:30 A.M. a few yards from the longest pier. The 610 filibusters were
delayed more than an hour disembarking over a long narrow plank in single
file. Titus and the Kentucky Regiment were the first to debark and assume
formation. Their color bearer carried "the only flag which the invaders had at
Cárdenas," which would later become the national emblem of Cuba. O'Hara
sent sixty Kentuckians under Lieutenant Colonel Pickett and Capt. John
Allen to occupy the railroad yard a mile and one-half on the edge of town.
López then ordered O'Hara to seize the local infantry barracks. The Kentuckians impressed a passerby to take them there, but unbeknownst to them,
the garrison was not at the central Quintayros Plaza, as they had assumed,
but three blocks farther away. O'Hara, believing that he was being led astray,
countermarched his force until encountering López and his general staff,
who gave them a new guide who led them to their objective. Meanwhile
the Louisiana Regiment was advancing on a parallel street to the right of the
Kentucky Regiment heading for Quintayros Plaza. The Mississippi Regiment
was headed in the same direction one block to the left of the Kentuckians.[26]

As Titus and the Kentucky Regiment approached Quintayros Plaza,
O'Hara thought that his frightened guide was confused regarding the location of the infantry barracks. The man insisted that the massive stone jailhouse building at the plaza was not the garrison. As he was being goaded
toward the prison gate, the sentry blurted out three quick challenges before
firing his musket. Titus and his comrades replied with a fierce fusillade and
the shrill "Old Kentuck'" yells heard in earlier wars. The fifteen soldiers in
the building answered with a precise volley. Titus survived unscathed, but
O'Hara was shot in the thigh and a few attackers were disabled. Command
of the Kentucky Regiment then passed to Major Hawkins, whom Titus
now served as adjutant. Colonel Wheat, upon hearing the gunfire, rushed
his regiment into the plaza and ran into a detachment of fleeing Spanish
soldiers who shot at them. Wheat, felled by a slight shoulder wound, bellowed, "Louisianans! Your colonel is killed! Go and avenge his death!" Command of his force passed to the one-armed Mexican War veteran Lt. Col.
William H. Bell. The Mississippi Regiment then arrived and battered down
the massive entrance doors as the Spaniards fled through the rear gate.[27]

López afterward attached to the Louisiana Regiment a company of Kentuckians and a company of Mississippians and ordered them to attack the

two-story rubble masonry Capitular House across from the jailhouse. It was the headquarters of Lt. Gov. Florencio Ceruti, who had barricaded himself with sixty soldiers on the second floor of the building. The Kentuckians occupied a residence across the street from the Capitular House and fired at it in a line of battle. Lt. Richardson Hardy remembered Titus as "'Gallant Harry!' Jovial and laughing even in the midst of a fight; and a perfect Ajax in courage and proportions." At 7:00 A.M. López ordered the torching of the Capitular House after a score of soldiers escaped out the back during a diversionary peace proposal. The rising smoke and flames prompted Ceruti an hour later to surrender with his men and capitulate Cárdenas. The U.S. consul at Havana later wrote to the Department of State that López had captured "about seventy soldiers." Lieutenant Hardy estimated the filibuster toll at "some six or eight killed, and twelve or fifteen wounded; the Spanish loss was probably about the same, notwithstanding that they had fought most of the time behind impenetrable walls." Major Hawkins indicated that the Kentucky Regiment "lost eight, killed and wounded," while Lieutenant Colonel Bell reported "some twenty" Louisianan casualties. The injured filibusters were returned to the *Creole* for treatment.[28]

Oil painting of filibusters forming ranks in the Cárdenas plaza in front of the cathedral on May 19, 1850, after the surrender of the city. The scene, copied by C. Gregory Stapko (1913–2006) from a contemporary Spanish sketch, depicts the burning of the Capitular House, headquarters of the Spanish lieutenant governor, and, flying from an upper window, the Cuban rebel tricolor. Adj. Lt. Henry Titus was remembered by a filibuster that day as "'Gallant Harry!' Jovial and laughing even in the midst of a fight; and a perfect Ajax in courage and proportions." From the author's collection.

The filibusters occupied Quintayros Plaza and stacked their arms while a burial detail carried the dead to the municipal cemetery. Others went scrounging for food, while some took a nap. Adjutant Titus accompanied López and two others to the Municipal Council office, where they expropriated $5,132.75. They proceeded to the customhouse, where Titus demanded the "availables" from the administrator and seized his horse. The "polite officers set out their wine and fruits, pointed out the safe," a three-key iron deposit box, and provided two slaves who carried it to the filibuster headquarters at the jail. Lieutenant Hardy recalled, "It was an amusing sight to see the gallant Adjutant guarding the safe several squares by himself, sword in hand, having thrown away his coat and hat in the heat of the engagement." The strongbox, requiring the keys of three different administrators, was opened with difficulty and rendered $1,492.00.[29]

López, assisted by Titus and others, ceremoniously raised the Cuban flag at Quintayros Plaza and called on the citizens to gather in the square. He had proclamations distributed, gave a patriotic speech announcing the establishment of a provisional government, and invited the crowd to fight for their country, but none joined the invaders. Afro-Cubans were the only ones who "had a holiday and they were singing and dancing, thinking they would be released from slavery." At 10:00 A.M. a frustrated López went to harangue the jailed Spaniards, twenty-five of whom stripped off their uniforms, donned filibuster red shirts, and swore loyalty to the former Spanish general. Resistance against the invaders by Spanish loyalists occurred with sporadic ambushes. López was unsure of his next move: His undisciplined troops were scattered; many were drunk, and seven had deserted; four of his leading officers, regimental leaders O'Hara and Wheat and staff members Ambrosio Gonzales and Captain Murry, lay wounded in the *Creole;* and the populace had not rallied to his cause. López hesitated about proceeding to Matanzas, but by noon he regretted not having quickly gone there.[30]

When the incoming tide refloated the *Creole* at 2:00 P.M., allowing it to dock properly, López ordered the ammunition and stores on board transferred to a nearby train for passage to Matanzas. This lasted an hour while López, escorted by Titus and others, rode around town on horseback inspecting his troops and monitoring the railroad station and the docks for possible enemy movements. At 4:00 p.m. a horseman arrived and told López that the entire Matanzas garrison and its artillery unit would arrive at Cárdenas by train in about nine hours. The general informed Titus and his officers of the situation and indicated that the expedition would depart for Vuelta Abajo, where there was an organized force awaiting them. He ordered the supplies on the train returned to the *Creole,* and a slave gang that performed the task attempted to remain on board but was "kept off the steamer by force." López recalled the Kentuckians under Pickett from the railroad yard in the suburbs and ordered them to hold the intersection at Pinillos Plaza, one block from the steamer wharf. The Louisiana Regiment on Quintayros Plaza started withdrawing to the steamer.[31]

An hour later López sent Titus to inform Major Hawkins that Spanish mounted lancers and infantry were entering Cárdenas. Hawkins was to hold Quintayros Plaza with his Kentuckians until the embarkation was complete. As the Louisianans and Mississippians were boarding the *Creole,* they "heard the firing of volleys of musketry in the Plaza." A Spanish force of fifty infantry soldiers, forty peasant militia lancers, and thirty civilian riders from nearby plantations were charging the invaders. The infantry advancing on the left side of the plaza engaged Lieutenant Dear's company. According to Major Hawkins, Dear "found some difficulty in repulsing" the superior force, but "by great exertion on his own part and the gallant assistance of Adjutant Titus and Sergeant Major McDonald, they were finally driven back with considerable loss." The local residents took to the rooftops around the plaza to witness the action for thirty minutes until the Kentuckians were signaled to return to the steamer.[32]

As the Kentuckians were falling back through the middle of the street, a platoon of lancers bore down on them. The filibusters scrambled onto the sidewalks and from there delivered a raking fire on the passing cavalry. A second line of more than thirty lancers repeated the charge at headlong speed past the gauntlet of musketry and ran into the regrouped Kentuckians one block from the steamer. In a final hand-to-hand encounter, Titus "cleft the skull of a colonel of lancers at a single blow." The filibuster toll was twenty-six dead, some sixty wounded, and seven deserters. The ten Spaniards who perished were interred in La Cabaña fortress in Havana under an obelisk bearing their names. The Cárdenas physician Antonio García Ortega attended fifteen wounded Spaniards.[33]

The invaders departed on the *Creole* at 9:00 P.M. with twenty-six Spanish renegades. Five filibuster deserters were soon captured by the Spaniards and executed. López held a war council to express his desire of landing in the Vuelta Abajo region and to "send the Creole back for General John Anthony Quitman and his troops and munitions." Titus joined Gonzales, Colonel Wheat, and Captain Allen in backing the plan, but "the greater part of the company officers and consequently nearly all the rank and file, would not assent." O'Hara "declared the proposition to be madness." The Hardy brothers regarded the idea as "desperate and reckless." Only a score of Kentuckians and seven Louisianans vowed to follow López. The dissenters cited "the scarcity of ammunition, the absence of artillery, the scant supply of coal for the vessel, the limited quantity of water, and the tardiness with which the Cubans at Cárdenas joined the liberating standard." The patrolling Spanish war steamer *Pizarro* spotted the *Creole* on the morning of the 21st and began a three-hour chase that ended at Key West when the filibusters docked one hundred yards ahead of their pursuers. The mail steamship *Isabel* arrived at midnight and took Titus, López, and other officers and men to Savannah. The rest departed the island within a week, except the badly wounded, some of whom languished there for months.[34]

O'Hara blamed the expedition failure on "the fatal consequence of an indiscriminate enlistment of men," especially the "blackguard rowdies" and "riffraff" in the Louisiana Regiment. Lt. Richardson Hardy faulted "the fatal error of landing at Cárdenas, instead of going to Mantua in the first place" and called the entire campaign "a harumscarum business." The impetuous López was largely responsible for the disastrous results. His military strategy in believing that disgruntled Cubans and Spaniards would join foreign invaders speaking a different language was improvised and illusive. On June 21 a New Orleans federal grand jury indicted Narciso López and fifteen filibuster leaders and supporters for violation of the Neutrality Law, and their trial was set for December.[35]

Titus, not named in the indictment, on July 18 returned to Savannah by steamer from Augusta, Georgia. Three days later López and Gonzales reached Savannah by train from Macon and registered at the Pulaski House that evening, finding that Titus had left earlier for Jacksonville. Gonzales remained in Savannah, while López went to New York via Charleston. Titus signed the Jacksonville Hotel register on the 21st and listed his hometown as Philadelphia. He soon after entered into an equal-shares partnership with the thirty-year-old South Carolina "speculator" Wyley G. Harris and John M. Cureton to run Empire Mills, Florida's first steam-powered circular-saw mill. The mill was located on Hazzard's Bluff at the mouth of Pottsburg Creek, two miles south of Jacksonville on the east side of the St. Johns River. Titus used the mill as a base of operations to prepare the next invasion of Cuba.[36]

In August, Titus returned to Wilkes-Barre, Pennsylvania, for a family visit. He stayed in the home of his twenty-year-old sister Sarah Mershon Bowman, who five years earlier had married Col. Samuel Bowman, a confectioner. The couple resided with their two young daughters, Sarah's twenty-five-year-old sister Marian Ann Titus, and a nineteen-year-old free African

American servant. Titus later proceeded to Willard's Hotel in Washington, D.C., accompanied by Marian, arriving on September 2, the day after Narciso López registered there. During their meeting López gave Titus the rank of colonel after Titus agreed to raise a filibuster contingent in Jacksonville before the end of the year.[37]

Titus, accompanied by his sister, returned to the Jacksonville Hotel on September 9, 1850. The dwelling, on the southwest corner of Adams and Newnan Streets, served as unofficial filibuster headquarters for the next year. It was recently renovated with an additional twenty rooms, lengthy piazzas in front and back, and a capacity for more than 150 guests. The proprietor was thirty-six-year-old Samuel Buffington, a Florida Militia colonel, who owned 17 slaves. He was a member of Masonic Solomon's Lodge No. 20, where Titus was initiated soon after arriving in Jacksonville.[38]

The Jacksonville Hotel register soon listed the frequent arrival of Titus and his local partisans. Titus was lodging there on September 29 with Henry R. Saddler and John N. Reeves, members of a nucleus that would frequently join him during the next twelve months. Saddler, a member of Solomon's Lodge No. 20, was a wealthy fifty-one-year-old Georgia-born planter who owned the fifty-two-hundred-acre Ortega plantation at the mouth of the Ortega River. His 170 slaves made him the second-largest slaveholder in Duval County in 1850. Reeves, a bachelor, was a forty-year-old bookkeeper from Augusta, Georgia.[39]

In late October the Titus cadre included fifty-year-old Florida Militia general Benjamin Hopkins; his twenty-two-year-old merchant son John L. Hopkins, destined to command a company of the filibuster Jacksonville Battalion; Georgia Militia colonel Henry H. Floyd; John F. Frink; and Jacob Rutherford, hired by Andrew J. Johnson to be his assistant engineer in the upcoming Cuba expedition. General Hopkins, a member of Solomon's Lodge No. 20, was born in South Carolina, raised his family in Georgia, and settled in a Putnam County plantation after Florida received statehood in 1845. Floyd was a thirty-two-year-old planter from adjacent Camden County, Georgia, whose neighbor David Bailey was also a filibusterer. Florida-born Frink was a twenty-three-year-old farmer from nearby Hamilton County. Among those who began frequently appearing in Jacksonville with the filibuster leadership were Florida Militia colonel John P. Sanderson, Daniel C. Ambler, and J. Henry Hawkins. Sanderson, a thirty-seven-year-old Vermont-born lawyer, member of Solomon's Lodge No. 20, and veteran of the Second Seminole War, owned a plantation with thirty slaves and had a partnership in a dry goods store. Ambler was a forty-five-year-old, New York-born, wealthy dentist practicing in Jacksonville. Hawkins was a thirty-two-year-old Kentucky-born attorney from Tallahassee. Titus became the military leader of this heterogeneous group.[40]

The Cuba invasion plans were postponed after the filibuster leadership trial began in the U.S. Circuit Court in New Orleans on December 16, 1850. The next day Titus purchased Wyley G. Harris's one-third share of Empire Mills for $3,500. His twenty-three-year-old brother Ellett Howell Titus arrived in Jacksonville from New Orleans on January 27, 1851, to work at the mill. While the court proceedings were in progress, López sent Gonzales, his second in command, to meet with Titus and coordinate organizing the next expedition in Florida and other leaders in Columbus, Macon, Atlanta, and Savannah, Georgia. Titus put Gonzales in contact with thirty-eight-year-old Charles H. Hopkins, son of General Hopkins, a McIntosh County planter and Georgia Militia colonel. Gonzales was in turn introduced to the local planters William Henry Mongin and Randolph Spalding. The thirty-four-year-old Mongin owned an eight-hundred-acre rice plantation on General's Island, opposite the town of Darien, with 164 slaves. Titus then mortgaged his two-thirds share of the mill for $8,967 to his brother Ellett to raise the cash for supplying his Jacksonville Battalion. Gonzales, from his Pulaski House headquarters in Savannah, recruited men and funds from planters in coastal Georgia.[41]

On March 4 Titus and Cureton paid $466 for forty and one-half acres adjacent to their sawmill to increment their timber supply. Three days later López and his co-conspirators had their charges dismissed after three mistrials, the last deadlocked eleven-to-one for acquittal. A few weeks later the *New Orleans Delta* published news of a rumored uprising in Cuba, which circulated widely in the southern press. This prompted on April 9 the premature departure of a filibuster force from Rome, Georgia. As they passed through Atlanta the following day, Jesse Reneau, the Whig editor of the *Atlanta Republican,* telegraphed President Millard Fillmore, "Our rail-roads are crowded with an army of adventurers destined for Cuba—by way of Savannah beyond all doubt." Six days later Spanish minister Angel Calderón de la Barca met with Fillmore, who apologized for "difficult to control" Americans and promised to neutralize the expedition. A Yankee sojourning through the South heard of the Cuba filibuster plot and denounced it to New York senator Hamilton Fish, who promptly relayed it to Fillmore on April 26. The informant provided details of the conspiracy and claimed that the plan "is probably favored by some of the large planters. His instrument with the rank and file, is a man known as Harry Titus a celebrated fighting

man." A week later Fillmore issued a Presidential Proclamation calling filibuster expeditions "adventures for plunder and robbery" in violation of U.S.
laws, and he ordered all civil and military officers to arrest the perpetrators.
Titus read President Fillmore's appeal in the Jacksonville press, but it did
not dissuade him.[42]

During the three days prior to the scheduled invasion departure, filibuster
activists arriving in the Jacksonville Hotel included Ambler, Reeves, Thomas
E. Buckman, Kingsley Beatty Gibbs, Joseph W. Hickman, and Solomon F.
Halliday, accompanied by Theodore O'Hara, who led the Kentucky Regiment in the Cárdenas invasion. Buckman, a twenty-seven-year-old Pennsylvanian and member of Solomon's Lodge No. 20, later became a Confederate
hero for building intricate torpedo mines that sank Union steamers in the
St. Johns River. Gibbs, a forty-one-year-old New Yorker, had been a Florida
Militia brigadier major in the Second Seminole War and a former alderman
of St. Augustine in 1835, and he owned a plantation on Fort George Island
with fifty-four slaves. Hickman was a twenty-year-old unemployed Floridian
residing in the Jacksonville Hotel. Halliday, a Presbyterian minister and slave
owner, was a member of Masonic Alachua Lodge No. 26 in Newnansville.[43]

The Jacksonville contingent led by Titus was comprised of northern
Floridians and southeastern Georgians and had "some 600 men, 50 of whom
were to be mounted." It would be a larger congregation than the entire Jacksonville population of some four hundred citizens. A letter from St. Mary's,
Georgia, to New Orleans stated, "Many have volunteered from the middle counties, mostly young men of respectability and good standing. Capt.
[William] F[isher], of Tallahassee, who has seen some service in the Indian
wars of Florida, and possesses talents, intelligence and influence, is, I learn,
to be colonel. Young D—, son of Gen. D—, has a commission; he is a genuine fighting cock. Dr. F—, son of Mayor F—, goes as surgeon. In truth,
most of the best young men of that section of the country have volunteered.
Many of them are wealthy."[44]

The *Newark Advertiser*'s Jacksonville correspondent wrote on April 25 that
the expedition would sail within thirty-six hours from rendezvous points
on the St. Johns River, in St. Marys, Georgia, and in New Orleans. He
had recently seen in a local warehouse "cannon, gun-carriages, rifles, muskets, ammunition and the furniture of an army equipment to a very large
amount." The writer also observed about four hundred bushels of oats for
horse feed and "large quantities of wood and resin for the fuel on board the
steamers, and horses and men are collected in this vicinity, ready for embarkation." He described the Jacksonville Battalion officers as "men of bravery

and military talent" and most of the privates as Mexican War veterans. The troops included Floridians of Hispanic descent, Cubans, and a few who had been previously engaged in the Cárdenas affair, unimpeded by the lack of a local federal marshal. The same correspondent found, "It is interesting to observe how enticing and contagious is the war spirit." The expedition had been regarded as wild and chimerical by the citizenry the previous day, but "the field pieces and the muskets seem to have turned the heads of some from whom more wisdom would be expected." The article was reprinted in numerous newspapers throughout the country, including the *Philadelphia North American* and the *Louisville Democrat*.[45]

The Whig *Florida Republican* (Jacksonville) indicated that the city had "much of the appearance of a rendezvous for one branch of the 'patriot' army. Strange arrivals have been unusually frequent, among whom are one or two personages of note, who served as officers in the Cárdenas expedition." The reporter of the Whig *Newark Advertiser* wrote on Sunday, the 27th, that the Jacksonville ladies had wrought pretty tri-color Cuban banners, and "half the town seems disposed to go if their wives would let them." In preparation for departure, the telegraph wires had been cut and the "Judge and District Attorney were persuaded a week ago to take an excursion to the wilderness, and are now where no telegraph or mail can reach them."[46]

That evening Savannah customs collector Hiram Roberts chartered the steamer *Welaka* after receiving arrest warrants issued by President Fillmore for López, Gonzales, and the filibuster leadership in Georgia. Titus and the Florida activists were not included on the list. Roberts departed at midnight for the port of St. Marys, Georgia, with Savannah port surveyor Thomas Burke, U.S. marshal William H. C. Mills, one deputy, and an inspector. They were accompanied by a reporter from the *Savannah Morning News*. Arriving in St. Mary's on Monday night, Burke heard that there were "from 500 to 1,500 persons collected at Jacksonville," and they proceeded there. The *Welaka* encountered the steamer *St. Mathews* coming from Palatka on the St. Johns River. A passenger from Palatka packing dual pistols boarded the *Welaka* assuming it to be the tardy Cuban expeditionary vessel. Inquiries in Jacksonville on Tuesday morning failed to disclose any evidence of weapon caches or a large congregation of men. The Savannah reporter wrote that according to "reliable information, obtained from respectable sources. . . . No principal officer of the contemplated expedition, has been in Jacksonville lately."[47]

Before departing with the federal posse that day, the correspondent talked to some thirty men "who expressed themselves willing to join the expedition." He surmised that at Jacksonville "there are but few persons who do not sympathize with, and would aid the expedition as far as possible." The arrival of the authorities "caused an apparent hiatus in the program of arrangements" of the filibusters. They did not find any corroboration in the city because Titus had transferred everything to Empire Mills two miles south on the opposite bank of the river. He then checked into the Jacksonville Hotel on Monday, the 28th, with Sanderson, Saddler, Halliday, and thirty-one-year-old Georgia-born John Madison, a Marion County farmer, but they aroused no suspicion. López and Gonzales, hiding on the Barstow plantation on Wilmington Island near Savannah, departed on May 2. The general returned to New Orleans, and Gonzales was concealed on the Beaufort district plantation of Gen. James Hamilton, a War of 1812 veteran and South Carolina politician.[48]

The two Jacksonville weekly newspapers favored Cuban liberty. The Democratic *Florida News* expressed its support and that of "a very large portion of the community" for the filibusters, hoping to "heartily rejoice to see Cuba in the full enjoyment of her liberty and independence." The Whig *Florida Republican* reprinted an article from the Arkansas *Washington Telegraph* chastising Horace Greeley's abolitionist *New York Tribune* for regarding the affair as "nothing but the extension of the area of slavery." The article argued that "the condition of both races would be improved by the independence of Cuba," especially for slaves, who would then be returned to colonize and civilize Africa. The *Florida Republican* warned that Cuban annexation, by strengthening the South, might "embolden the North to clamor for the acquisition of Canada, thus bringing in another world of free-soil, as the price of our repeated effort to preserve the balance of power to ourselves." It advised that Fillmore buy Cuba from Spain and urged that the island should be "enfranchised by purchase—by spontaneous revolution of her people—or by a revolution begun at their instance by foreign aid, and seconded and finished by themselves."[49]

In contrast, the northern Whig and abolitionist newspapers excoriated the filibuster expedition, with one Iowa paper calling it a "Slaveocratic Crusade." The temperance paper *Cayuga Chief* of Auburn, New York, where Titus had lived as a child, described the filibusters as "pirates" and "marauders." Some northern Democratic publications that espoused popular sovereignty, especially the free-soil *Cincinnati Nonpareil,* favored the Cuban annexation cause. One of its editors, Richardson Hardy, was a Cárdenas veteran. Democratic support was not unanimous, with some "locofoco" editors denouncing the Cuba expedition.[50]

Titus and his comrades abandoned the Jacksonville Hotel after the federal authorities left the city, but he was back on May 9 with company commanders David Province and Samuel St. George Rogers and with thirty-one-year-old Florida-born bachelor George Mooney, a member of Solomon's Lodge No. 20 and owner of Florida's first iron foundry. Province was a twenty-four-year-old Kentucky-born Mexican War veteran and attorney residing in an Ocala boardinghouse. Rogers was a twenty-six-year-old Tennessee-born attorney from Franklin County affiliated with Masonic Marion Lodge No. 19 in Ocala. The group was joined by Buckman, McQueen McIntosh, and apparent filibuster supporters Lewis F. Roux, Thomas Tumlin, twenty-seven-year-old Maine-born Charles E. Dunn, and Benjamin Kimball, the latter two affiliated with Empire Mills. Tumlin was a wealthy twenty-year-old Georgia planter. McIntosh, who later served as attorney for the filibuster leadership, was a twenty-four-year-old Georgian who had recently moved with his family from their native state into the Jacksonville Hotel.[51]

The *Savannah Morning News* reported on May 19, "During the past week there had arrived, in the neighborhood of Jacksonville, some three hundred men with upwards of 150 horses, from different parts of this State and Florida, whose intention it was to have joined the Cuban expedition." The newspaper estimated that since the start of the movement, "upwards of 1,500 men have from time to time arrived in the vicinity of Jacksonville, with a view to embark from that point." In late May, Titus gathered in the Jacksonville Hotel with O'Hara, Buckman, Sanderson, Saddler, Reeves, Hawkins, Kimball, Tumlin, Gibbs, John L. Hopkins, Charles H. Dibble, and Florida Militia major Benjamin A. Putnam, a forty-nine-year-old lawyer from St. Augustine, among others. Dibble, a Florida Militia cavalry veteran of the Second Seminole War, was a thirty-six-year-old New York–born merchant from Mandarin, where he owned a forty-acre farm and three slaves. Titus and the Jacksonville filibuster leadership agreed to wait until López notified them of a better opportunity to renew their efforts.[52]

Titus kept in contact with López and Gonzales through secret courier mail using code names. Gonzales arrived from Savannah at the Jacksonville Hotel on June 26, twenty-four hours after Buckman. He met with Titus and other conspirators, took inventory of the weapons and equipment, and discussed plans for the next endeavor. Six days later López wrote to Gonzales, who had been taking quinine to alleviate a malarial "severe bilious fever," advising that he recuperate his health in the sulfur baths of Virginia until further instructions.[53]

On July 22 American newspapers reported that an annexationist uprising occurred in Puerto Príncipe, Cuba, on July 4, led by thirty-four-year-old attorney Joaquín de Agüero, with forty-four followers. Although the group was captured within three weeks, after various clashes with Spanish troops, news of their defeat was not known until the following month because the Spanish government had suspended postal service in Puerto Príncipe. López immediately sent his secretary Cirilo Villaverde to inform Titus to make final preparations for departure. Villaverde arrived at the Jacksonville Hotel on July 28 with Leopoldo Turla, a thirty-six-year-old Cuban poet. Titus then invited Villaverde to join his Masonic fraternity, Solomon's Lodge No. 20, free of charge. Filibuster activists arriving at the Jacksonville Hotel that week included Buckman, Judge Farquahar Bethune, Peter Vantassel, and others mobilized by Titus. The seventy-year-old Florida-born Bethune, a Florida Militia veteran of the Second Seminole War, owned the New Ross plantation near Jacksonville. He later returned twice more to the Jacksonville Hotel, both times accompanied by Theodore O'Hara. Six days after Villaverde's arrival, Titus and Cureton took a loss in selling Empire Mills and its acreage to Hiram L. French for five thousand dollars through the attorney McQueen McIntosh. Titus invested his half of the proceeds in acquiring equipment for the expedition.[54]

Other conspirators, among them twenty-eight-year-old Dominican writer Alejandro Angulo Guridi and Cárdenas expeditionary Juan Manuel Macías, reached Jacksonville on July 30. Four days later another Cárdenas veteran, José Sánchez Iznaga, arrived from New York via Savannah to join them. Agustín Manresa also appeared that day with the last instructional letter from López in New Orleans, dated July 24, telling Titus and the others that his force would leave on the 31st, reaching Jacksonville four days later.[55]

The expedition would depart on the steamer *Pampero*, purchased for sixty thousand dollars by *New Orleans Delta* publisher Laurent J. Sigur. When the vessel arrived in New Orleans on July 29, Capt. Armstrong Irvine Lewis reported that "his boilers were burnt out" from a collapsed fifteen-inch exhaust pipe. An improvised replacement tube was installed while the steamer was being towed out to sea with 450 expeditionaries. The malfunction slowed the *Pampero* down to eight knots, instead of its usual fifteen. They reached Key West on August 10 at sunset and were told erroneous news that the Cuban insurrection had spread to thirteen towns. López held a war council, and his officers indicated that everyone was "now impatient to strike straight across for the nearest part of the Island, and unwilling to go round first to the St. Johns for the artillery, munitions and men there waiting." They agreed that after landing in Cuba the *Pampero* would be sent to retrieve Titus and the Jacksonville contingent.[56]

After disembarking in western Cuba, López ordered Captain Lewis to pick up the Jacksonville and Savannah battalions. The *Pampero* arrived in Key West in the early morning of August 13 displaying the rebel Cuban flag. Its name was obliterated from the hull, although its home port appeared as Washington, D.C., and the ship's furnishings were labeled *Pampero.* When customs inspector Alexander Patterson boarded to request the ship's papers, Lewis provided a clearance signed by López three days earlier, identifying him as a Cuban citizen and the vessel as the *Cuban Liberator,* cleared from the port of Cabañas to Savannah, with ballast, and listing the crew members. The inspector took the paper to the onshore customs collector, who immediately ordered the steamer seized, but Lewis quickly departed after being forewarned. The *Pampero* ran aground approaching the Cape Florida shore while trying to land a party to chop wood for fuel. Two days were lost before a salvage vessel dislodged them. Several recruits, described by the U.S. district attorney as "men of no character," boarded the steamer, which then headed for Jacksonville to embark the reinforcement expedition.[57]

Titus read in the Jacksonville press its support for the Cuban uprising. The *Florida News* voiced its "warm sympathy in the cause of that oppressed people" and denounced that "the dread of seeing the power and influence of the South augmented by the annexation of Cuba, which must inevitably follow the establishment of her independence, is sufficient to arouse all the energies of the Administration in support of the Spanish despotism." The Whig *Florida Republican* stated that "we cannot, now that we are justified in believing that Cuba herself has started the ball of revolution, withhold our warm sympathy with the patriots in what must resolve itself into a struggle between Republicanism and colonial vassalage," and forecast that "Cuban expeditions will start from a hundred points on the Atlantic."[58]

The Titus call to arms was heard throughout northern Florida, prompting droves of adventurous and idealistic young men to descend upon Jacksonville. Sánchez-Iznaga, Saddler and son, Buckman, Reeves, and Tumlin were back in the Jacksonville Hotel by August 13. In Ocala, David Province, Samuel St. George Rogers, and William Fisher mustered three companies, numbering about 180 men, many "good riflemen" from the Florida Militia, and marched to Jacksonville on the 16th. The next day the Cubans Villaverde, Macías, and Turla departed for Savannah by steamer to finalize arrangements there. The successful López landing was announced in

American newspapers on the 20th. The next day the *Florida Republican* printed two articles about the *Pampero,* lauding the vessel that "can run away from the whole American Navy" if it tried to intercept the vessel. That evening the steamer entered Doboy Sound, Georgia, and anchored by the lighthouse. On the morning of the 22nd the Darien collector Armand Lifils discovered that the *Pampero* needed fuel. Captain Lewis went to Sapelo Island that day and later proceeded by canoe to Darien.[59]

The following morning, the 23rd, Lewis took the mail steamer to Savannah, and it landed the next day. Arriving with him were the Cuban revolutionary priest Felix Varela, who traveled from St. Augustine on the steamer *St. Matthews* along with David Yulee, the Democratic Florida senator recently defeated for reelection by Stephen Mallory, who espoused Cuban annexation; and filibuster supporters Samuel P. Hamilton, attorney Bird Murphy Pearson, and planter William Henry Mongin. Lewis provided the filibuster conspirators in Savannah accounts of what had transpired, and they plotted their next move. The captain was instructed to retrieve the Jacksonville Battalion and proceed to Wilmington Island, where the Georgia Battalion awaited. Lewis left Savannah on Monday, the 25th, on the steamer *J. Stone,* reaching the *Pampero* that evening. He saw in the latest edition of the *Savannah Morning News* that up to four hundred filibusters were in Jacksonville and its immediate vicinity. At dawn the next day, Lewis piloted the *Pampero* to the St. Johns River. The waterway, unlike any other in America, flows north for nearly four hundred miles, with an average width of two miles, turning east at Jacksonville to empty into the ocean.[60]

Meanwhile, Gonzales heard of the Cuban uprising while nursing his health at White Sulphur Springs, Virginia. He quickly departed by stagecoach, train, and steamer, arriving on August 23 in Charleston, South Carolina, where he met Sigur, who had gone there to hire another steamer. Two days later the *Charleston Courier* reported that Gonzales, instead of Titus, was supposed to be leading the Jacksonville contingent, but the Cuban was headed to Columbia, South Carolina, by railroad. Gonzales met in the state capital with state senator James Hopkins Adams, a brigadier general of the South Carolina Militia; the attorney Maxcy Gregg, a major in the Twelfth U.S. Infantry in the Mexican War; Adley Hogan Gladden, commander of the Palmetto Regiment of South Carolina volunteers in the Mexican War; and the planter and politician David James McCord. Gonzales appealed to them for assistance before he returned to Charleston on the 26th. He then covertly traveled to Wilmington Island, Georgia, due to his outstanding arrest warrant from the president of the United States.[61]

The *Florida Republican* announced on the 28th that the *Pampero* was "now in the waters of Georgia, to receive reinforcements, and may momentarily pay this port a visit." Two accompanying articles reprinted from newspapers dated a week earlier erroneously claimed that "five hundred Creoles have left Havana to join López," that "López's force is gaining from twelve to fourteen hundred men daily," and that an entire Spanish regiment had defected to López, who was causing massive casualties to the enemy. It did accurately report that fifty filibusters had been captured and executed by Spanish soldiers, who "committed horrible brutalities on the bodies." These accounts inflamed passions against Spain, prompting Jacksonville residents to attend a "large and enthusiastic" meeting convened by trumpet call the next evening at the courthouse. Presiding over the gathering was Judge Felix Livingston, editor of the Democratic *Florida News*. The purpose of the rally was for the citizens to "express their sympathy for the struggling Cubans and their approbation of the course of those patriotic citizens who are about to embark for Cuba to join the liberating army."[62]

Thirty-six hours later, at 10:00 A.M. on Sunday, August 31, the *Pampero* arrived in Jacksonville to the cheers of a large crowd. Many were curious to see the vessel described a week earlier as "the fastest thing on the water." Titus immediately sent Macías to Savannah to relay the latest information. Temporary customs inspector George H. Smith boarded the steamer and demanded its license. Captain Lewis gave evasive replies and claimed that the law allowed twenty-four hours to produce it. Smith reported the situation to customs collector Isaiah David Hart, who urged him to stay on board the *Pampero,* but Smith replied that he "was not desirous to do so, as it was an unpleasant place." Smith returned to the vessel the following day and was told that the ship's papers had been in a box that was knocked overboard. Lewis again avoided answering the inspector's questions.[63]

The *Pampero* lacked documentation, bore no name on its hull, and flew an unregistered flag, and the newspapers had identified it as a Cuban filibuster vessel, but for unknown reasons Hart, the customs collector, failed to impound it. The fifty-eight-year-old Georgia-born Hart had participated in the 1812 Patriot Rebellion against Spain and founded Jacksonville a decade later. He had served as postmaster, court clerk, judge of elections, militia major during the Seminole War, and Florida territorial Whig senator. Hart owned downtown real estate, a two-story boardinghouse, and a plantation with forty-eight slaves.[64]

While the *Pampero* was in port, Titus gave instructions to have it "fitted out as a *transport vessel* by having some of the partitions knocked away

between decks and places prepared for troops." A visiting U.S. Army lieutenant saw "that the Cuban flag was flying in the streets of Jacksonville, and
that under that flag *daily drills* took place of men avowedly organized for
a Cuban expedition." The *Pampero* engine was repaired by Tuesday afternoon, September 2. Titus paid the four-hundred-dollar Jacksonville Hotel
bill for some fifty young volunteers who had signed the expedition muster
roll. The steamer was loaded at the wharf with wood fuel, stores, and provisions and embarked for Empire Mills during the late evening. The armament
was boarded from a scow on Pottsburg Creek in boxes marked with Titus's
initials, "H.T.T." It consisted of "two [twelve-pound brass] cannons, two
howitzers, 5 or 600 muskets, about 150 Yauger Rifles, about 150 cutlasses, 10
or 15 kegs of Powder, some Bombs and 50 or 60 kegs of cartridges and some
[thirty] saddles and also about 75 men." The mountain howitzers were fitted
on treenails on the *Pampero* ready for action. The military hierarchy that left
Jacksonville on the steamer was headed by Col. Henry Theodore Titus, Lt.
Col. Theodore O'Hara, and Maj. David Province. Captains Samuel Rogers
and Andrew Colvin commanded companies.[65]

Titus had the *Pampero* halt for an hour at a plantation on the Nassau
River north of Jacksonville. The only two plantations accessible by steamer
were on the upper bank and were owned by John Christopher and Samuel
Harrison. Since Col. John P. Sanderson, who frequently stayed at the Jacksonville Hotel with Titus and the filibuster leadership, was married to a Harrison, the *Pampero* probably stopped at the latter place. The expedition then
continued on the intracoastal waterway to Wilmington Island. There, Titus
located some seventy men of the Georgia Battalion, commanded by Captain
Williamson, who arrived from Savannah on the steamer *Jasper* with *Pampero*
owner Laurent Sigur and a stock of provisions.[66]

Ambrosio Gonzales, hiding from the federal marshal on Wilmington
Island, was frustrated to see that the Titus reinforcement expedition had been
delayed more than a week in going to Cuba, that the engine continued to
malfunction, and that there was no coal or water on board for a sea voyage to
the island. A dispute arose when Gonzales tried to take the leadership from
Titus and demote him to a lieutenant colonelcy. Titus, who had a large financial investment in the affair, argued that he had received a letter from López
in July, when Gonzales was ill, giving him command of the Jacksonville Battalion. The controversy was settled when Sigur sided with Titus. Gonzales
later wrote, "Without interfering with that movement already in the hands
of others, I at once proceeded to raise the promised reinforcement," and he
returned to Charleston on September 3.[67]

Titus meanwhile was refusing to recognize the orders and directions given by Sigur, who had the *Pampero*'s name restored to the hull and instructed Captain Lewis to take the steamer back to the Nassau River plantation. One third of the *Pampero* cargo was transferred to the *Jasper* and returned to Savannah. Adjutant John L. Hopkins, Capt. Andrew Colvin, and others departed on the *Jasper*. Hopkins later rejoined the *Pampero* at Nassau Sound, while Sigur told Colvin, who stayed in Savannah, that he might go on another boat, the *Monmouth*. The *Pampero* was towed out of Wassaw Inlet by the *J. Stone* before dawn on September 4. That morning Savannah U.S. attorney Henry Williams telegraphed the secretary of state about the recent events and ordered the U.S. revenue cutter *Jackson,* armed with six nine-pounder guns, to the mouth of the St. Johns River. The *Pampero* sailed to the Nassau River with the Jacksonville and Georgia battalions, which encamped inland, presumably on the Harrison plantation. Titus had the crated arms distributed and drilled the men for about three days, while waiting for more volunteers to arrive. The Democratic Jacksonville *Florida News* reported on September 6 that López had been arrested and executed and that his followers were either killed or captured. In consequence half of the Titus force disbanded and Gonzales ceased his reinforcement efforts in Charleston.[68]

The *Pampero* left the Nassau River at 4:00 P.M. on September 8 with Titus and some thirty filibusters and was spotted by the cutter *Jackson* about ten miles away. The *Jackson* deployed full sails, closed in on the steamer, and fired a warning shot that fell short. Titus ordered the *Pampero* to proceed, and the "crew gave three hearty cheers, put on all steam, and went ahead" up the St. Johns River. The cutter remained outside the river bar, with its guns loaded and its dozen crew members at battle stations, sealing off the escape to sea. The steamer passed Jacksonville at 8:00 that evening. One hour later Hart, the customs collector, sent a dispatch to St. Augustine customs collector John M. Hanson requesting assistance. Soon thereafter 2nd Lt. Dudley Davenport arrived on a barge from the *Jackson* to inform Hart of his vessel's position. The *Pampero* continued up the St. Johns, and Titus had its cargo secretly unloaded at the Benjamin Hopkins plantation near Palatka, seventy-five miles from Jacksonville. Captain Lewis later hid the vessel farther south in Dunn's Creek, four miles into a swamp, where the steamer "almost filled up the creek from side to side."[69]

At dawn the next day, Hart sent customs inspector Henry Drayton Holland in the revenue boat up the St. Johns to search for the *Pampero* in all creeks and lakes. The forty-five-year-old Holland was a physician from Charleston, South Carolina, who owned a one-thousand-acre plantation with eleven slaves. He arrived in Florida in 1835 to serve as a surgeon in the Seminole War and later settled with his wife and seven children in Jacksonville, where he joined Solomon's Lodge No. 20. Customs collector Hart used "every exertion to get other boats and crews" to join the pursuit but found only one willing to do so, and in it he dispatched an assistant. On September 10 U.S. Army lieutenant Anderson Merchant arrived in Jacksonville at 6:00 A.M. with twenty soldiers sent by the St. Augustine customs collector. Hart then telegraphed St. Augustine requesting two artillery pieces, to prevent the *Pampero* from escaping to sea, which arrived the next evening.[70]

On September 10 *Pampero* owner Laurent Sigur appeared in Jacksonville from Savannah accompanied by John L. O'Sullivan. Sigur asked the attorney McQueen McIntosh to help them find and surrender the vessel. Some one hundred filibusters balked and decided to commandeer the *Pampero* and went in the steamer *St. Mathews* up the St. Johns "making threats that they would resist to the last." The St. Augustine collector wrote to the Department of State asking "that an armed force of at least 50 men be sent immediately to Jacksonville." When Sigur and McIntosh arrived at Picolata, they found there Inspector Holland and his assistant lodged at the tavern and asked them to join their search for the *Pampero*. Upon reaching Palatka, the group learned the vessel's location, and they went to Dunn's Creek the next morning. Sigur surrendered the steamer to Holland, offering to produce later its coasting license issued in New Orleans. The inspector and his companion traveled on the *Pampero* to the Jacksonville wharf, where it was placed under guard at 8:00 P.M. on the 11th. The steamer crew and the filibuster leadership, including Titus and Gen. Benjamin Hopkins, checked into the Jacksonville Hotel.[71]

During the three days after the *Pampero*'s surrender, filibuster officers O'Hara, Macías, Rogers, Province, Reeves, Williamson, Saddler, and his son, registered at the Jacksonville Hotel. Customs collector Hart, alarmed by the arrival of more than one hundred filibusters in Jacksonville, ordered the captain of the revenue cutter *Jackson* to come into port, as "there are quite a number of desperate fellows, around here." He then informed Treasury secretary Thomas Corwin of their presence and asked if he should arrest them. The U.S. attorney for the Northern District of Florida, George W. Call, filed a libel suit against the *Pampero* on September 18 for violation of the revenue laws, and the trial was set for October 9 in the St. Augustine courthouse.[72]

Three days later Call informed Secretary of State Daniel Webster that Henry Titus had concealed the filibuster armament and recommended that "should any prosecution be deemed advisable I would point out this person as a proper subject; both because he was the leader of the expedition, and because his conduct since amounts to an almost open defiance of the law." The Democratic Jacksonville *Florida News* editorialized against a "purely vindictive" prosecution of the "unfortunate" men or the *Pampero,* who had "the sympathies and good wishes of this whole community."[73]

The *Pampero* libel trial was held in St. Augustine before U.S. District Court judge Isaac Hopkins Bronson, a former Democratic representative from New York. Sigur, as claimant of the vessel, was represented by McQueen McIntosh and Benjamin A. Putnam of St. Augustine, along with Robert Charlton, John Elliott Ward, and George S. Owens of Savannah. Witnesses testifying on October 11 included the expedition leaders Henry Titus, John L. Hopkins, Andrew Colvin, and Jacob Rutherford. That same day the provisions and stores confiscated from the *Pampero* were sold by the U.S. marshal in Jacksonville. The testimony of all the witnesses, including Samuel Buffington, concluded on October 14, and Judge Bronson adjourned court until December 1. Although the statements of Colvin did not greatly differ from those of the others, on the last day of testimony he filed charges against Titus in St. Johns County Circuit Court for "an assault and battery with intent to kill," in which case Hopkins and Rutherford had to post two-hundred-dollar bonds as material witnesses. The prosecutor was John P. Sanderson, a filibuster supporter, who dropped the charges against Titus eighteen months later when the witnesses failed to appear.[74]

Three weeks after the trial, Titus used a small schooner belonging to John Thompson, a member of Solomon's Lodge No. 20, to remove the expedition armament he left at the Hopkins plantation near Palatka. Customs collector Hart seized in Jacksonville the boat containing "sixty-nine boxes of fixed ammunition, a quantity of new harness, cavalry saddles, and one brass piece." Titus sued through the attorney James A. Peden to recover these articles, which he got back in December after the government failed to identify them. Four months later Titus sold the equipment to the Florida Militia.[75]

The final hearing of the *Pampero* trial began on December 1 with U.S. attorney Call summarizing that the steamer carried a false registry, had violated federal law by being used in an armed expedition against Cuba, and should therefore be forfeited according to law. The defense attorneys argued the technicalities of the Neutrality Law, alleging that the *Pampero* was not an armed vessel since no weapons were found in it but had "engaged in a mere transport service." The court ruled on December 11 against the steamer on both charges and ordered its sale at public auction. The *Pampero* was sold in Jacksonville on Saturday, January 17, 1852, to Capt. William Caldwell

Templeton of New Orleans for $15,525, one fourth of what Sigur paid for it. The steamer's furniture and apparel went for $425 to Thomas O. Holmes, a Jacksonville merchant. The local press reported, "There was little disposition by the public to bid high on the boat, as the friends of Mr. Segur [*sic*] expressed their wish to purchase for his interest."[76]

Titus remained in Jacksonville with his brother Ellett and in February 1852 established a grocery and provisions store. After Ellett returned from a business trip to Charleston, South Carolina, Titus began advertising in Jacksonville newspapers "The Cheap Cash Store of H. T. Titus" dealt in sundry goods including cigars, shotguns and Kentucky rifles, vintage wines and brandies, ladies' linen gaiters, boots and shoes, "Furniture, Hardware, Crockery, Glassware, &c." By the end of the year he was also advertising tools, chains, axes, and large quantities of flour, mackerel, pickled salmon, lard, sugar-cured hams, and cheese. Titus boasted that he would "sell lower for cash than can be bought in the southern country."[77]

Mary Evelina Titus.
From the author's collection

Edward Stevens Hopkins.
Courtesy of the State Archives of Florida

While in Jacksonville, twenty-nine-year-old Titus became romantically involved with nineteen-year-old Mary Evelina Hopkins, daughter of Florida Militia general Edward Stevens Hopkins. The Hopkins family had supported the Cuba filibuster expedition, and Titus had previously visited their home. They were "one of the best and most influential families" of Florida, and the patriarch was a Whig Party representative in the state legislature and owned a plantation with forty-six slaves. Titus and Mary Hopkins were married on Tuesday evening, March 16, 1852, at her birthplace of Darien, Georgia. The ceremony was performed in the residence of navy captain Robert Day by the Episcopalian clergyman Edward P. Brown of St. Simons Island. After their honeymoon, the newlyweds returned to Jacksonville.[78]

JUST RECEIVED,

AT H. T. TITUS' CASH GROCERY AND PROVISION STORE.

100 BARRELS best quality FLOUR; 20 kits No.1 MACKEREL, fresh; 15 kits No 1 PICKLED SALMON do 500 lbs LEAF LARD, best quality, 30 tubs RARIFIED LARD, for extra family use
1000 lbs sugar cured HAMS,
50 box CHEESE of superior quality.

ALSO,

A full assortment of Hardware, Planters, Tools and Implements of every description, including Corn Mills, Corn Shellers, Ploughs Hoes, Chains, Axes, &c. Also a large stock of

BOOTS AND SHOES,

Including men's coarse and fine Brogans, of every description. A large assortment of

Double-barrelled Guns,

of large size, KENTUCKY RIFLES,-full and whole stock. A large quantity of

WINES AND BRANDIES,

of older vintage than ever offered in this market, which I will sell lower for cash than can be bought in the southern country. Produce or good paper taken in exchange for goods.

N B—Planters and Lumbermen who wish large bills are respectfully invited to call and examine before buying elsewhere.   tier23

Ad for H. T. Titus's Cash
Grocery and Provision Store.
Jacksonville News, December 4, 1852

Titus was now part of a slave-owning family and became "more orthodox on the slavery question than Southern men themselves." He shared the belief of most chattel owners that slavery was a constitutional right and that abolitionist appeals to "the higher law" were transgressions against America's efficacious political, legal, and economic principles. On May 25, 1852, Titus participated in a public meeting at the Jacksonville courthouse of citizens desiring to defeat the projects of abolitionists trying to "entice our slave population to abscond." There had been a recent nocturnal attempt to assist three slaves working at the Bellechasse and Finegan sawmill into fleeing north on a vessel on the St. Johns River. The gathering was presided over by customs inspector Holland. Eloquent speeches were made by local notables who were chattel owners and supporters of Cuba filibustering, including Judge Felix Livingston; Colonels Bird Murphy Pearson, John P. Sanderson, and J. McRobert Baker; the Episcopal minister Isaac Swart; Stephen D. Fernandez; and Joseph Finegan. Titus, lacking the qualities of a public orator, did not address the crowd. The participants created a Committee of Vigilance and Safety, to which Titus, Finegan, Fernandez, Col. Samuel Buffington, and Capt. Joseph A. Barbee were appointed. The meeting adjourned for four days to allow the committee to present its report.[79]

On Saturday evening, May 29, Titus and other citizens advocating the protection of slave property met again at the Jacksonville courthouse. The officers of the previous meeting were at their seats when the report drafted by Titus and the vigilance committee was presented. It emphasized the Florida laws of 1832 and 1845 that punished slave stealing with death and punished those who enticed, aided, and abetted a runaway slave with a "fine not exceeding one thousand dollars, or standing in the pillory one hour, or be branded on the right hand with the letters S.S., or imprisoned for a term not exceeding six months." The problem was acquiring the proof against those who violated the laws. The committee was concerned that the expanding lumber trade and increased northern maritime commerce made Jacksonville "the most exposed and accessible point in the State for the operation of the abolitionists and their tools."[80]

Titus and the Committee of Vigilance and Safety warned that slaves allowed to go at large had greater opportunities for secreting themselves in vessels arriving and departing daily to load their cargo at remote and unfrequented points of the St. Johns River. They recommended that the city council pass ordinances for keeping the slave population "restrained within their proper limits" and "prohibiting masters from allowing slaves to hire their own time." The committee also recommended that the state legislature pass a law stating that finding a slave aboard a vessel for more than ten minutes without permission would charge the captain and crew with enticing the slave to run away. The committee requested that these resolutions be printed as a memorial and circulated throughout the county, urging the next General Assembly to adopt their suggestions. The Jacksonville newspapers were requested to publish the proceedings of the meeting. Two months later Titus participated in a Fourth of July banquet in the Buffington House, which assembled many local prominent citizens. After various toasts were raised, a drunken Titus, lacking oratory skills, bellowed, "Florida, for ever: Long may she wave."[81]

In late August 1852 newspaper accounts described how Theodore Titus and his son Ellett, who had nearly perished in a railroad accident a decade earlier, were survivors of a disaster collision between the steamer *Atlantic* and the propeller *Ogdensburg* on Lake Erie. The *Atlantic* was bound from Buffalo to Detroit when, at around 2:40 A.M. on August 20, it was rammed mid-ship by the *Ogdensburg*. The Tituses rushed from their cabin in the *Atlantic* to the upper deck and noticed that it was gradually sinking. There was panic on board as half of the 450 passengers were Norwegian emigrants who did not understand the English instructions given them. They cried out in terror in the darkness, and dozens jumped overboard. The Tituses donned life preservers, threw overboard a table, which they clung to once they were in the water, and drifted away for one hundred yards. Passengers around them who had lost their fortitude, especially children, were shrieking for help and drowning. After less than an hour, the *Ogdensburg* approached and rescued the Tituses along with 216 survivors, the other half of the passengers having perished. The names of "Mr. Titus and son, Detroit," appeared on newspaper lists of the cabin passenger survivors who were taken to Erie, Pennsylvania. Father and son testified at a coroner's inquest that morning regarding the accident. Ellett stated that he was from Jacksonville and was "awake and in conversation with my father when the collision took place." The night was "a little hazy, but it was star-light. Could see a long distance." Based on this visibility testimony and that of other witnesses, the jurors rendered a verdict of culpability against the first mate of the *Ogdensburg* for gross carelessness and recommended the case to a grand jury.[82]

Six months later Henry Titus published the last newspaper advertisement of his Jacksonville grocery store and ended the business. He turned to land speculation and the lumber business that he learned from his father. On July 1, 1853, he sold 306 acres in Jacksonville to John Roberts Jr. The next day he bargained an additional 33 acres to John H. Gardiner for forty dollars but reserved a six-month "privilege of cutting timber." Titus soon departed on the steamer *Carolina* for Charleston, seeking other business prospects. A month prior to the expiration of his timber agreement with Gardiner, Titus purchased 159.6 acres from Charles Craig in what today is West Jacksonville. Two months later Titus bought from the family of James Haskins an additional 80 acres adjacent west of his timberland, which included present-day Gregory Community Park.[83]

In October, Theodore Titus attended an exhibition in New York City, where he demonstrated a planing machine invented by Aretus Andrews Wilder of Detroit. The machine was described in *Scientific American* as differing from the others "in having the knives placed horizontally, and in a reciprocating frame, by the backward motion of which the board is drawn in. While the planes are acting upon it, it is held by clamps to the main bed. There is a table at the rear end of the machine, upon which are knives for matching the lumber if required." Henry Titus went into business with his father as "Proprietor and Agent for the sale of Rights" in the southern states of Wilder's Improved Planing Mill. His newspaper advertisement in the Jacksonville *Florida Republican* on December 15, 1853, boasted that the "Improved Planing and Tongueing and Grooving Machine" will "dress more lumber in ten hours, with less amount of power, than any Machine now before the public." All communications were to be addressed to him at "North River Planing Mill, 28th Street, New York."[84]

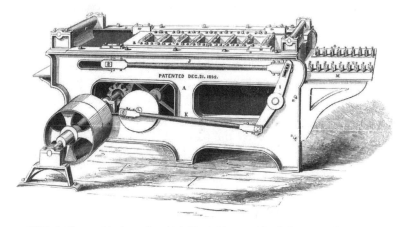

Wilder's Planing Machine, for which Henry Titus and his father were sales agents.
From *Scientific American,* March 26, 1853

Henry Titus and his wife departed by steamer for New York in mid-January 1854. They landed in Charleston, South Carolina, where he ran another advertisement in the *Courier.* It described the planing mill as "peculiarly adapted for Southern Pine" and requiring little power and repairs when compared to others. All communications were to be addressed to his father at "Mathawan, N.Y., or to H. T. Titus, care of J. Holmes, 100 Wall St.," New York. His father's address, by error or maliciousness, was wrong, as such a place did not exist and Theodore Titus resided in Matawan, New

Jersey. Henry Titus and his wife stayed in the North about a week and on the return trip to Jacksonville checked into the National Hotel in Washington, D.C., on January 26, 1854. Four days later they stopped in Charleston on the steamer *Wilmington* before reaching home.[85]

Henry Titus sometimes neglected his debts or settled business disagreements with violence. While in New York City, he contracted a debt for $88.75 with the coal dealer Denton Smith Halstead that he failed to pay. Halstead hired a law firm, which six months later obtained a ruling from the New York Supreme Court in favor of its client. In another court case in Jacksonville, Joseph Finegan, a thirty-nine-year-old Irish immigrant and lumber mill operator who owned fourteen slaves, testified in court that due to Titus's "reputation in this community, *I could not believe him under oath.*" In consequence Titus located Finegan on Sunday, February 19, 1854, at the Jacksonville steamboat wharf and pistol-whipped him. The next day, Finegan posted a handbill throughout the city denouncing Titus as a coward.[86]

The newspaper advertisements for the planing mill ceased on March 9, 1854. The next day Mary Titus received from her father a gift of ten acres on the south bank of the St. Johns River known as the "Ship Yard," launching Titus on a new sawmill venture. Two weeks later Theodore Titus received numerous impudent letters from his daughter-in-law. He wrote to his son on March 29 stating that the language in that correspondence "I know to be yours from the writing and the spirit they breathe." A family feud exploded over property settlements after the patriarch remarried. He chided his son in another letter for "language in reference to your second Mother that *few men, however base, in any way,* connected with their parents." The elder Titus claimed that all of his son's transactions had been a disadvantage to him. His entire investment in southern property had only rendered one thousand dollars in North Carolina. Titus was admonished by his father: "If your intention is only to benefit yourself, without risking a thing, all I ask of you is for you to cancel all the papers, and come to a fair settlement, and for the future go your own road. . . . Never did I expect to be taunted by my own children!"[87]

The following month, on April 5, 1854, a fire swept Jacksonville, destroying seventy buildings valued at more than three hundred thousand dollars. The entire business district, comprising twenty-three stores, was in ruins. The next day Titus departed on the steamer *Carolina* for Charleston, where the Southern Commercial Convention was meeting. On April 8 Henry Titus wrote to his father while in transit to New York for the summer. The family feud continued after he threatened to settle his accounts with his father through an attorney and affirming that "henceforth we are strangers." The patriarch responded on April 17, "Be it so . . . I blush for you to think you are so depraved." Henry Titus was warned that "vengeance of an overruling God may overtake you" because "your ungovernable temper leads you to acts I am sure you must be ashamed of on reflection, *or else there are few so base.*"[88]

Five days later, in another letter, the elder Titus revoked his son's agency for the sale of Wilder's Improved Planing Mill. He accused him of "purloining a deed intrusted to his care, and with making misstatements in relation to their business transactions." The patriarch again complained in a missive of June 18, "After having built up a business by which I was in hopes to have benefitted my children; and to be overreached by my son in the very first transaction. . . . If I could not take the word and honor of my own son, whose could I?" He then offered an olive branch to his firstborn by saying, "If I can see that you have regrets for your former conduct, I am willing to overlook the past and trust you again. . . . This is the last appeal I shall ever make to you to do me justice in our transactions."[89]

Henry Titus on August 13, 1854, returned to Charleston, where he purchased a thirty-five-year-old slave named Peter for $650 from the Jewish auctioneer Benjamin Mordecai. He then settled as an overseer on his father-in-law's 1,250-acre cotton plantation, "situated on Pablo Creek, eight miles from St. John's Bar, and adjoining the Diego Plains" in Mayport Mills. In September the Duval County Whig Convention elected Gen. Edward Stevens Hopkins as state senator. Titus was nominated by proxy to a seat in the convention, representing the St. John's Bar District, by the Freemason and former U.S. district attorney George Call, his nemesis during the *Pampero* trial. On October 4 Titus participated in another Whig meeting at the Duval County courthouse, where he proposed and headed a committee appointed "to gather information in regard to illegal votes in this county."[90]

Henry Titus continued expanding his economic affairs while frequently traveling in and out of Jacksonville. He is listed among the arrivals at the Buffington House the first week of January 1855. On May 1 Titus bought 240 acres along the west shore of the St. Johns River in Clay County to provide timber for his sawmill. The land encompassed what today is Knollwood Road on the north and west, Decoy Road on the south, and the river on the east, in Green Cove Springs. Six months later Titus enlarged his business venture at the "Ship Yard" by purchasing for two hundred dollars from his wife's uncle Benjamin Hopkins twenty acres adjacent to the ten his wife owned.[91]

The following year Titus renewed his political activism by participating on March 21, 1856, in a public meeting of the American (Know-Nothing) Party at the Jacksonville courthouse, backing the presidential electoral ticket of Millard Fillmore. The Whig Party was disintegrating after the passage of the Kansas-Nebraska Act, and many southern followers had regrouped in the new organization. In Florida the Know-Nothings avoided the anti-immigrant and anti-Catholic rhetoric of their national organization and emphasized the protection of slavery and loyalty to the Union. On a motion from Col. Samuel Buffington, forty-three activists were appointed delegates to attend their party's upcoming convention in Tallahassee that summer to nominate candidates for presidential electors, governor, member of Congress, and state officers. These included Titus, his father-in-law, former filibuster supporters, plantation owners, and other renowned citizens. Titus, however, would not be attending the assembly.[92]

The first half of Henry Titus's life had been filled with thrills and adventures. He had resided in five states and the bustling cities of Wilkes-Barre, Philadelphia, Louisville, and Jacksonville and had traveled widely. Titus acquired an education and worked as a sawyer, postal inspector, steamer clerk, grocer, land speculator, and plantation overseer. The Cuba expedition gave him notoriety and experience in combat. However, Titus avoided the John Quitman Cuba filibuster conspiracy of 1853–55, which was dismantled in the United States after the arrest and execution of Ramón Pintó and their counterparts on the island. Titus became an avowed defender of states' rights and slavery after marrying into a wealthy planter family. His bad business deals ended in lawsuits and fisticuffs with his creditors and a feud with his father. Titus dabbled in Whig politics but never transcended the grassroots level, lacking the skills of a public speaker. In the spring of 1856 he conceived an idea that would trump attending the Know-Nothing convention that summer.

★ *Chapter Two* ★

Bleeding in Kansas
1856

The *Florida Republican* announced on April 2, 1856, that Henry Titus "proposes to leave for Kansas in a few weeks." The article predicted that Titus would be successful in the new territory due to his "adaptation by experience, as well as by physical proportions for a frontier life." During the spring season river transit to Kansas was renewed, and thousands of new migrants were heading there. Titus had various motivations for moving, including a desire for cheap preemptive land, economic profit, and the defense of slavery.[1]

The Kansas-Nebraska Act of May 30, 1854, had opened both those territories to settlement and allowed for the status of slavery to be decided by popular sovereignty, annulling the Missouri Compromise of 1820. To keep the balance of power in Congress, the South "was willing to give Nebraska to the north, [and] they asked and demanded that Kansas should be ceded to the south." Preemptors began pouring into the Kansas river valleys and rolling prairies in search of fertile soil, land speculation, and government jobs. Northern free-soilers were encouraged by the abolitionist press, pulpit, and emigrant aid societies. Proslavery men, mostly from neighboring Missouri and dubbed "Border Ruffians" by their opponents, were driven by the political rhetoric of border leaders. Both sides eventually made "Bleeding Kansas" a battleground over slavery and land acquisition. By the summer of 1855, some twelve hundred armed New Englanders had arrived in the new territory. Sectional violence erupted in Kansas after the dubiously elected territorial legislature passed laws legalizing slavery and making Lecompton the territorial capital and the seat of federal authority. Free-soil settlers refused to succumb or pay taxes and in the fall of 1855 fraudulently elected a rival government at Topeka under a constitution outlawing slavery. In a special message on Kansas to Congress, President Franklin Pierce backed the Lecompton legislature and denounced the free-state movement as being "engaged in revolutionary acts which must be suppressed." Republican leaders made the status of Kansas the focal point of the 1856 presidential campaign.[2]

In the midst of this political controversy, Titus headed for Kansas with his "wife, children and servants" and "a colony of white men and a dozen slaves" from Florida and Georgia. Mary Titus had a strong character and personality, and she and her husband held deep convictions and beliefs. After traveling on the Mississippi River to St. Louis, Missouri, a bustling city of more than 120,000 people, the emigrants boarded a double side-wheel steamboat on the Missouri River bound for Kansas City, Missouri, with freight and passengers. A similar five-day voyage was later described by Mark Twain as "climbing over reefs and clambering over snags patiently and laboriously all day long." The upward struggle against the turbid current of the Missouri included repeated stoppages at various town landings to disgorge passengers and cargo and take on wood and freight. At Kansas City the Tituses lodged overnight in the American Hotel, on the corner of Wyandotte Street and the Levee. The brick four-and-a-half-story structure, on a high bluff overlooking the Missouri River, was the only hostelry in town. The next day the Titus party boarded another steamer at the levee, which took them fifty miles west on the Kansas River to Lecompton, located on a bluff on its southern bank. The town contained a legislative assembly hall and twenty-five dwellings, including a few taverns, and Irishmen were busy erecting the foundation of the capitol. Lecompton was flanked by the free-state river communities of Lawrence, twelve miles eastward, and Topeka, ten miles to the west.[3]

The Titus coterie arrived on May 1, 1856, and the next day the Buford expedition, some four hundred men mostly from Alabama, South Carolina, and Georgia and led by Jefferson Buford, entered Kansas and scattered about to make squatter claims. Titus established a homestead on a 160-acre tract of preempted land one mile south of Lecompton, along the west side of present-day Douglas County Road 1029. The land today is occupied in part by twenty-six tanks of the Heetco propane gas dealer. Titus constructed a four-room log house that had a loft with gables facing north and south, rifle portholes, a portico, a stable, rail fences, and a hedge of stones defending the entrance. The logs, less than six inches in diameter, were "hewn and laid close together." Some of the men and the slaves who accompanied him lived in nearby tents. The dwelling, four hundred yards east of the road, was on a ridge where a farmer presently keeps more than four hundred bales of rolled

hay. The free-soilers called the residence Fort .
camp in Douglas County, the others being a blo⌐
the village of Franklin five miles southeast of Lawren⌐
house of Capt. James P. Saunders, called "Fort Saunders,
of Col. B. F. Treadwell, on a high bluff on the south side ⌐
Creek, twelve miles southwest of Lawrence. Free-soilers regarde⌐
strongholds as a threat to "cut off Lawrence from help and from sup⌐
Fort Titus was "the strongest and most annoying of the three forts." ⌐ne
abolitionist press indicated, "From these strongholds they would sally forth,
'press' horses and cattle, intercept the mails, rob stores and dwellings, plunder travelers, burn houses, and destroy crops."[4]

The antislavery *New York Tribune, New York Times,* and St. Louis *Missouri Democrat* were the only newspapers that had regular "correspondents" in Kansas during the troubles. Southern journals, outmatched in resources, and small-town editors relied on the gossipy missives of local immigrants for news. Both sides bombarded editors with real or imagined atrocity tales in ferocious hues. The abolitionist propagandists were James Redpath, Thomas Wentworth "Worcester" Higginson, William Addison Phillips, and Hugh "Potter" Young, of the *Tribune;* William B. "Randolph" Hutchinson, James M. Winchell, and Samuel F. Tappan wrote for the *New York Times.* Other abolitionists who sporadically wrote fiery rhetoric from Kansas were Richard J. "Kent" Hinton of the *Boston Traveller,* the *New York Post,* and the *Chicago Tribune;* John Henry Kagi, correspondent for the *New York Post,* the *New York Tribune,* and the *Washington National Era;* and Richard Realf of the *Illinois State Gazette.* Redpath also published in the *Missouri Democrat* and the *Chicago Tribune,* and he along with all the others were "earnest supporters" and apologists for free-state depredations and the fanatical abolitionist John Brown. Redpath, Phillips, Hinton, Young, and Realf were British immigrants. All of these journalists became active participants in the free-state movement. The twenty-two-year-old Redpath had the rank of major in James H. "Jim" Lane's "Army of the North" and later acknowledged that he went to Kansas "to precipitate a revolution." Hutchinson praised free-state violence: "If it must take blood to wash our skirts of Slavery—blood it is." Kagi and Realf two years later became cabinet members in Brown's insurrectional government.[5]

The free-state propagandists constantly derided their opponents in print, and Titus was a lightning rod for their vituperation. Border Ruffians were vilified as vulgar, degraded, loafers, squalid, and murderous villains. Their alcoholic proclivities were rife in the Bleeding Kansas literature and cartoons, which did not mention tosspot free-soilers, even though there were grog

...awrence, the Free State Hotel kept "a good stock" of "wines and ... uors," a Lawrence Temperance Association was organized, and the *Herald of Freedom* denounced "dead drunk" Indians roaming the town and said that "our friends Allen & Gordon, at Topeka, were engaged in the liquor traffic." Gov. Wilson Shannon, committed to popular sovereignty, was depicted as being drunk "at every opportunity" since taking office. In contrast, Shannon's biographer indicated that "throughout his life he seldom consumed alcoholic beverages of any kind." Proslavery editors minimized the violence in Kansas to avoid discouraging the recruitment of southern emigrants and largely directed their attacks at free-soil leaders. The contending writers promoted sectional hatred and alienation and made a major contribution to the excitement and suspicion of the race to settle Kansas.[6]

The northern press had boasted for months that the free-state capital of Lawrence, population three hundred, was an armed camp. Redpath reported in the *Missouri Democrat* that "two thousand stands of rifles and twenty breech-loading cannon" had been smuggled into Lawrence. The "fortified city" was surrounded by four large circular earthworks one hundred feet in diameter and seven feet high with a four-foot timber walk on top and several lines of ditches and entrenchments engineered by Jim Lane. The Eldridge House, called the Free State Hotel, was administered by thirty-nine-year-old Col. Shalor Winchell Eldridge. It was described as a "fortress" with sentinels on the roof behind a parapet wall "three and a half feet, with four port-holes in each side—making in all sixteen—large enough to admit the mouth of an eighteen-pounder gun. The mouths of the holes were concealed from view by a thin coat of lime that could be easily knocked out when desired." The "strongly constructed three-story stone building," with thick walls fifty feet by seventy feet in length and an addition of twenty-four by forty-five feet, a basement, fifty rooms, and a hallway in each floor, was built for twenty thousand dollars by the abolitionist New England Emigrant Aid Company. It had "30 or 40 port-holes in the walls, [so] that the building may be converted into a citadel in case of further invasion." According to Phillips, "Two chambers in the third story, in the south-east corner of the building, were the council-room and the general's quarters. Many of the companies had their quarters in the hotel. Below, the dining-hall was used as a general place of reception for the soldiers. Two sentinels guarded the door, to let none in but those who had business or had the password." The facility never opened as public lodging.[7]

On May 11, 1856, ten days after Titus arrived in Kansas, U.S. marshal Israel D. Donalson called on Douglas County sheriff Samuel J. Jones and all "law-abiding citizens" to help him execute eight writs in Lawrence in a legally constituted posse authorized by Governor Shannon. The orders had been issued by territorial supreme court chief justice Samuel Dexter Lecompte against free-state Kansas Volunteers commander in chief Maj. Gen. Charles L. Robinson, his second in command Brig. Gen. Jim Lane, and six other free-state leaders. They had been indicted by a Douglas County territorial grand jury for high treason for usurping office and levying war against the government. The accused were previously summoned as witnesses before the judicial body but did not appear. Jones had on three previous occasions gone to Lawrence, where he was disarmed, punched in the face, and shot in the back while trying to serve the warrants. U.S. deputy marshal William Perry Fain, a thirty-one-year-old from Calhoun, Georgia, had likewise been prohibited by a mob from making an arrest there two weeks earlier. Free-state colonel John A. Perry tried to intimidate Fain by saying that his superior, Gen. Samuel Clarke Pomeroy, wanted him to know that he had two thousand men under his command at Lawrence. Donalson had "every reason to believe that any attempt to execute there writs will be resisted by a large body of armed men."[8]

The grand jury also issued an order to abate the Free State Hotel stronghold and the presses of the antislavery newspapers *Herald of Freedom* and *Kansas Free State,* characterized as nuisances. The hotel "had been used as a fortress" and an "arsenal" for military occupation and defense "as a stronghold of resistance to law." The "seditious" newspapers were indicted because "they had urged the people to resist the enactments passed" by the territorial governor. Shannon determined that the Free State Hotel garrison and the fortified houses of George Washington Brown, editor of the *Herald of Freedom,* and Josiah Miller, editor of the *Kansas Free State,* and the store of George W. and William B. Hutchinson and Co., which supplied the free-state Volunteers, were "forts" and "nuisances" that "must go down—they can't be tolerated any longer."[9]

The call for assistance from the authorities prompted Titus quickly to organize the Douglas County Militia company with 180 mounted riflemen. They enrolled in the marshal's posse comitatus, and Governor Shannon, the commander in chief of the territorial militia, provided them with U.S. Mississippi rifles and bayonets. The enticement was more economic than political with the offer of a dollar a day plus rations and a portion of whiskey for service. Militia camps "were formed at different points along the highways and on the Kansas River" to interdict assistance to Lawrence. Titus and his men proceeded to the camp of various proslavery militias on the 1,109-foot summit of Coon Point, at the head of Coon Creek, five miles southwest of Lecompton and eight miles west of Lawrence, where Oregon Trail settlers rested on their westward trek.[10]

The encampment was headed by Col. John H. Stringfellow, a physician and editor of the *Squatter Sovereign* newspaper, who commanded the Third Regiment of Kansas Territorial Militia. Different flags fluttered on the windy hilltop, including the South Carolina Company of Maj. Warren D. Wilkes, a twenty-six-year-old attorney and newspaper publisher from Anderson, South Carolina. His sixteen followers wore red shirts and had a red flag with a white star in its center emblazoned "Southern Rights" on one side and "South Carolina" on the other. The company was sponsored by the Kansas Committee of Columbia, South Carolina, chaired by former senator William Ford De Saussure, a trustee of South Carolina College (now the University of South Carolina) in Columbia. The Buford Company displayed a banner bearing the motto "The Supremacy of the White Race" on one side and "Kansas, the Outpost" on the reverse. Other standards included the United States flag and another with a white background and black stripes, and the Doniphan Tigers from Doniphan County flew a white banner with purple stripes depicting in the upper corner a tiger couchant surrounded by stars.[11]

On the night of May 14, the pickets of a proslavery militia camp near Franklin stopped and searched a wagon headed for Lawrence. They found a secret compartment containing "thirty-eight guns and some half dozen sabres," which were seized and distributed among the Alabamians. Two days later free-state colonel John A. Perry was taking a letter from the Lawrence Committee of Safety to Marshal Donalson and Governor Shannon in Lecompton when he "was stopped about four miles from Lawrence by Col. Titus, with some fifty horsemen armed with United States muskets, shotguns, pistols, bowie-knives, &c., and questioned very closely" regarding his business and destination before being allowed to proceed. After delivering the message, Perry was again halted by Titus and his company on his return to Lawrence. Titus requested to see his pass, and Perry showed him the one he had received from Shannon. The free-state activist told Titus that "he and his men had better be at work instead of riding around there, for they would earn enough to buy a farm each while they were fussing around there." Titus replied, "Your people of Lawrence won't let us."[12]

That evening, Friday the 16th, two Yankees without identification papers, William Mitchell and Dr. Joseph Pomeroy Root, were riding their mules near the Coon Point proslavery camp when they were detained by pickets. Both were leaders of the free-state Prairie Guard Militia of Wabaunsee who had been sent by the Connecticut Kansas Company, also called the Beecher Bible and Rifle Colony, to investigate rumors of disturbances in the vicinity of Lawrence. Mitchell and Root were taken before Capt. William F. Donalson, the twenty-five-year-old son of Marshal Donalson, acting on his father's behalf, who confiscated their weapons and remitted them to a tent under guard. The next morning the strangers were separately queried by Stringfellow. Titus participated in the interrogation, which the detainees described as "close and vulgar, and overbearing." He asked them "if they would steal niggers" and questioned the condition and purposes of their colony, their number of rifles, and what they intended to do with them. The northerners were afterward remanded to custody. That afternoon, as the *New York Herald* correspondent was leaving Franklin, he saw that "Col. Titus' company of mounted riflemen passed through it on a scout. We learn that in going through Lawrence, Col. Titus' men produced no little stir, as the free State people got on the housetops to see the Border Ruffian cavalry ride by."[13]

By May 19 the proslavery forces answering Donalson's call had arrived at Douglas County from every quarter. The Lecompton encampment contained "about 50 tents and upward of 400 men" with eight captives, including two fugitive free-state men recently seized in Missouri by a proslavery militia. The next morning, wearing a grayish hickory shirt, Titus appeared at the entrance "with a huge knife in his hand" and stared at those inside trying to make identification. When the new detainees were about to address him, Titus "hissed through his closed teeth: 'G--d d--n you, don't speak to me, if you do I will cut your G--d d--n throat for you.'" Titus was seen early that afternoon leading a cavalry drill of his 180 mounted men, who were "dashing over the hills at the clear tones of their commander's voice." At 3:00 P.M. Donalson ordered all the militias to march under "the martial notes of a drum and fife" to a camp at Franklin, five miles from Lawrence. They were joined there at 6:00 by an additional 150 men with three cannons.[14]

On May 21 at 3:00 A.M. Titus and "at least two hundred men, mounted on fine horses," escorted a cannon to Mount Oread, three quarters of a mile from Lawrence. The artillery piece was positioned on a ridge about five hundred yards southeast of the free-state earthworks. During the next few hours, hundreds more proslavery men on foot and horseback arrived at Mount Oread. The force included Dr. Stringfellow's militia regiment from Coon Point; former Missouri senator David Rice Atchison with seventy men of his Platte County Rifles and two artillery pieces; Gen. George Washington Clarke's militia company; Capt. Alex H. Dunning's Doniphan Tigers; the Kickapoo Rangers under Capt. Charles Dunn; and a Fort Leavenworth dragoon company.

Colonel Buford temporarily commanded the Franklin force, and Titus had charge of the cavalry, while the U.S. marshal controlled the whole. At dawn a free-state leader was seen haranguing some 150 men gathered in front of the Free State Hotel. Titus and his cavalry "were relieved by the infantry and marched off to breakfast." The federal posse seized as headquarters the abandoned hillside two-story frame house of Charles L. Robinson, the chief resident agent of the New England Emigrant Aid Company and illegally inaugurated "governor" of the free-state party, who was under indictment for high treason. Free-state colonel John A. Perry abandoned his fortified residence on Mount Oread and went to Lawrence, later claiming that he was looted out of money, a rifle, and clothing. The proslavery force occupied all the roads leading to Lawrence and cut off communication or assistance.[15]

After 10:00 Marshal Donalson sent his deputy William Perry Fain with eight men to the Free State Hotel. The posse was comprised of Capt. John "Jack" Donaldson and members of his red-shirt Lecompton Guards. Free-state militants Col. George Washington Deitzler and Judge George W. Smith peacefully surrendered in the hotel as Colonel Eldridge informed the deputy that the other indicted men were gone. Eldridge conveyed the prisoners in his hack to the U.S. marshal at Mount Oread, where Titus and his cavalry returned at noon. The posse was then told that "Sheriff Jones had some processes to serve, and that they would hold themselves in readiness to go with him." Dr. John H. Gihon described Jones as six feet tall, with light hair and "his features irregular and unprepossessing." William Phillips added that he "was a strongly-built man" with "a slightly sinister expression." In contrast, *Herald* correspondent G. Douglas Brewerton found the sheriff "a fine-looking young man." A historian portrayed Jones as "a man of great energy, noise, violence, courage and sincerity."[16]

The sheriff, who was "quite weak and much bent" with "pale countenance and emaciated form" from a bullet in his back during a prior assassination attempt at Lawrence, "was received with loud and deafening cheers" as he rode along the line. He gave Titus command of a posse of eighteen mounted men mostly from Capt. Robert De Treville's Palmetto Rifles of Charleston, South Carolina. They arrived at the free-state barracks at 1:00 P.M. carrying Mississippi rifles with bayonets. The sheriff gave General Pomeroy five minutes to surrender all his "cannon and rifles." Pomeroy along with free-state lieutenant governor William Y. Roberts and others soon relinquished a brass twelve-pounder mountain howitzer, dubbed the "Abbott howitzer," and "one 8-pounder and two 6-pounder" swivels. Phillips claimed that the latter were instead "four other small brass breech-loading cannon, carrying a pound ball," that "were nearly useless." The number of Sharps rifles seized ranged from a few up to two hundred, depending on the pro- or antislavery press, while Pomeroy received a receipt for the confiscated weapons.[17]

At 3:15 P.M., with the temperature ranging above ninety degrees, Sheriff Jones told Colonel Eldridge that he had a grand jury order to destroy the stronghold and the presses inside and gave him two hours to remove his furniture. When the hotel administrator balked, the posse dumped most of the furniture on the street. Eldridge and his family placed some personal effects in carriages and were escorted out of town. Lawrence residents began fleeing for the nearby woods when, according to the free-soiler Samuel C. Smith, some five hundred proslavery militia, including two companies commanded by Titus, poured into the streets "yelling like savages." James Redpath acknowledged that "no resistance was attempted." According to Dr. Gihon, "Titus had been one of the most active of the assailants in the sacking of Lawrence. On that occasion he rode through the town, giving his orders in a loud voice, and urging on his men to the work of destruction." The colonel "declared boldly that the printing presses must be destroyed, to satisfy the boys from South Carolina." They first headed for the *Kansas Free State* printing office on the second floor of a concrete building. Its antislavery editor Josiah Miller was a South Carolinian accused by his proslavery provincials of treason against their native state. Volunteer officer Colonel Perry, who had retreated to Mount Oread, saw the "printing presses and furniture" being thrown out in the street. Simultaneously the Carolinians entered the Free State Hotel and broke the platen, weights, and movable parts off the heavy cast iron *Herald of Freedom* press. The streets in front of both newspaper offices were strewn with papers, books, hundreds of pounds of lead type, and broken machinery.[18]

Colonel Perry saw the South Carolina red flag with a lone star first hoisted over the *Kansas Free State* office before it later waved over the hotel. Two Carolinians had "planted it on one of the small chimneys on top of the hotel." The prodigious effect was "one tremendous and long-continued shout burst from the ranks." The *Lecompton Union* boasted, "Thus floated victoriously the first banner of Southern rights over the abolition town of Lawrence, unfurled by the noble sons of Carolina, and every whip of its folds seemed a death-stroke to Beecher propagandism and the fanatics of the East. O! That its red folds could have been seen by every Southern eye!"[19]

Jones had four small artillery pieces placed 150 feet across the street from the Free State Hotel at 5:00 P.M. and announced to Eldridge that the bombardment would start in five minutes. The artillery discharged between a dozen and thirty-two shots, depending on conflicting accounts, doing little damage and proving too slow a method of destruction. According to Redpath, who was absent, the posse simultaneously fired "by platoons" at the windows. Three kegs of powder were placed in the cellar, but only one ignited and without the desired effect. When James F. Legate, a twenty-seven -year-old Massachusetts native, allegedly questioned the sheriff's authority to wreck the presses and the hotel, Jones cited the court order he received based on the grand jury findings. Legate described Titus as the military commander of the posse and heard him give the order "to set the building on fire." The conflagration started at 5:30 P.M. in the newspaper office in the center of the edifice and in other areas, which were quickly consumed by the flames. The walls "trembled and fell" to the accompanying "shouts and yells of the mob." Titus proceeded to the store of G. W. and W. Hutchinson and Co. and shouted, "I think there are some Sharps rifles in there; stave her in boys, if she is locked." Ten Carolinians broke the front door window to enter, while others ransacked Legate's boardinghouse. Legate claimed that he lost all his clothing, $538 in cash, and many of his private letters.[20]

A room in the store serving as the post office was looted, and Colonel Stringfellow seized some of its contents looking for incriminating abolitionist correspondence to publish in his _Squatter Sovereign_. All "the houses of the Free state men were pillaged, except the Cincinnati Hotel," which was owned by two women. The floor in the home of the editor George Washington Brown, who was imprisoned in Lecompton for treason, burned before locals extinguished it. While Titus allegedly urged "the destruction of the whole town," Senator Atchison, who "was conspicuous amongst the mob," advised moderation, while "Col. [Zadock] Jackson, of Georgia, with many others, were opposed to the burning of the hotel." Colonel Buford "also disclaimed having come to Kansas to destroy property, and condemned the course which had been taken." That evening the Mount Oread home of Charles L. Robinson was torched. Col. Peter T. Abell, who was "over six feet tall and weighed almost 300 pounds," detailed a company to snuff the fire. When another blaze started, "Sheriff Jones had the flames suppressed, and the boys guilty of the act were sent immediately to camp." However, the house fell to arson a third time about 10:00. When the posse began dispersing an hour before sunset, Titus allegedly declared "that if ever he came into the place again he would kill every damned Abolitionist in it."[21]

The "sack of Lawrence" provided the antislavery press the first opportunity to depict the conflict as "a general reign of terror in the Territory," although not one free-soiler was harmed. Redpath, reporting from Leaven-worth, wrote in the St. Louis Missouri *Democrat* that "upwards of $200,000 worth of property in and about Lawrence was destroyed or carried off," even though the cost of the Free State Hotel was twenty thousand dollars. His article in the *New York Tribune* was headlined "From Kansas: Lawrence in Ashes." The yellow journalist, who was thirty-five miles away, decried that the nighttime fire at Lawrence could be seen from fifteen miles away, indi-cating "no doubt but that the town is in ashes and many of its inhabitants butchered." It was reported that the wail of helpless and abused women rose to heaven, and Redpath said that there were two rapes a few days prior to the attack and "two hundred horses and large herds of horned cattle" stolen. Phillips wrote of "frightful stories of outrages, and of women being ravished." A letter to the editor in the *Boston Telegraph* alleged that a gentleman recently arrived from Lawrence stated that a party of "white savages" went to the nearby claim of "a matronly woman and her two daughters; that they vio-lently abused the mother in her own house, and took her daughters to their tent and kept them during the invasion!" In contrast, the *New York Herald* correspondent in Westport wrote that members of the New England Emi-grant Aid Company, which owned the Free State Hotel, "have done their utmost to stir up this war—they have kindled the fire, and should not com-plain now that they have scorched their hands."[22]

Some three hundred Lawrencians "were greatly exasperated at their lead-ers, because they had deserted in the hour of their difficulties." The forti-fied Free State Hotel and the four earthworks around the town had been abandoned without a shot fired. No free-state Volunteer companies in the territory went to Lawrence in its time of need. The two thousand men whom Pomeroy told the marshal he commanded never appeared, and their repu-tation for courage was lost. Eldridge "estimated his loss at $10,000–$1,800 of which was in groceries, wines, segars, &c. . . . He declines to have any-thing to do with the furniture saved, as he expects Congress will have to remunerate him for the loss." Instead the federal government a few days later paid $17,600 to the members of the marshal's posse for services during twenty-two days. Governor Shannon immediately requested that the army station dragoon companies of one hundred men each at the trouble spots of Lecompton, Lawrence, and Leavenworth, which was promptly done. The abolitionists used the Lawrence incident to call publicly on antislavery advo-cates for help after turning a military defeat into a moral and political victory. The independent *New York Herald* warned, "It is natural that the people of the Northern States should be opposed to slavery, and that the people of the Southern States should be in favor of it. But no civil war need necessarily flow out of this difference in opinion."[23]

The next day, May 22, Dr. Joseph Root and William Mitchell went to Marshal Donalson's office in Lecompton to recover their seized property. Titus entered with a man named Elliot, cursing about free-state captain Samuel Walker, leader of the eighty-six-member Bloomington Guards, and boasted that "he would have his head, on or off his shoulders, and for it he would give any man five hundred dollars." In contrast, the abolitionist Phillips wrote that Titus "offered three hundred dollars for his head." Titus afterward led a posse of sixty men who surrounded the home of fifty-nine-year-old John Allen Wakefield, the free-state territorial treasurer elect under the Topeka Convention, and took him prisoner. Wakefield had the previous month traveled to St. Paul, Minnesota, to recruit among Republicans for volunteers, weapons, and funds. When Wakefield appeared before Judge Samuel Lecompte, he used his lawyer's skills to demand "the indictment, affidavit or other legal document" authorizing his arrest. The judge asked who had arrested him, and Wakefield identified Titus. Attorney General Andrew J. Isaacs stated that he would go ask Titus what charges were made against the prisoner. He soon returned to announce that no writ had been issued against Wakefield, who was immediately released. Wakefield claimed three years later that Titus's men took from him two large horses and that when he recovered them ten days later, they "were damaged to the amount of over fifty dollars."[24]

In reprisal for the Lawrence raid, Dr. Gihon wrote that parties of desperate free-state men "attacked the proslavery men in the roads and at their dwellings, and committed most flagrant outrages." Their motivation was "in many instances as much by a disposition to plunder as from a spirit of retaliation and revenge for insults and injuries they had received." On the night of May 24, the zealot John Brown carried out the Pottawatomie Creek massacre of five proslavery men, including a father and his two sons and a member of the territorial House of Representatives. The northern press refuted the account that the abolitionists had used broadswords and "literally cut and hacked them to pieces, cutting off their ears and faces, and mangling them in the most shocking manner." Brown told his followers that it was necessary to "strike terror into the hearts of the Proslavery party." The next day Hutchinson wrote from Lawrence to the *New York Times* that "Brown is a man of most desperate courage, and when the time comes he will gain for himself much distinction." He also stated that the radical abolitionist was not in the vicinity when a proslavery "mob" called on a free-state man in the night and threatened to hang him, prompting his comrades to rally and shoot five of their enemy dead.[25]

Redpath tried to justify the murders with a phony "eye-witness" account in the St. Louis *Missouri Democrat* and the *Chicago Tribune* claiming that the five were ambushed and killed while trying to hang a free-state man. Phillips described Brown as "a strange, resolute, repulsive, iron-willed, inexorable old man" and alleged that "the frightful stories about mutilations were unfounded, as applied to this affair," since Indians, whom he despised, did the atrocities. He blamed "the corrupt government and perverted official authority" for the Pottawatomie Creek slaughter. Hugh "Potter" Young in the *Tribune* called Brown a "venerable hero" and said that "the expression of his countenance indicates anything else than the ferocious character in which the Border newspapers paint him." Free-soilers later tried justifying the murders as retaliation for the attack on Lawrence even though no homicides occurred there. Until that moment "Bleeding Kansas" had been virtually bloodless after two years of agitation. The Pottawatomie Creek massacre started a war in which contending armed bands roved the territory committing depredations and murders.[26]

Six days later, on May 30, Titus and his Douglas County Militia rode with Governor Shannon, Marshal Donalson, other militia companies, and Capt. Samuel Davis Sturgis with about fifty soldiers to the homestead of free-state captain Samuel Walker, seven miles west of Lawrence. The previous night a U.S. deputy marshal accompanied by the governor's son, the Lecompton postmaster, and others had been fired on when arriving at the Walker house, wounding one man and killing a horse. Shannon had warrants for treason against Walker, James Redpath, John Wakefield, William Hazeltine, and six other free-state participants. The Republican *Kansas Tribune* accused Titus, twenty-two-year-old John Shannon, and others of attacking Walker's residence. However, Walker's memoirs excluded Titus from the incident and mentioned that the governor's son, who was taken prisoner and released the next day, had been reported killed. Shannon posted a five-hundred-dollar reward for the capture of the fugitive Walker, and after not finding him at home, the posse headed for the Hazeltine farm later that night. As they approached the homestead, Walker was proceeding down the road in the same direction and saw them coming. He later reminisced, "I jumped into a clump of bushes not ten feet from the path and cocked my rifle, determined to kill the governor at least, if I was discovered." The posse did not see him and arrested Hazeltine at home.[27]

According to *Tribune* correspondent Phillips, the governor then gathered a dozen dragoons, who were part of Companies F and K of the First Cavalry camped near Lecompton, and a proslavery staff, with "Colonel Titus being its chief pillar and ornament, his Fidus Achates, and legal and military adviser to boot." They went about for two days in the Bloomington area, whose free-soil residents had formed a Volunteer force and helped slaves escape via the Underground Railroad. Shannon, towering at six feet, six inches tall, stout, with iron-gray hair and "a deep, strong voice," personally disarmed anyone with a Sharps rifle, which he defined as "used only for war purposes." The weapon, dubbed "Beecher's Bible," was a 52-caliber carbine, breech-loading and self-priming, renowned for high accuracy at five hundred yards while firing eight to ten shots per minute. Walker claimed that Titus later returned to his home and gave his thirty-one-year-old wife Marian two hours to clear out the furniture, which she and her six children placed along the road. He gives no explanation for this purpose, since his property was not destroyed. The Walker family spent the night at the neighboring Wakefield home, whose patriarch was escorted by Capt. George A. Cutler and thirty free-state men to Lawrence. Walker admitted that he then bushwhacked an armed Alabamian heading to Lecompton. He tied him to a tree and "stripped off everything valuable he had." After the man escaped and had Walker indicted for highway robbery, in reprisal "Captain Abbott's company attacked the fellow's store in Franklin and cleaned him out of everything."[28]

A month later, on the evening of June 26, Titus participated in a public meeting held in Kendall's Hall at Lecompton. Presiding over the gathering was Col. Ely Moore of New York, the register of the local U.S. land office, who announced that postmaster Dr. Aristides Rodrique had received a letter from his brother in New York inquiring into the possibility of obtaining claims for up to five hundred proslavery settlers. On a motion by Titus, it was agreed that "a committee of five be appointed to prepare suitable resolutions, expressive of the sense of the citizens of Lecompton." Titus and four others were named to the committee, which drafted a unanimously approved preamble and resolutions. They called for assisting the newcomers "in selecting desirable locations" and rendering services "as may be conducive to their welfare and comfort." Orators praised conservative northerners who sided "with the South upon the great principle of non-interference in the domestic institutions of the States and Territories."[29]

M. H. Dozier, a twenty-two-year-old Kentuckian who arrived in Kansas with the Titus party, on July 12 surveyed a claim a mile and one-half from Lecompton that lacked a dwelling or cultivated land and erected his own shack on it. A few days later the free-soiler Jacob Smith appeared and began framing a lean-to, telling Dozier that he had located the claim a year earlier but left it "for the purpose of making money." According to the preemption law, a settler had to build and live in a house on the claim and make improvements on it such as fencing or plowing. The uncertainty about inchoate land titles and boundaries prompted many personal confrontations during the territorial period. The *New York Tribune* claimed that Governor Shannon had previously tried to negotiate with Smith to purchase the claim but that the deal failed when the free-soiler demanded the astronomical sum of one thousand dollars. Dozier alleged that he and Titus went to see Smith to make an arrangement to purchase the claim but that "Smith became excited and boasted that he would hold his claim in defiance of Law, [and] that he intended to raise enough men to put me off of my claim." Dozier claimed that Smith "made demonstrations of fight" toward the brawny Titus, who then "caught him by the shoulders and jerked him down, and told him if he did not behave himself he would give him a whipping." Dozier later gave a sworn statement saying that Titus did not strike Smith and that they did not burn his house. He alleged that it was Smith who "set my house on fire, but I reached there just in time to extinguish the flames" and that Titus did not incinerate Smith's dwelling.[30]

In contrast, an unsigned correspondence on July 20 to a Massachusetts Republican newspaper claimed that Titus and Dozier beat Smith "most cruelly, stamping him with their feet, and leaving him partly covered with blood. Titus then directed his accomplice to burn down Smith's house which accordingly was done. . . . This doughty Titus declared that no d--d Yankee should live in that vicinity." Smith's friends notified Governor Shannon that "unless justice shall be done to Titus by the authorities, *they will take it into their own hands.*" The anonymous writer issued a foreboding threat: "Col. Titus may yet meet with the punishment due to his crime, rather more summary perhaps than he would desire." Redpath described Titus as "a very powerful man" who along with a companion "administered a persuasive beating to inculcate resignation" to the claim. Titus refuted the accusation, saying that Smith had voluntarily left his claim earlier, "when it was jumped by a citizen of Lecompton, who never took possession of it." Afterward, Dozier "in the latter part of July entered upon it."[31]

Titus was demonized by Redpath in the *Tribune* article "Brutality of Col. Titus," which repeated and grossly exaggerated the assault on Smith. The account was reprinted in abolitionist newspapers for weeks. Titus was called a "hound" and "Gov. Shannon's right-hand man and the same one that offered $500 for the head of Capt. Walker." Redpath claimed that it was Titus, instead of Dozier, who desired the property and that the colonel "had plenty of his crew to back him" so as to "be perfectly safe in attempting a fistfight" with the free-soiler. After "pounding Smith to his heart's content," Titus ordered a reluctant underling to burn his building and "drew his revolver and threatened to shoot him unless he obeyed." When Smith's friends protested to Shannon, the governor ordered "a company of U.S. dragoons, to defend Titus in his assumed right to the claim and improvements." No mention was made that Dozier, and not Titus, had been living on the disputed land for the previous two weeks. Redpath repeated this version in the *Tribune* for the third time in a month eight days later, which had free-state militants clamoring for revenge against Titus.[32]

The *New York Times* correspondent Samuel F. Tappan accused Titus on July 21 of taking "a leading part in every outrage committed against Free-State people." He blamed Titus for assaulting Smith and burning his cabin. The Republican *Kansas Tribune* claimed that Titus also had "charge of the stores in Lecompton to feed the mob." Redpath alleged in the Missouri *Democrat* that Titus suggested to Governor Shannon that he call out the territorial militia to enforce the tax laws that the free-soilers refused to recognize and that Shannon replied, "I *understand* this calling out of the militia of Kansas. It means calling over the State of Missouri here, which I won't do." Shannon was the scapegoat of the national press and politicians for the Kansas turmoil during the previous year. He was a liability to the Democrats four months before the presidential election. On July 28 President Pierce appointed John Geary, a Mexican War veteran and former mayor of San Francisco, to replace him. Before leaving office, Shannon, who like Titus was a Freemason, commissioned Titus as colonel of the Second Regiment, First Brigade, Southern Division, Kansas Territorial Militia, on August 5.[33]

Five days later, according to Redpath, Titus went to the home of his free-state neighbor, fifty-seven-year-old Pennsylvanian Benjamin S. Hancock, with a group of subordinates and demanded pay for cattle that he accused him of butchering. The neighbor denied the charge, to which Titus "told him that he must pay for them or he would have his life on the spot." Hancock allegedly slammed shut his house door, abandoned his twenty-four-year-old wife Margaretta, and fled out the back to seek help at the army camp about a mile distant. The *Tribune* reported that Titus and his men then "broke open the door, a scuffle ensued between Titus and Mrs. Hancock, during which she disarmed him of his revolver. He promised to leave if she would return his revolver. She did so, and he left in time to save himself from the dragoons." It seems highly doubtful that Hancock would be so cowardly as to forsake his young spouse to the mercy of armed opponents or that the stalwart Titus could be easily disarmed by her while his companions did not intervene. In addition it is unlikely that the assailed woman whose home had been broken into would not have shot Titus immediately after taking his handgun and would trust him enough to return it after he had threatened to kill her husband on the spot. This was apparently another fabricated attempt by Redpath to ridicule Titus.[34]

Another controversial account arose regarding the death of thirty-five-year-old free-state major David Starr Hoyt, a land surveyor and Mexican War veteran from Massachusetts. According to the *New York Times* correspondent, Hoyt left his camp at Wakarusa on August 11 to reconnoiter the proslavery Treadwell settlement with only a bowie knife. Captain Walker confirmed that "Hoyt proposed to go into the fort in order to find out the strength of the border ruffians," saying that "he was a Mason, and that he had no fears." The proslavery *St. Louis Republican* called him a spy. Colonel Treadwell had previously received written notice from the free-soilers that if his colony did not leave Kansas in ten days, they would be driven out. His neighbors were also threatened not to assist the southerners. In contrast, Redpath alleged that Hoyt went to remonstrate the plundering of nearby free-state cornfields and poultry yards. The major had told his comrades that if he did not return by 2:00 P.M., "they might consider him dead or a prisoner." An apocryphal account claimed that Hoyt was a Freemason who received a letter from professed southern Freemasons to meet and that they then murdered him. Hoyt was "riddled" with three to ten shots, according to various conflicting reports, two and a half miles from the proslavery camp. Another story has a youth appearing at the Wakarusa camp the next morning to report finding a dead man shot in the bushes, "his pocket rifled, and turned wrong side out, and his boots off; his throat was cut from ear to ear, and the upper part of his face covered and concealed with a paste of some kind." A conflicting northern version stated that after Hoyt was shot, his killers "proceeded to pound his head with the breeches of their muskets."[35]

When Hoyt did not return by the next morning, his comrades found his partially buried remains on the prairie on the old Santa Fe Road "a little South East of Lawrence." He was "doubled up with his boots on" and "his face very much mutilated & disfigured by some chemical preparation." A New York newspaper affirmed that Hoyt's face was "blackened, to prevent recognition." Another free-soiler account alleged that after they overran the Treadwell settlement, the women there were questioned about Hoyt and after being threatened "told where the man was buried." Twenty-five years later the "ultra abolitionist" John Ritchie, who helped find the body, erroneously alleged that "Titus' command had shot and buried" Hoyt. Captain Walker's memoirs stated that in the morning, Hoyt's body "was found about a mile from the fort, with a little dirt thrown over it—not enough however, to cover the feet." Walker made no mention of the condition of the corpse's face or wounds. The *New York Times* alleged that Hoyt's corpse "remained unprotected upon the prairie" for "nearly three days." Jim Lane said that Hoyt was "hacked to pieces, and a few sods throw[n] over him, leaving his arms and feet projecting from the earth, prey for wolves." These inconsistent reports elucidate the difficulty of separating fact from fiction in sectional accounts, especially when blaming Titus, who was not present. After the corpse was retrieved, the twenty-four-year-old New York teacher S. P. Hand recalled, "All in camp were permitted to look at him but could scarcely recognize him."[36]

Lane had recently arrived in Topeka after a four-week journey from Iowa City with his emigrant expedition ominously dubbed by the press the "Army of the North," whose progress was publicly noted and heralded as numbering "from 300 to 800 men." They carried no agricultural or artisan tools for settlement but were heavily armed "for the purpose of controlling the political destinies of the Territory." The force was comprised of a Massachusetts unit led by Dr. Calvin Cutter and the Chicago Company under Lane and James A. Harvey. The Chicago Company agent, thirty-three-year-old abolitionist Joseph Medill, co-owner of the *Chicago Tribune,* agreed in writing to provide local volunteers with a thirty-dollar bounty or its equivalent in provisions and support them in Kansas up to a year if necessary. Their opponents dubbed them "Free State free-booters" and "emigrant aid hirelings."[37]

Lane was more than six feet tall, exceedingly slim, with a long, narrow, hollow-cheeked and bearded face, topped by a swirl of long hair. He was described in the *New York Times* as being "noted more for his impulsive rashness than for wise caution." Phillips called Lane "hot-headed, rash, regardless of consequences, but not wanting in bravery . . . a cross between a Western mountaineer and a Broadway dandy." Harvey was "a short, small man, quick in movement, with a dark complexion, large eagle eyes and a large Roman nose." He was twenty-nine years old and had left his wife Eunice and four-year-old daughter in Chicago, where he owned three thousand dollars in real estate and personal property. The new arrivals rendezvoused at Rock ʼeek with a force led by Capt. Samuel Walker. When the bloated remains ʼoyt were displayed, the men became "so indignant at the outrage, that they begged to be led immediately to seek his revenge" by attacking "Fort Saunders" four miles away.[38]

The "Army of the North" assaulted the proslavery settlement at Franklin around 11:00 P.M. on August 12. Lane was using the cognomen "Col. Cook" due to his pending arrest warrant for high treason. The *New York Times* indicated that there were 60 attackers, Redpath claimed they numbered about 100 men, while resident R. S. Crane and Governor Shannon said that there were about 250 raiders. Decades later Samuel Walker gave a contradictory version in his memoirs, first saying that the attack was carried out by Captain Cutler and only fifteen men without casualties and then claiming that Lane had captured Franklin and "a number of his men had been killed and wounded." Thirteen southerners were barricaded in a blockhouse from where they fired rifles "through the chinks between the logs." They were flanked by the post office log building and on the opposite side by the large two-story log hotel of postmaster and justice of the peace Samuel Crane Sr. The assailants had to retreat twice during three hours after sustaining one killed, "two very dangerously wounded, and five or six slightly." Their leader, however, determined that since Lawrence had lost its cannon and "their future operations against these log forts depended upon having one, that they would never go home without the one in the fort," a bronze eight-pounder Mexican War cannon called "Old Sacramento." The free-soilers then pushed a double wagon with blazing hay against the blockhouse, forcing its occupants to surrender. Phillips provided a contrasting account, claiming that the raid by fifteen men, none of whom was wounded, was only to assail the guardhouse and liberate a free-state prisoner.[39]

The abolitionists, however, ransacked all six dwellings and seized "all the bed blankets and clothing they could find" and "robbed the Post office of about $70 worth of stamped envelopes." At the home of Samuel Crane Jr., they took thirty U.S. muskets and seized "Old Sacramento" and three cannonballs. The *Westport Border Ruffian* reported that "Mrs. Crane was knocked down by one of the assailing party." The *St. Louis Republican* alleged that the attackers "maltreated her, and threatened to violate her person, and took her off for that purpose." Another account said that she "was knocked down by an Abolitionist." The temperance fanatics destroyed two barrels of whiskey. They expropriated from Capt. Samuel R. Ruckle $125 in cash, a gold watch, and clothing. They also "took a large lot of clothing" from a Mr. Barnes; accounts, notes, and clothing worth more than $1,200 from R. S. Crane; and a "fine horse" from William Perry Fain, the county assessor for Douglas County, who was shot in the shoulder. The free-soilers had previously declared that Fain "should not make any assessments in Lawrence, and if he attempted it, it would be at the peril of his own life."[40]

According to R. S. Crane, they "killed seven of the Abolitionists and wounded a great many. No one touched on the Pro Slavery side." In contrast, northern newspapers reported that three defenders were wounded and the attackers lost Edward Sackett from Detroit killed and seven wounded. The raiders were accused by their opponents of stealing "horses to mount the invading army" and "the assassination of individuals, the pillage, the burning of isolated dwellings." However, one of the abolitionists admitted that they also expropriated "about twelve hundred pounds of bacon, besides a quantity of flour, sugar, coffee, &c." The assailing parties "ordered all the inhabitants of Franklin to leave, threatening to kill them if they did not." *New York Times* correspondent William B. "Randolph" Hutchinson praised the assault: "If it must take blood to wash our skirts of Slavery—blood it is." The next morning Governor Shannon went to Franklin accompanied by the deputy marshal and a company of dragoons. Five of Lane's men who lost their way were arrested on a complaint from Postmaster Samuel Crane, for assault with intent to kill, robbery, and arson. The attack on Franklin had begun the most intense and destructive period of the Bleeding Kansas saga.[41]

The next day, August 13, Mary Titus wrote to a relative in Georgia that the previous evening they had received information from a reliable source that their house "was to be attacked by about *sixty* Abolitionists." She had been unable to sleep since then and was very nervous. Upon hearing this, twenty young friends of Titus appeared wearing militia red shirts and holstered revolvers and "nobly offered their services." Titus sent out a scout to look for free-state troops who "reported seeing a number of them at the appointed place." However, instead of going to the Titus homestead, the abolitionists attacked Franklin fourteen miles away, and the Tituses were told that everyone there had been slaughtered. Mrs. Titus additionally wrote, "They have sworn vengeance against Mr. Titus for taking such a bold stand against them, and they say all they want is his head." She described her cabin as having "15 U.S. muskets in one corner, a half dozen guns and Sharps rifles in another, and any quantity of revolvers lying about here, there, and everywhere."[42]

In consequence of the imminent danger, the next day Titus advertised in the *Lecompton Union* his Order No. 1 as commander of the Second Regiment, First Brigade, Southern Division, Kansas Territorial Militia. It was cosigned by his adjutant Capt. William F. Donalson and called for a general parade of his troops at Wheatland or Spicer's Post Office at 10:00 A.M. on the first Monday of September. All men subject to the militia law were "ordered to attend, or be dealt with according to law." They were instructed to organize into companies of at least thirty men, elect their officers, and report to Titus before the day of muster.[43]

On Friday afternoon, August 15, the "Army of the North" planned a nocturnal surprise attack on the Treadwell settlement, located on a high bluff on Washington Creek, where Col. B. F. Treadwell and twenty-five southerners had taken claims around the farm of Capt. James P. Saunders and made "Fort Saunders" their headquarters. The "two-story log blockhouse, about twenty-five feet square, with port-holes above and below" and an attic, had wide cracks between the logs covered with nailed fence rails. The house was "enclosed with a low rail fence" turned into a slight breastwork with sod. There were "two or three large tents" on each side of the structure. Jim Lane insisted on an immediate assault. He expropriated a dozen wagons and "had poles cut about as long as a man, and then tied hay to one end of them; placing them in the wagons, it produced the impression that they were filled with men." The hay wagons would be used to burn out resistance at "Fort Saunders." Captain Walker recalled making "a big show in front with our mounted men behind the wagons, and, still further behind, the men on foot. At a distance it looked like an army of 1200 men."[44]

The sentry with a spyglass on the roof saw some five hundred riders coming with "Old Sacramento" from the free-state camp three miles away. Colonel Treadwell sent a woman with an urgent message to Governor Shannon stating that they were "surrounded by 385 abolitionists, who swear that no quarter shall be given." At 2:00 P.M. Treadwell and forty companions scattered and safely made their way to Lecompton. They left behind forty muskets in boxes, three kegs of powder, their personal baggage, and a few provisions, while Hoyt's pony was found nearby. A flag emblazoned "Enforce the Laws" was discovered in the bushes. Another free-state account claimed that "they found a breakfast table set most temptingly" but believed the food had been poisoned for them. Lane's men "tore up the floor and found underneath" an eighteen-year-old male slave "who had prepared dinner for a large company." Twenty-four-year-old abolitionist Hugh "Potter" Young, the *Tribune* reporter, "told him he was free" but assumed that the youth went to a proslavery camp after departing. The settlement, composed of several southern families engaged in farming with their slaves, was then plundered and torched.[45]

After the men returned to their Rock Creek encampment with the spoils, Lane turned command of his force over to Walker and departed with fifteen men without giving an explanation. He went to Nebraska and was not heard from for two weeks. Walker disbanded the five hundred men, many of whom went to Lawrence, but they were heralded back a few hours later when word arrived that free-state emigrants who were lost and entered Lecompton "were going to be hung in the morning." The "Army of the North," under Captains Walker and Harvey, Dr. Cutter, and thirty-year-old Hoosier lawyer Henry J. Shombre, headed for the territorial capital to release the prisoners and seize the Abbott howitzer. Meanwhile, Colonel Treadwell and his company had barricaded themselves in the foundations of the un-finished territorial capitol building.[46]

When late word that "Fort Saunders" was under siege reached Titus that evening, he notified forty-four-year-old militia general George Washington Clarke, the Pottawatomie Indian agent and slaveholder who resided three miles from Lecompton, to round up as many mounted men as possible and go assist the Treadwell settlement. Titus left his homestead accompanied by eighteen men, including twenty-five-year-old Richmond native Charles W. Otey, who recalled that due to the lack of horses, some men had to mount double until "pressing horses into service" along the road to "Fort Saunders." Upon reaching the home of John D. Lehay, a proslavery man who lived eight miles from Lecompton, Titus learned that the Treadwell settlement had been destroyed. He decided to return home, but after riding back four miles, the colonel told his followers that in reprisal they would burn the home of free-state major John Allen Wakefield, a half mile distant, whom he had arrested three months earlier.[47]

Upon sighting the house under a full moon at about 11:00 P.M., Titus saw a dozen men there, and moments later two of them left at full gallop toward Lecompton. The colonel ordered Otey and three other riders on fast horses to follow them. The pursuers fired a few times at those fleeing until running into the "Army of the North" hidden from view by a fence along the road to the territorial capital. As the four proslavery men retreated, they encountered the rest of their group who had caught up to them. Titus gave the order "to form with a view of charging into them, but after taking a full survey of the party, it was decided that it would be best to return at once to Lecompton and prepare for defence." Otey recalled that the free-soilers "had strung themselves guerrilla fashion all along the road for a distance of about three hundred yards, and as we passed them we received their volley, and some of our men returned it." Titus and his red shirts retreated until losing their pursuers after a three-mile chase. Otey wrote that they then "found two of our men missing, and three wounded—one of them shot through the leg while riding by my side—Col. Titus shot through the hand, to say nothing of the hats shot off our heads, and the horses killed." The colonel's thumb and middle fingers on his right hand were badly maimed but not "shot off," as reported. The red shirts lost one killed and several wounded, while Walker reported that Titus had "400 men" and that no free-soilers were seriously hurt. On the spot the Volunteers found a militia man's hat, labeled Cramer, with a bullet hole in it.[48]

According to N. W. Spicer, when his free-state force approached Wakefield's home, they clashed with a "gang of Horse Thieves" led by the "desperado" Titus. They killed one of Titus's men, wounded another, seized two of their horses, and took as a prisoner the Alabamian W. H. Clowes, editor of the *Southern Advocate*. At 2:00 A.M. that Saturday, the Reverend Ephraim Nute began ringing the large bell at his Unitarian church in Lawrence with "a deep and earnest peal, which brought together immediately what fighting men remained in town." They quickly went on the march to join Captain Walker for the attack on Lecompton. Spicer claimed that Titus, expecting an imminent assault on his home, sent a dispatch to Lecompton for assistance and that a large force soon arrived at his homestead but returned to town at daybreak.[49]

At dawn on August 16, an anxious Captain Shombre started awakening his company, "saying if he could raise sixty cavalrymen he could take Titus's Fort." Some fifty riders departed without breakfast, leaving behind the main body, racing to the Titus blockhouse to reap the glory. Titus was accompanied by a score of young men who were camped around his residence. He described them as mostly former clerks who "were waiting for business to open, so as to obtain employment." A raider stated that the majority were Germans who had been working on the capitol at Lecompton, "had been passed into service," and "could scarcely speak English." Approaching from the west, John Ritchie was riding in the lead with Shombre when he saw "all those outside took to the woods or into the Fort, Titus with the rest. There was a window in the North gable end of the Fort, and a fire was opened upon us from that, and Captain Shombre fell mortally wounded," shot through the groin and the bowels. According to the *New York Times* correspondent, "seven or eight ran from the tent towards the log-house, and were taken prisoners on the way, after an exchange of several shots." He stated that Titus "with his own shot" hit Shombre. The southern prisoner Clowes took "advantage of the confusion, broke from his captors, and rushed to the arms of his friends," but he was gunned down. When the skirmish started, F. Becker, a German, "was shot dead as he ran from the camp to the house." The attackers then retreated to await the main force led by Walker, Harvey, and Dr. Cutter. When a raider falling back encountered the advance, he told them "to push on saying there was plenty of fun ahead." Titus decided to stay and defend his home instead of fleeing as Treadwell and the Lawrencians had done. He reported that "about five or six hundred" attackers soon arrived armed with "Sharps rifles, Colts repeaters and bowie knives" with the intent of "wiping out the proslavery party and taking possession of the Territory by force of arms." In one account Walker acknowledged that he had "500 determined men," and the *New York Times* reported the number at "nearly five hundred."[50]

Walker gave a completely different story forty-four years later. He said that he had instructed Capt. Joel Grover with ten men to get between the Titus house and the dragoon camp in order to impede any messenger reaching there. Walker gave another ten men to Captain Shombre to take position "along a fence that ran in front of Titus's house, and about 200 yards from it." He then took some thirty riders and "attacked the camp, a short distance from the house, and drove them out of the grove." Just then "Titus was standing in his door, and he called to his men to come into the house." Shombre and his men mounted their horses and dashed to the door, and when they were within six feet "the first round killed the captain and wounded every man but one." Walker wrote that "in a short time we had eighteen out of the forty now comprising the attacking party wounded" and that he was wounded by buckshot in the breast.[51]

After a two-hour skirmish the free-soilers wheeled up "Old Sacramento," the eight-pounder cannon seized with three round shot at Franklin four days earlier. Capt. Thomas Bickerton, a Scottish forty-year-old machinist from Portland, Maine, had additionally molded various six-pound round slugs from "some of the type in 'pi' which remained of the destruction of the *Herald of Freedom* Office." The abolitionists renamed the cannon the "Herald of Freedom." Since the blockhouse's strongest defense points were on the west and the north, the artillery piece was placed to the east. According to one participant, the cannon stood two hundred yards away, while Walker claimed that it was located "within 300 yards" of the house. Harvey's riflemen took positions behind a rail fence. A free-state account said that "Harvey ordered us to fire low. At the first fire the U.S. Troops bugle sounded a retreat. Harvey thinking they were coming up out of the ravine to attack us ordered us to form in line facing the ravine to receive them. After discovery that this was not their intention he ordered us back to our old position."[52]

They then called on Titus "to surrender or digest the last issue of the *Herald of Freedom*." Yankee cannoneer Richard Baxter Foster wrote that when

Bickerton fired the first shot, the crew shouted, "*The Herald of Freedom was issued again!*" Bickerton asked Foster to stand close by, on the windward side, "to report the effects of the balls. Two of them struck the ground; the other four the house." One shot "knocked the ridge pole higher than a kite." Bickerton "got the range right and the sixth ball plumped through the center" just above the first floor. A raider said that "the shot entered & passed through a trunk over which a slave woman had her arm lying: this colored woman came nearer being white on this occasion than at any previous period in her life. And coat, one of Titus's best, at this time also lost a part of its tail & the end of the warrior sword was also cut off. A slave boy the day before had helped Titus grind this very sword."[53]

The abolitionist John Brown Jr., imprisoned in the military camp nearby, said that "they fired six balls, out of seven shots, through Colonel Titus's house," knocking out the logs on the back side. Titus stated that they "fired seven times, the balls going through the house, shattering every thing in their passage." The *New York Times* reported "eight shots." Walker said that the fort was hit "nine or ten times" but that "it could not be battered down." The raiders then loaded a wagon with hay and ran it against the blockhouse, like they had done at Franklin, in preparation for burning them out. Titus wrote, "At the firing of the Seventh cannon, we hung out a flag of truce, seeing the impossibility of holding out against the cannon and fire." Spicer saw that "a white Flag was suspended from a window" before the nineteen men in the house were taken prisoner. Another free-soiler recalled, "The besieged fought like tigers, and had the advantage of walls, with port-holes for the rifles, but were compelled to cry for quarter, which was readily granted." The attackers had "nine or ten" casualties, including Shombre, who died that night, and Absalom White, whose arm was amputated. Walker later exaggerated that twenty-seven proslavery men were captured, six badly wounded, and that one was found dead. The *New York Times* claimed that "two dead bodies were found in the house. . . . It is supposed they were killed in the skirmish the night previous."[54]

Walker asked the prisoners who was in command, which was acknowledged by Capt. William F. Donalson, who denied knowing the whereabouts of Titus. One of Harvey's men, Jerome Hazen, stated that "our company were the first men in: one of us Mr. [James] Hall arrested Titus & [Alexander] MacArthur was placed guard over him by Harvey. The brave Col Titus was found secreted under the floor boards in a corner. The entire floor had been taken up & an excavation made down in the earth & the earth thrown up against the sides of the house: the loose boards were piled up in a corner of the room & under these we found Titus looking very much surprised & very pale. He held up his hand streaming with blood exclaiming I surrender as a prisoner of war & ask to be treated as such." Northern newspapers claimed that "Titus fought bravely at the commencement of the action, and was wounded in three places." He was hit "in the upper part of his chest near the shoulder" by a Sharps rifle minié ball, which permanently lodged there. The abolition press relished in reporting that he was found "concealed in a closet, and when dragged out by order of Captain Walker, begged piteously for his life." Harvey seized Titus's pearl-handled sword and gold-plated scabbard as war trophies. Foster said that he got the colonel's sword and a musket. Walker later wrote that Titus emerged "all covered with blood" when "a hundred rifles were leveled at his head and he shook like a leaf." When Titus saw Walker mounted, he cried out, "For God's Sake, Walker, save my life! You have a wife and children; so have I. Think of them and save me."[55]

Col. Henry Titus, kneeling, when captured by abolitionists after the Battle of
Fort Titus, was spared from death when he gave the Masonic
grand hailing sign of distress. From Albert Richardson,
Beyond the Mississippi (1869)

According to the Republican *Milwaukee Daily Sentinel,* when Titus "surrendered, he gave the masonic sign of distress" that identified him as a brother Mason in need of sworn fraternal assistance. Dr. James Malachi Pelot, the grand lecturer of the Masonic Grand Lodge of Kansas, who resided at Lecompton, stated three years later that "it was confidently expected that his life would pay the forfeit of his unenviable notoriety. An officer who knew him to be a brother Mason declared that he would die before the prisoner should be injured." Walker later wrote that he "promised him his life, and that I would defend it with my own" but never mentioned their Masonic ties. Titus acknowledged that among the attackers "only one or two of their captains seemed to posses any principles of honor." According to the records of the Masonic Grand Lodge of Kansas, Titus was never affiliated with a lodge in the territory.[56]

Col. Henry Titus's surrendered sword and scabbard and the captured South Carolina red flag of "Southern Rights" are on display in the Kansas Museum of History at Topeka. From the author's collection

Walker took Titus into the stable because "the men were intent on his life, and I had to knock one fellow down to keep him from shooting the poor wretch on the spot." As the crowd outside grew angry and restless, Walker feared for his own life. He went outside and appealed to the mob: "Colonel Titus sits here wounded and bleeding. He can make no resistance. I love him as little as you do, but in his present condition I should be ashamed to touch him. But if in the crowd of brave men there is one sneaking and brutal enough to shoot a wounded and defenseless man, let him step up and do the deed." The challenge went unanswered.[57]

The raiders queried the prisoners about the location of Mrs. Titus, and "they informed them that she was not there, but had been sent away for safety the day before. They accused the prisoners of lying; that they knew she was there, and swore they would find her, and continued their search, and ripped up the floor of the house, and searched under it for her." In a trunk that "a cannon ball had riddled from end to end," the raiders found the "uniform stolen from Col. Topliff at the sack of Lawrence." Harvey claimed that the tents on the property were taken from him two months earlier when the Chicago Company was turned back at Weston by a proslavery force. Titus denied it, but "Harvey replied in characteristic fashion that it made 'no difference as long as we thought so.'"[58]

Titus stated that after he and his men surrendered, the abolitionists drove up several empty wagons they had with them and "commenced pillaging the premises; they took every moveable article of any value, trunks, bedding, clothing, plows, crockery ware, axes, our arms, &c.," and even his wife's clothing. The free-soilers also seized the clothing of his slaves and told them "that they were free, and advised them to go to Topeka." Titus also lost his wagon, his buggy, and all the horses and mules that were in his stable, three of them belonging to him and the others to his guests. Also expropriated were "private papers, drafts, carpet bags and trunks" belonging to Titus and his friends. He accused the raiders of stealing all the money in the house, including a carpetbag with ten thousand dollars that Col. Thomas H. Rosser, of Sen. David Atchison's militia, had left there for safekeeping. Joseph C. Anderson subsequently filed a notice that three land warrants of 120 acres each that he owned were either stolen or destroyed at the blockhouse.[59]

Titus's adjoining neighbor, twenty-five-year-old New Yorker Sherman J. Waful, whose house was one-half mile distant from the colonel's home, abhorred the sectional violence swirling around him. He wrote to his father, a physician in Pamelia, New York, that Titus's "private dwelling was made a target of by 500 desperaders [sic] armed with Sharp's rifles and one piece of cannon" that "battered in the walls carrying off part of the roof." To protect Titus, "some ten of his neighbors volunteered to guard his house, as the outlaws had made repeated threats against him." The defenders lost "one man killed being shot through the head" who "had his pockets rifled of $80 in gold." The looters "even went so far as to carry off Mrs. Titus' bonnets, dresses, daguerreotypes which were regarded as sacred momentoes [sic] . . . stripping him of his gold watch, cutting off his boots in their search for gold." Waful indicated that the attackers "went so far as to robb [sic] the negroes belonging to Col. T. of what little they possessed, and yet these are the men who profess so much sympathy for the negro." The New Yorker emphasized, "I do not want it understood that I hold to either party for I do believe there never was another such a corupt [*sic*] set congregated together, I shall not fight for either party. . . . There has been about one thousand troops stationed all on my place, they robb [*sic*] corn-fields, kill hogs, and chickens. My house has been broken open lately and robbed. I was robbed of $45 by the free soil party, and now both parties." He hoped for "peace, but that cannot be, for each party say they can't live together."[60]

Walker recalled that while the house was in flames, one of his men dashed out with a satchel but that he grabbed it and threw it back inside. The robber got it again and ran off. Titus told Walker that the carpetbag "contained $15,000" sent from Virginia. Walker indicated, "The thief got away with the swag, but it did him little good. He died a miserable death in the far West." The *Milwaukee Daily Sentinel* informed readers that a certain raider was seen with the carpetbag in Lawrence talking to a lady. They both quickly departed for the East by different routes, and the man "was pursued but the money was not found with him."[61]

The northerners captured a total of nineteen men, twenty horses, a fine two-horse buggy, "30 muskets and about a dozen other guns and Sharpe's rifles," a fair stock of provisions, and fifteen thousand dollars. Walker's memoirs exaggerated the numbers to "400 muskets" and "thirty-four prisoners taken." The attackers claimed that some of this property "had been stolen from the Chicago Company on the Missouri River." Some of the personal documents and correspondence taken from Titus were sent to Boston abolitionists, and Redpath published six of them in the *Tribune*. The northern press justified the attack and destruction of the Titus homestead. The *New York Times* correspondent described him as "obnoxious to our Free-State men, especially since horse-stealing has become his trade. He has always taken an active part when any of our citizens have been prisoners in their hands, and has often talked of hanging, shooting, and the like." The *Chicago Tribune* called Titus "one of the most violent and dangerous of the Southerners who emigrated to the territory this summer." The Republican *Daily Cleveland Herald* said that he "had been the terror of the whole neighborhood for months. He and those under him robbed, pillaged and plundered every party that was unfortunate enough to fall into their path." The abolitionist *Springfield Republican* of Massachusetts falsely claimed that the attack was "in order to rescue eight recent emigrants from Illinois, seized while passing peaceably on the road, whom he held and threatened to hang." The Republican *Alton Weekly Courier* of Illinois alleged that Titus "with his own hand" had "fired Governor Robinson's house in Lawrence at the time of the siege" and that the burning of his home was in retaliation. This contradicts the fact that when Titus had the opportunity to burn Walker's home, he did not do so. In contrast, the *Savannah News* published a letter from a citizen in Kansas to his brother back home saying, "Titus' bravery commands the admiration of every one—the enemy say they never saw such a man."[62]

According to Titus, Walker told him that their initial intention was to attack Lecompton but that because the night before Titus had gone with a group to assist Colonel Treadwell, the raiders determined to assault Titus at home first and then march on Lecompton. The colonel was further informed that the attack on his residence was in reprisal for his having burned the house of neighbor Jacob Smith, which he adamantly denied. The cannonading had prompted the bugler at the camp of U.S. dragoons, one mile west, to sound the alarm. "Very many" of the raiders, especially the newcomers flushed with victory, wanted to give a "drubbing" to the federal troops, but their officers canceled the plan to attack Lecompton. The bugle call and cannonading mobilized the Lecompton women and children to flee across the Kansas River. Dr. Gihon called the attack on the Titus log house "one of the boldest strokes of the Kansas war."[63]

During the skirmish some free-soilers rode in with David Kendall, whom they had arrested and whose horse they had seized while he was taking a dispatch from Governor Shannon to U.S. Army major John Sedgwick, commanding the First Cavalry dragoon camp near Lecompton. Kendall saw the blockhouse "completely enveloped in flames" as he was herded with the other prisoners. He noticed the raiders "carrying off a dead man from the house that was burning" and others removing "a clock, a landscape painting, bed clothes, trunks," a woman's shawl, along with "five horses, one carriage and harness, all belonging to Col. Titus." Kendall, threatened by his captors with being hung or shot, was made to walk with six or eight detainees behind the wagon that held Titus and the rest of the captives.[64]

While Titus was under attack, Tennessean Lewis H. Morgan took an express message to Major Sedgwick asking for army protection, but the officer "refused any assistance." John Brown Jr., detained in the army camp, saw the messenger arrive with news that the wounded "Titus and several others were taken prisoners." Brown had earlier heard the attack on Titus's house and saw the flames from more than a mile distant. The next day Sedgwick wrote to his superior and indicated that upon hearing the cannonade, he had only thirty soldiers and placed them between the Titus house and Lecompton. He stated that he had "received no instruction how to act in a conflict with citizens, or when an officer is authorized to fire upon them." After Governor Shannon appeared, the dragoons proceeded to the Titus home, arriving after it had been destroyed and the prisoners carried off. Four decades later the first history of Lawrence alleged that Major Sedgwick had "become thoroughly incensed at the insolence and outrages of Colonel Titus and his gang." When Sedgwick learned that the free-soilers were about to attack the Titus homestead, "he quietly told Captain Walker a few days before, that if 'they wanted to gobble up old Titus and would do it quickly, he did not think he should be able to get over in time to hinder him.'" Walker's memoirs described Sedgwick as "one of our best friends" who had previously told him that if they "could attack and capture Titus before the governor sent orders to him that he would not interfere."[65]

Walker provided an incredulous account trying to justify his actions by stating that after "having plundered Titus's house in the presence of governor and troops, my boys felt well satisfied with their morning's work, and willing to leave the rest of Lecompton alive." It was at this time, he said, that "200 or more of the Lane party had come in" and that they "filed slowly out of town, 'escorted' by Major Sedgwick, his troops, and the noble governor, who kept urging the major to attack us. The major declined, however, saying that we were too strong for him." Dr. Gihon wrote a contradictory version claiming that Shannon was prevailed upon by Sedgwick "to accompany the dragoons in pursuit of Walker, and after proceeding a few miles, he saw him and his army leisurely crossing the prairies. Major Sedgwick asked for orders to make an attack and rescue the prisoners. But the governor, looking at the formidable force before him, thought it better not to venture an engagement, and gave orders for an immediate return to Lecompton."[66]

As Walker was leading the prisoners to Lawrence, he stopped at his home to announce to his wife and children that he had survived the assault on Fort Titus. Maj. John Allen Wakefield, whom Titus had previously arrested, was there and "made a violent speech, urging his immediate execution." Marian Walker retorted, "Stand off, don't touch me, any man that will take 'Old Titus' and not kill him needn't come around me." Walker pointed to the state of his wounded prisoner, hoping to arouse her feelings of mercy, but she insisted, "Clear out. I never want to see you again. You needn't think you can come around me. Take Old Titus and not kill him! You are a nice man ain't you?" The raiders got restless again, but Walker controlled the situation to prevent Titus being "torn limb from limb." The *New York Tribune* correspondent who described this incident clarified that Titus was "comparatively a young man—not over 28 years old—and is decidedly the handsomest man in Kansas."[67]

While he was approaching Lawrence, a delegation from the Committee of Safety gave Walker an order to hand over Titus immediately, but he refused. Upon entering the town at about 2:00 P.M., Walker "compelled Titus to sit up in the wagon and look around him, and as he carried him past the ruined buildings, would stop and ask him to contemplate his work." The prisoners were halted in front of the debris of the Free State Hotel. An excited mob surrounded them and clamored to lynch Titus. After being "sufficiently tormented," all the detainees except the wounded Titus and M. M. Halsey were confined in the basement of the building housing the *Herald of Freedom*. The injured were taken to another place, where a mail carrier saw that Titus "was treated rudely and harshly by those around him, and was lying on a bare floor without mattress or pillow." His badgerers, including John Brown, who was called the "Osawatomie murderer" in the press, would "strike him with their feet, and tear his clothes from him, and curse him, and spit tobacco juice upon him" as he lay on the floor. Those who erroneously blamed Titus for the murders of David Hoyt and George Williams of Massachusetts were crying out, "Hang him on the spot." The Committee of Safety formed a kangaroo court, which sentenced Titus to death, with "John Brown and other distinguished men urging the measure strongly," according to Walker, who appeared before the committee at 4:00 P.M. that day and stated that Titus had surrendered to him and that he had promised Titus his life. Walker further stated he would defend Titus's life with his own. Titus had told Walker that he would "leave the Territory if liberated."[68]

When Walker left the room, Carmi William Babcock followed him to ask if he was firmly resolved. Upon a positive reply, the committee by a new vote decided to postpone hanging Titus indefinitely. Walker went to check on his prisoner, and as he opened the door of the confinement house, pistol shots rang out in Titus's room. Walker rushed in and "found a desperado named 'Buckskin' firing over the guards' shoulders at the wounded man as he lay on his coat." Walker gave the assailant a blow with his dragoon pistol that sent him "heels-over-head to the bottom of the stairs." Walker found that John Brown and Dr. Avery, a sixty-year-old Hoosier physician who had attended the dying Shombre and had possession of his papers, were outside haranguing an excitable crowd to hang Titus and accusing Walker of being a public enemy for opposing the Committee of Safety. However, the sight of Walker's three hundred men held the mob in check.[69]

Meanwhile, Mary Titus and her children had fled at dawn on August 16 on the four-horse mail stagecoach to Westport, Missouri, four miles from Kansas City and with a population of eight hundred, the eastern portal of the three western trails. Later that morning she received an express mail from Lecompton postmaster Dr. Aristides Rodrique announcing "the attack on Colonel Titus's house, and the probable murder of the entire party." Another report said that it was feared that since Titus "was not summoned to surrender that he was executed on the spot." Mrs. Titus was under great anxiety and despair until further news arrived that her husband had been seized and sent to Lawrence. She wrote to her father, Edward Stevens Hopkins, saying that her home had been assailed by "five hundred Abolitionists—our property destroyed and our all taken." Mrs. Titus planned on heading to Lawrence the next day even "if they kill me on the way." The northern press claimed that her husband had sunk twelve thousand dollars of her wealth "in trying to introduce slavery into Kansas."[70]

On Sunday, the 17th, Governor Shannon went to Lawrence with the Freemason Dr. Rodrique, Major Sedgwick, and an army escort. The trio met with the Committee of Safety and free-state Volunteer officers, including Dr. Cutter, in the Cincinnati Hotel. The governor was rebuffed when he demanded "the unconditional surrender of the prisoners, as being held without any authority at law." The abolitionists made various requests, including that the authorities "dislodge and oust all bands of Southerners throughout the Territory." The six-hour negotiations behind closed doors concluded with an agreement to exchange Titus and his eighteen comrades for the five free-state men arrested at Franklin by civil process and the dispersal of all the armed camps by U.S. forces. The Massachusetts and Chicago Companies of the "Army of the North" agreed to leave the territory, and the governor acquiesced returning to Lawrence the Abbott howitzer surrendered to Sheriff Jones in May. The *New York Times* editorialized that it was a "signal triumph" for free-state men. Outside, Shannon addressed the crowd that had gathered to hear the outcome of the meeting. He complained of having been misrepresented in the press and professed "no ill feelings against any man in this territory." Shannon stated that as his term in office would end the next day, he wanted to bring peace to Kansas. The mob was "very much excited, and much diversity of opinion existed in reference to the arrangement, many insisting that Titus and Donalson ought not to be set at liberty on any terms." They wanted to lynch Titus immediately, but he was constantly kept under guard.[71]

When Shannon returned to Lecompton, he wrote to Gen. Persifor Frazer Smith, commander of the Department of the West at Fort Leavenworth, indicating that the territorial capital was "threatened with utter extermination by a large party of free State men." He had seen at Lawrence "at least eight hundred men, who manifested a fixed purpose to demolish" Lecompton "in a very short time." The free-soilers had more than a thousand other armed men nearby "with several pieces of artillery." Lecompton was protected by "eighty or a hundred dragoons, and some hundred and twenty citizens, poorly armed, and badly supplied with ammunition." The women and children had evacuated the town, and there was "a general panic among the people." Shannon urgently requested a few infantry companies and some light artillery. General Smith quickly complied, sending thirteen hundred men of the Second Cavalry dragoons from Fort Riley, troops from Jefferson Barracks, a battalion of the Sixth Infantry, and Capt. Albion Parris Howe's company of the Fourth Artillery.[72]

In pursuance of the prisoner exchange agreement, the five free-state prisoners held at Lecompton arrived at Lawrence in a carriage at noon on Monday, August 18, escorted by a company of dragoons. They had appeared that morning before a Lecompton judge and were discharged after no witnesses appeared against them. Some one thousand "very excited" people in Lawrence crowded the streets to see the exchange, with many objecting to Titus and Donalson being freed. The nineteen proslavery prisoners were placed in wagons and escorted out of town by Captain Walker with a company of free-state Volunteers and footmen in a wagon alongside the dragoons. Walker later erroneously asserted, "They held about thirty of our men and we forty of theirs." The soldiers took Titus's men to Lecompton, while the Volunteers went to the army camp and retrieved the Abbott howitzer. Mary Titus, who had gone to Lawrence with the military escort, accompanied her wounded husband on the return to Lecompton. She notified her father on the 19th of their situation, stressing, "The Abolitionists stole every thing we had—even my dresses. Mr. Titus is left without shoes or hat." Six days later Titus gave a sworn four-page declaration to Douglas County justice of the peace Robert P. Nelson detailing the attack on his home and his losses. He claimed being "born & raised in Luzerne County, Pennsylvania." A few days later two men recognized as raiders of the Titus homestead were arrested near Leavenworth while driving a wagon containing some of his stolen property.[73]

When Governor Shannon left Lecompton on August 27, without awaiting the arrival of his successor, he was spotted fifteen miles away by 150 riders of Lane's force. They gave chase, but he managed to escape on a swift horse. Titus had departed Lecompton with Sheriff Jones for Missouri to assist in raising proslavery volunteers. On September 5 Lane reappeared and with Captain Walker descended on Lecompton with about 500 men. The free-state Volunteers formed in line on the bluff east of town, and Capt. Thomas Bickerton positioned two artillery pieces within range. They demanded the surrender of five abolitionists, including Dr. Avery, detained on their way to Leavenworth. The "Army of the North" retreated when a company of U.S. troops marched out to protect the town. Deputy Marshal Samuel Cramer and the territorial militia retaliated by torching seven free-state dwellings in Douglas County, including the homes of Walker, Wakefield, and John J. "Ottawa" Jones, one of the "Old Sacramento" cannoneers. Secretary of State William L. Marcy wrote on September 9 to newly appointed territorial governor John White Geary, "The insurrectionary invasion of the territory by the way of Nebraska, and the subsequent hostile attacks on the post-office at Franklin, and on the dwellings of Titus and of Clarke, seem to have stimulated the unlawful acts of the same character on the borders of Missouri." Marcy indicated that in order to disperse the armed groups rebelling against the territorial government, the governor should "have the militia of the Territory completely enrolled and organized."[74]

Geary arrived in the territorial capital the next day. He was an imposing man who stood six feet, six inches tall, weighed 260 pounds, and had been wounded five times during the Mexican War. The governor immediately issued a proclamation disbanding all militia organizations and warning all armed groups to disperse or leave Kansas. A simultaneous decree ordered all male citizens of the territory between the ages of eighteen and forty-five to enroll in a new militia controlled by Geary "for the maintenance of public order and civil government." Meanwhile the free-soilers preparing for a siege had fortified Lawrence with earthen embankments, stone walls, and various forts built by hundreds of arriving volunteers at Mount Oread, Blanton's Bridge, and the Wakarusa crossing at Blue Jackets. Those without arms received pitchforks and were placed behind breastworks by John Brown. Lane assumed command of the various entrenched regiments estimated at "from fifteen hundred to three thousand" and was "determined to make an assault on Lecompton."[75]

Lawrencians sent desperate letters to their friends and newspaper editors in New England begging for assistance. A Yale graduate wrote to abolitionist Massachusetts senator Henry Wilson, "Will our friends of the free States stand by and see us shot down and scalped and butchered, or will they rally to our defense? We want more men and ammunition." Reverend Nute sent a missive that was read from a Boston pulpit, and his appeal for relief "was promptly answered by the collection of $289."[76]

In the meantime Titus attended a large proslavery meeting in Kansas City, Missouri, where it was agreed to raise two thousand men to overrun Lawrence. Secretary of War Jefferson Davis instructed General Smith on

September 9 "to maintain order and to suppress the insurrection." Three days later Geary sent a special messenger to Lawrence with a copy of his proclamation. On September 13, at 1:30 A.M., the governor received a dispatch from his agent in Lawrence that free-soilers were preparing for battle after hearing that a large body of Missourians six miles away was going to attack them. An hour later the governor left for Lawrence accompanied by Lt. Col. Philip St. George Cooke with three hundred soldiers of the Second Dragoons and four artillery pieces. Upon arriving they discovered that "the danger had been exaggerated, and that there was no immediate necessity for the intervention of the military." Geary addressed the citizenry, who agreed to abide by the terms of his proclamations. After Geary returned with the troops to Lecompton, he was informed that "a large army from Missouri was encamped on the Wakarusa River" waiting to assault Lawrence at any moment. These men "had been called into service by the late acting-governor who gave them authority as the duly constituted militia of the territory." Geary sent a three-man delegation with orders for them to disband.[77]

Upon arriving at the militia camp, half of it on the bluff west of Franklin and the Missourians tenting a mile to the right on the Wakarusa shore, the delegates were introduced to Sen. David Atchison, commander in chief of the armies of Kansas; Colonel Titus; Sheriff Jones; Brig. Gen. William P. Richardson, leading the Northern Division of the Kansas Territorial Militia; and other proslavery leaders in charge of twenty-seven hundred men. This formidable force was comprised of Atchison's large force of Missourians with four artillery pieces; Brig. Gen. William A. Heiskell and his one thousand men of the First Brigade, Southern Division of the Kansas Territorial Militia; Titus with the Second Regiment of the same brigade; and Gen. John William Reid, a Missouri state representative and Mexican War veteran, with four hundred Missourians flush from a recent victory against John Brown at Osawatomie, where one of Brown's sons was killed. Other groups of volunteers were led by Gen. Benjamin Franklin Stringfellow, a former Missouri attorney general; Gen. L. A. MacLean, a tall and stout Scotchman who was the chief clerk of Surveyor General John Calhoun; Gen. John Wilkins Whitfield, territorial delegate to Congress; Gen. George W. Clarke, the Pottawatomie Indian agent; and Capt. Frederick Emory, a twenty-seven-year-old engineer from Maryland and a U.S. mail contractor leading a company of Leavenworth Regulators. Three years earlier Emory had been secretary of state of the filibusterer William Walker's fleeting Republic of Lower California. The proslavery army planned to destroy Lawrence in revenge for the attacks on Franklin, the Treadwell settlement, and the Titus homestead.

Their outposts were already skirmishing with their adversaries, prompting the governor's delegation to ask Geary to appear there as soon as possible.[78]

Geary, however, before receiving the message had already left Lecompton with Lieutenant Colonel Cooke's force, arriving at Lawrence early Sunday evening, September 14. He "neither saw Lane nor any body of armed forces" and stationed the army outside of town in defensive positions. At midnight militia general Heiskell received information that Cooke had positioned a large force of U.S. troops in front of Lawrence. The next morning Cooke sent Heiskell a note to that effect and warned of the consequences of an attack. The governor then assured protection to the local citizenry and at sunrise on the 15th proceeded with Cooke and an escort three miles to the pro-slavery militia camp.[79]

Geary met in a storehouse with a council of proslavery military leaders and through coded signs, words, and handshakes identified himself as a brother Freemason to Titus and Atchison. The governor read to them his instructions from the president "to maintain the public peace, and bring punishment upon all acts of violence and disorder, by whomsoever the same may be perpetrated." Geary declared that he was "prepared to enforce the laws; to arrest offenders; to crush insurrection, and to suppress disorder with the assistance of the troops under his command." The army had just arrested near Lecompton that morning Capt. Thomas Bickerton with "Old Sacramento" and 101 of Colonel Harvey's men who had attacked Capt. John Robertson's force at Hickory Point. The horses seized included two stolen from Titus that he later recuperated. Geary stated that the prisoners would be tried in court for first degree murder and advised the proslavery militia to disband and abandon their projected attack on Lawrence. The governor warned "that if they persisted in their mad career," the destruction of Lawrence would provoke "so fierce an indignation throughout the entire North" that Kansas would be "entirely over run by a Northern army," igniting the flames of civil war. Lieutenant Colonel Cooke urged them "to submit to the patriotic demand that they retire"; otherwise it would be his "painful duty" to sustain Geary "at the cannon's mouth."[80]

Atchison denounced the "outrageous conduct of the Abolitionists," concluding that although it was "a painful duty," he would comply with the governor's request. Most of the council members expressed their opinions, and "Col. Titus also addressed the meeting, urging with much feeling the outrages and infamies that he had suffered at the hands of the marauders. He told the Gov. of the cannonading his home, of its burning, of the from 5 to 10,000 dollars of which they had robbed him, and held up his mutilated

arm in proof of their desperate efforts to destroy him." Titus denounced how
the abolitionists "even took and kept the oil-painted portrait of his wife's
mother, who is now dead. . . . In her far-off home Mrs. T. valued as very
precious the portrait of her dead mother. Was it not cruel to take from her
the last emblem of maternal love?" Titus concluded by saying "that his heart
beat tumultuously for revenge; but he was willing to await the result of the
efforts about to be made to bring the outlaws to justice." The conference then
closed, and Geary retired after authorizing "Col. Titus to raise three companies of volunteers, to be mustered into service, consisting of eighty men each,
two companies to be mounted." The council met in private and agreed to
yield to the governor's policy.[81]

Titus, Atchison, and Reid then returned to camp and addressed their
troops that evening. They "urged compliance with the Governor's proposal"
and enrolled about one hundred recruits into the new militia. Atchison
chaired an assemblage in which a committee was appointed "to prepare resolutions expressive of the sense of the meeting." The panel was comprised of
Titus, Sheriff Samuel J. Jones, George W. Clarke, and others. Four resolutions
were passed affirming that the Missourians would disband and return home
as a result of the protection promised by the governor to peaceful settlers;
that the governor should distribute various mounted companies throughout
the territory to protect settlers; recommended to the governor that he station
a company of one hundred mounted men at Potawatomie Creek in Franklin,
Anderson and Lykins counties to protect homesteaders in that section; and
recommending Titus Titus "as commander of the Territorial militia now to
be mustered into service." The *Kickapoo Pioneer* pronounced that Gen. John
Reid should not have delayed the attack on Lawrence when he was "within
4 short miles" and that "the South was sold . . . by having a hybrid species
of political military leaders at the head of her affairs." Reid responded that
the arrival of Geary with instructions from the government "not only superseded the necessity for our action, but the prompt measures taken by him to
suppress the wrongs complained of and to bring the wrong-doers to justice,
took from us the justification we before had for taking redress into our own
hands." He indicated that "Lane and his marauders" had already fled Lawrence and that only "defenseless people" were left there.[82]

Titus accompanied the retreating Missourians to Westport, where on
September 18 they held a "large and enthusiastic meeting of Southern men"
presided over by B. F. Treadwell. They passed resolutions acknowledging that
since they were "unable to enter the Territory as armed, organized companies," they should make claims in Kansas and occupy them "in defiance of

Yankee guerrillas and Lane's banditti." Representatives would be appointed "to canvass the Southern States and collect means, so as to secure our colonies in Kansas against want during the coming winter, and for the benefit of future emigration to Kansas." Numerous appointments were made to represent fifteen states, with Titus being one of the five Florida delegates. An executive committee of five members was chosen "to receive and disburse all moneys collected by the representatives in their respective states." Titus was one of two Lecompton representatives.[83]

The previous day Gen. Persifor Smith had requested that Governor Geary provide two militia infantry companies to be mustered into U.S. service. Each company was to consist of "one captain, one first-lieutenant, four sergeants, four corporals, two musicians, and seventy-four privates." The Titus militia received from the army on September 21 the 101 Hickory Point prisoners, who were handed over outside Lecompton and marched to the local jail. The following day Governor Geary went to Lawrence "trying to raise a company of volunteers to serve, like Titus, under Gen. Smith." On the 28th Smith requested from Geary an additional militia cavalry company. The next day Titus participated in the Law and Order Party County Convention for Douglas County at Lecompton. The colonel was appointed delegate from Lecompton Township along with Sheriff Jones and eight others. Twenty-one additional delegates represented Lake Township, Washington Creek, Willow Springs, and Hickory Point. The gathering then elected five candidates to be supported by the Law and Order Party for the offices of Douglas County representatives. The convention closed after unanimously renominating Gen. John Wilkins Whitfield for delegate to Congress from the Kansas Territory.[84]

A few days later Governor Geary called Titus and Samuel Walker to the executive chamber. The *St. Louis Republican* wrote that their "start of surprise and their sudden flush of hate was only repressed by the Executive presence." Geary told both Freemasons, "Gentlemen, you have been enemies long enough, men of such generous natures and true instincts should be friends. I require the services of you both to assist me in restoring peace to this beautiful but distracted territory. For my sake, and for the sake of the country you must shake hands and be friends." The article claimed, "From that moment they were friends, and it would have done you good to see the manly tear roll down their cheeks as they recounted the story of their wrongs, and pledged eternal friendship to each other." Geary, who had recently written a letter to the *St. Louis Republican,* was most likely the source of this information.[85]

The visitors were attended to by the slave woman Ann Clarke, property of Titus and George W. Clarke, who had been hired out to Geary to superintend the gubernatorial mansion. Geary officially "appointed Col. Titus to form volunteer battalions to preserve peace in the neighborhood of Lecompton, and Capt. Walker upon the same duty for the vicinity of Lawrence." Titus replied to the *St. Louis Republican* that he had been "most foully misrepresented" and that he spoke to Walker when introduced but only as a "courtesy to Gov. Geary . . . I am wounded and disabled, and could not have struck the dastard down if I had been so inclined." He claimed not to be "in the habit of 'mingling manly tears' with tears from the eyelids of thieves. Honorable men are not in the habit of 'pledging eternal friendship' to robbers and murderers—to men who have been reared in the sinks of iniquity, and in the moral cesspools of abolitionism." Titus admitted being "willing to submit to anything to keep the peace and heal the wide breach which now exist between our friends and our abolition invaders except being placed upon an equality with them." The *Lecompton Union* reprinted the letter in two subsequent editions and wrote that its opinion of Titus "has always been exalted, but we now think more of him. . . . He speaks to the point—he tells the truth—the whole truth, and nothing but the truth."[86]

In contrast, John Henry Kagi wrote to the *Washington National Era* that during the meeting, the marshal arrived to arrest Walker. The governor stated that Walker was there under his safe conduct and should not be molested. Titus responded by "putting himself between the Marshal and his desired victim, declared that the Captain should be arrested only over his dead body! The Marshal and his friends then withdrew, and Colonel Titus himself escorted Captain Walker out of town." Walker responded to the Titus letter, calling himself a humble farmer, denouncing "Col. Titus' free use of dirty epithets," accusing him of "brutal inhumanity" toward the free-state men, and claiming that the attack on his house "was with the full determination of taking his life." He said that "Col. Titus was found concealed in a closet; he was brought out, and seeing me, he appealed to me for protection." Walker claimed that it was against his wish or agency that the Titus home was set on fire. He made no mention of their Masonic brotherhood or the fact that Titus did not previously burn his residence when he had the opportunity to do so. Walker also did not address the accusation of the ten thousand dollars stolen from Titus or their meeting with Governor Geary. The abolitionist *Tribune* concluded, "Through the Governor's intervention, a pacific meeting occurred, a better understanding took place, mutual concessions were made, and pledges of friendship were passed; and, late in the afternoon, Walker left Lecompton in company with and under the safeguard of Col. Titus."[87]

As a result of the meeting, Geary administered the oath to one infantry company of free-state men raised in Lawrence, called the "Geary Guards," commanded by Capt. Samuel Walker with James A. Harvey as lieutenant and second in command. They received U.S. army uniforms, government muskets, rations, and twelve dollars monthly pay. The two other companies were organized with proslavery men and camped near the territorial capital. Capt. John Wallis led the mounted company, and Capt. John Donaldson commanded the infantry unit. His first lieutenant was twenty-two-year old South Carolina physician James M. Pelot. All three companies, numbering nearly 250 men, were mustered into service for three months. Titus was given "special direction of these troops." His first assignment was during the October 6 elections for members of the Territorial Assembly and a delegate to Congress. The free-state men abstained from what they regarded as a bogus contest. The Titus militias "were ordered to the ballot-box and all voted for the Pro-Slavery candidates as there were no others." John Wilkins Whitfield was reelected territorial delegate to Congress without opposition.[88]

Five days later Geary abided by the recommendation of the proslavery meeting the previous month and commissioned Titus as his special aide-de-camp "with the rank, title and emoluments of colonel, to take effect from and after the fifteenth day of September, 1856." The governor gave "special direction of these troops" to Titus, outranking Walker. The colonel, who had not yet recovered from his wounds, had "an ounce of 'free soil lead' in his body, at this time and has but partially recovered the use of his hands and arms." On October 17 the *New York Times* correspondent "Literal" saw "Col. Titus and his company, riding out to air their new equipments and uniform. These chivalrous gentlemen looked imposing enough in the fine clothes and on the good horses which our Governor has kindly given them: I noticed, too, that they have Sharpe's rifles." Lieutenant Colonel Cooke of the Second Dragoons received orders to supply them with rations.[89]

The abolitionist prisoner John Henry Kagi claimed that on Friday night, October 17, a group of drunken soldiers heading back to their camp from Lecompton "fired off their revolvers." He then heard people shouting, "Lane's coming, Lane's coming" and claimed that "Titus ran through the streets like a lunatic, screaming out orders to his men, as though the safety of the Union depended on the capacity of his lungs." The colonel had his militia formed in line of battle and "sent messengers to the people residing in the adjoining buildings, requesting them to go into their cellars, or to some other place of safety." Kagi claimed that the "disgraceful drama consumed three or four hours" and referred to his guards as the heathen "*mule* itia."[90]

The free-state prisoners, guarded by ten men, were held in a one-and-a-half-story cottonwood log house with a cooking stove and utensils and the captured "Old Sacramento" pointing at it. The dwelling had been previously used by the Titus militia as a "fort." Other accounts described the prison as "more like a stable than a house," a "plank house," a "dilapidated house," and "a frame house, poorly inclosed, without windows," surrounded by militia with two cannons planted on elevated ground. Capt. John Donaldson commanded the artillery. A delegation from Lawrence daily attended the inmates "by supplying many of the neglected necessities of life," including "pies and cakes." One elderly prisoner received a bed and a chair that his daughter sent him, together with "other little articles of comfort." After a prisoner died of intermittent fever, physicians from Lawrence visited the jail "every day or two." A room "between the guard room and the prison" was established as a hospital. Governor Geary "several times" visited the detainees. A photographer "took a daguerreotype of the prison and its inmates, who were grouped before it."[91]

A prisoner named E. R. Moffet managed to escape at night by cutting a hole in the floor and passing through the wall elevating the building. Titus "got out his regiment, and scoured the hills until daylight, but to no purpose." To prevent further escapes, Titus gave orders "that no letters shall pass to or from the prisoners, without first being read by him or the officer of the day." One inmate acknowledged that "Titus himself has been kind enough to us. . . . But his duty is only to prevent our escape." In spite of the amenities afforded the prisoners, decent treatment from Titus, and the frequent visits by the governor, physicians, and supporters providing food and comfort items, the abolitionist propaganda called the jail "a foul dungeon," a "den of horror," a counterpart of the British "Jersey prison ships," a "place that deserves commemoration with the Bastille and the Black Hole of Calcutta," and "Titus's black-hole." The accused were later tried in the first-district court, and while some were acquitted, twenty were convicted of manslaughter and sentenced to five years confinement at hard labor.[92]

The noted "John Smith," a pseudonym of the "special correspondent" of the antislavery St. Louis *Missouri Democrat,* wrote on October 29 that he had an interview with Colonel Titus, who said that in the upcoming presidential election "if Freemont is elected, he will 'take up his bed and walk.'" He did not doubt that James Buchanan would be chosen chief executive and "would advise every Free-State man in the Territory to do the same thing." Titus affirmed that "Buchanan was pledged to the South to make Kansas a Slave State, and that would be the result." The colonel "believed Kansas was not adapted for Slave Labor, but that it must be made a Slave State to preserve the balance of power, and that the South would have it at any cost." The correspondent called Titus "a good-looking man" with a life of "reckless adventure" and a believer "that might makes right. Hence he is a dangerous man." However, he found the colonel "polite and courteous to strangers, that he would listen to adverse sentiments and arguments with perfect composure. He spoke of his losses during the war with the coolness of a martyr, but he seemed to look upon the whole question here as a grand scheme in the lottery of life, and that the drawing of the 4th of November would decide who were the winners. My opinion is, that there are worse men among the Ruffians than Titus."[93]

Kansans awoke on November 4 to a sharp frost and a snowy blanket over the landscape from the previous afternoon's storm. The Kansas River had been quite high, and there was concern that navigation on the Missouri River would close in a week or two. That day, two weeks before the first public sale of territorial land occurred at Leavenworth, Mary Titus purchased a parcel on the southeast quarter section south of Lecompton that had been acquired by the Lecompton Town Company. The territorial capital had sprouted some one hundred buildings and had a population of six or seven hundred people. Mrs. Titus paid one hundred dollars and agreed to the further sum of one thousand dollars after the property deed was issued. The witness signing the agreement was Douglas County sheriff Samuel J. Jones, secretary of the Lecompton Town Company. The Fort Titus land was bought a year later by William M. Nace, who with his neighbor L. McKinney established the Battle-Ground Distillery. It was advertised as being "on the site of Old Fort Titus" and manufacturing "the very best double rectified and pure malt whiskey, which will be sold as low as in any city in the West."[94]

On November 8 Governor Geary was back in Lecompton after a three-week absence, and he wrote to Titus after reading Titus's letter in the *St. Louis Republican* stating, "Gov. Geary is doing his duty to all. He is a firm, resolute and commanding patriot, and skillful Chief Executive, and if any man could bring together these discordant elements, he might; but he knows the impossibility of such a thing, and will never undertake it." Geary admonished him: "As you are my special Aid de Camp, and as such, supposed to understand my policy and your own position, I deem it my duty to inquire of you, in order that I may do you no injustice, whether the document referred to is a genuine letter emanating from you." Titus replied the same day admitting authorship to defend his honor and vindicate himself from misrepresentation. In regard to the governor's policy, he assured Geary that he was intent on "carrying out your views in your absence in strict accordance with your wishes and would regret in an especial manner to lose your confidence in connection with the discharge of any of my duties as your Special Aid de Camp."[95]

In early November, Charles Hays, a member of the proslavery Kickapoo Rangers, was jailed in Lecompton for the murder of free-state Volunteer Sgt. David C. Buffum six weeks earlier. The defendant was released on a one-thousand-dollar bail bonded by Sheriff Jones. Governor Geary, who had offered a five-hundred-dollar reward for Hays's apprehension, nullified the bail on November 10 and ordered U.S. Marshal Israel B. Donalson to detain Hays, alleging that murder was not a bailable offense. The marshal refused to contravene a court order and presented his resignation. Geary gave the arrest warrant to Titus and sent him at midnight "with orders to take a file of men and execute it without delay." Samuel F. Tappan, the *New York Times* correspondent who had earlier falsely implicated Titus's underlings in the murder of Buffum, now wrongly predicted that the colonel would purposely never find the proslavery man and detain him. Titus, with six men, arrested Hays at his home and returned him to the Lecompton jail under his watch within forty-eight hours. A week later Titus received a writ of habeas corpus from Chief Justice Lecompte ordering him to bring Hays before the court. The judge immediately released the prisoner upon proof of exoneration. Titus then wrote to Geary explaining why Hays was again at large.[96]

On November 12 all the military troops guarding Lecompton except two companies of the First Cavalry and Company A of the Sixth Infantry were withdrawn. Three days later the forty remaining free-state prisoners were being transferred by U.S. troops to Tecumseh to stand trial on change of venue. As Titus was counting the prisoners under his charge, he told twenty-nine-year-old Kentuckian Martin J. Mitchell to fall in line. Mitchell, appointed aide to Jim Lane after serving as captain of Company F, Topeka Free State Volunteers, had participated in the Hickory Point attack. When he ignored Titus, the colonel "seized him by the collar and dragged him into line." Insults were exchanged, and Mitchell seized Titus by the beard, prompting the guards to intervene. After the prisoner was bound, the affront continued. The inmate John Ritchie recalled twenty-five years later that Mitchell "said to Titus damn you, when you were our prisoner you cried like a baby and you were fed on the best the good women could get. You feed us on fly-blown beef necks your own men would not eat and moldy side meat."[97]

Titus had Mitchell "bucked and gagged" for thirteen hours. This military punishment, forcing into a man's mouth a stick tied to a band around his head, was common. While in a seated position, the prisoner's legs were flexed to his chest, a rod would be passed under his knees and over his elbows, and his wrists and ankles were tied together to prevent movement. In contrast, the prisoner Thomas Bickerton, who cannoned Titus's home, never complained of being mistreated by his jailer. Mitchell, Ritchie, and seven others soon after escaped and sought refuge in Lawrence. The Free State Convention in Lawrence later issued a manifesto "to the people of the United States and Kansas" in which they asserted, "The political Free State prisoners, under indictments for treason and murder, were treated with revolting barbarity by Col. Titus and his Southern ruffians."[98]

In mid-November, after the news of Buchanan's presidential victory was confirmed, Titus and a large group of proslavery men participated in a public gathering of Douglas County citizens in the Virginia Saloon in Lecompton. They were going to name delegates to a convention of the Law and Order Party meeting at Leavenworth on December 1. Surveyor General John Calhoun was unanimously called to chair the assembly. Titus was selected with five other men to a committee to draft resolutions expressing their opinion. It was agreed to send fifteen representatives from Douglas County to the convention at Leavenworth, and Titus was among those chosen. They pledged "to resist every effort that Abolition Aid societies and Black Republicans may make to prevent the proper execution of the laws of the Territory."[99]

The previous month Titus had received two letters inviting him to "leave Kansas and take command of an expedition for Central America." One was from Gen. John Quitman, and the other was from his Cuba filibuster comrade Chatam Roberdeau Wheat, who said that he was in New York organizing a brigade for Central America that would gather in New Orleans in mid-November. Wheat wanted to know if Titus could provide five hundred armed men, like those under his command, to assist William Walker in Nicaragua. If so, Wheat would furnish transportation for them to the Crescent City. He offered Titus command of the new regiment and requested that he reply to him in Louisville, Kentucky. Wheat assured Titus "that it is the best expedition that I have ever been engaged in" and enticed him to join by stressing, "Fortune awaits."[100]

In a recruitment effort, Titus showed the letter to some of the detainees and allowed Capt. Thomas Bickerton to "read it aloud to the prisoners" twice. According to the inmate John Henry Kagi, who was corresponding with the *Washington National Era*, Bickerton, "who once resided in Nicaragua, remarked in the presence of Titus . . . that he should like to return to that country and inquired if some of the others would not accompany him.

Several expressed their willingness to go, in case Kansas became a slave State, and a few replied that they would go anyhow, for the sake of adventure." Titus said that after conquering Nicaragua and El Salvador, "everything was arranged to strike a blow at Cuba." Kagi sent a copy of the letter to the *National Era* and alleged that Titus "read the 'Appeal to the American People,' sent out by the prisoners a few weeks since, and now declares himself our open enemy." The document accused Titus of "robbing houses and stealing horses" and called the greatest portion of their guards "drunken, brawling demons, too vile and wicked for portrayal." The *Leavenworth Weekly Herald* later denounced the purported Titus offer as "an Abolition lie." Titus "never had confidence enough in the free state prisoners to take their word for anything, much less to go with him to join Walker" and fight for slavery. The detainee O. M. Marsh, who called Titus "the life and soul of the Ruffian party," wrote that the colonel told the inmates "that they were getting ready the *ball* and *chain,* and the convicts' striped garb, as rapidly as possible, for those who had been convicted."[101]

Col. Henry Titus, left, at Lecompton prison in November 1856, reading a filibuster proclamation to recruit volunteers for Nicaragua among free-state prisoners. From John Speer, *Life of Gen. James H. Lane* (1896)

Titus accepted the Nicaragua offer after the *Lecompton Union* announced on November 6 that Walker was "firmly established" and was preparing Nicaragua "for admission into the Union" as a slave state. He decided to send his wife to her family in Jacksonville and "offered liberty and a free passage to Nicaragua to all of the prisoners who will join him in that expedition."

Two weeks later the *Lecompton Union* reprinted an article from the *New Orleans Delta* praising four hundred Nicaragua volunteers departing their city and destined for "brilliant deeds." On the night of November 22, Bickerton and thirty free-state prisoners guarded by the dragoons in Tecumseh escaped from the new courthouse basement cells. They picked out the bricks with musket bayonets used for candlesticks. Most of them went to Lawrence, and none joined Titus. The two soldiers guarding the prisoners were later "sentenced to wear a chain and ball for one year." Two days later a newspaper correspondent in Lecompton heard that Titus would soon depart with his militia companies after petitioning Governor Geary that he and his men be discharged "so that they may embark for Central America, and enlist under the banner of Walker." Titus claimed to have received "very flattering offers" from Walker, and as "he was born, as he says, a filibuster[er], and there is nothing more to be done in this Territory, it is destiny for him to go to Central America." The colonel anticipated "a fine opportunity to distinguish himself there, and is in excellent spirits at the thoughts of going." The news was widely disseminated as far as Honolulu, Hawaii.[102]

The next day Captains Donaldson and Wallis and their entire command requested that Geary dismiss them since peace prevailed in the territory. The governor quickly consulted with Gen. Persifor Smith and concurred that all three militia companies would be mustered out with pay on December 1, with Walker's company at Lawrence and the two proslavery companies at Fort Leavenworth. Seventy of Titus's men enlisted to go to Nicaragua and agreed to rendezvous in St. Louis in a fortnight. On November 27 the *Lecompton Union* denounced a story in the *New York Times* that Gen. John Quitman had urged Titus in a letter to "leave Kansas and devote his energies to the cause of the South in Central America." The newspaper indicated that Quitman did not give such advice, "nor has Col. Titus any idea of leaving Kansas for the purpose of going to Central America. He will go South this winter, upon matters of a purely private nature, and will return early in the Spring." The *Lecompton Union* recognized that some local "spirited young men" intended leaving shortly to join Walker and advised, "Kansas needs Southern men more than Nicaragua. . . .Think gentlemen twice before you act, Kansas should not be sacrificed for the sake of Nicaragua."[103]

Titus, however, had already made a decision the previous day when he and his men crossed the Kansas River at Lecompton and proceeded to Leavenworth to receive their militia severance pay. Before leaving Lecompton, the colonel released the free-state prisoner William Butler of New Hampshire "on condition that he would meet him at St. Louis and enlist for

Nicaragua." Titus also dismissed another inmate, thirty-five-year-old Edmund Root Falley, a saddle and harness maker from Mt. Gilead, Ohio, who had nursed and attended the wounded colonel three months earlier in Lawrence. Titus called on Falley at the prison, "led him through the guards and out of Lecompton, and pointing with his finger as he turned to Falley, said, 'That is the way to Lawrence—go.'"[104]

Nicaragua had been embroiled in a civil war between liberals and conservatives since the previous year, when the losing side asked thirty-one-year-old Tennessean William Walker and his filibusters to assist them. Walker captured the city of Granada and rigged a local election to declare himself president of Nicaragua on July 12, 1856. Two months later the neighboring countries of El Salvador, Honduras, Guatemala, and Costa Rica allied to invade Nicaragua. Walker sent an appeal to American volunteers for assistance. Titus responded once again to the filibuster cause by giving public notice in Kansas that anyone desiring free passage to Nicaragua should rendezvous at the St. Louis Hotel on December 10. He declared that "it is useless for the South to attempt to establish slavery in Kansas." Titus added that after the Central American affairs were settled, "he intend[ed] going over into Cuba, and revolutionize that island, and gain it for the South." The colonel was in a hurry to leave Kansas before winter would freeze the Kansas and Missouri Rivers and paralyze steamboat traffic.[105]

On Wednesday, December 3, a cotillion was held at 9:00 P.M. in the Leavenworth Hotel, on the corner of Main and Delaware Streets in Leavenworth, Kansas, in honor of Colonel Titus and his militia captains John Donaldson and John Wallis. Formal invitations were printed by the seven managers of the affair. The next day Titus departed from Leavenworth, forwarding forty volunteers in wagons 180 miles to Jefferson City, Missouri, as the ice forming in the Missouri River made the prospects of a vessel uncertain. Twenty-four hours later the colonel sent the remainder of his followers thirty miles southeast to Parkville, Missouri, where they boarded the steamer *Australia.* Passage from Leavenworth to St. Louis was fifteen dollars per person. The *Leavenworth Weekly Herald* bid farewell to Titus, calling him a "meritorious citizen and gallant soldier" who "acted a prominent part in our Territory, and is known and recognized as a talented gentleman, and brave soldier." The newspaper wished, "Success to him and his gallant comrades wherever they go."[106]

Titus arrived with nine companions in Kansas City, Missouri, on December 8 and lodged in the American Hotel. The town was immensely crowded with Kansas residents heading east for the winter, land speculators hastening home, and disheartened filibusters seeking a steamboat ride down the Missouri River before it froze in order to avoid the hardships of the stage route. The Jackson County sheriff tried to serve Titus with a capias for an unpaid boarding bill at the Harris House in nearby Westport contracted by one of his men. Titus became defiant, exploded with "energetic expletives," and said that "he was a gentleman, and would not be called upon to pay debts in such a public manner." The sheriff withdrew after Titus bragged that he had enough men to turn the town "bottom-side-up in two minutes; and that the Almighty himself had not the power to put him in durance!"[107]

Journalists saw Titus, Jefferson Buford, and some Border Ruffians at the American Hotel having dinner with their former abolitionist enemies, including the free-state advocates Governor Charles Robinson, Lt. Gov. William Y. Roberts, Gen. Samuel Clarke Pomeroy, and Col. Shalor Winchell Eldridge, whose Free State Hotel in Lawrence had been destroyed by Titus and the proslavery forces. Titus sent "round his champagne bottle to those who had held him prisoner in Lawrence" and toasted them, "Kansas, a Free State!" Former adversaries "pledged each other's health in the choicest Heidsieck." This prompted the *Richmond Whig* to denounce Titus as lacking sincerity and patriotism, advising "Gen. William Walker to keep a vigilant eye on the renowned Col. Titus, and be sure to put him in no position of power or influence," as he "would no doubt sell friend or country any day for thirty pieces of silver."[108]

During the dinner Titus held up a "much deformed" left hand and claimed that it was "probed with a Spanish lance while in Cuba." Titus had a penchant for dramatic exaggeration, and his withered thumb and index finger were probably results of a sawmill accident severing tendon muscles and nerves, as no Cuba filibuster accounts include him with those wounded. Titus then displayed his right hand, which was gnarled even worse, and roared that "the damned Yankees shot a Sharpe's rifle ball through that one, and into his shoulder also." Titus, called "the gallant Floridian" by his men, was described by a *New York Times* correspondent in Kansas City as "a figure by no means displeasing to the romantic vision," with "his burly form cased in a military suit, his red cheeks and glowing eyes shaded by his Magyar hat" with its long black feather plume "à *la Kossuth*." The *Cincinnati Gazette* said that Titus was "a fine looking military man, and is very proud of his trappings and attire. . . . He is about six feet high, with a full broad face, a clear healthy complexion of white and red, a large black eye, jet black hair and beard." Unknown to the public, the colonel's health began to fail, as he developed a rheumatic condition that would worsen with age.[109]

Much of what was reported regarding the Kansas troubles is of doubtful reliability. Samuel Walker's memoirs, written forty-six years later, had versions that contradicted themselves and those of contemporary newspaper accounts. The abolitionist press did not chide Governor Geary for appointing their nemesis Titus as his aide-de-camp and ranking him as a colonel above Captain Walker and the Lawrence militia company. They also did not demonstrate that Geary had hired Titus's female slave as a servant. Northern and southern newspapers were biased and full of exaggerated accounts and figures, both sides claiming that they were attacked by overwhelming odds while decreasing the amount of their forces and losses. The *St. Louis Intelligencer* denounced "a device of one or the other party of agitators and factionists in the Territory to get up an excitement among their respective sympathizers, and induce prejudiced, misguided men to go into the Territory with a view of keeping alive the disturbances. The design of each is mainly to affect the Presidential canvass." A Missourian writing to a friend predicted, "I fear that the end will be a general war all over the Union . . . a war that will destroy the Union, I have no doubt." Free-soilers and proslavery men accused each other of indecency and dishonor toward women, along with being characterized by brutality, lust, and cowardice. The sectional press published sensationalist accounts defining the conflict as a civil war against tyranny and oppression.[110]

A number of Kansas emigrants arrived for the purpose of affecting the elections. There were fanatics on opposing sides committing depredations, expropriating horses and provisions, and taking plunder. Each group accused the other of pillage and murder. Abolitionists felt morally obliged to assist slaves in the territory escape their masters and thereby promote free-soil labor. They were regarded by their opponents as "Negro thieves" violating a constitutional right. Both sides, rejecting each other's legal system and therefore having no redress for wrongs in the courts, drove off troublesome neighbors by threats and force. Dr. John H. Gihon, Governor Geary's private secretary, summed up the situation: "The one party burned houses, and robbed and murdered unoffending people; and the other, in retaliation, committed the same atrocities." He also indicated, "Many of the personal rencontres in Kansas, grew out of the unsettled condition of affairs in regard to the possession of lands."[111]

Titus was accused by the *New York Times* of taking "a leading part in every outrage committed against Free-State people." This was disproved the following year when scores of citizens made government claims against losses occasioned during the Kansas troubles. Some implicated Titus. Claims of $100 each were made by G. W. and W. Hutchinson and Co. for "Damage on store building, May 21, 1856, by order of Titus" and by Edward S. Jewett for a gray mare that "was greatly damaged by Titus and Clark's company." George G. Brayman demanded $100 for his father's wagon taken by Titus's men at Lecompton after the elder Brayman was arrested for participating in the Hickory Point battle. John A. Wakefield asked for $50 for injury to two horses stolen and recovered in May 1856 by "a body of armed men, said to be commanded by Colonel H. Titus." Erastus Heath petitioned for $175 for a horse that was shot and killed when ridden by Captain Shombre when he assaulted Fort Titus. Absalom White, who lost his arm when he attacked the Titus homestead, put in a victim claim for $2,000, which was supported by his comrades Thomas Bickerton and S. B. Prentice. This case was quickly dismissed by the government commissioner upon the ground that Smith "was engaged in rebellion and making unwarranted attack upon the person and property of a private citizen, not in obedience to the laws of the country, or commands of any legal authority." There were no direct accusations against Titus, who never made his own claim, and no acknowledged rewards were ever paid by the government.[112]

Titus had gone to Kansas with his family to start a new life as homesteaders, but his involvement in proslavery militancy marred his prospects. He did not shirk confrontation or danger when called upon to defend his cause. While Titus blustered and bullied his enemies and probably pummeled his free-state neighbor during an argument, there is no evidence that he murdered anyone, in spite of the unsubstantiated abolitionist claims that he killed David Hoyt and George Williams. When he had the opportunity to burn the home of Capt. Samuel Walker, after forcing his family to evacuate their furnishings, he withheld from doing so, perhaps because of the pitiful pleadings of Mrs. Walker and her children and/or the possible sighting of Masonic emblems in the residence. When captured, Titus was aware that Walker was a Freemason, and he used the brotherhood's grand hailing sign of distress to plead for sworn fraternal assistance. Walker, in turn, was unable to spare Titus's home from a vengeful mob bent on retribution and was barely able to save his life. The colonel's enemies acknowledged that he fought like a tiger to defend his hearth. This made him a hero to proslavery men. Lecompton attorneys A. W. Jones and Robert H. Bennett listed him among the references in the newspaper advertisement of their law office. Titus's defeat resulted in an economic loss of $12,000, the equivalent of an income value of $4,480,000 today, with the forfeiture of his home, personal belongings, and slaves and the permanent impairment of his right hand. He now realized that his political activism had been a folly, but he did not bitterly hold a grudge. Titus released from jail in Lecompton a free-state man who had nursed him during captivity in Lawrence. He dined with his former enemies in Kansas City and toasted their free-state electoral triumph. Titus's only lasting achievement for such a perilous seven-month undertaking was that two territorial governors officially gave him the title of colonel, which he proudly flaunted thereafter. Nicaragua now beckoned with the greater economic and military opportunities that had proved fleeting in his Cuba and Kansas adventures.[113]

★ *Chapter Three* ★

Nicaragua Filibuster
1857

In mid-December 1856 Col. Henry Titus and some one hundred followers left Kansas City, Missouri, by steamer on the Missouri River for Jefferson City and from there boarded the Pacific railroad to St. Louis. The 125-mile ride, at speeds of up to eighteen miles an hour, cost five dollars per passenger. Upon arriving on December 16, Titus checked into the fashionable Barnum's Hotel, where an antislavery traveler saw him "in full feather, inveigling sundry simpletons into his Nicaragua net." The colonel and his coterie departed three days later on the steamer *Maria Denning* down the Mississippi River 1,280 miles to New Orleans. Reaching Memphis on December 23, they transferred to the *John Simonds* as it was about to leave for the Crescent City. The filibusters did not arrive in time at their destination, and the steamship *Texas* left for Nicaragua without them on the 28th with 250 volunteers. Titus reached New Orleans two days later with 120 followers, who were joined by another 20 volunteers from Texas. There was no possibility for the latecomers to proceed to Nicaragua until the *Texas* returned to sail again a month later.[1]

While in the Crescent City, N. C. Harney, a filibusterer from Missouri, was shot in the lower leg by a feuding party due to mistaken identity. He died from gangrene at the Charity Hospital on January 13. Eight days later "a large and influential meeting of citizens" was held in New Orleans, with Judge Edward Rawle presiding. Resolutions were unanimously approved supporting William Walker as the man of "manifest destiny" and the "heroic efforts" to rescue Central America from "tyrannical and oppressive rule"; denouncing British military intervention in the region; censuring the U.S. government's "timorous and peevish policy" toward the region; and inviting the "generous cooperation" of Americans toward "men combating for freedom . . . for the spread of republican principles." Achilles L. Kewen, a captain in the 1850 López expedition, gave a "forcible and eloquent speech" justifying Walker's "patriotic" intervention in Nicaragua. Recruits were also enticed with the pay offer of twenty-five dollars monthly in script and the promise of "150 acres of good land" after a year's service. A committee raised subscriptions for the next steamer leaving for Nicaragua in a few days. Col. Maunsel White, one of the wealthiest planters in Louisiana with nearly two hundred slaves, offered $500. Titus subscribed with $250, and Col. Shadrach F. Slatter followed with $500. R. W. Sheldon, a slave owner who had a boardinghouse, signed up for $500. A total of $1,750 was raised for the expedition.[2]

Titus left New Orleans with 120 filibusters on the steamship *Texas* on January 28, 1857, headed for San Juan del Norte (known in English as Greytown), Nicaragua. He was accompanied by Col. Anthony Francis Rudler, who had "seen a great deal of service in Nicaragua" on behalf of William Walker and had gone to the Crescent City the previous month to raise volunteers. The officers of Titus's command were Capt. William Moon, Company A; Capt. William Seaton West, Company B; Captain Williams, Company C; 1st Lts. John G. Starr and G. E. Conkling; and 2nd Lts. Emery and J. Mulholland. Titus's aide-de-camp E. S. Baker described his contingent as being "about two hundred and fifty men many of them from Kansas and Missouri." Baker carried a rifle, two Colt repeaters, and an "Arkansas Toothpick" dagger. Titus's second in command, twenty-five-year-old Capt. William M. Brantley, was leading the "Alabama Rifles" he had recruited in his state. He described Titus as "being unusually imposing. He weighs 220 pounds and is finely proportioned. For mental calibre, however, he says he has not two well-defined ideas in his head. His chief characteristics he defines as want of courage, and immense brag and a selfish tyrant." Titus claimed that "his sole object was to open the San Juan River, and that accomplished, he should return whence he came; that he was not desirous of obtaining any command, and would accept none, but as a mere temporary necessity. He had urgent business in the States, whither he should proceed as soon as his special object was secured."[3]

William Walker, nearly encircled in Rivas, Nicaragua, by the allied armies of Central America, was anxiously expecting the Titus reinforcements to regain control of the San Juan River. The waterway was the boundary between Nicaragua and Costa Rica, serving as a transit route between the Atlantic Ocean and Lake Nicaragua and by land carriage beyond to the Pacific. It was Walker's lifeline for men, weapons, and supplies from the eastern United States, but he had left the 150-mile river poorly protected at its three vital points. These were Fort San Carlos, on a bluff at the north bank of the head-waters of the San Juan River at Lake Nicaragua, and forts El Castillo and Sarapiquí at midway points along the southern shore. Costa Rican president Juan Rafael Mora had raised an additional levy of one thousand men, which allowed his army easily to occupy the three bastions during fifteen days in late December. They had also seized the four steamers of the Accessory Tran-sit Company, one loaded with the last rifles and howitzers sent to Walker. Mora declared the waterway closed and issued an English-language procla-mation "To the Soldiers of Walker's Army" offering them "free and safe pas-sage to Greytown and from thence 'per' Steamer to the City of New York."[4]

Fort Sarapiquí was located at La Trinidad hamlet, on Hipp's Point, where the Sarapiquí River flows into the San Juan River. It was thirty-five miles from Punta Arenas, a narrow sand strip jutting out several miles into the Greytown bay, at the mouth of the San Juan River. El Castillo was another fifty-five miles upstream, and Lake Nicaragua was thirty-five miles farther west from there. The Costa Rican military line of communication between their base and the San Juan River was the San Carlos River, twenty-five miles west of La Trinidad running parallel to the Sarapiquí. The San Juan River had a varying width that did not exceed six hundred feet. It had a slow stream, and the whole country for twenty miles inland was "a miserable swamp, cut up by lagoons and creeks and covered more or less with a dense growth of shrubbery."[5]

The Sarapiquí River, center, flowing into the San Juan River. Alvarado's Point is on the left, and Hipp's Point, with Costa Rican garrison, is on the right. From *Frank Leslie's Illustrated Newspaper,* June 21, 1856

A filibuster company that had left New Orleans in late December was bivouacking at Punta Arenas, three miles across the bay from Greytown. The latter was a town of some three hundred inhabitants, composed of a variety of Europeans, Americans, Central Americans, Jamaicans, and other nationalities. They mostly made their livings exporting beef hides, deerskins, Brazilwood, cacao, indigo, and gum elastic. Greytown had "about two or three dozen old houses or shanties," lacked a customhouse or a constabulary, and had various drinking establishments. The filibuster encampment was headed by twenty-eight-year-old Col. Samuel A. Lockridge, who had arrived the previous month as Walker's emigration agent. An Alabama native, he was described as "a robust six-footer, browny-complexion," with "a fine military presence." Lockridge had previously resided for six years in Costa Rica "and still considers himself a citizen of that country." The Greytown correspondent of the abolitionist *New York Tribune* described him as "a sensible, sober and brave man." The nonpartisan *New York Herald* called Lockridge "clear-headed, cool and of undoubted courage." His force had been under incessant rain for a week. The river had crested, and the planks the filibusters slept on "were floating at every full tide."[6]

Near the camp, since the previous July, there was a British naval force directly from England consisting of the screw ship HMS *Orion* with ninety-four guns, the corvettes HMS *Cossack* with twenty guns and *Tartar* with twenty-one guns, and the steam sloop gunboats HMS *Intrepid, Victor,* and *Pioneer,* each with six guns, along with more than two thousand men. The squadron commander, Capt. John E. Erskine, had a fortnight earlier received a letter from Costa Rican general in chief José Joaquín Mora requesting that he seize the filibuster vessels at Punta Arenas. Erskine responded that he had been instructed by his government "to preserve a perfect neutrality between the contending parties." He warned that since the future disposition of Greytown and Punta Arenas was still the subject of negotiations, he would "not recognize the right of Costa Rica to a military possession or occupation of the same" and would not permit "a blockade of the port of Greytown." Erskine then sent an officer from the HMS *Cossack* to the filibuster camp offering protection and free passage home to any British subjects wanting to leave. A dozen Irishmen quickly departed amid the groans and shouts of their comrades. Lockridge authorized anyone else who desired to go to do so, but none did.[7]

Gen. Chatham Roberdeau Wheat, who had been Titus's superior officer in the 1850 López expedition and now commanded the artillery, had recently arrived from New York City with Col. Frank Palmer Anderson, Maj. Charles William Doubleday, and some fifty men. He climbed on a barrel to harangue the filibusters and denounced British intervention in their affairs. Wheat was "in fine condition and as fat as a mackerel," and when he ended his tirade, the volunteers cheered for Walker and Nicaragua. On the evening of January 22, repair work was completed on the abandoned iron-hull steamer *Clayton*, dubbed the *Rescue*, in the factory of the Accessory Transit Company at Punta Arenas. The seventy-five-ton burthen vessel, powered by a 350-horsepower engine and side wheels eighteen feet in diameter, could hold two hundred men. Lt. A. C. Allen of Company B went on it for a trial run and determined that it went "pretty well." Jean Mesnier, a French merchant at Greytown, immediately informed the Fort Sarapiquí commander that the filibusters had just tested their steamer in preparation for attacking La Trinidad with 180 men, two cannons, and some eighteen landing rafts. Maj. Máximo Blanco, a thirty-two-year-old career officer, had received command of Fort Sarapiquí on January 21. Gen. Mora then assigned Capt. Damian Soto as his second in command and shipped him "100 American rifles and 10 thousand bullets" from Fort San Carlos.[8]

Lockridge, concerned about Fort Sarapiquí receiving further reinforcements, decided not to await the arrival of Titus and his men before launching an attack. The Costa Rican government *Boletin Oficial* (Official Bulletin) mockingly dubbed him the "new El Cid the Champion" and the "new Fierabras." At 7:00 A.M. on January 23, the *Rescue* steamed up the San Juan River with about two hundred men, towing several large bungos and a barge with a four-pounder cannon and a six-pounder cannon, arms, ammunition, and stores. Six filibusters afflicted with fever and measles were left behind. Pvt. Milton Shauman remembered that upon departing, "three cheers were given for Walker, three for Col. Lockridge, and three times three for Gen. Wheat, who was a great favorite among us." A half hour later and five miles upstream, at the inlet of the San Juanillo River, Lockridge transferred to the steamer a cannon, one hundred men, and two days' provisions from the scow, which was left anchored in the middle of the river with the bungos and twenty-five men. The *Rescue* went reconnoitering up the winding San Juanillo River. A fifty-man party, with information from a Nicaraguan "Indian" named Felipe Mena, nicknamed Petacas, disembarked to search for a Costa Rican sentinel but did not find him. Mena also told Lockridge that two Costa Rican soldiers were on a bungo on the San Juanillo River headed for Greytown. They were taking a letter from Major Blanco to Jean Mesnier for purchasing on credit two boats for Fort Sarapiquí. Mena had misinformed Blanco that the filibuster expedition had disbanded and told the invaders of the deplorable condition of the garrison.[9]

That same day, January 23, a Costa Rican contingent of 4 officers and 85 privates arrived at La Trinidad by raft from the town of Muelle de Sarapiquí, sixty miles up the Sarapiquí River. Sixteen soldiers absconded en route. The La Trinidad garrison of 263 men was "demoralized by being in the middle of a swamp" with many sick soldiers and increasing desertions. A number of Costa Ricans were prostrate with malaria and cholera. A sergeant and 21 men had fled a fortnight earlier due to hunger. The previous week a platoon from Cartago had briefly mutinied in support of a sergeant who refused to work.[10]

The *Rescue* returned to the barge that night and dropped anchor after searching the San Juanillo River as far as it was navigable. Lt. A. C. Allen found it "extremely unpleasant" to spend the night there, "as there is hardly room for us to stand up, not to speak of laying [*sic*] down; and it is raining, and the water is pouring through the old rotten roofs of our crafts, in a thousand different streams. And we are rather hungry." The following morning, the 24th, the steamer continued up the San Juan without the scow, stopping after five miles to question two natives coming down in a canoe. The strangers said that they were returning to Greytown after acquiring fruit and that they had not seen any Costa Ricans. They were "furnished a pass to enable them to go below the barge." The expedition continued five miles more until signaled by "a loud whistle" at Petacas Point, a north bank projecting point, where Mena had a "good-sized hacienda" on a clearing eight miles from Sarapiquí and twenty-four miles from Greytown. The filibusters disembarked and dug an entrenchment by the shore, naming it Fort Anderson, after the popular Colonel Frank Anderson, a thirty-two-year-old New Yorker who had been wounded at the first battle of Rivas in 1855. Most of the expeditionaries slept in the steamer that night to keep out of the rain after not finding sufficient shelter on shore. According to William Brown and Lieutenant Allen, their daily ration was "two pilot crackers" and "half a pound of beef" or "a slice of raw fat bacon." Twenty-five filibusters suffered from diarrhea "caused by eating green corn and green limes and lemons, and by drinking the brackish, unwholesome water of the San Juan River."[11]

The *Rescue* left Petacas Point early on Sunday, January 25, to retrieve the scow with the rest of the expedition and returned with them at 5:00 P.M. to the point of departure. That evening, while Private Devine was mounting guard, he accidentally shot Colonel Anderson on the shoulder. Devine was "bucked and gagged" to await punishment, but the colonel pardoned him for the slight wound. Pvt. William Henry Wilkins, a sixteen-year-old Natchez native, was also "bucked and gagged" for "refusing to go on duty." Three days later at 9:00 A.M., the steamer approached the Sarapiquí River inlet, which was strongly fortified on both banks of the San Juan River. At that point the San Juan River, which runs in a west-to-east course between Costa Rica and Nicaragua, dips south for one thousand yards, and the Sarapiquí River, making an S turn, flows into it from the west. Fort Sarapiquí was "strongly built of logs and earth" with four brass six-pounder cannons and a British nine-pounder iron gun. Major Blanco's headquarters was a palm-frond hut detached from the stockade. There were two defensive right-angle trenches, each twenty yards long by three yards wide, one on the north shore of the Sarapiquí River and the other parallel to the San Juan River. Across from the latter, on Cody's Point, was a small Costa Rican detachment behind an earthwork. Blanco later wrote to President Mora that it would be easy for the enemy to cut off their Sarapiquí River supply line but that he would hold his position instead of dividing them on both shores. When Blanco sighted the *Rescue*'s plume of smoke approaching between the trees, he ordered the bugler to call the troops to arms.[12]

Upon hearing the signal, General Wheat fired from the barge three six-pounder cannonballs that arched fifty yards high over the woods, and one hit a hut in the fort. Sylvanus M. Spencer, who had recently arrived at the garrison in transit to Fort San Carlos, returned fire with the long iron gun. Two more artillery shots forced the *Rescue* to retreat to Fort Anderson after Lockridge decided that it was safer to await the arrival of Titus and his force before renewing the attack. Spencer then sent a bungo with scouts to locate the position of the *Rescue,* and they returned at noon to report that the steamer was gone. Blanco claimed in his revised diary that he then ordered a corporal and two privates to establish an advanced post on the north bank of the San Juan on a bend one thousand yards away, "from where they could distinguish a good length of the river." He sent a squad of twenty men, commanded by Lieutenants Desiderio Selva and Dionisio Jiménez, downstream on the Nicaraguan shore to await in ambush at a spot where he presumed that the invaders would land. Blanco's troops lacked food, fevers and dysentery had spread, and four days earlier he stopped frequent desertions by "severely punishing" those caught fleeing. The major then had the Fort Sarapiquí trenches, previously capped with banana stalks, deepened and fortified with logs.[13]

After Lockridge returned to Petacas Point, he left Anderson in charge and went to Punta Arenas on the *Rescue* with 15 men to retrieve lumber and materials for building a breastwork and shelters. He posted a public notice in Greytown on January 26, responding to President Mora's proclamation, stating that he would "immediately proceed to open" the San Juan River. Meanwhile a few filibusters escaped from Fort Anderson by drifting downriver on logs after complaining of exposure to the elements, bad food, and being knee-deep in water in the encampment. The British consul at Greytown provided deserters with funds for food and passage to Panama on the English mail steamer. Desertion and disease had by then reduced Lockridge's force by about one third, to some 200 men. It was under these deplorable circumstances that on February 4, after the HMS *Orion* had left Greytown, the steamship *Texas* arrived after a week from New Orleans with Titus and some 250 volunteers.[14]

The *New York Times* correspondent at Greytown was impressed with the good physical appearance of Titus and his Kansans, "who seemed eager for a fight." William Walker later wrote in his memoirs, "Many of the persons with Titus had been his companions in Kansas, and probably most of them were made of better stuff than their leader. But his swaggering air had imposed on many people." Walker's *El Nicaraguense* newspaper had three months earlier mentioned Titus's appointment as commander of the Kansas Militia. The colonel arrived with "the prestige of a successful military chief, whose exploits in Kansas had invested his name with glory in the eyes of Southern men . . . there was no doubt felt of his military skill and conduct." A filibusterer described him as "a very fine looking man, tall, well made, with handsome face and the air of a gentleman."[15]

The *Rescue* stopped alongside the *Texas* and transferred the filibusters and their war materiel on board, including a six-pounder brass cannon, Mississippi rifles, plenty of Sharps rifles and Colt navy revolvers, and provisions for three months. Titus gave Lockridge letters "from nearly all the distinguished men of the South, recommending him both as a gentleman and officer, worthy of my highest consideration." Lockridge claimed that Titus "seemed to have very little command over his men," and he therefore placed the seasoned Col. Anthony Francis Rudler in charge of Titus's battalion. Titus replied with a note "refusing to give Col. Rudler any command in his battalion, stating that his authority for coming to this country emanated from higher authority" than Lockridge and that he would control them until Walker gave him orders. Walker explained that "Lockridge organized Titus and his men in a separate body, and soon a jealousy rather than rivalry sprang up between the new-comers and those acting under Anderson." The *Tribune* indicated that "a strong feeling of jealousy arose between the three leading officers," and "Titus also considered he had an equal right to the position of commanding officer."[16]

Titus and his Kansans departed Greytown on the *Rescue* that day at 3:00 P.M. and joined the other volunteers at Fort Anderson before sunset. There were 434 men in the camp, 23 being sick or wounded. Germans made up an entire company commanded by Capt. C. T. Sleight. Many filibusters had participated in international conflicts, including Hungarian revolutionaries who had fought at Szeged in 1848; Italian veterans of the Battle of Novara in 1849; Prussians from the Schleswig-Holstein campaigns of 1848–51; Frenchmen who had served in Algeria; English artillerymen who were in the Crimean War; Americans who had joined the López expeditions to Cuba and had been imprisoned in Ceuta for a year. Others were Mexican War veterans; and some officers had served in Nicaragua since the previous year and were returning from leaves of absence. According to Pvt. Martin Schroeder of St. Louis, "at least one-fourth of Lockridge's army were less than 17 years of age, and some were not more than 12 years old." He described Lockridge as "a man of energy and great endurance" who lacked "military skill."[17]

That same Wednesday, February 4, General Mora wrote from Fort San Carlos to Major Blanco warning that he was unable to support him and recommended that Blanco establish a strong line of communications with Muelle de Sarapiquí, inspect and constantly improve his fortifications, take care of the troops, and keep vigilant. The filibusters in Fort Anderson spent the next day "cleaning arms" and "trampling around through the slush to the disgust and horror of all." It was "a most miserable place reeking in filth knee deep in mud." Two men sent out as scouts never returned. The following morning a search party "found two newly made graves" but did not open them, assuming that their missing comrades had been killed by Costa Ricans lurking in the vicinity. At 8:00 A.M. on February 6, the filibusters headed to Fort Sarapiquí on the *Rescue,* towing the artillery barge and leaving behind 50 men to guard Fort Anderson. The volunteers were divided into three columns: Anderson led the First Battalion with 100 recruits; Titus followed with the Second Battalion of 150 mostly Kansans; and twenty-seven-year-old Maj. Robert H. Ellis commanded the rearguard with 100 men. The Kansans were distinguishable in their blue flannel militia shirts, while Anderson's men "were dressed in every conceivable irregularity of costume."[18]

Major Blanco later wrote to General Mora that at 6:00 that afternoon the invaders disembarked on the opposite bank two thousand yards away, where the hamlet of El Paraíso is today. According to Lockridge's aide, John Marks Baldwin, who was a correspondent for the *New Orleans Picayune,* they landed "about three miles" below Sarapiquí, but another anonymous report in the same newspaper claimed that it was "within half a mile of the enemy." Pvt. Milton Shauman stated that they sailed "within about two miles of Fort Sarapiquí and landed secretly among the bushes." Colonel Rudler asserted that they stopped "within one mile of Fort Sarapiquí." Their objective was Cody's Point, a high hill overlooking Fort Sarapiquí from 150 yards across the river. The plantation and furnished houses there were owned by Dr. Thomas Cody, an American citizen and former chief justice of the Supreme Court of San Juan del Norte. The property contained "a wood yard with sheds for supplying the river steamers with wood" and employed eight laborers.[19]

The landing party was allowed ninety minutes to arrive at their objective, and by that time the *Rescue* would reach the fort and draw their fire, "while Titus was attacking the post on the opposite shore." Colonel Rudler guided the force parallel to the riverbank, which was "too heavily overgrown with underbrush for them to proceed." A dozen men with machetes began cutting a path but made little progress since the shore had been mired by the "recent unusually heavy rains." The filibusters made a circuitous route inland on firm ground through the woods for some two miles, and after "some four or five hours of fatiguing traveling through marshes, they reached high land, behind Cody's point." The three battalions had difficulty going in the right direction due to the dense thicket. Eventually "the whole command reached the Plantain Patch about the same time" at Cody's Point. The forces regrouped and rested at 3:00 P.M. for thirty minutes before attacking the earthwork below the hill.[20]

Meanwhile, as the steamer approached Fort Sarapiquí at 1:00 P.M., Blanco's forward sentinel fired two rifle shots as a warning signal. When the *Rescue* was some fifty paces from Hipp's Point, it came under round shot artillery fire from Fort Sarapiquí and a hail of minié bullets from twenty men commanded by Lieutenant Selva entrenched on the opposite shore. There was no material injury, but the danger of being sunk made the *Rescue* retreat eight hundred yards to a bend in the river beyond enemy range. Wheat responded with two artillery pieces mounted on the barge in tow. He could see "the effect of almost every shot, and regardless of the danger he incurred, would get upon a prominent position and cheer every time the wall was injured or a roof destroyed." Blanco indicated in his diary that the enemy artillery fire "wrecked the main house" that was his headquarters.[21]

At 4:00 P.M. Blanco sent the officer of the day, Capt. Rafael Zarret, in a bungo with oarsmen to check Lieutenant Selva's barricade on the opposite riverbank and to warn him against a surprise attack. When Zarret advanced ten steps from shore, Titus's command unleashed their first volley. The lieutenant jumped into the river unscathed while his subalterns ran for the hills. Colonel Anderson, accompanied by Colonel Rudler, led the charge from the hilltop on Cody's Point to the Costa Rican entrenchment by the shore. Titus and his battalion followed "with a shout and hurra." According to George W.

Sites, a twenty-four-year-old medical student from Philadelphia serving as an orderly in Lt. John Coghlin's Company of Anderson's battalion, "Some of our men rushed madly into the attack and acted very unadvisedly and without orders." He recalled that Anderson's column followed around the hill while Titus's blue shirts, keeping in course, marched over the top. Sites stated that the Kansans did not recognize Anderson's men in the distance, "and supposing us to be Costa Ricans they fired. All the Americans who were killed or wounded in that attack, with one exception, were shot by Titus's battalion." Most of the Costa Rican raw recruits fled when they noticed their opponents approaching and began "crossing from Cody's to Hipp's Point as rapidly as they could" and "were immediately killed or driven to the wilds." They "fled in all directions, some jumped into the river and others took to the woods."[22]

Alvarado's Point, lower left, with Hipp's Point behind it across the Sarapiquí River. A Nicaraguan military post, right, occupies the shore of the San Juan River on Cody's Point. Titus and his filibuster company occupied the hill behind it on the right. From the author's collection

On the opposite shore, six Costa Ricans "sprang upon the embankment which surrounded their camp, shouting 'carajo,' and uttering cries of indignation and contempt." Blanco's soldiers unleashed "grape shot and canister, and a perfect hurricane of minnie balls" during a ten-minute duel. Others described the exchange as lasting up to half an hour. The filibuster muskets were no match for the greater accuracy and distance of the Costa Rican minié rifles. Capt. W. W. Berrington was wounded, and Major Ellis was grazed on the forehead by a ball when he left his shelter to observe the movement of a cannon. The three filibuster doctors, instead of attending the wounded, hid behind a log in the marsh. Titus ordered a cease-fire after seeing that their shots were doing little damage and that his men were "exposing themselves unnecessarily." He withdrew them out of range and "began to fortify himself on the hill" under cover of a ridge bearing down on Fort Sarapiquí. The abolitionist *Tribune,* when reporting this battle, continued its vilification campaign by accusing "Col. Titus and his Border Ruffians" of "robbing Indians and stealing plantains."[23]

After occupying the Costa Rican earthwork, Colonels Rudler and Anderson went down the trail alongside the San Juan River to notify Lockridge on the *Rescue.* When they hailed the steamer in the middle of the waterway one thousand yards away, Lieutenant Selva's advanced picket guard fired on them and the vessel. The Costa Ricans were behind a chaparral, "well entrenched, and brush thrown over the work so as to completely hide it." Blanco had expected the filibusters to land at this point, but they had taken the circuitous route behind the hill. Rudler was hit from eight feet away on the right thigh, and a steamer passenger was wounded. Wheat, afraid to return fire lest he shoot his comrades, withdrew the *Rescue* farther down the river. The officers quickly returned to Titus's position for assistance to repel the attackers. Rudler, "exhausted with fatigue and loss of blood," collapsed as he reached his unit. Capt. Robert Harris, commanding Company B of Anderson's battalion, sallied forth with twenty men whose rifles lacked bayonets. Lt. John P. Homan, a Texas Ranger in Captain Berrington's company, "drew his sword and endeavored to rally the men to charge" but was killed by a bullet to the head. Company B "lost their courage and retreated in a disorderly manner," after firing a close volley. Harris was said to have "acted cowardly in the affair." The platoon fled on the same path by which they had arrived, and it was not until two hours after dark that they rejoined Titus's force.[24]

E. S. Baker, Titus's aide-de-camp, stated that their total losses for the day were "seven killed and as many wounded" while "killing eleven of the enemy who were on our side of the river." Another account claimed that the Costa Ricans had "seven killed and a large number wounded" and that the invaders had "four Americans killed and ten wounded." Colonel Rudler inflated enemy losses to "twenty killed and about thirty wounded. Our loss is but trifling." According to Lt. Col. Edmund H. McDonald of the Second Rifles, "it was useless to attempt anything on the opposite side of the river without artillery." Baker acknowledged that enemy cannons kept them at a distance. Orderly Sites recalled that they left in such haste "that we had no time to bury the dead, and we were refused permission to do this." A filibusterer who later deserted claimed that before departing, the officers "appropriated to their own use the contents of the pockets of our dead comrades." The men had a "slow and laborious march" eight miles back to Fort Anderson under a rain storm, arriving at 3:00 A.M., and "spent a wretched night ashore." Sites recalled, "We wrapped ourselves in our blankets, and without shelter, drenched to the skin, enjoyed a good night's rest after the severe labor of the day."[25]

After daybreak on February 7, the *Rescue* transferred the filibusters back upstream to what is now El Paraíso. They disembarked "all the forces and artillery, except one company, which was left at Fort Anderson." The place was dubbed Fort Titus, due to the rivalry between Titus and Anderson, who, "by mutual arrangement, had command on alternate days." Major Blanco that day wrote to Capt. Faustino Montes de Oca, commanding El Castillo fortress, informing him that "the enemy is fortifying 2,000 yards from here" and that his situation was "very bad." McDonald erroneously claimed that their position was "500 yards below Sarapiquí," which would have been too dangerously close to Blanco's artillery. The filibusters spent four days cutting down trees, erecting breastworks and flimsy huts covered with broad plantain leaves, positioning cannons, and sending out reconnoitering parties to locate the enemy. Titus had the post built "large enough to require 500 men for its defense," to render Fort Anderson obsolete.[26]

Titus had his men spend February 8 cutting a hidden trail parallel to the San Juan River and bridging a creek to roll the artillery to Cody's Point. Wheat simultaneously directed the construction of a concealed breastwork for three cannons across from Fort Sarapiquí. The next morning the *Rescue* returned to Punta Arenas for boiler repairs, while Colonel Rudler and some wounded were evacuated to New Orleans. Fifty filibusters had arrived the previous day from New York commanded by Capt. John Egbert Farnum and Col. George Bolivar Hall. The latter wore the "Nicaragua uniform, with the emblem of the State—the five volcanoes—on the button" and "fashionable long-legged waterproof boots." The only weapons they brought were "some half dozen rifles and shot guns." As the uniforms were being issued to the newcomers on the 10th, seven English and Irish recruits refused to board the *Rescue* and defected to the British gunboat *Victor.* The rest were ferried that afternoon to Fort Titus, where Lockridge appointed Hall to head the commissary department. The illiterate Lockridge also assigned Hall to write his dispatches for him. Meanwhile, Major Blanco had sent a captain with a spyglass to observe Fort Titus from across the river. The officer reported that "its trenches are made with logs and a bronze cannon is on the bow of a scow.

The steamer goes back and forth every day, even making two trips, that are probably to San Juan [del Norte]."[27]

The news prompted a stampede of desertions at Fort Sarapiquí. Blanco wrote to General Mora on the 9th, "With the greatest disgust I announce to you that this troop is not of men it is less than women: it is impossible for me to contain desertions, all the enlisted men have left and I only have the sick . . . there is much fear in these soldiers." He further complained that these were "men who had never handled a rifle, and they know less of duty: when the enemy fires a cannon, there are men who bury their face in the mud." All his troops complained of hunger, some had "long faces due to fear of bullets," and others were malingerers who trembled when forced to hold a rifle. Blanco stressed that he had not been provisioned on time, he had victuals for only two days, and that "the situation in the camp is very pitiful." The major wrote that he had only six good officers to count on and had sent a sergeant after a corporal and five soldiers who fled and would be executed upon their capture. He felt "embarrassment and regret at seeing what people he had to fight with" but would hold on to La Trinidad.[28]

On Wednesday afternoon, February 11, Titus and the filibuster officers called their troops before them and distributed each a minié rifle and ammunition. Sites recalled how "we were told that we must prepare for a hot engagement the next day, and each company was informed that with them it was confidently believed would rest the honor of the victory." At 3:00 A.M. the next day, Titus's command began dragging three brass six-pounder cannons on their carriages to Cody's Point. Colonel Anderson and 130 men on the *Rescue* were transported across the San Juan River "a mile or two below the fort," according to Maj. Charles Doubleday. They slashed with machetes a path up to Alvarado's Point at the inlet across from Fort Sarapiquí. Lockridge sent a courier to Greytown requesting that the steamer *Texas,* scheduled to depart at 8:00 A.M., wait until 2:00 P.M., as he was about to attack Fort Sarapiquí and "desired to forward accounts of the results." The *Texas* stayed until 3:00 P.M. and left without the dispatches, which arrived three hours later.[29]

According to Colonel Hall, the attack strategy was planned by Wheat, Anderson, and Titus. Wheat directed the mounting of the artillery on an entrenchment behind a chaparral on the shore opposite Fort Sarapiquí. Capt. William Seaton West's company occupied the rifle pits on the left of the battery, and Captain Brantley's Alabamians were "on the right, on the brow of a hill." Titus commanded all the riflemen, and the artillery was under Wheat. Sites, an orderly in Anderson's battalion, indicated that on Friday, the 13th, "Gen. Wheat commenced the attack about sunrise, at the reveille of the Costa Ricans—they being mustered in a line in the fort at the town" of La Trinidad. Major Blanco wrote that he was unable to see the enemy due to the darkness and the fog. He exaggerated in his diary that they were greeted by some "five hundred rifle bullets and three artillery bar shots," since Titus had only 150 men and Anderson's force had not yet reached its objective. Wheat's cannoneers and Titus's riflemen fired at Fort Sarapiquí and its more than 200 defenders under a heavy rain that made flintlock muskets difficult to discharge. Wheat had "devised a kind of chain-shot composed of melted leaden balls connected by short chains." A filibusterer claimed that their artillery "threw 400 round-shot" at Fort Sarapiquí, but Walker wrote that it did not make "a serious impression on the enemy." Captain West's riflemen focused on picking off Blanco's gunners manning four brass six-pounder cannons and a British nine-pounder iron gun. A Costa Rican six-pounder was dismounted by a shot, and their iron piece was never fired because Brantley's sharpshooters impeded approaching it.[30]

According to Major Doubleday, Colonel Anderson's force reached Alvarado's Point near daylight and met no resistance. That morning Blanco saw a lieutenant and four soldiers posted there fleeing across the Sarapiquí upstream. Doubleday described the area as a "small clearing of felled timber, which had recently been cut down," assuming it was "to destroy the cover which the standing timber made for an enemy in attacking the fort." However, Montes de Oca the previous month had ordered men to "cut plenty" of the wood there to supply their steamers on the San Juan River. Doubleday was also contradicted by McDonald and the orderly Sites, who stated that they arrived there at noon without being seen by their opponents, who were "much weakened by sickness." Anderson established a line behind the downed tree trunks that extended along the Sarapiquí shore for two hundred yards, with his right flank near the mouth of the river. Four companies under Doubleday "fired volley after volley" into the side and rear of the fort's right-angle trenches. Doubleday recalled, "The firing for about an hour was really very sharp." The attackers succeeded in dislodging Blanco's men and "driving them from their barricades to the main building up the San Juan River." James Ryan, an Irishman in Anderson's force, stated that many of the Costa Rican soldiers were inexperienced marksmen, "firing at haphazard, and generally too high." He saw that "many of them would avert their faces at the moment of pulling the trigger" to avoid the blowback of spent gunpowder and smoke. The filibuster assault from both riverbanks continued until nightfall.[31]

An anonymous filibuster letter to the editor of the *Aspinwall Courier* of Panama indicated that the battle started at 6:00 A.M. and that "in ten hours we threw 400 round shots among them, knocking the fort and houses to pieces." Lt. Vicente Salazar, sixty miles away at the town of Muelle de Sarapiquí, heard incessant cannonading until 1:00 that afternoon. Lieutenant Colonel McDonald stated that the garrison commander fled at 2:30 P.M. and that he later "saw the enemy running away into the woods, leaving their blankets and throwing their guns away." Blanco, however, wrote in his revised diary that he departed after dark. Another filibusterer stated, "The enemy retired in small parties during the day, and in the night entirely deserted the fort." Two of Anderson's Germans who "needlessly exposed themselves to the enemy" were killed, while the orderly George W. Sites was hit by a minié ball in the thigh and buckshot in the knee and Capt. F. Schlicht "had a ball through the shoulder, which the doctor extracted from behind." Colonel Titus's command had "two wounded and none killed—and the artillery none." During the heat of battle, Titus discarded his uniform coat, just like he had done at Cárdenas. Lockridge remained on the *Rescue* the entire day "without landing or conducting in person any portion of the engagement." Titus never crossed the river during the engagement or got close to the Costa Ricans as did Anderson's force. According to E. S. Baker, Titus's aide-de-camp, the colonel "as usual claimed the credit of whipping them and the language he used on the occasion was ridicule and vain as well as vulgar. Why he looked so buoyant that I think that if his suspenders would have been cut he would have went up like a balloon."[32]

At 5:00 A.M. on Saturday, February 14, Wheat's artillery lobbed a few more shells at the garrison, which were heard by Lieutenant Salazar at Muelle de Sarapiquí. After daylight Capt. Julius De Brissot, "a little bow-legged, bullet headed, sandy haired, red eyed, individual" from New Orleans, and John King, called "Kentuck," paddled a canoe to Fort Sarapiquí, removed the Costa Rican flag, and hoisted Walker's Lone Star of Nicaragua banner. Colonel Anderson's command crossed in the *Rescue* from Alvarado's Point to the stockade and found thirteen corpses inside, mostly artillery victims, and two injured soldiers. A Costa Rican "severely wounded in the leg" said that he was a silver mine laborer and got conscripted because "Mora compelled the natives to fight or suffer the garrote." He was "highly pleased with the lenient treatment he received," having been told that the filibusters were "a band of blood-thirsty villains, giving no quarter, and roasting all they didn't choose to hang." The prisoner complained that during the previous month the garrison had been "badly treated and worse fed, living on beans and plantains alone." He added that during their evacuation, his commander "left the place at noon, about 150 men left in the afternoon, and the rest during the night, after destroying their ammunition and whatever else they could." The captive indicated that they "lost 14 killed and 30 wounded" and that many of their dead were "thrown into the river."[33]

In contrast, the *New York Times* quoted the same prisoner as saying that their casualties were "7 killed and 20 wounded," and he omitted mention of their watery grave. Doubleday, however, claimed that the filibuster dead "were decently buried, but Lockridge conceived the novel idea of notifying the British, who had persecuted us so much in the harbor of Greytown, of our victory, by throwing the dead of the enemy into the river, whose rapid current, when the tide set outward, soon carried to the sea those spared by the alligators." McDonald affirmed that Anderson assigned fifty men to bury thirty-three of the enemies. The abolitionist *Tribune* selectively copied McDonald's account from the *Aspinwall Courier*, without naming him, and changed the word "burying" of the enemy dead to "burning" them.[34]

As the filibusters were posting their picket guards around Fort Sarapiquí a wounded Costa Rican lying on the grass raised himself up. A sentinel "leveled his musket and blew his head off." Sites claimed, "He would not have been killed had not our men at that time feared an ambuscade, and the guard-house being full of Costa Ricans" who were local civilians. The other wounded prisoner "afterwards died of fever or cholera." Anderson sent a squad along the Sarapiquí River trail for six miles. A half mile away they found a hut that served as an outpost containing the corpse of a Costa Rican who had died from his wounds. At different places they recovered two minié rifles and ten flintlock muskets discarded during flight. Three of Anderson's men, McDonald, Sites, and William Brown, affirmed that the enemy threw into the river three cannons without spiking, including the nine-pounder and some cannonballs, and everything was recovered later.[35]

According to McDonald, they also occupied "upwards of 400 stands of English Minié muskets that were left scattered on the ground," along with "fifty thousand rounds of Minié rifle cartridges, in good condition, and a large quantity of damaged ammunition, 250 pairs of pantaloons, 40 bushels of beans, and six barrels of salt, but enough kettles and pans for 2,000 men." The pants were canvas trousers with a red stripe that the Costa Ricans had seized from Walker's Commissariat when they gained control of the San Juan River. Ryan raised the number of abandoned weapons inside the stockade to "near one thousand stand of arms, several of them rifles." Sites stated that they also found "a quantity of female clothing" and that "the officers left their trunks and mosquito bars, the luxury of which we appreciated," along with "money and bijouterie." Brown complained, "All the plunder was appropriated by the officers; the privates did not get the first thing." Sites saw an "elegant sword" inscribed to General Mora and a parcel of letters from him to the Costa Rican president, his brother; to the minister of war requesting more troops to hold his position; and to the commander of the British squadron at Greytown.[36]

Blanco had retreated along the Sarapiquí River bank sixty miles to Muelle de Sarapiquí, where during the next forty-eight hours he regrouped seventy of his more than two hundred men. He wrote to President Mora explaining the motivations for his withdrawal. Mora approved his actions and asked the major to bring his force to the capital "in the greatest order, cheering the government and shouting death to the filibuster[er]s." Blanco was ordered to outfit his soldiers with the extra uniforms at his location "so that they enter well dressed."[37]

According to Doubleday, who erroneously wrote that Titus arrived in Nicaragua at this time, Lockridge proposed that Anderson should command an expedition to seize El Castillo fortress fifty-five miles upstream. Titus was "claiming as a privilege" the right to go first. Doubleday wrote that Titus, who "was blown full of pride by the cheap reputation he had acquired in burning defenseless houses on the Missouri-Kansas frontier, refused to serve under anyone, but offered to capture the 'blank place' with his company alone." Titus was anxious to seize a larger fortification than the one his rival had just taken. According to Walker, the contest as to rank between Anderson and Titus "had increased the disorganization and disorder already existing in Lockridge's command." Captain Brantley claimed that Lockridge possessed "neither decision, firmness, nor tact" and had "no elements of a good commander." He described him as "an unlettered man, uncouth in his manners, but with some ambition for notoriety, with great energy and industry."[38]

Lockridge gave Anderson charge of Fort Sarapiquí, and the filibusters spent the next two days repairing the fortification and remounting the guns. Anderson "occupied a thatched cottage, about 30 yards distant from the walls, formerly the quarters of the Costa Rican Commandant of the fort." In contrast, his men were "sleeping on logs and the ground without a blanket, being on guard at night pretty often, and laboring hard during the day." The area was prone to yellow fever and malaria "to an alarming extent—four or five persons dying a day from fever and general debility." On Saturday evening, the 14th, Lockridge took the *Rescue* with Titus and his command and a four-pounder gun to Providencia Island (also called San Carlos Island), twenty miles from El Castillo at the confluence of the San Juan and San Carlos Rivers, which was occupied without opposition. The steamer returned to Sarapiquí, retrieved Colonel Hall and the stores needed at the new post, and went back to the island. Meanwhile the thirty-two-year-old, red-headed Englishman Capt. George Frederick Cauty, director general of all the Costa Rican vessels, was heading downstream on the transit steamer *Charles Morgan* under orders from Gen. José Joaquín Mora to assist Blanco. Three miles from Fort Sarapiquí, two fleeing Costa Rican soldiers signaled him and informed him of their defeat. The steamer reversed course and was ahead by four hours when spotted by the *Rescue,* which gave chase. Cauty arrived at El Castillo on Sunday, the 15th, at 6:00 A.M., appraised Capt. Faustino Montes de Oca of the situation, and offered his services.[39]

The hamlet of El Castillo, on the San Juan's southern shore, had a couple of hundred inhabitants residing in "a dozen well-built frame houses, besides numerous structures of lesser pretensions." River steamers disgorged passengers and cargo on the eastern wharves in front of the Transit Company house that was flanked ten yards apart by two hotels, the cheaper and smaller Nicaragua Hotel on its left and the National Hotel on its right. The latter was a two-story frame house containing fifteen bedrooms, a parlor, a barroom, a dining room and a pantry, and an additional "story and a half kitchen and bake house with oven." The bedrooms each had double bedsteads with straw mattresses and mosquito bar, cotton sheets and pillow cases, curtains, a mirror, a table and chair, and a washbowl and pitcher. The parlor contained a sofa lounge, center and side tables, six cane-seat chairs, a chess set, two large mirrors, curtains, floor mats, and a china tea set. The kitchen had a stove and an extra boiler, a coffee mill, waffle irons, graters, a grindstone, a butcher's cleaver, eighteen tin pie plates, and utensils. The National Hotel, worth $20,950, was owned by Thomas Townsend, who resided in one room with his wife and annually rented the property for $1,500 to New Yorkers Samuel S. Wood and his son Alexander M. C. Wood. The proprietor of the Nicaragua Hotel was twenty-seven-year-old John Edward Hollenbeck, and the building and furnishings, including a bar and eighteen beds, were valued at $8,498.[40]

The hotels served as the terminus of a mule-drawn portage railway that snaked along the riverbank beyond the Castillo Rapids to a western dock. The lightened iron-hull steamers then endeavored passage through the interstices of large, loose stones obstructing the river by using hawsers trailed around stumps on the shore. Overlooking the rapids is the Nuestra Señora de la Inmaculada Concepción fortress, dubbed El Castillo, completed in 1675 by the Spanish Crown to impede Caribbean pirate attacks on Granada via the water route. It crowns a steep hill, with almost perpendicular sides, whose northern slope runs down to the rail line along the shore. The castle is 117 feet above the river, providing a two-mile view in either direction. It is surrounded by a moat with a drawbridge entrance facing west, opposite the water approach. The castle was in disrepair after the British seized and destroyed large parts of it in 1780. Its damp and wet vaults prohibited the storage of victuals or gunpowder. The ramparts initially mounted thirty-six guns, and there was an abandoned water battery by the river.[41]

Nuestra Señora de la Inmaculada Concepción fortress, El Castillo, Nicaragua.
Below is the San Juan River steamer landing in front of the National Hotel.
From *Frank Leslie's Illustrated Newspaper*, May 17, 1856

Seven weeks earlier Captain Montes de Oca arrived at El Castillo with thirty sappers and an officer. The forty-six-year-old officer, a farmer who had recently volunteered for military service, owed his rank to being married to the sister of President Mora and the general in chief. He received command of the fortress under the dire warning by General Mora that "with his neck he would respond for the security of the Castle." The fall of El Castillo would give Titus and the filibusters complete control of the San Juan River and cut off the Costa Rican line of communication between the San Carlos River and Lake Nicaragua. Montes de Oca took lodging at the Nicaragua Hotel. The sappers, mostly conscripted prisoners, dug a trench where the portage railway curved around the fortress hill. The captain placed a six-pounder cannon aimed at the hamlet thoroughfare leading to the eastern dock and hotels and another cannon pointed in the opposite direction. He asked General Mora for artillerists to handle the pieces. The captain built other defensive points and had his troops doing daily drills and target practice. Mora later sent Capt. Rafael Rojas, assigned as second in command to Montes de Oca, along with a lieutenant, twenty privates, and four boxes of munitions. A bilingual proclamation issued by Mora was posted in the hamlet instructing all to obey his orders transmitted through Montes de Oca and warning that anyone aiding or speaking in favor of the filibusters "would be immediately shot."[42]

When Cauty arrived on the *Charles Morgan* at dawn on Sunday, February 15, Montes de Oca, whose command had been reduced to twenty-two men, assigned him with ten sappers to the artillery trench by the river. The captain then evacuated John Hollenbeck, his sister, his twenty-six-year-old German wife Elise, and their son John Jr. along with all the local families to Fort San Carlos on the steamer. Hollenbeck told Montes de Oca that he and his troops were welcome to everything he left behind in his hotel. The captain assigned six foreigners, "four Nicaraguans, an American, and a Frenchman," to the breastwork under duress. Another resident, Englishman Charles M. Stewart, who owned a small inn, had earlier joined the Costa Rican army and was stationed at Fort San Carlos. Montes de Oca then had the boiler valves removed from the steamers *J. N. Scott* and *Machuca,* which were chained to the eastern wharves in front of each hotel. Walter Harris, an American working on the vessels, deposed that Cauty ordered him "to see to preparing the steamers with fuel which would easily ignite." The ships were packed with firewood and dry grass soaked with tar and turpentine. A sapper with a matchbox stood on each boat with orders that upon hearing the warning shots from the sentries two hundred yards downriver, they were to torch the steamers and return to Cauty's trench.[43]

That morning Titus disembarked from the *Rescue* two miles below El Castillo with a detachment that he claimed had 1 officer and 72 men. Walker and Lockridge indicated that this force consisted of 140 men. A private accompanying Titus said that there were 150 troops "worn out by labor and three days' exposure in the rain and open field at Sarapiquí." Montes de Oca estimated that he was "attacked by 150 filibuster[er]s." Lockridge ordered Titus to charge the castle "at once, and save the steamers if possible." His command was "to march round through the woods and enter it on the other side, while he went up to cannonade it from the river with his remaining force." An anonymous apologia for Titus in the *New York Herald,* dated three months later from Panama, headlined "Doings of Col. Titus at Rivas," and similar to an exculpatory letter that the colonel afterward sent to newspapers, claimed that Lockridge refused to give him two of the ordnance pieces on the steamer. Titus wrote that he and his men "landed without proper means of defense, having neither artillery, no axes, and short of provisions." They also lacked a guide "who understood the construction of the works or the approaches to them." Half a mile from the fortress, Titus sent his second in command, Captain Brantley, "with a small detachment to make his way around to the upper side" west of El Castillo and begin shooting "to withdraw attention from Titus, who was to attack from below."[44]

Brantley's journal indicates that his squad stealthily advanced through the plantain trees, "taking a wide circuit in order to avoid the enemy's pickets." They passed a mile-long range of three hills covered with thick shrubbery parallel to the river and flanking the castle. The last one, Nelson's Hill, had an old earthwork called Fort Nelson that encircled its crown. It overlooked from a side angle the entrance to the fortress from thirty feet high and one hundred yards away. The redoubt was built in April 1780 by Capt. Horatio Nelson, of future Trafalgar fame, to attack the castle during Britain's war with Spain. Fort Nelson has since disappeared, and today the El Castillo village cemetery occupies the hilltop. Titus's aide-de-camp E. S. Baker surmised that the bastion was "capable of holding 800 men." Before a surprise charge could be effected on the fortress, "Col. Titus *saw a big bull* at a short distance. Regarding it as a prize too valuable to let get out of their way, he ordered two or three men to fire their pieces." The beast bellowed and collapsed under the crackling shots, alarming the garrison and giving them time to resist the assault. Baker described how after crossing a bayou "lined with a dense thicket," they were seen when emerging near the fort. He thought that "instead of rushing on the fort as he should have done, Titus gave them time to set the *J. N. Scott* and the *Machuca* on fire."[45]

According to Captain Montes de Oca, the attack started on the 15th at 2:30 P.M. as the *Rescue* simultaneously appeared at six hundred yards in the middle of a bend in the river. He used a spyglass to see that the steamer was towing "a scow with something like a howitzer, and I did not doubt for a moment that they would bury us alive." General Wheat fired a cannonball over the fortress, and the men inside responded with a massive twenty-four-pounder gun. Baker recalled that the loud booms made "the hills tremble with every shot," forcing the steamer to retreat quickly two miles downriver. Cauty recalled that he had just placed his two "six pounders into position, when the filibuster's steamer hove in sight. At the same moment our advanced sentries came in, having been fired upon on all sides by the thieves in the woods" on the flanking hills. The six conscripted foreigners ran upon hearing the first detonation, leaving Cauty with ten men. Baker saw them flee to the fortress from "behind a barricade which they had thrown up across the road at the upper end of the rapids." When Titus spotted Cauty's position, instead of leading a charge, he "appealed to the chivalry of some of the boys to put the fire out" on the steamers. A renegade filibusterer later claimed that Titus offered one hundred dollars to anyone who would extinguish it.[46]

Two volunteers dove into the river "under a perfect hurricane of grape and canister shot, fired from the castle," boarded the *J. N. Scott,* and doused the flames, "although the machinery was much injured." Titus never paid them "a cent of the promised reward." The stern-wheel steamer, "the largest and finest boat on the river," measuring 140 feet long by twenty-five feet wide, had a large hole in the deck where the fire started, its woodwork was riddled with shot, and its boiler valve was gone. Cauty, accompanied by two men, ran down to release the docking chain on the burning *Machuca,* which then drifted into the *J. N. Scott.* Titus's men cut the mooring lines on the latter, letting it float fifty yards downriver until it grounded on rocks. The smoke billowing from the steamer dropped cinders on the adjacent houses and provided cover for Cauty and his helpers to return safely to their trench. Montes de Oca recalled that the vapors ascending beyond El Castillo impeded him from seeing the enemy below and they in turn could not discern the fortress, initially limiting the action to Cauty's trench.[47]

Several filibusters went behind the National Hotel and "kept up a sharp fire on the barricade." According to Baker, "the boys now began to flock in like so many lazy men at a fight with our redoubtable Colonel at their foot, there was no regard to order and company A. B. and C. were mixed up as promiscuously as you could mix a pint of corn and beans with a quart of punkinseed [*sic*]." Ten minutes after the shooting started, Cauty fired a six-pounder at the *J. N. Scott* as it drifted downstream. Baker saw how "the shot made the splinters fly and brought down a couple of the boys and frightened some of the rest overboard." The report made some twenty or thirty filibusters behind the National Hotel run off and hide in the woods, while others swam out to the steamer.[48]

The embers from the *Machuca* had ignited a shed attached to the National Hotel. Baker believed that if Titus had charged Cauty's position, "which kept up a fire all the time so that no one dared to go in the street," they could have overrun it and then extinguished the flames. Titus, "being afraid to charge the battery," instead gave the order to snuff the blaze. Several filibusters ran to the structure, "and some tried to punch the shingles off" while others provided a covering fire from the corner of the adjacent kitchen building. When the shingles would not give, Baker and a companion went in the kitchen, got a kettle of water, and emerged onto the street to pour it on the shed. Cauty, anticipating their return, from ten yards away fired a shrapnel blast that bowled them over. Baker was unhurt except for a burning pain on his right thigh where a ball tucked and tore off part of his pants. His companion had both his legs blown away and was carried to safety, dying of his injuries at midnight. Baker wrote that it was "the last attempt to put out the fire and the National Hotel was soon in a blaze." Some of the hotel furniture and bedding was saved, but all the other houses and their contents were destroyed.[49]

After the smoke dissipated, Montes de Oca was sniping at the filibusters from the fortress when he noticed that his ten sappers were poor marksmen who would "lower their head[s] as they fired" to avoid the blowback into their eyes. He ordered them to stop shooting and instead load muskets for him and his second in command Capt. Rafael Rojas. Both officers were positioned behind parapets, but only Montes de Oca took the precaution of building an embrasure with bricks, leaving a two-inch-square gap to insert his weapon. Rojas, neglecting such protection, died of a bullet to the forehead, and a corporal too was killed.[50]

Cauty manned his artillery pieces until 7:00 P.M., under a constant "rain of bullets," sparingly firing "shot, grape, chain-shot and stones" whenever the attackers attempted to form and charge. Two defenders were wounded in the redoubt, and the gun embrasure was splintered under fire. Lt. Col. Edmund H. McDonald stated that the position was "taken by storm by Capt. West's company of Col. Titus's command." In contrast, the Englishman alleged that when the enemy fire slackened and his gunpowder was spent, he spiked the cannons and retreated with his crew into the fortress, carrying the artillery implements and lynchpins, under cover of darkness. Lacking shelter in the hamlet, some filibusters retired to the *J. N. Scott* and others to the hills. A neutral American who visited the fortress days later said that the defenders had "just *twenty-one men*." Titus failed to encircle the castle, "withdrew among the plantain bushes, threw up a light breastwork during the night, and at daylight withdrew." He later admitted that Cauty "displayed considerable bravery" and that his shooting was "very steady and sure."[51]

At dawn on Monday, February 16, Titus ordered Capt. William Moon to move the grounded *J. N. Scott* to the landing two miles downriver out of the reach of the fortress gun. Cauty, upon hearing from the castle rampart that the enemy "sounded a retreat," focused a spyglass on the steamer and assumed that the men prone on deck were wounded. Montes de Oca, using the same instrument, could not determine if the filibusters were sleeping or injured and saw three others struggling to free the stuck vessel, which a strong current carried away at 9:00 A.M. He noticed that the hamlet below was all "in ashes." In contrast, Walter Harris deposed that Montes de Oca later told him that "the Costa Ricans had set fire to the 'Company's Office' in order to keep the filibuster[er]s from occupying it" and that the flames leaped to the adjacent Nicaragua Hotel and destroyed it. Cauty estimated that fifty filibusters remained facing the castle "to keep us inside, firing with great precision at the least visible object." They were Brantley's men in Fort Nelson, unaware of what had transpired on the other side. Brantley sent messengers to locate Titus, but they were unable to find him. In consequence, Brantley withdrew his company from the redoubt at noon and went searching for Titus at the disembarkation point. During the interim Montes de Oca had the two men who had been killed the previous day interred in El Castillo and appointed Cauty as his second in command.[52]

Titus had gone to meet Lockridge, who was on the *Rescue* at the landing two miles away, and they "held a long parley." According to Colonel Hall, Lockridge told Titus to "hold his position for twenty-four hours, in which time he promised to return with reinforcements." Lockridge, before departing for Fort Sarapiquí to retrieve Capt. Robert Harris's Company B, ordered Titus to charge the fort. He then went on the steamer to get provisions at Greytown. Montes de Oca spotted the attackers returning on Monday, the 16th, at 6:00 P.M. and hurriedly wrote to General Mora at Fort San Carlos detailing the events of the previous twenty-eight hours. He emphasized, "I have only 20 men and some of them are sick. I have little rifle ammunition and less for the cannon. I am short of provisions." The captain requested that an auxiliary steamer should ring its bell six times upon approaching and said that the fortress would respond with the signal agreed to with Capt. Jesús Alvarado. Cauty added a postscript to the letter affirming that "with fifty men and provisions they will never take this place . . . I remain until reinforcements come as I consider the place of the highest importance, and if they take it now, never again will Costa Rica have it." He advised that reinforcements should land one mile distant. Father Rafael Brenes, the chaplain of the Costa Rican army, stated that a messenger was lowered by rope from the castle. Montes de Oca and Cauty both later concurred that a "mail boat" was sent out Monday night.[53]

After returning to El Castillo, Titus "backed out" of effecting the charge ordered by Lockridge and instead posted Brantley's company in Fort Nelson, "cleared out the trenches," and positioned the two other companies on the ridge below. The filibuster encampments were concealed within the forested hills. Titus then had the captured "two cannon planted so as to command the entrance to the fort." On Tuesday morning the Costa Ricans had just finished butchering a cow for breakfast when the shooting renewed from Nelson's Hill. Montes de Oca recalled that "everyone ran to their posts, leaving the rest of the cow there. From that time on, no one could show their hat without it being pierced by a bullet; we were under siege and what is worse is that we could not see the enemy because they were covered in the forest."[54]

At midday on Wednesday, the 18th, Montes de Oca heard his name being called from the woods flanking the fortress. Although the captain spoke English, he told his subaltern Cauty to ask what they wanted. The reply was a request to meet under a flag of truce. There are various contradictory accounts of what transpired next. Cauty days later wrote a vainglorious version, omitting Montes de Oca, in the San José *Album Semanal* bilingual newspaper that he began editing with J. Carranza on September 12, 1856, and whose financial manager was his father, Thomas Henry Horatio Cauty. The English-language article was reprinted in the American press. Montes de Oca's viewpoint was unknown until his diary and a letter he wrote to his son after fifteen years were published together 150 years later. However, both of his narratives contain discrepancies.[55]

When Cauty saw filibuster officers leaving Nelson's Hill and heading for the Transit Company house, he requested permission to go speak with them. Montes de Oca was concerned that his emissary would be taken hostage to force the surrender of the garrison, but Cauty expressed confidence that that would not happen. Before departing with an officer, the Englishman suggested that if he were seized, the captain should shoot and kill him. Montes de Oca years later told his son that he was the one who under a white cease-fire flag parlayed with the filibusters after they requested to speak to the commander. He did not mention this meeting in his diary, and it contradicts his concern for the welfare of the messenger. It also differs from a letter he penned to President Mora indicating that he met Titus "face to face" for the first time two months later. Cauty alleged that he "went down to the lines of the fortification and took a drink with Col. Titus." Filibuster captain John W. Patterson stated that after the flag of truce was displayed, "two officers, believed to be Englishmen, came out and invited Col. Titus into the fort, which invitation he accepted of, and, as it is believed, also partook of their hospitalities if nothing else." It is highly unlikely that the distrustful Titus would have gone into the fort alone, and he probably just conferred at a picket line.[56]

Montes de Oca recalled that "Colonel Titus then appeared demanding the unconditional surrender of the fortress because he had large caliber artillery and said that he could knock down the ruins since he had 300 men for the assault but first wanted to propose peace." A "long private conversation ensued" in which Cauty "read an order from the President of Costa Rica, that all Americans who should fall into his hands should be put to death." The Briton wrote that Titus claimed "he had a large battery of cannon, of great caliber, mounted for the attack" and that he had upward of one thousand men on the river, completely surrounding the fort. Cauty dismissed the threat as "too bombastic" and "lay in hope of relief, but determined to hold out to the last" awaiting the assistance requested by messenger two days earlier. Titus told his adversaries "to unconditionally surrender the castle within half an hour because it was useless to sustain it without shedding further blood since they had already received artillery capable of bringing down the fort."[57]

Montes de Oca, in the letter to his son, said that he "responded laughing that he would not surrender and to do so it was precise to have an order from the general." Titus gave him twelve hours to suspend hostilities and extended it to twenty-four hours when the captain said that it was not sufficient time to get a reply from General Mora at Fort San Carlos thirty-four miles away. Cauty claimed that he was the one who refused to capitulate "without the General's consent." Montes de Oca wrote that after Titus agreed "without much difficulty, and hostilities were suspended, I then sent a black youth who had just arrived as a messenger from the fort and who had passed by them without being seen." Doubleday wrote that Titus "granted the request" because he was "an untried man" and "had no real soldierly knowledge or qualifications."[58]

The truce agreement kept the filibusters behind the forest line and the Costa Ricans in the clearing around the fortress with access to the river. One account claimed that Titus agreed to the truce "on condition that they would surrender next day at noon" and "permitted a messenger to pass through his lines," even though many of his officers and men demanded an immediate attack. The officers "gave vent to their dissatisfaction in very audible language." Baker affirmed that "Titus the ineffable fool allowed him to do it." A *New York Times* correspondent, writing from Aspinwall, Panama, three weeks later, indicated that Titus said that the defenders had promised to evacuate the next day. The colonel "then lay back upon the laurels won by him in Kansas, using the anticipatory evacuation of Castillo in the morning as a pillow." According to Pvt. Martin Schroeder, of Major Ellis's Company B, "Col. Titus sent down a small bungo to Greytown, to Lockridge, with word that he had surrounded Fort Castillo, and had given the enemy twenty-four hours to surrender." Lockridge later wrote that Titus had made "arrangements with the enemy in the fort granting them permission to leave as prisoners on 'parole.'"[59]

A different version indicates that after Titus agreed to the proposition, "his men rested on their arms, while the Costa Ricans had free communication with the river above the rapids, and by that means with Fort San Carlos." William Walker wrote that with the acceptance of Cauty's proposal, "it was not difficult for him to send a courier to Fort San Carlos with news of his position." The *Panama Star* reported that "Titus held a parley with the Costa Ricans at Castillo, and permitted a messenger to pass through his lines from their forces, on condition that they would surrender the next day at noon." Titus later admitted to Captain Brantley, his second in command, that he had the courier shot. He tried to trick Montes de Oca into thinking that his requested assistance would not be forthcoming and therefore that he should surrender the fort according to their agreement. Brantley later denounced Titus as "guilty of a cowardly and brutal treachery" for killing the messenger "without the ability to turn it to any advantage. At any rate, this miserable man reposed in security, flattering himself that all was right." Titus was unaware that the first dispatcher had already reached General Mora and therefore "took no steps to secure himself against a surprise or to cut off communication of the fort with the country above." At midnight the fortress sentinel reported a distant dim light in the upper river. Cauty used the spyglass to identify it as a steamer with bow and stern illumination. Everyone in the garrison cheerfully agreed that it probably carried troops coming to their assistance.[60]

Meanwhile, Lockridge that same day, Wednesday, the 18th, entered the Greytown harbor on the *Rescue* with twenty men. The steamer was quickly surrounded by armed boats from the British squadron with two hundred marines. The officers demanded to question each filibusterer separately as to their willingness to return to Castillo Viejo and assured them protection if they wished to defect. Capt. Algernon Frederick Rous De Horsey, commander of the HMS *Victor*, boarded the *Rescue* when it docked at Punta Arenas and told Lockridge that he could not leave until an investigation was completed about a rumor that "two Englishmen had been hanged on board the last river boat that went up." The captain dropped the demand when Lockridge requested "a copy in writing of the charges and by whom made &c." The filibusters were ordered to present themselves, and four accepted De Horsey's offer of free exit passage and boarded the *Victor*. An hour later Lockridge was informed that he could depart. Before leaving, the colonel posted a proclamation at Greytown, dated the previous day at Castillo Rapids, announcing that the water battery below the fort had been taken and that the San Juan River was now opened up to that point, and he offered protection to "all those who wish to trade or pass on the river." The *Rescue* left that night, was grounded on a bar, and broke its rudder, prompting a twelve-hour delay. The steamer before dawn reached Machuca Rapids, twelve miles from El Castillo, losing another twelve hours, and Lockridge blamed British intervention for delaying his appointment with Titus.[61]

On Thursday morning, the 19th, Montes de Oca felt anxious inside El Castillo when the expected reinforcements had not appeared by 7:00. The entire garrison, on the verge of "starvation and thirst," was "desperate" an hour later, "believing that by their not having made a signal, those coming had returned thinking that the castle was held by the filibuster[er]s." When the soldiers sat down to eat at 9:00 A.M., bullets tore through their mess tent. The commander assumed that the cease-fire had been violated but then heard increasing cries of "Viva Costa Rica" and it "seemed that they were [coming from] 500 men." Cauty recalled that it was 10:00 A.M., two hours before the truce expired, when they "heard firing in the hills and loud shouts and *vivas* for Costa Rica, which we answered." It was a company of sixty-two men led by Captains Jesús Alvarado and Joaquín Ortiz, sent by General Mora from Fort San Carlos, that had disembarked four and a half miles away the previous night. Brantley recalled that the reinforcements "having landed above made their way around through the thick brush wood unobserved, until they were upon us." The filibusters did not see the attackers until they were eighty yards away "on account of the thick bushes." Baker recalled that the Costa Ricans drove in the filibuster pickets and scattered those on the bottom ridge "like sheep through the woods" while others "made for the redoubt."[62]

Titus was in Fort Nelson with Brantley's company when "some stragglers came running in and told him that the enemy numbered 500, and he immediately ordered a retreat." An apocryphal account in the *New York Times* sent from San Juan del Norte six weeks later claimed that when one of the fleeing pickets told Titus that the Costa Ricans were upon them, he was "told to go back to his company and give them fight." The soldier replied that there were more than five hundred of them, to which Titus responded, "The hell there is! Then we had better run—save yourselves, boys." The newspaper, heaping further ridicule on Titus, reported that a filibusterer exclaimed "that he never saw so fat a man run so fast before!" George W. Sites heard Titus give the order to withdraw "and ran away himself first. His men remained and fired a few rounds, and finding that they had no commander, of course retreated.

They did not shoot him for cowardice because he was a colonel, and nobody was above him in rank." E. S. Baker claimed that there were three hundred reinforcements and believed that the Americans in the redoubt "might have held out against one thousand men here but the moment the firing commenced Titus gave the order to retreat."[63]

Baker nearly got lost running through the forest and came upon a Costa Rican "streaking it through the woods for the fort." The two filibuster companies camped out of sight below the hill "did not get the order to retreat." According to the *New York Times,* these units "fought the Costa Ricans well, and after killing some of the enemy, and losing themselves a few men, they succeeded in driving the enemy back." Both companies, "in danger of being flanked, fell back to where they supposed the reserve with Titus would be found," but it had vanished. When one of the men asked where Titus was, someone responded that he had left "three-quarters of an hour ago,—whereupon they all retreated," leaving behind their ammunition and provisions. As Baker reached Fort Nelson, his comrades "were all gone but two or three," who quickly departed with him. The *Herald* reported that "Titus gave the order to retire, and set the example," creating a "stampede." He abandoned the wounded, who had to fend for themselves. An "old man named Washington was lying in camp" recovering from his wounds, "and when last seen was crawling off—the enemy no doubt put him to death." This was forty-three-year-old Lewis Miles Hobbs Washington, a writer and veteran of the Texas Revolution, with a wounded foot. The press reported that after he was captured, his last words were, "I am an American—shoot me."[64]

Walker wrote, "Titus retreated in great disorder and confusion. The retreat was made before the number of the relieving party was even approximately ascertained; and the fact, that the Americans were able to escape without any protection to their rear, shows the enemy did not arrive with much force." Montes de Oca and Cauty agreed that "the filibuster[er]s fled, throwing away their arms, ammunition, and provisions, so that the road two miles down the river was strew[n] with them." The former wrote that the skirmish lasted "less than half an hour." Cauty exaggerated that "the filibuster[er]s lost 40 men" in contrast to his "trifling" loss of one private. Montes de Oca wrote in his diary that all the fleeing filibusters "must have died of hunger" in the mountains and that Titus "was the only one who escaped." However, in the letter to his son fifteen years later he affirmed finding only two dead Americans and that his own loss was two dead and one slightly wounded. Brantley estimated that the filibusters at El Castillo had "in killed and missing, some ten men." Lockridge tallied four dead: James Peacock, B. C. Lang, Peter Mann, and

Lewis M. H. Washington. The correspondent of the *Herald* gave a "moderate estimate" of perhaps twenty-five filibuster[er]s killed and 150 deserted during the entire river campaign."[65]

Titus's own anonymous apologia in the *Herald* claimed, "After waiting fifty hours without aid, being short of provisions, and satisfied with the impossibility of taking the fort with small arms, and the enemy flanking his party to cut off his retreat, he (Col. Titus) determined to go on board the other steamer and drop down the stream." The filibusters fleeing Nelson's Hill found Titus at the *J. N. Scott* landing two miles away. The colonel tried to rally his men by saying, "Now, boys, let us stand and fight the enemy like brave men, or die in the attempt." Seeing that the Costa Ricans had not pursued them, the filibusters boarded the vessel. Captain Montes de Oca heard the *J. N. Scott's* whistle blow a few times and some distant shots. He sent Captain Alvarado with twenty-five men to seize the steamer, but it was gone when they got there.[66]

The boat drifted twelve miles down to Machuca Rapids and remained there until the *Rescue* arrived at noon on Friday, the 20th, with Capt. Robert Harris's Company B and provisions. Lockridge boarded the *J. N. Scott*, objurgated Titus for leaving El Castillo, and branded him a coward. Titus replied "that he allowed no man to call him a coward; that Lockridge played the coward at Sarapiquí, and seizing Lockridge by the throat, was about to throw him overboard, when some friends interfered and separated them. Col. Lockridge apologized to Titus." Lockridge later wrote to B. Squire Cotrell, the U.S. commercial agent at Greytown who had consular duties, that Titus "considered it prudent to fall back on the steamer" to "Machucha for want of provisions & munitions of war." According to Baker, after Titus and his men boarded the *Rescue*, "Lockridge could not make Titus go back again and we went down to San Carlos river and we threw up a fort until the next reinforcements arrived." That day Montes de Oca received forty more soldiers and assigned them to fortify Nelson's Hill, letting them keep the American rifles found there.[67]

The filibusters returned to Providencia Island and built "a slight breastwork" dubbed Fort Slatter, in honor of Col. Shadrach F. Slatter of New Orleans, "who had largely contributed to the filibuster cause." Lockridge soon revoked "the commission that he gave to Titus, for cowardice and total incompetency." Titus made no mention of being routed and instead claimed that he had been "awaiting the return of Lockridge, who agreed to return with reinforcements in twelve hours" after landing. His own anonymous apologia stated that after boarding the steamer with his force, Lockridge's "jealousy" of Titus manifested itself on February 21 "to such an extent that the officers of Col. Titus' command became disgusted with the whole proceedings in Nicaragua, and tendered their resignations." Titus responded with a note rejecting their action. In their written reply, the dozen dissenters insisted that since they had not yet regularly mustered into Walker's army and held rank "by the voluntary consent of the men of our battalion," they had the right to leave. The officers concluded that "we would like to sustain the cause of the State of Nicaragua, but wish to promote it under different auspices."[68]

Captain Brantley, who resigned as Titus's second in command, said that Titus's "blundering was most disastrous—dissatisfaction and mutiny began to prevail—Titus lost the confidence and respect of his men." He emphasized, "War is a science, and such men as Lockridge and Titus cannot carry it on." Colonel Anderson "used a very strong term . . . not at all complimentary to Colonel Titus as a commander." Doubleday indicated that the undisciplined Kansas volunteers deserted in large numbers. They "constructed rafts during their night watches, and men and officers floated down the river to Greytown, leaving the camp unguarded." According to Walker, the "shameful" repulse at Castillo demoralized "the whole command on the river, and desertions accordingly increased. Such, too, was the feeling against Titus that he gave up his command and left for San Juan del Norte." Titus, instead of returning to the United States after his officers left him, agreed to act "as a special agent and bearer of despatches" from Lockridge to Walker via Panama. His troops were then transferred to General Wheat's command. Captain Montes de Oca believed that "if Titus had taken El Castillo like he took La Trinidad, the [San Carlos] Fort could not resist him and four days later the entire river would have returned its control to the filibuster[er]s and all of Central America would not have been able to wrest it from them."[69]

The northern antislavery press highlighted the "cowardice" in battle of their Kansas archenemy. The *Tribune* wrote that Titus had gone to Nicaragua "to *civilize* the country by robbery and cutting people's throats." The *New York Times* asserted that Colonel Lockridge had been thwarted "by the stupidity (not to say the cowardice and treachery) of Col. Titus." The newspaper weeks later editorialized, "If we cannot propagate 'Americanism' by any more decent agents than 'Colonel' Titus or 'General' Wheat, it were better that the eagle should furl his wings. The voice of a great nation should not make itself heard through the stammerings and belchings of drunkards." The *Daily Chronicle* of New London, Connecticut, excoriated Titus: "So consummate a villain could hardly be anything else but a coward." Southern newspapers expressed outrage and dismay. The New Orleans correspondent of the

Democratic *Baton Rouge Daily Advocate* denounced how "Col. Titus, cuts rather a sorry figure in the accounts of his operations on this side of the Isthmus. If he did not actually betray cowardice, he showed a total want of judgement, and an unworthiness to be trusted with any important command." John Marks Baldwin, Lockridge's aide, wrote to the *New Orleans Picayune* of the Titus defeat: "This disaster has ruined everything, and places things in a worse position than they were, previous to the taking of Sarapiquí; all Titus's officers have resigned . . . I fear that this part of the enterprise is lost."[70]

There were allegations that since Titus retreated "without firing a gun or offering any opposition to the advancing column or waiting to ascertain its force," he "had been bought by the enemy." Pvt. Martin Schroeder said, "It was supposed by many of us that Titus sold out to the enemy." Aide-de-camp E. S. Baker stated that Titus "was so badly seared after the retreat that one could easily see that there was not mixed work in it. I do not believe though that he is too good to be bribed." He called Titus "the most arrant coward that ever went to Nicaragua." The *Herald* asserted that the bribery supposition was "probably unjust" but that "it will be difficult for him to satisfy his brother officers and the men that the name of coward does not fairly belong to him." *Frank Leslie's Illustrated Newspaper* of New York dismissed the bribery charges and affirmed that Titus "was completely out-generaled" due to cowardice. Walker blamed the "incapacity of Titus" for losing the "opportune moment for taking Castillo." Titus accused Lockridge for not properly supporting him and stressed that "the climate, heat, and incessant wet" weather discouraged his men.[71]

After stopping at Providence Island, Lockridge had the steamer *Rescue* tow the *J. N. Scott* for repairs to the factory of the Accessory Transit Company at Punta Arenas. He was accompanied on the trip by Colonels Titus, Anderson, and Hall; Lieutenant Colonel McDonald; Captain Farnum; and some thirty men. A few miles downstream, the *J. N. Scott* was "grounded on a rock, and was not got off till three days after. One of the sections of her hull was torn off, and other parts injured." When the steamer reached Punta Arenas on March 3, it was surrounded by three British gunboats. Captain De Horsey again appeared on a barge alongside the *Rescue,* announced that he had orders to seize both steamers "engaged in an unlawful enterprise," and offered protection to anyone leaving Walker's army. Brantley recalled that "Titus gave vent to sundry threats, and much gasconade and coarse abuse." The colonel threatened to shoot De Horsey, cursed the Queen of England, and "endeavored to create a disturbance, by using most exciting language to the people aboard the river steamer." Lockridge said that "he never heard language so vile and foul from anyone, gentleman or boor." Titus later wrote that he replied "with all the venom of my nature," prompting the officer to menace him with arrest, flogging, and punishment if he did not immediately shut up. Titus announced "that he alone was responsible for his acts" and "responded in the language of a wounded and oppressed American." De Horsey returned to his vessel with two defectors and signaled his superior officer on the corvette HMS *Cossack*.[72]

De Horsey returned with a fleet of boats manned by British marines with a demand from Capt. James H. Cockburn, senior officer at Greytown, for Lockridge to turn over Titus to them. He seized both steamers and tied the *Rescue* alongside the *Victor*. The wily colonel had already absconded for Punta Arenas and was crossing the harbor toward Greytown in a boat "under the American flag" when he was arrested and disarmed by the Britons. Titus "announced himself an American citizen" and was taken under protest aboard the *Cossack*. He claimed that he was "accosted in the most brutal manner before the entire crew." Capt. James H. Cockburn told Titus that he would be tried for insulting an English officer. Lockridge demanded the release of the steamers to him, but Cockburn replied that since Titus had not been delivered to him and was seized while "attempting to escape," the vessels would be held until the return of his superior officer. Lockridge decried that "Titus was not in commission, and had no authority on the steamers or connection with them" and demanded their immediate recovery. Before Titus was taken below deck under guard, he asked Lieutenant Colonel McDonald to solicit his protection from the American consular agent B. Squire Cotrell. Captain Cockburn immediately sent a gunboat to explain the situation to Capt. John Erskine, the commander of the British squadron aboard the ninety-one-gun HMS *Orion*, anchored eighty miles northeast at Corn Island.[73]

The next morning, March 4, McDonald called on Cotrell and requested that he visit Titus. The American representative declined, believing he had no right "to claim Col. Titus as a citizen entitled to the protection of the United States, as it was clearly evident that he had been engaged with Col. Lockridge, in command of an armed force on the San Juan River." Cotrell indicated that the State Department was aware that he had always avoided taking sides in the present difficulties and could not begin now. McDonald replied offensively before leaving. At noon the U.S. sloop of war *Saratoga* under Capt. Edward G. Tilton appeared on the coast and "exercised the 1st Division at the great Guns and the 2nd with small arms; fired three rounds with blank cartridges." Titus and the steamers were released that afternoon after Erskine reprimanded Cockburn for their seizure. The colonel then sent a letter from Greytown to the *New Orleans Delta,* which was reproduced in other southern newspapers, appealing to the American people, "in the name of our sacred Constitution and the precepts of our institutions, to call for the rights of her citizens, and from such outrageous insults from the hands of the English coxcombs that infest this coast." Lockridge wrote to Cotrell that day and enclosed his exchange of notes with the British officers protesting that English government intervention was giving assistance and encouragement to Costa Rica. In consequence, he was resigning his position commanding the San Juan River after bringing his men to Greytown for obtaining passage to the United States and would join Walker as a volunteer.[74]

On the morning of March 5, as Cotrell was leaving his house, he was approached by McDonald, Farnum, and Titus, who demanded to know why the consular agent "had not interfered on his behalf." While expressing his neutrality in the armed conflict, Cotrell recalled that Titus "broke out into the most foul mouthed abuse that I ever remember to have listened to; his companions, all of whom were armed with revolvers, forming a half circle around me." The consul walked away from what he perceived as a premeditated provocation. After the *Saratoga* anchored at noon in the harbor, Cotrell reported the conduct of Titus and the filibusters to Commander Tilton and requested "some protection." The abolitionist *Tribune* falsely claimed that in consequence, Titus was briefly taken prisoner by the officers of the *Saratoga* before being released. However, the log book of the Saratoga, Captain Tilton's official letters, and Cotrell's diplomatic correspondence do not sustain this. According to the *Herald,* Titus while at Greytown "made enemies of everybody by his abusive language and violence, which are none the less when he is under the influence of liquor." He was "perpetually in a drunken and riotous state."[75]

Captain Farnum and Colonel Hall "were in the streets in a state of intoxication." The former provoked a general melee that lasted "three or four hours" with black Jamaicans and local natives until it was suppressed by British marines. Lockridge then gave Anderson command of Punta Arenas while he recovered from pleurisy and dismissed Hall, Farnum, and Lt. James Smith from the service for "intemperance, and for conduct unbecoming officers and gentlemen." Lockridge forwarded to Captain Tilton the names of eleven American filibuster deserters and hoped that he would disregard their applications. The USS *Saratoga* left for Key West on March 19 after Tilton reported to the U.S. secretary of the navy, "Our citizens here are unmolested in their lawful pursuits." When the steamer *Texas* arrived from New Orleans that day, Jean Mesnier, a local French merchant, quickly wrote to the Costa Rican minister of war. He reported that the vessel brought "150 filibuster[er]s, many munitions of war and some 400 barrels of provisions," along with "15 boxes of rifles," and that they were immediately going to attack El Castillo. Captain Brantley, after departing on the *Texas*, blamed "the almost universal intemperate character" of the filibuster officers for their misfortune and inefficiency. He told a *New York Times* correspondent that "he never saw such drunkenness—it was terrible. *Nearly all the men were drunkards and gutter-birds.*"[76]

The officers expelled by Lockridge left on the *Texas* the next day and returned to New York City. There, dressed in their military raiment, they lounged at the St. Charles Hotel saloon at the corner of Broadway and Leonard Streets, which was owned by the Nicaragua colonization agent Alexander C. Lawrence. Hall and Farnum had drinks with Col. Alexander Jones, filibuster recruiter Appleton Oaksmith, and a *New York Times* reporter. There was a consensus that Titus "is a man of unquestioned bravery, but destitute of some of the requisite qualifications of a military commander." They agreed, "At Castillo he committed a grave blunder, but it was an error of judgement rather than an instance of disaffection to the cause." Titus was described as "very much of a gentleman, and is the man to enforce respectful treatment from all." The clique had "a poorer opinion of Colonel Lockridge," who was "horribly illiterate." They claimed that he "had no military experience, and is regarded as altogether incompetent. He acts like an Irishman hired by the hour, and is good at carrying logs, or knocking down a refractory private." The officers chastised Lockridge for leaving the brunt of the battle at Sarapiquí to Anderson and Wheat. In contrast, the *Tribune* correspondent at Greytown weeks later described Lockridge as "a hard-working, sober man, civil and respectful in his intercourse with all whom he meets."[77]

The disgruntled officers wrote letters to the editor and gave reporters accounts of their versions of what transpired during the San Juan River campaign. Farnum penned a 2,000-word missive published in the *New York Times* and the *Herald* detailing his "complicity" since January 1856, justifying his behavior, and denouncing Lockridge and his "dastardly baseness." The letter derided Lockridge as "notoriously ignorant of every detail of military science, notoriously ignorant of everything else but manual labor: overbearing, coarse, insolent, and not *notoriously* brave." Farnum emphasized that Lockridge "was not under fire throughout the entire fight" at Sarapiquí. He praised General Wheat, saying that "a nobler soldier does not live," and alleged, "It was through either the negligence or culpable ignorance of ~ckridge, that Col. Titus retired from Castillo. I have the word of Gen. ~ for it, that Col. Titus is as brave a man as ever trod on Nicaragua

soil." Farnum claimed that Lockridge had asserted "that failing to receive reinforcements, Col. Titus deemed it prudent to retire, and did so orderly, and
without the loss of a man." He concluded by indicating that "not one of the
recent calumniators of Col. Titus dared to wag their tongues to his discredit"
until after his departure from Greytown. Hall, in a 750-word letter to the
Herald about his role, also praised Titus. He blamed Lockridge's "incompetency" for the loss of El Castillo, "for if he had returned with the reinforcement in twenty-four instead of fifty-six hours, as he did, Colonel Titus would
not have retired."[78]

Titus took passage on Sunday, March 8, on the steamer *Tennessee* to
Aspinwall, Panama, arriving there the next day. The British steamer *Clyde*
had just put ashore twenty-two filibuster deserters. Upon hearing that Titus
was on the *Tennessee,* they bitterly called him "a coward and a brute" and
menaced that he would never cross the isthmus alive. Titus replied that "he
was not afraid of them" and displayed "two revolvers in his belt." The colonel, however, decided to remain on board the *Tennessee* with other passengers until the next day, when they departed at 10:00 A.M. on the railroad to
Panama City. The *Tribune* reported that "Titus went about Aspinwall with a
loaded revolver in his fist, expecting that his outraged men would really take
his life." A traveler described Titus as "a splendid looking man."[79]

The colonel then boarded the Pacific steamer *Sierra Nevada* to San Juan
del Sur, Nicaragua. The once vibrant community of seven hundred inhabitants was now nearly a ghost town. It had fewer than seventy-five people,
and the houses were "doorless and windowless," with the buildings "going to
ruin." On March 10 the one-armed Col. W. P. Caycee and a detachment of
thirty Rangers from Texas escorted Titus to Walker's camp near Rivas. The
seventeen-mile trip lasted three hours as they carried "a large quantity of provisions and ammunition" on mules. The filibusters now had some six hundred men at San Juan del Sur and Rivas. According to Walker, Titus did not
hand him Lockridge's official report "describing the whole course of events
on the river for the last two months" and instead provided a verbal account
"of very inaccurate character."[80]

Before the hoax was discovered with a duplicate account sent by the
next steamer, Titus briefly replaced one of Walker's ailing aides. He initially
"requested to be sent to the United States with authority to act for Nicaragua" but was denied because Walker considered him as having "too much the
air of the bully, to gain credit for either honesty or firmness of purpose." At
dawn on March 17, Walker left Gen. Charles Frederick Henningsen holding
Rivas with fifty men and advanced three miles to attack the village of San

Jorge on Lake Nicaragua. After seizing the plaza, he heard that Henningsen was besieged by twelve hundred troops led by Nicaraguan general Fernando Chamorro. Walker sent Titus to reconnoiter the front lines, but Titus, "not venturing within range of the enemy's fire, received a statement from a soldier and brought it to headquarters as a report of facts." Soon after, Henningsen arrived and "reported to Walker a state of facts entirely the reverse of Titus' report."[81]

Before dawn on the March 23, allied generals Chamorro and José M. Cañas assailed the Rivas fortifications from different angles with a combined force of twenty-five hundred troops. After hours of fighting, they briefly penetrated the plaza but were forced to retreat. Titus claimed that "Walker desired him to act in his staff, and on being refused Colonel Titus was ordered to his quarters, where he was compelled to remain." The six hundred filibusters in Rivas were "reduced to feed on mule meat and dogs, seasoned with sugar in default of salt." The next day the allies occupied San Juan del Sur, cutting off any further assistance to the filibusters. On March 25 Walker offered terms for capitulation, which the Central Americans rejected, insisting on unconditional surrender. Attempting to reinforce Walker, Lockridge took another expedition on the *Rescue* and the *J. N. Scott* up the San Juan River to assault El Castillo. They were astonished to find that the castle and Fort Nelson "had been strongly fortified; trenches had been dug, barricades had been built and water batteries erected, rendering the place absolutely impregnable to the force that Lockridge could bring to bear against it." Lockridge called a council of war and informed the officers that he had received a letter from Walker's agent in New Orleans "stating that the New York steamers had ceased bringing emigrants, and that we need not expect another steamer from New Orleans, nor provisions." He also declared that neither one of their steamers was powerful enough to pass Castillo rapids to join Walker at Rivas, that they would lose about one hundred men in taking Nelson's Hill and the castle, and that they had "meat for fifteen days, and bread for twenty-five days, and no chance of getting any more from any quarter."[82]

In consequence, Lockridge announced that he was abandoning the San Juan River and gave the filibusters the option of going with him to Rivas via Panama to join Walker or returning home. He refused to take along Germans. The Kansans who had accompanied Titus were divided, but his former aide-de-camp E. S. Baker decided to stay. One hundred volunteers gave three cheers to accompany Lockridge, while 275 uttered three groans expressing their desire to leave. Two Americans left a scrawled message on a paper fastened to a tree with a bayonet: "James Bowie and E. J. Calhoun present their compliments to the Commander of Fort Castillo. Good bye, friends. Warriors remain in peace—the war is over." When the filibusters retreated on April 1, the *J. N. Scott* was grounded on a sandbar a mile and a half from Sarapiquí. Doubleday was on the upper deck when he was suddenly "hurled into the air with terrific force." He indicated, "The engineer had pumped cold water into the superheated cylinder, and the boiler had burst, tearing the entire front of the boat into fragments." Sixty filibusters were killed; seventeen, including Doubleday, were badly scalded; and eight were slightly wounded. Baker wrote home that he was "scalded from my waist to my shoulders on my back the skin all came off and in some places the flesh to the depth of half an inch. I never experienced such excruciating pain in all my life."[83]

Many of those who had previously agreed to accompany Lockridge decided to leave. The colonel then disbanded the filibusters and left their armaments with Joseph N. Scott, the agent of Morgan and Sons of New York, who would not accept them as collateral for payment toward steamer passage to the United States. Senior British officer Capt. James H. Cockburn then made himself responsible for transporting the Americans to Panama, "for twenty dollars a head," with "the money to be raised from the sale of the arms." The British warships *Cossack* and *Tartar* took 375 filibusters from Greytown and left them at Aspinwall on April 11. Two days later the weapons were taken by Col. George F. Cauty after he seized Punta Arenas. They included 6 small brass cannons with their carriages, 269 muskets and rifles, 1,000 pounds of lead balls, 20 small barrels and boxes of lead balls, 43 boxes of munitions for small arms, 1 box of cannonballs, 2 boxes and a trunk with percussion caps, and 197 half and one-fourth barrels of gunpowder, weighing two and a half tons, among other sundry items, in addition to shoes, pickaxes, shovels, and frying pans. Five of the artillery pieces and all the muskets and rifles had been abandoned by the Costa Ricans at Sarapiquí. Three days later fifty of Lockridge's men arrived in New York on the steamship *Tennessee*. Among the mementos of the San Juan campaign that someone kept was the "coat of Col. Titus, left at Sarapiquí, which he wore in Kansas—buttons and all." The *Tribune* reported that "the majority were beardless boys, some of them not yet 13 years of age! All of them were worn down with hunger, fever and exposure, and most of them had no other covering on their shivering bodies than filthy rags, fastened around them with pieces of string." Some "had run away from their parents, and falling short of money, rather than return home enlisted in Walker's service."[84]

On April 22 Capt. Charles Henry Davis, commanding the twenty-two-gun sloop of war USS *St. Mary's*, anchored at San Juan del Sur since early

February, received permission from General Mora to send a messenger across his territory to Rivas. Twenty-seven-year-old navy lieutenant Thomas Truxton Houston, a Mexican War veteran, accompanied by a marine sergeant, retrieved forty American women and children from the Walker camp and escorted them to San Juan del Sur three days later. Titus wrote that after another allied attack against Rivas, he became determined to "save Walker," and "at all hazards" he left their camp on April 28 for San Juan del Sur. There he solicited assistance, "in the name of humanity," from Captain Davis "in behalf of the sick and wounded who might be exchanged for Costa Rican prisoners then in possession of Walker." In contrast, Walker and the Panama correspondent of the San Francisco *Daily Evening Bulletin* wrote that Titus disappeared from Rivas on the 26th, in spite of his claim to the contrary. The official correspondence of Captain Davis does not mention Titus, nor does his name appear in the logbook of the *St. Mary's*.[85]

At noon on April 28, Titus approached an outpost commanded by Maj. Horace Bell at the Santa Ursula cacao plantation, a mile south of Rivas. He was allowed to pass the picket to acquire fruit in the field. Four hours later B. Bostwick, Walker's attorney general and acting secretary of state, appeared and made inquiries about Titus. As Bell accompanied him to the farm to gather cacao, they spotted Titus and another filibusterer, who motioned both men toward them. When Bell and Bostwick were within twenty yards of Titus, some thirty enemy soldiers appeared. Bell recalled that upon questioning Titus, "he answered, that he had been taken prisoner, and that now we were prisoners too. I protested, and accused him of treachery." Titus and all the detainees were taken to the quarters of Gen. Fernando Chamorro, who sent them to Costa Rican president Mora. According to the *San José Crónica,* among the deserters were "the most celebrated, Titus, two Majors, two Captains, one Lieutenant, one Surgeon, a German Engineer and lawyer, and some seventy men more presented themselves to the General in Chief Mora." The filibusters received passports for Punta Arenas de Costa Rica, where they embarked on the steamship *Panama* for the isthmus two weeks later. The rate of desertions greatly increased after the Costa Rican government started giving each defector "$12 in addition to paying his passage to the States."[86]

In stark contrast to Bell's account, another filibusterer's version indicated that there was "a conclave held at Major Bell's quarters, consisting of Colonel Titus, Bostwick, Dr. Johnson, Lt. [H. C.] Miller, General [Edward J.] Sanders and Capt. [Thomas] Farrel. Titus, however, had so completely lost his head from fear that he sneaked off before the others were ready, which drew attention to Bell's quarters, and probably prevented the betrayal of those quarters to the enemy." Walker accused Titus, Bostwick, Johnson, and Bell of deserting to the enemy. Titus had immediately gone to San Juan del Sur and told Captain Davis of the *St. Mary's* that "he had been cut off with Judge Ware." He then wrote to Bell's quarters to say that "all was right" and "was last seen under the protection of one of the allied generals or colonels, a truculent gentleman of color, at whose beck and call he seemed proud to find himself." Capt. Faustino Montes de Oca wrote to President Mora on April 30, "I have had the pleasure of seeing face to face the famous boaster Colonel Titus, and I regret not being the one taking him to Tortuga to remind him of his run from Castillo; the night before last I saw him speaking with the general, as humble as if he could not break a plate."[87]

Captain Davis, accompanied by his ship's surgeon, Dr. John Winthrop Taylor, and two sailors, went to General Mora's camp on the afternoon of April 30 to mediate Walker's capitulation. He spoke with Mora for thirty minutes and exchanged several notes with Walker on the terms of evacuation. Davis and Taylor then had three interviews with General Henningsen and Col. John P. Waters, representing Walker, before agreeing to the terms of withdrawal that were completed on the morning of May 1. Davis and his coterie, accompanied by Gen. José V. Zavala and his staff, entered Rivas at 4:00 P.M. General Henningsen announced the terms of the capitulation to 240 filibusters formed in the plaza and stated that they were now under the protection of the American flag and were expected to obey Commander Davis. Walker and sixteen of his officers were immediately escorted by Zavala on horseback to San Juan del Sur, where they boarded the *St. Mary's* for Panama. The other filibusters were led by Dr. Taylor to Virgin Bay on the way to Punta Arenas de Costa Rica and in June by steamer to Panama. The rest of the Americans, including sixty sick and wounded and a few women and children, were later taken on a Costa Rican steamer to Greytown, where they boarded the USS *Cyane* a month later for passage to Aspinwall. Captain Davis quickly turned over the plaza of Rivas to Gen. José M. Cañas. Days later crowds were beckoned to the streets of San José by the peeling of bells and a one-hundred-gun salute announcing the surrender of the filibusters and the reestablishment of peace. The celebrations were followed by parties, balls, and congratulatory dinners.[88]

Titus arrived at Panama City on the steamship *Panama* on Sunday morning, May 17, after leaving Punta Arenas de Costa Rica three days earlier. The vessel unloaded "5,100 hides, 2,300 bags coffee, some cochineal, sugar and other merchandise." The *St. Mary's* anchored there the same day with Walker and thirty filibusters, who remained on board two days waiting for the

Atlantic steamer to arrive at Aspinwall. A dozen marines accompanied Walker's party on the railroad across the isthmus to assure their safety from angry locals who had killed fifteen Americans and wounded twenty others during a riot the previous year. The filibusters received "steerage tickets to New Orleans at $10 each." Titus left Panama City on the 18th and the following day was seen about Aspinwall "denouncing Walker as a murderer, and said he quitted him when he found out what a villain he was." Capt. John W. Sevier, Lockridge's aide who had been wounded at Rivas, "challenged him, but did not obtain a meeting."[89]

Titus and General Henningsen boarded the steamer *Illinois* on May 19 and stopped at Kingston, Jamaica, three days later before arriving in New York City on May 28 with 781 passengers. A large crowd, including General Wheat, Capt. Frank Anderson, and William Leslie Cazneau, was there to greet them and to see Henningsen, the "hero of Granada." Henningsen was received with "three hearty cheers and repeated the number in tigers." He was the first to descend the gangplank, and the rest of the passengers poured out and filled awaiting cab after cab. The *Herald* described "the confusion, the crowding, surging, stepping on toes, dragging trunks, hallooing of commands, jabbering of passengers, and the reckless, headstrong plunging and insolent officiousness of the cab drivers." Reporters asked questions of every man "who looked like a filibuster[er]" and carried "trunks, boxes, bundles, carpet bags, and every imaginable etcetera." Those waiting for Henningsen took him to celebrate at the St. Charles saloon. Titus was not mentioned in the press and did not accompany Henningsen; nor was he received by his comrades Wheat and Anderson. He most likely waited until the crowd left before departing in anonymity. Titus remained with his sister in Queens for a month, receiving mail care of the post office, which published his name in their list of letters in the *Herald*.[90]

The day Titus left Panama, he wrote an anonymous apologia that was published in the *Herald* eleven days later under the title "Doings of Col. Titus at Rivas." He alleged that "Walker's bloody drama in Central America was finally brought to a close on the 1st of May, at the instance of Col. H. T. Titus." This self-serving account stated that Titus left Walker's camp "and in the name of humanity appealed to Capt. Davis to go up and, if possible, save the sick and wounded." The article, subheaded Titus's "Contributions and Labors for the Cause," emphasized his "brilliant victory" at Sarapiquí and blamed Lockridge for the disaster at El Castillo. The last paragraph of the article, entitled "Titus' Courage Undoubted," claimed that it was "Walker's minions" who charged him with cowardice. No one other than Titus could have written the following: "The courage and firmness of Col. Titus is too well known to be doubted by those who know him, and his character for a brave and generous officer has been too long established to be injured by the attacks of Lockridge."[91]

The war of the reminiscences continued days later when Captain Brantley, Titus's second in command, after reaching his home in Selma, Alabama, wrote a letter to the *New Orleans Delta* that was reprinted in various southern newspapers. He stated that "Lockridge and Titus are two of the most miserable humbugs that accident ever placed into position. Conceited, selfish, vain, they know no more of war as a science than they do of Sanscrit." He blamed them for "time, money, ammunition, blood, and life . . . thrown away to no purpose." Titus then tried to justify his actions in Nicaragua in a letter to the editor of the *Herald* on June 6, 1857, responding to an article that he said had assailed and committed calumny on his character. The missive was reproduced with editorial commentaries in newspapers for and against the filibusters. Titus claimed to have responded "to the call of Nicaragua for aid" to "maintain a liberal government" and "for assistance in their efforts to put down the tyranny and oppression of their aristocratic and corrupt officials." He said that Walker "disgraced" the cause when he "lost sight of the real interest of the State in contemplating and planning for the realization of his own high and selfish ambition."[92]

Titus claimed that his conduct at El Castillo was misrepresented by Walker's "contemptible hounds." He reported being attacked there by "500 Costa Ricans," that his force "made a determined resistance, and drove the enemy back into the fort," but that he ordered a retreat after "finding it impossible to take the fort without the aid of artillery." Titus blamed his defeat on Lockridge for not keeping his word to provide reinforcements or artillery. He accused Lockridge of "total ignorance" in military matters and said his "contemptible jealousy" prompted him to be "low, mean and cowardly."[93]

The colonel stressed that he gave his service to the cause "without being mustered into the army of Walker, or in any way identified with his operations, except for the general interest of Nicaragua." He determined to leave for the United States after being "deceived in relation to Walker's position in the country," but after his friends insisted that he meet with Walker, he went to Rivas via Panama. Titus claimed that he was "unlawfully detained" by Walker for two months after he "declined service in Walker's staff." He called Walker a tyrant and Lockridge his minion, and he denounced Col. Edward J. C. Kewen as a liar. Two months earlier a letter from Kewen to a friend in Memphis published in the *New York Times* and the *Herald,* referred to the "cowardice of Titus—a thing almost incredible." Titus concluded his version by telling the "Young men of the South" to ask the sick and wounded filibusters soon to be arriving from the isthmus "whether they can rely on the magnanimity of the 'grey eyed man'; then decide."[94]

Colonel Lockridge's official report of the San Juan River operations submitted to Walker had selected paragraphs mentioning Titus published in the *Tribune* on June 19. Lockridge accused Titus of "treachery and cowardice" at El Castillo. He described how he found the *J. N. Scott* in the San Juan River without steam while Titus and his battalion were in "full retreat" and "complete disorganization." Titus's men were "all saying he had acted cowardly, while they openly declared that he had sold the fight to Vanderbilt before leaving New Orleans." Lockridge regretted not having placed Colonel Rudler in command of Titus's force when he arrived in Nicaragua, and if Titus had interfered, he would "have hung him from the nearest tree."[95]

General Wheat wrote his own anonymous autobiographical note in the *New York Times,* and it was reprinted in other newspapers. The piece exalted his own heroics and briefly mentioned that after "the delays of Col. Lockridge, and the peculiar retreat of Col. Titus from before Castillo," the dispirited men expressed that had Wheat been commander in chief, El Castillo would have fallen. A historian wrote decades later, "The incompetence of Titus and Lockridge lost the key to Nicaragua and her transit practically forever. A fool and a coward cost what would have been so simple for Walker or Henningsen to achieve."[96]

Titus went to Nicaragua enticed by Wheat's offer of awaiting fortune. His Kansas venture had been disastrous, and he sought new entrepreneurial opportunities. As a future officer in Walker's Army of Nicaragua he was expecting to obtain the reward missed in Cuba of a substantial salary and a confiscated large plantation. However, not only was the filibuster scheme elusive, but Titus lacked the military knowledge and forethought of field tactics required of a martial leader. He proved to be a reckless strategist, jealous of those more capable than he was, and made costly wrong choices due to his intemperate character.

Titus had a rivalry with Colonel Anderson, a Mexican War veteran, for rank and prestige. He needlessly built a massive defensive position on the river dubbed "Fort Titus," like his former blockhouse in Kansas, to outdo "Fort Anderson." On the field he had no control of his troops, whose indiscipline caused friendly fire at Cody's Point and pandemonium at El Castillo.

El Castillo imploded the filibuster San Juan River campaign. Titus made the tactical mistakes of losing the surprise element by killing a bull; not charging the fortress or Cauty's artillery trench, which was later carried by Captain West's command; and expecting to bluff a fortress into surrender. He hastily retreated without resistance from Fort Nelson when mistakenly believing that he faced a larger enemy force. When Walker made another failed attempt to invade Nicaragua in December 1857, Colonel Anderson and forty-five filibusters proved that skilled tactics and leadership were all that were needed to seize El Castillo. Titus failed to show courage in battle at Sarapiquí and El Castillo, always shooting from a distant safe position. He did not venture within range of the enemy's fire at Rivas and refused to serve as Walker's aide. Titus had to abandon his command in disgrace after the reprobation of his subordinates and disappointing those who had high military expectations of him.

The colonel's braggadocio, intimidating personality, and loud, abusive, and profane language were scorned by many, including his aide, and mocked in the northern press. His barroom buddies, especially Colonel Hall and Captain Farnum, were the only ones who publicly defended Titus, but they did so more to disparage Colonel Lockridge. Titus's defeat at El Castillo prevented Walker from receiving further assistance from the eastern United States and led to his defeat three months later. Walker should have listened to the foreboding of the *Richmond Whig* six months earlier by keeping a vigilant eye on Titus and giving him "no position of power or influence."

Titus's claims upon reaching Nicaragua that he exclusively desired to open the San Juan River under temporary mandate and that upon success he would immediately return to America due to pending urgent business proved false. After his command was rescinded and all his officers resigned, Titus did not immediately go home. Instead he took a costly twelve-hundred-mile route through Panama to ingratiate himself with Walker in an attempt to redeem his reputation and military career and return to the United States in a diplomatic mission. When Titus perceived Walker's imminent collapse, he defected to the enemy for passage home and behaved gentlemanly toward his captors to assure his survival. His tarnished filibuster venture ended in disgrace after six months, and he returned to America to ponder his next career move after another costly and dangerous adventure.

★ *Chapter Four* ★

Arizona Silver Miner
1858–1860

Henry Titus was staying at his father's residence at Lambertville, New Jersey, along the Delaware River in July 1857. After his wife, Mary, joined him, Titus publicly announced that he was soon leaving for Kansas. He wrote to Samuel J. Jones, who had resigned as sheriff the previous winter, "directing him to erect a large warehouse for him at Lecompton, and stating that he will soon return to Kansas with a stock of goods and commence trading." Titus complained about his depiction in the press by the Nicaraguan correspondents and claimed that he would redeem his reputation for bravery if the opportunity arose in Kansas. Titus said, "The Northern abolition papers will have enough to do to keep track of me." The colonel and his wife went to Kansas via a steamer to New Orleans and then up the Mississippi and Missouri Rivers. Martin J. Mitchell, the free-state prisoner whom Titus had "bucked and gagged" the previous November, "followed him to New Orleans for the purpose of shooting him." After they spotted each other in Kansas, James Redpath, correspondent for the St. Louis *Missouri Democrat,* stated, "If Titus should be suddenly sent to the spirit world, some day—and at an early day—you need not be surprised at the intelligence. He had better be careful of his health."[1]

Under the heading "Lynch Law in Leavenworth," a correspondent for the *New York Tribune* wrote from Leavenworth, Kansas, on August 1, "The famous or infamous Col. Titus, of Nicaraguan fame, has returned to bless the Territory with his presence, and to sustain 'law and order.'" In contrast, the *Kansas National Democrat* newspaper, which had superseded the *Lecompton Union,* made no mention that Titus had returned to Kansas. The Tituses proceeded by riverboat to Lawrence on the night of the 2nd, accompanied by

Col. Joseph C. Anderson of Lexington, Missouri, a member of the territorial legislature and the Constitutional Convention. Titus and his wife afterward visited recently appointed governor Robert John Walker and traveled part of the way with him on the Kansas River as he conveyed troops one hundred miles west to assist Fort Riley against Indian attack. The Tituses disembarked at Lecompton and met with former sheriff Samuel Jones, who due to mounting debt had been selling all his real estate properties. On August 4 Mary Titus purchased land adjoining Lecompton from William E. Thompson. The town was in decline and businesses were relocating to the expanding free-state communities of Lawrence and Topeka, the future state capital.[2]

The *Leavenworth Weekly Herald* announced on September 5, 1857, that Titus had "located at Kansas City, and is going into the commission and lumber business." Ten days later the colonel was staying at the grand five-story Planters' House in St. Louis. The hotel had 150 lavish rooms with call bells connected to the main desk, coal heaters, and Venetian window shutters. It served as the winter quarters of wealthy cotton and tobacco planters with their families and cadre of slave servants. There were shops and offices on the ground floor and a roof observatory providing a view of the city and the Mississippi River. The grand ballroom on the second floor had an eight-foot-high orchestra platform, and the large dining room had a beam-paneled ceiling and classical pilasters.[3]

Titus proceeded to the hotel saloon accompanied by friends. While drinking and discussing the Nicaragua situation Titus began "talking in a violent and excited manner, thumping the counter with his fists, and swearing roundly." The commotion prompted a nearby, maudlin guest to address Titus with offensive remarks. The colonel cursed and "pushed him away, causing him to fall." Assisted by others, the man arose and continued his drunken tirade against Titus, who gave him a severe blow to the head with a loaded cane, cutting his ear. The hotel porter intervened and took up the quarrel, saying that "it was a damned shame, and that no gentleman would act as Titus had." The bellhop angrily rushed toward Titus, who drew his revolver and fired just as his hand was pushed down by the bartender. The shot went into the floor near the porter, prompting a stampede of patrons. No damage was done, but according to the deriding abolitionist press, Titus "narrowly escaped shooting his own foot." A Republican newspaper mockingly indicated, "This is the bravest act of Titus on record, and is explained by the fact that he had just come from the bar, where he had fired up liberally." The *New York Times* announced that "Col. Titus cannot exist without notoriety." There was great excitement as several people separated the quarreling parties. While Titus was being jostled toward the door, "he again leveled his pistol but did not fire." The police intervened and took the colonel and the tosspot to the station. Titus claimed, "as a 'soldier of fortune,' special privileges regarding the persons and property of honest men." He was charged with assault with intent to kill and was afterward released when a friend posted bail for him to appear before the recorder.[4]

Returning to Kansas days later on a Missouri River steamer, Titus was jubilant in telling a fellow passenger about the elections for the territorial legislature members and their delegate to Congress scheduled for October 5–6. He said they had "the thing all fixed and success is certain" for the Constitutional Convention to pass a proslavery charter afterward. The convention would then "submit it under restrictions that the mass of free-state men will not comply with, and we have the assurance of our friends in Congress that we shall be admitted under it." Titus claimed that they would carry the election with the Indian vote, that proslavery judges would receive the vote of a thousand Missourians with claims in the Shawnee Reserve across the border in Johnson County, and that para-Masonic blue lodges had been organizing thousands of Missourians since the previous spring quietly to claim residence in the territory and vote. The U.S. Army, under orders from Governor Walker, protected the polls. The day prior to the election, Walker sent an artillery battery and three companies totaling thirteen hundred men, commanded by Col. Horace Brooks, to Shawnee, eleven miles from Kansas City, "the supposed point of danger, to prevent illegal voting, especially from Missouri." Brooks stated that he was called upon by Titus and a Mr. Anderson, of Westport, Missouri, "who complained bitterly of the stationing of the troops there, and said that 'the people would be compelled to vote at the point of the bayonet.'"[5]

On the first day of elections, Titus was with Samuel Jones at Lecompton. The abolitionist *Tribune* wrote that the next day both men went to the Oxford precinct, a village with six houses, including stores, twelve miles from Shawnee in Johnson County on the Missouri border, and met with the judges and clerks of elections after 70 votes were cast. The judges then spent the second day of elections registering 1,548 fraudulent votes that gave their district a proslavery majority, although the county had 890 inhabitants of whom only 496 were registered voters. Protests over the illegality of the votes prompted Governor Walker and territorial secretary Frederick Perry Stanton to visit the contested precinct, and they ruled that the Indian Reserve, which was "not yet subject to settlement or preemption, can give no such vote as that which is represented to have been polled." They issued a report stating that the poll books were not original and therefore were inadmissible as a "gross and palpable fraud." The report ominously concluded that the pacification of Kansas could be achieved only through honest elections. Otherwise "civil war would immediately be recommenced in this Territory, extending, we fear, to adjacent States and subjecting the Government of the Union to imminent peril." Titus's efforts at rigging a county election were blatantly amateurish.[6]

The contest gave the free-state representatives twenty-two of the thirty-seven House seats. For the next few weeks Titus remained in Lecompton, where a proslavery Constitutional Convention reconvened on October 19 to conclude the delegates' futile task. Many of them were intimidated by a large crowd of angry free-soilers who thronged outside Lecompton's Constitution Hall to hear James H. Lane deride the assembly as "outlaws, bloodhounds, villains, devils, rascals, recreants, scoundrels, usurpers, murderers, and thieves, and their schemes as atrocious, disgraceful, hellish, and damnable, and he himself was in favor of cutting their throats then and there." The constituents met during numerous sessions until November 3, when they charted the Lecompton constitution that protected chattel property and prohibited free blacks from living in the state. Governor Walker resigned before the document was submitted to a territorial plebiscite on January 4, 1858.[7]

That day Titus appeared in a two-horse buggy at Shawnee to cast his vote, although special mail agent John D. Henderson, who recognized him, "did not see him vote." Around noon Titus and two companions got into an argument with a hotel keeper, whom Titus knocked down after he refused to reveal his vote. The marshal was called to quell the disturbance and immediately sought backing from 2nd Lt. A. J. Harrison, who was stationed with a company of the Sixth Infantry Regiment half a mile from town to keep the peace during the elections. The Lecompton constitution was defeated by more than ten thousand votes, with fewer than two hundred approving ratification. Six months later a third Lecompton constitution referendum in Kansas mandated by an act of Congress resulted in defeat by a wider voter margin, ending slavery in Kansas and Titus's aspirations in the territory.[8]

Weeks earlier Titus had rented a restaurant/billiard/saloon, "furnished like a palace," in a three-story building on what is now the southwest corner of Main and W. Commercial Streets in Kansas City, Missouri. The Boston abolitionist newspaper the *Liberator* described it as "a fashionable saloon and gambling shop, which is the resort of great numbers of the citizens; and with the support of his gang he [Titus] manages to rule the town by bullying and bravado." A *New York Times* correspondent called Titus's establishment "a fashionable hell, where drinking, fighting and gambling are the favorite amusements. He is assisted by some dozen of the worst despera-does who have in times past infested the Territory." Titus obtained a ninety-day, three-thousand-dollar mortgage from Joseph C. Ranson on March 23, 1858, for his property, including "Liquors, Groceries, Furniture, Pictures, Billiard Tables, Cigars, and every other thing."⁹

Three weeks later forty-two-year-old free-soil leader Gen. Samuel Clarke Pomeroy, mayor of Atchison, Kansas, arrived in Kansas City to attend a legal matter on the sale of his interest in the Free State Hotel. While descending the courthouse stairs at midday, he was confronted by Titus, flanked by companions, regarding severe reflections "to his courage and personal character in the *Squatter Sovereign* while Gen. Pomeroy was one of the proprietors of that paper." Pomeroy denied what was attributed to him and announced that he was unarmed. Titus uttered "the foulest abuse," threw his pistol on the ground, and challenged Pomeroy "to take it, and shoot if he dared." As a crowd of spectators gathered, Titus struck Pomeroy on the neck with a loaded cane. The general instinctively raised his left forearm to ward off the next blow, which fractured his ulna. It happened "in the immediate presence of a large number of the influential citizens, none of whom offered to interfere either to prevent the attack, or shield the victim."¹⁰

Kansas City mayor Milton J. Payne happened upon the scene and ordered city marshal Jonathan Richardson to arrest Titus, but he refused. The deputy marshal intervened and detained Titus while Pomeroy was taken to a physician. According to the *New York Times,* as the deputy marshal was escorting Titus to the courthouse, the colonel "acted more like a master followed by his nigger, as he walked off, than like a culprit in charge of an officer of the law." The local citizenry manifested "great excitement" in consequence of the occurrence. During his trial Titus "conspicuously displayed" his holstered revolvers. The jury could not agree on the verdict. One sympathetic juror suggested "a fine of *one dollar!*" The *Atchison Freedom's Champion* called for "a just retaliation" against Titus. The Kansas *Herald of Freedom* regretted that Titus was not killed when taken prisoner two years earlier and prognosticated, "Unless dispatched in some affray in which he is concerned, he will end his days on the gallows." Shortly thereafter a "Massachusetts gentleman" visiting Kansas wrote to a friend in Boston that he saw Colonel Titus and Sheriff Jones and had "quite a chat" with the former. He found Titus to be "a very quiet, unassuming gentleman, besides one of the finest looking men I ever saw."¹¹

In May 1858 Titus and his thirty-one-year-old brother Ellett started recruiting laborers in Kansas City, Missouri, for the "Southwestern Pioneer and Mining Company," which would soon leave for Arizona. Gold had recently been discovered in southwestern Arizona, and prospectors were rushing to the territory. Newspapers proclaimed the success that American companies were achieving with silver mining in the Gadsden Purchase region. Titus lost his saloon to the unpaid mortgage; sent his pregnant wife, Mary, to her family in Georgia; and departed from nearby Westport on June 10, accompanied by some thirty armed men. Another group of fifty free-state men were organizing in Lawrence to ride soon to Arizona. The *New York Times* proposed that the political adversaries meet at a central place in Kansas "and have a general fight." That way, "It will cost less to kill each other here, and agitate the nation less than it will after killing each other in Arizona."[12]

The following week Kansas territorial governor James W. Denver arrived at the frontier town of Barnesville, along the Missouri border near Fort Scott, with an infantry company. As Denver was conversing with the settlers about their concerns, "a stranger rode into town, who said that he was direct from the western part of Vernon Co., Missouri, and that Col. Titus was then in his neighborhood with some three hundred men, preparing for a fresh invasion of the Territory." The public was aware that the Titus expedition was heading south through western Missouri, "but it was not generally believed he meditated an invasion of the Territory, and there was not much in the appearance of the stranger to strengthen the suspicion." William P. Tomlinson, a twenty-five-year-old Pennsylvania abolitionist and Kansas correspondent for the *New York Tribune,* who was accompanying the governor, decided to inquire into the matter.[13]

Tomlinson claimed that free-soilers living near the Missouri border were "greatly agitated by fears of danger" that Titus "was waiting for a favorable opportunity to invade the Territory." He claimed that as a result the settlers pursued their daily avocations armed and scarcely in an isolated manner. On June 21 Tomlinson left Osage and headed eastward to Titus's camp on a fleet Indian pony and armed with a brace of heavy pistols. While he was crossing Vernon County, residents pointed him in the direction of the emigrant company, until he stopped at a settler's home for the night. The family stated that Titus was camped ten miles south, but they were unaware of his intentions. Tomlinson left early the next morning and at noon reached the campground abandoned by Titus in a cove of timber near Dry Wood Creek. The reporter ran into the rear guard of the expedition, "who were busied in loading the heavier camping furniture on some wagons preparatory to following the main body."[14]

The abolitionist pretended to be a new recruit to their company and was told, "The camp broke up hours ago, and the men are miles ahead by this time, so if you wish to overtake them you must hurry on after them!" Desiring to learn of their objective, the correspondent replied, "Well, I don't know whether it will pay to join your leader or not. I don't know that I fairly understand what is to be done, any how. What are the first objectives of the enterprise?" The group leader approached the stranger and said, "I expect you are a *friend* to our company, but I may as well be sure of the fact," and he flashed a cryptic para-Masonic greeting. Tomlinson wrote that he had recently learned the countersign from a free-state settler and "was thus able to return the secret test of brotherhood."[15]

The *Tribune* correspondent stated that the stragglers told him they would "soon be joined by Capt. [Charles] Hamilton and his party, who are to come up the Arkansas River. We will then proceed to Arizona, which our leader, Hamilton, and others, say they are determined to make a Slave State at all hazzards. They say that the 'abolitionists' got ahead of them in Kansas, but they defy them to compete with them in Arizona." Tomlinson was maliciously trying to link Titus to Hamilton and his band, wanted for the Marais des Cygnes Massacre of five free-soilers the previous month. The writer claimed that he also heard that the Titus party was "going to try the mines first, and if mining don't pay, we are going South to Sonora and other places, and plunder the rich churches and convents." Tomlinson replied that he was unable to join them that day but would think the matter over and if in agreement would overtake them the next day. This was as close as Tomlinson supposedly got to Titus. He probably sent a sensationalistic report of this incident to the *New York Tribune,* but it was never published in the paper. Instead it appeared in his book *Kansas in Eighteen Fifty-Eight,* published a year later.[16]

The Titus emigrants followed the new Butterfield Overland Mail Company route, which stretched from St. Louis, Missouri, to San Francisco, California, via the Southwest. Their destination, Sonoita Valley, Arizona, was eighteen hundred miles away. The Butterfield line merged old and new western roads and generally followed Captain Randolph Marcy's 1849 trail across Texas. Main stops along the way were Springfield, Missouri, and a chain of military posts including Fort Smith, Arkansas; Fort Washita, Indian Territory (Oklahoma); Forts Belknap, Chadbourne, and Bliss in Texas; and Fort Fillmore and Tucson in New Mexico Territory. The expanse between Fort Smith and Fort Bliss in El Paso was "a thousand miles of wilderness, arid plains, deserts, and mountains, inhabited only by bands of roving Indians." The Comanches had been making predatory raids in the region, and the U.S. Cavalry tried keeping them in check. The Titus expedition set out with covered wagons and accompanying mules loaded with essential provisions of flour, bacon, dried beef, beans, salt, coffee and other victuals, water barrels, chicken coops, bedding, durable clothing, rugged boots, a cookstove, house-keeping utensils, a few furnishings, tools, mining equipment, rifles, and ammunition boxes. Extra oxen, cows, and dogs accompanied the sojourners, who hunted abundant game along the way.[17]

In late June, as the "southern emigrants" passed Neosho Valley in south-eastern Kansas, fifteen horses were stolen from local farmers. The county sheriff and a small posse trailed their hoof prints to the Titus encampment near the Osage Catholic Mission. When Titus did not surrender the steeds, the sheriff departed and sought assistance from the staunch abolitionist Col. James Montgomery, who refused to intervene after abiding by Governor Denver's territorial pacification plan. By the first week of July, the Titus party had grown to one hundred men. They crossed the Oklahoma border into Texas at Colbert's Ferry on the Red River, eight miles below Preston, a rowdy frontier town seventy-four miles north of Dallas. The wily Titus claimed that he was headed for Oregon, but the press reported that the emigrants were going to filibuster for Gen. José Santiago Vidaurri, the governor of Nuevo León and Cohauila, during the War of the Reform. The Nicaragua filibus-terer Samuel Lockridge in March had published a letter in the *Galveston News* calling for Texas recruits "for the purpose of emigrating to Northern Mexico," in an apparent filibuster expedition.[18]

The Titus sojourners then headed 146 miles to Fort Belknap near the Brazos River, at present-day Newcastle, Texas. It was the northern anchor of a second line of fortifications built in the 1850s through Comanche terri-tory, from the Red River to the Rio Grande, that protected emigrants, mail coaches, and freight wagons traveling west. The garrison was comprised of sixteen houses and lacked defensive works. Its two companies of the Second Cavalry, with 7 officers and 134 troops, were commanded by Maj. George H. Thomas. The Titus party followed the emigrant trail on a southwestern route for 136 miles to Fort Chadbourne, Texas, arriving on July 20, 1858. The frontier post on Oak Creek, 11 miles northeast of Bronte, garrisoned two companies with 95 men of the U.S. First Infantry Regiment, which had been suppressing local Indian hostility. Capt. John Haskell King, commanding the fort, immediately wrote to his superior at Army Headquarters for the Department of Texas in San Antonio, indicating that the notorious filibuster colonel was headed for Arizona, "for the purpose, ostensibly of mining." He added that Titus "expects to be joined on the route by over one hundred men which force will be further increased to twelve hundred, concentrating at or near Tucson." King believed that Titus was leading a filibuster force that would "move into Sonora with hostile intentions towards the Govt. of Mexico." Bvt. Maj. Gen. David E. Twiggs, the Department of Texas commander, endorsed the communication, saying, "It will be impossible for the troops in Texas to prevent persons crossing the Rio Grande: There is not one mile of the stream that cannot be passed by a body of men at any time." The letter was then forwarded to Secretary of War John Floyd, who took no action. The *San Antonio Herald* reported the event on August 12, and the *New York Times* reprinted it a fortnight later.[19]

A week earlier the Republican *Fremont Journal* in Sandusky County, Ohio, promulgated a rumor from Kansas that "the notorious Col. Titus has been hung in the Indian Territory, for horse stealing. The news is too good to be true we fear." According to other gossip, "the Colonel had 'raised a row' with the Cherokees, and came off second best, having seven of his men killed, and report says, himself taken prisoner." The Titus company and their lumbering oxen pulling creaky wagons proceeded from Fort Chadbourne in a southwestern direction across the Colorado River until fording 130 miles later the muddy Pecos River at Horsehead Crossing. The emigrants reached the safety of Fort Davis, Texas, in early September. The area from the Pecos to the garrison was in "full possession" of Comanche and Apache warriors who were killing and scalping travelers and seizing their horses. The post, with 126 soldiers of the Third Infantry, was the major link in a line of forts on the San Antonio–El Paso Road. The Titus party camped near the garrison and bought provisions from the sutler. They gathered wood for their campfires, and some nestled under the wagon covers that flapped in. The trek continued on the scenic San Antonio–San Diego Mail Line, which in Texas was safer from Indian attack and had a series of springs and wells fifteen miles apart that provided a continuous supply of water.[20]

The *San Diego Herald* reported that the Titus group of "seventy-five filibuster[er]s" was "destined for Sonora," although "they profess to intend settling as farmers in Arizona. They were well provided with such agricultural implements as Sharps rifles and six-shooters. Rumor had it that two hundred and fifty men were on the way from Santa Fe, and two hundred were expected from California." Due to Titus's notoriety as a filibuster leader in Cuba and Nicaragua, it was generally assumed that he would invade Mexico during its ongoing civil war. The previous year Henry A. Crabb, a former

California state senator who married into a prominent Sonora family, had led a seventy-man filibuster expedition into that territory from Arizona. The invaders were besieged for five days at Caborca, and all but one teenager were executed after surrendering. Crabb was riddled by a one-hundred-man firing squad, and his decapitated head was exhibited in a jar of mescal for preservation. The southwestern press and local citizens still clamored for "avenging Crabb" long after Titus had settled in Arizona.[21]

The Titus emigrants proceeded from Fort Davis to El Paso on the Davis Mountains route, called the military road, which was protected from Indian raids. They headed sixty miles west to newly established Fort Quitman, on a barren and sandy plain four hundred yards east of the Rio Grande. The entourage followed the principal watering places before reaching the garrison, which was manned by two companies with 83 men of the Eighth Infantry Regiment. The remaining trek north to Franklin, today El Paso, ran parallel to the Rio Grande, which provided a refreshing dip for travelers and draft animals and water for washing dusty clothes and refilling drinking barrels and canteens. The Titus expedition stopped at Franklin, a community of a few hundred inhabitants who were protected by the adobe-walled Fort Bliss and its 125 soldiers of the Eighth Infantry and Mounted Riflemen.[22]

The sojourners continued on the recently built road from El Paso to Fort Yuma, which had been cleared of trees, boulders, and steep grades and widened eighteen feet on straight stretches and twenty-five feet on curves. The dusty route, 350 miles from El Paso to Tucson, Arizona, starting parallel to the Rio Grande into New Mexico, was mostly without water except for that available at the Butterfield stations. Fort Fillmore, consisting of six adobe buildings, was the first stop 40 miles north and 6 miles southeast of Mesilla. When the Titus expedition arrived, the garrison had fewer than fifty soldiers of the Third Infantry after sixty-five troops had gone out to patrol the vicinity of Albuquerque. The Butterfield route diverted west a few miles north of Mesilla, a city of some three thousand Mexican inhabitants with "a few speculating Yankees," and then followed a series of springs in the Mesilla Valley into the Gadsden Purchase region.[23]

The Gadsden Purchase had acquired a 45,535-square-mile area in southern New Mexico in 1853 to obtain a suitable route for a southern Pacific railroad. The region was first colonized in 1687 by Spanish Jesuit missionaries who established missions along the Santa Cruz River and at Tucson. In 1752 a presidio was built at Tubac after silver and gold were discovered in the Santa Rita Mountains. The settlement was vacated during the Mexican war of independence in the 1810s and the Jesuits left after blocking the entrances to the mines with timber and stones. Mexicans returned to the mines from 1828 to 1830 but soon fled due to Apache ravages. The area was nearly deserted when Charles Debrille Poston established the headquarters of his Sonora Exploring and Mining Company at the former presidio in 1856. Tubac was located fifty-two miles south of Tucson on the old Spanish road to Sonora, Mexico. It was a "God forsaken village" in the Santa Cruz Valley that became the business district of silver mining within a twenty-mile radius. The only buildings in tolerable repair were those of Poston's enterprise, occupying a portion of the plaza and flanked by the old mission church. The lure of mineral wealth and the rich farmland of Arizona soon attracted farmers, miners, and speculators to the region. New prospectors clung to the tale that "great riches had been covered up" in an estimated 150 abandoned silver mines.[24]

Titus and his men entered the Gadsden Purchase region in southwestern New Mexico on the El Paso–Fort Yuma Road, which ran through three treacherous canyons in the Chiricagua mountains: Cooke's Canyon, Doubtful Canyon, and Apache Pass, notorious for frequent Indian ambushes. The emigrants, with weapons ready, listlessly scanned the rocky hills on their flanks for any signs of Indian movement. They silently marched through the second canyon, more than a mile long, between steep mountain gorge walls. Dragoon Springs appeared thirty-seven miles beyond Apache Pass. The fortified station, enclosed by a ten-foot-tall stone wall, had three employees recently murdered by Mexican laborers. The road then gradually descended for twenty-five miles through deep gullies and creek beds to the San Pedro River, fifty miles east of Tucson. When the Titus company reached Tucson in October 1858 after a four-month trek, they had "lost a large number of their animals, by the Apaches, and owing to dissensions that had arisen among them, the party had divided, some returning to Texas, and others to the new gold diggings."[25]

Tucson, the capital of the territory, contained "houses built of sun-dried mud [and] bordered a vista that opened upon a vast, yellow-brown, desert plain." It had some six hundred inhabitants, who were described by a contemporary traveler, Samuel Cozzens, as "nearly one half of which were Mexicans, the balance consisting of a mixture of Apaches, Pimos, Papagoes, and cut-throats. . . . a complete assortment of horse-thieves, gamblers, murderers, vagrants, and villains." Cozzens met the infamous Philemon Thomas Herbert, a former U.S. representative from California, who had killed an Irish waiter in Willard's Hotel in the capital two years earlier when he was refused breakfast at 11:00 A.M. Cozzens was disgusted at seeing "dilapidated bake ovens, old sheds, broken pottery, dead horses, tumble-down corrals, live dogs, drunken Indians, mules, pigs, and naked children." He concluded that "if there ever was a place closely allied to old Sodom, it was Tucson." After Titus arrived there, his expedition awaited for promised assistance from Fort Buchanan, fifty miles southeast, before crossing Apache country to his new homestead.[26]

Fort Buchanan, built the previous March, was the first permanent military post in Arizona. It was located on a small, sloping plateau three and a half miles southwest of the present town of Sonoita and on the north side of today's Highway 82 and the parallel Sonoita Creek, a tributary of the Santa Cruz River. The Sonoita Valley, originating there and extending eleven miles southwest, with a width of from fifty feet to half a mile, was "studded with large trees of live oak and cottonwood" and "matted with a luxuriant growth of clover." The garrison lacked form or shape. Its "cabins of upright logs chinked with adobe," each with a flat roof covered with dirt, were scattered over half a mile, surrounded on three sides by marshes that fed Sonoita Creek and proved unhealthy. Its southern point lay "between two hills which form a funnelshaped gorge." The fort, resembling a Mexican village, contained "stables, corrals, pig-pens, root-houses, open latrines," and two adobe buildings that served as officers' quarters and a post hospital. The garrison was commanded by Capt. Richard S. Ewell, with 138 men of Companies D and G, First Dragoons, most of whom had contracted malaria and dysentery. The post also employed 13 civilians: a carpenter, a blacksmith, an Apache interpreter, a guide, a mail rider, and eight herders.[27]

The population of Arizona was described by the geologist Raphael Pumpelly as being "made up of outlaws," excepting "a few widely separated American ranch owners and miners." The riffraff included those fleeing "from the vengeance of the San Francisco Vigilance Committee, and from the States, and there were escaped convicts from Australia. The labor element consisted of Mexicans, largely outlaws from Sonora." The territory lacked constituted civil authority, making every man "judge, jury, and sheriff; back of him was the quickly formed Vigilance Committee." According to Edward Ephraim Cross, editor of the Tubac *Weekly Arizonian,* there were some 250 Americans, including 16 women, along with some 8,000 Mexicans and Indians in Arizona. Horse stealing was so prevalent that the newspaper recommended a discouragement: "If citizens would adopt the plan of shooting, on sight, all strange and suspicious Mexicans found lurking about their premises, it would doubtless have a salutary effect."[28]

Soon after arriving in Arizona, Titus entered into an agreement with George D. Mercer, a twenty-seven-year-old civil engineer and surveyor from the District of Columbia, William J. Godfroy, and John Y. Bryant to search for hidden silver mines to exploit. After prospecting for a fortnight, Bryant returned east and sold his interest to Bernard John Dowling Irwin, a twenty-eight-year-old Irish army surgeon at Fort Buchanan. The partners then formed the Union Silver Mining Company and included Elias Brevoort, a thirty-six-year-old army sutler and mail rider. Irwin, as secretary and treasurer of the company, drafted the articles of agreement. Each company member received a copy signed by all participants and guaranteeing them "an equal share in the right, title, interest, emoluments, and profits," in consideration of "each one regularly paying their equal portion of the expenses of the company."[29]

A contemporary letter from Fort Buchanan to the *Texas Republican* said that Titus and Mercer had discovered in mid-November 1858 the Compadre and French Mines after a "long and painful search." The "shafts were found carefully concealed, partially filled with rubbish; and thirteen [adobe] furnaces in tolerable preservation, prove how extensively the mines were once worked" by the Jesuits who had abandoned them due to Apache raids. The French Mine, also called the Trench Mine, was located on the north slope of a mountain in the Patagonia range about five miles from the Sonoita Valley, "in a well wooded and watered region." The main shaft was 240 feet deep, with a 6-foot-wide vein containing "low grade argentiferous galena ore, excellent for smelting and easily mined." The lode stretched for more than 20,000 feet and yielded from 30 to 80 percent lead. Each ton of ore produced from thirty to one hundred dollars of silver. Both mines were located in the San Rafael de la Zanja land grant, purchased by Ramón Romero in 1825, which consisted of four square leagues (17,474.06 acres) north of the United States–Mexico border intersected by the Santa Cruz River. Romero and his family had fled to California due to Apache depredations a decade before the Americans arrived.[30]

Titus quickly departed for Tucson and filed claims for his mines. In mid-December a news dispatch informed readers that the colonel had left Tucson for the Patagonia Mine, 48 miles from Tubac and 3.5 miles southeast of the Trench Mine. The open pit mine and the ruins of its stone buildings are today located 1,000 feet north of the intersection of Harshaw and Apache Roads, in the Patagonia Mountains, which are part of the Coronado National Forest. The Patagonia Mine had three large and well-defined veins, with "a splendid quality of argentiferous galena and carbonate ores, in a formation of limestone, ironstone, and manganese inclosed in a granitic primary formation." Each ton of ore contained 50 percent lead and reportedly rendered "from forty to seventy-five ounces of silver." The mine, 10 miles from the Mexican border, occupied five hundred acres of land at 6,160 feet above sea level. Its laborers lived a mile away in the village of Commission along Commission Creek.[31]

An 1864 drawing by J. Ross Browne of the open-pit Patagonia (Mowry)
Mine in the Patagonia Mountains of Arizona. From J. Ross Browne,
Adventures in the Apache Country (1871).

The Patagonia Mine recently had been rediscovered by a Mexican herder, who sold the location for "a pony and some other traps" to U.S. Army captain Ewell; Lts. J. N. Moore, George M. Randall, and Richard S. C. Lord; former colonel James W. Douglass; and a Mr. Doss. Ewell described it as "the darkest, gloomiest looking cavern you can imagine . . . about 50 feet deep." Contemporary images show that the mine was worked by retrieving the galena ore with a windlass. It was then processed with the Spanish *arrastra* grinding system. The ore was dumped into a large sunken stone-enclosed circle with a turnstile in its center. The turnstile had grinding stones attached to it within the circle, and its outer arm was hitched to a draft animal that would tread around the circumference. The deposits rendered "from 15% to 60% for lead and 5oz. to 1000oz. silver per ton." Those with high silver content were smelted in furnaces, and the lead derived from them was deemed worthless due to the high cost of transporting it to market. The silver was hammered into bars and cut into pieces called "planchets," which were stamped according to value, from twenty-five cents to a dollar or more. Some of the silver was sold to the Mexican government and sent under strong convoy "to Hermosillo, and there coined into money." According to a report thirty-five years later, the mine contained "the *very best smelting ores ever found in Arizona*." In late 1858 Elias Brevoort bought out two of his partners and became the principal owner and superintendent of the mine. The remaining original owners sold their entire shares to Titus in 1859 after personal disagreements and operational failures due to badly constructed furnaces and Apache raids that killed their Mexican mine workers. The labor difficulties continued "on account of the payment of the purchase money" by Titus, who also owned the Union Exploring and Mining Company.[32]

The Titus brothers resided in the old San José de Sonoita Mission, an adobe "church and house for the visiting priest" built in the late 1740s on a bluff on "the south edge of Sonoita Creek." It overlooked a broad valley that was "shaded by magnificent live-oaks," two hundred yards from today's Highway 82 and two miles southwest of the town of Patagonia. The ranch also had a blacksmith shop, a livestock corral, and a garden. The buildings were on "the lower southwest extremity" of what today is the Patagonia-Sonoita Creek Preserve. A contemporary map of the Sonoita and Santa Cruz river valleys drawn by the metallurgist and mining engineer F. Biertu indicates that between Calabasas and Casa Blanca, in a northeastern direction along Sonoita Creek, were the farms of William H. Finley, C. B. Marshall, Joseph Ashworth, John Ward, Henry T. Titus, Felix Grundy Ake, and William C. Wadsworth, the latter being four miles from Fort Buchanan. Titus and his neighbors were squatters on the Spanish land grant "San José de Sonoita," containing "one league and three fourths" (7,591.61 acres) along Sonoita Creek, purchased by León Herreros on May 15, 1825. The property was sold to Joaquín V. Elias on December 26, 1831, and remained unoccupied between 1833 and 1853. José Antonio Crespo purchased the land for $1,950 on August 21, 1856, but did not settle on it.[33]

Ake was a forty-nine-year-old Alabamian farmer with eighty-five hundred dollars in personal and real estate property. He had lost a bid for a seat as a Democrat in the Arkansas legislature in 1846. Ake, his pregnant Scotch-Irish wife, and two children settled near Fort Buchanan in June 1857, and he provided lumber, hay, and beef to the garrison under contract. Ake hired neighboring Mexican teamsters to drive his lumber loads to the fort, nearby mines, and expanding hamlets. On his property resided William Ward, a twenty-two-year-old shoemaker from Arkansas; a laborer from

New York and another from Mexico; and his "hard-living, hard-fighting" twenty-two-year-old nephew William W. "Bill" Ake and his wife. Bill arrived from California with a group of filibusters who were late for their intended role in the ill-fated Henry Crabb expedition. He had killed several men in California over a mining dispute and became "the worst outlaw" in the Sonoita Valley.[34]

William C. Wadsworth was a thirty-one-year-old Mississippi lawyer with personal and real estate assets worth eight thousand dollars. He was a Mexican War veteran and had been a schoolteacher and a court clerk in Jefferson, Texas. In 1853 Wadsworth had a wife and children when he met seventeen-year-old Esther Saxon, a married woman with a baby girl. Their affair prompted them to abandon their families and flee to Fort Smith, Arkansas, where they boarded with the Akes. Esther was pregnant when they arrived in Arizona. The couple were assisted on their farm by a cook and a worker from the North, three Mexican laborers, a stock raiser, and a maid. Wadsworth made five thousand dollars from a recent barley crop and purchased in Mexico fifteen hundred head of cattle, at five dollars each, which he was selling to the army at a profit with cattle drives as far as Fort Bliss, Texas.[35]

William H. Finley was a forty-nine-year-old Virginia farmer with property worth four thousand dollars. He had the largest ranch in the valley with nearly two hundred acres and a gristmill. Kentuckian C. B. Marshall owned "160 acres of good land and timber," where Mexican laborers produced "some of the best crops in the region." Joseph Ashworth, a twenty-four-year-old Arkansas farmer, had arrived from California with Bill Ake and the filibusters and was a partner in a sawmill operation. Ashworth's farm produced that year a barley crop worth five thousand dollars that was used as fodder for the Fort Buchanan horses. John Ward was a fifty-three-year-old illiterate Irish glassblower and farmer with a two-thousand-dollar personal estate. He was living with an illiterate Mexican peasant, twenty-eight-year-old Jesús María Martínez, and raising her children Félix Telles and Teodora Rangel and their baby daughter Mary Ward. His ranch had a sixty-by-sixteen-foot, three-room adobe house with a dozen glass-pane windows and a blacksmith shop at the bottom of a hill on a bluff overlooking today's Highway 82. It was "abundantly supplied with water, and produced good crops." Charles Debrille Poston described Ward as "a castoff from the Vigilance Committee in San Francisco, and who was, in all respects, a worthless character." Ward "hauled timber from the Santa Rita mountains and the Patagonia Hills for the Mowry, San Antonio and other mines" and provided hay for Fort Buchanan.[36]

William W. Wrightson, a thirty-one-year-old British surveyor, Cincinnati newspaperman, and agent of the Santa Rita Silver Mining Company, visited Fort Buchanan on January 2, 1859, and conversed with Titus and other locals who were being entertained by Captain Ewell. Titus acknowledged that "political excitements don't pay" and that he "lost a great deal of money and more of reputation by the Kansas squabbles." He was now determined to "mind his own business, and stick to law and order, and legitimate Democracy." Wrightson wrote that Titus had forgotten "his threat to come over and clean out our people and I concluded that I should not very soon be under the necessity of using a spare Lariat to suspend the famous Col. if he interfered with us." He added that Titus was "without men and without means" and that the colonel and his partners had recently begun working what they called the Union Mine, believing it to be rich in lead ore. Edward Ephraim Cross concurred when reporting to the *Cincinnati Times* that "Col. Titus has abandoned all his ideas of fillibusterism, and settled down to hard work." He saw "very fine" specimens produced by the Union Mine.[37]

The Akes celebrated a wedding reception at their ranch for their eighteen-year-old daughter Annie and her husband George P. Davis on March 1, 1859. Guests arrived from as far away as Tucson, there were soldiers from Fort Buchanan, and Titus most likely partook in drinking and celebrating with his neighbors. The outdoor tables were crowded with "all the sumptuous dishes of the Castilian menu." The demijohns of whiskey flanking the woodpile provided a gathering spot for the men. The brash Bill Ake in all likelihood regarded Titus as a heroic figure, and the colonel entertained the participants with tales of filibustering and adventure in foreign lands and fighting abolitionists in Kansas. Soon after the feast, Apaches absconded with Ake's cattle, which he and his new son-in-law retrieved after giving chase and confrontation. The Indians also killed Ake's neighbor Wadsworth's cow, and the Titus property was likewise affected by theft.[38]

Titus left for New York the first week of April 1859. Soon thereafter a disgruntled member of his emigration party, twenty-eight-year-old William M. Thatcher, wrote from Tucson to his hometown newspaper the *Border Star* in Westport, Missouri, to "warn the public against one Col. Titus." He pronounced him "a thief and a black-hearted villain. . . . He has stolen money from myself, if not from others, and hired an assassin to murder certain members of his company who had entrusted themselves and property to him to emigrate to his country." Thatcher requested that his letter be copied by "all papers in the States and territories," but it was exclusively reprinted in Republican newspapers.[39]

Disagreements between American settlers and their Mexican laborers resulted in the murder of the Calabasas rancher Greenbury Byrd on May 6, 1859, over late wages and mistreatment. He was mortally wounded in his sleep by ax blows from two hired hands, who stole his horses and fled to Mexico. The killers, who had worked for George D. Mercer, Titus's mining partner and manager at the Reventon ranch on the Santa Cruz River, nine miles north of Tubac, had committed an infraction a few days earlier. Mercer had them whipped and their hair shorn as punishment. Byrd was present and probably participated in the lashing. In retribution for Byrd's death, Billy Ake and six other vigilantes terrorized the Mexican laborers in the Sonoita Valley, murdering five in a neighboring farm and panicking hundreds of others into fleeing across the border. Workers deserted Titus's mines, and other local economic interests were affected. The settlers quickly captured three of the vigilantes and handed them over to the military, while a fourth was arrested by the soldiers. A hearing was later held in Mesilla before Probate Judge Rafael Buelas, who upon hearing arguments and evidence, dropped the murder charges and fined all four the aggregate amount of nine hundred dollars.[40]

That summer Ellett Titus was working the Patagonia Mine "energetically and with much success" but was "sorely annoyed by the Apache Indians, who were constantly coming in for provisions and frightening away the laborers." The Apaches, in violation of their treaties, robbed him "of several thousand dollars worth of property," including all the animals. The raiders, bound for Sonora to escape pursuit, passed through the valley. They also halted the mail coach near Tucson, "levied a tribute of Tobacco and corn," and committed a murder at the copper mines. In consequence, the Patagonia Mine advertised in the *Weekly Arizonian* for Mexican workers under "the highest wages paid." The continued violence in the region prompted a sharp decrease in the white population. Col. Benjamin L. E. Bonneville took a census that summer of Americans west of the Mesilla Valley, including the overland mail stations, and counted only 180 citizens.[41]

Henry Titus arrived in New York City on May 24, 1859, to buy mining supplies and smelting machinery, and he lodged at the elegant St. Nicholas Hotel on Broadway, between Broome and Spring Streets. The six-story building had 350 rooms, marble interiors, a carved white-oak staircase, and fresco ceilings. Titus was in the hotel saloon talking with his father and friends on the night of the 30th when he was confronted by Col. Frank B. Anderson, veteran of the San Juan River campaign. Anderson, who had led the attack on Fort Sarapiquí and captured El Castillo after Titus failed, was in the city with other filibuster officers meeting with Gen. William Walker. Anderson, accompanied by comrades, tried to start a fight with Titus over an old feud, but failing to do so, he left at about 9:30 P.M. Titus returned to his quarters, but an hour later, thinking that his opponents had departed, returned to the barroom, which contained more than two hundred patrons.[42]

A police captain who had been notified of trouble there appeared accompanied by a sergeant. As they entered the barroom, Anderson returned with the filibusters Gen. Chatham Wheat, Maj. George Bolivar Hall, Lieutenant Peel, and two others, who were "considerably under the influence of liquor." Titus was distracted in conversation when he got sucker-punched in the face, and in turn he knocked the aggressor across the marble floor with one blow. The attackers started beating Titus over the head with loaded canes and, according to a correspondent of the San Francisco *Daily Evening Bulletin,* they "were amusing themselves quite jollily with trying to beat his head into a jelly." The police captain drew his club and caught a cane thereon, but it glanced off and struck the sergeant in the eye, "making a bad bruise." Wheat was reported to be "only an accidental spectator" who was "a personal friend of Col. Titus." As the violence escalated, a number of frightened guests jumped out the back windows onto Mercer Street. Titus attempted to draw a revolver, but when the authorities intervened and took him away, he shouted that Anderson was a "damned coward, and a man who did not dare to cross the lines and fight him with pistols." That was the only manner "to settle the differences between them in a gentlemanly way." The police ordered the lounge closed and led Titus back to his room by a rear door. It was believed that "the whole affair was started in order to kill Titus by shooting him." More than a dozen national newspapers commented on the filibusterer "collision," with northern newspapers vituperating the participants. The *Boston Traveller* chastised that it was not chivalrous for "a score" of filibusters to attack one man and suggested, "Why can't the rascals go to Cuba, and get caught?"[43]

The next evening Anderson and his cronies returned to the saloon looking for Titus. Anderson was "excessively annoyed at being publicly branded as a coward, and swore to have revenge at any and every cost." One of the hotel proprietors, John P. Treadwell, told Anderson that any further improprieties would prompt police intervention. Anderson "became greatly enraged" and responded with "opprobrious epithets." The police captain, who had stationed a dozen of his men in mufti about the hotel in anticipation of renewed hostilities, quickly arrested Anderson for disorderly conduct and assault. Anderson spent the night in jail before appearing in police court the next morning. Titus refused to press charges, "alleging that Southern men were not in the habit of obtaining satisfaction for ill-treatment in that way." Treadwell complained of being "fearful of personal violence" because Anderson had "called him a liar and a thief" and had threateningly shaken his finger at him. The accused had to pay a ten-dollar fine and post a one-thousand-dollar bail to keep the peace toward Treadwell for six months before being released.[44]

According to an Illinois newspaper, the "redoubtable" Titus was in New York City "trying to organize companies to work the mines, and to induce emigration" to Arizona. His former filibuster nemesis Col. Samuel Lockridge was supposedly helping him, and they were being assisted by Manhattan Democrat and alderman William Wilson, an Englishman and emigrant runner. Wilson had applied to Secretary of War John Floyd "for permission to take a body of armed emigrants across the frontier of Texas," which was refused in the belief that "its object was simply to obtain governmental sanction to a filibustering expedition." The newspaper indicated that "both Titus and Lockridge are operating with a view to sell out bogus mines, and the statements which they and their associates are putting forth through the public prints" are phony.[45]

A week after the barroom fracas, Mary Titus arrived in New York City on the steamship *Augusta* from Savannah, accompanied by her five-month-old son Edward Hopkins Titus and a slave servant. The colonel was overjoyed at seeing his son for the first time, and the family stayed with their relatives in Queens. There are two newspaper references to the Tituses previously having their children with them in Kansas, but they apparently did not survive. Soon thereafter Titus sold his interest in the Union Exploring and Mining Company to a New York enterprise presided by Alvah Clark for "a handsome compensation." He used twenty-five thousand dollars of it to acquire capital and "an immense mass" of "supplies and machinery necessary for prosecuting mining and smelting operations." Titus, as manager of the New York and Compadre Mining Company, departed for Arizona accompanied by Elias Brevoort and various business partners, "including the cashier and a smelter of ore," stopping in St. Louis, Missouri, for a few days. The colonel commented to reporters that the population of Arizona was so meager that any attempt at territorial organization was premature. He favored its actual status as a judicial district of New Mexico, with "proper provisions for Courts, ministers of the law and other officers."[46]

Titus shipped his mining machinery, including a steam engine and a six-thousand-pound boiler transported in three parts, by riverboat from St. Louis to New Orleans. It was then forwarded to San Antonio, Texas, by way of Port Lavaca, before arriving at its destination. The Apaches "not only kept a respectable distance from it, but could not be induced to approach it, believing it to be a huge cannon." The colonel and his entourage continued to Arizona on July 25 with smaller freight on the Butterfield Overland Mail Company route. The fare from St. Louis to San Francisco was $150.00, which did not include meals costing $1.00. Way passengers such as Titus, who did not travel the entire route, were charged $0.15 per mile. Each rider was allowed forty pounds of baggage free of charge. Freight cost was $1.00 per one hundred pounds per one hundred miles and traveled by slower ox-wagon caravan. Each coach carried an average of five thousand letters, whose postage was $0.10 per half ounce.[47]

Titus began the semiweekly trip by railroad 168 miles from St. Louis to Syracuse, Missouri, followed by 143 miles on a Concord coach to Springfield, Missouri. Travelers then transferred to spring wagons and later switched again to coaches for the 175 miles to Fort Smith, Arkansas. The Concord coach, pulled by four horses, was five feet wide and eight feet long, weighed forty-eight hundred pounds, and "was painted red or green, with designs and pictures painted on the lower panels of the doors." Bilateral wire pattern candle lamps hung outside for illumination. The interior had russet leather lining, side curtains, and cushions on three seats that usually filled to capacity with nine people. Those sitting in the middle had no back support and interlocked their knees with the occupants in front of them. A dozen passengers could ride on top dangling their legs over the side. A heavy mail in the trunk, portmanteaus, and baggage would weigh down the rear of the coach, keeping the front seat passengers uncomfortably bent forward without back support. Mark Twain would later describe a similar coach ride as "a cradle on wheels," due to its swinging and swaying on its three-inch-thick leather thoroughbraces instead of bouncing on steel springs. Titus, much taller than the average contemporary, had a cumbersome sojourn. He carried a rifle, revolvers, and a knife and must have insisted on riding outside part of the way. The coach horses were exchanged for fresh ones at stations usually about twelve miles apart.[48]

The Butterfield Overland Mail Company had "home stations" that housed a station masters, blacksmiths, harness makers, wheelwrights, herders, and cooks and contained eating accommodations. The "swing stations" were maintained by only two or three men who changed the horses during stops lasting less than ten minutes. Titus and other passengers would briefly debark to stretch their legs at every opportunity. Most of the travelers "did not change their clothes or shave during the entire journey lasting nearly three weeks." Each station had corrals, stables, ample water, and a two-month supply of hay and grain. The transports stopped for morning, noon, and evening meals at designated home stations. The fare consisted of "bread, tea, and fried steaks of bacon, venison, antelope, or mule flesh—the latter tough enough." Mark Twain complained that what was billed as tea had "too much dish-rag, and sand, and old bacon-rind in it to deceive the intelligent traveler." Drivers were assigned routes some 60 miles long and lived at the end stations of their sections. The conductor, accompanying the driver, was responsible for the safety of the mail and passengers and rode the coach during a 120-mile stretch. He would notify their approach to a station with a brass bugle that could be heard two miles distant.[49]

From Fort Smith to Arizona, Titus rode for fifteen hundred miles in Celerity wagons, each of which had a light frame structure with a canvas roof and a wide wheelbase and was designed as a sleeper for nine passengers, with three seats that converted into a bed. The average rate of speed was "about four and a quarter miles an hour." Most passengers who kept journals complained that they could not sleep the first week due to the hard seats and the constant bouncing and jolting. A *New York Herald* correspondent complained of "inhaling constant clouds of dust." In the Arizona mountain and desert region, the wagons were pulled by mules, with an additional team hitched for steep grades. This route across Comanche territory was beset with anxiety and fears of Indian attacks. The stations were ten miles apart in this dangerous region and were "guarded by from twenty to twenty-five men" with an escort on six horses accompanying the coach. The stagecoach traveled without lights at night to avoid detection, increasing the possibility of an accident.[50]

Titus, Brevoort, and their companions arrived at the La Cienega stagecoach station on August 12, 1859, after "a rough passage of 23 days, owing to high water." The way stop, southeast of Tucson on Frontage Road, was near today's South Sonoita Highway 83, leading to Fort Buchanan. Titus told a *New York Herald* reporter on the 17th that he would "at once commence work with a strong force of Mexicans, build houses and furnaces and prepare his machinery for smelting" at the Compadre and French Mines of the New York and Compadre Mining Company. Titus expected to "reduce about eight tons of ore per day." The next day a correspondent of the *New York Tribune* divulged rumors that Titus intended to jump claims. The colonel allegedly "threatened to seize the Longarina Mine, owned by two respectable and intelligent German gentlemen, on the ground that under the old Mexican Mining Laws, which still prevail here, no foreigner can hold a mine." The writer, however, dismissed the gossip, claiming that he knew Titus well and he was "not the soldier of fortune, or freebooter, he is usually represented." The colonel was "a real acquisition" to Arizona, where "he has been a good citizen, quietly and industriously pursuing his legitimate business in an honorable way, meddling with no one, but always ready to lend assistance in maintaining law and order." On August 20 a *New York Times* correspondent at Fort Buchanan wrote that "Col. Titus & Co." were prospecting the Compadre and French Mines, which "contain ore adapted to the smelting process" for which "extensive furnaces" were being built in Sonoita Valley, "about ten miles from the post." In reducing silver ores, smelting could be used only with ores containing lead, or that will combine with lead, which is used as a flux. Titus was "laboring vigorously for success."[51]

The reporter had recently had to retract himself after writing the previous month that the "veritable Col. Titus," who was expected to arrive at Tubac "with anywhere from 1,000 to 1,900 men," had appeared "with less [*sic*] than ten men who immediately disbanded on their arrival. All such enterprises will fail." He apologized by saying that "Col. T's friends think the letter spoke of him in a disrespectful manner. Your correspondent had no such intention." The writer stressed that Titus was "a man of great energy and enterprise" who, since arriving in Arizona, "has been actively engaged in mining, in exploring and opening old and new workings, and has really done more than any individual to develop the country. He has now some of the best mines in the country, and I believe is on his way out with plenty of material for working them."[52]

Titus along with George D. Mercer, Christopher C. Dodson, Robert Phillips, Henry Jenkins, George W. Redding, and Elias Brevoort, at the latter's Reventon Ranch, signed a document on August 29, 1859, staking a claim to a silver mine located about two-thirds of a mile southwest of the Cerro Colorado Mine, owned by the Sonora Exploring and Mining Company. The seven partners agreed to call it the Redding Mine, whose main vein ran east and west, with an additional five veins whose extent was unknown. The petition concluded, "Should there be more veins discovered upon the usual quantity of land allotted to such mines, the company claim the right & title to them by possession." Three days later Brevoort mailed the claim from Tubac to Gen. William Pelham, the surveyor general of New Mexico at Santa Fe, requesting the registration of the silver mine and a returned certified copy. The postscript on the letter stated, "The ore in this mine is worth from $9.50 to $28.00 per ton, and a mountain of it."[53]

Violence and death periodically shadowed Titus in Arizona. On August 31 Apaches attacked the Patagonia Mine, resulting in the mortally wounding of an American mine worker and an Indian. Weeks later Captain Johnson, a Nicaragua filibusterer, arrived in Arizona from the East "for the avowed purpose of fighting a duel" with Titus. However, before locating his rival, Johnson was shot and killed by Colonel Robinson over a gambling table drunken dispute. Then on November 1 Titus was settling payroll accounts of his New York and Compadre Mining Company at his office in his hacienda when a Mexican laborer "got excited" over his rightful share. The peon "raised a large stone-hammer as if to strike Titus when the latter, taking a pistol from the belt of a bystander shot at but missed the Mexican." A second shot in the groin mortally wounded the man. That month the *Mining Magazine and Journal of Geology* announced, "The Compadre and French mines are now being worked, under the direction of Col. Titus and company. Furnaces for melting are being erected ten miles from the fort." By the end of November, a local newspaper correspondent wrote that "the Union Mining Company, under the management of Col. Titus, is laboring vigorously for success."[54]

In March 1860 newspapers in St. Louis and Cincinnati reported that Titus, manager of the New York and Compadre Mining Company, had passed through their cities headed for New York and had "kindly submitted to our inspection over 50 lbs. pure silver, the product of his mine, together with a large number of fabulously rich specimens of the ores." The colonel had sold for forty thousand dollars his share of the Compadre Mine that he owned with Brevoort. Robert L. d'Aumaile, a member of the Geological Survey of Sonora, wrote in the *Daily Evening Bulletin* that the Titus mine and others in the Sonoita Valley were "completely paralyzed. . . . The managers and employees are constantly prostrated by the endemic fevers so prevalent in the valley." He claimed that Titus was able to get only five dollars of silver to the ton from the Compadre ores, "which are a mixture of argillaceous peroxide of iron with calc-spar, a little oxide and carbonate of lead."[55]

D'Aumaile had been previously arrested in San Francisco for forgery and threats, and a grand jury determined that he had "monomania." He called the San Antonio Mining Company "one of Titus' abortive humbugs." D'Aumaile accused Titus of buying eight hundred dollars worth of silver from the Patagonia Mining Company, managed by his brother Ellett, and secretly dumping it with his excavated ore in a smelter furnace, whose operator gave him a high-grade certificate. The article claimed that Titus got another favorable silver evaluation from a treasurer "elicited through the medium of a loaded revolver." The colonel then used these bogus documents in New York to raise the value of his mining stocks. Titus countered the negative stories with his own letter to the St. Louis *Missouri Republican* claiming that these statements, along with reports of increasing Indian attacks, were "greatly exaggerated." He stopped in Jacksonville to join his wife and child in early March 1860 and accompanied them on the steamer *St. Johns* to Savannah, from where Mary Titus proceeded to New York City, checking into the St. Nicholas Hotel on March 16.[56]

Titus was back in Arizona by mid-April 1860 to find that there had been "no cessation of Apache depredations in the settlement," including the murder of two Mexican wood choppers, the theft of animals, crop burning, and the abduction of females and children. The region, with temperatures of 130 degrees Fahrenheit, was "literally swarming with roving bands" of Indians, "whose footprints are seen in the vicinity of every ranch" in the area. Apaches stole all the horses from the Santa Rita Mine on May 28 and the next day absconded with the cattle from a farm near Fort Buchanan. Titus and his partner in the Patagonia Mine sold their interests to twenty-eight-year-old Sylvester Mowry for twenty-five thousand dollars cash. Mowry was a Rhode Islander who had graduated from the U.S. Military Academy in 1852 as an artillery officer. After frontier duty in California for five years, he was reassigned to Fort Buchanan before resigning in July 1858. Mowry appears in the 1860 census as a "Retired U.S. Army Officer" with real estate valued at fifty thousand dollars and a personal estate of twenty-five thousand dollars. The Patagonia Mine, subsequently called the Mowry Mine, soon fell prey to the Indians. On June 6 "a band of Apaches drove off all the company's stock, and murdered the superintendent and many of the miners." Captain Ewell, Lieutenant Lord, and forty-three men immediately left Fort Buchanan "on a scout against the Chiricahua Indians and returned on the 16th." Nine days later the officers departed again on the same mission with seventy-three men for the Chiricahua mountains for three weeks. Upon their return they were joined by a new arrival, Bvt. 2nd Lt. Joseph Wheeler, assigned to Company D, First Dragoons, who went on to earn the sobriquet "Fighting Joe," which made him renowned as a Confederate Civil War cavalry general.[57]

That summer Titus returned to visit his family at their home in the Jamaica neighborhood of Queens, New York. He was enumerated in the federal census on June 20, 1860, along with his wife, Mary, and their one-year-old son Edward; his sixty-five-year-old father, Theodore; his thirty-five-year-old sister Marian Ann Titus; and two Irish servants. Henry Titus appeared as a merchant with real estate valued at ten thousand dollars and a personal estate worth five thousand dollars. By the following month, Titus had returned to his Arizona ranch accompanied by the forty-year-old Italian Charles Garibaldi.[58]

On August 5 Titus held a public meeting at his Sonoita Valley hacienda. All participants went "armed and on horseback, ready for any emergency." The gathering was presided over by Edward Ephraim Cross, editor of the *Weekly Arizonian,* who recounted the numerous atrocities committed in the region by Mexicans and paid homage to the memory of the pioneer victims. Two weeks earlier eleven Sonora peons at the new San Pedro Mine, thirty-five miles east of Fort Buchanan, had plundered it and murdered three Americans employees of the St. Louis Mining Company, which owned the shaft. The teenagers Will and Jeff Ake, Titus's neighbors, discovered the massacre when they arrived there to deliver provisions. Ellett Titus was at the meeting representing the Patagonia Mining Company. The group drafted resolutions that in part called on the Mexican authorities "to extend all proper efforts to bring the murderers to justice and restore the stolen property" and agreed to establish armed patrols to protect the miners from Mexican bandits.[59]

Titus and four other participants were elected to a committee to report on a plan of action. The gathering then discussed the regulation of Mexican labor and settled on meeting soon with all miners and farmers "to agree upon all matters pertaining to the employment of peons." Titus then gave "an excellent speech" advocating creating separate judicial and land districts and denouncing the "complete failure" of the so-styled provisional government. The group unanimously supported a resolution drafted by Titus, on behalf of the "citizens of Western Arizona," utterly repudiating the provisional government and petitioning Congress "for the organizing of a judicial and land district" because "there were no legal officers to whom the authorities of Sonora could give up the prisoners if they were arrested." Titus then announced that he had "just struck very rich mineral in his Eagle mine," half a mile from the Patagonia Mine, which he had been "prospecting for some time back." He added that there was a New York company waiting for this event and anxious to purchase a local mine.[60]

That month Titus wrote various letters to Surveyor General Alexander Perry Wilbar at Santa Fe, New Mexico, signing them as "Agent of the New York and Arizona Exploring Company." He enclosed several documents intended as denouncement claims of abandoned Spanish mines in New Mexico. Wilbar refused to record the claims and forwarded the Titus letters and documentation to Joseph S. Wilson, commissioner of the General Land Office in Washington, D.C. Wilson cited federal statutes of 1853 indicating that "the Executive has no authority to recognize any claim to mines in virtue of present discovery, or denouncement" in the New Mexico Territory because the United States Congress had not "passed any Act of legislation on the subject." He ordered Wilbar to extend consideration only to "private claims lawfully derived from the former governments [of Spain and Mexico], and to Donation claims." The commissioner concurred with the surveyor general in not validating the Titus claims.[61]

The federal census of the Sonoita Valley settlement on August 27, 1860, enumerated the Titus brothers among one hundred residents, fifty-two of whom were Mexicans. There were seventeen adult women living in the valley, twelve of them Mexicans. The Tituses were included among eight people identified as "Compadre Silver Mining Works."[62] The dwellings on both sides of the Titus property were listed as "unoccupied." The colonel appeared as a thirty-seven-year-old "Miner," with thirty thousand dollars in real estate and fifty thousand dollars in personal assets. His brother Ellett was listed as having real estate valued at five thousand dollars and personal property worth three thousand dollars. The following week the colonel left Arizona on the overland mail stage, arriving at Fort Smith, Arkansas, at noon on Saturday, September 15. The passengers reported that the Indians in New Mexico had renewed hostilities. The previous mail coach had been attacked by Navajos while traveling between Mesilla and Santa Fe. The driver and conductor were killed and the coach and mails destroyed.[63]

Lawlessness increased in the Sonoita Valley that fall after Captain Ewell left Fort Buchanan in September for Fort Bliss, Texas, and was replaced in command by Lt. Col. Pitcairn Valleau Morrison of the Seventh Infantry Regiment. On the 13th eight Apaches killed Titus's neighbor Joe Ashworth as he and two companions were driving fifteen head of cattle near Wadsworth's ranch. The Indians approached making gestures of friendship, gunned down Ashworth when they noticed that he was the only one armed, and made off with the herd. By December the post office at Tubac was closed by the government and "investors were spurning Arizona mines." On the 27th two lieutenants and fifty-six enlisted men of Company K, Seventh Infantry, departed Fort Buchanan "to Santa Cruz river and vicinity of the Heintzelman Mine, for the protection of settlers, depredations being apprehended on the citizens in that vicinity from bands of disorganized Filibuster[er]s."[64]

Titus meanwhile had gone to New York to assure investors that his mining operations represented a safe investment. He had spent the previous two and a half years trying to get rich with his mining schemes in Arizona. The colonel entered into partnerships for owning the Compadre, Patagonia, Trench, Redding, and Eagle Mines and was a stockholder of the Union Silver Mining Company and the Union Exploring and Mining Company and managed the New York and Compadre Mining Company. His detractors accused him of dishonest dealings with investors. Titus had labored hard while under the constant danger of Indian attacks and disgruntled employees, killing one in self-defense.

The colonel's previous entrepreneurial schemes had floundered. There had been no awaiting enterprise back home after leaving Nicaragua, since he stayed with his father for six weeks and then summoned his wife from Florida before moving to Kansas seeking new fortune. His Kansas City business ventures were unsustainable. Titus initially planned a lumber business but apparently lacked the necessary capital. He rented a saloon but lost it after a few months by defaulting on the mortgage. The colonel tried to revive his political fortunes by lobbying with Governor Walker, but the magistrate's early resignation nixed it. After sectional violence ended in Kansas, Titus conspired to rig the election for a proslavery constitution, but it was soundly defeated twice at the polls. He also looked forward to an opportunity to restore his reputation for bravery, which had been damaged by the negative northern press. However, examples of his prowess were limited to drunken barroom brawls in St. Louis and New York City, a violent political argument with a hotel keeper, and the assault of a free-soiler, which resulted in his expulsion from Kansas City. In the fall of 1860 Titus was back in New York City, where the three major metropolitan newspapers, as well as others from Cincinnati to San Francisco, had been closely following his activities in Arizona and deriding him.

★ *Chapter Five* ★

Florida Pioneer
1861–1881

enry Titus arrived in New York City in mid-October 1860, established
residence at 117 W. Fortieth Street, and worked as an agent for a firm
at 506 Tenth Avenue. Abraham Lincoln's presidential campaign was in full
swing, with Republican "Wide-Awake" supporters marching in nighttime
torchlit parades throughout the city. Lincoln won the four-candidate election with 39.65 percent of the popular vote and 59.4 percent of the electoral
college, without receiving a single southern vote. The following month Titus
was present when his daughter Catherine Howell Titus was born in Jamaica,
Queens, New York, on December 2. Eighteen days later South Carolina was
the first state to secede from the Union, and Florida followed suit on January
10, 1861. Titus had another opportunity to defend the southern cause when
Hinton Rowen Helper was scheduled on the 14th to deliver the antislavery
lecture "Two Systems of Labor" in Clinton Hall at the Mercantile Library of
New York. Helper, a thirty-two-year-old North Carolinian, was the author
of *The Impending Crisis of the South: How to Meet It,* which blamed slavery
for southern backwardness and incited poor whites to oppose bondage and
planter dominance. The book was widely popular in the North, especially
during the 1860 elections, when the Republican Party used it as a campaign
document. In contrast, the work was banned as treasonous in the South,
where it was subjected to book burnings.[1]

Hours before the scheduled lecture, Titus joined a hostile mob awaiting
Helper outside Clinton Hall. The sponsors of the event posted a note on the
building entrance canceling the presentation "owing to the excited state of
the public mind." The protesters then dispersed except for a rowdy group
that "gave three cheers for South Carolina and groans for Helper, and all who

held with him." Titus was branded "ringleader" of this group, which included former police captain William L. Wiley and a Colonel Van Zandt. A police captain with a twenty-seven-man platoon emerged from the hall and scattered the crowd. Titus was arrested for disorderly conduct and defying the officer. As he was being conveyed to the Fifteenth Ward police station, a large mob followed, cheering for the Union and for Maj. Robert Anderson, the commander of Fort Sumter.[2]

Titus initially stated that "his name was H. H. James, and that he was from New Jersey, that he was 35 years old and was married, and that he had no business in particular." Before being booked, Titus asked to be released, but the police captain replied, "You must not get yourself into such business. The laws must be sustained." The officer then asked his prisoner if he was carrying any weapons and received a negative reply. When the captain frisked Titus and "pulled forth a loaded revolver from his pocket, he said he had no arms except those he always carried." Captain Wiley then offered the police officer one thousand dollars for the release of the prisoner, who was remitted to a cell in the Tombs for the night. Titus appeared the next day before the Jefferson Market police court and was released after three "respectable gentlemen" said that they were present at the protest and did not see the accused commit any overt act. They described the incident as an "unprovoked outrage" by the police captain who arrested him. The *Springfield Republican* of Massachusetts believed that Titus "is probably one of the agents sent to New York by the disunionists to organize the desperate classes for a riot. The police should keep an eye on him."[3]

After Florida seceded from the Union, Titus and his family went back to the San Pablo plantation in Jacksonville, Florida. There was nothing to return to in Arizona, where Apache depredations had devastated the Sonoita Valley. On January 27, 1861, the Indians raided the ranch of Titus's neighbor John Ward, taking his twelve-year-old Mexican stepson, Felix Telles, and twenty head of cattle. Two days later Ward accompanied 2nd Lt. George N. Bascom and fifty-four mounted soldiers of Company C, Seventh Infantry, who searched for his son. When negotiations with the Indian leader Cochise failed, a skirmish ensued on February 5, in which Ward and a sergeant were wounded. Thus started the Apache wars of reprisals and murders that lasted more than two decades.[4]

The Apaches then burned the Wadsworth and Marshall homesteads before the overland mail was abandoned, cutting off the lifeline to the territory and encouraging further Indian depredations. On the night of April 25, emboldened Apaches descended upon the cattle herd at Fort Buchanan and fled under fire from two military herders. Two days later Ellett Titus died during an Apache raid on his ranch. Raphael Pumpelly, a metallurgist at the Santa Rita Mines, who arrived at the hacienda soon thereafter, described how "as we came to the principal house a scene of destruction met our eyes. The doors had been forced in, and the whole contents of the house lay on the ground outside, in heaps of broken rubbish." Supplies and victuals were strewn about. Heavy flour sacks were slashed and dumped on the ground. Everyone on the property had been killed or committed suicide to avoid capture and torture by the Indians, who rarely seized male prisoners. After the army razed Fort Buchanan in July, the Sonoita Valley settlers fled, and Apache attacks kept nearly all white settlers out of the region for the next fifteen years.[5]

After the Civil War started in April, the former filibuster veteran and Bleeding Kansas colonel enlisted as assistant quartermaster of the Florida Militia on detached service in Jacksonville. His father-in-law, Col. Edward Stevens Hopkins, who had been a candidate for Florida governor the previous year under the antisecessionist Constitutional Union Party, joined the Confederate army. His brother-in-law Coriolanus Hopkins joined the Eighth Field Battery, Texas Light Artillery, as a sergeant and was later promoted to second lieutenant. The first Titus state payroll form, on June 15, 1861, indicated that he was receiving a monthly salary of $130.00 plus an extra $11.00 for the services of his black servant Plato. Titus economically profited from the war by supplying the army with victuals from his plantation. Foreign commerce was suspended after the Union navy blockaded the mouth of the St. Johns River. On November 2 Titus delivered to Joseph Remington, the Confederate commissary inspector of beef at Fernandina, fifty barrels of mess meat. Ten barrels were forwarded to the troops at St. Augustine, and the rest were assigned to the soldiers at Fernandina. Titus received $41,537.50 for 15,375 pounds of beef. Two weeks later Remington weighed and inspected in Jacksonville another sixty-two barrels of meat provided by Titus, complying with contract specifications.[6]

The war went well for Titus until March 7, 1862, when Jacksonville mayor Halsted H. Hoeg, a forty-one-year-old transplanted New York merchant and sawmill owner, issued a public proclamation stating that inasmuch as all Confederate forces were being withdrawn from eastern and southern Florida in the face of a Union expedition, Jacksonville would be surrendered upon the approach of the enemy. Responding to rumors of an imminent enemy incursion, he advised all citizens "to remain at their homes and pursue their usual avocations." Many of the city's economic enterprises were owned by northerners. The Confederates had no fortifications in the city and "neither naval forces nor batteries at the time on the river." That day Titus sent a letter to his father-in-law, Colonel Hopkins, commanding the Fourth Regiment of Florida Volunteers and headquartered at Fernandina. The regiment, comprised of 812 men, was scattered in other, western parts of Florida at St. Vincent's Island, at St. Marks and the lighthouse near there, and at Cedar Keys. Three-fourths of its Company C was made up of teenagers.[7]

Titus wrote, "Instead of the enemy taking our property, they protect it and the rights of the citizen." He indicated that his wife, who was eight months pregnant, was unwell and refusing to leave. Titus stressed that after being left without a government or protection, he did not intend to follow a retrograde army and instead would "remain on my place and pursue my peaceable avocations, and submit to the power of the U.S. Government." He added, "The negro property of all persons are safe, and the rights of all citizens are respected." Titus concluded his letter saying, "I may be denounced for my course, but, after mature reflection, it will be my course. You well know it has been my opinion that this State could not, under any circumstances, sustain herself against the strong power of the Government." Titus forwarded the letter via the Reverend Richard M. Tydings, a thirty-nine-year-old Pennsylvanian Methodist and Freemason, who was sent by the Yankees under a flag of truce to the Confederate camp with a proposition. The Federals offered to evacuate Jacksonville, providing Confederate troops should be sent to protect local Unionists from guerrilla reprisals. Colonel Hopkins resigned from the Confederacy two months later when his Fourth Regiment of Florida Volunteers was ordered to Corinth, Mississippi, and he refused to leave his state. Titus did not join the army when all the state militia units were disbanded and many of its ranks transferred to Confederate service.[8]

On March 11 a Confederate special battalion under Maj. Charles Floyd Hopkins arrived in Jacksonville and carried out orders to destroy everything of value to the enemy. Fire was set to thirteen large sawmills owned by northern men, four million feet of lumber, the foundry, a gunboat on its stocks, the Judson House owned by a Bostonian, and a few other buildings. The next day four Federal gunboats and two transports of Commodore Samuel Francis Du Pont's squadron anchored in the St. Johns River off Jacksonville. Six companies of the Fourth New Hampshire Regiment debarked while their band played "Yankee Doodle." One of their officers wrote from Jacksonville on the 14th that "none of us know who are friends or enemies, with the exception of the poor class, who have nothing to gain or lose. Col. Titus, of Kansas notoriety, is here, professedly Union, but who believes it?" Six days later thirty-three-year-old Vermonter Calvin L. Robinson, a local wealthy merchant with a wife and two children, presided over a public meeting that passed resolutions calling for organizing a state government loyal to the Union and requesting a northern military presence in the city. Titus did not attend the meeting, and he is not mentioned in Robinson's journal.[9]

Soon thereafter three slaves on the San Pablo plantation fled to Union lines. Two belonged to Titus, and the other was twenty-four-year-old Sharper owned by Jesse Gresham. Titus requested from the military occupiers that his runaway slaves be returned to him. On April 3 U.S. Navy lieutenant T. H. Stevens, on the gunboat *Ottawa* off Jacksonville, wrote to his superior officer, Cdr. Percival Drayton, a Charlestonian whose brother was a Confederate general, that "Colonel Titus has been informed that two of his slaves have been left by the *Wabash* at Fernandina. Can they be sent in one of our vessels to him?" Titus went to the Union camp with an order directing Col. Gilman E. Sleeper to deliver the remaining slave to his master. According to the abolitionist general Rufus B. Saxton, "On receiving this negro Col. Titus put a slipping noose rope around the negro's neck, with a timber pitch at his arm, mounted his horse and dragged the poor victim off in the presence of our troops." The return of the slave was possible because the previous summer the U.S. Congress had passed a nearly unanimous resolution affirming that the purpose of the war was to preserve the Union and not change southern domestic institutions. In consequence slaves were considered contrabands of war and the Fugitive Slave Act was enforced by some Union officers. Three months after Titus had his runaway slave returned to him, Congress authorized the confiscation of slaves whose masters supported the Confederacy.[10]

The Union concession to Titus prompted some fleeing refugees to tell the *Gainesville Cotton States* newspaper that the "traitor" Titus "had gone over to the Federals, and had made an effort to recruit a company in Jacksonville for the Lincolnites." The false account was reprinted in various southern publications. Meanwhile the U.S. Army announced on April 7 that troops would evacuate Jacksonville, prompting pandemonium among those who had recently sworn loyalty to the Union, who hurriedly boarded the military transports. The merchant Calvin L. Robinson, his family, and his female slave were among the 125 loyalists who left with the troops. Ten days prior to the departure, a number of slave owners went to Jacksonville under a flag of truce to claim their absconded chattels, and "in every instance they were given up and restored to their masters." As Jacksonville was being evacuated, General Wright ordered that the runaway slaves on the transports be left behind, and 52 who reached Fernandina were "returned to Jacksonville and delivered to Confederate troops under flag of truce."[11]

Titus responded to accounts of his defection with a letter addressed "To the Public" on April 11 from San Pablo, saying that he had been at his plantation with his "family and negroes and effects, without means of transportation," when he was "informed by officers of the Confederate army that orders were received to leave the State of Florida." Titus was "indignant at the course to be pursued without a moment's warning." He stressed that in the absence of the Confederate army, he had "no other prerogative" than to submit, suffering "deep humiliation." Titus reminded his readers that he had "struck the first blow and fought the first fight" for "Southern rights on the plains of Kansas!" He emphasized that he and his parentage before him were "born in a slave State," since New Jersey never fully abolished slavery until the enactment of the Thirteenth Amendment after the Civil War. Titus claimed to be "no politician" and would "at all times, stand ready, under the proper military organization, to defend my hearth stone against any invasion, come from what quarter it may. Nor will my zeal grow less; no reverses of our arms will change my position in regard to the welfare of my country." Eighteen days later his third child, Mary Evelina, called "Minnie," was born on the San Pablo plantation.[12]

The Confederate defenders spent that summer mounting ten guns on opposite banks of the St. Johns River east of Jacksonville at Yellow Bluff and St. Johns Bluff, the latter commanded by Lt. Col. Charles Floyd Hopkins, a graduate of the U.S. Naval Academy at Annapolis. On October 1, 1862, a Union flotilla of six gunboats and four transports with fifteen hundred troops appeared at the mouth of the river and landed troops on the St. Johns Bluff flank and rear at Mount Pleasant Creek, about five miles north of the San Pablo plantation. The outmaneuvered and outgunned Hopkins and his troops abandoned their position, allowing Jacksonville to be occupied again on the 5th. The gunboats sailed 205 miles up the St. Johns River to its headwaters at Enterprise, capturing the disabled steamer *Governor Milton*. The expeditionary force departed Jacksonville after four days with 276 contrabands, leaving behind a detachment at the bluff.[13]

Meanwhile, Titus evacuated his plantation, taking his family and some in-laws, slaves, and property. U.S. Navy commander M. Woodhull, on the USS *Cimarron* at Jacksonville, wrote on October 11, 1862, to the commander of the St. Johns Flotilla that Titus, "one of [William] Walker's men," had crossed the St. Johns River to the mainland "some 10 miles below this and has gone to Tallahassee. He is an able soldier and may have gone to that place to get means to arm that point." Woodhull was mistaken since Titus was interested only in profiting from the war and was exempt from the Confederate Conscription Act as a plantation overseer. The colonel and his entourage followed the Confederate retrograde movement on the Florida, Atlantic and Gulf Central Railroad to Lake City, sixty miles west of Jacksonville.[14]

Titus continued supplying the Confederacy from his new location. On February 26, 1863, he sold 5,420 pounds of bacon, 7,025 pounds of pickled pork, and 10,875 pounds of cornmeal packed in 236 bushels for $5,874.62 to Maj. Antonio A. Canova, the Confederate commissary of subsistence at Lake City. A fortnight later Jacksonville was invaded by the Federal First and Second South Carolina Regiments, comprised of freed slaves and led by the abolitionist Bleeding Kansas veteran colonels Thomas Wentworth Higginson and James Montgomery. The five hundred whites in the city were in "perpetual fear" upon seeing some of their former slaves in the occupation army that was giving them orders. A Private Jake sought out his former master A. M. Reed desiring revenge for the sale of his wife to Georgia. Jake was arrested by the military police after he "publicly threatened to burn down the Reed home, and then put a loaded gun against the head of a white man who had shot at him the night he escaped." Higginson delighted in confronting his uniformed and armed former slaves with their previous owners. The colonel introduced a man he described as the "ignorant" and "heavily built" Cpl. Robert Sutton to his prior mistress, the fifty-two-year-old widow Ernestine Alberti, at Woodstock Mills on the St. Marys River in Nassau County and enjoyed watching the "unutterable indignation" on her face. The abolitionist doctor Esther Hill Hawks, an army nurse on Hilton Head, South Carolina, was pleased to write in her diary about "the great rage to the good dame" when the African American corporal placed a picket of black soldiers around her home and gave "the order to shoot anyone who attempted to leave the house without his permission." These abolitionist accounts allude to the widow as a southerner, when in fact she was born in New York and her late husband, Edwin R. Alberti, the sawmill proprietor, was a Philadelphian.[15]

The whites accused "the blacks with misconduct and abuses of authority," and four hundred of them left the city under a flag of truce. Gen. Rufus Saxton reported to Secretary of War Edwin Stanton that "scarcely an incident in the war has caused a greater panic throughout the Southern coast than this raid of the colored troops in Florida." The Confederates sporadically clashed with Union pickets, having at Camp Finegan, eight miles west of Jacksonville, ten infantry companies, four of cavalry, and three of artillery, including a sixty-four-pounder rifled gun on a railroad car. When the invading force withdrew on March 28 after failing to meet their objective of massive slave recruitment, they plundered Jacksonville and torched some two dozen buildings, including the Catholic church, as the remaining Union families left with them. Three weeks later Titus provided eight mules, two four-mule iron axle wagons, one six-mule secondhand wagon, one cart, and eight sets of single harnesses for fifty-four hundred dollars to Maj. H. R. Teasdale, the Confederate quartermaster at Lake City.[16]

By early May, Titus had moved with his family and chattels by railroad fifty-two miles farther northwest to Madison, where he purchased a home. He then sold the Confederate commissary a pair of platform scales for $81.00 and 743 pounds of bacon for $510.00. On June 10 Titus hired out to Maj. R. C. Williams a two-mule team and driver for three days for $36.00. Two days later he charged $6.00 for half a day's work in hauling six loads of sacks from a military warehouse to the Madison railroad depot. On the 20th Titus made $12.00 for contracting his two-mule team and driver to deliver sacks to various plantations for one day. Ten days later he hired out the same driver and team for $24.00 to haul corn from various plantations over two days. During the previous four months Titus received a total of $11,943.62 in payments from the Confederacy, making the war very profitable for him. It was the greatest sum of money he had made in his life in such a short period.[17]

Titus spent $300.00 of his profits on August 26 purchasing a lot in Baldwin, Florida, that had been confiscated from the Jacksonville merchant Calvin L. Robinson, "an alien enemy of the Confederate States." It was sold under the Sequestration Act of the Confederate States by George R. Foster. The land, which was on the southeast corner of the Alligator Plank Road (U.S. Highway 90) and Chesnut Street, measured thirty feet along the former and ninety feet on the latter. It is the present site of the First United Methodist Church. Baldwin, considered "the key to the Peninsula," was the railroad junction extending lines eleven miles east to Jacksonville, north to Georgia and Fernandina on the Atlantic, south to Gainesville, and to Cedar Keys on the Gulf. The hamlet contained a railway station, a warehouse, a hotel, a tavern, and a few shabby unpainted wooden buildings. Titus did not settle there and remained with his family at Madison.[18]

By New Year's Day in 1864 the Titus clan was divided by the war, as were many other American families. The Titus sisters Marian, Sarah, and Julia remained with the patriarch in Wilkes-Barre, Pennsylvania; Helen was in Brooklyn, New York; and Carrie was in Philadelphia. Seventy-year-old Theodore Titus died in Wilkes-Barre on January 16, 1864, and was interred in the St. Stephen's Episcopal Church graveyard. Three weeks later, on February 7, nearly deserted Jacksonville was occupied by the Union army for the fourth and last time. The soldiers erected fortified walls with gates around the city, and all unauthorized personnel were ordered off the streets at night with a daily bugle call. U.S. Maj. Gen. Quincy Adams Gilmore, commander of the Department of the South headquartered at Hilton Head, South Carolina, had indicated that he wanted "to redeem Florida from the rebels with Colored troops if permitted by the Government." Brig. Gen. Truman Seymour landed in Jacksonville with some 7,000 men of a division of troops from the Tenth Corps in Port Royal, South Carolina, to secure Federalist enclaves, destroy the railroad junction at Baldwin, and conscript freed slaves into colored regiments. Two days later a detachment of the Fortieth Massachusetts Mounted Infantry occupied Baldwin. Seymour advanced 5,115 troops from Baldwin westward along the railroad tracks toward Lake City, where Gen. Joseph Finegan had concentrated 5,000 troops. On February 20 the adversaries clashed at the Battle of Olustee, forty-seven miles west of Jacksonville. The conflict, Florida's only major engagement of the Civil War, lasted all day, and Seymour retreated to Jacksonville with 1,861 casualties, leaving behind 5 artillery pieces, 1,600 small arms, and 130,000 rounds of ammunition, while Finegan had 946 losses.[19]

The following month Titus purchased two Confederate bonds totaling $1,100 at 4 percent annual interest from the Bank of St. Johns depository office in Lake City. He afterward endorsed both certificates to "D. J. McMullen, District Collector of the Confederate States for 11th District in the State of Florida in payment of Taxes due by me to the Confederate States." That summer the Federals recaptured Baldwin and carried out plundering expeditions along the St. Johns River and as far south as Gainesville. The Confederates responded with a torpedo campaign that sank various Yankee steamers on the river and "effectively limited the upriver mobility of Union naval vessels and minimized the threat of raids into the interior of Florida." Titus remained at Madison, where on October 1 he hired out two of his slaves, Bob and George, as laborers for seventy days to the local Confederate Quartermaster Department. In turn he received $156.00 remuneration from the assistant quartermaster Capt. R. R. Reid on December 16, 1864. By then all major infantry and artillery duels in northeast Florida were finished.[20]

When the war ended four months later, Titus was at Lake City, "a quiet little hamlet of 700 inhabitants, with no appearance of thrift or business." Cuba filibuster veteran Frances Calvin Morgan Boggess, now a Confederate lieutenant, found him there, and "it was like two brothers meeting after a long separation." When the surrender of Gen. Robert E. Lee was announced,

"100 shots were fired" in his honor, and "there were more men intoxicated than Lieutenant Boggess ever saw at one time, bewailing the surrender of General Lee," including Titus. The colonel lost all his chattel property after the formal emancipation of Florida's slaves on May 14, 1865. Many freedmen believed "that the end of slavery meant the end of labor" and around Lake City began "taking possession of plantation lands and threatening violence to their former owners." The mayor wrote to the provost marshal in Jacksonville that "the whites of Lake City feared for their personal safety and needed to be protected from blacks by the military."[21]

A *New York Times* correspondent who stopped at Lake City in July on his way to Tallahassee by train wrote that Titus "still cherishes his old hatred of the North and free institutions." The colonel expected the state government to return to "the hands of the 'chivalry,' and boasts that their bowie-knives and revolvers may be used by 'gentlemen' without fear of law." On July 15 Titus's father-in-law, Edward Stevens Hopkins, took the amnesty oath at Lake City, swearing to abide by federal laws and proclamations "with reference to the Emancipation of Slaves." There is no record of Titus taking the oath or receiving a presidential pardon, since he never wore a Confederate uniform and was proud of his northern birth. A recent arrival at Lake City was Confederate brigadier general Jesse Johnson Finley, who had commanded all of the Florida infantry in the Army of Tennessee and had twice been severely wounded in the Georgia campaigns of 1864. Finley established a law practice after receiving a presidential pardon, and his friendship with Titus would prove rewarding the following decade.[22]

The Titus family was residing in Madison when the couple's fourth child, Howell Theodore, was born on August 11, 1865. The colonel was seeking to rebuild his finances in a devastated economy controlled by the North that left him with worthless Confederate notes. That summer Titus apparently turned down a proposition by Francis F. L'Engle, a Duval County planter and lumber man, who was recruiting in Madison to establish a colony in Brazil under the Florida Emigration Society. Instead, Titus was interested in an offer by fifty-five-year-old Virginian James Paine, a former police captain in Charleston, South Carolina, who seven years earlier had taken his wife and five children to a farm at Fort Capron, opposite the Indian River inlet. Paine gave Titus "glowing accounts" of south Florida and its business opportunities. They made a partnership with Dr. John Westcott to run a cannery on Morris Creek, where they kept a green sea turtle hatchery. The trio agreed to "ship fish in ice, live turtle and canned oysters to New York in a fresh state; and to preserve fish in salt for commerce." The oysters would be opened by steam apparatus, and refuse fish would be compressed into fish oil. Ten men, blacks and whites, were employed to catch fish, turtles, and oysters. Titus returned to New York with his family and created a bevy of shareholders in the New York and Indian River Preserving Company, selling shares of capital stock at one hundred dollars each. Thirty-eight-year-old Irish iron dealer Henry Finnegan Hamill, of the New York Fishing Company, purchased the former USS *Clyde* side-wheel steamer gunboat and renamed it the *Indian River* after it was conveyed to him at the New York customhouse on November 16, 1865. The vessel had one deck and two masts; measured 199 feet in length, 19 feet in breadth, and 9 feet in depth; and had a 294ton burthen. It was fitted out with "ice bunkers capable of storing forty tons of fish" and temperature-controlled compartments for preserving large numbers of green sea turtles.[23]

Titus recruited more than sixty colonists in New York City to work for him in Florida. He departed with his wife and three children from Manhattan for Florida on November 22 on the *Indian River* with a crew of nineteen. The trip was pleasant and uneventful except for a stop at Jacksonville to retrieve a sawmill. When the Jacksonville agent of the U.S. Army's Bureau of Refugees, Freedmen, and Abandoned Lands heard that ship captain S. A. Emerson endeavored to obtain laborers there, "suspicion was excited and the steamer left without the desired hands." The vessel approached the Indian River inlet on December 3, 1865, and Emerson sent sailors in a bateau to sound the depth of the bar and assess the amount of clearance. The channel was "capable of admitting vessels not drawing more than four feet" as it was filled with sand and oyster shells. The crew reported back as the tide was receding. Minnie Titus, three years old at the time, stated in her memoirs that when Captain Emerson asked instructions from her father, who was ill with a rheumatic recurrence, he replied, "You are the Captain, I leave it to your judgement." However, due to the adventurer's impatient character, he most likely gave the order to proceed. The master ordered "full speed ahead" and tried to ram the nine-foot-deep steamer through four feet of water, but it "sunk fast into the sand." A portion of the damaged cargo was landed and sold at auction on the 12th. Three weeks later the Columbian Coast Wrecking Company of New York sent the schooner *Elizabeth White,* with a full complement of men and materials, to dislodge the vessel but failed.[24]

The nineteen crew members of the *Indian River* lost all their possessions and immediately departed for Fort Reid (today Sanford), traveling 34 miles in forty hours. The military provided food and shelter before they proceeded on the St. Johns River another 205 miles to Jacksonville. Once there, the men were "refused assistance from several parties to whom they applied." The stranded sailors were eventually taken on board the *Helen Getty* and conveyed to Savannah. Some left for New York on the steamer *Zodiac,* while the engineers Ralph Lewis and Anthony French took passage on the steamer *Constitution.* After the latter vessel struck the outer shoals of Cape Lookout, North Carolina, on December 26, Lewis was one of the few survivors and French perished. Dr. Esther Hill Hawks, working in Jacksonville as a teacher, saw the crew "begging chances to work their passage back to N.Y." She jotted in her diary that it was "shrewdly surmised that the old blockade runner Clyde would be used in running negroes over to Cuba" to be sold into slavery. Hawks believed that Titus lacked the morals to avoid "such adventures."[25]

In consequence of the hearsay, Lt. David M. Hammond of the Thirty-fourth United States Colored Troops (USCT) was "sent along the coast of East Fla. in disguise to ascertain if possible the truth of the rumors." Hammond reported that "there is nothing at Indian River to indicate any purpose on the part of the owners or crew of the Stmr. Indian Queen [*sic*], to kidnap negroes, except the previous character of Titus the cmdr. of the party. The steamer is now a perfect loss." A Mr. Brantly of Mellonville told Hammond in mid-February 1866 that "he had visited the camp of Titus where he found persons engaged in preparing for market fish and oysters in hermetically sealed cans" numbering about "eight thousand." The steamer was "hard aground in the sand and had been abandoned by Titus and his party and was in charge of the agent of the underwriters who was making preparations to get her off." The *Indian River* was scrapped after its hull was discovered broken. A small tug that was on board was also lost. A fortnight later a Dr. James "visited the camp of Titus and his party" and "found only eleven persons engaged in putting up fish and oysters." He was informed "that Titus would soon leave with the entire party for the north as the warm weather would end the fishing season."[26]

While the Tituses were at Fort Capron, Seminole Indian women took hogs into their camp for sale. Minnie Titus vividly recalled how their braves "would come in the dining room while we were eating and sit down on the table. They would eat anything my mother gave them, but their manners left much to be desired and I was very afraid of them." Titus purchased at Fort Capron the schooner *Live Yankee* with two sails and a crew. He headed north on the Indian River with his family looking for a navigation point in which to settle. The 121-mile waterway of brackish saltwater with a varying width from one mile to four miles and separated from the ocean by a narrow strip of land averaging a half mile wide, is now part of the Atlantic Intracoastal Waterway. Its western shore, some ten to twenty feet above the ocean, was described as "marshy, with hammocks. About half a mile from the water runs a ridge, averaging half a mile across, covered with pines, oak, and palmettos." The banks of the Indian River were lined with trees producing oranges and semitropical fruits. The waterway was "perfectly alive with every variety of fish that inhabit the Southern waters, and the woods abound in game of every description." The Indian River was landlocked fifteen miles north of Sand Point, a sandy hammock with palmettos projecting a few hundred yards into the river. The opposite shore on the north end of Merritt Island was seven miles distant and the Cape Canaveral lighthouse was thirty miles north.[27]

The *Live Yankee* dropped anchor at Sand Point, and the Tituses camped ashore even though the vessel had bunks. They pitched "a large tent and slept on beds of green palmetto fans, covered with blankets and under mosquito bars." Minnie Titus recalled that the area "was mainly pine and scrub palmetto. The pines were very tall and some were three feet or more in diameter" with "eagle's nests in the tops." The land had been settled since 1828, when Douglas Dummett began commercially shipping oranges from his grove on northern Merritt Island. During the Civil War, Confederates established at Sand Point a saltworks, which was destroyed by a Union cavalry force. The abandoned old arches and broken evaporation kettle remained near the shore. British investors of the Florida Provision Company had recently purchased land there to establish a cannery for fruits, vegetables, and seafood. The southern financial crisis of 1867 scuttled their plans. After scouting the area for a few days, the Tituses sailed in the *Live Yankee* ten miles to the Haulover canal, a cut through the soft coquina rock of a narrow strip of land two hundred yards between the Indian River and Mosquito Lagoon. They went "up the Halifax to New Smyrna and out the Inlet into the Atlantic and on to Jacksonville." Upon arriving they discovered that the Thirty-fourth USCT, which had garrisoned the town during the previous year, had been withdrawn after Maj. Gen. Ulysses S. Grant ordered the removal of all black troops from the South. After a short visit with the Hopkins family, the Tituses took steamer passage back to Queens. According to the *Tallahassee Floridian* of April 24, 1866, Titus's Indian River enterprise was "progressing encouragingly. Large quantities of oysters have been canned and very many fine turtles caught, which would be shipped North at an early date." The goods were shipped to Wells, Provost and Co. in New York, "who were largely interested in the enterprise from the first." Weeks later the cannery caught fire and the insurance company too failed, with Titus's vision of prosperity going up in smoke.[28]

Titus recruited his brother-in-law James Black Hodgskin, a prominent Brooklyn capitalist, into his money-making schemes. On July 28, 1866, the colonel left Manhattan on the steamship *Alabama* for Savannah, where four days later he checked into the Screven House accompanied by a servant. Titus continued by steamer to Jacksonville, which had become a thriving town "with a main street of some dozen good brick blocks and warehouses along the water, with half a dozen or more stunted wharves and three or four saw mills." A visiting Bostonian discovered that "Southern spirit is as bitter in most parts of the State as in South Carolina and Georgia."[29]

On August 20 President Andrew Johnson issued a proclamation declaring that the insurrection had ended and restored the supremacy of the civil law over the military throughout the nation. A few days later, while Titus was in the barroom of the Taylor House on the corner of Bay and Market Streets in Jacksonville, he got into a political argument with Myron L. Mickles, a dentist and former Union private in the Second Illinois Light Artillery. Mickles overheard Titus tell C. D. Lincoln that Florida had been promised by Johnson through his appointed provisional governor William Marvin "that if the state would do certain things it would be admitted into the Union, etc. The state had complied and the promise had not been fulfilled." The governor had urged whites to take the oath of allegiance, register as voters, and elect state constituents who would draft a new constitution to bring Florida back into the Union. The new charter instituted the Black Codes, which denied African Americans their civil rights and suffrage. The U.S. Congress rejected the Florida constitution, refused to seat the state delegation that included Marvin as senator, and imposed a military reconstruction program that lasted more than a decade.[30]

Mickles intervened in the conversation by responding that "the President could not bind Congress, that he could only bind himself, and that he had fulfilled to the best of his ability." An "extremely agitated" Titus told Mickles that "Congress was a dammed set of abolition sons of bitches and any one that upheld that radical congress in this state ought to be hung up to the lamp post. They have no business here." The dentist replied that he had the right to express his own opinions since he "was in the United States and under the protection of its flag," and he added that "Negroes are as good as white people." Titus responded that he "would see about that" and struck Mickles "on the head twice with a heavy hickory cane," causing severe wounds. As Mickles lay on the barroom floor, Titus bellowed that "the citizens of Jacksonville were a set of poltroons or they would not allow these damned abolitionists to talk as they did here." He exclaimed that the dentist "ought to be hung up to the lamp post, and he would be one of twenty five to do it."[31]

The next day Mickles entered a complaint before a justice of the peace, and Titus had to provide $300.00 for bail to appear before the Duval County court on August 30 at 10:00 A.M. on assault and battery charges. The colonel declared to the mayor's court, "I had a political discussion with this fellow . . . he used some language that did not suit me and I knocked him in the head with my stick." The complainant alleged that he had been "unable to prepare for trial on account of ill health" and that the only witness who "could prove the assault was absent from the city and had not been subpoenaed." Mickles wrote to the prosecutor claiming that he "was unable to attend on account of ill health." The sheriff then went to get Mickles in his room and told him that he "must go sick or well." After the dentist testified at the trial, the jury blamed him for throwing the first punch and acquitted the defendant. The judge, former Confederate captain Aristides H. Doggett, who was also an agent of the Freedmen's Bureau, fined the complainant $45.46 in court costs, the equivalent of three months' army pay. The next day Mickles wrote to Capt. Charles C. Rawn, commanding the military post at Jacksonville, claiming that justice was not done because he was compelled to testify while sick and without witnesses, and he blamed the prosecutor for not doing his duty. He demanded that "the civil authorities be distrained from collecting the above mentioned costs and the said Titus be tried by the military authorities." Rawn wrote to his superior that Mickles was attacked "by Colonel Titus, of Nicaraguan notoriety, on account of a difficulty growing out of a difference of opinion in regard to the acts of the President and Congress. As the matter was taken in hand by the civil authorities and properly dealt with, I did not interfere."[32]

The next day Mickles wrote to Bvt. Maj. Gen. John Gray Foster, who commanded the military administrative Department of Florida, appealing to "the military authorities to have justice done him." Foster indicated in his semimonthly report on September 11, 1866, that his previous communication there had been "only one breach of the peace on account of political sentiments." It "was by the notorious Col. Titus at Jacksonville, who was arrested & fined by the Civil authorities for the offence." Three days later Foster wrote to Maj. Gen. Oliver O. Howard, commissioner of the Freedmen's Bureau, "A case of violent attack and beating occurred at Jacksonville upon an inoffensive white man by the notorious Col. Titus of Kansas fame. I sincerely believe that the continued presence of U.S. Troops is absolutely required to give proper protection to Union men." According to Orloff M.

Dorman, a fifty-six-year-old Jacksonville lawyer, a rumor circulated in Jacksonville on October 8 that "the military are going to re arrest Titus, and try him over again by a military court" for the assault on the "white negro" Mickles. Gov. David S. Walker had "sent down for the papers, describing Titus in his despatch as of 'Kansas notoriety.'" Dorman was concerned that the governor, "with the assistance of the military, will be able to scare and revise the judgments."[33]

Walker then on October 10 forwarded the court documents to Major General Foster, who responded that a "great injustice had been done" and that the judge, prosecutor, and jury failed in their duty. The general told the governor that "Titus is well known to have been a violent secessionist and is now a violent hater of Union-men." Foster described the incident as a "cowardly attack" and requested that the governor remit the costs of the case against Mickles. Five days later Mickles gave the Jacksonville deputy sheriff copies of the letters from Governor Walker to Foster saying that Mickles should not pay the court costs and one from Foster to Col. Andrew Mahony to the same effect. The deputy sheriff referred Mickles to Judge Doggett, "who refused to return the amount."[34]

Three weeks later, on November 6, the circuit court for the Middle District of Florida rendered a judgment against Titus in favor of William Wilson for $76.90 in principal and $11.00 in costs for an unpaid debt. When Titus did not respond to the ruling, the Madison County sheriff was ordered a year later to seize the colonel's town lot in Madison. The confiscation was publicly advertised for thirty days, and the property was auctioned off on the courthouse steps. Titus had another brush with the law in February 1867, when he was arrested for attempting "to drive a harpoon through a revenue officer when in the discharge of his duty." He was remanded to the custody of the U.S. marshal at St. Augustine "but finally was cleared in the United States court."[35]

Six months later, on August 15, 1867, a suit in assumpsit by attachment began in the Duval County circuit court by W. A. Work and Son against Titus for not paying an outstanding bill. Ward A. Work and his son George were commission merchants and wholesale provision dealers at 27 Front Street, New York City. An affidavit, bond, and praecipe were filed, a writ of attachment issued to which certain goods of the defendant were applied. The affidavit was made by the agent of the plaintiffs, George D. Gilchrist, a twenty-three-year-old New Yorker operating a lumber mill in Jacksonville, who also executed the bond with two sureties. Defense attorneys responded that "the bond was not in compliance with the statute" because Gilchrist was not named as the agent. The plaintiffs moved to amend by adding the word "agent" after Gilchrist's name on the bond. The judge ruled that Gilchrist had to make the amendment in person, "and as he was not present, the attachment was dissolved and the case dismissed."[36]

Titus returned that summer to Wilkes-Barre, Pennsylvania, where his wife gave birth to their fifth child, Henry Theodore, on August 25, 1867. The family then moved to Jacksonville to stay with her relatives for the winter. The city was sustaining a business revival while Edward Stevens Hopkins and his son Coriolanus operated a grocery and provisions store. Titus decided to establish a similar venture and on January 1, 1868, borrowed from his brother-in-law "two thousand dollars in cash and goods to carry out my business at Sand Point." As security he provided a lien on all his personal effects, including the *Live Yankee* and "also the stock of goods now at Sand Point." Titus agreed to start paying the loan "from time to time" after one year. On the 25th Mary Titus purchased twenty acres on Alligator Plank Road in Baldwin, Florida, for five hundred dollars. Two months later the *New York Commercial Advertiser* reported that "the hundreds of immigrants to the Indian River" were planting orange groves. These would yield at present prices "a thousand dollars an acre within four years." That spring Edward Stevens Hopkins was elected Democratic mayor of Jacksonville, and he would serve for two years. Titus did not follow his father-in-law into the Democratic Party and instead tried to reconcile his former Whig ideology with the dominant Republican Party in the emerging nation. On June 10, 1868, Mary Titus paid two hundred dollars to the Florida Provision Company in Jacksonville for seventy-three and one-third acres at Sand Point in Volusia County. Her brother Coriolanus and F. N. Hopkins witnessed the document.[37]

The easiest way to reach Sand Point from Jacksonville was to take a steamer on the St. Johns River 205 miles to its terminal at Enterprise, the seat of Volusia County. The trip, including time for stoppages, lasted thirty-six hours. The fare, with meals and a stateroom, was nine dollars. Travelers would then "row to Lake Harney in two days" and take a hack 22 miles to Sand Point for a four-dollar fare. The land abounded "in valuable timber, of which live oak, other species of oak, hickory, ash, beech, cedar, magnolia, sweet bay, gum, cypress, constitute a great proportion." The Titus family initially lived in tents while the patriarch began cutting red cedar planks to build their residence and make magnolia wood furniture. Since there was no sawmill, "the lumber had to be split out by hand and then allowed to dry in the sun." The house had floors "of narrow curled pin boards that were polished," but "soon after it was built, it burned down." Pioneer life on the wild frontier was grueling for all. The experienced Mary was well accustomed to the tasks of food preparation and preservation, cooking, laundering, and child caring. The family survived by gathering a variety of wild fruits, fishing, raising hogs and fowl, and cultivating their own garden and crops. Minnie Titus recalled, "The country around Titusville abounded in huckleberries, blueberries, gooseberries and bear berries." The pioneers "raised cassava, corn, sweet potatoes, cabbage, cowpeas, etc. They cut the cassava into small pieces and parched it and after it was boiled, it was 'coffee.' Cassava was also used in lieu of flour. The bud of the palmetto was cooked and called 'swamp cabbage.'" The settlers would hunt "bears, deer, wildcats, panthers, otters, raccoons, possums and smaller animals," including wild turkeys. Ship wrecks off the Florida coast washed cargo ashore and prompted the Tituses and other families to scrounge for goods. Salvaged items included clothing, furniture, canned goods, lumber, and other stores. The wreck of the Mallory Line steamer *Victor* off Jupiter provided the Pierce family with a Wheeler and Wilson sewing machine.[38]

The year after the Titus family settled at Sand Point, Congress approved on March 3, 1869, a fifty-mile post road between Enterprise and Sand Point. The following month a post office was established at Sand Point three-fourths of a mile from the west bank of the Indian River under postmaster John W. Harvey, a sixty-four-year-old house carpenter from New York. The mail route was via a small sailboat from New Smyrna down the Indian River, stopping at Sand Point and Jupiter and continuing by ocean vessel to Miami and Key West, 576 miles and back, twice a month. The Tituses expanded their holdings on June 7, 1869, when Mary purchased forty acres at Sand Point for $1.25 each from the state trustees of the Internal Improvements Fund in Tallahassee. Two months later Dr. Daniel G. Brinton printed in Philadelphia *A Guide-Book of Florida and the South, for Tourists, Invalids and Emigrants,* which announced, "Titus has a store and dwelling at Sand Point, and accommodates tourists either with his team or his table." That fall the colonel's sixth offspring, Ellett Livingston Titus, was born at Sand Point.[39]

The Sand Point post office was discontinued in October 1869 and reestablished on June 16, 1870, with a new postmaster, Lawrence J. Carlile, a thirty-year-old farmer from Mississippi with a wife and two children. The position, appointed by the president, received a twelve-dollar monthly salary, and the Sand Point mail was delivered three times a week on horseback. Carlile resigned at the end of the year, and William M. Lanehart, a twenty-nine-year-old New Yorker, replaced him. In July 1870 the Board of County Commissioners of Volusia County ordered the construction of a road from

Enterprise to Sand Point. Titus established a mule-team wagon line between the towns, carrying passengers, freight, and correspondence. Minnie Titus recalled that during the forty-mile route, two creeks about fifty feet wide were traversed, and "water often came into the wagons of the mule teams as they crossed."[40]

The colonel also used the *Live Yankee* to create another delivery route between Daytona Beach and Jupiter ferrying cargo, mail, and travelers and taking a week if the weather allowed it. The local goods exported to Jacksonville included "fish, venison and honey." Titus built a sawmill powered by a windmill, a general store, and a hotel at Sand Point. His sawmill "had a machine to make shingles, and also all kinds of fancy canes, cups and saucers, and napkin rings out of the native wood. Lignum vitae, crabwood, palmetto and black mangrove were among the woods used." Lanehart ran the sawmill, which also cut red cedars for the Faber Company, manufacturers of Faber lead pencils, whose New York branch was headed by James Black Hodgskin, Titus's brother-in-law. The Florida logs were shipped to New York and forwarded to the pencil factory in Nuremberg, Bavaria, Germany. The hollow lead holders were later made in America and sent to Germany to save on bulk and freight.[41]

The Titus House, completed in 1870 in tropical style, became famously known as "one of the finest combinations of saloons and hotels on the east coast of Florida." It had "a large main building with two long wings, all one story high, forming three sides of a square neatly laid out in a garden, and with the rooms opening off of the wide verandas like a row of houses in a city block." The hotel had a dozen rooms, each with a bedroom set, pillows, blankets, washing bowls and pitchers, and additional cots and mattresses. Five rooms were equipped with tubs. The parlor contained a piano, a billiard table, four china candlesticks, a card table, and a clock. The dining room had two water coolers, called Mexican Monkey Jugs, which were large stoneware vases with a handle on top flanked by twin spouts. The three dining tables mostly served the local cuisine of "oysters, clams, fish, shark-steaks, turtle-steaks, etc., with many strange and familiar fruits and vegetables." The only commercial competition was a small boardinghouse accommodating sportsmen and offering meager meals. Titus then began advocating changing the name of the town. According to the forty-four-year-old abolitionist Dr. John Milton Hawks, former surgeon with the First South Carolina Volunteers and husband of Esther Hill Hawks, "*Indian River City,* is the name proposed for Sand Point by Col. Titus, who is the leading spirit here. There is a post-office and two stores in the neighborhood."[42]

That summer several northern newspapers wrongly reported, "The death of Col. Titus, a well-known Kansas 'border ruffian,' is confirmed. He was tortured to death by Indians in Arizona." One publication gleefully added, "His end was an appropriate one."According to the June 1870 federal census, Titus, his wife, and their six children resided in three dwellings in division 17 of Volusia County. The colonel was listed as a merchant with real estate assets worth $5,000.00 and personal property estimated at $2,500.00. Titus operated a dry goods store and saloon with John Wesley Joyner, a forty-seven-year-old house carpenter from South Carolina. It was the only grocery along the coastline of Volusia and Brevard Counties selling "a line of staple groceries and supplies." Titus also had a mercantile partnership at Enterprise with sixty-year-old Carolinian Elijah Watson and fifty-five-year-old Englishman Thomas Mason. His Volusia County tax records show a different property net worth. The 113 acres were priced at $125.00 with $500.00 in improvements on five acres, household furnishings were worth $1,500.00, and there was a cash value of $1,850.00 on personal property. Titus owned a horse and three mules. His annual taxes were $2.47 for a sinking fund, $12.88 state tax, $12.88 county tax, and $2.47 school tax.[43]

The 1870 Volusia County federal census enumerated 1,723 residents in the towns of Volusia (800), Enterprise (523), Sand Point (200), Port Orange (160), and New Smyrna (40). The county had 421 families residing in 514 dwellings. Dr. Hawks described the typical Volusia County residences as "rude affairs" built of logs, without glass windows, and with roofs thatched with palm leaves. The population consisted of 724 white males, 672 white females, 168 black males, and 159 black females. Among the white folks there were 28 foreign-born males and females, all British citizens except for three Italians and a German doctor. At Sand Point the Tituses were among 61 families who resided in seventy-eight dwellings. The town population consisted of 179 whites and 21 blacks. The foreigners were a forty-year-old German physician, a fifty-five-year-old Canadian ship carpenter, 3 Italian agriculturalists, 2 Irish farmers, a housewife, and a West Indian fruit grower. Those employed at Sand Point included 43 farmers, 13 farm laborers, 3 physicians, 3 hunters, the Cape Canaveral lighthouse keeper and his assistant, a fruit grower, a stock minder, a ship carpenter, a house carpenter, a clerk, and a boatman. All the adult females were homemakers. Maria Peckham, a twenty-year-old South Carolina native wed to a New Yorker farmer, maintained a private school in LaGrange, two miles northwest of Sand Point, where Minnie Titus received a rudimentary primary education and learned to make patchwork quilts and featherstitching. She recalled that one day on her way to school, "I met a heard of deer, about 25 in all, I clapped my hands and gave a rebel yell and away they ran through the pines." According to Minnie, many South Carolina families migrated to the region in ox carts after the Civil War because "they feared a Negro uprising."[44]

Dr. John Milton Hawks, who resided at Port Orange, described Volusia County in 1870 as having no public schools and lacking a clergyman. He wrote, "We have no politicians; offices go begging; two of my neighbors who have commissions as Justices of the Peace decline to act; the office of County Treasurer has been vacant for two years, seeking a man to accept it. We have no jail and little need of one." Hawks had created the Florida Land and Lumber Company in October 1865. More than twenty thousand dollars "was thrown away in a vain attempt to build and run a large steam saw mill." Some five hundred African American families from the vicinity of Columbia, South Carolina, migrated there under a homestead investment scheme created by former Union colonel Ralph Ely. Both ventures went bankrupt by late 1868, leaving only nine black families at Port Orange.[45]

After the Titus family was firmly established at Sand Point and intent on catering to the tourist trade, Mary Titus purchased 40 acres at Salt Lake on January 10, 1871, for $1.25 an acre from the state trustees of the Internal Improvements Fund in Tallahassee. She now owned 153 ⅓ acres in Volusia County. Part of the new land was used for planting sugar cane, but a hurricane just prior to harvest time destroyed the crop. Two days later the Tituses sold their Baldwin property, without a profit, to a Jacksonville bank cashier after Mary relinquished her separate estate. She did so because the law protected married women in the ownership and control of property apart from their husbands. On January 14 the Tituses borrowed $500.00 from the New York merchant Theodore Tracy Edgerton at 3 percent monthly interest for three months, using their land as collateral. A New Yorker visiting Sand Point in mid-January reported how on the Indian River "the people fish, hunt, raise a little patch of cane, for a living, get their clothing mostly from vessels which are so unfortunate as to be wrecked on the coast." He described "the magnificent grandeur of the scenery in these primeval old forests, anon interspersed with the rude cabin of the hardy pioneer." The winter weather was the most pleasant he ever saw with "the air soft and balmy." The tourist called the Indian River region the "celebrated resort of the sportsman." After the Florida legislature took active measures to induce immigration, it was estimated that at least fifty thousand people visited Florida that winter, of whom about a fourth were invalids.[46]

To liquidate their pending $500.00 loan, the Tituses on March 1 mort-gaged five acres of their lot 2 for $1,172.23 to the Empire Windmill Manufac-turing Company of Syracuse, New York, for three years. The land included a twenty-four-foot windmill that Titus had purchased from them, with attached "shafting pulleys & machinery of different kinds." Three months later, on June 5, 1871, the Volusia County Board of Commissioners met at the Enterprise courthouse to assess the worth of twenty-two properties for tax purposes. The Titus holdings were ordered raised in value from $1,225.00 to $3,000.00. In consequence, his taxes tripled to $34.80 for the state and $39.70 for the county. Titus no longer had a horse but owned three mules.[47]

Due to the proximity of Sand Point to the Florida shore, it became a place of refuge for shipwrecked passengers whose vessels succumbed to hur-ricanes or the prevalent Gulf Stream gales. On the morning of August 18, 1871, the steamship *Lodona,* traveling from New York to New Orleans, struck the coast six miles north of the Cape Canaveral lighthouse during the worst hurricane to hit the region in three decades. The vessel turned on its beam and broke up, and the waves scattered its cargo and fourteen corpses for thirty miles. Twenty crewmen, including the captain, were lost, and thirteen survivors "reached Col. Titus' house." They "were, through the kindness of that gentleman, enabled to reach Fernandina in safety." Minnie Titus recalled that her "father gave them food and clothing and money to pay their way back to New York." During the previous ten days, three brigs and a bark also wrecked nearby, with loss of life and cargo. In consequence of previous efforts to rescue goods or ascertain their losses, Titus was appointed agent of the Board of Underwriters, Coast of Florida, for the Atlantic Mutual Marine Insurance Company in New York. His job was to collect from wrecked vessels salvageable cargo.[48]

Capt. Mills Olcott Burnham, the fifty-four-year-old Cape Canaveral lighthouse keeper, reported the effects of the storm at Sand Point: "Houses were unroofed and blown down; immense trees—oak and pine—two and three feet in diameter, blown down and broken off like carrots; all the orange plantations destroyed and fruit rotting on the ground." Minnie Titus remem-bered that the "giant pines were thrown down as though they were sticks." The entire section of the coast was "a scene of desolation and ruin—no com-munication with the interior; no prospect of getting to Jacksonville or St. Augustine; everyone compelled to look out for themselves; no provisions along the coast." Mary Titus weathered the storm while seven months preg-nant with her seventh child, Theodore Titus, born on October 23, 1871, amid the rebuilding of their lives and property once again.[49]

When Mary heard that the Episcopal bishop of Florida John Freeman Young would be touring the region, she insisted on having her baby baptized together with her two-year-old son Ellett and invited the reverend to stay at the Titus House. It was "the first Episcopal visitation of the Florida East Coast, south of Palatka." The fifty-one-year-old bishop went accompanied by thirty-five-year-old Rev. Francis R. Holeman of Palatka, whose mission territory was the St. Johns River area. They arrived by steamer at the Salt Lake landing on December 9 and followed the road eight miles to Sand Point. Young recalled, "The scream of our steam whistle soon brought settlers to the shore. In due time we effected our landing; and after a ride of nine miles we reached the residence of Col. Titus, and received a very cordial welcome. Notice of our coming had been sent on before us, and the information, we were told, had been well published."[50]

The next morning was Sunday, and "a congregation of nearly fifty" assembled in the large dining room of the Titus House. Holeman said the morning prayer, and the bishop preached a sermon and baptized Theodore and Ellett Titus and another child. Afternoon services were announced for nearby LaGrange, where some fifty additional people gathered at the log schoolhouse. A Sunday school regularly taught by twenty-eight-year-old Englishman Thomas Johnson was in session. Johnson, who was Titus's nearest neighbor, was a cooper with a wife and child. The participants were not only the children but also "most of the adults of the neighborhood, who, after the catechizing is over, unite for some time in singing, reading the Holy Scriptures and prayer, this whole region being totally destitute of ministerial services of any denomination, or character, whatsoever." Bishop Young recalled, "Such a manner of spending the Lord's day speaks well for the character of the settlers in this far off region, and I could not forbear saying to them before proceeding with my sermon, how much gratified I was at learning these facts, encouraging them to persevere in their good ways and bidding upon them the blessing of God. After service, though our forms were new and strange to them, they expressed an earnest desire, as had been done after the Morning Service, that our visit might be soon repeated, and I promised to do what I could to give them regular services." The bishop and his companion spent the night at the Titus House and the next morning departed in a large sailboat heading north for the coastal settlements on Mosquito Lagoon and the Halifax River.[51]

That month a New York sportsman traveling in the region referred to "a post office called Sand Point, on the Indian River." He described the mail to Fort Capron as being "carried as nearly once a week as the carrier sees fit, in a small sailboat, which will run when the wind is favorable, or stay hitched to a post when the carrier is drunk—just as circumstances may require." The mail between Sand Point and Enterprise was "carried across the country by a man on horseback, who starts Sunday afternoon, and returns Wednesday, quite regularly." The postmaster was George Bond, who after resigning was superseded by John Varner on March 15, 1872. Government records indicate that two months later a post office was simultaneously opened at Titusville with Postmaster William M. Lanehart, who had held that position at Sand Point the previous year. It appears that irregular mail service and political squabbles prompted the dual presidential appointment of postmasters for Sand Point and Titusville.[52]

On April 1, 1872, the Tituses borrowed six hundred dollars from New Yorker Charles R. Gill, mortgaging seventy-three acres at Sand Point for five years with interest. Four months later the colonel wrote to the Light House Board in Washington, D.C., flaunting his title as "deputy agent for underwriters," to complain about James Arango Armour, the forty-six-year-old lighthouse keeper at Jupiter Inlet, and his first assistant Charles Carlin, a thirty-one-year-old Irishman. The one-hundred-foot brick lighthouse stood on a bluff fifty feet above the ocean, at the confluence of the Indian and Locohatchee Rivers. It had a "first-class, revolving light, made in France, and shows a succession of flashes, followed by a somewhat prolonged, steady light." Titus indicated, "The Light of late is frequently out long before day light whilst this man Armour is away at Sand Point charging most of the time as long as six weeks at a time." He described Armour as "a man totally unworthy of so vital and important a situation" who bartered off the lighthouse oil and spent most of his time on the beach with Carlin salvaging from wrecked ships. Titus claimed that Armour was convicted for piracy by the U.S. government at Key West and sentenced to two years, but "by some turn he got out and is a man of the very worst character and should be removed at once." He offered to send affidavits and cited as personal references the Republican Florida senator Thomas W. Osborn and Republican representatives Charles St. John of New York and Hon. Lazarus Denison Shoemaker of Wilkes-Barre, Pennsylvania. Twelve days later the secretary of the Light House Board, Rear Adm. Charles Stewart Boggs, ordered an investigation of the allegations if the inspector had "implicit confidence" in the accusations. The affidavits were then requested from Titus.[53]

The colonel responded on September 23, enclosing the sworn testimony of Daniel O'Hara, who had resigned the previous year after fourteen months as assistant keeper under Armour. Titus insisted that "the evil should be removed as soon as possible for there is too great a risk to the lives & property depending upon this important Light House." He claimed to have no motivation other than "being a Special Agent of the Underwriters and a supporter of General Grant and to see all things appertaining to the Government in accordance with the Laws." He closed his letter by again naming Senator Osborn as a reference. The O'Hara affidavit stated that Armour would send him and the other assistant keeper, O. P. Barnes, to forage for two or three days for wrecked goods washed ashore and then the items would be divided among the trio. Meanwhile, Armour would work the light alone at a low flow so that it would burn out in the night and then skimmed off the oil for his own profit. O'Hara added, "Armour often leaves the light house for six weeks at a time which the said light house is left in charge of the two assistants and that the two assistants also go away frequently and be gone from the post for weeks." He reiterated that during the Civil War, Armour was convicted for "felony and piracy" and "sentenced to two years imprisonment" but got out after serving some time. O'Hara concluded by indicating that first assistant Charles Carlin was "a foreign man not a citizen of the United States." The deponent's good character was attested to by Titus, Isaac Dunlin Parkinson, and J. C. C. Feaster, the justice of the peace who notarized the document.[54]

One afternoon around December 1, Titus arrived at the Jupiter Inlet lighthouse dock on his sailboat accompanied by his son Howell and his sawmill employee Postmaster William M. Lanehart. The teenager Charles W. Pierce recalled, "They said they were on their way to Lake Worth for a load of crabwood, a certain sort of very close-grained wood that was extremely hard and not found in any of the hammocks north of the lake. They used this wood in making fancy walking canes and cuff buttons." Titus was spying on Armour to see if his written complaints had resulted in his dismissal. He returned from Lake Worth after ten days with a cargo of crabwood and reported that the old sailor Charlie Moore from Miami had settled there. The colonel was irked at finding Armour at his post. Two weeks later Lanehart heard that his rival postmaster at Sand Point had been replaced by the thirty-eight-year-old Enterprise farmer William S. Abbott.[55]

The following month, after Armour appeared at Titusville to buy supplies, Titus again wrote to the Light House Board. He indicated that nothing had been done about the "outrageous acts of the Jupiter Light House Keepers" and that if the board failed to act, he would take another course. The colonel complained that Armour and Carlin continued "to steal goods from stranded vessels on the coast," recently "trading and selling goods taken from the steamer Victor," wrecked at Jupiter Inlet under a gale the previous October. Its lost cargo of assorted merchandise was worth $250,000. Titus stated that Armour frequently remained in Titusville for a month and that after returning to his post, Carlin would leave for three weeks in violation of "the Law and the rule of the Light House Board." Carlin, considered "the most famous of the Indian river sailors," was also employed as a tourist guide, keeping him absent from the lighthouse for long periods.[56]

During the winters the Titus House became an annual attraction for infirm northerners seeking health in warmer climates. In 1873 a Yankee who had resided in Florida for two years recommended they visit Sand Point, where "the hunting and fishing are fine," although it was "not easy of access for extreme invalids." The steamer voyage from the upper St. Johns River to Enterprise was via "coffee-colored waters, winding and turning, so as to puzzle the best pilots; with alligators sleeping on its marshy banks, and eagles' nests on its tall cypresses, and palmetto groves on its higher banks." Small steamers fitted with staterooms would leave Jacksonville for Enterprise and return in three days. Enterprise accommodations included "a large hotel and a few boarding houses."[57]

Minnie Titus described the Indian River at Titusville as "teaming with fish of many kinds: bass, trout, mullet, and snook, being only a few. Many kinds of wild duck wintered there and great rafts of them were on the water at all times during the winter. The river was beautiful, clear as crystal, and a beautiful white sand beach stretched for miles. Along the shore blue and white herons, Ibis, and other kindred birds could be seen, daily wading on their long legs, getting their meals by plying the fisherman's trade. The osprey was to be seen also, and the bald eagle." She recalled, "Just as plentiful was the wild life in wood and field. Bears, deer, wildcats, panthers, otters, raccoons, 'possums, and smaller animals roamed in ever increasing numbers. It was a veritable poor man's paradise and flocks of wild turkeys were a common sight."[58]

When Minnie was ten years old, her father considered her a good rider and allowed her to ride any of his horses or mules. She reminisced, "My cousins Ida, Frank and brother Henry and I once took a mule named old Dave, putting a bridle on him, and rode him out into the woods. He ran away and bounced us all off. Ida and I broke our arms but this did not cure me." Minnie was a prankster who made a mask out of dough, "cut out the eyes and nose in it and put it on," and wrapped herself in a bed sheet. She "sneaked out to the corral where the horses and mules were behind a rail fence." Minnie remembered, "It was a moonlight night and I took down the bars and went in and began to wave my arms and prance around. The horses were plenty surprised and frightened, they stampeded and knocked down the

rails and ran for about six miles. I sneaked back to the house and put everything away and next morning when the horses were discovered absent, none
could guess what had happened in the night to cause them to break out."
She and her sister Kate once anxiously went looking for a gopher down the
Capron Trail. They got lost in the woods after about three miles and started
crying and calling out, but no one responded. She then realized that it would
be easy to follow their footprints back to Titusville.[59]

The Titusville post office was discontinued on May 27, 1873, and sixty-
one-year-old Englishman Isaac Dunlin Parkinson was appointed postmaster
at Sand Point after William S. Abbott was removed. The following month
Titus and his wife sold a one-acre lot on the west bank of the Indian River,
adjacent to the Mary Carlile property, for twenty-five dollars to thirty-three-
year-old Frances "Fanny" G. Joyner, the widow of his former business partner. Mary Titus executed a deed of conveyance to relinquish her right of
dower to the sold property. This meant that she could not make a widow's
claim on the assets that were part of the land transaction. The document was
notarized by Justice of the Peace Isaac Dunlin Parkinson. Mrs. Titus, who
was forty years old, gave birth to their eighth and last son, Pierre Soule Titus,
on August 16.[60]

Three days later Mary Titus and her husband sold to Bartholomew Einig
for $37.50 an acre-and-a-half lot fronting Indian River in the township
"known as Titusville, old Sand Point," north of the W. Lewis Newton house.
The witnesses to the deed were Newton and former postmaster Lanehart.
Mary also relinquished her right of dower to this property. On October 3 the
Tituses sold another acre and a half to Einig for the same price. The buyer,
a forty-seven-year-old widowed German, "started a small sawmill soon after
his arrival" and three months later married twenty-one-year-old Charlotte J.
Smith. The duality of post offices maintained during the previous seventeen months ended on October 16, when the Sand Point post office name
was changed to Titusville and Parkinson was reappointed as postmaster. Two
months later Titus was commissioned as a notary public for Volusia County
for a term of four years by Florida Republican governor Ossian B. Hart, a
Jacksonville native and former slave owner whose father was the city founder
and customs collector who neutralized the *Pampero* expedition.[61]

By the spring of 1874, the economic depression called the Panic of 1873,
which had began the previous September, had affected eastern Florida.
There was a slump in business that drastically decreased railroad expansion
and tourism to the region. In consequence, on April 27, 1874, the Tituses
sold forty acres to New Yorker H. W. Van Buren for $650. Mary, as was

customary, renounced her future widow's claim on the land. Two months later the colonel joined in conveying his wife's separate estate in selling to John J. Harris, a thirty-nine-year-old physician from Brunswick, Georgia, ten acres of lot 1 on the Indian River shore, bordering Main Street on the north and land owned by Mrs. Titus on the south, "at a place commonly known as Titusville or Sand Point," for $4,600. The sale included the Titus House and all its furnishings, "excepting one side board, one dining table, six cane chairs, six paintings and two sets of furniture." The Tituses acknowledged responsibility for a $600 mortgage on the property pending with Charles R. Gill. The witnesses signing the document, which Mary notarized as "separate and apart from my said husband," were her father, Edward Stevens Hopkins; the Jacksonville attorney Aristides H. Doggett; former postmaster Lanehart; and twenty-five-year-old Moses Backster Metzger, a farm laborer recently arrived from Effingham County, Georgia. After two months Dr. Harris still owed Mrs. Titus $3,600, and on August 25 he and his wife signed two three-year promissory notes, with interest, for the pending debt and returned the Titus House for $1. The Harrises later sold the lot to Thomas Walker Lund.[62]

By 1874 Titus had developed a routine of planting in the spring and hunting green sea turtles and their eggs for six weeks during the summer. He showed a visitor a sweet potato he raised "that weighed eighteen pounds and three-quarters." A northern traveler saw Titus on the beach below Cape Canaveral with tents and servants, camping out "like an old veteran." The tourist noted, "As he is entirely crippled by bullets and rheumatism he can do but little besides overseeing the job. I hear that he is one of the most successful turtlers on the Indian river." The green sea turtles, weighing 150 to 400 pounds, were "captured in nets a hundred feet long, sunk for three days at a depth of twelve to fourteen feet." They were also "caught at night when coming ashore to deposit their eggs and were seized by the hunters and turned on their backs until the entire catch was made." Their meat was worth "six cents a pound on the river, and from twenty-eight to thirty-five cents in New York City," with annual profits of about six hundred dollars. During the approaching winter season, a tourist wrote how "Indian river is difficult of access, but swarms of travelers are now finding their way there."[63]

The Volusia County Board of Commissioners met on September 7 and 8, 1874, and for the upcoming elections "ordered that Election Precinct No. 5 be changed to Titusville Post Office from Sand Point." They appointed as inspectors of elections the former postmaster Lanehart, the twenty-seven-year-old farmer William S. Norwood, and Charles Norman. Two months later the Tituses sold to James A. Russell a half acre on the Indian River shore for seventy dollars, in a deed with covenants against the grantor only and with Mary relinquishing her dower. Russell, a thirty-nine-year-old "beach comber" from North Carolina, also owned a turtling camp opposite Fort Capron. The tourist handbook *Camp Life in Florida* recommended Russell as being "thoroughly posted upon the game and fish of Indian river, and will be found of great value to any party contemplating a winter's camp there."[64]

Another visitor, Thomas Sedgwick Steele, a thirty-year-old outdoorsman, writer, and photographer from Hartford, Connecticut, in the spring of 1875 described Titusville as having "one church and seven houses, and to the long wharf which extended out into the water some distance, were moored a number of sailing craft." He noticed that the Titus sawmill was producing "beautiful walking sticks of crabtree, mangrove and other woods," which were sold in "the curiosity shops which abound at all the ports on the St. Johns River." Steele claimed that Titus would be "long remembered," after two decades, for "ways that are dark, as concerned in the past outrages of bleeding Kansas." He portrayed the fifty-three-year-old colonel as "very cross looking, with florid complexion, heavy gray hair and beard, but the twinkle of his bright black eyes shows that a little of the old fire remains." Steele alleged that Titus had "managed to break the company . . . canning and shipping of turtle and oysters . . . but retired rich himself, and with his gains now luxuriates in case and comfort." This was a spiteful falsehood, as Titus was unable to recover his loss in the venture and had not retired. Five years earlier the New York Supreme Court had ordered that ninety-nine shares of capital stock in his New York and Indian River Preserving Co., valued at $100.00 each, and company property worth $10,413.03, belonging to James H. Moran and others, be sold at public auction along with dozens of other assets and claims of other businesses.[65]

The Titus family at the time lived comfortably from the rewards of their hard labor, various successful business ventures, and profitable land speculation; land they had purchased for $1.25 an acre was now going for $300.00 each. The colonel and his wife that summer sold to Perry E. Wager, a fifty-five-year-old teacher from Cambridge, New York, for $300.00 "one lot in the town of Titusville" on the riverbank next to that of Isaac D. Parkinson. Mrs. Titus relinquished her right of dower for $1.00. Legal document references to Titusville as formerly being Sand Point no longer appeared. Wager opened "The Headquarters" grocery store with an extended river dock, and five years later he and his son Ellis B. Wager published Titusville's first newspaper, the *Florida Star.* Wager also bought a ten-acre sugar cane plantation with a grinding "mill of three iron rollers, worked by a mule," on "a lagoon on Banana Creek, six miles southeast of Titusville."[66]

Titus redeemed his political reputation on May 1, 1875, when he was appointed justice of the peace, "during good behavior, subject to removal by the Governor at his own discretion," for Volusia County by Republican governor Marcellus L. Stearns, a former Union army lieutenant and the last Reconstruction governor of Florida. In August thirty-seven citizens of Titusville petitioned Stearns to remove the colonel from his post. The document stated that Titus had refused to issue an arrest warrant for J. M. Hopkins, accused of assault and battery, because he "had no constable and had no authority to appoint one." The *Cedar Keys Journal* opined that the petitioners would gain nothing, "as nonfeasance, malfeasance, or any other misconduct in office, will not be regarded by Gov. Stearns as wrong if committed by a Radical."[67]

Titus's appointment as justice of the peace of Volusia County, Fla., May 1, 1875.
Courtesy of the State Archives of Florida

During the 1875 winter tourist season, George B. Christian, his uncle, and two male companions traveled from Ohio to Florida for sporting activities. They boarded a steamer at Jacksonville for Salt Lake, "a rather small swamp surrounded body of water a few miles west of Titusville." On the final stretch, the sojourners "were compelled to pass through a winding branch, known as Snake creek. This creek meandered through a veritable jungle." Upon their arrival, Christian recalled, "Circling about in the blue sky were innumerable game birds that had risen from their haunts disturbed by the advent of our ship." On the shore were long lines of both crimson and white flamingoes interspersed with cranes. Seventeen-year-old Edward Hopkins Titus appeared with "two mules hitched to an open spring-wagon for passenger service, and a heavier vehicle for the transportation of baggage and freight." The teenager drove the mules into two feet of water and brought the wagon up alongside the boat for the passenger transfer to the Titus House. Christian was introduced to the colonel by his uncle, who had previously corresponded with him.[68]

Titus stated that he "had been forced to reside in this southern climate from an unrelenting foe—muscular rheumatism," also called fibromyalgia. Christian noted that "notwithstanding the ravages of illness," Titus "had been a man of wonderful proportions and splendid appearance." The colonel shared sparkling vintages with his guests. "As he related some incidents of adventurous career, his dark eyes flashed, and this, associated with a choice selection of vituperative adjectives, disclosed what manner of a man he must have been." Titus boasted about his saloon fights and how his disagreement with William Walker resulted in an attempt by the filibuster general and his adherents to place him "in front of a firing line of rifles." The colonel gave his guests "a rather optimistic view of the country." He said that the lands lying between the Indian River and the St. Johns "would reach values of $200 to $300 an acre; that below on both banks of the river were large areas of the finest lands for orange culture in the world." Christian later heard from town residents that the colonel's "daily habit included several hours of sitting on his veranda with a loaded rifle across his lap waiting to locate one or more of his local enemies, who might carelessly invade the territory covered by the range of his gun." The visitors concluded that Titus was "a fine old gentleman, however, interesting and hospitable."[69]

A northern traveler arrived by sail in Titusville on February 28, 1876, and later wrote, "The place amounts to nothing at present." It was "the residence of Col. Titus, by reputation a cowardly old bully who figured conspicuously among the border ruffians of Kansas." He called Titus "a bad egg" and found

him "prostrated by what he is pleased to call 'rheumatic gout.'" *1.*
Stoneman Douglas, a granddaughter of abolitionists, who moved to Florida
in 1915 to work for the *Miami Herald,* later described Titus as "a crippled old
reprobate" who "dominated" the town "from a wheel chair on the veranda of
his long, low hotel, a shotgun across his lap. People were attracted as much
by his wild tales as by the lavish meals of venison, oysters, fish, and rum
punches. . . . A huge, mustachioed blusterer, he swaggered even in a wheel
chair among his admiring tourists."[70]

Titus's daughter Minnie stated that her father "spent his days in a wheel
chair and was a great sufferer." She never heard him "complain of his lot or
blame the Almighty. Neither did he resort to drugs to deaden his pain, but
when it was too severe, he would say, 'God have mercy on my soul.'" According to Minnie, her father "had an idea his rheumatism might have been
caused or helped by his mother never letting him go barefoot as a child, so he
insisted we go barefoot part time." The colonel believed that early morning
swimming was beneficial and at 6:00 A.M. moved about in his wheelchair
to awake his children by knocking on their bedroom doors. He had a bath-
house built on the river in about five feet of water. Minnie remembered that
"there was a platform inside and steps that led down to another platform just
above the water." One morning she "jumped in and saw an alligator under
the lower platform." The sickly Minnie was encouraged to be outdoors as
much as possible. A cedar bateau was built for her to row every morning on
the Indian River. Minnie recalled that at the Titus House, "Lord and Lady
Parker, from England, were among the visitors and slaughtered many of the
numerous deer; taking their hides back to England and allowing the venison
to go to waste."[71]

Another guest was forty-two-year-old New Yorker Charles Hallock, a
noted author, publisher, and former proprietor and associate editor of the
New York Journal of Commerce. He indicated that "Titusville owes all of its
present prosperity to the indefatigable energy of its proprietor, Colonel H.
T. Titus. This place is only noteworthy as a point of the arrival and departure for more interesting points on the river." Hallock described the Titus
House as "the only one on the river, and is said to be well kept; $3 per day
is charged for transient boarders." The writer stated, "Very fine specimens
of native woods may be procured here, such as the crabwood, royal palm,
mangrove, palmetto, and iron wood, made into canes, etc." The author of
Guide to Florida indicated in 1876 that "Col. Titus, of Kansas and Nicaragua
fame, keeps a good hotel." Titusville served as the northernmost of four post
offices on the Indian River. The mail was scheduled for weekly arrival and

departure, but it really came and went depending on the sailing winds. To regulate postal service, the government opened bids, and on March 6, 1876, Titus won the contract to deliver the mail from New Smyrna to Titusville, forty-five miles and back, twice a week on Route 16160. He gave the lowest of nine bids, at $720 per annum, and had to post a $1,200 bond. The mail departed Titusville Monday and Thursday at 6:00 A.M. and arrived at New Smyrna the next morning. It then left New Smyrna on Tuesday and Friday at 1:00 P.M., reaching Titusville the following days by 5:00 P.M.[72]

Titusville continued expanding that year when on September 18, 1876, Mary Titus leased to William B. Hatter, a forty-three-year-old grocery clerk from Alabama, and forty-five-year-old Florida farmer John M. Dixon, "for the use of mercantile purposes," a plot about one hundred feet in length south of Broad Street between the river and the stable. The firm of Hatter and Dixon agreed to erect a substantial building worth $350.00 and keep it in good repair in exchange for having free rent for seven years. The structure and land would then revert to the ownership of Mrs. Titus. The colonel was also involved in a lawsuit against James R. Avielher and Company and won a $482.90 settlement. He was represented by the Jacksonville attorney Eleazer Kingsbury Foster Jr.[73]

The following month, in preparation for the November 7 general elections, the Volusia County Board of Commissioners met and on a motion from William Allan ordered the establishment of voting precinct "No. 13 Titusville, at the Titus Store." They appointed the fifty-one-year-old Carolinian fruit grower Adger C. McCrorey, the grocer Perry E. Wager, and Justice of the Peace Theodore Bartles as inspectors of elections there. Forty-six male citizens voted at Titusville. Most Florida native whites were Democrats adamant in overthrowing the Republican carpetbagger regime. Titus ran for constable as a Republican against the Democrat Moses Backster Metzger and received only five ballots compared to nineteen for his opponent, with twenty-two abstentions. Many voters were still resentful that Titus had not ordered the arrest of J. M. Hopkins the previous year. The gubernatorial election resulted in a victory for Democrat George Franklin Drew against Republican Marcellus L. Stearns. Most white northerners had by then stopped backing federal support of Republican regimes in the South.[74]

By the winter of 1876–77, according to the pioneer Charles W. Pierce, "Sand Point had blossomed out as a real town, now named Titusville," and the winter tourists at the Titus House "were becoming more numerous each succeeding season." On January 17, 1877, Titus purchased for $500 from forty-six-year-old Thomas Walker Lund and his wife a section of town lot 1 along the Indian River that the colonel had previously sold to John J. Harris. Lund was a pilot of the Jacksonville and Salt Lake Line steamers. He established the Lund House on Washington Avenue and Main Street, near the Titus House, with a wharf on the river and a building for packing oranges. The Lund family resided in Jacksonville, and the hostelry was administered by S. A. Merrill of Lynn, Massachusetts. A year later Volusia County tax records indicated that Titus owned a hotel on two acres, a private residence on a one-acre lot, wharf property, and a store. The value of his five town lots was $1,800. That year his fifteen-year-old daughter Minnie had a relapse of typhoid fever and was sent to recuperate in New York, where she remained for three years with her aunt Marian.[75]

The Tituses augmented their real estate profits and value on June 1, 1878, when they sold a town lot of one-quarter acre between Washington Avenue and Hopkins Street, neighboring John M. Dixon's property, for seventy-five dollars to William Woodmansee, a forty-six-year-old bachelor shoe-maker from New Jersey. In the front and rear of the lot there were areas "left reserved for side walks in common for the use of the said citizens of the town of Titusville." Mary notarized the execution of the deed separate from her husband, in the presence of Justice of the Peace Theodore Bartles, doing so "freely and voluntarily and without any compulsion, constraint, apprehension or fear of or from my said husband." Three months later the colonel and his wife sold a one-quarter-acre lot on the corner of Main Street and Washington Avenue to former postmaster Lawrence Carlile for one hundred dollars. The document was witnessed by the colonel's daughter Kate H. Titus and thirty-eight-year-old English farmer William Watton. Mary, according to law, renounced future claim to the property as witnessed by Kate and notarized by Bartles.[76]

Six months later, at the start of the winter tourist season, Dr. James A. Henshall, a forty-four-year-old Marylander, reached Salt Lake on the morning of December 24, 1878, on a steamer from Jacksonville with five northern patients seeking the warmer Florida climate to improve their health. These were "two dyspeptics, one incipient consumptive, one bad liver, one nasal catarrh." On the lake shore the party boarded the St. Johns and Indian River Railroad wooden tramway, "drawn by two mules who travel outside of the track, one on each side," which took them eight miles to Titusville, with arrival in time for dinner. Henshall described the "small village" as "a place of considerable importance in East Florida, being the emporium for the entire country south for a distance of two hundred miles." The weather was "at 75

degrees, with the birds singing merrily, and tuberoses and hyacinths bloom-
ing in the open ground; while all around were trees and shrubs luxuriant
in their green and graceful foliage." Titusville had "two hotels and a half-
dozen stores, and is the distributing and shipping point for South-east Florida." The Titus House, expanded to twenty-four rooms with plastered walls,
was rented the previous winter to forty-year-old farmer Joseph H. Bodine
of Enterprise and thirty-nine-year-old Irish ship carpenter John F. McCarty
of Oak Hill. Mrs. Titus reverted to running the hotel after Bodine and
McCarty went north.[77]

Titusville had a brisk trade in local products being shipped to Jacksonville via Salt Lake, "such as oranges, limes, pineapples, bananas, cane syrup,
early vegetables, green turtle, oysters, venison, skins, hides, etc.," while "the
return cargoes consist of groceries, provisions, clothing, household goods,
etc." At the various local stores, including the colonel's, there were "self-rising
flour, bacon, coffee, sugar, canned goods of every description, and the great
Florida staple, hominy, or grits," available at reasonable prices. Dr. Henshall recommended that the sportsman "take his ammunition and fishing
tackle with him, or at least procure them in Jacksonville." He spent Christmas night at the Titus House, where "everyone was now in a thoroughly
good humor, and we were 'swapping yarns' and retailing old jokes." A vio-
lin was passed around, and the physician played *Devil's Dream, Gray Eagle,
Arkansas Traveler,* and other lively tunes and then used the parlor piano to
accompany another fiddler.[78]

Titus resumed his real estate dealings on January 1, 1879, when he rented
to William B. Moore, at one hundred dollars for two years, a one-hundred-
foot-long parcel of land between the Indian River bank and Washington
Avenue, between the Titus House and the Lund House hotels. The contract
stipulated that Moore had four months to clear the lot and build on it "a
store house for the purpose of trading and carrying on mercantile business."
The agreement could be renewed for three years with an annual rent of seventy-five dollars. Titus would then purchase the store from Moore for cash at
a value established by three disinterested persons. Two days later the Tituses
sold for one hundred dollars, with Mary relinquishing her dowry for one
dollar, a town lot of one-eighth acre on block 6 of Main Street, next to that of
Lawrence Carlile, to Lucy Brennan, a twenty-eight-year-old Irish American
spinster, who established a dry goods store there.[79]

That year Titus was instrumental in having the southern section of Volusia County that included Titusville annexed to Brevard County. He was
supported by Volusia County assemblyman and Florida assembly speaker

Charles Dougherty, who on March 8, 1879, passed a law allowing Brevard County voters after a thirty-day notice to "locate and establish a county site or court-house" by majority vote. Three days later Dougherty passed "An Act to Define the Boundary Lines of Volusia and Brevard Counties." The entire Indian River was now embraced in the county, with the exception of about twenty miles above Jupiter Inlet. Titus then donated land to Brevard County under the stipulation that it be used "only for county or public purposes." As a result, Titusville was voted the county seat, over Eau Gallie and Rockledge, making it the colonel's crowning achievement for the community. This move entailed political and economic rewards. Governmental business was shifted to Titusville, and the price of town lots increased. The colonel had the streets "beautified with shade trees and shrubs, bringing in hibiscus and other plants" and "had to direct his work from a wheel chair." He also "hired out boats and sent down the Indian river to get shells for the streets." The new courthouse handled probate and judicial matters, while county officials set and administered local taxes and supervised the construction and maintenance of public works. There was political patronage for the distribution of county officers, including sheriff, constable, jailer, clerks, justice of the peace, surveyor, coroner, and assessor. A "full and efficient organization of the County was made by the appointment of a full set of county officials," and for the first time "taxes were systematically collected."[80]

In January 1880 a "Special Correspondent" of the *Augusta Chronicle* visited Titusville, which he described as "the *entrepot* for the whole region." The town had "a packing house, a post office, several stores, a church that is never opened, and a comfortable hotel." Titus was described as "the builder and principal owner of the town" and a "character" who "has been everywhere." The colonel loved to tell his reminiscences full of anecdotes of Kansas and filibustering. He was "still a man of indomitable energy and pluck" whose "magnificent physique, his unflinching courage, and his air of authority and power have given him great influence, which he seems not to have abused." The article indicated that Titus had "accomplished a great deal" for his community as magistrate and agent for the underwriters and general regulator of wreckers. Titus boasted that the region had "the finest and healthiest climate" and that now was the time to buy land as the railroad line was approaching.[81]

An *Augusta Chronicle* reporter wrote that the region produced oranges that were "of superior quality and command the highest prices in the Northern markets." Many fine orchards were scattered along the riverbank. The waters abounded with fish, the woods were filled with game, and "living costs but a trifle." However, it was still an isolated area without telegraph, railroad, or steamboat traffic, and the mail was transported weekly on a small sailboat on the river. Schools were "almost an impossibility." The writer found the mosquitoes, gnats, fleas, sand flies, and other insects that swarmed about in myriads to be Titusville's worst problem. The poorer townspeople would "extinguish their lights and fill their houses with smoke" to avoid the insects, while those who could afford it used wire screens on their windows and doors.[82]

Railroad depot for Sandpoint and Titusville (1870–90).
Courtesy of the State Archives of Florida

A sportsman who visited Titusville in January 1880 later wrote a lengthy account in the *Cazenovia Republican* of New York under the pen name "Friar Tuck." After fishing and hunting ducks, turkeys, quail, and venison for three weeks around Lakes Jessup and Harney in his own boat, the sportsman and his retinue "decided to run direct to Salt Lake and thence via Sand Point to Indian river." It took them three days to reach the lake, and they shot with rifles more than one hundred alligators that "were on all sides." Upon reaching Salt Lake at noon, the manager of the mule-drawn wooden tramway to Titusville told the group that "the road had not been in operation for some time, as it was undergoing repairs," but that he would transfer their "boat and traps to Indian river the following morning." At sunrise it was discovered that "through the maliciousness of some rival stock-holder, or other conscienceless cuss, the long-eared motors used had been turned loose." Suspicion fell on Titus because the tramway company was involved in a lawsuit against him. The colonel was again represented by Jacksonville attorney Eleazer Kingsbury Foster Jr.[83]

"Friar Tuck" wrote, "As the next best thing, Colonel Titus had sent his colored boy, 'Alec,' with three mules and a wagon rigged for the purpose." The visitors unloaded from their boat "provisions for a long cruise, an armory of firearms, and an arsenal of ammunition, together with cooking utensils, clothing and camp fixtures." The wagon was driven into the lake until the mules refused to go deeper, and everyone tugged to get the boat on the wagon. Twice "the mules started prematurely, leaving the boat behind." After the vessel was pulled out of the water and strapped down on the wagon, the men walked beside it for eight miles, "in order to prevent the boat from being racked off." The group made the Titus House their headquarters for the weekend before sailing down the Indian River. "Friar Tuck" stressed, "With no axe to grind, or interest to serve, but writing simply for the benefit of my brother sportsmen who may journey South, I say this is the best regulated hotel south of Enterprise, and as good as any on the St. Johns River. The table was one that any hotel man might well be proud of, and all the house appointments are in good style, and everything in thoroughly comfortable." He added, "Sportsmen will meet with a warm welcome from the proprietor, Col. H. T. Titus, and can rely on the Colonel's knowledge of the country— no man knows it better."[84]

Titus and his family appeared in the 1880 federal census that listed 1,486 inhabitants in Brevard County. The district east of the St. Johns River, which encompassed Titusville, contained 895 residents, including 66 farmers, 62 farm laborers, 33 horticulturalists, 32 fruit growers, 6 sawmill workers, 6 schoolteachers, 5 store clerks, 4 carpenters, 4 U.S. mail carriers, 2 blacksmiths, 2 physicians, and a Methodist Episcopal preacher, among other professions listed. There were 73 African Americans, whose occupations included a dozen servants, 8 farm laborers, 3 of the 4 postal carriers, and 2 sawmill workers. Titusville had its first major crime on June 28, when Samuel Moore, a thirty-five-year-old bachelor store clerk, was robbed of a large sum of money and was found dead with a crushed skull. Henry Metzgar was arrested with some of the missing money and jailed in Enterprise to await trial. He confessed to having killed 7 men and died unrepentant on the gallows at Titusville the following year.[85]

Titus, who listed his occupation as "Hotel Keeper," was disabled with "Rheumatic Gout." Four sons were living at home, and the oldest worked as a teamster. Fourteen-year-old Howell was in school at Jacksonville and residing with his grandfather. Mary's employment appeared as "Keeping house," but in fact the forty-eight-year-old woman was running the Titus House. Twenty-two-year-old John Joyner Jr., the son of Titus's former partner, was the saloon keeper. The hotel had two waitresses, a nineteen-year-old Irish American female and an illiterate thirty-year-old African American single mother with three children, both of whom lived nearby. Titus was confined to a "chair with rollers," in which he was propelled around town by an African American servant. He spent most of his time on the hotel piazza entertaining guests with stupendous tales. The colonel's health was failing when on July 1, 1880, he wrote a one-paragraph note, witnessed by seventy-three-year-old Englishman Abraham Parkinson and his wife, bequeathing all his property to Mary and in the case of her death dividing it equally among their children.[86]

Titus was the local representative of the Board of Underwriters of the Atlantic Mutual Marine Insurance Company of New York when on September 2, 1880, he informed Charles Denis, the company secretary, of the losses to the steamer *City of Vera Cruz*, which four days earlier foundered at dawn off Cape Canaveral due to a severe gale. The vessel, bound from New York to Havana, was a six-year-old wooden brigantine-rigged steamship of 1,874 tons with two compressed cylinder engines and screw. It was "296 feet long, 37 feet beam, and 26 feet deep, and had three decks." The steamer was valued at $200,000 and insured for $150,000. Its cargo, worth up to $150,000, consisted of "dry goods and provisions, including a large quantity of potatoes, railway machinery, tools, etc., partially insured." Twenty-nine bags of mail and newspapers were lost with a State Department dispatch bag. There were twenty-eight cabin passengers on board, including a dozen Cubans, and forty-nine officers and crew, of whom fourteen survived, including an African American who swam to shore with a life preserver. One of the corpses that washed ashore was that of forty-seven-year-old Civil War Union brigadier general Alfred T. A. Torbert, the former U.S. consul general to Paris. Titus rendered two reports of the disaster and had to pay ten dollars to a boatman to post them thirty-four miles away at Sanford, the nearest mail, telegraph, and steamship communication point. His father-in-law, Edward Stevens Hopkins, collector of the Port of Jacksonville, served as a pallbearer when Torbert's coffin arrived by steamer to await another vessel going north.[87]

Two months later Titus was advertising himself in newspapers as a "General Marine Underwriter's Agent, American and Foreign, also Notary Public at Large for the State of Florida." He also announced that he was a "Dealer in Pure Liquors, Imported wines, ales, etc. Old Port and Sherry wines kept expressly for invalids, warranted pure." The hotel barroom was stocked with seventy pounds of plug tobacco, cigars, and dozens of bottles of cherry and peach brandies; claret, perry, and East India madeira fine wines; classic Heidsieck and other cheaper champagnes; twenty gallons of whiskey; and scores of bottles of gin, beer, and ale. The ad concluded, "The Titus House is now open for the winter and Hacks will connect with the boats at Salt Lake." The steamer *Wekiwa* ran twice a week between Salt Lake and Enterprise, where other steamers made the trip to Jacksonville.[88]

In early December 1880 the colonel wrote to the editor of the Titusville *Florida Star* denouncing the incendiary acts of arson by those whose nefarious purposes were to collect insurance premiums. His angry tone suggests that the arson personally affected him as it was "endangering the property of others in this town." The lack of investigation prompted Titus to question if there was "not manhood left in the people and no interest left for the future prosperity of the town." Soon thereafter he leased his store/saloon to a Mr. Smith of Mosquito Lagoon, who stocked it with his own general merchandise for sale. The new billiard table in the saloon was moved into the office of the Titus House.[89]

The betterment that Titus wanted for his settlement had been steadfastly increasing with tourism to the region. The "Arrivals at the Titus House" weekly notices in the *Florida Star* showed that a growing number of visitors were arriving at the hotel that winter. By late February 1881 there were thirty guests at the Titus House in one week. They were mostly northerners, but some came from as far away as Canada, England, and China. A number of dignitaries that winter enjoyed Titus's hospitality, including various physicians, Florida senator William Hamilton Sharpe, Reps. Henry Parker and R. B. Potter, and Ercole Tamajo, the Duke of Castelluccia and hero of the Crimean War, with his new wife and servants. Some visitors were "seeking permanent homes" in the Indian River area, including Tamajo, who contracted to build a new villa after purchasing the Dummett property. When the tourist season ended in May, Titus began "enlarging his commodious hotel for next winter's travel," including "a large cistern capable of holding 12,000 gallons of water." The following month Titus's notoriety was revived when chapters of *Reminiscences of Gov. Robert J. Walker,* written by George Washington Brown, former editor of the free-soiler *Herald of Freedom,* were reprinted in newspapers across the country. One paragraph referred to Titus as "now an incurable paralytic of Titusville, Florida, the redoubtable pro-slavery ruffian."[90]

Earlier that year Republican Horatio Bisbee Jr. contested the Florida election held the previous November 2, which gave a victory to former Confederate general Jesse Johnson Finley, Titus's friend since 1865, as representative to the Forty-seventh Congress. Bisbee, who had been colonel of the Fifth Massachusetts Volunteer Infantry Regiment during the Civil War, listed irregularities in sixteen Florida counties and claimed that in Brevard County the election "was held & conducted as if there were no laws requiring registration of electors. That no ballot-boxes were furnished the inspectors of election, and the ballots at the so-called election were deposited in unsafe and insecure boxes improvised for the occasion; that the returns of the so-called election were not made and conveyed from the several polls as required by law, and are wholly void." Bisbee requested the annulment of the election in the precincts with irregularities and in all the polls in Brevard County. He claimed that in some counties ballot boxes were stuffed against him, Republican electors were denied the right to vote, ballots were destroyed, poll books were falsified, nonresidents and aliens were allowed to vote, and polls did not open and close at the required times, among other anomalies. The accusations prompted a congressional investigation even though Finley denied all the charges.[91]

Bisbee had testimony taken of election officials in numerous counties to contest the election. In Titusville depositions were taken of James A. McCrory, county judge and deputy clerk of court, and Brevard County sheriff W. F. Richards. Their affidavits were taken in the presence of Henry Titus, notary public for the State of Florida, on behalf of the contestant. Twenty-six-year-old McCrory testified on May 2, 1881, that there were a dozen election precincts in the county and that some of the lists of registered electors, on loose sheets of paper, were returned to the clerk's office before the day of the election and others were not. Not all the sheets had the required heading, oath, or the number or name of the election precinct printed on them. Two of the precincts sent their returns to the clerk's office by registered mail.

He acknowledged being a Democrat and that as justice of the peace he was a member of the board of the county canvassers for the general election. McCrory affirmed, "The canvass was made from the returns made to the clerk. The returns made to the county judge were not canvassed." Titus notarized and sealed the document after reading to McCrory his statements.[92]

Three days later Brevard County sheriff William F. Richards, a twenty-nine-year-old ship carpenter from New Jersey, testified before Titus that a few days before the last general election he received from his county clerk of court ballot boxes and lists of registered voters to be delivered to the inspectors at the twelve election precincts. Richards stated that he delivered everything except at Fort Prince precinct 5, which he "was unable to reach in time." Titus repeated the process of taking and reading his testimony over to the witness, who swore to and subscribed it. Counsel for the contestant then offered in evidence four exhibits that consisted of a notice of examination of the two witnesses at Titusville and the poll lists for precincts 2, 9, and 10 containing eighty-four names. The colonel and his twenty-one-year-old son Edward Hopkins Titus appeared as voters of the second precinct, where Finley received twenty-eight ballots and Bisbee got twelve. The congressional investigation concluded that in Brevard County the several irregularities were limited to the distant precincts west of Titusville. The final Brevard County tally was 222 votes for Finley and 74 for Bisbee. The latter successfully contested the election and as a result was seated in the Fortyseventh Congress.[93]

The Florida pioneer Charles W. Pierce described Titusville in 1881 as "not large in any sense of the word but was quite busy for a place so far removed from civilization. As the county seat of Brevard County, it was the most important town on the lower east coast south of Daytona and north of Key West. Titusville's business houses at this time consisted of three general stores, a hotel, and a saloon. The saloon appeared to be doing more business than all the other concerns combined, but this is what one would expect from a frontier town." In contrast, a resident of Cape Malabar, fifty miles south of Titusville, wrote in the Jacksonville *Florida Dispatch* on June 29, 1881, under the pen name "Will-o'-The-Wisp," that Titusville was "a dreary waste of white sand. I felt when I first beheld it I had certainly come to the poorest place on earth." He indicated that farther down the river there were "rich lands" and that the growing town of Rockledge "is a most beautiful place, and would make a magnificent winter resort." The anonymous writer questioned why the railroad planners wanted to make Titusville instead of Rockledge a terminus. Titusville had "no scenery, nothing but white sand banks, and when the river is low or a west or north wind, a boat of any size can't get within half a mile of shore, and if the railroad company makes a wharf out to deep water the chances are that it will be destroyed in the first gale." The writer gave "several good reasons why the railroad company would do well to make Rock Ledge their Indian river terminus."[94]

Titus waged his last battle, with a clear and responsive mind, when replying to his adversary in the *Florida Dispatch* of August 3. He ridiculed him as an "imbecile," like "all such liars and itinerant quill drivers," in need of "a 'wet nurse' to keep them out of mischief." The colonel indicated that the Enterprise and Titusville Railroad would be completed by the end of the year and that the Coast Canal Company was commencing operations at once to expand the Haulover Canal. He described Titusville as the "grand center of all trade and will so continue to be. No slanderous article from any irresponsible person will change or alter its destiny. Her motto is 'to live and let live.'"[95]

Four days later, on a Sunday morning, fifty-nine-year-old Titus peacefully passed away in his bed surrounded by his family, having escaped the hangman's noose in Bleeding Kansas, a filibuster firing squad in Nicaragua, a Comanche ambush while crossing Texas, and the Apache destruction of his Arizona ranch. Minnie Titus recalled that her father's "character and courage was [*sic*] such that he carried on daily, almost to the hour of his death." The colonel died intestate, leaving property worth two thousand dollars that was settled in probate court. The local *Florida Star* reported, "Titusville has lost an energetic citizen in the death of Col. H. T. Titus . . . after a prolonged illness." The Jacksonville *Florida Union* editorialized, "There are few men more widely known in this State than was the deceased gentleman." His demise was reported in numerous newspapers throughout the nation, especially in Florida, Georgia, and Kansas, and as far north as Portland, Maine. He was remembered mostly for his "remarkably adventurous career." The Republican *Lawrence Western Home Journal* praised its former enemy, saying, "He was at best notable for a dogged kind of courage which manifested itself in several encounters with the free-soil men." The article recalled that during the attack on Titus's home, "His manly bearing and courageous manner inspired a feeling of respect in the hearts of even his deadly foes." Other obituaries highlighted his participation in the López expedition, being "in the thick of the quarrel in Kansas," joining the Walker expedition, leading "a wild life" in Arizona, and "in his old age found[ing] the flourishing Florida town that bears his name."[96]

Epilogue

Episcopalian funeral rites for Henry Theodore Titus were held in the La Grange Church in Titusville, followed by a solemn interment in the family plot in the churchyard cemetery. His marble tombstone, erected years later, has no epitaph, and his birth year erroneously appears as 1823. The colonel did not live to see his dream come true during the next decade. In 1882 a "new and handsome court-house" was completed and the U.S. Department of Agriculture described Titusville as "a thriving town." The arrival of the railroad in 1886 made Titusville "the transportation hub of the Indian River country." During the next three months, nine new buildings were erected. The following year Titusville was incorporated as a city with some two hundred citizens and "claimed 20 businesses, three real estate agents, two lumber yards, two newspapers, and had plans for a bank." The city served as the shipping point for Indian River citrus products. A new steamer, the *Indian River*, "was making regular round trips to Melbourne each day." Before the end of the decade, Titusville had several hundred buildings and was the "metropolis of the Indian River Country."[1]

A northern visitor in 1891 saw Titusville as exceedingly clean and neat. The piers, depots, and their surroundings were "kept free from tramps and dead rubbish." Indian River's "unrivaled water facilities, its peculiar and romantic scenery, its superb fishing, hunting and yachting, its unexcelled fruits, its delightful climate, and its clean bill of health, all combine to make it the Mecca of the tourist, whether he comes for health or for pleasure." Three years later a British tourist described Titusville as having "a population of about sixteen hundred, its streets 'shelled,' lit by electricity, with good stores in brick buildings, a bank, half-a-dozen churches, and a jail—is a go-ahead,

lively little town, doing a business with all parts of the river and back-coun-
try; and while the East Coast Line passes right through, it is the terminus
of the Jacksonville, Tampa and Key West Railway, here connecting with the
Indian-River Steamboat Company, which acts as a feeder, and carries freight
to and from all parts of the river."[2]

Titus family plot in La Grange Church cemetery, 1575 Old Dixie Highway, Titusville,
Fla. Henry Titus's grave marker, in the right forefront, is adorned with an American flag.
From the author's collection

    The widowed forty-eight-year-old Mary Evelina Titus remained in Titus-
ville and frequently traveled to visit her family in Jacksonville. Her charitable contributions helped build the Carpenter Gothic St. Gabriel's Episcopal
Church, where a stained-glass window, which is still there, was dedicated to
the memory of her husband. She also donated the land on which a six-hun-
dred-foot city dock was built on the river. Management of the Titus House
passed to William H. Moore of Lake Worth in 1884 and later to John A.
McRae, formerly of Sanford. In December 1889 Mrs. Titus sold thirteen lots
on the west end of town to sixty-three-year-old Canadian Thomas Wetmore
and fifty-eight-year-old Stephen Gladwin, "mechanics of ability and considerable experience, who will erect an ice factory." She was also advertising
"several building lots for sale either on the installment plan or for cash." Six
years later, on December 12, 1895, a fire swept across the Titusville business
district along Washington Avenue. Mary Titus lost four buildings, including
the Titus House, and the Lund House was destroyed. She then went to live

with her recently married son Theodore in Thomasville, Georgia, until her death at the age of seventy-eight in November 1911. Mary was laid to rest beside her father, Edward Stevens Hopkins, in the family plot at Evergreen Cemetery in Jacksonville. Her grave marker has no epitaph. By then two of her eight offspring had preceded her in death and four others had sought their fortunes far from Titusville.[3]

Edward Hopkins Titus (January 19, 1859–1934) briefly married Joanna Combs in the 1880s and after their divorce worked as a carpenter in Brooklyn. In 1896 he married Kate, a thirty-three-year-old German American. By 1910 he was single and residing in the Salvation Army's Rescue Mission in Paterson, New Jersey. A decade later Edward was a carpenter in what is now Ponte Vedra Beach, Florida. He was interred in the Titus family plot in LaGrange Cemetery.[4]

Catherine Howell Titus (December 2, 1860–February 3, 1883) was married on May 20, 1882, to James McComb Jr., a clerk of the Brock House in Enterprise, Florida. She died in Titusville while giving birth to premature twins who did not survive. The three were interred in the Titus family plot in LaGrange Cemetery.

Mary Evelina "Minnie" Titus (April 29, 1862–April 1949) married George F. Ensey, a Merritt Island farmer, on December 27, 1882, and they had five children. She dedicated her life to being a homemaker.

Howell Theodore Titus (August 11, 1865–May 21, 1937) practiced law and served as Titusville city marshal and U.S. deputy marshal. He departed for Jacksonville in 1895 after being "charged with embezzling funds" and left "a bad reputation behind him." Howell was arrested in Jacksonville for operating a gambling house "and thrown in jail. By some means or other, he got out of this trouble" due to family influence. Howell was detained in Charlotte, North Carolina, in 1897 for passing worthless checks, which his mother repaid to obtain his release. He "moved to Washington, D.C. and obtained a license to practice law," gaining a reputation as an ineffective lawyer "absolutely devoid of honor or principle."[5]

In February 1900 Howell was convicted for claiming that for fifteen dollars he could get a case dismissed against a client. He fled to New Orleans, where the following month he surrendered after stating that "he does not know how he got to that city, that he has been drinking heavily and using morphine." His sentence was annulled, and Howell was disbarred from practicing law. He moved to Savannah, where on September 21 he "was charged with swindling W. B. Sturtevant out of $25 on a fraudulent draft." Three days later he was released after the case was nol-prossed. Howell went to

Montgomery, Alabama, where he was arrested on February 4, 1901, "for obtaining money under false pretenses." He remained in jail nine months until the prosecutor quashed the charge. His mother's money and influence probably prompted the dismissal of his repeated cases. Howell returned to New Orleans, where in January 1902 he enlisted for three years in Company C, Fifteenth Infantry, U.S. Army and deserted nine months later.[6]

On July 26, 1903, Howell married Mary Randle in Jefferson, Alabama; moved to Chattanooga, Tennessee; and "made application to practice law and stated to the court that he had been practicing for several years in the state of Florida, and the judges, knowing nothing of his record of crime in other cities, admitted him to practice." In the fall of 1906 Howell entered into a law partnership in Chattanooga with his brother Pierre Soule Titus. A year later Pierre sued Howell "to recover certain alleged fees due him by his brother" and challenged him "to go before a doctor and be examined as to sanity." In a public letter, Pierre accused Howell of "many serious misdeeds, among others being the misappropriation of funds and practices not in accord with the ethics of the legal profession."[7]

Howell was disbarred in Tennessee in October 1908 "after one of the most sensational hearings on record in that state. He was proven a bigamist and finally found guilty of using the names of moneyed men on criminal bail bonds without due power of attorney." During his five years in Chattanooga, "among the various charges against him there was one of bastardy; numerous cases of obtaining money under false pretenses; passing worthless checks" for from five to fifty dollars; resisting an officer; "drunkenness, disorderly conduct, and assault and battery." Howell fled before being indicted for embezzlement.[8]

He drifted to San Diego, California, where in March 1909 he was arrested for issuing several worthless checks amounting to about one hundred dollars to various merchants. Howell blamed "wine and cards for his downfall" and was said "to be a sufferer from a loathsome disease." He did not remain in jail for long before appearing in Texas in 1910. A year after his mother's death, Howell married thirty-five-year-old Mississippian Lucy D'Barbour. By 1920 he had settled down as a hotel keeper in Water Valley, Mississippi, and four years later he ran the Hotel Munger in Daytona Beach. In 1925 Howell managed the Columbia Hotel in Jacksonville, where he passed away in 1937.[9]

Henry Theodore Titus Jr. (August 25, 1867–October 21, 1946) at the age of twenty-three owned a boot and shoe store, "an ice cream saloon, and soda water and candy stand" on Washington Avenue in Titusville. He wed Inez Campbell in 1888, and only one of their three offspring survived childhood.

Inez was in poor health by 1900 and passed away in 1902. Two years later Henry married Blanche V. Osborn in St. Augustine, Florida, and they had three children. The family moved to Daytona Beach and opened a billiard parlor and the Crystal Theater. Henry, with only a sixth-grade education, was elected justice of the peace in 1908, the first paid fire chief in 1909, tax collector the following year, and was mayor, municipal judge, and city commissioner from 1911 to 1922. By 1944 he was dock master of the Municipal Dock before his retirement.[10]

Ellett Livingston Titus (November 25, 1869–October 16, 1894) left Titusville in 1887 to reside with his aunt Helen Catherine Hodgskin at 440 Clinton Street in Brooklyn and was employed by the brokerage firm Floyd and Walsh on Wall Street. He was engaged to twenty-three-year-old Mary S. Duff, whose father was a wealthy carriage maker. Their dead bodies were discovered at her father's beach boathouse at Seacliff, Long Island. She died from a heart attack induced by a whiff of chloroform administered by Ellett, without evil intentions, "to allay a severe headache" while they were on a nightly stroll on the beach. Miss Duff had a history of "heart trouble" and "violent headaches." After failing to resuscitate his fiancée, the frenzied twenty-four-year-old Ellett arranged her dress "neatly and tidily," folded her hands across her breast, lay prone beside her, and shot himself in the head with a .38-caliber revolver. A half-full two-ounce chloroform vial was found in his pocket. Private funeral services were held for Ellett at Christ Protestant Episcopal Church and were attended by his aunt and his brother Theodore, who traveled from Georgia. Their mother was unable to attend, but under her instructions Ellett was interred in the Hodgskin family plot in Green-Wood Cemetery in Brooklyn.[11]

Theodore Titus (October 23, 1871–July 4, 1959) went to Thomasville, Georgia, as a boy to study at the Fletcherville Institute. In 1890 he began a law practice that would last more than sixty years. Five years later he married Francis Carara Hopkins, and they had three sons. He was a member of the Board of Aldermen of Thomasville and served as city attorney for several years.[12]

Pierre Soule Titus (August 16, 1873–August 30, 1956) wed Margaret Frances Martin at her birthplace of Hopkinsville, Kentucky, in 1892, and the couple soon returned to Titusville, where their three children were born. Margaret died in 1903 and was buried with other Titus family members at LaGrange. In 1910 Pierre was working as a fisherman and residing with his two young daughters in a boardinghouse in Hawks Park, today Edgewater, Florida. Five years later he was living in Jacksonville with his second wife, Louise Woodman. In 1918 they resided in Los Angeles, California, and he labored as a mining engineer for Quincy Junior Mining Company, Salt Lake City, Utah. Pierre afterward was married to the widow Ida J. Davidson, who preceded him in death in Los Angeles by three years. He was interred in Altadena, California.[13]

The life of Col. Henry Theodore Titus should be perceived within the context of nineteenth-century American society intersecting the convulsive antebellum, Civil War, and Reconstruction epochs, which produced drastic changes. Titus and other young Americans carving out a future were allured by the possible economic, political, and landed opportunities of filibuster expeditions to Cuba and Nicaragua, preemptive land in Kansas, and gold and silver mining in the western mountains. Titus tried his hand at more than a dozen occupations, including sawyer, postal inspector, steamer clerk, soldier of fortune, grocer, planing mill salesman, farmer, slave overseer, miner, canner, turtler, insurance underwriter, mail contractor, liquore dealer, and hotel keeper, but his skill as a sawyer and land speculator that he learned as a child from his father endured and helped develop Titusville. The colonel inherited from his father the will to persevere and succeed after bankruptcy. The patriarch had rebuilt his finances with a sawmill partnership and hard work after the Panic of 1837. His son likewise quickly recuperated from his financial disasters in Kansas and Arizona and during Reconstruction with diligent labor through a series of business associations.

Titus had leadership qualities that allowed him quickly to organize the Douglas County militia company with 180 mounted riflemen, most of whom followed him to Nicaragua, and he created entrepreneurial partnerships with northerners who entrusted him with their investments. His mining and canning businesses failed due to uncontrollable circumstances. The colonel's military skills were improvised and deficient. At Cárdenas he strictly followed orders and fought bravely; at his homestead in Kansas he courageously led a score of desperate men under siege against an overwhelming force; and in Nicaragua he demonstrated a lack of tactics and had little control of his troops. His close brush with death in Kansas resulted in severe wounds and less agile, mangled hands that made him more cautious and less assertive at filibuster combat in Nicaragua. After his crippling injuries, the colonel resorted to head bashing with a loaded cane to settle arguments with strangers who provoked him in saloons or in print. This skull-caning tactic was common among political opponents in the antebellum era. It gained notoriety in 1856 when House speaker Albert Rust attacked *Tribune* editor Horace Greeley in January and four months later South Carolina representative Preston Brooks assaulted Sen. Charles Sumner. Titus killed no one during seven months in Bleeding Kansas, and the only deaths that can be attributed to him were those of a Spanish officer in hand-to-hand combat in Cuba and the shooting in self-defense of a Mexican mining employee who lunged at him with a stone hammer. When the Civil War began, the colonel at the age of thirty-nine was done with warfare. He did not take up arms for the Confederacy, which represented everything he had championed the previous decade, and instead, after a brief stint as assistant quartermaster in the Florida Militia, returned to civilian life for the remainder of the conflict.

Titus, emulating his father, had a profound commitment to his large family. The memoirs of his daughter Minnie, whom he called "his little sunbeam," portray him as a dedicated and loving patriarch who doted on his children and turned to prayer during physical affliction. Mary, his remarkable wife, had all her children baptized in the Episcopal church to which she gave charitable donations. Religious faith helped the family endure the hardships and privations of economic dislocation and pioneer life. Mary was a partner in all her husband's endeavors, bore him at least ten children (two of whom apparently died in infancy), followed him whenever she could, and purchased the land in Jacksonville, Lecompton, and Sand Point that allowed them a new start each time. When she heard that her spouse was a wounded prisoner at Lawrence, Mary fearlessly rushed to his side. Unfortunately there is little personal information about her life to have made a joint study valid.

Would Titus have upheld the institution of slavery had he not wed into a wealthy planter family? It is questionable, since his father had manumitted his own slaves in 1824 and Titus had no need for chattels before moving South and marrying into landed aristocracy. Slavery was not a moral concern to him but rather was a political issue and an economic necessity guaranteed by the Constitution, a document penned by patriots who included slaveholders. Titus accepted servitude as normal and as a slave owner sought slavery's legal protection. He lived in the context of his era and was shaped by the national events over which he had no control. After advocating for the legalization of slavery in Kansas, Titus became a lightning rod for the antislavery movement, which did not miss an opportunity to ridicule or denounce him even after his death. In contrast, unlike the fanatical abolitionists who never forgave him, he did not harbor perpetual animosity toward his political adversaries. Titus displayed gratitude when releasing a free-state prisoner under his charge who had nursed him during his captivity. Prior to leaving Kansas for Nicaragua, he sent a bottle of expensive Heidsieck champagne to his former free-state enemies at a dinner in Kansas City and gave a hearty toast to their health and political triumph. The colonel was also a Good Samaritan to destitute shipwreck survivors on the Florida coast, whom he provided with food, clothing, and cash. He became a civic leader dedicated to beautifying the streets of his city.

The youthful Titus had followed his father into the Whig Party and in 1856 accompanied his father-in-law, Edward Stevens Hopkins, a slave-owning Unionist, into the dissolving Know-Nothing Party. A lack of intellectual and oratorical skills limited his political advancement. His postwar family and business travels to New York and Pennsylvania demonstrated the economic and political benefits available under the corrupt Grant administration, which had the support of the Supreme Court and Congress. Titus quickly established contacts with northern Republican politicians, whom he later cited as personal references. During Reconstruction he pragmatically adhered to the Whig-Republican ideology of modernization and economic protectionism that had a major role in shaping the state governments. When most native white Floridians, including his in-laws, were voting for Democrats, Titus regarded the Lost Cause of the Confederacy and its antinorthern sentiment as a moot endeavor. Two Florida Republican governors rewarded him, with positions as notary public and justice of the peace. Titus ran as a Republican in the 1876 elections for the post of Titusville constable and suffered a landslide defeat when half of the local electors, who were overwhelmingly Democrat, abstained from voting.

Although Henry Titus is remembered as the founder of Titusville, it was Mary Titus who purchased for three hundred dollars a total of 153 ⅓ acres in Volusia County. She shrewdly invested her assets, borrowed funds with her husband during financial difficulties, and profitably liquidated their various mortgages. The colonel was able to overcome the economic catastrophe of Reconstruction and the Panic of 1873 due to his acumen in business matters, the contacts his brother-in-law James Black Hodgskin facilitated in New York, and the assistance of the Hopkins family, which had quickly recovered its wealth and influence in Jacksonville. Titus reaped in Florida the land speculation success that eluded him in Kansas due to the political troubles. His vision that the Indian River community would extend for forty-five miles as a continuous megalopolis from Titusville to Eau Gallie was probably considered hyperbole at the time. That dream became a reality after Henry Flagler expanded the Florida East Coast Railway from Jacksonville in 1885 to Key West by 1912. Fourteen years later U.S. Route 1 was completed from Miami, Florida, to Fort Kent, Maine, traversing Titusville and facilitating settlers' arrivals by automobiles in the Indian River community.

Henry Titus was not a paragon of virtue, but it is unfair to remember him as villainous based on the outpouring of abolitionist propaganda. He should not be expected to have lived up to the social standards of the twenty-first century. Titus was not endowed with any particular intellectual talent, and by his own design he was a product of his times. This included his profanity, braggadocio, duplicity, and explosive temper, which exasperated anyone who would be sympathetic. However, these were not uncommon traits for many leading men of his era. During his lifetime the colonel interacted with many renowned political and military leaders. Titus survived difficult and dangerous situations by being cunning in various unstable environments. His character was shaped by the tragedies of the accidental death of his mother and the murder of his brother; his painful experiences with the premature deaths of his first children and the crippling wounds and rheumatism that left him handicapped in his later years; his violent confrontations with his ideological opponents and a volatile relationship with his father; the humiliations of unconditional surrender to his enemies in Kansas and Nicaragua and experiencing Confederate defeat; the human and economic failings of pioneering in Kansas and silver mining in Arizona; and pursuing vindication and success through the founding and development of Titusville and his gubernatorial appointments. During the last decade of his life Titus strived to redeem his reputation. He entertained hotel guests with stories of his adventures but did not write about them as had other filibuster and Bleeding Kansas veterans who penned their memoirs. His obituary in the *Kansas City Journal* stated, "He was by no means a great character, but he was at one time a noted one, and the fact that his death at this time only recalls his memory to many who had entirely forgotten that such a man ever lived, only illustrates how quickly men and their deeds are forgotten in this fast age." The greatest legacy this controversial American left was the city that bears his surname. Titus borrowed $2,000, the equivalent of $541,000 today, to invest in a grocery and sawmill business on a hurricane-endangered frontier settlement that later would be popularly voted a county seat and grow into the city that became the tourist gateway to the Kennedy Space Center.[14]

★ NOTES ★

Abbreviations

AABD Archibald Abstract Book 1, Duval County Courthouse, Jacksonville, Fla.
AHS Arizona Historical Society, Tucson
ANCR Dirección General del Archivo Nacional, Departamento Archivo Histórico, San José, Costa Rica
ANHC Archivo Nacional, Havana, Cuba
DSJN Despatches from United States Consuls in San Juan del Norte, 1851–1906
FDMA Florida Department of Military Affairs, State Arsenal, St. Augustine, Fla.
KSHS Kansas State Historical Society, Topeka
LOC Library of Congress
LRDF Letters Received, 1866, Department and District of Florida, 1865–69, U.S. Army Continental Commands, 1821–1920
MFA Manuscripts and Folklife Archives, Western Kentucky University, Bowling Green
MLDS Miscellaneous Letters of the Department of State
NARA National Archives and Records Administration
OR Official Records of the Union and Confederate Armies
RG Record Group
RMP Returns from U.S. Military Posts, 1800–1916
SAF State Archives of Florida, Tallahassee
SDTP State Department Territorial Papers, Kansas, 1854–61
VCCT Volusia County, Clerk of the Circuit Court, Records Management Center, Deland, Fla.

Introduction

1. John Calhoun (October 14, 1806–October 13, 1859), a Boston native, was raised in New York, where he studied law. He then settled in Springfield, Illinois, in 1830 and became a schoolteacher. Two years later he served in the Black Hawk War in Capt. L. W. Goodman's company of mounted volunteers. Calhoun served in the Illinois State Legislature and was three times elected mayor of Springfield. After the defeat of the Lecompton constitution, he moved to St. Joseph, Mo., where he passed away. See Beezley, "Land-Office Spoilsmen in 'Bleeding Kansas,'" 67–78. For an excellent biography of John Quitman, see May, *John Anthony Quitman*.

2. "The Kansas War," *New York Times,* September 3, 1856, 3; Gihon, *Geary and Kansas,* 94.

3. "Obituary Notes," *New York Herald,* August 17, 1881, 5; *Portland (Maine) Daily Press,* August 26, 1881, 1, "Personal and Otherwise," *Duluth (Minn.) News-Tribune,* August 26, 1881, 2; *New Hampshire Sentinel,* September 15, 1881, 2.

4. "A Rare Southern Patriot," *Richmond Whig,* January 2, 1857, 1.

5. Mackie, "Dugald Dalgetty," 221; "Early Recollections of Minnie Titus Ensey, Youngest Daughter of Colonel Henry Theodore Titus, as Told to Her Daughter Fedora Ensey Grey" [1945], Henry Theodore Titus Collection, North Brevard Public Library, Titusville, Fla., 1, 13.

6. Patricia Cohen, "Technology Advances; Humans Supersize," *New York Times,* April 26, 2011; "How Capt. Walker's Wife Scolded Him Because He Didn't Kill 'Old Titus,'" *New York Tribune,* December 10, 1856, 7.

7. In 1882 the St. Stephen's Episcopal Church parish building was erected upon a portion of the old burying ground. The only burial records available were the twenty-five gravestones remaining, none of which belonged to the Tituses. All unclaimed remains found "were removed to a common lot in the City Cemetery, in North Wilkes-Barre." More unidentified skeletons were found when the edifice was enlarged in 1897. See "Cemetery in the Rear of St. Stephen's Church, So. Franklin Street, Wilkes-Barre, Penna.," St. Stephen's Cemetery File, Luzerne County Historical Society, Wilkes-Barre, Pa.

8. Cabrera Geserick, "Legacy of the Filibuster War," 2013.

9. Argilagos, *Próceres de la Independencia de Cuba;* Morales, *Iniciadores y primeros mártires de la revolución cubana,* 3 vols.; Portell Vilá, *Narciso López y su época,* 3 vols.; "Cuban 'Ambassadors' Attend Unveiling of Bust of National Hero," *Louisville Courier Journal,* August 13, 1955, 1B; Sheryl Edelen, "Effort Aims to Restore Shively Park Statue of Cuban Poet, Hero, José Martí," *Louisville Courier Journal,* May 26, 2010.

10. Blackmar, ed., *Kansas,* 809; Sanborn, ed., *Life and Letters of John Brown,* 312–13; Villard, *John Brown 1800–1859,* 231–34; Wilson, *John Brown,* 156–58; Karsner, *John Brown Terrible "Saint,"* 201; Warren, *John Brown,* 204–5; Abels, *Man on Fire,* 98–99, 106; Christian, *My Lost Millions,* 10.

11. The schooner *Charm,* with a ten-ton burthen and worth $950, had on board its master; four crew members; seven passengers, most of whom were fleeing the Confederate draft; and twenty-one bales of Sea Island cotton valued at $8,450. It arrived under confiscation at Key West on March 16, 1863, and was subjected to auction by the Admiralty Court. According to an e-mail on February 3, 2014, from the U.S. Coast Guard historian Bob Browning, there are no further research leads other than those cited in this book to fully identify the mysterious Captain Titus from Nassau. See U.S. War Department, Official Records of the Union and Confederate Armies (hereafter cited as OR), 1:17, 372–75; gunboat *Sagamore* and bark *Gem of the Seas,* February 23–24, 1863, Logs of U.S. Naval Ships, 1801–1915, Records of the Bureau of Naval Personnel, Record Group (hereafter cited as RG), 24, National Archives and Records Administration (hereafter cited as NARA); "Our Key West Correspondence," *New York Times,* March 25, 1863; "Blockade Runners Caught," *Washington Daily National Intelligencer,* March 26, 1863, 3; "The Key West Prize Cases," *New York Herald,* June 16, 1863, 2; U.S. vs. the Schooner Charm and cargo, Admiralty Docket, April 1861–April 1867, Admiralty Final Record Books, 1829–1911, No. 121, 143–48, Southern District of Florida, Key West Division, U.S. Circuit Courts, RG 21, NARA; Admiralty Order Books, April 1861–July 1863 and November 1863–March 1865, ibid.; Voucher No. 15, February 26, 1863, Citizens File, H. T. Titus, Box 1162, RG 109, ibid.

12. Douglas, *Florida,* 217; Manning and Hudson, *North Brevard County,* 56.

13. Elisha Higgerson Rice (1841–September 20, 1892) is called "Captain Rice" by his grandson, but the rank is dubious. His illiterate widow collected his $1.75 monthly Confederate private's pension. See Mrs. E. H. Rice, June 5, 1906, Confederate Pension Applications, 1880–1940, Alabama Department of Archives and History, Montgomery; Newman, *Stories of Early Life along Beautiful Indian River,* 52; 1860 Texas Federal Census, Victoria Co., 82; 1870 Alabama Federal Census, Township 3, Lauderdale Co., 603; 1880 Florida Federal Census, Concord, Gadsden Co., 197; 1885 Florida State Census, Titusville, 334; 1900 Florida Federal Census, Cotton Plant, Marion Co., 11.

14. Hawks, *Florida Gazetteer,* 130; Nance, ed., *East Coast of Florida,* 259; Record of Appointment of Postmasters, 1832–September 30, 1971, Volusia County, Fla., M841, Roll 21, 362, RG 28, NARA.

15. Eriksen, *Brevard County,* 62–63, 69; Titus, *Titus,* 491–94; Snyder, *Light in the Wilderness,* 203, 209, 253–55.

16. "Henry Titus: Hero or Hoax?," *Today's Sunrise,* April 8, 1973, 6–7; Dave Heath, "Henry Titus: Scurrilous Pioneer," *Today,* July 1, 1974, 1B; "Old Henry T. Was Quite a Character," *Star-Advocate,* December 20, 1978; "Henry Titus: The Revolutionary Rheumatic Who Settled Brevard County," *Florida Trend,* September 1981, 129–131; Bob Hudson, "Man for Whom Titusville Is Named Had Scandalous and Colorful Past," *Star-Advocate,* September 15, 1986, 2.

Chapter One: The Road toCuba Filibustering, 1849–1855

1. Tilton, *History of Rehoboth Massachusetts,* 23–24, 29; Titus, *Titus,* 5; Ianthe Bond Hebel, "Robert Titus – Emigrant to Massachusetts, 1635 to Henry Theodore Titus, Founder of Titusville, Florida," typed ms. in Henry Theodore Titus Collection, North Brevard Public Library, Titusville, Fla.

2. Tilton, *History of Rehoboth Massachusetts,* 27–28; Titus, *Titus,* 6.

3. Family records indicate that Henry Theodore Titus was born on February 18, 1822, while his grave marker erroneously lists the year as 1823. His siblings were Marian Ann (August 3, 1824–July 20, 1899), a spinster; Ellett Howell (1827–April 27, 1861) a bachelor; Sarah Mershon (October 15, 1826–May 14, 1864), married in 1845 to Samuel Bowman (October 31, 1818–April 19, 1889) of Wilkes-Barre, Pa., where she passed away; Julia Eliza (June 1830–January 29, 1901), married Samuel G. Miner (1816–October 1, 1847) of Wilkes Barre, Pa.; Helen Catherine (July 1836–August 29, 1902), married James Black Hodgskin (March 4, 1831–June 28, 1879) of Brooklyn; and Catharine "Carrie" Eugenia (October 1842–February 27, 1903), born in Philadelphia, first husband Col. Eugene Provost of Philadelphia, second husband Rev. Edward P. Heberton of Bridgeton, N.J. The New Jersey State Lunatic Asylum was built on the former Titus farm near Trenton. See Sons of the American Revolution Membership Applications, 1889–1970, Michael Louis Regan membership 89952, March 28, 1963, National Society of the Sons of the American Revolution, Louisville, Ky.; "Married," *Philadelphia Franklin Gazette,* June 29, 1820, 3; "Titus," *New York Tribune,* December 15, 1856, 7; "New Jersey State Lunatic Asylum," *Baltimore Sun,* November 11, 1842, 1; "New Jersey Lunatic Asylum," *New York Commercial Advertiser,* July 9, 1845, 2; "Report of the Commissioners to Build the Lunatic Asylum," *Newark Centinel of Freedom,* January 26, 1846, 4; Hebel, "Robert Titus"; "Early Recollections of Minnie Titus Ensey, Youngest Daughter of Colonel Henry Theodore Titus, as Told to Her Daughter Fedora Ensey Grey" [1945] and photocopy of genealogy page of family Bible, Henry Theodore Titus Collection, North Brevard Public Library, Titusville, Fla.; "Henry Theodore Titus: Famous or Infamous," ibid.

4. Montour Falls was called Catharines Town when its post office was established on October 13, 1802. The name was changed to Havana on June 9, 1828. Its current name was adopted in 1890. Amasa Dana (October 19, 1792–December 24, 1867) was born in Wilkes-Barre, Pa., and was elected to the New York State Assembly in 1828–29. He served as a Democrat in the U.S. Congress in 1839–41 and 1843–45. David Ayers (August 10, 1793–October 25, 1881), a War of 1812 veteran, was a merchant in Ithaca, N.Y., who moved to San Patricio, Tex., with his family in May 1834, taking a cargo of Bibles to settlers on behalf of the American Bible Society. He settled in Galveston in 1847, becoming a successful business, civic, and religious leader. See Morrison, *Early History,* 5, 21, 38, 90, 94; Whitford, *History of the Canal System,* 607–19; Emerson, *Link in the Great Chain,* 20–22, 25, 32; *History of Tioga, Chemung, Tompkins, and Schuyler Counties, New York,* 32, 645, 657; *Havana Observer,* April 1, 1830.

5. Harmon Pumpelly (August 1, 1795–September 28, 1882), born in Salisbury, Conn., and an early inhabitant of Owego, Tioga Co., also owned large tracts of land in Havana but never resided there. He made a fortune in land, lumber, and cattle before moving to Albany in 1841 and leaving an estate worth a million dollars. The lots purchased by Titus in Havana were 38,

40, 44, 50, 53, 67, 68, 69 and 76. See "Death of an Albany Millionaire," *Troy (N.Y.) Times,* October 5, 1882, 3; Morrison, *Early History,* 21, 34, 43, 51; Indenture, April 30, 1830, Deeds 2, 253–54, Chemung Schuyler County Records, vol. 1, Roll 95, Schuyler County Clerks' Office, Watkins Glen, N.Y.; Indenture, May, 1, 1830, Deeds 2, 271–72, ibid.; 1830 New York Federal Census, Tioga Co., Catharine, 198; Emerson, *Link in the Great Chain,* ix, 29; *Cooperstown (N.Y.) Watch-Tower,* July 26, 1830, 3.

6. Jonathan Paul Couch (August 7, 1792–July 25, 1853) was a member of the New York State Assembly from Chemung County in 1839. He was promoted to major general and commander of the Seventh Division of the N.Y. State Militia. Couch was also a Freemason, a ruling elder and deacon of the Presbyterian Church, and president of the village of Havana in 1847. See *Albany (N.Y.) Evening Journal,* August 9, 1853, 2; "Men of Note in Kansas: Col. Titus," *Ripley (Ohio) Bee,* February 7, 1857; Emerson, *Link in the Great Chain,* 25–26, 36–37; Indenture, November 9, 1830, Deeds 2, 288–89, Schuyler County Clerks' Office, Watkins Glen, N.Y.; Indenture, March 4, 1831, Deeds 3, 333–34, ibid.; Morrison, *Early History,* 27, 73; New York State Census 1855, 126, New York State Archives, Albany.

7. James Talcott Gifford (January 1, 1800–August 10, 1850) removed to Illinois in 1835 and helped establish what would become the city of Elgin. He temporarily left there to found the hamlet of Port Ulao, Wis., in 1847 and returned to Elgin a year before he died of cholera. Ransom B. Rathbone (April 10, 1780–July 17, 1861), a War of 1812 veteran, state militia general, and slave owner, in 1842 settled as an entrepreneur in what later became the town of Rathbone, N.Y. See *History of Tioga, Chemung, Tompkins, and Schuyler Counties, New York,* 325, 357; Indenture, March 8, 1832, Tioga Deeds, Chemung Co., vol. 9, 496–97, Chemung County Clerk's Office, Elmira, N.Y.; Emerson, *Link in the Great Chain,* 33–34, 39, 45; Morrison, *Early History,* 90, 94, 319; "List of Letters Remaining in the Post Office," *Morning Courier and New-York Enquirer,* August 20, 1832, 1; "Notice," *Geneva (N.Y.) Courier,* September 5, 1832, 3; Indenture, February 22, 1833, Deeds 2, 484–85, Schuyler County Clerks' Office, Watkins Glen, N.Y.; "List of Letters," *New York Evening Post,* September, 3. 1833, 1; Indenture, September 9, 1833, Tioga Deeds, Chemung Co., vol. 10, 164, Chemung County Clerk's Office, Elmira, N.Y.

8. "Rail-Road Convention," *Geneva (N.Y.) Gazette,* December 31, 1834, 2; "Men of Note in Kansas: Col. Titus," *Ripley (Ohio) Bee,* February 7, 1857; Indenture, November 22, 1837, Deeds 4, 115, Schuyler County Clerks' Office, Watkins Glen, N.Y.; Morrison, *Early History,* 45.

9. Miscellaneous Book A, Steuben Co., 292–94, Steuben County Clerk's Office, Bath, N.Y.; "To Exonerate from Imprisonment," *Albany Argus,* December 22, 1837, 3; "List of Letters Remaining in the New-York Post Office," *New York Evening Post,* April 28, 1838, 1.

10. "Opening of the Lehigh and Susquehanna Rail Road," *Philadelphia North American,* August 17, 1840, 2; 1840 Pennsylvania Federal Census, Luzerne Co., Wilkes-Barre, 132; "Titus," *New York Tribune,* December 15, 1856, 7.

11. The Ashley Planes, south of Route 81 and west of Route 309 along Solomon Creek, were closed on July 1948 and added to the National Register of Historic Places in 1980. Today they are part of the Delaware and Lehigh National Heritage Corridor of the U.S. National Park Service. See "National Register of Historic Places Inventory: Ashley Planes," Ashley Planes File, Luzerne County Historical Society, Wilkes-Barre, Pa.; "Fatal Accident," *New York Spectator,* July 15, 1843, 3; "Dreadful Railroad Accident," *Charleston (S.C.) Southern Patriot,* July 17, 1843, 2; "A Frightful Accident," *Washington Daily National Intelligencer,* July 17, 1843, 3; *Philadelphia North American,* July 27, 1843, 2; "Railroad Accident," *Boston Liberator,* July 28, 1843, 120; Mrs. Theodore Titus, July 8, 1843, Old Ground, in Hayden, ed., "Parish Register of St. Stephen's Protestant Episcopal Church," 200.

12. "Men of Note in Kansas: Col. Titus," *Ripley (Ohio) Bee,* February 7, 1857; U.S. Department of State, *Register of All Officers and Agents,* 432; "List of Letters Remaining in the Phil-

adelphia Post Office," *Philadelphia Public Ledger,* October 27, 1847, 4; Hardy, *History and Adventures,* 22; "Further Particulars Relative to the Loss of the Germantown," *Sandusky (Ohio) Register,* September 29, 1849, 2; 1850 New York Federal Census, New York City, Ward 9, 3rd District, 431.

13. Presidencia de la Comisión Militar Ejecutiva Permanente, October 28, 1849, Gobierno Militar de Cuba, Expediente 1748, Archivo General Militar de Segovia, Spain; de la Cova, *Cuban Confederate Colonel,* 8–11, 30; de la Cova, "Taylor Administration versus Mississippi Sovereignty," 296–97; de la Cova, "Kentucky Regiment," 572.

14. de la Cova, "Filibusters and Freemasons," 95; de la Cova, "Kentucky Regiment," 579; de la Cova, "Taylor Administration versus Mississippi Sovereignty," 295.

15. "Arrivals at the Hotels," *Washington Republic,* November 22, 27, 1849, 3; de la Cova, *Cuban Confederate Colonel,* 16, 28, 30; "Early Recollections of Minnie Titus Ensey," Henry Theodore Titus Collection, North Brevard Public Library, Titusville, Fla., 1.

16. Theodore O'Hara (February 11, 1820–June 6, 1867), an inveterate bachelor born in Danville, Ky., was the son of Kane O'Hara, an Irish political exile and educator. After the Cárdenas expedition, he was one of the six editors of the *Louisville Times* and got involved in the John Quitman filibuster conspiracy to invade Cuba that was disbanded in 1855. O'Hara was then appointed captain in the U.S. Army's Second Cavalry but resigned on December 1, 1856. He afterward edited the *Mobile Register* until the Civil War, when he was appointed Confederate colonel of the Twelfth Alabama Regiment. O'Hara later served on the staffs of Maj. Gens. Albert Sydney Johnston and John C. Breckenridge until August 1863. After the cessation of hostilities, he engaged in the cotton business in Columbus, Ga. He died of bilious fever at a friend's plantation near Gerrytown, Ala. In 1874 O'Hara's remains were transferred to the state cemetery at Frankfort, Ky. and buried beside Thomas Theodore Hawkins, amid the graves of the Mexican War casualties for whom he had written the poem "The Bivouac of the Dead." See Morton, "Theodore O'Hara," 49; Johnston, "Sketch of Theodore O'Hara," 67; Hardy, *History and Adventures,* 20–21; Hughes and Ware, *Theodore O'Hara,* 22, 25, 29, 33. John Thomas Pickett (October 9, 1823–October 18, 1884) was born near Maysville, Ky. His great-grandfather William S. Pickett was a Virginia planter and a captain in the American Revolution. His grandfather Gen. Joseph Desha (1768–1842) was a veteran of the Indian War of 1794 and the War of 1812, served as U.S. representative during 1807–19, and was governor of Kentucky during 1824–28. His father, John Chamberlayne Pickett (1793–1872), was an army artillery captain in the War of 1812, a lawyer, and editor of the *Congressional Globe,* and he served as an American diplomat in South America during 1829–33 and 1838–45. After the Cuba invasion, Pickett resided with his uncle Dr. John R. Desha and his family in Lexington, Ky. He later settled in Newport, Ky., and in 1853 was appointed U.S. consul to Veracruz, Mexico. Pickett married Catherine "Kate" Keyworth (1836–88) of Washington, D.C., on October 18, 1853. She was the daughter of Maj. Robert Keyworth, a War of 1812 veteran, Masonic grand master of the District of Columbia, and a clock and watch maker and jeweler. They had four children, only two of whom survived to adulthood. Pickett resigned his post after Abraham Lincoln's election and in May 1861 was assigned as Confederate commissioner to Mexico. A year later Pickett was appointed colonel and chief of staff of Gen. John C. Breckenridge, and he retired in 1863 due to poor health. In 1864 he lost the election to represent the Confederate Eighth Congressional District of Northern Kentucky. After the war, Pickett practiced law in Washington, D.C., and resided with his family at 2142 Pennsylvania Ave., N.W. He was afflicted with paralysis in 1878 and died of apoplexy six years later. See Quisenberry, *Lopez's Expeditions to Cuba,* 37–40, 44; Hardy, *History and Adventures,* 21; "Suspicious Military Enterprises," *New Orleans Commercial Bulletin,* September 8, 1849, 2; "The Cuban Expedition," *Daily National Intelligencer,* January 16, 1850, 3; 1850 Kentucky Federal Census, Fayette Co.,

189; Paxton, *Marshall Family,* 56; "To the Army and the People of Kentucky," John Hunt Morgan Papers, Southern Historical Collection, University of North Carolina, Chapel Hill; de la Cova, "Kentucky Regiment," 579.

17. Quisenberry, *Lopez's Expeditions to Cuba,* 121; Hardy, *History and Adventures,* 19.

18. John A. Quitman had been the first president of the Aztec Club, which included his Mexican War brigade quartermaster Theodore O'Hara. He was Masonic grand sovereign of South West, grand inspector general of the 33rd Degree of the Southern Division of the United States, for the State of Mississippi, and a founder of the Supreme Council. Quitman had been elected grand master of the Grand Lodge of Mississippi during 1826–38, 1840, and 1845–46. See May, *John Anthony Quitman,* 197–99; Ambrosio José Gonzales, "On to Cuba," *New Orleans Times Democrat,* March 30, 1884, 9; *New Orleans Crescent,* January 13, 1851, 2; *New Orleans Delta,* January 3, 1851, 3, and January 14, 1851, 2; Denslow, 10,000 *Famous Freemasons,* 4:3; Pike, "John Anthony Quitman," x–xvi, 626; U.S. vs. Narciso Lopez et al., U.S. District Court, Eastern District of Louisiana, New Orleans Circuit Court, General Case Files (E-121), Case 1965, "Enrollment No. 183," RG 21, NARA.

19. McDonough J. Bunch (1824–November 2, 1857) was appointed on August 18, 1846, as assistant commissary, with the rank of captain, in the Commissary Department of the U.S. Army. He was discharged on June 30, 1847, and then served as major of the Fourth Regiment Tennessee Volunteers until August 1848. After the Cárdenas invasion, Bunch engaged in a duel with *Creole* captain Armstrong I. Lewis, with pistols at ten paces, near the Louisiana race track in New Orleans on July 23, 1850. Lewis was shot through the fleshy part of both thighs, and Bunch was unhurt. Bunch then practiced law in Aberdeen, Miss., where he was a Democrat Party activist. He was elected secretary of the Mississippi State Senate in January 1854. Four months later, while gambling at cards with the forty-six-year-old Irishman Michael Fannin, a veteran of the Army of the Republic of Texas, 1838–40, from Austin, Bunch lost a large sum of money, his horse and buggy, and a slave servant. When Fannin went to collect the next day, Bunch killed him with shotgun blasts to the face and abdomen. It was called "one of the most cold blooded murders ever committed in the annals of Mississippi." Bunch was arrested and held to bail for "$1,000 cash for himself and two securities," but the outcome of the trial was not reported before his death three years later. Chatham Roberdeau Wheat (April 9, 1826–June 27, 1862) in 1852 joined José M. Carbajal in the separatist insurrection to create the Republic of Sierra Madre in northern Mexico and was twice wounded during skirmishes. Two years later, during the Mexican Revolution of Ayutla against Antonio López de Santa Ana, the rebel leader Juan Alvarez invited Wheat to command his artillery with the rank of brigadier general. Wheat was appointed military governor of Veracruz and was in command when the San Juan de Ulloa fortress was taken from insurgents. He resigned the Mexican service in August 1856 to join William Walker in Nicaragua. After Walker's defeat, Wheat returned to New Orleans in June 1857 to practice law. Wheat joined Giuseppe Garibaldi's revolutionary forces in Italy in October 1860 but returned to New York in February 1861. At the outbreak of the Civil War, he organized in New Orleans the First Louisiana Special Battalion, called the "Louisiana Tigers," some five hundred mostly Irish and German riffraff. Wheat and his unit fought at First Manassas, where he was shot through both lungs; in Jackson's Valley Campaign; and in the Peninsula Campaign, where he was mortally wounded by a rifle bullet to the head at the Battle of Gaines' Mill. He is interred in Hollywood Cemetery, Richmond. See "The House Organized," *Washington Daily Union,* October 16, 1845, 2; "Tennessee," *Washington Daily Union,* October 29, 1848, 3; 1850 Mississippi Federal Census, Hinds Co., 223; John H. Goddard to Thomas Ewing, June 17, 1850, Records Concerning the Cuban Expedition 1850–51, Box 145, Entry 142, Office of the Secretary of the Interior, RG 48, NARA; "Mississippi Legislature," *Mississippi Free Trader* (Natchez), January 10, 1854, 2; "Mike Fannin Killed," *Texas State Gazette* (Austin), June 10, 1854, 303; "Michael Fannin Killed," *San Antonio*

Ledger and Texan, June 15, 1854, 2; *Baton Rouge Daily Advocate,* June 7, 1854, 2; *Baltimore Sun,* November 17, 1857, 1; Biographical sketch of Chatham Roberdeau Wheat by his father John Thomas Wheat, John Thomas Wheat Papers, Southern Historical Collection, University of North Carolina, Chapel Hill; Dufour, *Gentle Tiger,* 37; Robarts, *Complete Roster of the Regular and Volunteer Troops,* 73; "Appointments by the President," *Boston Daily Atlas,* December 26, 1846; "Official," *Daily National Intelligencer,* August 11, 1847; "A Card," *Mississippian* (Jackson), August 9 and September 6, 1850; "Gen. Wheat," *Alexandria Gazette,* July 4, 1857, 2.

20. *Louisville Courier,* April 6, 1850, 2, 3; "Markets and Marine," *New Orleans* New Orleans *Evening Picayune,* April 11, 1850, 1; "Arrivals at the Principal Hotels," New Orleans Evening *Picayune,* April 12, 1850, 2.

21. The four Cuban expeditionaries were the merchant Juan Manuel Macías Sardina (1826–92); the planter José Sánchez Iznaga (1811–87); the journalist and educator Francisco Javier de la Cruz Rivero (1804–94); and José Manuel Hernández Canalejos (1826–56), who later joined the Cuban contingent of William Walker's filibusters in Nicaragua, where he accidentally died. See "Arrivals at the Principal Hotels," New Orleans *Picayune,* April 12, 1850, 2; "Arrived," *Picayune,* April 12, 1850, 1; *Daily National Intelligencer,* April 12, 1850, 4; de la Cova, *Cuban Confederate Colonel,* 37–39; U.S. Senate, *Message of the President of the United States, Transmitting Reports of the Several Heads of Department Relative to the Subject of the Resolution of the Senate of the 23d May, as to Alleged Revolutionary Movements in Cuba,* Exec. Doc. 57, 31st Congress, 1st session, June 19, 1850, 23–24.

22. John "Jack" Allen (October 25, 1811–November 5, 1871). After the failure of the López expeditions of 1849–51, Allen was indicted in the United States for being a leader of the José Carbajal filibuster movement against Mexico. He afterward "organized fifteen hundred Kentuckians, eager to avenge the death of Crittenden, Logan, and other brave men" who perished in Cuba. The plot was headed by Gen. John A. Quitman, but its followers were disbanded in 1855 after their conspirators on the island were arrested and executed. On May 21, 1856, Allen left Louisville with some 150 Kentucky volunteers for William Walker's filibuster army in Nicaragua. When he arrived in Granada on June 29 with 104 men, Walker appointed him colonel of the Second Battalion of Rifles, replacing Hungarian Louis Schlessinger, a former Cuba filibusterer. Allen returned to Louisville on August 16 on furlough, going back to Nicaragua on October 6 with some 100 more recruits. A week later Allen and his force, wielding a howitzer, fought at the battles of Masaya and Granada, repulsing a body of lancers at the latter. Allen returned to the United States soon after and on December 30, 1856, was married by a Baptist minister to twenty-five-year-old Ruth M. Thomas at her father's home in Taylorsville, Ky. He went back to farming in Shelby County, where his daughter Mildred was born two years later. In December 1857 Allen, his brother Joseph, and five other men were acquitted in a Louisville court of the murder the previous year of Paschal D. Craddock, a counterfeiter and horse thief. John Allen appears as captain on the rolls of Company B, Second Kentucky Cavalry Regiment, of the Confederate army, organized in October 1861 under Capt. John Hunt Morgan. He was promoted on June 1, 1862, to lieutenant colonel of the First Kentucky Cavalry Regiment. After the Civil War, Allen returned to his farm, which he sold in 1870, and then moved with his family to Louisville. He died while on a visit to Sulphur Springs, Tex. The Allen farm, located today at 2581 Fisherville Road, Finchville, Ky., still has the family cemetery with nine grave markers, including those of six children. See Will of John Allen, June 25, 1835, Will Book 11, 176–77, Marriage Book 5-B 1838–43, No. 1046, and Deed Book B3, 535–36, all in Shelby County Courthouse, Shelbyville, Ky.; 1850 Kentucky Federal Census, District 2, Shelby Co., 387; *Louisville Journal,* September 20, 1851, 3; *Florida Republican* (Jacksonville), November 3, 1854, 2; May, *Manifest Destiny's Underworld,* 282; *Daily National Intelligencer,* August 6, 1853; William C. Smeades to unidentified recipient, January 10, 1857, and Jack Allen to Thomas Marshall, February 24, 1857, Marshall Family Papers, Filson Historical Society,

Louisville, Ky.; *Columbus (Ga.) Enquirer,* May 29, 1856, 2; Walker, *War in Nicaragua,* 230, 290; *El Nicaraguense,* July 12, 1856, 2, October 11, 1856, 3, October 18, 1856, 3, 6, November 1, 1856, 1; John Allen, Certificate No. 1061, Mexican War Service Case Files, Records of the Department of Veterans Affairs, RG 15, NARA; *New Albany (Ind.) Daily Ledger,* December 5, 1857, 2; 1860 Kentucky Federal Census, Shelby Co., 159; *Report of the Adjutant General of the State of Kentucky, Confederate Kentucky Volunteers, War,* 1861–65, 1:486, 548–49, 594; 1870 Kentucky Federal Census, Louisville Sixth Ward, 84; "An Old Filibuster," *Trenton Daily State Gazette,* November 13, 1871, 1; "Report of Col. O'Hara, Kentucky Reg't.," New Orleans *Evening Picayune,* June 28, 1850, 1; Hardy, *History and Adventures,* 16, 18–19; "Col. M. C. Taylor's Diary," 81; "Cuban Expedition," *Cincinnati Nonpareil,* June 17, 1850, 2; U.S. House of Representatives, *Barque Georgiana and Brig Susan Loud,* March 23, 1852, 32nd Congress, 1st Session, Ex. Doc. 83 (Washington, D.C.: United States Government Printing Office, 1852), 96, 116; "United States Circuit Court," *Delta,* January 14, 1851, 2; "U.S. Circuit Court," *Crescent,* January 11, 1851, 2.

23. "The Cuba Expedition," New Orleans *Evening Picayune,* May 23, 1850, 1; Thomas R. Wolfe to John Thomas Wheat, May 9, 1850, John Thomas Wheat Papers, Southern Historical Collection, University of North Carolina, Chapel Hill.

24. O.D.D.O., *History of the Late Expedition to Cuba,* 19, 31, 44–45; Hardy, *History and Adventures,* 32, 35, 53, 56, 83; Gonzales, "On to Cuba"; "Col. M. C. Taylor's Diary," 84–85; Hellberg, *Historia Estadística de Cárdenas,* 62; "Official Reports of the Expedition to Cuba," New Orleans *Evening Picayune,* June 28, 1850, 1.

25. The U.S. Model 1841 Harpers Ferry (Yager) Rifle was the first issued percussion cap rifled-barrel musket. It got its sobriquet as a result of its excellent performance in the hands of Jefferson Davis's Mississippi Regiment at the battle of Buena Vista. See O.D.D.O., *History of the Late Expedition to Cuba,* 26, 50, 64; Hardy, *History and Adventures,* 34; Gonzales, "On to Cuba"; "Col. M. C. Taylor's Diary," 85; Boggess, *Veteran of Four Wars,* 10–11; Steamer *Creole,* June 19, 1850, Admiralty Final Record Books, 1829–11, no. 4, 443–50, Southern District of Florida, Key West Division, U.S. Circuit Courts, RG 21, NARA.

26. Theodore O'Hara penned "Primus in Cuba" on the battle flag carried by the Kentucky Regiment at Cárdenas after returning to America. The banner was safeguarded by the expeditionary Juan Manuel Macías, who draped it over the casket of Francisco Vicente Aguilera at his funeral at City Hall in New York City on February 26, 1877. Aguilera's family gave the flag to Gen. Mario García Menocal, who later passed it on to Gen. Manuel Sanguily. The flag became a permanent fixture in the Cuban Chamber of Representatives in the late 1940s. See "Report of Col. O'Hara"; "Report of Lieut. Col. Pickett, Ky. Reg't.," New Orleans *Evening Picayune,* June 28, 1850, 1; "The Late Piratical Assault on Cuba," *Daily National Intelligencer,* May 29, 1850, 3; "Primera página de la historia de la revolución de Cuba," *La Verdad,* July 7, 1850, 1; John H. Goddard to Alexander H. H. Stuart, December 12, 1850, Records Concerning the Cuban Expedition 1850-51, Box 145, Entry 142, Office of the Secretary of the Interior, RG 48, NARA. Sumario, May 22, 1850, Legajo 43, no. 52, Archivo Nacional, Havana, Cuba, hereafter cited as ANHC; Hellberg, *Historia Estadística de Cárdenas,* 63; O.D.D.O., *History of the Late Expedition to Cuba,* 65–66, 68; Hardy, *History and Adventures,* 7, 39; "Col. M. C. Taylor's Diary," 85; Portell Vilá, *Narciso López,* 2:137–38, 308–10; Gonzales, "On to Cuba."

27. Hardy, *History and Adventures,* 39–40, 75–78; O.D.D.O., *History of the Late Expedition to Cuba,* 66–67; "Report of Col. O'Hara"; Portell Vilá, *Narciso López,* 2:308–10; Portell Vilá, *Historia de Cárdenas,* 90; Boggess, *Veteran of Four Wars,* 14; "From Cardenas," New Orleans *Evening Picayune,* June 8, 1850, 1; "The Late Piratical Assault on Cuba," 3; "Cuban Expedition," *Cincinnati Nonpareil,* June 17, 1850, 2; Ahumada, *Memoria Histórico Política,* 272; Gonzales, "On to Cuba"; "The Attack on Cardenas," *Missouri Republican* (St. Louis), June 23, 1850, 2.

28. Boggess, *Veteran of Four Wars,* 15, 17; O.D.D.O., *History of the Late Expedition to Cuba,* 68, 70–71; "Report of Major Hawkins, Kentucky Reg't.," New Orleans *Evening Picayune,* June

28, 1850, 1; "Report of Lieut. Col. Bell," ibid.; "Primera página de la historia de la revolución de Cuba," *La Verdad,* July 7, 1850, 1; Hardy, *History and Adventures,* 44–45, 77; "The Attack on Cardenas," 2; "Col. M. C. Taylor's Diary," 85; Portell Vilá, *Narciso López,* 2:314–15; Sumario, May 22, 1850, Legajo 43, no. 52, ANHC.

29. Consul Robert Campbell wrote that the money seized from the customhouse was twenty-four hundred dollars and that about sixteen hundred dollars was taken from the city hall. See Robert Campbell to John Clayton, May 22, 1850, Despatches from United States Consuls in Havana, RG 59, NARA; Zaragoza, *Las Insurrecciones en Cuba,* 1:596; "Recortes de periódicos de Cuba sobre los sucesos de Cárdenas," *Boletín del Archivo Nacional de Cuba,* July–December 1920, 194; New Orleans *Evening Picayune,* June 8 and 28, 1850, 1; *Daily National Intelligencer,* May 29, 1850, 1; *New York Tribune,* May 30, 1850, 6; New Orleans *Picayune,* May 26, 1850, 1; *La Verdad,* September 25, 1850, 2; Portell Vilá, *Narciso López,* 2:317, 371, 374; Hellberg, *Historia Estadística de Cárdenas,* 64–65; W. Grayson to John Clayton, May 25, 1850, Miscellaneous Letters of the Department of State, RG 59, NARA, hereafter cited as MLDS; "Reseña oficial de lo ocurrido en Cárdenas," 155; Sumario, May 22, 1850, Legajo 43, no. 52, ANHC; O.D.D.O., *History of the Late Expedition to Cuba,* 70–71; Hardy, *History and Adventures,* 44.

30. Hardy, *History and Adventures,* 41–42; "Recortes de periódicos de Cuba sobre los sucesos de Cárdenas," 194; "Reseña oficial de lo ocurrido en Cárdenas," 153; Portell Vilá, *Narciso López,* 2:312, 317, 324–28, 342–47; Boggess, *Veteran of Four Wars,* 16–17; *La Verdad,* September 25, 1850, 2; Hellberg, *Historia Estadística de Cárdenas* , 48–49, 65; Zaragoza, *Las Insurrecciones en Cuba,* 1:596; New Orleans *Evening Picayune,* June 8, 1850, 1.

31. O.D.D.O., *History of the Late Expedition to Cuba,* 72–73; Hardy, *History and Adventures,* 42; *Mississippian,* September 6, 1850, 3; *Daily National Intelligencer,* May 29, 1850, 3; "Recortes de periódicos de Cuba sobre los sucesos de Cárdenas," 195; Boggess, *Veteran of Four Wars,* 17–18; *Cincinnati Nonpareil,* June 17, 1850, 2; Portell Vilá, *Historia de Cárdenas,* 111, 113; Portell Vilá, *Narciso López,* 2:349; New Orleans *Evening Picayune,* June 8, 1850, 1; Robert Campbell to John Clayton, May 22, 1850, Despatches from United States Consuls in Havana, RG 59, NARA.

32. New Orleans *Evening Picayune,* June 8, 1850, 1; Hardy, *History and Adventures,* 42–43; Zaragoza, *Las Insurrecciones en Cuba,* 1:597; Portell Vilá, *Narciso López,* 2:353–56.

33. De la Cova, "Kentucky Regiment," 609–11; de la Cova, *Cuban Confederate Colonel,* 64; *New Hampshire Sentinel,* September 15, 1881, S2; New Orleans *Evening Picayune,* May 31 and June 8, 1850, 1; Hardy, *History and Adventures,* 78; Boggess, *Veteran of Four Wars,* 19.

34. Hardy, *History and Adventures,* 31, 46–47, 57, 59; O.D.D.O., *History of the Late Expedition to Cuba,* 77–80; Sumario, May 22, 1850, Legajo 43, no. 52, ANHC; "Report of Lieut. Col. Pickett"; "The Late Piratical Assault on Cuba," 3; "Statement of the Kentucky Regiment," *Florida Sentinel* (Tallahassee), June 11, 1850, 2; "Col. M. C. Taylor's Diary," 86; "The Attack on Cardenas," 2; Quisenberry, *Lopez's Expeditions to Cuba,* 62; John H. Goddard to Thomas Ewing, June 17, 1850, Records Concerning the Cuban Expedition 1850–51, Box 145, Entry 142, Office of the Secretary of the Interior, RG 48, NARA.

35. Those indicted in New Orleans with Narciso López were Ambrosio José Gonzales, Theodore O'Hara, Chatham Roberdeau Wheat, Thomas Theodore Hawkins, John T. Pickett, McDonough J. Bunch, William H. Bell, and Peter Smith and the supporters John A. Quitman, John L. O'Sullivan, Laurent Sigur, Jean Baptiste Donatien Augustin, Judge Cotesworth Pinckney Smith, John Henderson, and J. A. Hayden. See Theodore O'Hara to William Nelson, March 18, 1854, John A. Quitman Papers, Mississippi Department of Archives and History, Jackson; Theodore O'Hara to Quitman, December 17, 1854, ibid.; Hardy, *History and Adventures,* 57, 72.

36. During the Civil War federal occupation of Jacksonville in 1864, the Union army dismantled Holme's Mill on the Nassau River and transferred it to "the former site of Empire

Mills," which had been burned, to "turn out from 40,000 to 50,000 feet of lumber daily." See OR 1:35, pt. 1, 410; "Passengers," *Savannah Morning News,* July 19, 1850, 3; *Georgian* (Savannah), July 22, 1850, 2; *Savannah Morning News,* July 22, 1850, 2; "Arrivals at the Jacksonville Hotel," *Florida Republican,* July 25, 1850, 3; 1850 Georgia Federal Census, Richmond Co., 900; "Dissolution and Formation of Copartnership," *Florida News* (Jacksonville), April 19, 1851, 4; "Milling," *Florida Republican,* April 24, 1851, 2; T. Davis, *History of Jacksonville,* 95.

37. 1850 Pennsylvania Federal Census, Luzerne Co., Wilkes Barre, 887; "Arrivals at the Hotels," *Republic* (Washington, D.C.), September 3, 1850, 3; "The Pampero Trial," *Florida Republican,* November 20, 1851, 1.

38. Samuel Buffington (June 7, 1815–June 2, 1866), born in Milledgeville, Ga., was a representative from Duval County in the Florida legislature in 1856 and three years later moved to St. Augustine after his hotel burned down. He established the Magnolia House in St. Augustine, where he was arrested on March 29, 1862, under suspicion of being disloyal to the Union. Buffington received a Masonic interment in the Old Jacksonville City Cemetery. See "Arrivals at Jacksonville Hotel," *Florida News,* September 14, 1850, 3; 1850 Florida Census, Duval Co., 92; 1850 Florida Slave Schedules, Duval Co., 79; "Jacksonville Hotel," *Florida Republican,* June 5, 1851, 4; *Proceedings of the Grand Lodge of the Most Ancient and Honorable Fraternity of Free and Accepted Masons, of the State of Florida,* 1859, 855; "Death of a Distinguished Floridian," *Columbus (Ga.) Daily Sun,* July 13, 1866, 2; "Dissolution and Formation of Copartnership," *Florida News,* March 1, 1851, 4; "Milling," *Florida Republican,* April 24, 1851, 2; Martin, "River and Forest," 22.

39. "Arrivals at the Jacksonville Hotel," *Florida Republican,* October 3, 1850, 3; 1850 Florida Federal Census, Duval Co.; 1850 Florida Agriculture Census, Duval Co., 59; 1850 Florida Slave Schedules, Duval Co., 101; 1850 Georgia Federal Census, Richmond Co., 499.

40. "Arrivals at the Jacksonville Hotel," *Florida Republican,* October 31, November 28, 1850, 3; "The Pampero Trial," *Florida Republican,* November 20, 1851, 1; 1850 Florida Federal Census, Duval Co., 184, 252, Leon Co., 106, and Putnam Co., 39; 1850 Georgia Federal Census, Camden Co., 386; Gonzales, "Cuban Crusade," 9; 1860 Florida Census, Hamilton Co., 577; 1850 Florida Slave Schedules, Duval Co., 83; *Florida News,* August 7, 1850, 1.

41. "U.S. Circuit Court," New Orleans *Evening Picayune,* December 17, 1850, 2; de la Cova, *Cuban Confederate Colonel,* 77, 80; Office No. 1403, Book H, 336, December 17, 1850, Office No. 1434, Book H, 404, and Office No. 1529, Book I, March 4, 1851, Archibald Abstract Book 1, Duval County Courthouse, Jacksonville, Fla., hereafter cited as AABD; "Arrivals at the Jacksonville Hotel," *Florida Republican,* January 30, 1851, 3; de la Cova, *Cuban Confederate Colonel,* 76; "Executor's Sale," *Charleston Courier,* November 25, 1851, 3; 1850 Georgia Federal Census, Chatham Co., 658; 1850 Georgia Slave Schedules, District No. 13, Chatham Co.

42. "The Cuban Prosecutions Abandoned," New Orleans *Evening Picayune,* March 7, 1851, 1; Logan Hunton to Daniel Webster, March 7, 1851, in Manning, *Diplomatic Correspondence,* 11:101; "The Late Cuba State Trials," *Democratic Review,* April 1852, 307; "Cuba: Rumored Outbreak," *New Orleans Delta,* March 29, 1851, 1; "Another Cuban Expedition," *Rome (Ga.) Courier,* April 10, 1851, 2; J. Reneau to President of the U. States, April 10, 1851, MLDS; Hamilton Fish to Millard Fillmore, April 26, 1851, ibid.; Angel Calderón de la Barca to Captain General, April 15, 1851, Legajo 217, No. 17, ANHC; de la Cova, *Cuban Confederate Colonel,* 86; "The President's Message," *Florida News,* May 3, 1851, 2; "Proclamation by the President of the United States," *Florida Republican,* May 8, 1851, 2.

43. Kingsley Beatty Gibbs (July 25, 1810–October 15, 1859) was born in Brooklyn Heights, N.Y. He married Ana Eduarda Teresa Hernández on February 7, 1833, and she died three years later. Gibbs later wed Laura Williams and purchased the Fort George Island plantation in 1839 from his uncle Zephaniah Kingsley, selling it in 1852. Solomon Freelig Halliday (December 25, 1811–1888) was born in Schraalenburgh, N.J.; graduated from Union College in Schenectady,

N.Y., in 1825; and for the next three years attended Princeton Theological Seminary. He was ordained as a minister in 1833 and was pastor of the Presbyterian church in Huntington, Long Island, until April 1836, when he went to preach in Philadelphia. Halliday was sent as a missionary to Jacksonville, where he wed Mary J. Fleming on July 6, 1840, purchased a middle-aged female slave, and acquired 160 acres at Lake Weir. In 1849 they settled in Newnansville, Fla., where he was a Whig appointee as receiver of public moneys at the land office and served as postmaster from November 1851 to November 1852. Halliday enlisted in Company A, Florida Tenth Infantry Regiment on September 3, 1861, at Starke and was mustered out on May 11, 1862, at Rico Bluff. He afterward endorsed the Union occupation of Jacksonville, became a Republican, and was a machinist and part owner of a steam mill in Jacksonville during 1866–67. Halliday then settled in Gainesville as a preacher, land agent, and attorney until his demise. See *Biographical Souvenir of the States of Georgia and Florida*, 359; "From a Correspondent," *New York Spectator*, August 1, 1825; Prime, *History of Long Island*, 257; 1840 Florida Federal Census, Duval Co., 145; Peter G. Washington and Columbus Alexander, eds., *The United States Postal Guide and Official Advertiser* 1, no. 4 (October 1850): 102; Record of Appointment of Postmasters, 1832–September 30, 1971, RG 28, M841, Roll 17, 114, NARA; compiled service records of Confederate soldiers who served in organizations from the State of Florida, M-251, Roll 4, RG 109, NARA; R. G. Dun & Company Credit Report Volumes, Florida, vol. 2, Duval Co., 54, Baker Library, Harvard University, Boston, Mass.; U.S. House of Representatives, *Finley vs. Bisbee*, 378–79; *Webb's Jacksonville and Consolidated Directory*, 1886, 404; "Arrivals at the Jacksonville Hotel," *Florida Republican*, May 1, 1851, 3; 1860 Florida Census, Duval Co., 260; Holland, Manley, and Towart, *Maple Leaf*, 26; 1850 Florida Federal Census, Duval Co., 92, 230; 1850 Florida Slave Schedules, Duval Co., 125; Florida Department of Military Affairs, Special Archives Publication Number 67, Florida Militia Muster Rolls, Seminole Indian Wars, (Vol. 1), State Arsenal, St. Francis Barracks, St. Augustine, Florida, hereafter cited as FDMA; *Charleston Courier*, November 20, 1835, 2.

44. Twenty-six-year-old William Fisher had joined Captain Johnson's Company at Fort Brooke, Tampa, in 1847 as second lieutenant to fight in the Mexican War, but his unit served stateside, relieving a regular army force that went to Mexico. When Johnson's Company was discharged after one year, Fisher reorganized many volunteers into Fisher's Company, which he commanded with the rank of captain at Fort Brooke until their disbandment six months later. See Publication 9, Compiled Muster and Service Records Florida Militia Volunteers, War with Mexico 1846–48, FDMA; "That Cuba Expedition," *Savannah Republican*, May 6, 1851, 2; Esgate, *Jacksonville*, 16; "The Cuba Affair," New Orleans *Evening Picayune*, May 20, 1851, 1.

45. "The Descent on Cuba," *New York Tribune*, May 2, 1851, 5; "Invasion of Cuba," *Louisville Democrat*, May 8, 1851, 3.

46. "Cuban Invasion," *Florida Republican*, May 1, 1851, 2; "The Cuban Expedition," *Savannah Morning News*, May 10, 1851, 2.

47. Hiram Roberts to W. L. Hodge, May 3, 1851, MLDS; "The Welaka," *Florida News*, May 3, 1851, 2; "The Cuban Expedition-Cruise of the Welaka in Search of the Expeditionaries," *Savannah Morning News*, May 3, 1851, 2.

48. "The Cuban Expedition-Cruise of the Welaka in Search of the Expeditionaries," *Savannah Morning News*, May 3, 1851"; "Cuban Invasion," *Florida Republican*, May 1, 1851, 2; "Arrivals at the Jacksonville Hotel," *Florida Republican*, May 1, 1851, 3; 1850 Florida Census, Marion Co., 243; Portell Vilá, *Narciso López*, 3:228–29; de la Cova, *Cuban Confederate Colonel*, 88–89.

49. "The Cuban Expedition," *Florida News*, May 3, 1851, 2; "The Invasion of Cuba" and "Cuba Invasion," *Florida Republican*, May 1, 1851, 2; "Cuba," ibid., May 15, 1851, 2.

50. Locofocos were a radical group of New York Democrats organized in 1835 in opposition to the regular party organization. See "The Cuban Invasion," *Burlington (Iowa) Hawk-Eye*,

May 30, 1850, 2; *Auburn (N.Y.) Cayuga Chief,* May 21, 1850, 2; *Cincinnati Nonpareil,* May 15, 1850, 2; Hardy, *History and Adventures,* 7; *Louisville Democrat,* May 19, 1851, 2.

51. 1850 Florida Federal Census, Duval Co., 92, Franklin Co., 324, and Marion Co., 230; "Jacksonville Foundry," *Florida News,* August 30, 1851, 2; *Florida Sentinel,* September 9, 1851, 2; "Arrivals at the Jacksonville Hotel," *Florida Republican,* May 15, 1851, 3; 1860 Georgia Federal Census, Cass Co., 687.

52. "From Florida—More Arrivals of Troops at Jacksonville," *Savannah Morning News,* May 19, 1851, 2; "Arrivals at the Jacksonville Hotel," *Florida Republican,* May 29, 1851, 3; 1850 Florida Federal Census, St. Johns Co., 399, and Duval Co., 203; 1850 Florida Federal Agriculture Census, Mandarin District, 61; 1850 Florida Slave Schedules, 109; Special Archives Publication Number 69, Florida Militia MusterRolls, Seminole Indian Wars, (Vol. 3), 18, 21, FDMA.

53. Portell Vilá, *Narciso López,* 3:228–29; "Arrivals at the Jacksonville Hotel," *Florida Republican,* July 3, 1851, 3; Gonzales, *Manifesto on Cuban Affairs,* 10–11; Gonzales, "Cuban Crusade," 9; de la Cova, *Cuban Confederate Colonel,* 91; N. L. to D. German [Ambrosio Gonzales], July 2, 1851, Keith M. Read Collection, Hargrett Rare Book and Manuscript Library, University of Georgia, Athens.

54. Leopoldo Turla y Denis (1815–March 20, 1877), born in Havana to an Italian tailor father and an American mother, began his literary work at the age of nineteen in various Cuban publications. He arrived in Charleston, S.C., as a political exile in 1850, then moved to Savannah, and two years later was working in New Orleans as a teacher, translator, and cigar vendor to support his wife and four offspring. During the Civil War he served in the Confederate Louisiana First Regiment Chasseurs a pied Militia, the First Battalion Infantry (State Guards), and Co. B of the Louisiana First Volunteers Infantry Regiment. He passed away in his New Orleans residence and was interred in the tomb of Cuban filibuster Julio Chassagne (1827–53), Saint Vincent De Paul Cemetery #1 (Louisa), Plot: Piety Alley, Left Vault 39. See "Turla, the Poet," New Orleans *Times*-New Orleans *Picayune,* March 22, 1877; Calcagno, *Diccionario Biográfico Cubano,* 627–28; 1860 Louisiana Federal Census, New Orleans Ward 9, 424; Index to Compiled Service Records of Confederate Soldiers Who Served in Organizations from the State of Louisiana, M378, Roll 29, RG 94, NARA; "Cuba to Honor Turla, New Orleans Poet," New Orleans *Times-Picayune,* March 20, 1927, 3. Hiram L. French sold Empire Mills to William Harrell and William H. Aiken a year later for five thousand dollars. See Office No. 1538, Book I, 17, August 2, 1851, and Office No. 1731, Book I, 343, November 2, 1852, AABD; Conspiración en Puerto Príncipe; Partidas de paisanos armados y montados; Causas instruídas en Cuba, Puerto Príncipe y Trinidad, No. 378, Subcarpeta 19:13.1, Caja 2542, Ultramar, Cuba, Archivo General Militar, Madrid, Spain; Juárez Cano, *Hombres del 51,* 7, 58; "Further Cuban News," New Orleans *Evening Picayune,* August 18 and 21, 1851, 1; "Arrivals at the Jacksonville Hotel" and "Dissolution," *Florida Republican,* August 7, 1851, 3; Portell Vilá, *Narciso López,* 1:76–77; Portell Vilá, *Narciso López,* 3:483, 656.

55. Alejandro Angulo Guridi (May 3, 1822–January 17, 1906) was born in Santo Domingo, Dominican Republic, and then moved to Puerto Rico as an infant and afterward to Cuba with his family. He acquired a judicial and literary education and wrote for various publications. Angulo founded the monthly *El Prisma* in Havana in 1846, and its collaborators included the separatists Gaspar Betancourt Cisneros and Miguel Teurbe Tolón, who involved him in their conspiratorial activities. He went into exile in the United States in 1848 and became involved in the López revolutionary movement. Angulo returned to Santo Domingo in 1852 to teach law and literature at San Buenaventura College. Four years later he founded the newspaper *La República* in support of the government of Gen. Pedro Santana, who annexed his nation to Spain in 1861. After the restoration, Angulo settled in 1866 at Ciudad Bolívar, Venezuela, as a teacher and secretary to the federalist general José L. Arismendi, chief of the custom-

house and president of the state of Guyana. He returned to Santo Domingo in 1875 to establish the newspaper *El Demócrata* and briefly served as interim secretary of foreign relations. Angulo moved to Nicaragua in 1886 and later went to Chile, where he directed the Saint Rose Lyceum of Tacna for seven years, before passing away in Masaya, Nicaragua. He published a dozen books during 1841–1902. See Balaguer, *Literatura dominicana,* 55–67; *Cuba en la Mano,* 676; Portell Vilá, *Narciso López,* 2:59; 1850 Florida Federal Census, Duval Co., 102; Special Archives Publication Numbers 67 and 69, Florida Militia Muster Rolls, Seminole Indian Wars (Vols. 1, 3), FDMA; Davis, *History of Jacksonville,* 67–68; "Arrivals at the Jacksonville Hotel," *Florida Republican,* August 7, September 18, and October 9, 1851, 3; "Dissolution," *Florida News,* August 16, 1851, 3; Portell Vilá, *Narciso López,* 1:76–77; Portell Vilá, *Narciso López,* 3:483, 656.

56. Freret, *Correspondence,* 8, 45; Schlesinger, "Personal Narrative," September 1852, 217–19.

57. United States vs. The Steamer Pampero, District Court of the United States for the North District of Florida, Opinion and Decision on Libel & information for violation of the Revenue Laws, December 12, 1851, RG 206, Solicitor of the Treasury, Letters Received, U.S. Attorneys, Clerks of Courts, and Marshals, Florida 1846–April 1863, Box 19, NARA; William R. Hackley to Daniel Webster, August 23, 1851, MLDS; "The Pampero Trial," *Florida Republican,* November 20, 1851, 1; "The Cuba Expedition," *Charleston Courier,* August 25, 1851, 2; "The Pampero's Trip to Cuba," *Cincinnati Nonpareil,* September 5, 1851, 1; "The Pampero Case," *New Orleans Delta,* December 23, 1851, 4.

58. "The Cuba News," *Florida News,* August 2, 1851, 2; "The Cuban Revolution," *Florida News,* August 9, 1851, 2; "Cuba Revolution," *Florida Republican,* August 14, 1851, 2.

59. "Arrivals at the Jacksonville Hotel," *Florida Republican,* August 28, 1851, 2; "More Troops for Cuba," *Savannah Morning News,* August 22, 1851, 2; "Passengers," *Savannah Morning News,* August 18, 1851, 2; "Landing of Gen. Lopez," New Orleans *Evening Picayune,* August 20, 1851, 1; "The Steam Ship Pampero," *Florida Republican,* August 21, 1851, 2; Armand Lifils to Henry Williams, August 28, 1851, MLDS.

60. "The Pampero's Trip to Cuba," *Cincinnati Nonpareil,* September 5, 1851, 1; "Passengers," *Savannah Morning News,* August 25, 1851, 2; Rauch, *American Interest in Cuba,* 45; Armand Lifils to Henry Williams, August 28, 1851, MLDS.

61. "The Cuba Expedition," *Charleston Courier,* August 25, 1851, 2; "Arrivals at the Charleston Hotel," *Charleston Courier,* August 25 and 26, 1851, 2; de la Cova, *Cuban Confederate Colonel,* 96–97; Gonzales, *Manifesto on Cuban Affairs,* 10.

62. Felix Livingston (1817–February 9, 1876), born in South Carolina on July 20, 1836, enrolled as a private in Lt. James Livingston's Co., First Regiment (Warren's), Florida Mounted Militia during the Seminole War. He remained in Florida after the conflict, married, and had two sons. Livingston was elected judge of probate for Duval County during 1849–55 and owned five slaves. He was appointed editor of the *Florida News* in April 1851 after Gen. Charles Byrne bought the newspaper but resigned after nine months. Livingston moved to Fernandina, Fla., where President James Buchanan appointed him collector of the port, a post that he held until the Confederacy evacuated the town in February 1862. His home was confiscated and sold by the Lincoln administration. Livingston was a lieutenant in the Fernandina Volunteers State Militia, which occupied Fort Clinch. In May 1863 he was appointed captain and assistant commissary of subsistence in the Confederate army, and he held that post until the end of the war. Livingston applied for a presidential pardon in August 1865, took the Union oath on May 8, 1867, and returned to practicing law in Fernandina until his death. He was interred in Saint Peters Episcopal Cemetery, Fernandina. See Compiled Service Records of Volunteer Soldiers Who Served in Organizations from the State of Florida during the Florida Indian Wars, 1835–58, M1086, Roll 10, Records of the Adjutant General's Office, 1780s–1917, RG 94, NARA; 1850 Florida Federal Census, Duval Co., 92; 1850 Florida Slave Schedules,

Duval Co., 79; *Floridian and Journal* (Tallahassee), October 10, 1851, and January 31, 1852; 1860 Florida Federal Census, Fernandina, Nassau Co., 409; Case Files of Applications from Former Confederates for Presidential Pardons ("Amnesty Papers"), 1865–67, Florida 1865, M1003, Records of the Adjutant General's Office, 1780s–1917, RG 94, NARA; Minute Book 1846–67, U.S. District Court, Northern District, Florida, Tallahassee, RG 21, NARA; 1870 Florida Federal Census, Fernandina, Nassau Co., 400; "The Cuba News" and "Important Cuba Intelligence," *Florida Republican,* August 28, 1851, 2; "Cuban Meeting," *Florida News,* August 30, 1851, 2.

63. "Ho, for Cuba!," *Florida News,* September 6, 1851, 2; "The Pampero," *Charleston Courier,* September 6, 1851, 2; "Rumored Plans of Gen. Lopez," *Florida News,* August 23, 1851, 2; "Passengers," *Savannah Morning News,* September 1, 1851, 3; "The Pampero Trial," *Florida Republican,* November 20, 1851, 1.

64. Isaiah David Hart (November 6, 1792–September 4, 1861). See 1850 Florida Federal Census, Duval Co., 90; 1850 Florida Slave Schedules, Duval Co., 77; Special Archives Publication Number 67, Florida Militia Muster Rolls, Seminole Indian Wars, (Vol. 1), FDMA; Davis, *History of Jacksonville,* 53–54, 57–58; Craig, "Isaiah David Hart," 1–6; Snodgrass, "A Remarkable Man," 42–46; Brown, *Ossian Bingley Hart,* 12–22.

65. The muster rolls used in the López expeditions have not been found and are not in the Archivo General Militar de Madrid. See Henry Williams to Secretary of State, September 4, 1851, MLDS; "Ho, for Cuba!," *Florida News,* September 6, 1851, 2; "The Pampero Trial," *Florida Republican,* November 20, 1851, 1; United States vs. The Steamer Pampero, December 11, 1851.

66. "The Pampero—The Finale," *Florida News,* September 13, 1851, 2; "The Pampero Trial," *Florida Republican,* November 20, 1851, 1; Harrison Family Papers, Amelia Island Museum, Fernandina Beach. Fla.

67. "The Pampero Trial," *Florida Republican,* November 20, 1851, 1; Gonzales, *Manifesto on Cuban Affairs,* 10; "Arrivals at the Charleston Hotel," *Charleston Courier,* September 4, 1851, 2.

68. "Important from Cuba!," *Florida News,* September 6, 1851, 3; Henry Williams to Secretary of State, September 4, 1851, MLDS; "The Pampero Trial," *Florida Republican,* November 20, 1851, 1; Correspondence on the Lopez Expedition to Cuba, 1849–51, State Department Miscellaneous Correspondence, 1784–1906, Box 1, Entry 121, RG 59, NARA.

69. "Chasing the Pampero," *Florida Republican,* September 11, 1851, 2; *Savannah Republican,* September 14, 1851, 2; Isaiah D. Hart to Secretary of the Treasury Thomas Corwin, September 13, 1851, MLDS.

70. Dr. Henry Drayton Holland (1805–November 9, 1860) graduated from the Medical College of South Carolina in 1830 and moved to Camden County, Ga., the following year. His plantation, Mulberry Grove, seven miles south of Jacksonville on the St. Johns River, is the present site of the Jacksonville Naval Air Station. Holland was elected mayor of Jacksonville in 1852. See Merritt, *Century of Medicine,* 17–18; 1850 Florida Federal Census, Duval Co., 92; Isaiah D. Hart to Treasury Secretary Thomas Corwin, September 13, 1851, MLDS; J. M. Hanson to Acting Secretary of State W. S. Derrick, September 9, 1851, MLDS; "Chasing the Pampero," *Florida Republican,* September 11, 1851, 2; "Arrivals at the Jacksonville Hotel," *Florida Republican,* September 18, 1851, 3; *Charleston Courier,* September 15, 1851, 2; "Capture of the Pampero," *Georgia Journal and Messenger* (Macon), September 17, 1851, 2.

71. J. M. Hanson to Acting Secretary of State W. S. Derrick, September 11, 1851, MLDS; Isaiah D. Hart to Treasury Secretary Thomas Corwin, September 13, 1851, MLDS; "The Pampero" and "Arrivals at the Jacksonville Hotel," *Florida Republican,* September 18, 1851, 2, 3.

72. "Arrivals at the Jacksonville Hotel," *Florida Republican,* September 18, 1851, 3; Isaiah D. Hart to I. J. Morrison, September 12, 1851, and Isaiah D. Hart to Treasury Secretary Thomas Corwin, September 14, 1851, MLDS; "Notice," *Florida Republican,* October 2, 1851, 3.

73. George W. Call to Daniel Webster, September 21, 1851, MLDS; "The Pampero," *Florida News,* September 27, 1851, 2, repr. in *New Orleans Delta,* October 9, 1851, 1.

74. *New Orleans Delta,* October 18, 1851, 2; "The Pampero," *New Orleans Delta,* October 21, 1851, 1; "The Pampero Trial," *Florida Republican,* November 20, 1851, 1; "From Florida," *Savannah Morning News,* October 14, 1851, 2; The State of Florida vs. Henry T. Titus, October 14, 1851, Circuit Court Papers, St. Johns County, Florida, Box 163, Folder 41, St. Augustine Historical Society, St. Augustine, Fla.

75. "Fillibusterism," *Florida Republican,* November 13, 1851, 2; "The Pampero Case," *New Orleans Delta,* December 23, 1851, 4; "Payments to Titus, April 3, 1852," *Florida Senate Journal,* 6th Session, November 22, 1852, 116.

76. "The Pampero Case," *Florida News,* December 6, 1851, 3; "Pampero," *Florida Republican,* December 18, 1851, 3; "Sale of the Steamer Pampero," *Florida News,* December 20, 1851, 3; "Sale of the Pampero," *Florida Republican,* January 22, 1852, 2.

77. Titus store advertisements in *Florida Republican,* February 19, 1852, 3, and *Florida News,* April 24, June 19, and December 4, 1852, 3; "Passengers," *Florida Republican,* February 12, 1852, 3.

78. Edward Stevens Hopkins (February 11, 1809–September 28, 1887) was born in Belville, McIntosh County, Ga. and married Mary Evelina DuFour (August 10, 1814–September 21, 1840) in St. Marys, Camden County, Ga., on August 25, 1832. They had three offspring who survived to adulthood. In 1836 Hopkins was a major in the Eighth Battalion, First Brigade, Georgia Militia, before becoming a U.S. Army officer and settling in Florida a decade later. He had a spectacular duel in October 1837 over a cattle feud with Georgia Militia brigadier general Charles Rinaldo Floyd, his neighbor and brother's father-in-law, on Amelia Island. The contenders were armed with "double-barreled shotguns, heavily loaded with buckshot, a brace of pistols and a bowie-knife." At the appointed hour they immediately began shooting, ignoring the customary preliminaries, and both were badly wounded and bedridden for months. Hopkins, hit in the left thigh and right calf, was left with a severe limp. He was the Constitutional Union candidate for governor of Florida in 1860. On July 27, 1861, Hopkins enlisted as a Confederate colonel of the Fourth Regiment of Florida, and he resigned on May 12, 1862. He afterward was brigadier general of the Forty-first Florida State Troops. Hopkins served as Democratic mayor of Jacksonville from 1868 to 1870 and was appointed U.S. collector of customs for St. Johns District in 1879. The patriarch is interred in the Hopkins family plot at Evergreen Cemetery in Jacksonville. See "Col. Titus Turned Up," *New Orleans Daily True Delta,* April 22, 1862, 4; Huxford, *Pioneers of Wiregrass Georgia,* 5:212–14; 1850 Florida Slave Schedules, St. Johns Bar District, Duval Co., 123; "A Remarkable Duel Recalled," *Philadelphia Inquirer,* October 22, 1887, 10; "Married," *Florida Republican,* March 25, 1852, 3; 1850 Georgia Federal Census, Glynn Co., 4A; "Early Recollections of Minnie Titus Ensey," Henry Theodore Titus Collection, North Brevard Public Library, Titusville, Fla., 1.

79. "Men of Note in Kansas: Col. Titus," *Ripley (Ohio) Bee,* February 7, 1857; 1850 Florida Slave Schedules, Duval Co., 77, 79, 83; 1850 Florida Agriculture Census, Jacksonville, 55; "Public Meetings," *Florida News,* June 5, 1852, 1; Schafer, *Thunder on the River,* 9–11.

80. "Public Meetings," *Florida News,* June 5, 1852, 1.

81. Ibid.; "Fourth of July Celebration," *Florida Republican,* July 8, 1852, 2.

82. "Another Terrible Steamboat Disaster, and Loss of Two Hundred Lives!," *Daily National Intelligencer,* August 21, 1852, 3; "The Lake Erie Disaster," *Albany Evening Journal,* August 21, 1852, 2; "The Atlantic—The Coroner's Inquest, and the Verdict of the Jury," *Cleveland Plain Dealer,* August 25, 1852, 3; "Terrible Steamboat Disaster on Lake Erie," *Connecticut Courant* (Hartford), August 28, 1852, 1.

83. The acreage Titus purchased from Craig today borders Jammes Road on the east, Firestone Road on the west, Miss Muffet Lane on the north, and Cinderella Road on the south in Jacksonville. See "Just Received," *Florida News,* December 4, 1852, 3; Office No. 1827, Book I,

533, July 2, 1853, and Office No. 1911, Book J, 119, July 1, 1853, AABD; "Passengers," *Charleston Courier,* July 6, 1853, 4.

84. "Wilder's Planing Machine," *Scientific American,* March 26, 1853, 217, and October 29, 1853, 54; "Wilder's Improved Planing Mill," *Florida Republican,* December 15, 1853, 3.

85. "Wilder's Improved Planing Mill," *Charleston Courier,* January 6, 1854, 3; "List of Arrivals at the Hotels," *Washington Evening Star,* January 27, 1854, 4; "Passengers," *Charleston Courier,* January 31, 1854, 4.

86. Joseph Finegan (November 17, 1814–October 29, 1885), born in Ireland, moved to Fernandina, Fla., in 1854 and joined Sen. David Yulee in railroad construction. Appointed by the governor to Florida's secession convention in 1861, the following year he was commissioned as a Confederate brigadier general in charge of the District of Middle and East Florida. At the Battle of Olustee in 1864, he stopped the Union advance on Tallahassee. After the war Finegan was a cotton broker and commission merchant in Savannah in 1868 before moving with his second wife to an orange grove in central Florida, where he passed away. See 1850 New York Federal Census, New York City, Ward 16, District 3, 225; 1850 Florida Slave Schedules, Jacksonville, 81; "New York Supreme Court," *New York Evening Post,* October 2, 1854, 4; "The Heroes of the South in Kansas: Col. H. T. Titus," *New York Tribune,* January 5, 1857, 6.

87. Office No. 4212, Book A, 210, March 10, 1854, AABD; "The Heroes of the South in Kansas: Col. H. T. Titus," *New York Tribune,* January 5, 1857, 6.

88. Martin, *City Makers,* 16; "Great and Disastrous Conflagration," *Florida Republican,* April 6, 1854, 1; "Passengers," *Charleston Courier,* April 7, 1854, 4; "The Heroes of the South in Kansas: Col. H. T. Titus," *New York Tribune,* January 5, 1857, 6.

89. "The Heroes of the South in Kansas: Col. H. T. Titus," *New York Tribune,* January 5, 1857, 6.

90. Ibid.; *Florida Republican,* September 7 and 21, 1854, 2; "Whig Meeting," *Florida Republican,* October 12, 1854, 2.

91. *Florida News,* January 6, 1855; Henry T. Titus, May 1, 1855, Florida, St. Augustine Land Office, Documents 781–84, Records of the Bureau of Land Management, General Land Office, RG 49, NARA; Office No. 2305, Book K, 275, November 7, 1855, AABD.

92. "Ratification Meeting," *Florida Republican,* March 27, 1856, 2; Schafer, *Thunder on the River,* 14–15.

Chapter Two: Bleeding in Kansas, 1856

1. "For Kansas," *Florida Republican,* April 2, 1856, 2.

2. Wilder, *Annals of Kansas,* 35–38, 45; Holloway, *History of Kansas,* 106–9; Gihon, *Geary and Kansas,* 43–44, 129; de la Cova, "Samuel J. Kookogey," 3, 147; Day, "Life of Wilson Shannon," 178, 247.

3. "Poor Shombre," *New Haven Columbian Register,* October 25, 1856, 2; "Men of Note in Kansas: Col. Titus," *Ripley (Ohio) Bee,* February 7, 1857; Twain, *Roughing It,* 1:3; Gihon, *Geary and Kansas,* 122; "Kansas News Items," *New York Reformer* (Watertown), May 22, 1856, 3.

4. Fort Titus was located at 39°1'19.71"N 95°23'42.37"W, which appears on a map at NE 1/4; see Section 10, Range 18 East, Township 12 South, Kansas Tract Books, vols. 22, 23, 24, p. 184, MS-328, Roll 8, Kansas State Historical Society, Topeka, Kans., hereafter cited as KSHS. B. F. Treadwell (1808–?) was born in South Carolina, where in 1836 he was commissioned by Gov. George McDuffie as colonel of the Fourteenth Regiment of the South Carolina Militia and ordered to assemble at Orangeburg for review on October 13, 1836. In 1840 he was farming in Barbour County, Alabama, where a decade later he owned fifty-five slaves. Treadwell arrived in Kansas with the rank of colonel in the Buford expedition in May 1856. He received an honorary membership in the City Guards of Eufaula, Ala. In 1860 Treadwell owned $123,000 in land and ninety-seven slaves. See 1840 Alabama Federal Census, Barbour County, 57; 1850 Alabama Slave Schedules, Division 23, Barbour, 489–90; 1860 Alabama Federal Census, Eastern

Division, Barbour, 452; Fleming, "Buford Expedition to Kansas," 43; "Glorious Victory," *Milwaukee Daily Sentinel,* August 28, 1856, 2; "Block Houses," *Leavenworth Weekly Herald,* October 4, 1856, 1; "Letter from Col. Titus," *Florida Republican,* November 5, 1856, 2; M. H. Dozier, sworn statement, August 22, 1856, State Department Territorial Papers, Kansas, 1854–61, Official Correspondence, May 30, 1854–April 30, 1861, M-218, Roll 1, RG 59, NARA, hereafter cited as SDTP; John Ritchie to F. G. Adams, September 30, 1881, John Ritchie folder, Miscellaneous Collection, KSHS; He enlisted in Co. K, Alabama 46th Infantry Regiment on May 2, 1862. Cordley, *History of Lawrence, Kansas,* 112–15; Gihon, *Geary and Kansas,* 93.

5. James Henry Lane (June 22, 1814–July 11, 1866), born and raised a Hoosier, married Mary E. Baldridge in Pennsylvania on November 29, 1841, and had four children. He became a lawyer, joined Indiana volunteers in the Mexican War, and served as Democratic lieutenant governor of Indiana (1849–53) and congressman (1853–55), during which time he voted for the Kansas-Nebraska Act. Lane immigrated to Kansas in April 1855 and invested seven thousand dollars mostly in real estate. His father-in-law accused him of abandoning his family for a mistress, which prompted a divorce on May 12, 1856. That month the *Washington Daily Union* published that Lane had been "for some time laboring under symptoms of insanity." Two years later Lane reconciled with his former wife and remarried her. In 1859 Lane was charged with the "willful murder" of his free-state neighbor Gaius Jenkins over a land dispute. Wilson Shannon was one of three lawyers who obtained Lane's acquittal. During the Civil War, Lane served in the U.S. Senate and as a Union army general. He was the third member of his family to commit suicide, shooting himself in the mouth after being accused of financial corruption and demonized for voting against the Civil Rights bill. See Speer, *Life of Gen. James H. Lane;* "Jim Lane," *Lecompton Union,* August 30, 1856, 1; "A Kansas Hero Unmasked," *Jeffersonian Democrat* (Monroe, Wis.), September 25, 1856, 2; "Mock Heroic Gladiatorial Honors to Jim Lane," *Washington Daily Union,* May 31, 1856, 3; "Twice Married," *Lowell (Mass.) Daily Citizen and News,* July 25, 1866, 2; Brewerton, *War in Kansas,* 339–41; Weisberger, "Newspaper Reporter and the Kansas Imbroglio," 636–41; Day, "Life of Wilson Shannon," 192–93; McKivigan, *Forgotten Firebrand,* 27.

6. Wilson Shannon (February 24, 1802–August 30, 1877) was a lawyer and Democratic governor of Ohio (1838–40, 1842–44), minister to Mexico (1844–45), and congressman (1853–55) before becoming the second governor of the Kansas Territory on September 7, 1855. He has been demonized as servile to the slaveocracy in Kansas, but his biographer indicates that Shannon advocated the implementation of his party's popular sovereignty policy to resolve the slavery issue. He was both praised and condemned by proslavery adherents. The *New York Herald* called him a "nincompoop." The abolitionist William Phillips purported that when Wilson Shannon was a congressman, his daughter temporarily "kept him sober, and even, it is stated, wisely counseled him on his public course." Shannon denounced the frequent false accusations of intemperance in the antislavery press with a character reference signed by sixteen prominent friends, including three former congressmen, a former U.S. senator, a Methodist preacher, and a renowned abolitionist lawyer, Thomas H. Henin. After Shannon was removed from office on July 28, 1856, he returned to Kansas to practice law until his demise. See Phillips, *Conquest of Kansas,* 116, 299; "Gov. Shannon's Defence," *Washington Daily National Intelligencer,* November 28, 1856, 2; Day, "Life of Wilson Shannon," 194, 253, 290–91; *Kansas Herald of Freedom,* January 12, March 22, April 5 and 12, and December 27, 1856.

7. "Later from Kansas," *Boston Traveler,* April 25, 1856, 2; *Missouri Democrat* (St. Louis), quoted in "Letter from Kansas," *New York Tribune,* February 15, 1856, 3; Brewerton, *War in Kansas,* 340, 351–52, 367; Gihon, *Geary and Kansas,* 85; "Affairs in Kansas," *New York Times,* June 6, 1856, 1; Phillips, *Conquest of Kansas,* 203, 231, 309.

8. The federal indictment is reproduced in Phillips, *Conquest of Kansas,* 351–54. Samuel J. Jones (1819–December 10, 1885) while serving as Douglas County sheriff was also assistant

postmaster at Westport, where his father-in-law, Col. Albert Gallatin Boone (1806–84), was the postmaster. Samuel Clarke Pomeroy (January 3, 1816–August 27, 1891) was born in Southampton, Mass., and served in the state House of Representatives 1852–53. An antislavery activist, he was organizer and financial agent of the New England Emigrant Aid Company and led two hundred migrants to Kansas in August 1854. Pomeroy was mayor of Atchison, established the largest steam flouring mill in the state, was the president at the Atchison Bank, and was a U.S. senator from Kansas from 1861 to 1873. Charles Lawrence Robinson (July 21, 1818–August 17, 1894) was born in Hardwick, Mass., where he studied and practiced medicine in his state until going to California in 1849 via the land route. The next year he was a leader of the Squatter' Riot in Sacramento after erecting his shack on private land. During an armed confrontation with the authorities, Robinson and the mayor of Sacramento were gravely wounded and five others were killed. While under indictment for conspiracy and murder, Robinson was elected to the California legislature, and the charges were dismissed. He left Sacramento in July 1851 by ship for New York, and after a shipwreck and other delays crossing Panama, he arrived in Havana in time to witness the public execution of Narciso López on September 1, 1851. Robinson reached Manhattan eight days later and returned to practicing medicine in Fitchburg, Mass., until migrating with his family to Kansas in June 1854. See U.S. Congress, *Biographical Dictionary,* 1660; Empire City, September 8, 1851, Passenger Lists of Vessels Arriving at New York, New York, 1820–97, M237, Roll 104, Records of the U.S. Customs Service, RG 36, NARA; Brewerton, *War in Kansas,* 302; Day, "Life of Wilson Shannon," 262–66; Phillips, *Conquest of Kansas,* 252, 255–56, 269; "Report," *Lecompton Union*—Extra, April 28, 1856, 1; "Summary of the Kansas News," *New York Weekly Herald,* May 31, 1856, 171; "Incidents of the Glorious Victory," *New York Tribune,* June 9, 1856, 6; Gihon, *Geary and Kansas,* 54, 77–79; "Affairs in Kansas," *New York Times,* June 6, 1856, 1.

   9. Phillips, *Conquest of Kansas,* 269; "From Kansas: Facts of the Last Invasion," *New York Tribune,* July 25, 1856, 6; Gihon, *Geary and Kansas,* 77–78; Receipt, D. A. Clayton Jr. to G. W. Hutchinson and William Hutchinson, July 25, 1856, James Blood Collection, Box 1, Folder 4, KSHS.

   10. Day, "Life of Wilson Shannon," 2, 236; "From Our Kansas Correspondent," *Milwaukee Sentinel,* June 6, 1856, 2; "Affairs in Kansas," *New York Times,* June 6, 1856, 1; "Notes to and from the Siege of Lawrence," *Leavenworth Weekly Herald,* August 23, 1856, 1; "Affairs of Kansas," *New York Herald,* October 16, 1856, 1.

   11. "Executive Committee Kansas Association," *Charleston Courier,* June 25, 1856, 2; ibid., October 25, 1856, 2; "Kansas Meeting," *Charleston Mercury,* June 27, 1856, 2; Phillips, *Conquest of Kansas,* 289–90, 296–97, 305; "Affairs in Kansas," *New York Times,* June 6, 1856, 1; Gihon, *Geary and Kansas,* 78, 82; 1860 South Carolina Federal Census, Anderson, 261; "Kansas— Sacking of Lawrence," *St. Albans (Vt.) Messenger,* September 3, 1857, 1; Fleming, "Buford Expedition to Kansas," 43; "Trailing in the Dust," *Kansas Herald of Freedom,* November 1, 1856, 1; "From Kansas: Facts of the Last Invasion," *New York Tribune,* July 25, 1856, 6.

   12. John A. Perry (September 1824–May 1903) was born in Massachusetts and was a stone cutter residing with his wife and three children in Providence, R.I., before arriving in Lawrence on April 18, 1856. He speculated in land and managed Charles L. Robinson's quarrying business. Perry was appointed to the Lawrence Committee of Safety and was the first person cited using the term "Bleeding Kansas" when he attended the Republican Party nominating convention in New York City in mid-June 1856. By 1860 he had returned to Rhode Island as a clergyman. During the Civil War, Perry was a chaplain lieutenant in the First Regiment Rhode Island Light Artillery. After the war he took up farming in Rhode Island. See 1850 Rhode Island Federal Census, Providence, Ward 6, 466; 1860 Rhode Island Federal Census, Coventry, 5; 1900 Rhode Island Federal Census, Foster Town, 220-B; "Affairs in Kansas," *New York Herald,* May 30, 1856, 4; "The Presidency," *New York Herald,* June 14, 1856, 7; "From Kansas: Facts of the Last Invasion," *New York Tribune,* July 25, 1856, 6.

13. U.S. House of Representatives, *Kansas Claims,* 787–88, 1377, 1386, hereafter cited as *Kansas Claims;* Fleming, "Buford Expedition to Kansas," 45; "The 'Blister' of the United States," *New York Herald,* July 12, 1856, 3; *Connecticut Courant* (Hartford), July 12, 1856, 1.

14. "Affairs in Kansas," *New York Herald,* May 30, 1856, 4; "Col. Titus," *Kansas Herald of Freedom,* May 2, 1857; Phillips, *Conquest of Kansas,* 304; "The 'Blister' of the United States," *New York Herald,* July 12, 1856, 3; Phillips, *Conquest of Kansas,* 304–5.

15. David Rice Atchison (August 11, 1807–January 26, 1886) was born in Fayette County, Ky., and studied law before moving to Clay County, Mo., in 1830. He was elected to the Missouri House of Representatives, serving there in 1834–38 and in the U.S. Senate from 1843 to 1855. Atchison was a Missouri militia major general during the Mormon War of 1838 and a member of Masonic Platte Lodge No. 56, Platte City, Mo. The inveterate bachelor resided in Platte City until 1856, when he moved to his Clinton County plantation, residing there until his death. Warren D. Wilkes permanently returned to South Carolina in June 1856 due to bad health. The red shirt would be revived as a paramilitary political symbol in South Carolina by Wade Hampton's followers in 1876. James Redpath, from Leavenworth, put the number of proslavery militia at "about 400," as did three fleeing Lawrencians cited in northern papers. William Phillips said they numbered "from five to eight hundred men," and James F. Legate saw "some seven or eight hundred" men. The *Albany Evening Journal* purported that "two thousand . . . Missouri, Carolina and Alabama adventurers" plundered Lawrence. See Paxton, *Annals of Platte County,* 833; Denslow, *10,000 Famous Freemasons,* 1:36; Ingalls, *History of Atchison County, Kansas,* 186–88; "Affairs in Kansas," *New York Herald,* May 30, 1856, 4; "Destruction of Lawrence," *Cleveland Plain Dealer,* May 26, 1856, 3; Gihon, *Geary and Kansas,* 83; Phillips, *Conquest of Kansas,* 289–92, 305; *Kansas Affairs,* 1386; "The History of Lawrence," *Albany (N.Y.) Evening Journal,* May 29, 1856, 2; "From Kansas: The Sack of Lawrence," *New York Tribune,* June 7, 1856, 8; Brewerton, *War in Kansas,* 364; "The Outrage at Lawrence, in Kansas," *Daily National Intelligencer,* June 5, 1856, 2; "The Sacking of Lawrence," *Massachusetts Spy* (Worcester), June 25, 1856, 3; "Summary of the Kansas News," *New York Weekly Herald,* May 31, 1856, 171; "Affairs in Kansas," *New York Times,* June 6, 1856, 1; "From Kansas: Facts of the Last Invasion," *New York Tribune,* July 25, 1856, 6.

16. George Washington Deitzler (November 30, 1826–April 11, 1884) was born in Pennsylvania and moved to Illinois and California before settling in March 1855 in Lawrence, Kans., where he became a land speculator and antislavery activist. He smuggled Sharps rifles into Kansas from Massachusetts and partly commanded free-state forces during the bloodless Wakarusa War of November–December 1855. Deitzler served in the territorial legislature and was mayor of Lawrence in 1860. He helped raise and was appointed colonel of the First Kansas Volunteer Infantry Regiment and was wounded at the Battle of Wilson's Creek in August 1861. Dietzler was promoted to brigadier general of volunteers in April 1863 and commanded the First Brigade, Sixth Division, Seventeen Corps during the Vicksburg campaign. He resigned on August 27, 1863, while on sick leave at Lawrence and the following year was commissioned as a major general of Kansas militia. He moved to San Francisco with his family in 1872, and in 1884, while visiting Tucson, Ariz., to arrange settling there, he died in a buggy accident. George W. Smith (1806–78), a transplanted Pennsylvania attorney, was colonel of the Fifth Regiment of the First Brigade of Kansas Volunteers in the Wakarusa War. After he, Deitzler, and Jenkins were arrested, they were imprisoned with George W. Brown, John Brown Jr., Charles L. Robinson, and Henry H. Williams in the U.S. Army's Camp Sackett, located 3.5 miles southwest of Lecompton, until released on bail of five thousand dollars each by Judge Lecompte after the district attorney did not appear in court in October 1856. In 1858 Smith was a founder and vestryman of Trinity Episcopal Church in Lawrence. After the Civil War he represented Douglas County in the Kansas legislature and was elected Speaker of the House. See "Affairs in Kansas," *New York Herald,* May 30, 1856, 4; Gihon, *Geary and Kansas,* 51, 83,

135, 163–64; Phillips, *Conquest of Kansas,* 188, 291–92, 306; Brewerton, *War in Kansas,* 136; "The Sacking of Lawrence," *Massachusetts Spy* (Worcester), June 25, 1856, 3; Day, "Life of Wilson Shannon," 270; "Summary of the Kansas News," *New York Weekly Herald,* May 31, 1856, 171; "Kansas Affairs," *New York Herald,* June 2, 1856, 3; "The Outrage at Lawrence, in Kansas," *Daily National Intelligencer,* June 5, 1856, 2; "Affairs in Kansas," *New York Times,* June 6, 1856, 1; "From Kansas: Facts of the Last Invasion," *New York Tribune,* July 25, 1856, 6.

17. "The Outrage at Lawrence, in Kansas," *Daily National Intelligencer,* June 5, 1856, 2; "Affairs in Kansas," *New York Herald,* May 30, 1856, 4; Gihon, *Geary and Kansas,* 74, 83–84; Phillips, *Conquest of Kansas,* 292–95, 306–7; "The Sacking of Lawrence," *Massachusetts Spy* (Worcester), June 25, 1856, 3; "Summary of the Kansas News," *New York Weekly Herald,* May 31, 1856, 171; "Affairs in Kansas," *New York Times,* June 6, 1856, 1.

18. Josiah Miller (November 12, 1828–July 7, 1870), born in Chester County, S.C., to a farming family, graduated from Indiana University in 1851 and later studied law in Poughkeepsie, N.Y. He arrived in Kansas in August 1854 seeking preemptive land and business opportunities. Miller partnered with Robert G. Elliott of Cincinnati to establish the free-soil newspaper *Kansas Free State* in Lawrence on January 5, 1855. Two years later he was elected probate judge of Douglas County, and in 1859 he served in the Kansas Senate. Miller was Lawrence postmaster from 1861 to 1863, when he was appointed army paymaster with the rank of major. He was elected to the Kansas House of Representatives in 1866 and passed away in Lawrence four years later. See Josiah Miller to his parents, September 10, 1854, Josiah Miller Collection, Kenneth Spencer Research Library, University of Kansas, Lawrence; "Affairs in Kansas," *New York Times,* June 6, 1856, 1; "The Sacking of Lawrence," *Massachusetts Spy* (Worcester), June 25, 1856, 3; "Affairs in Kansas," *New York Herald,* May 30, 1856, 4; "From Lawrence," *New York Tribune,* May 30, 1856, 6; "Summary of the Kansas News," *New York Weekly Herald,* May 31, 1856, 171; Stephenson, *Publications of the Kansas State Historical Society,* 3:68; Phillips, *Conquest of Kansas,* 290, 295, 298–99, 308; Gihon, *Geary and Kansas,* 96; "From Kansas: Facts of the Last Invasion," *New York Tribune,* July 25, 1856, 6; "Affairs in Kansas," *New York Times,* June 6, 1856, 1; Day, "Life of Wilson Shannon," 270; "From Kansas: The Sacking of Lawrence," *New York Tribune,* June 9, 1856, 6.

19. The South Carolina red flag emblazoned "Southern Rights" was captured four months later by Col. James A. Harvey at Easton. It was sent to Boston to be exhibited as a war trophy and today is displayed at the Kansas Museum of History at Topeka. The *Lecompton Union* was a "Southern rights and Democratic principles" weekly newspaper published by the attorneys A. W. Jones and Robert H. Bennett beginning on April 28, 1856. Its twenty-five surviving issues can be read at http://www.latinamericanstudies.org/kansas-newspapers.htm. See "Curiosities from Kansas," *New York Times,* October 8, 1856, 3; "Kanzas Notes," *Springfield (Mass.) Republican,* September 24, 1856, 4; "From Kansas: Facts of the Last Invasion," *New York Tribune,* July 25, 1856, 6; "Summary of the Kansas News," *New York Weekly Herald,* May 31, 1856, 171; "The Outrage at Lawrence, in Kansas," *Daily National Intelligencer,* June 5, 1856, 2; *Lecompton Union* quoted in Phillips, *Conquest of Kansas,* 307.

20. "Affairs in Kansas," *New York Times,* June 6, 1856, 1; "The Sacking of Lawrence," *Massachusetts Spy* (Worcester), June 25, 1856, 3; "Newspaper Accounts," *New York Herald,* May 30, 1856, 4; "Civil War in Kansas!," *Milwaukee Sentinel,* May 30, 1856, 2; "Summary of the Kansas News," *New York Weekly Herald,* May 31, 1856, 171; "The Outrage at Lawrence, in Kansas," *Daily National Intelligencer,* June 5, 1856, 2; "From Kansas: The Sacking of Lawrence," *New York Tribune,* June 9, 1856, 6; McKivigan, *Forgotten Firebrand,* 28; Gihon, *Geary and Kansas,* 85; Phillips, *Conquest of Kansas,* 299; "From Kansas: Facts of the Last Invasion," *New York Tribune,* July 25, 1856, 6; Weisberger, "Newspaper Reporter and the Kansas Imbroglio," 644.

21. Peter T. Abell (July 29, 1813–January 16, 1874), born in Bardstown, Ky., was orphaned as an infant. He lost sight in one eye as the result of an infection as a teenager and by the age

of twenty was merchandising with his cousin in Keytesville, Mo. In 1835 Abell married E. M. Cabell, and they had six children. He studied law under Gen. Benjamin Franklin Stringfellow, and they formed a partnership at Brunswick, Mo., in 1849 that lasted until he moved to Weston in 1853. The following year Abell was elected president of the town company that founded Atchison, Kans., with Dr. John H. Stringfellow as secretary. In 1854 one of his slaves, an "intelligent mulatto," fled to Canada. Five years later Abell incorporated the Atchison & Topeka Railroad Company with Samuel Clarke Pomeroy and eleven other men. He moved from Atchison during the Civil War years and returned afterward to promote railroading, being elected president of the Atchison and Nebraska Railroad Company in 1871. See Bay, *Reminiscences,* 215–16; Ingalls, *History of Atchison County, Kansas,* 65; Peter T. Abell Miscellaneous Collection, KSHS; "Affairs in Kansas," *New York Times,* June 6, 1856, 1; "Newspaper Accounts," *New York Herald,* May 30, 1856, 4; "The Sacking of Lawrence," *Massachusetts Spy* (Worcester), June 25, 1856, 3; Brewerton, *War in Kansas,* 260; Phillips, *Conquest of Kansas,* 298, 300–301, 308; "Summary of the Kansas News," *New York Weekly Herald,* May 31, 1856, 171; "The Outrage at Lawrence, in Kansas," *Daily National Intelligencer,* June 5, 1856, 2; "From Kansas: The Sacking of Lawrence," *New York Tribune,* June 9, 1856, 6.

22. "Later from Kansas: Reign of Terror in the Territory," *New York Tribune,* May 22, 1856, 5; *St. Louis Democrat* quoted in "Affairs in Kansas," *New York Herald,* May 30 and 31, 1856; McKivigan, *Forgotten Firebrand,* 28; *St. Louis Democrat* quoted in "Affairs in Kansas," *New York Times,* June 6, 1856, 1; "From Kansas: Lawrence in Ashes," *New York Tribune,* May 30, 1856, 6; "From Kansas: The Sacking of Lawrence," *New York Tribune,* June 9, 1856, 6; Phillips, *Conquest of Kansas,* 300–301; Day, "Life of Wilson Shannon," 271; Weisberger, "Newspaper Reporter and the Kansas Imbroglio," 645; "The 'Blister' of the United States," *New York Herald,* July 12, 1856, 3; "Violence to Women in Kansas!," *Cleveland Leader,* June 12, 1856, 2; "Kansas Affairs," *New York Herald,* June 2, 1856, 3.

23. *St. Louis Democrat* cited in "Affairs in Kansas," *New York Herald,* May 30, 1856, 4; "Summary of the Kansas News," *New York Weekly Herald,* May 31, 1856, 171; *St. Louis Democrat* quoted in "Affairs in Kansas," *New York Times,* June 6, 1856, 1; "From Our Kansas Correspondent," *Milwaukee Sentinel,* June 6, 1856, 2; "From Kansas: The Sacking of Lawrence," *New York Tribune,* June 9, 1856, 6; Phillips, *Conquest of Kansas,* 300–301; "Kansas Affairs," *New York Herald,* June 2, 1856, 3; Day, "Life of Wilson Shannon," 271; Weisberger, "Newspaper Reporter and the Kansas Imbroglio," 645; "The 'Blister' of the United States," *New York Herald,* July 12, 1856, 3.

24. John Allen Wakefield (January 22, 1797–June 18, 1873), a native of Richland County, S.C., moved to St. Claire County, Ill., in 1808 and was a scout for the Illinois Militia in the War of 1812. He later studied medicine in Cincinnati and St. Louis and after studying law was admitted to the Illinois Bar in 1818. Six years later Wakefield was elected to the Illinois House on an antislavery platform. He attained the rank of major in the Black Hawk War in 1832 and befriended Abraham Lincoln. Wakefield moved to Wisconsin in 1846 and later to St. Paul, Minn., where he owned the Tremont House and was the first justice of the peace. In 1851 the Wakefield family went to Iowa, and three years later they were among the first squatters at Kanwaka, Kans., where he was the drill master for the Bloomington Guards militia. Wakefield was a candidate in the November 1854 election for a territorial delegate to Congress. He served as a major in the free-state Volunteers under Brig. Gen. James H. Lane during the bloodless Wakarusa War of November–December 1855. Wakefield was elected free-state Kansas treasurer in 1856 and served in the Kansas State Legislature in 1864, passing away in Lawrence. See "From Kansas: The Sacking of Lawrence," *New York Tribune,* June 9, 1856, 6; Phillips, *Conquest of Kansas,* 320; Robinson, *Kansas,* 255; "From Kansas," *St. Paul Daily Pioneer,* April 28, 1856, 3; *Kansas Claims,* 161.

25. Gihon, *Geary and Kansas,* 86–87; Day, "Life of Wilson Shannon," 275; Andreas, *History of the State of Kansas,* 604; "From Our Kansas Correspondent," *Milwaukee Sentinel,* June 6,

1856, 2; "Affairs in Kansas," *New York Times,* June 6, 1856, 1; "Kansas: Military Movements," *New York Tribune,* September 19, 1856, 5; Watts, "How Bloody Was Bleeding Kansas," 126.

26. *Missouri Democrat* article repr. in "The Slaughter of Five Pro-Slavery Men," *New York Tribune,* June 9, 1856, 6; *Chicago Tribune* quoted in "A Reign of Terror in Kansas," *Cleveland Leader,* June 11, 1856, 1; Phillips, *Conquest of Kansas,* 317, 332.

27. Samuel Davis Sturgis (June 11, 1822–September 28, 1889), born in Shippensburg, Pa., graduated from the U.S. Military Academy at West Point in 1846 and was commissioned as a second lieutenant in the Second U.S. Dragoons. He was captured during the Mexican War while doing reconnaissance at Buena Vista and freed eight days later. At the start of the Civil War, Sturgis was promoted to major, and in 1862 he became a brigadier general of volunteers. He led his forces at the battles of South Mountain, Antietam, and Fredericksburg, being soundly defeated by Confederate major general Nathan Bedford Forrest at Brice's Cross Roads on June 10, 1864. Sturgis spent the rest of the war "awaiting orders" and reverted to his regular army rank of lieutenant colonel. He was promoted to colonel in 1869 and received command of the Seventh U.S. Cavalry, whose lieutenant colonel was George Armstrong Custer. Sturgis was on detached duty when part of his force under Custer was destroyed at the Battle of the Little Big Horn. He resigned in 1886 and passed away in St. Paul, Minn. Samuel Walker (October 22, 1822–February 6, 1893) was a cabinet maker born in Franklin County, Pa. He moved to Ohio in 1848 and settled in Kansas in April 1855 with his wife Marian and six children. In May 1855 he organized the Bloomington Guards company with eighty-six free-soilers. Walker was arrested in Lawrence by U.S. Deputy Marshal A. W. Pardee on February 13, 1857, and taken before a Lecompton judge on a grand jury indictment for murder, arson, robbery, and assault with intent to kill in connection with the destruction of Fort Titus the previous summer. Walker posted a fifteen-thousand-dollar bail. The case was dropped after Gov. John White Geary granted a blanket amnesty for all 1856 acts of violence. In 1860 Walker was the sheriff of Douglas County, a post that, along with that of city marshal, he held for decades. See Faust, *Historical Times,* 729–30; Gleed, "Samuel Walker," 6:249–50, 253, 262–63, 270; "Kansas," *New York Tribune,* June 11, 1856, 5; "Still Later from Kansas," *Baltimore Sun,* June 11, 1856, 1; "From Our Kansas Correspondent," *Milwaukee Daily Sentinel,* June 12, 1856, 2; "Lecompton Quiet," *Kansas Tribune,* August 16, 1856, 2; Phillips, *Conquest of Kansas,* 321–22, 326.

28. Phillips, *Conquest of Kansas,* 323–24; Gleed, "Samuel Walker," 263–64; Day, "Life of Wilson Shannon," 25; "Kansas," *New York Tribune,* June 11, 1856, 5; "Still Later from Kansas," *Baltimore Sun,* June 11, 1856, 1; "From Our Kansas Correspondent," *Milwaukee Daily Sentinel,* June 12, 1856, 2; "Wilson Shannon," *Connecticut Courant* (Hartford), February 23, 1856, 2.

29. Dr. Aristides Rodrique (1810–June 11, 1857) was born in Philadelphia to French parents who owned a sugar plantation with slaves in St. Domingue and fled during the revolt. Rodrique, sometimes spelled Rodrigue, studied medicine at the University of Pennsylvania. He married Ann Caroline Bellas of Sunbury, and they had nine children born in various counties of the state between 1835 and 1850. Rodrique was a founding member of Masonic Juniata Lodge No. 282, Blair County, Pa., on December 7, 1853. He moved his family to Kansas the next year and with Col. Albert G. Boone founded Lecompton. Rodrique became the first postmaster and built the three-story Rowena hotel. The physician was described as "a short, slenderly-built, keen-eyed and almost raven-haired man, with military whiskers, and an intellectual brow." Rodrique died of gastritis in 1857, and within a year his son Andrew was killed in a fight outside the Star Saloon. His widow took the rest of the family back to Woodridge, N.J. See "Dr. Aristides Rodrigue," 1; 1850 Pennsylvania Federal Census, Hollidaysburg, Blair Co., 90; Africa, *History of Huntingdon and Blair Counties,* 78; "Death of Dr. Rodrigue," *Lecompton Union,* June 12, 1857, 2; Brewerton, *War in Kansas,* 242; "Pro-Slavery Kansas Emigrants from New York," *New York Herald,* July 23, 1856, 8.

30. "Kansas," *New York Tribune,* July 30 and August 1, 1856, 6; "Pre-Emption Law," *Lecompton Union,* April 11, 1857, 1; *Lowell Daily Citizen and News,* August 5, 1856, 2; 1860 Kansas Territory Census, Arapahoe County, 525; M. H. Dozier statement, August 22, 1856, SDTP.

31. "Interesting Letter from Kanzas," *Springfield Republican,* July 30, 1856, 1; "Kansas," *New York Tribune,* July 30 and August 1, 1856, 6; H. T. Titus, sworn statement, August 25, 1856, SDTP.

32. "Brutality of Col. Titus," *New York Tribune,* August 15, 1856, 7, *Liberator* (Boston), August 22, 1856, 137, and *Holmes County Republican* (Ohio), September 11, 1856, 1; "Kansas: The New Outbreak," *New York Tribune,* August 23, 1856, 3.

33. Wilson Shannon (February 24, 1802–August 30, 1877) was governor of Kansas Territory from September 7, 1855, to August 18, 1856. He had been governor of Ohio, 1838–40 and 1842–44; U.S. minister to Mexico, 1844–45; and Ohio representative to Congress, 1853–55. Shannon became a Freemason in Belmont Lodge No. 16, St. Clairsville, Ohio, in 1846. In February 1849 he organized a mining company that went to the California gold fields but disbanded after finding only two thousand dollars in gold in one year. See Day, "Life of Wilson Shannon," 170–72, 283–84; "Executive Minutes," 3:323; "Affairs in Kansas," *New York Times,* July 31, 1856, 8; *St. Louis Democrat* quoted in "From and About Kanzas," *Springfield Republican,* September 15, 1856, 2; Denslow, 10,000 *Famous Freemasons,* 4:125.

34. "Kansas: The New Outbreak," *New York Tribune,* August 23, 1856, 3; 1860 Kansas Federal Census, Douglas County, Lawrence, 32; 1865 Kansas State Census, Leavenworth, Ward 2, Roll 5, KSHS;

35. Massachusetts State Census, Deerfield, June 1, 1855, New England Historic Genealogical Society, Boston, Mass.; "The War in Kansas," *New York Times,* August 25, 1856, 1; *St. Louis Republican* repr. in "Kansas Affairs," *New York Herald,* September 7, 1856, 8; "From Kansas," *Albany Evening Journal,* August 22, 1856, 2; Gleed, "Samuel Walker," 268–69; Gihon, *Geary and Kansas,* 93–94; "Civil War Renewed in Kansas!," *Lowell Daily Citizen and News,* August 22, 1856, 2; "The War in Kansas," *New York Times,* August 26, 1856, 1; "The War in Kansas," *New York Herald,* August 25, 1856, 2; "Kansas: Details of the Fight at Fort Saunders," *New York Tribune,* August 29, 1856, 3; "Affairs in Kansas," *New York Herald,* September 1, 1856, 8; "The Murder of Hoyt, and Consequent Disturbances," *Springfield Republican,* September 2, 1856, 2; "Attack on Col. Treadwell," *Leavenworth Weekly Herald,* September 6, 1856, 1; "Matters in Kansas," *Cleveland Leader,* September 11, 1856, 2.

36. David Starr Hoyt (February 17, 1821–August 12, 1856), born in Deerfield, Mass., was initially buried at Rock Creek. On June 23, 1857, his remains were exhumed and then interred with military honors between the graves of Thomas Barber and Henry Shombre at what is now Pioneer Cemetery on the West Campus of the University of Kansas at Lawrence. See "Funeral of Major Hoyt," *Kansas Herald of Freedom,* June 27, 1857; "From Our Kansas Correspondent," *New York Reformer* (Watertown), September 18, 1856, 2; "The War in Kansas," *New York Times,* August 26, 1856, 1; Testimony of S. P. Hand, December 2, 1856, Thaddeus Hyatt Collection, Box 1, Folder 5, KSHS; Testimonies of Alexander McArthur, James Hall, and Jerome Hazen, December 5–7, 1856, ibid.; John Ritchie to F. G. Adams, September 30, 1881, John Ritchie folder, Miscellaneous Collection, ibid.; "Challenge from Gen. Lane to the Border Ruffians," *New York Times,* October 6, 1856, 2.

37. Calvin Cutter (May 1, 1807–June 20, 1872), born in Jaffrey, N.H., studied and practiced medicine in his native state and compiled the textbook *Cutter's Physiology.* He smuggled a supply of Sharps rifles into Kansas before returning with the Worcester armed company of sixty men. During the Civil War he was surgeon of the Twenty-first Massachusetts Infantry and was twice wounded and taken prisoner at Bull Run. See Malin, "Colonel Harvey and His Forty Thieves," 57–58; "Report of the St. Louis Kansas Committee," *New York Herald,* September

24, 1856, 4; "The War in Kansas," *New York Weekly Herald,* August 30, 1856, 275; "Later from Kansas," *Boston Herald,* August 22, 1856, 2; "Gov. Geary's Policy," *Lecompton Union,* November 6, 1856, 2; "Kansas Experience of J. A. Harvey," Thaddeus Hyatt Collection, Box 2, Folder 3, KSHS; "Who Are the Ruffians in Kansas?," *Washington (Pa.) Review and Examiner,* September 13, 1856, 2.

38. James A. Harvey (1827–December 22, 1857) died of heart disease. Although he has been described as a Mexican War veteran, there is no military record to corroborate this, nor is there a Mexican War widow's pension file. See Malin, "Colonel Harvey and His Forty Thieves," 58; "The Kansas War," *New York Times,* September 6, 1856, 1; Phillips, *Conquest of Kansas,* 139.

39. "Old Sacramento" was one of ten bronze cannons captured by Missouri volunteers on February 28, 1847, at the Battle of Sacramento during the Mexican War and deposited at the arsenal in Liberty, Mo. Missourians moved it from there for use during Bleeding Kansas. "Old Sacramento" has been variably described as a four-, six-, or eight-pounder cannon. The "Old Sacramento" Cannoneers Association has described it as "probably an 8 pounder." The cannon exploded when it was being fired in 1896, and the mangled relic is presently on display in the Watkins Community Museum of History in Lawrence, Kans. See "Gov. Shannon's Defence," *Daily National Intelligencer,* November 28, 1856, 2; "The Kansas War," *New York Times,* September 16, 1856, 1; "War in Kansas!," *Glasgow (Mo.) Weekly Times,* August 21, 1856, 2; "From Kansas," *Albany Evening Journal,* August 22, 1856, 2; Gleed, "Samuel Walker," 259, 268; Gihon, *Geary and Kansas,* 94; Phillips, *Conquest of Kansas,* 344–49; "The President's Message," *New Albany (Ind.) Daily Ledger,* August 22, 1856, 3; "Exciting News from Kansas," *Daily Ohio Statesman* (Columbus), August 24, 1856, 2; "The War in Kansas," *New York Times,* August 25, 1856, 1; Wilder, *Annals of Kansas,* 104; "Kansas: The New Outbreak," *New York Tribune,* August 23, 1856, 3; "The War in Kansas," *New York Times,* August 26, 1856, 1; "Kansas—Horrid Atrocities—Interesting Letter," *Lowell Daily Citizen and News,* August 30, 1856, 2; "Pro-Slavery Accounts," *New York Tribune,* September 8, 1856, 5; "The War in Kansas," *New York Weekly Herald,* August 30, 1856, 275.

40. "War in Kansas!," *Glasgow(Mo.) Weekly Times,* August 21, 1856, 2; "The President's Message," *New Albany (Ind.) Daily Ledger,* August 22, 1856, 3; "Exciting News from Kansas," *Daily Ohio Statesman* (Columbus), August 24, 1856, 2; "The War in Kansas," *New York Times,* August 25, 1856, 1; *St. Louis Republican* repr. in "Kansas Affairs," *New York Herald,* September 7, 1856, 8; *Charleston Mercury,* September 9, 1856, 2; "Kansas: The New Outbreak," *New York Tribune,* August 23, 1856, 3; "The War in Kansas," *New York Times,* August 26, 1856, 1; "Kansas—Horrid Atrocities—Interesting Letter," *Lowell Daily Citizen and News,* August 30, 1856, 2; "Pro-Slavery Accounts," *New York Tribune,* September 8, 1856, 5; *Westport Border Ruffian* quoted in "Civil War on the Border," *Philadelphia Inquirer,* August 25, 1856, 1; "Glorious Victory," *Milwaukee Daily Sentinel,* August 28, 1856, 1; "The War in Kansas," *New York Weekly Herald,* August 30, 1856, 275.

41. "From Kansas," *Albany Evening Journal,* August 22, 1856, 2; "The War in Kansas," *New York Times,* August 25 and 26, 1856, 1; "Kansas: The New Outbreak," *New York Tribune,* August 23, 1856, 3; "The War in Kansas," *New York Weekly Herald,* August 30, 1856, 275.

42. "From Our Kansas Correspondent," *Milwaukee Daily Sentinel,* August 29, 1856, 2.

43. "Attention—Regiment!," *Lecompton Union,* August 14, 1856; "Kansas: The New Outbreak," *New York Tribune,* August 23, 1856, 3.

44. "The War in Kansas," *New York Herald,* August 25, 1856, 2; Gleed, "Samuel Walker," 268–69.

45. Hugh "Potter" Young (December 14, 1832–Ocober 20, 1912) was a Scotch-Irishman born in Killyleagh, Northern Ireland. In 1850 he visited a brother in Potter County, Pa., and remained in America doing various jobs until becoming a correspondent for the *New York Tribune.* Young returned to Coudersport, Pa., in 1856 and three years later wed Lois Ann

Butterworth, with whom he had three sons. On July 6, 1863, after the Battle of Gettysburg, he enlisted in Company F, Thirty-fifth Pennsylvania Infantry Regiment as quartermaster. In 1876 Young was elected representative to the Pennsylvania legislature, and his twin brother, Thomas, served as governor of Ohio, 1877–78. Hugh then went into the banking business and held various posts until his death. See Col. Hugh Young file, Potter County Historical Society, Potter Co., Pa.; "Attack on Col. Treadwell," *Leavenworth Weekly Herald,* September 6, 1856, 1; "Kansas: Details of the Fight at Fort Saunders," *New York Tribune,* August 29, 1856, 3; Gihon, *Geary and Kansas,* 94; Testimonies of Alexander McArthur, James Hall, and Jerome Hazen, December 5–7, 1856, KSHS; "From Our Kansas Correspondent," *New York Reformer* (Watertown), September 18, 1856, 2; "Matters in Kansas," *Cleveland Leader,* September 11, 1856, 2; "Letter from Kansas," *Nashville Union and American,* September 6, 1856, 2; "Exciting News from Kansas," *Newark Daily Advertiser,* August 22, 1856, 2; "Civil War Renewed in Kansas!," *Lowell Daily Citizen and News,* August 22, 1856, 2; "Glorious Victory," *Milwaukee Daily Sentinel,* August 28, 1856, 2; "Kansas—Horrid Atrocities—Interesting Letter," *Lowell Daily Citizen and News,* August 30, 1856, 2; "Late News from Kansas," *Portland (Maine) Advertiser,* September 16, 1856, 4; "Report of the St. Louis Kansas Committee," *New York Herald,* September 24, 1856, 4.

46. The unfinished territorial capitol building at Lecompton was abandoned after Kansas became a free state. Lane University was erected on its foundation in 1882, and today the building is the Lane University & Territorial Capital Museum, 609 E. Woodson Avenue, Lecompton. See Malin, "Colonel Harvey and His Forty Thieves," 60; "The War in Kansas," *New York Times,* August 26, 1856, 1; "Civil War on the Border," *Philadelphia Inquirer,* August 25, 1856, 1; "The War in Kansas," *New York Herald,* August 25, 1856, 2; "Matters in Kansas," *Cleveland Leader,* September 11, 1856, 2; "Glorious Victory," *Milwaukee Daily Sentinel,* August 28, 1856, 2; "Kansas Correspondence of the Atlas," *Boston Daily Atlas,* September 24, 1856, 1; Andreas, *History of the State of Kansas,* 179; Gleed, "Samuel Walker," 270.

47. George Washington Clarke (1812–December 19, 1880) was born in Washington, D.C., and moved to Arkansas in 1832. He became associate editor of the *Van Buren (Ark.) Intelligencer* in July 1843. He married the following year and became sole proprietor and editor of the *Intelligencer,* a Democratic Party organ. In 1845 Clarke left the newspaper for two years after being appointed emigration agent for the Choctaw removing from Mississippi to western lands. After his return he was elected to the Arkansas State Senate in 1850. Three years later Clarke was named agent for the Pottawatomie Indians in the Kansas Territory, and he moved there with his slaves in 1855. He killed Thomas W. Barber, of the Bloomington Volunteers, during a shootout with free-state militants outside of Lawrence on December 6, 1855. Clarke escaped an assassination attempt in his Lecompton home in 1856. He was removed as Indian agent in December 1856 for participating in territorial violence. The following year Clarke worked at the U.S. Land Office in Fort Scott, and he settled in southwestern Missouri in August 1858. He joined the Confederate army in 1861 as a private in the Twenty-fifth Arkansas Infantry and at the end of the war migrated to Mexico. Clarke was editor and proprietor of the English-language newspaper *Two Republics* in Mexico City, where he passed away. See Brewerton, *War in Kansas,* 137; "Letter from Kansas," *Richmond Whig,* September 5, 1856, 4; Gihon, *Geary and Kansas,* 66–67; Day, "Life of Wilson Shannon," 227.

48. "Letter from Kansas," *Richmond Whig,* September 5, 1856, 4; "Miscellaneous News," *New York Times,* March 9, 1857, 2; "Civil War on the Border," *Philadelphia Inquirer,* August 25, 1856, 1; Testimonies of Alexander McArthur, James Hall, and Jerome Hazen, December 5–7, 1856, KSHS; "The War in Kansas," *New York Herald,* August 25, 1856, 2; "Glorious Victory," *Milwaukee Daily Sentinel,* August 28, 1856, 2; "The Recent Fights in Kanzas," *Springfield Republican,* August 30, 1856, 4; "Matters in Kansas," *Cleveland Leader,* September 11, 1856, 2; Gleed, "Samuel Walker," 270; "The Kansas War," *New York Times,* August 29, 1856, 1.

49. "Experiences of N. W. Spicer in Kansas," Thaddeus Hyatt Collection, Box 2, Folder 3, State Archives Division, Kansas Historical Society, Topeka; "Glorious Victory," *Milwaukee Daily Sentinel,* August 28, 1856, 2; "Matters in Kansas," *Cleveland Leader,* September 11, 1856, 2; "The War in Kansas," *New York Times,* August 26, 1856, 1.

50. "The War in Kansas—Attack on Titus' House," *Daily Cleveland Herald,* August 30, 1856; Cordley, *History of Lawrence, Kansas,* 118; "Civil War Renewed in Kansas!," *Lowell Daily Citizen and News,* August 22, 1856, 2; "The War in Kansas," *New York Times,* August 26, 1856, 1; John Ritchie to F. G. Adams, September 30, 1881, John Ritchie folder, Miscellaneous Collection, KSHS; Testimonies of Alexander McArthur, James Hall, and Jerome Hazen, December 5–7, 1856, ibid.; "Matters in Kansas," *Cleveland Leader,* September 11, 1856, 2; "The Kansas War," *New York Times,* August 29, 1856, 1; Titus statement, August 25, 1856, SDTP; "Glorious Victory," *Milwaukee Daily Sentinel,* August 28, 1856, 2; Gleed, "Samuel Walker," 270; "The War in Kansas," *New York Times,* August 26, 1856, 1; "The Kansas War," *New York Times,* September 3, 1856, 3.

51. Henry J. Shombre (1826–August 16, 1856) became wealthy after laboring in the California gold mines. He returned to Cincinnati and enrolled in Farmer's College and studied law. He then opened a law practice in Richmond, Ind. Shombre, described as "somewhat eccentric," declared his intention to make Kansas "a Free State or perish" during a public speech in which he raised eighteen volunteers, including his physician Dr. Avery. The company joined the so-called Army of the North at Iowa City. Shombre's military enthusiasm came from his British father, who had been a soldier in the Napoleonic Wars. Three days after arriving in Kansas, he was buried with military honors in Mount Oread, in a now unmarked grave next to the free-soil martyr Thomas W. Barber, in present-day Pioneer Cemetery. Northern newspapers gave contradictory accounts as to his final words to either his friends or to his nonexistent wife: "I die cheerfully—giving my life freely for Freedom and Kansas." They also purported that he had been "murdered" instead of mortally wounded in combat. See "One of the Fallen in Kansas," *Rockford (Ill.) Republican,* September 10, 1856, 1; "An Almost Forgotten Hero," *Kansas City Star,* January 22, 1913, 6; Gleed, "Samuel Walker," 271; "The War in Kansas," *Daily Cleveland Herald,* August 30, 1856; "The Recent Fights in Kanzas," *Springfield Republican,* August 30, 1856, 4; "Kansas—Horrid Atrocities—Interesting Letter," *Lowell Daily Citizen and News,* August 30, 1856, 2; "Meeting in Lawrence, Kanzas," *Springfield Republican,* September 10, 1856, 1.

52. Thomas Bickerton (June 16, 1816–January 22, 1901), born in North Berwick, Scotland, arrived in Norfolk, Va., in 1832. He was a machinist and locomotive builder by trade. On November 23, 1852, Bickerton married twenty-three-year-old Circia D. Clapp in Portland, Maine, and she died ten months later during childbirth. He became a naturalized American citizen in Portland on March 13, 1855. Bickerton married twenty-two-year-old Hannah Dutton in Boston on March 4, 1858. On July 23, 1861, he enrolled as captain of Company G, Third Battery Lane's Brigade, Kansas Light Artillery Volunteers at Fort Leavenworth. Bickerton was discharged on February 13, 1862, after the rheumatism that he had contracted in Kansas turned into dropsy, which was treated with surgery. He then resided on a farm in Kanwaka, Kans., with his wife, mother-in-law, and two adopted children until the 1880s, when he and Hannah moved to a twenty-acre farm in Deland, Fla. Bickerton began receiving a twenty-dollar monthly military invalid pension on May 22, 1888, after falling off a ladder and injuring his groin. See Index to New England Naturalization Petitions, 1791–1906, M1299, Roll 49, RG 85, NARA; 1865 Kansas State Census, Kanwaka, 82, Roll 3, KSHS; 1870 Kansas Federal Census, Kanwaka, 275; 1880 Kansas Federal Census, Kanwaka, 40; 1900 Florida Federal Census, Orange County, Orlando, 6; "Matters in Kansas," *Cleveland Leader,* September 11, 1856, 2; "Kansas," *Chicago Daily Inter Ocean,* April 25, 1888, 2; "The Kansas War," *New York Times,*

August 29, 1856, 1; "Kansas Correspondence of the Atlas," *Boston Daily Atlas,* September 24, 1856, 1; Gleed, "Samuel Walker," 271; "From Our Kansas Correspondent," *New York Reformer* (Watertown), September 18, 1856, 2; Gihon, *Geary and Kansas,* 94–95; Cordley, *History of Lawrence, Kansas,* 115.

53. Testimonies of Alexander McArthur, James Hall, and Jerome Hazen, December 5–7, 1856, KSHS; "Glorious Victory," *Milwaukee Daily Sentinel,* August 28, 1856, 2; "Block Houses," *Leavenworth Weekly Herald,* October 4, 1856, 1; "Kansas—Horrid Atrocities— Interesting Letter," *Lowell Daily Citizen and News,* August 30, 1856, 2; Cordley, *History of Lawrence, Kansas,* 115, 118.

54. Gleed, "Samuel Walker," 271; "Matters in Kansas," *Cleveland Leader,* September 11, 1856, 2; "From Our Kansas Correspondent," *New York Reformer* (Watertown), September 18, 1856, 2; Titus statement, August 25, 1856, SDTP; "The Kansas War," *New York Times,* August 29, 1856, 1; Gihon, *Geary and Kansas,* 95.

55. The minié bullet lodged in Titus's back since 1856 "came out just before he died in a large abscess." The widow of Col. James Harvey donated the Titus sword in 1884 to the Kansas State Historical Society, and it is now on display at the Kansas Museum of History at Topeka. See "Early Recollections of Minnie Titus Ensey," Henry Theodore Titus Collection, North Brevard Public Library, Titusville, Fla., 2; Testimonies of Alexander McArthur, James Hall, and Jerome Hazen, December 5–7, 1856, KSHS; "Men of Note in Kansas: Col. Titus," *Ripley (Ohio) Bee,* February 7, 1857; Gihon, *Geary and Kansas,* 95; "Glorious Victory," *Milwaukee Daily Sentinel,* August 28, 1856, 2; "Kansas—Horrid Atrocities—Interesting Letter," *Lowell Daily Citizen and News,* August 30, 1856, 2; "The Kansas War," *New York Times,* September 3, 1856, 3; Gleed, "Samuel Walker," 271–72; Cordley, *History of Lawrence, Kansas,* 119.

56. Dr. James Malachi Pelot (February 18, 1833–February 24, 1888) was a graduate of the Citadel, Charleston, S.C., in 1851. Four years later he received a degree from the Medical College of the State of South Carolina, Charleston. Pelot moved to Lecompton in 1856, practiced medicine, and in 1859 was a founder of the Kansas Medical Society. He returned to his native state after the Civil War began and enlisted as a private in Company D, Fifth S.C. Infantry, at Orangeburg. Pelot was wounded at the Seven Days Battles before Richmond in June 1862 and sent home to recuperate. The following year he was promoted to assistant surgeon at James Island, where he was captured on September 9, 1863, and exchanged three months later. Pelot then served as assistant surgeon at Fort Sumter, with the Third South Carolina (Palmetto) Battalion Light Artillery and at General Hospital No. 1, Savannah. He married Eleanor J. Bulkley in 1868 and two years later was practicing medicine at Elmwood, Saline Co., Mo. See F. T. Hambrecht and J. L. Koste, "Biographical Register of Physicians Who Served the Confederacy in a Medical Capacity" (November 24, 2013), unpub. database; 1880 Missouri Federal Census, Brownsville, Saline Co., 417; "Masonry in the Kansas Troubles," 184; Titus statement, August 25, 1856, SDTP; "Glorious Victory," *Milwaukee Daily Sentinel,* August 28, 1856, 2; Robert B. Pfuetze, grand secretary of the Grand Lodge AF&AM of Kansas, e-mail message to author, June 4, 2003.

57. Gleed, "Samuel Walker," 272; "The Kansas War," *New York Times,* September 3, 1856, 3.

58. Charles W. Topliff was falsely portrayed as a "West Point graduate" by Redpath in the *St. Louis Democrat* quoted in "Reliable from Kansas," *Albany Evening Journal,* May 30, 1856, 2, and in Phillips, *Conquest of Kansas,* 321. See "Report on Kansas," *Charleston Courier,* September 27, 1856, 1; "Glorious Victory," *Milwaukee Daily Sentinel,* August 28, 1856, 2; "Report of the St. Louis Kansas Committee," *New York Herald,* September 24, 1856, 4; Malin, "Col. Harvey and His Forty Thieves," 58, 61.

59. Titus statement, August 25, 1856, SDTP; "The Robberies by Lane's Band in Kansas," *Weekly St. Louis Pilot,* September 20, 1856, 2; "Notice," *Lecompton Union,* November 27, 1856, 3.

60. "Kansas Correspondence," *New York Reformer* (Watertown), October 2, 1856, 2.

61. "From Our Kansas Correspondent," *Milwaukee Daily Sentinel,* August 29, 1856, 2; Gleed, "Samuel Walker," 272.

62. "Glorious Victory," *Milwaukee Daily Sentinel,* August 28, 1856, 2; "The Heroes of the South in Kansas: Col. H. T. Titus," *New York Tribune,* January 5, 1857, 6; *Chicago Tribune* quoted in "Important from Kansas," *Jackson (Mich.) Citizen,* August 28, 1856, 1; "Kansas—Horrid Atrocities—Interesting Letter," *Lowell Daily Citizen and News,* August 30, 1856, 2; "The War in Kansas—Attack on Titus' House," *Daily Cleveland Herald,* August 30, 1856; "The Recent Fights in Kanzas," *Springfield Republican,* August 30, 1856, 4; *Alton Weekly Courier* cited in "Affairs in Kansas," *New York Herald,* September 1, 1856, 8; *Savannah News* cited in "Facts from Kansas," *Charleston Courier,* September 6, 1856, 2.

63. Malin, "Col. Harvey and His Forty Thieves," 61; "The Kansas War," *New York Times,* September 2, 1856, 2; Gihon, *Geary and Kansas,* 94.

64. John Sedgwick (September 13, 1813–May 9, 1864), born in Cornwall, Conn., graduated from the U.S. Military Academy in 1837 and served in the Seminole War as a second lieutenant in the Second Artillery. During the Mexican War he participated in all the major battles of the Veracruz to Mexico City campaign in 1847. Sedgwick was appointed brigadier general of Civil War Volunteers in August 1861 and was engaged in the Virginia Peninsula Campaign, where he was wounded in the arm and leg and promoted to major general. At the Battle of Antietam, he was hit by three bullets and disabled for three months. Sedgwick had a commanding role in the battles of Fredericksburg, Gettysburg, Rappahannock Station, and Mine Run in 1863 and in the Battle of the Wilderness in 1864. He was openly directing the placing of artillery for the Battle of Spotsylvania when shot below the eye by a sharpshooter after assuring his men that the enemy "couldn't hit an elephant at this distance." See Warner, *Generals in Blue,* 430–31; David Kendall statement, August 23, 1856, SDTP.

65. John Brown, Jr. to [John Brown?], John Brown Collection, Box 1, Folder 17, KSHS; "Letter from Kansas," *Nashville Union and American,* September 6, 1856, 2; "Affairs of Kansas," *New York Herald,* September 9, 1856, 8; Cordley, *History of Lawrence, Kansas,* 116; Gleed, "Samuel Walker," 270.

66. Gleed, "Samuel Walker," 272; Gihon, *Geary and Kansas,* 95.

67. "How Capt. Walker's Wife Scolded Him Because He Didn't Kill 'Old Titus,'" *New York Tribune,* December 10, 1856, 7; Gleed, "Samuel Walker," 272.

68. Carmi William Babcock (April 21, 1830–October 22, 1889) was born Franklin County, Vt., where he was a teacher until moving to St. Paul, Minn., in 1850. He then studied law before moving to Lawrence in September 1854. Babcock was the first postmaster and the second mayor of the town. He served in the Free State Legislature in 1856 and was taken prisoner five times. Babcock was appointed surveyor general in 1869 and 1878. See "Glorious Victory," *Milwaukee Daily Sentinel,* August 28, 1856, 2; Testimonies of Alexander McArthur, James Hall, and Jerome Hazen, December 5–7, 1856, KSHS; "Later from Kansas," *Cleveland Leader,* August 28, 1856, 3; Gihon, *Geary and Kansas,* 96; "Early Recollections of Minnie Titus Ensey," Henry Theodore Titus Collection, North Brevard Public Library, Titusville, Fla., 2; "The Murder of Hoyt, and Consequent Disturbances," *Springfield Republican,* September 2, 1856, 2; Gleed, "Samuel Walker," 272.

69. Gleed, "Samuel Walker," 273; "Kansas Affairs," *New York Herald,* September 7, 1856, 8; "The Kansas War," *Boston Daily Atlas,* September 9, 1856, 2.

70. Edward Stevens Hopkins is erroneously located in Kansas at this time in Schafer, *Thunder on the River,* 16. See "Florida and Kansas," *Charleston Courier,* September 15, 1856, 2; "The War in Kansas," *New York Times,* August 25, 1856, 1; "Affairs in Kansas," *New York Herald,* September 1, 1856, 8; "Kansas Affairs," *New York Herald,* September 7, 1856, 8; "Men of Note in Kansas: Col. Titus," *Ripley (Ohio) Bee,* February 7, 1857.

71. Maj. James Burnett Abbott (December 3, 1818–March 2, 1897) purchased the howitzer from the Ames Manufacturing Company of Chicopee, Mass., after a fund-raising tour in New York. It was smuggled from Kansas City to Lawrence by Thomas Bickerton and David and Robert Buffum and captured by proslavery forces on May 21, 1856. The howitzer was used during the Civil War by James H. Lane's brigade. Today it is on exhibit at the Kansas Museum of History at Topeka. See "The War in Kansas—Attack on Titus' House," *Daily Cleveland Herald*, August 30, 1856; "Important from Kansas," *Jackson (Mich.) Citizen*, August 28, 1856, 1; "Later from Kansas," *Albany Evening Journal*, August 25, 1856, 3; "Glorious Victory," *Milwaukee Daily Sentinel*, August 28, 1856, 1; "The Recent Fights in Kanzas," *Springfield Republican*, August 30, 1856, 4; "Fights in Kansas," *Semi-Weekly Raleigh Register*, August 30, 1856; "The Murder of Hoyt, and Consequent Disturbances," *Springfield Republican*, September 2, 1856, 2; "Matters in Kansas," *Cleveland Leader*, September 11, 1856, 2; "From Kansas," *New York Times*, August 29, 1856, 4; "The Kansas War," *New York Times*, September 3, 1856, 3; Gihon, *Geary and Kansas*, 96; Day, "Life of Wilson Shannon," 287.

72. Persifor Frazer Smith (November 16, 1798–May 17, 1858) was a Philadelphia lawyer and colonel of volunteers in the Seminole War, 1836–38. He was commissioned as a U.S. Army colonel during the Mexican War and distinguished himself at the battle of Monterrey and in the campaign for Mexico City. Smith commanded the Department of Texas during 1850–56. Albion Parris Howe (March 25, 1818–January 25, 1897), born in Standish, Maine, graduated from the U.S. Military Academy on July 1, 1841, and was assigned as a second lieutenant to the Fourth Artillery. He participated in the Mexican War battles from Veracruz to the fall of Mexico City during 1847–48 and in the Harper's Ferry Expedition to suppress John Brown's raid in 1859. During the Civil War, Howe commanded a brigade of light artillery throughout the Virginia Peninsula campaign, earning a promotion to brigadier general of U.S. Volunteers in June 1862. He participated in major battles at Antietam, Fredericksburg, Gettysburg, Rappahannock Station, and the Mine Run Operations. After the war Howe mustered out of volunteer service, reverted to his U.S. army rank of major, and served in various administrative positions until retiring as a colonel in 1882. See Cullum, *Biographical Register*, 2:9–10; "Affairs of Kansas," *New York Herald*, September 9, 1856, 8; Day, "Life of Wilson Shannon," 287; "The Kansas War," *New York Times*, September 8, 1856, 1.

73. "From Our Kansas Correspondent," *Milwaukee Daily Sentinel*, August 29, 1856, 2; "Matters in Kansas," *Cleveland Leader*, September 11, 1856, 2; Gleed, "Samuel Walker," 273; "Florida and Kansas," *Charleston Courier*, September 15, 1856, 2; Titus statement, August 25, 1856, SDTP; "Letter from Gov. Woodson," *New York Tribune*, September 15, 1856, 7.

74. John J. Jones, known as "Ottawa Jones" because he was half Indian and served as the interpreter of the tribe, appeared in a photo with "Old Sacramento" cannoneers James Redpath, August Bondi, Thomas Bickerton, George B. Gill, and John Brown's son Owen. See "Kansas Correspondence of the Atlas," *Boston Daily Atlas*, September 24, 1856, 1; "The Kansas War," *New York Times*, September 6, 1856, 1; "Kansas: Military Movements," *New York Tribune*, September 19, 1856, 5; "Report of the St. Louis Kansas Committee," *New York Herald*, September 24, 1856, 4; Gleed, "Samuel Walker," 273–74; Gihon, *Geary and Kansas*, 101, 196, 275.

75. John White Geary (December 30, 1819–February 8, 1873) served as the third governor of Kansas Territory from September 9, 1856, to March 12, 1857. At the start of the Civil War, he was colonel of the Twenty-eighth Pennsylvania Infantry, and he ascended to brigadier general in 1862. Geary participated in numerous major eastern battles and in Sherman's March to the Sea and the Carolinas Campaign. He served as governor (Republican) of Pennsylvania during 1867–73. See "The Kansas War," *New York Times*, September 6, 1856, 1; "Documents in Relation to Kansas," *Charleston Courier*, September 9, 1856, 2; "Affairs of Kansas," *New York Herald*, September 9, 1856, 8; Malin, "Colonel Harvey and His Forty Thieves," 74; "The Free State Force at Lawrence," *Rockford Republican*, September 10, 1856, 1; Gihon, *Geary and*

Kansas, 126–27, 273; "The Kansas War," *New York Times,* September 6, 1856, 1; "Interesting from Kansas," *New York Times,* September 27, 1856, 1; Speer, *Life of Gen. James H. Lane,* 115.

76. "Late News from Kansas," *Portland Advertiser,* September 16, 1856, 4; "Pressing Necessities of the Emigrants in Kansas—Letter from Rev Mr. Nute," *Springfield Republican,* September 30, 1856, 2.

77. Philip St. George Cooke (June 13, 1809–March 20, 1895) was born in Virginia and graduated from the U.S. Military Academy in 1827. He was a lieutenant in the Black Hawk War and during the Mexican War led the Mormon Battalion from Santa Fe to California. Cooke battled with the Second U.S. Dragoons against the Apaches and the Sioux during 1854–55 and participated in the Utah expedition of 1857–58, earning him a promotion to colonel. He was appointed U.S. Army brigadier general during the Civil War in 1861 and the following year ordered the disastrous uphill charge of the Fifth U.S. Cavalry at Gaines' Mill that Gen. Fitz John Porter blamed for their failure to hold the battlefield and withdraw all their guns and wounded. Cooke had no further field service. His son John Rogers Cooke and son-in-law Jeb Stuart became outstanding Confederate generals. Following the war, Cooke held various departmental commands until his retirement in 1873. See Faust, *Historical Times,* 164; "Affairs in Kansas," *Charleston Mercury,* September 8, 1856, 2; Gihon, *Geary and Kansas,* 137–38, 153–54; Mullis, *Peacekeeping on the Plains,* 224; "Kansas," *New York Tribune,* September 29, 1856, 6; "A Bulletin from Gen. Lane's Camp," *New York Tribune,* October 6, 1856, 5.

78. Gihon, *Geary and Kansas,* 100, 149–50, 152, 156; "Interesting from Kansas," *New York Times,* September 27, 1856, 1; "The War Ended," *Glasgow (Mo.) Weekly Times,* October 2, 1856, 3; "A Kansas Scene," *New York Times,* October 21, 1856, 3; "From Kansas," *Boston Evening Transcript,* September 29, 1856, 2; Mullis, *Peacekeeping on the Plains,* 224–25.

79. "Kansas," *New York Tribune,* September 29, 1856, 6; "Correspondence of Gen. J. W. Reid and Gov. Geary," *Lecompton Union,* November 6, 1856, 1; "The War Ended," *Glasgow (Mo.) Weekly Times,* October 2, 1856, 3; Gihon, *Geary and Kansas,* 151, 154; Mullis, *Peacekeeping on the Plains,* 225; "Kansas," *El Nicaraguense,* October 25, 1856, 5; "From Kansas," *Boston Evening Transcript,* September 29, 1856, 2; "Last of the Kansas Troubles," *Boston Herald,* September 29, 1856, 4; "The War Ended," *New York Tribune,* October 9, 1856, 6.

80. "Instructions to the Governor of Kansas," *Charleston Courier,* September 15, 1856, 2; "The War Ended," *Glasgow(Mo.) Weekly Times,* October 2, 1856, 3; "Kansas," *New York Tribune,* September 29, 1856, 6; Gihon, *Geary and Kansas,* 140–41, 152, 156; Malin, "Colonel Harvey and His Forty Thieves," 70; "Affairs in Kansas," *New York Times,* September 29, 1856, 1; Mullis, *Peacekeeping on the Plains,* 225; "Kansas," *El Nicaraguense,* October 25, 1856, 5; "From Kansas," *Boston Evening Transcript,* September 29, 1856, 2; "Last of the Kansas Troubles," *Boston Herald,* September 29, 1856, 4; "The War Ended," *New York Tribune,* October 9, 1856, 6.

81. "The War Ended," *Glasgow (Mo.) Weekly Times,* October 2, 1856, 3; "Kansas," *New York Tribune,* September 29, 1856, 6; "Kansas," *El Nicaraguense,* October 25, 1856, 5; "From Kansas," *Boston Evening Transcript,* September 29, 1856, 2; "Last of the Kansas Troubles," *Boston Herald,* September 29, 1856, 4; "The War Ended," *New York Tribune,* October 9, 1856, 6; "Gov. Geary's Pacification of Kansas," *Jackson (Mich.) Citizen,* October 9, 1856, 2.

82. "The War Ended," *Glasgow (Mo.) Weekly Times,* October 2, 1856, 3; "Kansas," *New York Tribune,* September 29, 1856, 6; "Kansas," *El Nicaraguense,* October 25, 1856, 5; "From Kansas," *Boston Evening Transcript,* September 29, 1856, 2; "Last of the Kansas Troubles," *Boston Herald,* September 29, 1856, 4; "The War Ended," *New York Tribune,* October 9, 1856, 6; *Kickapoo Pioneer* quoted in "The Late Kansas War," *Glasgow (Mo.) Weekly Times,* October 2, 1856, 3.

83. "Interesting from Kansas," *New York Herald,* November 15, 1856, 3; "Southern Preparations for the Subjugation of Kansas," *New York Times,* November 24, 1856, 3.

84. Gihon, *Geary and Kansas,* 276–77; "Kansas," *Washington National Era,* October 16, 1856, 167; "The Battle between Col. Harvey and the Border-Ruffians," *New York Tribune,*

October 3, 1856, 6; "Sufferings and Wrongs of the State Prisoners in Kansas," *Albany Evening Journal*, November 4, 1856, 2; "Law and Order County Convention," *Lecompton Union*, October 2, 1856, 2; Mullis, *Peacekeeping on the Plains*, 227.

85. *St. Louis Republican* quoted in "Peace in Kansas!," *Daily Ohio Statesman* (Columbus), October 5, 1856, 2; "Latest by Telegraph," *New York Times*, October 6, 1856, 2.

86. The slave Ann Clarke fled in 1857 to the home of a Mr. Howard near Topeka and hid there and at other places for a few weeks. She was found by friends of her master, who returned her to Lecompton, from where she later escaped to Chicago. See "Interesting from Kansas," *New York Times*, November 22, 1856, 2; Cory, "Slavery in Kansas," 240; "Later from Kansas," *Daily Ohio Statesman* (Columbus), October 4, 1856, 3; *St. Louis Republican* quoted in "Letter from Col. Titus," *Florida Republican*, November 5, 1856, 2, and *New York Tribune*, November 10, 1856, 6; "Col. Titus' Letter," *Lecompton Union*, November 6, 1856, 2.

87. "Kansas," *Washington National Era*, October 23, 1856, 169; "Kansas," *New York Times*, November 10, 1856, 3; "Additional Kansas Documents," *New York Tribune*, December 11, 1856, 6.

88. "From Kansas," *New York Times*, October 21, 1856, 3; Malin, "Colonel Harvey and His Forty Thieves," 74–75; "Disbanding of the Troops," *Leavenworth Weekly Herald*, December 6, 1856, 2; "Executive Minutes of Governor John W. Geary," 601; "Affairs in Kansas," *New York Herald*, October 26, 1856, 8; "From Kansas," *Rockford (Ill.) Weekly Gazette*, October 18, 1856, 3; Gihon, *Geary and Kansas*, 276–77; "The Election in Kansas," *New York Herald*, October 18, 1856.

89. *Barre (Mass.) Gazette*, October 31, 1856, 2; Mullis, *Peacekeeping on the Plains*, 227–28; "The Illegality of Whitfield's Election," *New York Times*, October 28, 1856, 1; "Interesting from Kansas," *New York Times*, October 6, 1856, 2.

90. John Henry Kagi (March 15, 1835–October 17, 1859), born in Bristolville, Ohio, was an agnostic autodidactic schoolteacher, attorney, correspondent, teetotaler, and entrepreneur. For his participation in the assault on Fort Titus, he was charged with arson, manslaughter, and murder. Inmate E. R. Moffet saw Kagi in the Lecompton prison at his writing desk busily penning articles for the *Washington National Era*. On January 31, 1857, after his release when charges were dropped, Kagi was slightly wounded in the chest in a shootout with the proslavery judge Rush Elmore in Tecumseh, Kans., over an article that he had written. The following year, when Kagi gave a speech at an abolition meeting in Cleveland, the local newspaper described him as looking "like a melancholy Brigand." John Brown appointed him secretary of war in his provisional government. During the Harper's Ferry raid, Kagi was second in command with the rank of captain. He seized Hall's Rifle Works with five men, but they all quickly fled, and he was shot and killed while swimming across the Shenandoah River. See Description of J. H. Kagi by E. R. Moffet, March 4, 1860, Richard Hinton Collection, Box 1, Folder 12, KSHS; *Arkansas Weekly Gazette* (Little Rock), November 5, 1859, 2; Featherstonhaugh, "John Brown's Men," 288–89; "Kansas," *Washington National Era*, November 13, 1856, 183.

91. "Kansas," *New York Tribune*, November 10, 1856, 6; "A Visit to the Free-State Prisoners," *New York Tribune*, December 10, 1856, 6; "Kansas," *Washington National Era*, October 16 and 30, November 13, 1856; Gihon, *Geary and Kansas*, 143; "The Free-State Prisoners at Lecompton Bound over for Murder," *New York Times*, October 17, 1856, 2; "Kansas," *Charleston Courier*, October 18, 1856, 1; Description of J. H. Kagi by E. R. Moffet, March 4, 1860, Richard Hinton Collection, Box 1, Folder 12, KSHS; "Wholesale Prison, Lecompton," *Washington National Era*, November 27, 1856, 191.

92. "Kansas," *Washington National Era*, October 16 and November 6, 1856; "A Kansas Dungeon," *St. Albans (Vt.) Messenger*, October 23, 1856, 3; "Sufferings and Wrongs of the State Prisoners in Kansas," *Albany Evening Journal*, November 4, 1856, 2; "Good Omens for Kansas," *Springfield Republican*, December 5, 1856, 2; "Names of Prisoners in Custody at Lecompton," William I. R. Blackman Collection, Box 1, Folder 2, KSHS.

93. *Missouri Democrat* quoted in "Kansas," *New York Tribune*, November 10, 1856, 6.

94. William N. Nace built the territorial Council Building in Lecompton in 1857, and three years later it became the U.S. Land Office. See Deed Record, vol. A, 60, Douglas County, Kans., Kenneth Spencer Research Library, University of Kansas, Lawrence; William M. Nace, November 25, 1857, Kansas Tract Books, 1854–1965, vols. 22–24, 184, Roll 8, MS-328, KSHS; "Lecompton," *Leavenworth Weekly Herald,* November 29, 1856, 2; 1860 Kansas Territory Federal Census, Lecompton Township, 188; "New Advertisements," *Kansas National Democrat,* May 10, 1860.

95. *St. Louis Republican* quoted in "Letter from Col. Titus," *Florida Republican,* November 5, 1856, 2, and *New York Tribune,* November 10, 1856, 6; John W. Geary to Col. H. T. Titus, November 8, 1856, John White Geary Papers, Sterling Memorial Library, Yale University, New Haven, Conn.; H. T. Titus to John W. Geary, ibid.

96. Samuel Dexter Lecompte (December 13, 1814–April 24, 1888), born in Dorchester County, Md., was appointed by President Franklin Pierce as chief justice of the Supreme Court, Kansas Territory and served from December 1854 to March 9, 1859. David C. Buffum (November 11, 1822–September 12, 1856), born in Salem, Mass., moved to Kansas in 1854 and was first sergeant in Capt. Samuel Walker's Company D, Second Regiment, First Brigade, Kansas Volunteers at Lawrence in 1855. He helped transport the Abbott howitzer to Lawrence. Buffum's original grave marker at Pioneer Cemetery is in the Kansas Museum of History at Topeka. See "Geary vs. Donaldson," *Lecompton Union,* November 20, 1856, 2; "Governor Geary and the Kansas Judiciary," *Baltimore Sun,* November 26, 1856, 2; "From Kansas," *New York Times,* October 15, 1856, 3; "Gov. Geary and the Judiciary," *Leavenworth Weekly Herald,* November 8, 1856, 4; "From Kansas," *New York Times,* November 28, 1856, 1; Muster Roll of Capt. Samuel Walker, Company D, Second Regiment, First Brigade, Kansas Volunteers, December 12, 1855, KSHS; Gihon, *Geary and Kansas,* 171–79; "Judge Lecompte vs. Gov. Geary," *Lecompton Union,* January 7, 1857, 2; "Judge Lecompte's Letter to Wm. L. Hearn, Esq.," *Easton (Md.) Star,* February 3, 1857, 2; "From Kansas," *New York Times,* December 10, 1856, 3.

97. Gihon, *Geary and Kansas,* 206–7; "Nicaragua Bail," *New York Tribune,* December 12, 1856, 7; "Affairs in Kansas," *Washington National Era,* December 4, 1856, 19; John Ritchie to F. G. Adams, September 30, 1881, John Ritchie folder, Miscellaneous Collection, KSHS.

98. "Nicaragua Bail," *New York Tribune,* December 12, 1856, 7; "Affairs in Kansas," *Baltimore Sun,* December 12, 1856, 1; "The Free-State Prisoners," *New York Times,* December 2, 1856, 2; "Affairs in Kansas," *Washington National Era,* December 4, 1856, 19; "The Manifesto of Free Kansas," *Belmont Chronicle* (St. Clairsville, Ohio), May 14, 1857, 2.

99. "Public Meeting," *Lecompton Union,* November 20, 1856, 2.

100. *Boston Daily Atlas,* October 28, 1856, 2; *Barre Gazette,* October 31, 1856, 2; "Wholesale Prison, Lecompton," *Washington National Era,* November 27, 1856, 191.

101. "Wholesale Prison, Lecompton," *Washington National Era,* November 27, 1856, 191; "From the Free State Men in Prison in Kansas," *Cleveland Leader,* November 4, 1856, 1; *Leavenworth Weekly Herald,* December 20, 1856, 2; "Letter from a Free-State Prisoner in Kansas," *New York Tribune,* December 10, 1856, 7.

102. "Nicaragua," *Lecompton Union,* November 6, 1856, 2; "General Walker's Recruiting Agent in Kansas," *Albany Evening Journal,* November 8, 1856, 2; "Kansas—Facts and Prospects," *Springfield Republican,* November 8, 1856, 4; "Kansas Intelligence," *Rockford Republican,* December 4, 1856, 2; "From Kansas," *New York Times,* December 5, 1856, 2; "Kansas," *New York Tribune,* December 12 and 15, 1856; "The Nicaraguan Volunteers," *Lecompton Union,* November 20, 1856, 1; "The March of the Ruffians," *Daily Cleveland Herald,* December 4, 1856; "Affairs in Kansas," *Washington National Era,* December 18, 1856, 202; "Foreign News," *Pacific Commercial Advertiser* (Honolulu), February 5, 1857, 3.

103. "Disbanding of the Troops," *Leavenworth Weekly Herald,* December 6, 1856, 2; "From Kansas," *New York Times,* December 5, 1856, 2; "Gov. Geary's Militia Disbanded," *New York*

Tribune, December 15, 1856, 7; *Nashville Union and American,* December 16, 1856, 2; "Kansas," *Lecompton Union,* January 15, 1857, 1; "Nicaragua," *Lecompton Union,* November 27, 1856, 2; Gihon, *Geary and Kansas,* 277–79.

104. "Affairs in Kansas," *Baltimore Sun,* December 12, 1856, 1; "Late Kanzas News," *Springfield Republican,* December 13, 1856, 4; "Kansas," *New York Tribune,* December 15, 1856, 6; "Affairs in Kansas," *Washington National Era,* December 18, 1856, 202; 1850 Ohio Federal Census, Mount Gilead, Morrow Co., 513.

105. "Buford and Titus Leave Kansas in Disgust," *Daily Cleveland Herald,* December 15, 1856; "Col. Titus Recruiting for Nicaragua," *New York Times,* December 5, 1856, 2.

106. The managers of the December 3, 1856, cotillion party were Col. T. F. Scott, Maj. L. S. Boling, Dr. W. S. Catterson, J. Tripplett, J. G. Spivey, J. W. Corser, and John D. Henderson. See cotillion party invitation in Miscellaneous Collection, James M. Pelot, M.D. folder, KSHS; "Kansas," *Washington National Era,* November 27, 1856, 191; "Buford and Titus Leave Kansas in Disgust," *Daily Cleveland Herald,* December 15, 1856; "What the Conspiracy Against Free Immigration to Kansas Has Cost the People of Missouri," *New Lisbon (Ohio) Anti-Slavery Bugle,* December 13, 1856, 3; "Col. H. T. Titus," *Leavenworth Weekly Herald,* December 6, 1856, 3.

107. Kansas City, Mo., statistical facts, May 1857, Special Collections Vertical File, Kansas City Public Library, Kansas City, Mo.; "Good News from Kanzas," *Springfield Republican,* December 24, 1856, 2; "Colonel Titus Short of Funds," *Bangor Daily Whig & Courier,* December 29, 1856; "From Kansas to St. Louis," *New York Times,* January 5, 1857, 1.

108. "Affairs in Kansas," *New York Times,* June 6, 1856, 1; "Kansas," *New York Tribune,* January 1, 1857, 5; "From Kansas to St. Louis," *New York Times,* January 5, 1857, 1; "The 'Lion' and the 'Lamb,'" *Boston Herald,* January 17, 1857, 2; "A Rare Southern Patriot," *Richmond Whig,* January 2, 1857, 1.

109. "Latest from Kansas," *Cleveland Leader,* December 29, 1856, 2; "Kansas," *New York Tribune,* January 1, 1857, 5; "From Kansas to St. Louis," *New York Times,* January 5, 1857, 1; *Cincinnati Gazette* quoted in "Men of Note in Kansas: Col. Titus," *Ripley (Ohio) Bee,* February 7, 1857; "Early Recollections of Minnie Titus Ensey," Henry Theodore Titus Collection, North Brevard Public Library, Titusville, Fla., 2.

110. *St. Louis Intelligencer* cited in "Affairs in Kansas," *New York Herald,* September 1, 1856, 8; "Affairs in Kansas," *New York Herald,* September 5, 1856, 2.

111. Gihon, *Geary and Kansas,* 47, 49–50.

112. Strickler, *Commissioner to Audit,* 118, 454–55, 556–58.

113. "Jones & Bennett, Attorneys at Law," *Lecompton Union,* November 6, 1856, 3.

Chapter Three: Nicaragua Filibuster, 1857

1. *Washington National Era,* December 25, 1856, 207; "Col. Titus en Route to Nicaragua," *Cleveland Plain Dealer,* December. 18, 1856, 3; "From St. Louis," *Daily Cleveland Herald,* December 18, 1856; "Emigrants for Nicaragua," *Washington Daily National Intelligencer,* December 27, 1856, 3; A. C. Allen, "Diary of Incidents & Events That Transpired during My Sourjourne in Central America," 11, A. C. Allen Papers, Dolph Briscoe Center for American History, University of Texas, Austin, hereafter cited as A. C. Allen Diary; "Col. Titus and His Recruits for Nicaragua," *New York Times,* January 7, 1857, 1; "From Kansas to St. Louis Overland," *New York Times,* February 14, 1857, 10.

2. Maunsel White (1781–December 17, 1863) was an Irish Protestant who arrived in America at the age of thirteen. He worked as a clerk in a counting house in New Orleans and during the 1815 Battle of New Orleans served as a captain of the Louisiana Blues under Gen. Andrew Jackson. After establishing the enterprise Maunsel White & Co., he was Jackson's cotton agent during 1826–45. White's property, including the Deer Range plantation in Plaquemines Parish, was valued at more than three hundred thousand dollars in 1849. See "Death of a

Nicaraguan," New Orleans *Picayune,* January 13, 1857; E. S. Baker to Dear parents, January 26, 1857, Manuscripts and Folklife Archives, Western Kentucky University, Bowling Green, hereafter cited as MFA; "A Run to Nicaragua," *Wooster (Ohio) Republican,* June 18, 1857, 1; "Nicaraguan Meeting New-Orleans," *New York Times,* February 3, 1857, 2; "Important from Nicaragua," *New York Times,* March 21, 1857, 1; 1850 Louisiana Federal Census, New Orleans District 3, 227; 1850 Louisiana Slave Schedules, New Orleans District 3, 378, and Plaquemines Parish, 587; R. G. Dun & Company Credit Report Volumes, Louisiana, vol. 9, 87, Baker Library, Harvard University, Boston.

   3. Anthony Francis Rudler (June 14, 1820–August 7, 1871) was born in France and migrated to Augusta, Ga., with his family, moving to New Orleans in 1845. He was a captain in the Second Louisiana Infantry during the Mexican War and in 1848 served as a clerk in the customhouse in Laredo, Tex. The following year Rudler joined William Cazneau's trading expedition to Chihuahua, Mexico, and he later went to California during the Gold Rush. He joined William Walker in San Francisco and was captain of Company F (California Rifles) under Col. Louis Schlessinger during the battle of Santa Rosa, Costa Rica, on March 20, 1856. Two months later he was appointed lieutenant colonel and given command of the posts on the San Juan River. After Walker fled Nicaragua in 1857, Rudler returned to Augusta. He served as colonel and second in command to Walker during the September 1860 invasion of Honduras. They surrendered to a British commander, who turned them over to Honduran authorities. Walker was executed, but due to the Briton's insistence, the Frenchman was spared the death penalty and was instead sentenced to four years at hard labor in the mines. After U.S. government intercession, Rudler was sent to New York and from there arrived in Charleston, S.C., the day Fort Sumter surrendered, on April 13, 1861. Returning to Georgia, he helped raise the Confederate Third Georgia Battalion and was appointed its major on October 31, 1861. Rudler led his regiment at the battles of Hoover's Gap, Chickamauga, and Missionary Ridge, where he was severely wounded on November 25, 1863. He never returned to the field and remained in bad health until his death. See "Later from Nicaragua," *New York Tribune,* February 23, 1857, 6; E. S. Baker to Dear parents, January 26, 1857, MFA; "Passengers by the Steamship Texas," New Orleans *Picayune,* January 28, 1857, 4; *Philadelphia Inquirer,* December 25, 1856, 1; "News from Nicaragua," *New York Times,* February 23, 1857, 1; "A Filibuster View of the San Juan River," *New York Times,* April 4, 1857, 1.

   4. "How the Expedition Against the San Juan River Was Organized," *New York Times,* March 9, 1857, 1; Recopilación Museo Histórico Cultural Juan Santamaría, *El Combate de La Trinidad* (San José: Imprenta Nacional, 1999), 8–12; Comisión de Investigación, *Proclamas y Mensajes,* 47–48; "News from Western Nicaragua," *New York Herald,* February 23, 1857, 1; "The President of the Republic of Costa-Rica to the Soldiers of Walker's Army," December 10, 1856, Despatches from United States Consuls in San Juan del Norte, 1851–1906, Microcopy T-348, Roll 2, RG 59, NARA, hereafter cited as DSJN; J. O. Harris to B. S. Cotrell, January 5, 1857, Letters Received by the Secretary of the Navy from Commanders, 1804–86, January 1–March 31, 1857, M-147, Roll 52, RG 45, NARA.

   5. Hipp's Point was named after Wilhelm Christian Hipp (January 9, 1827–March 8, 1876), born in Neuwied, Germany. He migrated with his parents and six siblings to Virginia in 1844, and the following year the family moved to St. Clair Township, near Cincinnati, Ohio. At the outbreak of the Mexican War, Hipp enlisted for one year in Company C of the First Ohio Volunteer Infantry on May 27, 1846, and fought at the Battle of Monterrey. He was discharged on June 13, 1847, at New Orleans and returned home to work as a clerk. Hipp then traveled overland to San Francisco in 1851. Two years later he acquired land at the mouth of the Sarapiquí River from the British protectorate Kingdom of Mosquito that was contested by Costa Rica. He had one acre under cultivation and made extensive clearings to sell firewood to the Accessory Transit Company steamers on the San Juan River. Hipp established a rustic

inn and an eatery for travelers on both rivers. On December 25, 1853, he married the German immigrant Frances Bebent at Kirkland's Island (Leefe's Island), where the Colorado and San Juan Rivers meet. Their daughter was born in Greytown the following September. Hipp's Point was occupied by Costa Rican troops and became a filibuster battleground on March 19, 1856, forcing Hipp to flee with his family to Cincinnati. He became a naturalized U.S. citizen on October 3, 1856, and had three more children. His claim of thirty thousand dollars in property damages against the Costa Rican government was rejected on October 29, 1862, for want of proof by a joint commission of arbitration. Hipp worked as a bookkeeper in Sohn's brewery. In 1870 he was elected as Democratic alderman of Cincinnati, and two years later he became a city councilman, serving until 1874. He then moved his family to Mt. Sterling, Ky., where he founded a dry goods store. While hunting with his twelve-year-old son, Hipp died after his rifle accidentally discharged during a fall. See Smith, *Early Nineteenth-Century German Settlers,* 30–31; Frances Hipp, Widow's Certificate 1828, Mexican War Service Case Files, Records of the Department of Veterans Affairs, RG 15, NARA; 1850 Ohio Federal Census, Butler Co., 242; Moore, *History and Digest of the International Arbitrations,* 2:1555–56; 1860 Ohio Federal Census, Cincinnati, 3rd Ward, 174; 1870 Ohio Federal Census, Cincinnati, 12th Ward, 32; "Nominations by the Democratic Reform Party of the Twelfth Ward," *Cincinnati Daily Enquirer,* March 25, 1870, 5; *Williams' Cincinnati Directory, June,* 1871, 345; "The New Common Council," *Cincinnati Daily Gazette,* April 9, 1873, 8; "Our Municipal Legislature," *Cincinnati Commercial Tribune,* April 12, 1874, 3; Squier, "San Juan de Nicaragua," 59–60; Obregón, *Costa Rica y la guerra contra los filibusteros,* 307–8; "The Position and Prospects of the Contending Forces in Nicaragua," *New York Times,* February 2, 1857, 4; "News from Western Nicaragua," *New York Herald,* February 23, 1857, 1.

6. Samuel A. Lockridge (1828–February 21, 1862) was born in Jefferson County, Ala., where his father worked in agriculture and owned two slaves. By 1840 the family had migrated two hundred miles west to a farm in Yalobusha, Miss., and had eleven slaves. Lockridge moved to Gonzalez, Tex., in 1850 and the following year migrated to the California gold fields, before going to Costa Rica. Lockridge announced in New Orleans on March 13, 1858, that he was recruiting "emigrants interested" in becoming citizens of the Sierra Madre States. Mexican president Ignacio Comonfort had arrived in New Orleans the previous month after being forced to resign during the War of the Reform, and his Liberal Party was fighting for a revolutionary return. After Lockridge and his followers arrived at Brownsville to aid the Liberal cause, he warned Mexican general Santiago Vidaurri that Gen. Charles F. Henningsen, who had recently reached Monterrey, was an agent of Walker intent on filibustering in Mexico instead of helping the Liberals. In consequence, Vidaurri ended all communication with Lockridge, who returned to New Orleans after visiting his father in Gonzalez, Tex. Lockridge had been hoodwinked into the enterprise by the leaders of the Knights of the Golden Circle (KGC), a secret annexationist organization that never advanced beyond rituals and conspiracies. In early 1861 Lockridge was frequently traveling between Texas, New Orleans, Montgomery, and Pensacola preparing an independent mounted Texas Ranger Company for Confederate service. On September 7, 1861, he was ordered to report as major in the Fifth Texas Mounted Regiment, which became part of Brig. Gen. Henry H. Sibley's Brigade. At the Battle of Valverde, N.Mex., Lockridge "with heart of iron" led the charge against a battery of four Union guns spewing grapeshot and died along with half of the cannoneers in savage hand-to-hand combat. In Hall, "The Formation of Sibley's Brigade and the March to New Mexico," 138n49, Lockridge is erroneously identified as the notorious Cincinnati swindler and forger William Kissane, an Irishman who joined Walker's filibusters as Lt. Col. W. K. Rogers. The Lockridge/Kissane mistaken identity is repeated in Hollister, *Colorado Volunteers in New Mexico,* 1862, 183, and in The Handbook of Texas online. See "William Kissane in Walker's Army," *Columbus Ohio State Journal,* June 10, 1857, 3; "Northern Mexico," *Daily Illinois State Journal*

(Springfield), April 6, 1858, 2; "Letter from Col. S. A. Lockridge to Governor Vidaurri," *Texas State Gazette* (Austin), May 22, 1858, 3; "Col. S. A. Lockridge," *New York Herald,* August 14, 1858, 8; "Interesting from Mexico and the Rio Grande," *New York Herald,* January 31, 1860, 2; May, *Manifest Destiny's Underworld,* 109; Dunn, "The KGC in Texas," 551–52; Keehn, *Knights of the Golden Circle,* 44–45; *Dallas Weekly Herald,* March 27, 1861, 2; New Orleans *Picayune,* June 5, 1861, 1; Alberts, *Rebels on the Rio Grande,* 48; George L. Kilmer, "The War Fifty Years Ago," *Daily Illinois State Register,* February 24, 1912, 13; Noel, *Campaign from Santa Fe to the Mississippi,* 121–22; S. A. Lockridge, Fifth Cavalry (Fifth Mounted Volunteers, Second Regiment, Sibley's Brigade), Carded Records Showing Military Service of Soldiers Who Fought in Confederate Organizations, Roll 34, RG 109, NARA; "Col. S. A. Lockridge of Nicaragua," *Frank Leslie's Illustrated Newspaper,* July 11, 1857, 11; B. Squire Cotrell to W. L. Marcy, December 31, 1856, DSJN; A. C. Allen Diary, 18, 26–28; "News from Western Nicaragua," *New York Herald,* February 23, 1857, 1; "News from Nicaragua," *New York Times,* February 23, 1857, 1.

7. John Elphinstone Erskine (July 13, 1806–June 23, 1887) was an inveterate bachelor who joined the Royal Navy in 1819. He commanded war ships in the Mediterranean, the West Indies, and the Pacific before his Central American assignment. Erskine served in the Crimean War before his promotion to admiral in 1869. He was elected to Parliament as a Liberal in 1865 and held the seat until 1874. See B. Squire Cotrell to W. L. Marcy, August 4, 1856, DSJN; "Later from Nicaragua," *New York Tribune,* March 21, 1857, 5; John Erskine to Jose J. Mora, January 15, 1857, Fondo: Guerra, Sig. 4784, Dirección General del Archivo Nacional, Departamento Archivo Histórico, San José, Costa Rica, hereafter cited as ANCR; Doubleday, *Reminiscences of The "Filibuster" War in Nicaragua,* 179; "News from Western Nicaragua," *New York Herald,* February 23, 1857, 1; "Later from Nicaragua," *New York Tribune,* February 23, 1857, 5; "Important from Nicaragua," *Philadelphia Inquirer,* February 7, 1857, 1; "Very Latest and Interesting from Nicaragua," *Memphis Daily Appeal,* February 24, 1857, 2.

8. Charles William Doubleday (January 28, 1829–November 4, 1912) was born in Leicestershire, England, and in the 1830s migrated with his parents and five siblings to a farm in Brooklyn Township, Cuyahoga County, Ohio. He had left the family farm for the California gold mining camps on the Tuolumne River in 1849. Five years later, "while loafing about the water front" in San Francisco, he departed for San Juan del Sur, Nicaragua, where a civil war was in progress between Liberals and Conservatives. Doubleday was hired' as captain in the faction of Liberal general Máximo Jerez during the failed attack on the Conservative stronghold of Granada. When the Liberals called on William Walker for military assistance, Doubleday was sent to Realejo to receive him. He participated with them in the first battle of Rivas, where he got a slight head wound, and he received a contusion on the side at the skirmish at Virgin Bay. Doubleday returned to Brighton, Ohio, in the summer of 1857 to nurse his wounds after being scalded in the explosion of the steamer *J. N. Scott.* In mid-October 1858 he received a signed notice from William Walker stating that a vessel of immigrants to Central America would leave Mobile on November 10 and that anyone interested should contact him. Doubleday gave the message to the editor of the *Cleveland Plain Dealer* for publication, and it was reprinted in various other national newspapers. Walker afterward denied that he had signed the circular. Doubleday appears in the 1860 census as a laborer on his father's farm. On September 5, 1861, he was appointed by the governor of Ohio as colonel of the Second Ohio Cavalry Regiment. The regiment had 1,141 "very superior men in twelve companies," when they were sent from Camp Dennison, near Cincinnati, by railroad to Fort Benton, Mo., in mid-January 1862. The following month an abolitionist officer in his regiment wrote to the *Cleveland Leader* denouncing that Doubleday was returning fugitive slaves to "disloyal owners." His troops were accused of burning civilian homes. In March, Doubleday was in command of Fort Scott, Kans. On June 6 the Second Ohio Cavalry attacked with artillery

the Confederate camp of Col. Stand Watie's First Cherokee Mounted Rifles at Grand River, Mo., and captured some five hundred horses and cattle. A week later the *Leavenworth Conservative* accused Doubleday of blundering by allowing "some fifteen or eighteen hundred of the enemy" escape. On June 16, 1862, Doubleday resigned his commission as a result of being "tired of the pastoral life" of his regiment during the previous five months. After returning to Cleveland, on September 3, 1862, he married twenty-two-year-old Sarah Louise Hubby, daughter of Leander M. Hubby, president of the Cleveland, Columbus and Indiana Central Railroad. In June 1863 Doubleday appeared in the draft registry, indicating that he was a soldier by profession and resided in the Cleveland suburb of Solon. On May 9, 1864, Doubleday was among sixty-one men conscripted as privates from Cleveland's Second Ward. Two weeks later he appeared before of the Board of Enrollment with a substitute to take his place. The 1870 census indicates that Doubleday was a sleeping car proprietor with a sixty-five-thousand-dollar estate. He lived in East Cleveland with his wife, two infant daughters, and two servants. The family traveled to England in October 1873 and returned a year later. The 1880 census shows that Doubleday was unemployed and living with his in-laws. He published his memoirs six years later and in 1900 moved with his wife, daughter, and son-in-law to the two-story Cedars Mansion, today at 2145 N. Twenty-fourth Street, Arlington, Va. Doubleday passed away in his home, where private funeral services were held for him. In 1978 the Doubleday Mansion, a historic landmark house, was purchased by the Fellowship Christian organization, sponsor of the annual National Prayer Breakfast. See 1840 Ohio Federal Census, Cuyahoga Co., 134; 1850 Ohio Federal Census, Cuyahoga Co., 125; "Two Survivors of Walker's Expeditions Now Reside Near This City," *Washington Evening Star,* November 21, 1909, 4:5; "Col. Wheat," *Alexandria (Va.) Gazette,* July 4, 1857, 2; Doubleday, *Reminiscences,* 1, 20, 28, 41, 104, 112, 126, 195, 176; "Another Expedition to Nicaragua," *Cleveland Plain Dealer,* October 21, 1858, 2; "The Central American Imbroglio," *New York Herald,* November 22, 1858, 1; 1860 Ohio Federal Census, Cuyahoga Co., Brooklyn Township, 424; "Military Appointments," *Cleveland Leader,* September 11, 1861, 4; U.S. War Department, OR, 1:4, 344, 1:8, 557–58, 1:13, 102, 398, 427, 446, 949, 2:3, 411, 3:1, 806; Reid, *Ohio in the War,* 754; "From Benton Barracks," *Cleveland Plain Dealer,* January 24, 1862, 2; "From Missouri," *Boston Evening Transcript,* June 17, 1862, 1; "Colonel Doubleday," *Cleveland Plain Dealer,* June 21, 1862, 3; Cuyahoga County, Ohio, Marriage Records, 1810–1973, September 3, 1862, vols. 10–12, 340, Cuyahoga County Archive, Cleveland, Ohio; "The Draft," *Cleveland Plain Dealer,* May 10, 1864, 3; "The Draft," *Cleveland Leader,* May 26, 1864, 4; 1870 Ohio Federal Census, East Cleveland, 265; Passport Applications, 1795–1905, October 10, 1873, M1372, Roll 199, RG 59, NARA; Passenger Lists of Vessels Arriving at New York, New York, 1820–97, Celtic, October 26, 1874, M237, Roll 394, RG 36, NARA; 1900 Virginia Federal Census, Alexandria Co., Washington District, 70; "Died," *Washington Evening Star,* November 6, 1912, 7; "Deaths," *Cleveland Leader,* November 6, 1912, 12; "Later from Nicaragua," *New York Tribune,* February 23, 1857, 5; "Very Latest and Interesting from Nicaragua," *Memphis Daily Appeal,* February 24, 1857, 2; "Arrival of the Tennessee," *New York Times,* April 17, 1857, 1; "News from Nicaragua," *New York Times,* February 23, 1857, 1; "A Steamboat Captain Experience in Nicaragua," *New York Times,* March 5, 1857, 5; S. A. Lockridge to B. S. Cotrell, March 4, 1857, DSJN; A. C. Diary, 57–59; J. M. to P. Bariller, January 20, 1857, Fondo: Guerra, Sig. 4784, ANCR; José J. Mora to Trinidad Commander, January 21, 1857, Fondo: Guerra, Sig. 9243, ANCR.

    9. "News from Nicaragua," *New York Times,* February 23, 1857, 1; *Boletín Oficial* (San José, Costa Rica), February 7, 1857, 3; "Later from Nicaragua," *New York Tribune,* February 23, 1857, 5–6; B. Squire Cotrell to W. L. Marcy, February 10, 1857, DSJN; Recopilación, *El Combate de La Trinidad,* 40; "Additional from Nicaragua," *New York Herald,* February 23, 1857, 1; "Important from Nicaragua," *New York Herald,* March 14, 1857; 1; Máximo Blanco to Minister of the Treasury and War, January 29, 1957, Fondo: Guerra y Marina, Sig. 4763, ANCR.

10. Obregón Quesada, *Diarios de Faustino Montes de Oca Gamero,* 26–27; Pedro Barill-
ier to Minister of War, January 15, 1857, Fondo: Guerra, Sig. 4753, ANCR; Rafael Bolandi
to Minister of War, January 9 and 23, 1857, ibid.; "Nicaragua," *New York Tribune,* March
23, 1857, 6.

11. "News from Nicaragua," *New York Times,* February 23, 1857, 1; "Later from Nicaragua,"
New York Tribune, February 23, 1857, 5–6; Thomas Cody statement, January 14, 1857, DSJN;
"Additional from Nicaragua," *New York Herald,* February 23, 1857, 1; "Important from Nicaragua,"
New York Herald, March 14, 1857; 1; "Later from Nicaragua," *New York Tribune,* April 17, 1857, 6;
A. C. Allen Diary, 60–61, 63; "Important from Nicaragua," *New York Times,* March 21, 1857, 1.

12. Maximo Blanco Diary (3rd rev.), January 28, 1857, in possession of Werner Korte, San
José, Costa Rica, hereafter cited as Blanco Diary; Máximo Blanco to Gen. President, January
24 and 29, 1857, Fondo: Guerra y Marina, Sig. 4763, ANCR; Doubleday, *Reminiscences,* 182;
"Important from the Seat of War," *New York Herald,* February 5, 1857, 2; "Later from Nica-
ragua," *New York Tribune,* February 23, 1857, 5; "Arrival of the Tennessee," *New York Herald,*
February 22, 1857, 1; "News from Nicaragua," *New York Times,* February 23, 1857, 1.

13. Sylvanus M. Spencer (1819–May 29, 1862) was born in New York and raised by the
Jenkins family in Manhattan's Lower East Side, where he was "one of the roughs." A seaman
by trade, he was described as "a very loquacious man" with "a Yankee twang." Spencer was five
feet, ten inches tall, with a slim figure, hazel eyes, long fair hair, "slightly freckled face, large
coarse fair whiskers, long face . . . uses very emphatic language, well spiced with good strong
adjectives." Spencer was the mate on the 170-foot clipper ship *Sea Witch,* bound from New
York to China on the coolie and tea trade with twenty-three seamen, when its captain George
W. Fraser was murdered at sea on June 6, 1855, while Spencer had charge of the deck. Fraser's
skull was pierced by three distinct blows from a marlin spike, which was later discovered in
Spencer's room. The ship's surgeon accused him of the murder and had the vessel diverted to
Rio de Janeiro. During the ten-day voyage, Fraser's body was preserved in a coffin filled with
whiskey. Spencer made an unsuccessful suicide attempt by stabbing himself in the left breast
before being taken ashore in irons by order of Mr. Scott, the American consul, along with
two other crew members. He was tried for murder in the U.S. District Court of New York on
December 19, 1855, but was acquitted two days later due to circumstantial evidence. Spencer
arrived in San José, Costa Rica, on October 9, 1856, with a power of attorney from the Accessory Transit Company, whose property had been confiscated by William Walker. The government assigned him troops, which he used to recover the steamers belonging to the company
during the December campaign on the San Juan River. He told the crew of the steamers that
he was seizing them on behalf of Cornelius Vanderbilt. After Walker was defeated, Spencer
demanded on behalf of the company the return of the steamers from President Juan Mora,
but this was refused. In consequence, George F. Cauty denounced Spencer as a traitor. Spencer
was back in New York in February 1859 and three years later died "after a sudden and severe
illness" in Williamsburg, Brooklyn. See "The Emigration to Nicaragua," *New York Herald,*
January 29, 1857, 1; "Murder at Sea," *Albany Evening Journal,* July 28, 1855, 2; "Murder on the
High Seas," *New York Times,* December 22, 1855, 3; Moore, *History and Digest of the International Arbitrations,* 2:1558–59; "The Passage of the River," *New York Tribune,* January 26, 1857,
6; "Who Is Sylvanus M. Spencer?," *New York Times,* January 28, 1857, 1; "Nicaragua," *New York
Herald,* February 28, 1858, 1; "Died," *New York Tribune,* June 2, 1862, 5; Deposition of William
W. Wise, June 13, 1857, DSJN; Sylvanus Spencer to Juan R. Mora, January 28, 1857, Fondo:
Guerra y Marina, Sig. 4763, ANCR; Máximo Blanco to Gen. President, February 1, 1857,
ibid.; Máximo Blanco to Minister of the Treasury and War, January 29, 1957, ibid.; Blanco
Diary, January 28–30, 1857.

14. "Later from Nicaragua," *New York Tribune,* February 23, 1857, 6; "Arrival of the Tennessee," *New York Herald,* February 22, 1857, 1; "News from Nicaragua," *New York Times,* Febru-

ary 23, 1857, 1; "Additional from Nicaragua," *New York Herald,* February 23, 1857, 1; B. Squire Cotrell to W. L. Marcy, February 10, 1857, DSJN.

15. "News from Nicaragua," *New York Times,* February 23, 1857, 1; Walker, *War in Nicaragua,* 357–58; "Kansas," *El Nicaraguense,* October 25, 1856, 5; "Our Greytown Correspondence," *New York Herald,* March 21, 1857, 1.

16. "News from Nicaragua," *New York Times,* February 23, 1857, 1; "Col. Lockridge's Apology," *New York Tribune,* June 19, 1857, 7; Walker, *War in Nicaragua,* 358; "Additional from Nicaragua," *New York Herald,* February 23, 1857, 1; "Later from Nicaragua," *New York Tribune,* February 23, 1857, 5; "Very Late and Interesting from Nicaragua," New Orleans *Picayune,* February 18, 1857, 1; "Nicaragua," *New York Tribune,* March 23, 1857, 6.

17. "Very Late and Interesting from Nicaragua," New Orleans *Picayune,* February 18, 1857, 1; "News from Nicaragua," *New York Times,* February 23, 1857, 1; "A Run to Nicaragua," *Wooster (Ohio) Republican,* June 18, 1857, 1; "Nicaragua—The Adventures of a Fillibustero," *Philadelphia Inquirer,* April 18, 1857, 1.

18. Robert H. Ellis (1829–?) a Washington, D.C., clerk, was a lieutenant in the 1850 and 1851 López expeditions to Cuba. See José J. Mora to Comandante de la Trinidad, February 4, 1857, Fondo: Guerra, Sig. 9248, ANCR; "News from Nicaragua," *New York Times,* February 23, 1857, 1; "Operations on the San Juan River," *New York Herald,* April 4, 1857, 1; "Later from Nicaragua," *New York Tribune,* April 17, 1857, 6; "Late and Important from Nicaragua," *Baton Rouge Daily Advocate,* March 14, 1857, 2.

19. John Marks Baldwin (October 1829–August 2, 1912) was born in Mexico to Dr. John M. Baldwin of Philadelphia, who three years later moved the family to New Orleans. They settled in San Francisco during the Gold Rush, where the patriarch was murdered by an Englishman, who was hanged by the Vigilance Committee. Baldwin's profession was listed as "Gentleman" in the 1852 San Francisco, Calif., state census. An inveterate bachelor and civil engineer, he spoke Spanish and French as fluently as he did English. Baldwin left San Francisco on September 20, 1855, on the *Cortés* and arrived in San Juan del Sur, Nicaragua, two weeks later as first lieutenant of Company C, First Rifle Battalion. The following month he was promoted to quartermaster of the First Battalion. On March 1, 1856, Baldwin was first lieutenant of Company B, First Light Infantry Battalion, in command of the El Castillo garrison. He was made captain of the company six weeks later and charged with strengthening the defenses of Fort Sarapiquí with one hundred men. In August, Baldwin was in charge of Company C, First Light Infantry, stationed at Virgin Bay. The following month he was appointed solicitor general of the treasury, and in October he participated in the final battle of Granada. Baldwin ascended to major on December 9, 1856, returned to the United States, and was back in Greytown as aide to Lockridge in 1857. During the Civil War, Baldwin enlisted in Galveston, Tex., on August 1, 1861, as a private in Company L, First Texas Infantry, and later that month was elected a second lieutenant when his unit went to Manassas, Va., as part of Longstreet's Corps, Army of Northern Virginia. He was slightly wounded at the Battle of Second Manassas and promoted to first lieutenant on September 17, 862. Baldwin became a captain in 1863. After the war he returned to California, where in August 1870 he was the city engineer at Los Angeles, a position that he held for more than two decades. That year he was appointed brigadier general commanding the First Brigade, State Militia. His brother Leon, a mining engineer, was murdered by bandits in Durango, Mexico, in 1887. Baldwin then went to live with his widowed sister-in-law in San Francisco, where he passed away. Dr. Thomas Cody, an American citizen who resided in Greytown, had purchased a land grant on August 2, 1851, signed by the British consul in Greytown and the Mosquito King, claiming that his property was on the Mosquito Territory, a kingdom not recognized by Nicaragua or the United States. It was located on the Nicaraguan shore of the San Juan River, starting at the confluence of the Sarapiquí River, extending five miles toward the Pacific and five miles inland, comprising five

square miles. See California State Census, 1852, C144, Roll 4, 293, California State Library, Sacramento, Ca.; 1900 California Federal Census, San Francisco, 5; 1910 California Federal Census, San Francisco, 6; "Jottings about Town," *San Francisco Chronicle,* August 23, 1870, 3; "Murdered in Mexico," *San Francisco Bulletin,* September 5, 1887, 1; "General John Baldwin Dies," *Denver Rocky Mountain News,* August 3, 1912, 14; "General J. M. Baldwin, Civil War Veteran and Pioneer, Passes Away," *San Francisco Chronicle,* August 3, 1912, 2; "Máximo Blanco to General in Chief of the Army of Costa Rica," February 1, 1857, Fondo: Guerra y Marina, Sig. 4763, ANCR; "News from Nicaragua," *New York Times,* February 23, 1857, 1; "Later from Nicaragua," *New York Tribune,* April 17, 1857, 6; "Additional from Nicaragua," *New York Herald,* February 23, 1857, 1; U.S. Senate, Message of the President of the United States, Exec. Doc. No. 8, 23, 28; Hertslet, *A Complete Collection of the Treaties and Conventions,* 13:668; "Very Late and Interesting from Nicaragua," New Orleans *Picayune,* February 18, 1857, 1; Thomas Cody land grant and statement, January 14, 1857, DSJN.

 20. "Additional from Nicaragua," *New York Herald,* February 23, 1857, 1; "News from Nicaragua," *New York Times,* February 23, 1857, 1; "Later from Nicaragua," *New York Tribune,* April 17, 1857, 6; "Operations on the San Juan River," *New York Herald,* April 4, 1857, 1; "Very Late and Interesting from Nicaragua," New Orleans *Picayune,* February 18, 1857, 1.

 21. Blanco Diary, February 6, 1857; "Very Late and Interesting from Nicaragua," New Orleans *Picayune,* February 18, 1857, 1.

 22. Blanco Diary, February 6, 1857; "Additional from Nicaragua," *New York Herald,* February 23, 1857, 1; "Later from Nicaragua," *New York Tribune,* February 23, 1857, 5, and April 17, 1857, 6; "News from Nicaragua," *New York Times,* February 23, 1857, 1; "Operations on the San Juan River," *New York Herald,* April 4, 1857, 1; "Very Late and Interesting from Nicaragua," New Orleans *Picayune,* February 18, 1857, 1.

 23. "Additional from Nicaragua," *New York Herald,* February 23, 1857, 1; "News from Nicaragua," *New York Times,* February 23, 1857, 1; "Later from Nicaragua," *New York Tribune,* April 17, 1857, 6; "Operations on the San Juan River," *New York Herald,* April 4, 1857, 1; *New York Tribune,* February 24, 1857, 4; "Very Late and Interesting from Nicaragua," New Orleans *Picayune,* February 18, 1857, 1.

 24. "News from Nicaragua," *New York Times,* February 23, 1857, 1; "Later from Nicaragua," *New York Tribune,* April 17, 1857, 6; "Operations on the San Juan River," *New York Herald,* April 4, 1857, 1; "Very Late and Interesting from Nicaragua," New Orleans *Picayune,* February 18, 1857, 1.

 25. E. S. Baker to Dear parents, August 2, 1857, MFA; "News from Nicaragua," *New York Times,* February 23, 1857, 1; "Late and Important from Nicaragua," *Baton Rouge Daily Advocate,* March 14, 1857, 2; "Later from Nicaragua," *New York Tribune,* April 17, 1857, 6; "Operations on the San Juan River," *New York Herald,* April 4, 1857, 1; "Glorious News from Nicaragua," *Columbus (Ga.) Enquirer,* February 24, 1857, 2; "Very Latest and Interesting from Nicaragua," *Memphis Daily Appeal,* February 24, 1857, 2.

 26. Faustino Montes de Oca Gamero (July 29, 1810–December 25, 1878), born in Rivas, Nicaragua, was raised in San José, Costa Rica. His family's biography describes him as autodidactic, a farmer, a miner, and a womanizer. He was promoted from captain to lieutenant colonel for his defense of El Castillo. After the National Campaign against the filibusters, Montes de Oca was appointed administrator of the San José Post Office. When his brother-in-law President Juan Rafael Mora was overthrown in 1859, Montes de Oca went into exile in El Salvador, where he worked building roads. He returned to Costa Rica in 1862 and resumed farming until his death. See Obregón, *Diarios de Faustino Montes de Oca Gamero,* 1–15; "Late and Important from Nicaragua," *Baton Rouge Daily Advocate,* March 14, 1857, 2; "Later from Nicaragua," *New York Tribune,* April 17, 1857, 6; "Operations on the San Juan River," *New York Herald,* April 4, 1857, 1.

27. John Egbert Farnum (April 1, 1824–May 16, 1870) was born in South Carolina, according to his marriage certificate and the 1860 federal census, and was raised in Pottsville, Pa. He was a sergeant major with the First Pennsylvania Infantry during the Mexican War. Farnum joined Walker in Nicaragua in January 1856 but returned to New York on July 13, 1856, afflicted with yellow fever. He left there on June 8, 1858, as the purser of the 104-foot schooner *Wanderer,* which was equipped for the clandestine slave trade. The vessel picked up some 490 mostly male teenage captives in the Congo River four months later and in November unloaded 409 of them on Jekyll Island, Ga. It was the last cargo of slaves that landed in the United States. Farnum soon returned home to the St. Nicholas Hotel, where he was arrested for piracy on December 9, 1859, and escorted to Savannah for trial. He pleaded not guilty on April 10, 1860, and the trial started on May 22. More than a dozen witnesses testified, and three days later, after deliberating for twenty-six hours without food, the jurors announced that they were deadlocked. Farnum was released on five thousand dollars bail on May 30 and soon returned to New York "in fine spirits." He was back in the Chatham County Jail in August 1860, and the federal census listed his occupation as "Adventurer" and his birthplace as Charleston, S.C., while his thirty-year-old wife Anna B. Farnum of New York City appeared as residing with the jailor's family. The federal prosecutor announced on November 12, 1860, that he was entering a nolle prosequi in the case against Farnum and three codefendants. During the Civil War, Farnum enlisted as a major in Daniel Sickles's Seventieth New York Infantry Regiment, and he ascended to the rank of colonel and regimental commander on December 1, 1862. During the Peninsula Campaign, he was wounded at the battle of Williamsburg, Va., on May 5, 1862. His brigade saw little action at Fredericksburg, with only four wounded. The Seventieth New York was routed at the battle of Chancellorsville on May 3, 1863, losing four killed, eleven wounded, and eighteen missing. Two months later the Seventieth New York was kept in the rear as the division's reserve at the battle of Gettysburg. Farnum was detached on duty at New York on July 27, 1863, and four months later led his regiment during the Mine Run Campaign in Virginia, losing one killed and seven wounded. In August 1864 Farnum was transferred to the command of the Eleventh Veteran Reserve Corps in the District of St. Mary's, Md. Four months later he was in charge of the Draft Rendezvous post at Louisville, Ky., until June 1865, afterward leading a detachment of U.S. troops at Albany, N.Y. until the end of the year. Farnum married his second wife, twenty-six-year-old Amanda Frances Ray, on December 19, 1868, in a Presbyterian church. He worked as a New York City customhouse inspector until passing away from Bright's disease. See "Letter from Captain Farnum of the Nicaraguan Army," *New York Herald,* April 15, 1857, 3; Welles, *The Slave Ship Wanderer,* 20, 29–31, 63–71; Jackson, *The Wanderer Case,* 40–42, 62–63; U.S. vs. J. Egbert Farnum, 1859, Mixed Cases, 1790–1860, U.S. Circuit Court, Savannah, Ga., Box 113 (D13), RG 21, NARA; Minutes 1857–69, U.S. Circuit Court, Savannah, Ga., 253, 276–86, 291, 317, ibid.; 1860 Georgia Federal Census, Chatham Co., Savannah, 264; "Personal," *Washington Evening Star,* May 4, 1854, 2; OR, 1:11, pt. 1, 482; 1:21, 134, 384–86; 1:25, pt. 1, 463–64; 1:27, pt. 1, 564; 1:29, pt. 1, 771; 1:43, pt. 1, 976; "Obituary," *New York Times,* May 17, 1870; "Death of Gen. J. E. Farnum," *Baltimore Sun,* May 18, 1870, 2; "Later from Nicaragua," *New York Tribune,* April 17, 1857, 6; "Late and Important from Nicaragua," *Baton Rouge Daily Advocate,* March 14, 1857, 2; Affidavits presented by Capt. John Erskine, February 10, 1857, DSJN; Depositions of Capt. John S. Crowell and J. M. Bockins, February 11, 1857, DSJN; "Operations on the San Juan River," *New York Herald,* April 4, 1857, 1; "Very Latest and Interesting from Nicaragua," *Memphis Daily Appeal,* February 24, 1857, 2; "News from Nicaragua," *New York Times,* February 23, 1857, 1; "The Emigration to Nicaragua," *New York Herald,* January 29, 1857, 1; "Letter from Colonel Hall, of the Nicaraguan Army," *New York Herald,* April 15, 1857, 3; "Máximo Blanco to General in Chief of the Army of Costa Rica," February 9, 1857, Fondo: Guerra y Marina, Sig. 4763, ANCR.

28. "Máximo Blanco to General in Chief of the Army of Costa Rica," February 9, 1857, Fondo: Guerra y Marina, Sig. 4763, ANCR.

29. "Affairs of Nicaragua," *New York Times,* March 19, 1857, 1; "Later from Nicaragua," *New York Tribune,* February 23, 1857, 5; "Important from Nicaragua," *New York Times,* March 14 and 21, 1857, 1; "Later from Nicaragua," *New York Tribune,* April 17, 1857, 6; "Operations on the San Juan River," *New York Herald,* April 4, 1857, 1; "Later from Nicaragua," *New York Tribune,* March 14, 1857, 7; "Late and Important from Nicaragua," *Baton Rouge Daily Advocate,* March 14, 1857, 2; "Important from Nicaragua," *New York Herald,* March 14, 1857, 1; Doubleday, *Reminiscences,* 182; Máximo Blanco to Minister of War, February 16, 1857, Fondo: Guerra, Sig. 4753, ANCR.

30. George Bolivar Hall (July 15, 1825–May 24, 1864) was the son of the first mayor of Brooklyn. He served in the Mexican War as a lieutenant, captain, adjutant, and quartermaster in the Second Regiment of New York Volunteers. Hall fought with distinction in the battles of Veracruz, Cerro Gordo, and Contreras, prompting the New York State Assembly to recommend that the governor reward him with a gold medal. Hall was a captain on the staff of Gen. Narciso López in the 1850 expedition and shot a Spaniard off the parapet of the Palace at Cárdenas. In August 1853 he offered his services to Gen. John Quitman, who was preparing a filibuster invasion of Cuba, which was disbanded two years later. Hall resigned as a customs agent in New York City when he was arrested in December 1855 for violation of the Neutrality Act, but the charges were later dropped due to lack of evidence. He was made colonel and commissary general of subsistence in Walker's army on July 15, 1856. Hall was a whetstone manufacturer with a nine-year-old son in April 1861, when he raised, with the rank of colonel, the Seventy-first New York Regiment of Infantry. The following year he participated in the various battles of the Peninsula Campaign. At the Battle of Malvern Hill his character and conduct underwent investigation for drunkenness. At the Battle of Fredericksburg he commanded Sickles's Second Excelsior Brigade, which included Col. John Farnum's Seventieth New York Infantry Regiment. The brigade saw little action, resulting in no deaths and sixteen wounded. Hall then left his command stricken with hepatitis and dysentery and received a disability discharge on April 28, 1863. He died the following year at his father's home in Brooklyn. His military funeral procession to Green-Wood Cemetery was "a large and imposing" one. See New York State, *Journal of the Assembly of the State of New York,* 2:934; O.D.D.O., *History of the Late Expedition to Cuba,* 69; Wilson and Fiske, *Appletons' Cyclopedia of American Biography,* 3:40; 1860 New York Federal Census, New York, Dist. 1, Ward 17, 603; G. Bolivar Hall to John Quitman, August 2, 1853, John Anthony Quitman Papers, Houghton Library, Harvard University, Boston, Mass.; "The Nicaragua Expedition," *Daily National Intelligencer,* January 2, 1856, 3; *Boston Post,* May 29, 1856, 4; "Register of the Army of the Republic of Nicaragua," Box 4, Folder 120, Callender Fayssoux Collection, Latin American Library, Tulane University, New Orleans, La.; OR, 1:11, pt. 1, 826–27; 1:12, pt. 2, 449; 1:21, 54, 134, 384–86; "Obituary," *New York Herald,* May 27, 1864, 4; "Funeral of Colonel George B. Hall," *New York Herald,* May 30, 1864, 8; "Important from Nicaragua," *New York Times,* March 14 and 21, 1857, 1; "Later from Nicaragua," *New York Tribune,* April 17, 1857, 6; "Operations on the San Juan River," *New York Herald,* April 4, 1857, 1; "Interesting from Nicaragua," *New York Herald,* March 21, 1857, 1; "Later from Nicaragua," *New York Tribune,* March 14, 1857, 7; "Letter from Colonel Hall, of the Nicaraguan Army," *New York Herald,* April 15, 1857, 3; Doubleday, *Reminiscences,* 182; "Late and Important from Nicaragua," *Baton Rouge Daily Advocate,* March 14, 1857, 2; "Important from Nicaragua," *New York Herald,* March 14, 1857, 1; Walker, *War in Nicaragua,* 358.

31. Doubleday, *Reminiscences,* 183–84; "Máximo Blanco to General in Chief of the Army of Costa Rica," February 9, 1857, Fondo: Guerra y Marina, Sig. 4763, ANCR; F. Montes de Oca to J. Joaquín Mora, January 5, 1857, Fondo: Guerra, Sig. 9269, ANCR; "Later from

Nicaragua," *New York Tribune*, April 17, 1857, 6; "Operations on the San Juan River," *New York Herald*, April 4, 1857, 1; "Important from Nicaragua," *New York Times*, March 14, 1857, 1; "Later from Nicaragua," *New York Tribune*, March 14, 1857, 7; "Late and Important from Nicaragua," *Baton Rouge Daily Advocate*, March 14, 1857, 2; Walker, *War in Nicaragua*, 358; "Important from Nicaragua," *New York Herald*, March 14, 1857, 1.

32. *Aspinwall Courier* quoted in "Nicaraguan Affairs," *Memphis Daily Appeal*, March 17, 1857, 2; Vicente Salazar to Minister of War, February 14, 1857, Fondo: Guerra, Sig. 4753, ANCR; "Col. Titus in the Field," *Richmond Whig*, February 20, 1857, 1; "Later from Nicaragua," *New York Tribune*, April 17, 1857, 6; "Operations on the San Juan River," *New York Herald*, April 4, 1857, 1; "Important from Nicaragua," *New York Times*, March 14 and 21, 1857, 1; "Later from Nicaragua," *New York Tribune*, March 14, 1857, 7; "The Fillibusters on the River," *New York Tribune*, March 21, 1857, 5; "Letter from Colonel Hall, of the Nicaraguan Army," *New York Herald*, April 15, 1857, 3; "Arrival of the Tennessee," *New York Times*, April 17, 1857, 1; "Late and Important from Nicaragua," *Baton Rouge Daily Advocate*, March 14, 1857, 2; "Important from Nicaragua," *New York Herald*, March 14, 1857, 1; "Doings of Col. Titus at Rivas," *New York Herald*, May 29, 1857, 1; E. S. Baker to Dear parents, August 2, 1857, MFA.

33. Vicente Salazar to Minister of War, February 14, 1857, Fondo: Guerra, Sig. 4753, ANCR; A. C. Allen Diary, 15; "Important from Nicaragua," *New York Times*, March 21, 1857, 8; "Nicaraguan Affairs," *Memphis Daily Appeal*, March 17, 1857, 2; "Late and Important from Nicaragua," *Baton Rouge Daily Advocate*, March 14, 1857, 2; "Later from Nicaragua," *New York Tribune*, March 14, 1857, 7.

34. Julius De Brissot was the chief engineer on the steamer *Apure* when he was killed during a civil war in Venezuela defending his vessel on the Apure River at Apurito on October 17, 1865. See "Important from Nicaragua," *New York Times*, March 21, 1857, 8; "Nicaraguan Affairs," *Memphis Daily Appeal*, March 17, 1857, 2; "Late and Important from Nicaragua," *Baton Rouge Daily Advocate*, March 14, 1857, 2; "Later from Nicaragua," *New York Tribune*, March 14, 1857, 7.

35. "Later from Nicaragua," *New York Tribune*, April 17, 1857, 6; "Late and Important from Nicaragua," *Baton Rouge Daily Advocate*, March 14, 1857, 2; "Important from Nicaragua," *New York Times*, March 21, 1857, 1.

36. "Late and Important from Nicaragua," *Baton Rouge Daily Advocate*, March 14, 1857, 2; "Interesting from Nicaragua," *New York Herald*, March 21, 1857, 1; "Important from Nicaragua," *New York Times*, March 21, 1857, 1; "Later from Nicaragua," *New York Tribune*, March 14, 1857, 7; Walker, *War in Nicaragua*, 358; "Nicaraguan Affairs," *Memphis Daily Appeal*, March 17, 1857, 2; "Affairs of Nicaragua," *New York Times*, March 19, 1857, 1; "Later from Nicaragua," *New York Tribune*, April 17, 1857, 6.

37. Juan R. Mora to Máximo Blanco, February 17, 1857, Fondo: Guerra, Sig. 9239, ANCR.

38. Doubleday, *Reminiscences*, 185; Walker, *War in Nicaragua*, 358–59; E. S. Baker to Dear parents, August 2, 1857, MFA; "The News from Nicaragua," *New York Times*, April 4, 1857, 1.

39. "Interesting from Nicaragua," *New York Herald*, March 21, 1857, 1; "Important from Nicaragua," *New York Times*, March 21, 1857, 1; "Later from Nicaragua," *New York Tribune*, April 17, 1857, 6; "Late and Important from Nicaragua," *Baton Rouge Daily Advocate*, March 14, 1857, 2.

40. Samuel S. Wood was president of the City Council of San Juan del Norte in 1853. John Edward Hollenbeck (June 5, 1829–August 28, 1885), born in Hudson, Ohio, was a machinist. He arrived in Greytown in March 1852 and worked on steamers on the San Juan River route. Hollenbeck settled at El Castillo on July 12, 1853, purchased half of the Nicaragua Hotel for three thousand dollars, and bought out his partner a year later. On January 30, 1854, he married the German widow Elizabeth Hatsfeldt (October 17, 1827–September 9, 1918). Hollenbeck also sold merchandise and liquors and owned a "comfortable building" on Hollenbeck's

Island, today La Juana Island, in the San Juan River, half a mile below Castillo Rapids. After fleeing El Castillo and spending three months at San Miguelito with his family, they went to Greytown after the filibuster defeat. In May 1857 Colonel Cauty requested that the government give Hollenbeck the Accessory Transit house at El Castillo in remuneration for the loss of his hotel. After two months of meetings with President Juan Mora, Gen. José María Cañas, and Colonel Cauty, Hollenbeck was told that Costa Rica was not responsible for his loss. He then filed a claim for $12,157.00 against the Costa Rican government with the U.S. State Department. On December 31, 1862, Hollenbeck was awarded $7,269.75 in property damages against the Costa Rican government by a joint commission of arbitration. He spent the next decade traveling with his wife between Central America, the United States, and Europe until finally settling in a mansion in Boyle Heights in Los Angeles, Calif., in 1876. He became an urban developer, banker, and rancher until his death from apoplexy. Charles M. Stewart was afterward rewarded with permission to operate a hotel that served the new transit company and received 1.7 acres that were five hundred yards from El Castillo in addition to 17.2 acres of his choosing for farming. See Deposition of John E. Hollenbeck, July 25, 1857, DSJN; Moore, *History and Digest of the International Arbitrations,* 2:1556–57; Deposition of Thomas Townsend, February 19, 1857, DSJN; Tenant's Agreement and Inventory of household furniture and fixtures remaining in the house of Thomas Townsend called the "National Hotel," March 17, 1856, DSJN; Protest No. 4, J. E. Hollenbeck, July 25, 1857, DSJN; "Death of J. E. Hollenbeck," *San Diego Union,* September 6, 1885, 3.

41. The portage railway was removed decades later, and some of the iron rails are on exhibit today at the El Castillo Museum. See "El Castillo de la Concepcion del Rio de San Juan de Nicaragua: Descripción por su castellano D. Juan Antonio Alonso de Arze, 20 Enero 1732," Fondo: Complementario Colonial, Sig. 5387, ANCR; Ibáñez Montoya, *Estudio asesor para la restauración del fuerte;* Stout, *Nicaragua,* 21–22.

42. George Frederick Cauty (June 29, 1824–August 1911) was born in St. James, Middlesex County, England and joined the British navy at the age of fifteen. He settled in Central America in 1851 and "was for some years in the service of the States of Costa Rica and Nicaragua." In March 1859, during a sojourn in New York, Cauty was accosted by Chatham Wheat on the sidewalk in front of his hotel for disregarding a previous challenge to a duel in Greytown. Wheat spat in his face, punched his left eyebrow and struck him twice on the head above the left temple with a knobbed stick. Wheat then kicked Cauty when he fell to the ground bleeding. The Englishman soon left for London where he wed fifteen-year-old Lucy Charlotte (1844-1922) in the fall of 1859. In January 1860, Cauty was the agent of Croakey and Company when he proposed to the Nicaraguan government a San Juan River transit monopoly for 75 years. The enterprise offered to pay $100,000 for 100,000 acres of land along the route but the contract was rejected. Cauty resided with his wife and child in San José, Costa Rica, during 1861-62 before moving to Maillard's hotel in New York City from March 1863 until his arrest on December 24, 1863. He was detained with Dr. Henry Segur, the former Salvadoran minister to the U.S. and his wife, their maidservant and Salvadoran D. Pérez, as they were about to sail on the steamer *George Cromwell* for New Orleans. An informant revealed that barrels of potatoes on board contained "powder and percussion caps." Segur carried a bill of lading for fifty kegs of lard hiding one thousand navy revolvers on a British vessel. The baggage of Segur and Pérez contained "revolvers and rifle and pistol cartridges." Mrs. Segur, her children and their nurse all had revolvers concealed in their clothing. The foreigners were suspected of "violating the neutrality laws" while "endeavoring to procure a war steamer, and to purchase arms and enlist men in the United States to be employed in the war. . .between Salvador on the one side and Guatemala and Nicaragua on the other." Cauty was imprisoned in Fort Lafayette, in the Narrows of New York Harbor, until March 25, 1864. A month after his release he met with exiled Salvadorean Liberal President Gen. Gerardo Barrios at the Continental Hotel in

Philadelphia. Cauty afterward visited two British subjects imprisoned in Fort Lafayette on April 28, 1864 and tried "obtaining from them an advance of money for his own use" by falsely peddling his influence to free them. That summer, Cauty returned to San José with his family and in September presented the government with a $200,000 proposal to pave the streets of the capital, illuminate them with gas and build sewers. When the project was dismissed, he and his family moved to St. George Parish, Middlesex, England, where his second daughter Mariah Lucy was born in 1867. Three years later, the family was living in London where Cauty worked as a "translator of languages." On March 12, 1872, Cauty filed a £30,000 claim against the United States for wrongful arrest and was eventually awarded $15,700. A decade later, he was an unemployed commercial clerk living in a boarding house. Costa Rica afterward awarded him a hefty pension, which was extended to his widow after his death. See Class HO107, Piece 61, Book 1, Langley Marish Parish, Buckinghamshire County, Enumeration District 11, Folio 4, p. 2, Census Returns of England and Wales, 1841, Kew, Surrey, England, National Archives of the UK, London; John Bassett Moore, *A Digest of International Law* (Washington: Government Printing Office, 1906), 4:500; Moore, *History and Digest of the International Arbitrations*, 4:3309–10; Obregón, *Diarios de Faustino Montes de Oca Gamero*, 23, 26, 47; Deposition of John E. Hollenbeck, July 25, 1857, DSJN; F. Montes de Oca to J. Joaquín Mora, January 5, 1857, Fondo: Guerra, Sig. 9269, ANCR; Ibañez Montoya, *Estudio asesor para la restauración del fuerte*; Bolaños Geyer, *Campana Rota*, 35–36; "Affairs of Nicaragua," *New York Times*, March 17, 1857, 1; Obregón, *Costa Rica y la guerra contra los filibusteros*, 220–21; "Affairs of Nicaragua," *New York Times*, March 19, 1857, 1; "Col. Cauty's Statement," *Daily Ohio Statesman* (Columbus), March 18, 1859, 1; "America," *The Times* (London), February 28, 1860, 5; "Local Intelligence," *New York Times*, December 25 and 29, 1863; Great Britain, Foreign Office, North America: 1864, No. 18, *Further Papers Respecting the Arrest and Imprisonment of Mr. James McHugh in the United States* (London: Harrison and Sons, 1864), 3; Proposición hecha por Mr. Cauty, September 7, 1864, Fondo: Gobernación, Sig. 29012, ANCR; Robert S. Hale to William Hunter, Aug. 19, 1872, MLDS.

43. Deposition of William D. Emmons, March 17, 1857, DSJN; Deposition of Walter Harris, July 23, 1857, DSJN; F. Montes de Oca to J. R. Mora, April 30, 1857, DSJN; Deposition of John E. Hollenbeck, July 25, 1857, DSJN; George F. Cauty to Juan Rafael Mora, May 27, 1857, Fondo: Guerra, Sig. 4784, ANCR; Charles M. Stewart to the President, July 21, 1857, Fondo: Hacienda, Sig. 6045, ANCR; Obregón, *Diarios de Faustino Montes de Oca Gamero*, 49–50.

44. Walker, *War in Nicaragua*, 358; S. A. Lockridge to B. S. Cotrell, March 4, 1857, DSJN; "Letter from Colonel Hall, of the Nicaraguan Army," *New York Herald*, April 15, 1857, 3; "Col. Lockridge's Apology," *New York Tribune*, June 19, 1857, 7; "Doings of Col. Titus at Rivas," *New York Herald*, May 29, 1857, 1; "Letter from Col. Titus," *Columbus Enquirer*, April 2, 1857, 2, and *Augusta Daily Chronicle & Sentinel*, April 9, 1857; F. M. de Oca to General in Chief, February 16, 1857, Fondo: Guerra, Sig. 4746, ANCR; "Interesting from Nicaragua," *New York Herald*, March 21, 1857, 1; "Operations on the San Juan River," *New York Herald*, April 4, 1857, 1.

45. After Spain declared war on England in June 1779, nine months later the British tried to seize the San Juan River route, capture Granada, and cut Spanish America in half. Brig. Gen. Stephen Kemble and Capt. Horatio Nelson of the eight-gun frigate HMS *Hinchinbrook*, with some 2,000 men and four small four-pounder cannons, obtained the surrender of El Castillo and its 160 Spanish defenders after a two-week siege. The British blew up the fort when they evacuated six months later after massive deaths due to disease. See Marley, *Wars of the Americas*, 326; Bolaños Geyer, *Campana Rota*, 35–36; "The News from Nicaragua," *New York Times*, April 4, 1857, 1; "Operations on the San Juan River," *New York Herald*, April 4, 1857, 1; E. S. Baker to Dear parents, August 2, 1857, MFA.

46. Obregón, *Diarios de Faustino Montes de Oca Gamero*, 29, 31, 50; E. S. Baker to Dear parents, August 2, 1857, MFA; F. M. de Oca to General in Chief, February 16, 1857, Fondo:

Guerra, Sig. 4746, ANCR; "Important from Nicaragua," *New York Times,* March 14, 1857, 1; "Interesting from Nicaragua," *New York Herald,* March 21, 1857, 1; "Operations on the San Juan," *New York Times,* March 30, 1857, 1.

47. "Later from Nicaragua," *New York Tribune,* March 14, 1857, 7; Obregón, *Diarios de Faustino Montes de Oca Gamero,* 29, 51; F. M. de Oca to General in Chief, February 16, 1857, Fondo: Guerra, Sig. 4746, ANCR; "Important from Nicaragua," *New York Times,* March 14, 1857, 1; "Affairs of Nicaragua," *New York Times,* March 19, 1857, 1; "Failure of Capt. Lockridge's Expedition," *Philadelphia Inquirer,* April 17, 1857, 2; "Interesting from Nicaragua," *New York Herald,* March 21, 1857, 1; "Operations on the San Juan," *New York Times,* March 30, 1857, 1; "A Filibuster View of the San Juan River," *New York Times,* April 4, 1857, 1; "Operations on the San Juan River," *New York Herald,* April 4, 1857, 1.

48. E. S. Baker to Dear parents, August 2, 1857, MFA.

49. Ibid.; Obregón, *Diarios de Faustino Montes de Oca Gamero,* 50–52; Deposition of Thomas Townsend, February 19, 1857, DSJN.

50. Obregón, *Diarios de Faustino Montes de Oca Gamero,* 51.

51. "Operations on the San Juan," *New York Times,* March 30, 1857, 1; "Letter from Colonel Hall, of the Nicaraguan Army," *New York Herald,* April 15, 1857, 3; "Important from Nicaragua," *New York Times,* March 14, 1857, 1; "Late and Important from Nicaragua," *Baton Rouge Daily Advocate,* March 14, 1857, 2; "Later from Nicaragua," *New York Tribune,* March 14, 1857, 7; "Interesting from Nicaragua," *New York Herald,* March 21, 1857, 1; "Arrival of the Tennessee," *New York Times,* April 17, 1857, 1; "Colonel Titus' Account of Affairs," *New York Times,* March 21, 1857, 1.

52. "Letter from Col. Titus," *New York Herald,* June 9, 1857, 8; Obregón, *Diarios de Faustino Montes de Oca Gamero,* 51–52, 56; Deposition of Walter Harris, July 23, 1857, DSJN; "Operations on the San Juan," *New York Times,* March 30, 1857, 1; "Operations on the San Juan River," *New York Herald,* April 4, 1857, 1; "Affairs of Nicaragua," *New York Times,* March 19, 1857, 1.

53. "Letter from Colonel Hall, of the Nicaraguan Army," *New York Herald,* April 15, 1857, 3; F. M. de Oca to General in Chief, February 16, 1857, Fondo: Guerra, Sig. 4746, ANCR; Recopilación, *El Combate de La Trinidad,* 16; Obregón, *Diarios de Faustino Montes de Oca Gamero,* 53; "Operations on the San Juan," *New York Times,* March 30, 1857, 1.

54. "Letter from Col. Titus," *Columbus Enquirer,* July 7, 1857, 2; "Important from Nicaragua," *New York Times,* March 21, 1857, 1; Obregón, *Diarios de Faustino Montes de Oca Gamero,* 52.

55. The English-language skills of Capt. Faustino Montes de Oca are evident in the letter he sent to John E. Hollenbeck, May 22, 1857, DSJN. Thomas Henry Horatio Cauty (1796–?) joined the British army in 1813 and married thirteen-year-old Ann Alder in London on August 10, 1818. His son George was born in 1824, the year he was left on half pay as a first lieutenant in the Bourbon Rifles. He was subsequently an "auctioneer, broker, dealer, and chapman" and after 1828 was in frequent litigation, bankruptcy, and debt. Cauty became unemployed after partly leasing a lead mine and slate quarry and in 1844 was sent to the Queen's Prison on creditors' petitions. The patriarch remarried and had a daughter in 1848. He was a gambler who "had ridden many a good jockey race and steeple chase" and "had occupied a prominent position in sporting society in England." In early 1852 Cauty in one of the London clubs met Nicaraguan general José Trinidad Muñoz, who induced him to take command of his rebel force in Central America. Upon arriving in Nicaragua, Cauty was dismayed to find a small ragtag guerrilla force instead of the large army alluded to, and he abandoned the enterprise. The Briton established a hotel at Rivas after the Accessory Transit Company started operations. Due to American competition, he moved to Costa Rica with his family and built for the government a small-size steamer for a large profit. Cauty subsequently moved to San Francisco and "opened a club house over Wells, Fargo & Co.'s express office but closed it again through

the advice of his son." Upon returning to San José, Costa Rica, he managed the Union Club and Hotel and edited the English-language section of the *Album Semanal* newspaper from September 12, 1856, until July 1857. The following month Cauty was appointed Costa Rican minister to Washington to negotiate the "boundary line, the resumption of the Transit route, and the making of a free port of entry of Greytown." The diplomat he replaced denounced him as "an exceedingly cunning and unscrupulous man" who fleeced three thousand dollars from the widow of a former Nicaraguan president. Cauty was involved in a failed dishonest deal for the transit route. In 1861 the Costa Rican government canceled contracts made with the Cautys to build a road from San José to Sarapiquí and for steamboat river navigation. See Guildhall, St. Botolph Aldgate, Register of Marriages, 1815–22, P69/BOT2/A/o1/Ms 9230/9, Church of England Parish Registers, 1754–1921, London Metropolitan Archives, London, Great Britain; War Office, Great Britain, *A List of the Officers,* 627; "Bankrupts," *Edinburgh Gazette,* December 30, 1828, 1; *London Gazette,* August 13, 1830, 1750; "Cauty v. Houlditch," *Law Chronicle,* April 24, 1844, 6; "The Court for Relief of Insolvent Debtors," *London Gazette,* June 4 and 21, 1844; "A Queer Minister," *Washington Evening Star,* August 17, 1857, 2; "The Successor to Mr. Molina," *Washington Evening Star,* August 18, 1857, 2; *Album Semanal* cited in *Jamestown (N.Y.) Journal,* April 3, 1857, 2; "La vida en San Jose a mediados del siglo XIX," 44n54; "Later from Costa Rica," New Orleans *Picayune,* October 17, 1856, 1; "The Minister from Costa Rica," *New York Weekly Herald,* August 15, 1857; "The Quarrel over the Transit Route," *New York Tribune,* August 18, 1857, 5; "Plots and Counterplots for the Nicaragua Transit Route," *San Francisco Bulletin,* December 17, 1857, 2; "Decreto del Senado," July 23, 1861, Fondo: Congreso, Sig. 5881, ANCR; "Declarada caducas las contratas," August 12, 1861, Fondo: Congreso, Sig. 5867, ANCR; "Important from Central America," *New York Times,* March 30, 1857, 1; "Col. Titus Cashiered by Lockridge," *Jamestown Journal,* April 3, 1857, 2; Obregón, *Diarios de Faustino Montes de Oca Gamero,* 53–54.

56. Obregón, *Diarios de Faustino Montes de Oca Gamero,* 53–54; F. Montes de Oca to J. R. Mora, April 30, 1857, DSJN; "Later from Nicaragua," *New York Tribune,* April 17, 1857, 6; "Operations on the San Juan," *New York Times,* March 30, 1857, 1.

57. Obregón, *Diarios de Faustino Montes de Oca Gamero,* 30; "Operations on the San Juan," *New York Times,* March 30, 1857, 1; "Arrival of the Tennessee," *New York Times,* April 17, 1857, 1.

58. Obregón, *Diarios de Faustino Montes de Oca Gamero,* 30, 53; Doubleday, *Reminiscences,* 185–86; "Operations on the San Juan," *New York Times,* March 30, 1857, 1.

59. Obregón, *Diarios de Faustino Montes de Oca Gamero,* 53; E. S. Baker to Dear parents, August 2, 1857, MFA; "Later from Nicaragua," *New York Tribune,* April 17, 1857, 6; "Operations on the San Juan River," *New York Herald,* April 4, 1857, 1; "Important from Nicaragua," *New York Times,* March 21, 1857, 1; "Later from Nicaragua," *New York Tribune,* March 21, 1857, 5; "Nicaragua—The Adventures of a Fillibustero," *Philadelphia Inquirer,* April 18, 1857, 1; S. A. Lockridge to B. S. Cotrell, March 4, 1857, DSJN.

60. "Our Greytown Correspondence," *New York Herald,* March 21, 1857, 1; "Later from Nicaragua," *New York Tribune,* March 21, 1857, 5; Walker, *War in Nicaragua,* 360; *Panama Star* repr. in "Arrival of the Tennessee," *Charleston Mercury,* March 24, 1857, 2; "Operations on the San Juan River," *New York Herald,* April 4, 1857, 1; Obregón, *Diarios de Faustino Montes de Oca Gamero,* 54.

61. S. A. Lockridge to B. S. Cotrell, March 4, 1857, DSJN.

62. Obregón, *Diarios de Faustino Montes de Oca Gamero,* 54; "Operations on the San Juan," *New York Times,* March 30, 1857, 1; F. M. de Oca to Gen. [Mora], February 19, 1857, Fondo: Guerra, Sig. 4746, ANCR; E. S. Baker to Dear parents, August 2, 1857, MFA.

63. E. S. Baker to Dear parents, August 2, 1857, MFA; "Operations on the San Juan River," *New York Herald,* April 4, 1857, 1; "Arrival of the Tennessee," *New York Times,* April 17, 1857, 1.

64. Lewis Miles Hobbs Washington (December 3, 1813–February 19, 1857) was born in Georgia and in 1835 moved to Texas, where he joined James W. Fannin's staff and participated in the siege of Bexar. In 1839 he wed Rebecca Landis Davidson, a thirty-year-old widow from Pennsylvania with four children, and they had four more of their own. The family eventually settled in Austin, where the patriarch wrote for various newspapers and received bounty land for participating in various skirmishes with Mexico. He joined the Lockridge filibuster expedition as a correspondent of the New Orleans *Picayune*. See Lewis Miles Hobbs Washington, Family Papers, Dolph Briscoe Center for American History, University of Texas at Austin; 1850 Texas Federal Census, Austin, 309; E. S. Baker to Dear parents, August 2, 1857, MFA; "Important from Nicaragua," *New York Times*, March 21, 1857, 1; "Operations on the San Juan River," *New York Herald*, April 4, 1857, 1; *Springfield Daily Illinois State Journal*, May 25, 1857, 3.

65. Obregón, *Diarios de Faustino Montes de Oca Gamero*, 31, 54–55; "Operations on the San Juan River," *New York Herald*, April 4, 1857, 1; "Interesting from Nicaragua," *New York Herald*, March 21, 1857, 1, 8; *Jamestown Journal*, April 3, 1857, 2; Walker, *War in Nicaragua*, 360; F. M. de Oca to Gen. [Mora], February 19, 1857, Fondo: Guerra, Sig. 4746, ANCR.

66. "Doings of Col. Titus at Rivas," *New York Herald*, May 29, 1857, 1; "Arrival of the Tennessee," *New York Times*, April 17, 1857, 1; F. M. de Oca to Gen. [Mora], February 20, 1857, Fondo: Guerra y Marina, Sig. 4763, ANCR.

67. "Arrival of the Tennessee," *New York Times*, April 17, 1857, 1; S. A. Lockridge to B. S. Cotrell, March 4, 1857, DSJN; E. S. Baker to Dear parents, August 2, 1857, MFA; F. M. de Oca to Gen. [Mora], February 20, 1857, Fondo: Guerra y Marina, Sig. 4763, ANCR.

68. The filibuster officers of the Second Battalion commanded by Titus who resigned on February 21, 1857, were J. A. Anderson, William M. Brantley, G. E. Conkling, Robert H. Footman, William T. More, J. Mulholland, T. X. Richardson, J. Austin Smith, John G. Starr, D. W. Vowls, W. S. West, and C. P. Wyckoff. See "Arrival of the Tennessee," *New York Times*, April 17, 1857, 1; "Important from Nicaragua," *New York Times*, March 21, 1857, 1; "Important from Central America," *New York Times*, March 30, 1857, 1; "Later from Nicaragua," *New York Tribune*, March 21, 1857, 5; "Doings of Col. Titus at Rivas," *New York Herald*, May 29, 1857, 1.

69. "Important from Nicaragua," *New York Times*, March 21, 1857, 1; "Doings of Col. Titus at Rivas," *New York Herald*, May 29, 1857, 1; Doubleday, *Reminiscences*, 187; Walker, *War in Nicaragua*, 360; Obregón, *Diarios de Faustino Montes de Oca Gamero*, 55.

70. "Later from Nicaragua," *New York Tribune*, March 21, 1857, 5; "Our Foreign News," *New York Times*, March 21, 1857, 1; "The Ethics of Fillibusterism," *New York Times*, April 10, 1857, 4; "Col. Titus," *New London (Conn.) Daily Chronicle*, March 23, 1857, 2; "Letter from New Orleans," *Baton Rouge Daily Advocate*, April 1, 1857, 2; New Orleans *Picayune* quoted in "Nicaragua," *San Antonio Ledger and Texan*, April 4, 1857, 2.

71. "Interesting from Nicaragua," *New York Herald*, March 21, 1857, 1; "Important from Nicaragua," *New York Times*, March 21, 1857, 1; "Nicaragua—The Adventures of a Fillibustero," *Philadelphia Inquirer*, April 18, 1857, 1; E. S. Baker to Dear parents, August 2 and September 13, 1857, MFA; "Nicaragua," *Frank Leslie's Illustrated Newspaper*, April 4, 1857, 6; Walker, *War in Nicaragua*, 362; "Colonel Titus' Account of Affairs," *New York Times*, March 21, 1857, 1.

72. J. H. Cockburn to Commander de Horsey, March 3, 1857, DSJN; "A Filibuster View of the San Juan River," *New York Times*, April 4, 1857, 1; "Operations on the San Juan River," *New York Herald*, April 4, 1857, 1; "Important from Nicaragua," *New York Times*, March 21, 1857, 1; "Later from Nicaragua," *New York Tribune*, March 21, 1857, 5.

73. S. A. Lockridge to B. S. Cotrell, March 4, 1857, DSJN; B. Squire Cotrell to W. L. Marcy, March 6, 1857, DSJN; "Important from Nicaragua," *New York Times*, March 21, 1857, 1; "Later from Nicaragua," *New York Tribune*, March 21, 1857, 5; "Arrival of the Tennessee," *Charleston Mercury*, March 24, 1857, 2; "Our Greytown Correspondence," *New York Herald*,

March 21, 1857, 1; Walker, *War in Nicaragua,* 361; "Operations on the San Juan River," *New York Herald,* April 4, 1857, 1.

74. B. Squire Cotrell to S. A. Lockridge, March 4, 1857, DSJN; B. Squire Cotrell to W. L. Marcy, March 6, 1857, DSJN; "Our Greytown Correspondence," *New York Herald,* March 21, 1857, 1; Walker, *War in Nicaragua,* 361; "Operations on the San Juan River," *New York Herald,* April 4, 1857, 1; "Letter from Col. Titus," *Columbus Enquirer,* April 2, 1857, 2, and *Augusta Daily Chronicle & Sentinel,* April 9, 1857; Logs of Ships and Stations, 1801–1946, Logs of U.S. Naval Ships, 1801–1915, Saratoga, January 3, 1857, to January 12, 1858, March 4, 1857, vol. 15, Records of the Bureau of Naval Personnel, RG 24, NARA; S. A. Lockridge to B. S. Cotrell, March 4 and 5, 1857, DSJN.

75. B. Squire Cotrell to W. L. Marcy, March 6, 1857, DSJN; E. G. Tilton to Secretary of the Navy, March 7, 1857, Letters Received by the Secretary of the Navy from Commanders, 1804–86, January 1–March 31, 1857, M-147, Roll 52, RG 45, NARA; "Later from Nicaragua," *New York Tribune,* March 21, 1857, 5; "Our Greytown Correspondence," *New York Herald,* March 21, 1857, 1; "Operations on the San Juan River," *New York Herald,* April 4, 1857, 1; "The Fillibusters on the River," *New York Tribune,* March 21, 1857, 5.

76. "Interesting from Nicaragua," *New York Herald,* March 21, 1857, 8; "Interesting from Nicaragua," *New York Herald,* April 14 1857, 1; "Nicaragua," *New York Tribune,* April 14, 1857, 6; S. A. Lockridge to Capt. Tilton, March 6, 1857, and E. G. Tilton to Secretary of the Navy, March 17, 1857, Letters Received by the Secretary of the Navy from Commanders, 1804–86, January 1–March 31, 1857, M-147, Roll 52, RG 45, NARA; Juan Mesnier to R. G. Escalante, March 19, 1857, Fondo: Guerra, Sig. 4784, ANCR; "Journal and Views of Captain Brontley, of the Nicaraguan Army," *New York Times,* April 4, 1857, 1.

77. "A Filibuster View of the San Juan River," *New York Times,* April 4, 1857, 1; "Nicaragua," *New York Tribune,* April 14, 1857, 6.

78. "Letter from Captain J. Egbert Farnum Concerning Colonel Lockridge," *New York Times,* April 15, 1857, 1.

79. "The Evacuation of San Juan del Norte," *New York Times,* April 30, 1857, 1; "Arrival of the Tennessee," *Charleston Mercury,* March 24, 1857, 2; "Later from Nicaragua," *New York Tribune,* March 21, 1857, 5.

80. Col. W. P. Caycee participated in the 1848 revolution of José Antonio Páez in Venezuela and then worked as a muleteer and monte gambler in Panama. He joined the Conservative general Fruto Chamorro in the 1854 war against Liberals in Nicaragua, where he lost his left arm. When the Conservatives invited William Walker to join their side the following year, Caycee sided with the filibusters. After Walker capitulated on May 1, 1857, Caycee took service under Nicaraguan general Tomás Martínez for a few months and then was second in command to Costa Rican general in chief José M. Cañas. See Walker, *War in Nicaragua,* 392; "Doings of Col. Titus at Rivas," *New York Herald,* May 29, 1857, 1; "Highly Important from Nicaragua," *New York Times,* April 3, 1857, 1; "Later from Nicaragua," *New York Tribune,* April 3, 1857, 5.

81. Walker, *War in Nicaragua,* 392–93; "Highly Important from Nicaragua," *New York Times,* April 3, 1857, 1; "The War in Nicaragua," *New York Times,* April 13, 1857, 5; "Highly Important from Nicaragua," *Frank Leslie's Illustrated Newspaper,* April 18, 1857, 6.

82. *Charleston Courier,* May 4, 1857, 1; "Doings of Col. Titus at Rivas," *New York Herald,* May 29, 1857, 1; "Later from Nicaragua," *New York Tribune,* April 17, 1857, 6; "Additional Intelligence," *New York Herald,* April 30, 1857, 4; "Highly Important from Nicaragua," *New York Times,* April 17 and 30, 1857, 1.

83. "Later from Nicaragua," *New York Tribune,* April 17, 1857, 6; Doubleday, *Reminiscences,* 188–91; B. Squire Cotrell to Lewis Cass, April 14, 1857, DSJN; "Highly Important from Nicaragua," *New York Times,* April 17, 1857, 1; E. S. Baker to Dear parents, June 28, 1857, MFA.

84. Robert G. Robb to Commander H. Paulding, May 13, 1857, Letters Received by the Secretary of the Navy from Commanding Officers of Squadrons ("Squadron Letters"), 1841–86, Home Squadron, January 1, 1857–March 19, 1858, NARA, hereafter cited as Squadron Letters; George F. Cauty to the Inhabitants of Grey Town, April 12, 1857, DSJN; "Inventory of Property Belonging to Col. Lockridge's Expedition," April 13, 1857, DSJN; "Inventario, Greytown," April 13, 1857, Fondo: Guerra, Sig. 8902, ANCR; "Arrival of the Tennessee," *New York Times*, April 17, 1857, 1; "News from Central America," *New York Herald*, April 10, 1857, 4; "Later from Nicaragua," *New York Tribune*, April 17, 1857, 6.

85. Thomas Truxton Houston (November 11, 1829–June 26, 1860) was appointed a midshipman in 1845 and the following year participated with Commodore Stockton in taking California. He entered the Naval Academy at Annapolis three years later, graduating with the rank of lieutenant. Houston died of remittent fever on board the U.S. sloop of war *Iroquois* in the Bay of Naples, Italy, and was interred in Oak Hill cemetery, Washington, D.C. See "Obituary," *Daily National Intelligencer*, July 18, 1860, 1; "Death of Lieut. Houston," *Charleston Courier*, July 19, 1860, 1; Charles Henry Davis to Lieutenant Thomas T. Houston, April 22, 1857, Pacific Squadron, July 10, 1856–November 16, 1857, Squadron Letters; Charles Henry Davis to General Jose J. Mora, April 22, 25, and 26, 1857, Squadron Letters; "Doings of Col. Titus at Rivas," *New York Weekly Herald*, May 30, 1857, 130.

86. "Surrender of Col. Titus and Others," *New York Weekly Herald*, May 30, 1857, 130; "Additional Nicaragua News," *San Francisco Daily Evening Bulletin*, June 17, 1857, 1; *San José Crónica* quoted in "Surrender of Col. Titus and Others," *New York Herald*, May 29, 1857, 8; "Later from Nicaragua," *New York Tribune*, April 3, 1857, 5.

87. "Our San Juan Correspondence," *New York Herald*, May 29, 1857; "Highly Interesting from Central America," *New York Weekly Herald*, May 30, 1857, 130; Walker, *War in Nicaragua*, 411; F. Montes de Oca to J. R. Mora, April 30, 1857, DSJN.

88. Dr. John Winthrop Taylor (August 19, 1817–January 19, 1880) was appointed assistant surgeon in 1838 and promoted to surgeon in 1852. He was on the U.S. steam sloop *Pensacola* during the Civil War at the capture of New Orleans and the Mississippi River campaign. Taylor served as U.S. surgeon general in 1878–79 and died of heart disease in his Boston home. See "Obituary," *Boston Journal*, January 19, 1880, 2; Charles Henry Davis to Commodore William Mervine, May 13 and 14, 1857, Pacific Squadron, Squadron Letters; Charles Henry Davis to General William Walker, April 30, 1857, Squadron Letters; Wm. Walker and Charles Henry Davis agreement, May 1, 1857, Squadron Letters; D. Porter McCorkle to William Mervine, June 18, 1857, Squadron Letters; William Mervine to I. Toucey, July 3, 1857, Squadron Letters; H. Paulding to Issac Toucey, June 16, 1857, Home Squadron, Squadron Letters; "Highly Interesting from Central America," *New York Herald*, May 29, 1857, 1; "Important News from Nicaragua," *San Francisco Bulletin*, June 16, 1857, 2; B. Squire Cotrell to Lewis Cass, June 3 and 18, 1857, DSJN; Doubleday, *Reminiscences*, 193.

89. *San Francisco Daily Evening Bulletin*, June 16 and 17, 1857; William Mervine to I. Toucey, June 2, 1857, Squadron Letters; William Mervine to Bartolome Calvo, May 17 and 18, 1857, Squadron Letters; "Bloody Riot at Panama," *New York Weekly Herald*, May 3, 1856, 130; "Highly Interesting from Central America," *New York Weekly Herald*, May 30, 1857, 130.

90. William Leslie Cazneau (October 5, 1807–January 7, 1876), born in Boston, was a cotton buyer and general store merchant in Matagorda, Texas, in 1830. He moved to Austin in 1839 as commissary general of the Texas Republic. Cazneau served three terms as a representative from Travis County in the Texas Congress during 1842–45 and was one of the signers of the Texas constitution. He served in the Mexican War until August 1847 and two years later married Jane McManus Storms (1807–78), a journalist, political adviser, and promoter of filibustering in Cuba and Nicaragua. Cazneau was appointed U.S. commissioner plenipotentiary to the Dominican Republic in 1853 and special envoy in 1859. He died at his Keith Hall

estate in Jamaica. See Hudson, *Mistress of Manifest Destiny; Charleston Mercury,* May 30, 1857, 2; "Arrived," *New York Times,* May 29, 1857, 8; "List of Letters," *New York Herald,* June 13 and 20, 1857, 3.

91. "Doings of Col. Titus at Rivas," *New York Herald,* May 29, 1857, 1.

92. "An Indignant Fillibuster," *Richmond Whig,* May 22, 1857, 1; "Letter from Col. Titus," *Columbus Enquirer,* July 7, 1857, 2; *Savannah Republican* cited in *Daily National Intelligencer,* July 7, 1857.

93. "Letter from Col. Titus," *Columbus Enquirer,* July 7, 1857, 2.

94. Ibid.; "Aid for Nicaragua—Rendezvous at Charleston," *New York Times,* April 10, 1857, 1, and *New York Herald,* April 11, 1857, 1.

95. "Col. Lockridge's Apology," *New York Tribune,* June 19, 1857, 7.

96. "Gen. Wheat," *Alexandria (Va.) Gazette,* July 4, 1857, 2; Wiltsee, *Gold Rush Steamers,* 225.

Chapter Four: Arizona Silver Miner, 1858–1860

1. *Lowell (Mass.) Daily Citizen and News,* July 29, 1857, 2; *New York Tribune,* July 24, 1857, 5; "Col. Titus," *Ripley (Ohio) Bee,* July 25, 1857; "Col. Titus Going Back to Kansas," *Rockford (Ill.) Republican,* July 30, 1857, 2; *St. Louis Democrat* quoted in "The Siege of Lawrence Raised," *Cleveland Leader,* August 12, 1857, 2.

2. Robert John Walker (July 19, 1801–November 11, 1869) was born in Northumberland, Pa., and graduated from the University of Pennsylvania in 1819 at the head of his class. He practiced law in Pittsburgh until moving in 1826 to Mississippi, where he was a slave owner and passionately defended the institution of slavery. Walker served as Mississippi senator from 1836 to 1845 and was then appointed U.S. secretary of the Treasury until 1849. He served as Kansas territorial governor from May 27 to November 16, 1857, when he resigned. Walker afterward practiced law in Washington, D.C., until his death. See U.S. Congress, *Biographical Dictionary,* 364; "Gov. Walker," *Lecompton Union,* April 11, 1857, 2; "Lynch Law in Leavenworth," *New York Tribune,* August 10, 1857, 6; "From Kansas," *Boston Traveler,* August 11, 1857, 4; "Kansas Affairs," *Springfield (Mass.) Republican,* August 11, 1857, 2; "The Siege of Lawrence Raised," *Cleveland Leader,* August 12, 1857, 2; "Movements of Individuals," *Lowell Daily Citizen and News,* August 18, 1857, 3; Index to Deeds Grantor/Grantee, August 4, 1857, Deed Record, vol. A, 60, Douglas County, Kans., Kenneth Spencer Research Library, University of Kansas, Lawrence.

3. *Leavenworth Weekly Herald,* September 5, 1857, 2; Treacy, *Grand Hotels of Saint Louis,* 7; Van Ravenswaay, *Saint Louis,* 325–26.

4. *Baltimore Sun,* September 18, 1857, 1; *Philadelphia North American and United States Gazette,* September 19, 1857; "Kansas Notes," *Springfield Republican,* September 21, 1857, 2; *Newark Centinel of Freedom,* September 22, 1857, 3; "Miscellaneous Items," *New York Times,* September 23, 1857, 5; "Col. Titus in the Calaboose," *Baltimore Sun,* September 18, 1857, 1; *New York Tribune,* September 19, 1857, 3, *Albany Evening Journal,* September 21, 1857, 3, and *Athens (Tenn.) Post,* September 25, 1857, 2.

5. Horace Brooks (August 14, 1814–January 13, 1894), born in Boston, graduated from the U.S. Military Academy in 1835 and served in the Seminole War as an artillery lieutenant. During the Mexican War, he participated in all the major battles from Veracruz to Mexico City in 1847 and was promoted to brevet lieutenant colonel for gallantry at Molino del Rey. Brooks spent the Civil War in command of garrisons and administrative duties without engaging in combat. His last command post was the Presidio at San Francisco. He retired on January 10, 1877, and moved to Baltimore. He passed away in Kissimmee, Fla., and is interred in Green-Wood Cemetery, Brooklyn. See Cullum, *Biographical Register,* 1:794; 1880 Maryland Federal Census, Baltimore, 642; "Col. Titus Makes Known Their Plans," *Albany Evening Journal,* October 5, 1857, 2, and *Cleveland Leader,* October 7, 1857, 1; "Definite Intelligence of the

Result of the Late Election in Kansas," *Washington Daily National Intelligencer,* October 29, 1857, 3; "The Mysteries of Kansas Politics," *Davenport (Iowa) Democrat and Leader,* October 30, 1857, 2; Brown, *Reminiscences of Gov. R. J. Walker,* 95.

6. "Stupendous Election Fraud," *New York Tribune,* October 24, 1857, 5; Wilder, *Annals of Kansas,* 195; "Kansas Election," *Rockford Republican,* October 29, 1857, 2; "Definite Intelligence of the Result of the Late Election in Kansas," *Daily National Intelligencer,* October 29, 1857, 3; *Connecticut Courant* (Hartford), October 31, 1857, 1.

7. U.S. House of Representatives, Kansas Constitution, May 11, 1858, 35th Congress, 1st Session, Report No. 377, Serial 966, 38–56; Stephenson, *Publications of the Kansas State Historical Society,* 3:90; Johannsen, "The Lecompton Constitutional Convention," 225–43; de la Cova, "Samuel J. Kookogey," 160–62; Nevins, *Emergence of Lincoln,* 269; "Gov. Walker Resigned," *Lecompton National Democrat,* December 24, 1857, 3.

8. *Kansas Herald of Freedom,* May 15, 1858; *Lowell Daily Citizen and News,* January 25, 1858, 2; U.S. House of Representatives, Kansas Constitution, May 11, 1858, Report No. 377, 35th Congress, 1st Session, Serial Set 966, 196–97, 225, 258.

9. "Personal and Political," *Springfield Republican,* December 29, 1857, 2; "Assault upon Gen. Pomeroy of Kansas," *Liberator* (Boston), April 30, 1858, 71; "Personal Attack upon General Pomeroy," *New York Times,* April 29, 1858, 5; Deed of Trust, Book 28, 512–13, Jackson County Recorder of Deeds, Kansas City, Mo.

10. "Assault upon Gen. Pomeroy of Kansas," *Liberator,* April 30, 1858, 71; "Personal Attack upon General Pomeroy," *New York Times,* April 29, 1858, 5; "Outrage at Kansas City," *Freedom's Champion* (Atchison, Kans.), April 24, 1858; "The Kanzas City Outrage," *Quindaro Chindowan* (Kansas City, Kans.), April 24, 1858, 3; Douglas, "A History of Manufactures in the Kansas District," 93n47. Pomeroy purchased a fourth of the Squatter Sovereign in 1857.

11. "Assault upon Gen. Pomeroy of Kansas," *Liberator,* April 30, 1858, 71; *Kansas Herald of Freedom,* April 24, 1858; "Personal Attack upon General Pomeroy," *New York Times,* April 29, 1858, 5; *San Francisco Daily Evening Bulletin,* May 31, 1858, 1; "Outrage at Kansas City," *Freedom's Champion,* April 24, 1858; "The Inland and 'Border Ruffians' of Kansas," *Concord New Hampshire Patriot & State Gazette,* June 9, 1858, 3.

12. New Orleans *Picayune,* June 3, 1858, 1; "Affairs in Kansas," *New York Herald,* June 12, 1858; "Emigrants for Arizona," *New York Times,* May 31, 1858; *San Francisco Daily Evening Bulletin,* June 29, 1858, 2.

13. William P. Tomlinson (1833–June 13, 1901) was active in many social causes, including abolition, temperance, woman suffrage, and Indian relief. Raised as a farmer in Upper Makefield, Pa., under the spell of Wendell Phillips he began publishing the *Anti-Slavery Standard* for the American Anti-Slavery Society. In New York, Tomlinson became proprietor and editor of the *Woman's Advocate.* In October 1859 he went to Europe as a correspondent of the *New York Tribune* and the *New York Post.* After returning to Manhattan, Tomlinson published *Poems of Home and Abroad* in 1866. Six years later he settled in Kansas, married, and became editor of the *Topeka Democrat,* opposing populism, until his passing. See Tomlinson, *Kansas in Eighteen Fifty-eight,* 240–41; "Indian Aid Association," *Liberator,* April 15, 1859, 60; William P. Tomlinson, October 7, 1859, U.S. Passport Applications, 1795–1905, M-1372, RG 59, NARA; 1880 Kansas Federal Census, Russell City, 16; "The Other Side of the Picture," *Springfield Republican,* April 16, 1889, 3; "Colonel 'Whoop' Tomlinson," *Hutchinson (Kans.) News ,* August 4, 1896, 5; "W. P. Tomlinson Dead," *New York Times,* June 14, 1901.

14. Tomlinson, *Kansas in Eighteen Fifty-eight,* 246–52.

15. Ibid., 252–53.

16. Charles Hamilton, a Georgian proslavery leader, carried out the last significant act of violence in Bleeding Kansas on May 19, 1858. He and thirty of his followers captured eleven

unarmed free-soilers and executed five of them in what became known as the Marais des Cygnes Massacre. See ibid., 253–54.

17. John Butterfield and associates on September 1, 1857, signed a six-year government contract for six hundred thousand dollars annually to carry the mail semiweekly between St. Louis and San Francisco within twenty-five days. The first mail stages left St. Louis and San Francisco on September 15, 1858. From September 1858 to March 1861 the twenty-seven-hundred-mile Butterfield Overland Mail Company route operated 164 stations, manned by some eight hundred employees, using one hundred coaches and eighteen hundred horses and mules. See Gard, *Along the Early Trails of the Southwest*, 28–29, 32–35; Moody, *Stagecoach West*, 97.

18. "News from South Kansas," *Farmers' Cabinet* (Amherst, N.H.), July 21, 1858, 3; *Dallas Herald*, July 17, 1858, 2; "Expedition for Northern Mexico," *Daily National Intelligencer*, March 27, 1858.

19. John Haskell King (February 19, 1820–April 7, 1888) was appointed as second lieutenant of the First U.S. Infantry at the age of seventeen. He served in the Seminole War and was a captain in the Mexican War. During the Civil War, he was a brigadier general of volunteers and fought in numerous battles, being wounded at Murfreesboro. After the war he was promoted to colonel of the Ninth Infantry, and he served on the western frontier until his retirement in 1882. Fort Chadbourne was named for 2nd Lt. Theodore Lincoln Chadbourne, who was killed at the battle of Resaca de la Palma in the Mexican War. See Warner, *Generals in Blue*, 268–69; John H. King to John Withers, July 28, 1858, Post Return of Fort Belknap, Tex., July 1858, Returns from U.S. Military Posts, 1800–1916, M-617, Records of the Adjutant General's Office, 1780s–1917, RG 94, NARA, hereafter cited as RMP; "Military Movements in Texas," *New York Times*, August 27, 1858, 5.

20. Five photos of Fort Davis and its officers in 1888 are in Miscellaneous Files, Box 1, Envelope 102, Entry 287, Records of the Adjutant General's Office, RG 94, NARA; Post Return of Fort Davis, Tex., September 1858, RMP; *Fremont (Ohio) Journal*, August 6, 1858, 2; *Daily Confederation* (Montgomery, Ala.), August 13, 1858, 2; "Latest from Texas," *Charleston Mercury*, August 25, 1858, 2; "Indian Murders in Texas," *New York Commercial Advertiser*, September 9, 1858, 1.

21. Sonora had been part of the frustrated filibuster designs of William Walker, who in 1854 invaded Baja California and declared himself president of the "Republic of Lower California and Sonora." See *San Diego Herald* quoted in *San Francisco Bulletin*, October 7, 1858, 3; May, *Manifest Destiny's Underworld*, 43; Stout, *Schemers & Dreamers*, 44–47; "Annihilation of H. A. Crabb's Party!!!," *San Francisco Daily Globe*, May 14, 1857, 2.

22. Post Return of Fort Quitman, Tex., September 1858, RMP; Post Return of Fort Bliss, September and October 1858, RMP; Gard, *Along the Early Trails of the Southwest*, 24; "Overland to California," *New York Herald*, November 11, 1858, 1.

23. Post Return of Fort Fillmore, New Mexico, October and November 1858, RMP; "Overland to California," *New York Herald*, November 11, 1858, 1.

24. Charles Debrille Poston (April 20, 1825–June 24, 1902) was born in Kentucky and went to California in 1850 as clerk of the San Francisco customhouse. He was appointed Indian agent in 1863 and elected the following year as Arizona territorial delegate to the U.S. Congress. See Charles Debrille Poston Papers, Arizona Historical Society, Tucson, hereafter AHS; *Report of the Sonora Exploring and Mining Co.*, 41; *Report of the Governor of Arizona*, 44–47; "The Silver Mines of Arizona," *New York Tribune*, August 20, 1859, 7; "From Arizona," *New York Times*, September 17, 1859, 1; Poston, "Building a State in Apache Land," 206–7; "Interesting Letter from Arizona," *Daily Ohio Statesman* (Columbus), February 6, 1859, 1; "Arizona—The Silver Mines," *Cleveland Leader*, March 9, 1959, 2.

25. "Overland to California," *New York Herald*, November 11, 1858, 1; "Additional from the South," *San Francisco Daily Evening Bulletin*, November 26, 1858, 1.

26. Philemon Thomas Herbert (November 1, 1825–July 23, 1864), born in Pine Apple, Ala., attended the University of Alabama before moving to Mariposa City, Calif., in 1850 and entering politics. He was elected democratic representative to Congress and took office on March 4, 1855. His first trial for murder ended in a hung jury, but he was subsequently acquitted in July 1856 by a second jury believing that he acted in self-defense. The incident ruined Herbert's political career, and he briefly turned to mining in Arizona before moving to El Paso, Tex., in 1859 to practice law. Herbert joined the Confederate army as a lieutenant colonel and raised three companies known as Herbert's Battalion. In May 1863 he received command of the Seventh Texas Cavalry. Herbert was wounded at the Battle of Mansfield, La., on April 8, 1864, and died from his injuries three months later. See U.S. Congress, *Biographical Dictionary*, 1177; "P. T. Herbert in Washington: Details of the Killing of Thomas Keating," *Sacramento Daily Union*, June 21, 1856, 1; Cozzens, *Marvellous Country*, 79–80, 204; Pompelly, *My Reminiscences*, 1:188.

27. Fort Buchanan, founded on November 17, 1856, was located off present-day Hog Canyon Road, Sonoita, Ariz., at 31°39'27.36"N110°42'25.44"W. During the Civil War, the fort was burned on July 21, 1861, by Union troops withdrawing to New Mexico to avoid its occupation by Confederate forces. A lengthy description of Fort Buchanan by assistant surgeon Bernard J. D. Irwin regarding its health, climate, flora, fauna, and native population is in U.S. Senate, *Report of the Affairs in the Department of New Mexico*, 207–20, 306. See also Post Return of Fort Buchanan, N.Mex., October 1858, RMP; "Interesting Letter from W. Wrightson, Esq.," *Daily Ohio Statesman* (Columbus), February 5, 1859, 1; "From Arizona," *New York Times*, September 17, 1859, 1; Barnes, *Arizona Place Names*, 314–15; Altshuler, *Starting with Defiance*, 19; Pfanz, *Richard S. Ewell*, 103, 106; Sacks, "The Origins of Fort Buchanan," 207–26; "Sonoita Valley," *Weekly Arizonian*, May 12, 1859, 2.

28. Edward Ephraim Cross (April 22, 1832–July 3, 1863), born in Lancaster, N.H., was a reporter for the *Cincinnati Times* before going to Arizona in July 1858 with investors of the Santa Rita Silver Mining Company. He was editor of the *Weekly Arizonian*, published at Tubac by William Wrightson, from March 3, 1859, to June 14, 1860. On July 8, 1859, Cross fought a bloodless duel with Sylvester Mowry, who challenged him after a series of virulent attacks in the newspaper. In 1860 he accepted appointment as lieutenant in the Mexican Liberal Army of Benito Juárez and was assigned to command the El Fuerte garrison in Sonora. Cross resigned and returned to the United States after the start of the Civil War and was appointed colonel of the Fifth New Hampshire Volunteer Infantry. He was wounded at the battles of Seven Pines and Antietam before being killed at Gettysburg. Cross was a member of Masonic North Star Lodge No. 8, Lancaster. See Edward E. Cross folder, AHS; Pumpelly, *My Reminiscences*, 1:200; Denslow, *10,000 Famous Freemasons*, 1:269; "Arizona—The Silver Mines," *Cleveland Leader*, March 9, 1959, 2; "Mexican Horse Thieves," *Weekly Arizonian*, March 3, 1859, 2.

29. Bernard John Dowling Irwin (June 24, 1830–December 15, 1917), born in County Roscomom, Ireland, arrived in America as a youth and graduated from the New York Medical College in 1852. Three years later he was appointed an acting assistant surgeon in the army and sent to Texas. Irwin was stationed at Fort Buchanan from December 1857 until July 1861. His distinguished gallantry in action at Apache Pass on February 13–14, 1861, earned him the Congressional Medal of Honor. Promoted to captain that year, as medical director in the Army of the Ohio at the Battle of Shiloh, Irwin created the first tent field hospital that became internationally emulated. He was captured in Kentucky four months later and after two months as a POW was promoted to major. After the war Irwin served as post surgeon in various western garrisons until 1880. During the next decade, he was promoted to colonel and was in charge of army medical depots in New York City and San Francisco. Irwin learned to speak five languages before retiring as a brigadier general in 1904. He passed away in Corbourg, Ontario,

and was interred at West Point, N.Y. See Bernard John Dowling Irwin Papers, AHS; 'To the Public," *Weekly Arizonian,* July 7, 1859, 3; George D. Mercer file, AHS; 1860 New Mexico Territory Federal Census, Arizona Co., Fort Buchanan, 28, Tubac, 50, Lower Santa Cruz Settlements, 52; Post Return of Fort Buchanan, Arizona, October 1858, RMP.

30. The Trench mine is located off Flux Canyon Rd., near the intersection with Harshaw Rd., at 31°27′48″N110°43′41″W. In 1880 the Hearst estate of California bought the mine and sank a four-hundred-foot shaft that produced "a great deal of rich ore said to average 40% lead and 60 oz. silver." See Dunning, *Rock to Riches,* 269; "The 'Trench' Mine," *Arizona Citizen and Weekly Tribune,* November 15, 1873, 2; "Mining News," *Weekly Arizonian,* March 3 and April 28, 1859; "From Arizona," *New York Times,* September 17, 1859; *Texas Republican* (Marshall), February 18, 1859, 2; Mowry, *Arizona and Sonora,* 27; Hinton, *The Hand-Book to Arizona,* 126; Hodge, *Arizona as It Is,* 125–26; San Rafael de la Zanja Land Grant Collection, 1880–87, University of Arizona Library Special Collections, Tucson.

31. The Patagonia Mine, later renamed the Mowry Mine, was originally located at 31°25′39.80″N110°42′18.29″W. See "Three Days Later from California," *New York Times,* January 8, 1859, 1; Blake, "Silver and Copper Mining in Arizona," 8; Hinton, *The Hand-Book to Arizona,* 126; Hodge, *Arizona as It Is,* 126; Cozzens, *Marvellous Country,* 86–87.

32. Elias Brevoort (September 22, 1822–March 12, 1904), a Detroit native and inveterate bachelor, was a trader in Kaw, Mo., in 1850 before moving that year to Santa Fe, N.Mex. In 1851 he served as a second lieutenant of a local volunteer outfit, and by 1853 he was a first lieutenant in the Los Angeles Ranger cavalry militia in California. Beginning in July 1854 Brevoort and Joab Houghton carried the mail from Santa Fe to San Antonio, Tex., for three months. Brevoort arrived in Arizona as an army sutler in 1856, purchased the Reventon ranch in February 1859 to provide beef for Fort Buchanan, and abandoned it after the army left the region. By 1869 he had a saloon in Las Vegas, N.Mex., he then became a general merchant in Socorro County, and by 1872 he was a real estate agent. In 1874 Brevoort published the 176-page *Brevoort's New Mexico.* He was appointed receiver of the U.S. Land Office in Santa Fe during 1877–81 and held the post of interpretership at the Pueblo Indian Agency in 1890. Brevoort then began spending his winters in Silao, Guanajuato, Mexico, where he passed away. See Elias Brevoort folder, AHS; 1850 Missouri Federal Census, Kaw, Jackson Co., 237; 1870 New Mexico Federal Census, Socorro Co., 475; 1880 New Mexico Federal Census, Santa Fe, 25; "Major Brevoort in Mexico," *New Mexican* (Santa Fe), January 23, 1896, 4; Palmer, *Early Days in Detroit,* 609; Mowry, *Arizona and Sonora,* 76; Barnes, *Arizona Place Names,* 320; Hodge, *Arizona as It Is,* 126; Pfanz, *Richard S. Ewell,* 104, 112; Wilson, *Islands in the Desert,* 152; Wehrman, "Harshaw," 23–24; Charles H. Swain, "Report on the Mines Known as the Old Mowry Mines," 1893, unpub. ms., AHS. The Swain account contains various factual errors regarding Sylvester Mowry.

33. The Titus ranch was located at 31°31′24.60″N110°46′42.69″W and appears as a "house" in T22 S. R15 E. Section 14 of the Theodore F. White 1876 Arizona map. It is also depicted as "San José de Sonoita" in the 4000′ contour line extending into Section 14 of the John L. Harris 1880 Arizona map. The location is shown in the George J. Roskruge 1893 Arizona map as the "Sonoita Ruins" in the same section. The remains of four adobe structures that were there in 1968 have since vanished. The F. Biertu map of the Sonoita and Santa Cruz river valleys is in the F. Biertu Journal, 1860–61, MS HM4367, Henry E. Huntington Library, San Marino, Calif. The Biertu map was the basis for the Sonoita Valley ranches depicted in the 1865 William B. Hartley map of Arizona. The Biertu map is reproduced in Roberts, *With Their Own Blood,* 71. Roberts describes in her book all the settlers in the Sonoita Valley who appear in the Biertu map but inexplicably omits Titus. See John C. Greenleaf to Edward Steele, May 16, 1968, correspondence file, Patagonia-Sonoita Creek Preserve Visitor Center, Patagonia, Ariz.; Pumpelly, *My Reminiscences,* 1:217; Farish, *History of Arizona,* 2:44–45; U.S. House of

Representatives, *Private Land Grants in Arizona,* 3; U.S. House of Representatives, *Certain Private Land Grants in Arizona Territory,* 3; Thornburg, "The Sonoita Valley," 4–6.

34. William Ward was killed by Apaches in 1860. See "Democratic County Convention," *Arkansas Intelligencer* (Van Buren), May 2, 1846, 2; Roberts, *With Their Own Blood,* 39–41; 1860 New Mexico Territory Federal Census, Arizona Co., Sonoita Creek Settlement, 30, 31.

35. Roberts, *With Their Own Blood,* 40, 69, 85, 104–5; William C. Wadsworth folder, AHS; 1860 New Mexico Territory Federal Census, Arizona Co., Sonoita Creek Settlement, 30; 1850 Texas Federal Census, Jefferson Co., 515.

36. The adobe remains of the John Ward hacienda are at 31°30'45.78"N, 110°47'49.82"W. They were archaeologically excavated in 1960–61 under the erroneous belief that it was the San José de Sonoita Mission, with "burials known to have been made beneath the floors." The findings included "wagon parts, horse harness trappings, horse and mule shoes, cartridges, and metal fastenings." The 115-page scientific report was published by Fontana and Greenleaf as "Johnny Ward's Ranch." The neighboring Titus ranch, which contained the sought mission church and building, is not mentioned in the essay. See "Sonoita Valley," *Weekly Arizonian,* May 12, 1859, 2; John Ward folder, AHS; C. B. Marshall folder, AHS; Roberts, *With Their Own Blood,* 68; 1860 New Mexico Territory Federal Census, Arizona Co., Sonoita Creek Settlement, 31, 32, 34; Farish, *History of Arizona,* 2:30; C. M. Palmer Jr., "What Became of Mickey Free?," 1950, ms. in Mickey Free folder, AHS; Radbourne, *Salvador or Martinez?,* 7; Radbourne, *Mickey Free,* 3, 5–6—a biography of Mickey Free that lists all of John Ward's Sonoita Valley neighbors except the Titus brothers.

37. William W. Wrightson (1827–65), born in York, England, was a *Cincinnati Enquirer* reporter. He first visited Arizona in 1853 while surveying the Gadsden Purchase boundary lines. He was secretary of the Sonora Exploring and Mining Company in 1856. The following year he organized the Salero Mining Company, which acquired the Salero mine. Wrightson began publishing the *Weekly Arizonian* at Tubac on March 3, 1859. Five months later his brother John Wrightson was murdered at his Tomocacan ranch by two of his Mexican workers, who fled to Sonora with four horses and a revolver. William was killed by Apaches on February 17, 1865, while doing surveying for the U.S. Land Office at Monkey Springs, Ariz. See "Interesting Letter from W. Wrightson, Esq.," *Ohio Statesman* (Columbus), February 5, 1859, 1; "Arizona—The Silver Mines," *Cleveland Leader,* March 9, 1959, 2.

38. Roberts, *With Their Own Blood,* 63; Charles D. Poston, "Early Matrimony in Southern Arizona," *Prescott Morning Courier,* May 28, 1891; *Weekly Arizonian,* March 3, 1859, 3.

39. "Going to the States," *Weekly Arizonian,* April 7, 1859, 2; "Col. Titus Again," *Kansas Herald of Freedom,* May 21, 1859; *Atchison (Kans.) Freedom's Champion,* May 28, 1859, 1; 1850 Missouri Federal Census, District 12, Callaway Co., 222.

40. George D. Mercer folder, AHS; Roberts, *With Their Own Blood,* 64, 66–68, 71–76; *Weekly Arizonian,* May 12 and 19, 1857; "Murder of Five Mexicans," *New York Times,* June 2, 1859, 1.

41. "Later from Arizona," New Orleans *Picayune,* May 24, 1859, 6; *Augusta Chronicle,* July 24, 1859, 2; "News by Telegraph," *New York Times,* July 14, 1859, 4; "Advertisements," *Weekly Arizonian,* July 7, 1859, 3; "Interesting from Arizona," *New York Herald,* September 12, 1860, 10.

42. "Personal," *New York Tribune,* May 25, 1859, 5; *Weekly Arizonian,* July 21, 1859, 2; *San Francisco Daily Evening Bulletin,* August 20, 1859, 1.

43. "Fillibuster Fight," *New York Tribune,* May 31, 1859, 5; *Weekly Arizonian,* July 21, 1859, 2; "Affray among Fillibusters at the St. Nicholas Hotel," *Albany Evening Journal,* June 1, 1859, 2; "Fillibuster Fight," *Charleston Mercury,* June 3, 1859, 1; *San Francisco Daily Evening Bulletin,* June 30 and July 2, 1859, 3; *Boston Traveler,* June 4, 1859, 2.

44. "Fillibuster Fight," *Charleston Mercury,* June 3, 1859, 1; *Newark Daily Advertiser,* June 2, 1859, 4; "Colonel Anderson Arrested," *New York Times,* June 1, 1859, 5; "The Fillibusters in

Court," *New York Tribune,* June 2, 1859, 7; "New York Matters," *Newark Daily Advertiser,* June 20, 1859, 2; San Francisco *Daily Evening Bulletin,* July 2, 1859, 3.

45. "The Silver Mines of Arizona," *Rockford (Ill.) Daily News,* June 2, 1859, 2.

46. Edward Hopkins Titus, named after his maternal grandfather, was born in Savannah, Ga., on January 15, 1859. See "Passengers Arrived," *New York Times,* June 8, 1859, 8; "Poor Shombre," *New Haven Columbian Register,* October 25, 1856, 2; *Weekly Arizonian,* June 30, 1859, 3; "From Arizona," New Orleans *Picayune,* July 22, 1859, 4; *Augusta Chronicle,* July 24 and August 2, 1859, 2; "The Silver Mines of Arizona," *New York Tribune,* August 20, 1859, 7; "Letter from St. Louis," San Francisco *Daily Evening Bulletin,* August 20, 1859, 1; "Our Arizona Correspondence," *New York Herald,* September 20, 1859, 5.

47. *Baltimore Sun,* July 29, 1859, 1; Cozzens, *Marvellous Country,* 86–87; "Col. Titus," *Augusta Chronicle,* August 2, 1859, 2; "Letter from St. Louis," San Francisco *Daily Evening Bulletin,* August 20, 1859, 1; Gard, *Along the Early Trails of the Southwest,* 35–36.

48. Gard, *Along the Early Trails of the Southwest,* 33–34; Moody, *Stagecoach West,* 98; Twain, *Roughing It,* 8; Pumpelly, *My Reminiscences,* 1:182–83; "The Overland Route to California," *Frank Leslie's Illustrated Newspaper,* October 28, 1858, 327.

49. Gard, *Along the Early Trails of the Southwest,* 34–35, 38; Moody, *Stagecoach West,* 100; Eaton, "Frontier Life in Southern Arizona," 176.

50. Gard, *Along the Early Trails of the Southwest,* 34, 38; Greene, *900 Miles on the Butterfield Trail,* 20–21; "The Overland Route to California," *Frank Leslie's Illustrated Newspaper,* October 28, 1858, 328; "Overland to California," *New York Herald,* November 11, 1858, 1.

51. The La Cienega stagecoach station was at 32°1'8"N,110°38'33"W. See "Personal," *Weekly Arizonian,* August 18, 1859, 2; "The Silver Mines of Arizona," *New York Tribune,* August 20, 1859, 7; "From Arizona and Sonora," *New York Tribune,* September 7, 1859, 6; "Our Arizona Correspondence," *New York Herald,* September 20, 1859, 5; "From Arizona," *New York Times,* September 17, 1859, 1.

52. "From Arizona," *New York Times,* June 30 and August 19, 1859.

53. Christopher C. Dodson folder, AHS; *Baltimore Sun,* July 29, 1859, 1; Elias Brevoort to Gen. Wm. Pelham, September 1, 1859, Letters Received by the Surveyor General of New Mexico 1854–1907, Records of the Bureau of Land Management, M-1288, Roll 2, RG 49, NARA.

54. Captain Johnson is described as Henry L. Kinney's "lieutenant in his celebrated Nicaragua expedition" in Cozzens, *Marvellous Country,* 205–6. See U.S. Senate, *Report of the Affairs in the Department of New Mexico,* 323–24; "Fatal Affray at Tucson," San Francisco *Daily Evening Bulletin,* September 26 and November 22, 1859, 3; *Missouri Republican* (St. Louis), November 22 and December 12, 1859; "Killing of Two Mexicans on the Sonoita," *Weekly Arizonian,* November 10, 1859, 2; Blake, "Silver and Copper Mining in Arizona," 8; *Daily Ohio Statesman* (Columbus), December 18, 1859, 2.

55. "Letter from St. Louis," San Francisco, *Daily Evening Bulletin,* March 17, 1860, 1.

56. Robert L. d'Aumaile, alias Le Moine Noir (The Black Hand), was a California miner in the early 1850s. He was arrested in San Francisco on February 2, 1857, for having sold in 1852 a city lot "with the forgery of a release of mortgage" under the name Rupert Le Chevalier. D'Aumaile was then indicted on March 23, 1857, for writing threatening letters to Louis E. Ritter. He later became a Sonora and Arizona correspondent of the San Francisco *Daily Evening Bulletin.* The newspaper reported that he was murdered in Sonora on March 7, 1860, apparently by his own servants, while on a visit to an old mine. It subsequently quoted a letter from Mazatlan, Mexico, stating that D'Aumaile had been seen at Arispe two weeks after his supposed death. See San Francisco *Daily Evening Bulletin,* January 29, February 3 and 6, March 23, June 27, 1857, 3; "Later from Arizona," San Francisco *Daily Evening Bulletin,* March 27, 1860, 1; "Still Living," San Francisco *Daily Evening Bulletin,* May 2, 1860, 2; Burnett,

Recollections and Opinions of an Old Pioneer, 383; "Passengers," *Savannah Morning News,* March 14, 1860, 1, and *Missouri Republican* (St. Louis), April 14, 1860; "Arrivals at the City Hotels," *New York Evening Express,* March 17, 1860, 2.

57. Sylvester Mowry (January 17, 1833–October 17, 1871) was arrested in 1862 by the U.S. Army after a mine employee accused him of providing lead for ammunition to the Confederacy. His mine and other property were confiscated and sold at auction. Mowry was released from the Yuma prison after a few months due to the lack of evidence against him. In 1868 he received forty thousand dollars in compensation from the federal government, and the following year he resumed operations at the mine. He died while visiting London in 1871 and was interred in his native Providence, R.I. See Cullum, *Biographical Register,* 2:314; Brownell, *They Lived in Tubac,* 26–27; *Missouri Republican* (St. Louis), June 3, 1860; Hodge, *Arizona as It Is,* 126; Roberts, *With Their Own Blood,* 23, 26, 82; *New York Times,* April 12, 1860, 5; Pumpelly, *My Reminiscences,* 1:182–83; Pfanz, *Richard S. Ewell,* 118; Farish, *History of Arizona,* 2:69; Cozzens, *Marvellous Country,* 87; Mowry, *Arizona and Sonora,* 77; 1860 New Mexico Territory Federal Census, Arizona Co., Sopori Settlement, 38; Florin, "Mowry, Arizona," 37; Post Return of Fort Buchanan, New Mexico, June–August 1860, RMP; Faust, *Historical Times,* 818.

58. 1860 New York Federal Census, Jamaica, Queens, 808; "Interesting from Arizona," *New York Times,* September 17, 1860, 2.

59. "Letters from Arizona," *San Francisco Daily Evening Bulletin,* August 21, 1860, 1; Pumpelly, *My Reminiscences,* 1:202; Roberts, *With Their Own Blood,* 86; "Arizona Correspondence," *Missouri Republican* (St. Louis), August 27, 1860; "Interesting from Arizona," *New York Herald,* September 12, 1860, 10.

60. "Arizona Correspondence," *Missouri Republican* (St. Louis), August 27, 1860; "Interesting from Arizona," *New York Herald,* September 12, 1860, 10.

61. Alexander Perry Wilbar (1824–1876), whose father was a hatter in Alexandria, Va., arrived in the Southwest in 1850 as assistant surveyor to map the Rio Grande border with Mexico. Five years later he went to Santa Fe to work on the public land surveys of New Mexico. A Freemason and Confederate sympathizer, Wilbar was removed as surveyor general in 1861 after serving less than a year and left Santa Fe the following year with Gen. Henry Sibley's retreating army. He was living in San Antonio, Tex., when in June 1864 he was listed as a sergeant major in the Fourth Arizona Brigade of Baird's Regiment of Texas Cavalry and was later ascended to adjutant and captain of the unit. Wilbar moved in 1867 to Los Angeles, Calif., where he later passed way. Arizona was not attached to the Surveying District of New Mexico by an act of Congress until July 2, 1864, allowing for surveying operations. See Carded Records Showing Military Service of Soldiers Who Fought in Confederate Organizations, Roll 181, RG 109, NARA; Joseph S. Wilson to A. P. Wilbar, October 3, 1860, Letters Received by the Surveyor General of New Mexico 1854–1907, Records of the Bureau of Land Management, M-1288, Roll 2, RG 49, NARA.

62. According to the 1860 census, the Compadre Silver Mining Works was composed of miners Henry and Ellett Titus, 24-year-old C. Tompkins of Georgia, 37-year-old William Devers of Virginia and 40-year-old Charles Garibaldi of Italy; 27-year-old clerk George McDowell of New York; 24-year-old blacksmith John Drolet of Canada; and 45-year-old merchant Henry Jenkins from New York. 1860 New Mexico Territory Federal Census, Arizona Co., Sonoita Creek Settlements, 31.

63. 1860 New Mexico Territory Federal Census, Arizona Co., Sonoita Creek Settlements, 30–32; "Arrival of the Overland Mail," *New York Times,* September 17, 1860, 5.

64. Post Return of Fort Buchanan, New Mexico, September, October, and December 1860, RMP; Roberts, *With Their Own Blood,* 87–88; Radbourne, *Mickey Free,* 11.

Chapter Five: Florida Pioneer, 1861–1881

1. Hinton Rowan Helper (December 27, 1829–March 8, 1909) was appointed by Lincoln in 1861 as U.S. consul in Buenos Aires, Argentina. He committed suicide by inhaling illuminating gas in his Washington, D.C., boardinghouse room. See Pfanz, *Richard S. Ewell,* 119; *Missouri Republican* (St. Louis), October 4 and 15, 1860; Faust, *Historical Times,* 238, 357; Nevins, *Emergence of Lincoln,* 2:312–13; Dickison, *Confederate Military History of Florida,* 5.

2. "Letter from New York," *San Francisco Daily Evening Bulletin,* February 12, 1861, 1.

3. "Mr. Helper's Lecture Postponed" and "News of the Day," *New York Times,* January 15, 1861, 4, 5; *Charleston Courier,* January 19, 1861, 1; "The Clinton Hall Row," *New York Herald,* January 16, 1861, 5; "City Intelligence," *New York Commercial Advertiser,* January 15, 1861, 3; "Personal and Political," *Springfield (Mass.) Republican,* January 16, 1861, 2.

4. Felix Telles (1848–1914) after being kidnapped was acculturated by White Mountain Apaches. John Ward died in 1867 before his stepson reappeared as Mickey Free when he was mustered into service at Fort Verde on December 2, 1872, as one of forty-seven Indian scouts, receiving the rank of sergeant two years later. During the next decade he married and had four offspring and served as a scout, translator, and policeman on an Indian reservation. In July 1886 Mickey Free was interpreter for a Chiricahua Apache delegation visiting President Grover Cleveland at the White House. After his 1893 discharge, he lived quietly in the Fort Apache reservation until his death. See Roberts, *With Their Own Blood,* 90–91, 98; Post Return of Fort Buchanan, New Mexico, January, February, and March 1861, RMP; C. B. Marshall folder, AHS; William C. Wadsworth folder, AHS; Radbourne, *Mickey Free,* 9–12; "Apaches at the White House," *Macon (Ga.) Telegraph,* July 31, 1886, 5.

5. Minnie Titus provided a secondhand, puzzling account eighty-four years later about her uncle's death. She stated that her father, his brother, and others had gone out on a trail and that Ellett and a friend, Delevaset Joe, "ventured ahead of the party." The two were ambushed by Indians, and Joe was instantly killed, but her uncle "escaped on his horse and hid in a ravine. He stayed there until dark and thinking the Indians had gone, he came out and was getting on his horse when they shot him. He was mortally wounded and his horse killed. He had said he would never be taken alive by the Indians, so when he realized all hope was gone he took his revolver and shot himself. . . . A Mexican who was a prisoner of the Indians escaped and told my father about it and led him to the body. This so saddened my father he came back east and never returned as he felt responsible for his brother, although he had ridden ahead of the party against my father's wishes." See Post Return of Fort Buchanan, New Mexico, April 1861 and May 1862, RMP; Pumpelly, *My Reminiscences,* 1:218; Barnes, *Arizona Place Names,* 314, 325.

6. Coriolanus Hopkins (December 12, 1835–July 31, 1910) was appointed special deputy collector of the port of Jacksonville in 1881 under his father. See "Our Florida Correspondence," *New York Herald,* November 5, 1860, 2; Schafer, *Thunder on the River,* 22, 45; Voucher No. 93, Payrolls for Officers 1861–62, Quartermasters, Series 43, Carton 3, Folder 7, State Archives of Florida, Tallahassee, hereafter cited as SAF; 1861 Report of Pay Master General, Miscellaneous Military Expenditure Documents, 1840–69, RG 350, Series 43, Box 3, Folder 9, SAF; Voucher No. 34, H. T. Titus (Subsistence), November 9, 1861, Citizens File, H. T. Titus, Box 1162, RG 109, NARA.

7. Davis, *History of Jacksonville,* 116–17; OR 1:14, 488; Dickison, *Confederate Military History of Florida,* 20, 26–27, 32; *Columbus Enquirer,* April 23, 1862, 3; "Early Recollections of Minnie Titus Ensey," 2, Henry Theodore Titus Collection, North Brevard Public Library, Titusville, Fla.; Schafer, *Thunder on the River,* 46; Martin and Schafer, *Jacksonville's Ordeal by Fire,* 57, 65–66; Washington M. Ives Journal, 1860–62, SAF.

8. Richard M. Tydings (July 1, 1823–December 27, 1890). See *Columbus Enquirer,* April 23, 1862, 3; OR 1:14, 512.

9. Calvin L. Robinson (June 3, 1828–July 4, 1887), born in Reading, Vt., was educated in the Springfield Wesleyan Seminary in his state and at the University of Vermont until his junior year. After marriage, in the fall of 1858 he began enterprises in Jacksonville that included two large two-story merchandising stores, a two-hundred-foot-long warehouse and a steam sawmill on the waterfront, a lumber yard, a tin shop, and a retail outlet for stoves. Robinson's net worth in the 1860 census was $18,000, yet he claimed in his memoirs that he had $125,000 in assets at the start of hostilities. He was a member of the Republican National Committee from Florida during 1866–68. In 1870 Robinson was a real estate agent in Jacksonville and with his Canadian wife had $81,000 in assets. In the 1880s he was a Jacksonville attorney and a land developer. See Clancy, *A Yankee in a Confederate Town,* 17–18, 27, 36, 42–45, 56, 60, 100; 1860 Florida Federal Census, Duval Co., 251; 1880 Florida Federal Census, Duval Co., 499; Davis, *History of Jacksonville,* 117–20; Martin and Schafer, *Jacksonville's Ordeal by Fire,* 73–74, 77, 81–83; Schafer, *Thunder on the River,* 29, 58, 61, 64, 69; Davis, *The Civil War and Reconstruction in Florida,* 157, 250–52; "Our Army Correspondence," *Farmers' Cabinet* (Amherst, N.H.), April 10, 1862, 1.

10. Titus's neighbor Jesse Gresham lost twenty-seven slaves from his plantation on the St. Johns River, near the mouth of Clapboard Creek, during the Union occupation of Jacksonville. He afterward became a private in Company A, Tenth Florida Infantry Regiment. See Jesse Gresham, August 28, 1863, Claims for Slaves Lost, Florida, No. 1076, Confederate Papers Relating to Citizens or Business Firms, M346, Roll 380, RG 109, NARA; OR, 1:12, 705; Schafer, *Thunder on the River,* 87; Gen. Rufus B. Saxton to Edwin M. Stanton, August 20, 1862, Rufus and S. Willard Saxton Papers, Sterling Memorial Library, Yale University, New Haven, Conn.

11. When Calvin L. Robinson returned to his father's house in Reading, Vt., with his female slave, there was "quite an excitement" when some citizens, "averring that she was held as a slave, petitioned the Court to have her put under a guardian." Robinson alleged that he purchased her for manumission and "that he was educating her, claimed no right as owner, but did as guardian." A judge appointed a guardian, who wished her to remain in Robinson's care unless he could be her legal guardian. Robinson's journal calls her the "young colored nurse" of his two boys but omits that she departed Jacksonville with them. Orloff M. Dorman accused Robinson of being an opportunist who collaborated with whoever controlled Jacksonville. See *Vermont Journal* (Windsor), July 5, 1862, 8; Clancy, *A Yankee in a Confederate Town,* 41, 71–72, 77; Shofner, *Nor Is It Over Yet,* 14; Schafer, *Thunder on the River,* 73–74; Martin and Schafer, *Jacksonville's Ordeal by Fire,* 86–88, 99; "Evacuation of Jacksonville, Florida, by the Federals," *Augusta Daily Constitutionalist,* April 15, 1862, 1.

12. New Jersey, the Titus birthplace, abolished slavery by statute in 1846. However, the law did not grant manumission, and slaves continued to be bound to their masters as apprentices for life. The 1860 federal census listed eighteen slaves owned by New Jersey citizens. See Cooley, *A Study of Slavery in New Jersey,* 28–29; "The Yankees in Jacksonville, Florida," *Charleston Mercury,* April 8, 1862, 1; "Personal," *Savannah Morning News,* April 21, 1862; "Col. H. T. Titus," *Columbus Enquirer,* April 26, 1862, 2; "Early Recollections of Minnie Titus Ensey," Henry Theodore Titus Collection, North Brevard Public Library, Titusville, Fla., 1.

13. Charles Floyd Hopkins (December 1, 1824–January 17, 1898), born in McIntosh County, Ga., was the son of Gen. Benjamin Hopkins. He was appointed midshipman on October 19, 1841, and graduated from the U.S. Naval Academy in 1848, resigning in 1852. He entered Confederate service in September 1861 as major of infantry and was paroled at Appomattox Court House, Va., on April 13, 1865, with the rank of colonel. See Case Files of Applications from Former Confederates for Presidential Pardons ("Amnesty Papers") 1865–67, Florida 1865, M1003, Records of the Adjutant General's Office, 1780s–1917, RG 94, NARA;

OR 1:14,127–43; Davis, *History of Jacksonville,* 126–27; Martin and Schafer, *Jacksonville's Ordeal by Fire,* 98, 102–3, 108, 113, 116; Davis, *The Civil War and Reconstruction in Florida,* 170–71, 278; Schafer, *Thunder on the River,* 106, 109, 118.

14. OR Navy, 1:13, 360.

15. Edwin R. Alberti was a West Point graduate who served in the Seminole War in 1835–36. In 1850 he had fifty-two slaves at his sawmill, and a decade later he owned twenty slaves and was the agent for forty-one others belonging to five different masters. See Files 1–108 and Unnumbered, 1814, U.S. Military Academy Cadet Application Papers, 1805–66, M688, Roll 1, Records of the Adjutant General's Office, 1780s–1917, RG 94, NARA; Returns from U.S. Military Posts, 1800–1916, M617, Roll 1548, ibid.; Compiled Service Records of Volunteer Soldiers Who Served in Organizations from the State of Florida during the Florida Indian Wars, 1835–58, M1086, Roll 26, ibid.; 1850 Florida Federal Census, Nassau Co., 178; 1850 Florida Slave Schedules, Nassau Co., 853; 1860 Florida Slave Schedules, Nassau Co., 379; Voucher No. 15, February 26, 1863, Citizens File, H. T. Titus, Box 1162, RG 109, NARA; OR 1:14, 226; William H. Nulty, *Confederate Florida: The Road to Olustee* (Tuscaloosa, Ala.: University of Alabama Press, 1994), 50; Higginson, *Army Life in a Black Regiment,* 48, 66; Schwartz, *A Woman Doctor's Civil War,* 43.

16. Camp Finegan was built beside a railroad track near today's Lenox Avenue and Normandy Boulevard intersection in Jacksonville. See Voucher No. 12, May 10, 1863, Citizens File, H. T. Titus, Box 1162, RG 109, NARA; OR 1:14, 226, 233; Martin and Schafer, *Jacksonville's Ordeal by Fire,* 139–46, 158–65; Nulty, *Confederate Florida,* 51; Shofner, *Nor Is It Over Yet,* 6; Schafer, *Thunder on the River,* 144, 147–48, 155–63.

17. Deed Record H-1, Madison County, Fla., 604–5, Madison County Courthouse, Madison, Fla.; Voucher No. 38, May 10, 1863, Voucher No. 15, May 29, 1863, and Voucher No. 78, June 30, 1863, Citizens File, H. T. Titus, Box 1162, RG 109, NARA.

18. Calvin L. Robinson omits mention in his journal of his confiscated Baldwin property. He returned to Union-occupied Fernandina, Fla., in December 1862 and started a business on property seized from a Confederate citizen. Three months later, when Union troops occupied Jacksonville for one month, Robinson was in charge of inventorying and distributing "abandoned property," including the confiscated home of Judge Felix Livingston. The house of Joseph Finegan, valued at thirty-five hundred dollars, was sold to a New Yorker for twenty-five dollars. In late 1863 Robinson speculated with expropriated Confederate lands on behalf of northern creditors and purchased for his wife "a half-dozen fine lots with buildings" in St. Augustine. See Clancy, *A Yankee in a Confederate Town,* 87, 90–91, 102, 112–13; Shofner, *Nor Is It Over Yet,* 7; Office No. 3037, Book M, 516, AABD; Nulty, *Confederate Florida,* 91.

19. *Philadelphia Illustrated New Age,* January 22, 1864, 2; Hayden, ed., "Parish Register of St. Stephen's Protestant Episcopal Church," 210; Lyman Stickney to Salmon P. Chase, December 11, 1863, Salmon P. Chase Papers, Historical Society of Pennsylvania, Philadelphia; Davis, *The Civil War and Reconstruction in Florida,* 278; OR 1:35, pt. 1, 295–98, 330–37; Dickison, *Confederate Military History of Florida,* 34–44; Martin and Schafer, *Jacksonville's Ordeal by Fire,* 178–85, 192–96; Nulty, *Confederate Florida,* 81, 94, 126, 203, 218; Schafer, *Thunder on the River,* 178–80, 186–89, 242–44.

20. Certificates 1909 and 1910 issued to Henry Titus, March 30, 1864, Certificates for Stocks & Bonds ("Box 11"), April 1861–February 1865, weekly reports of stock certificates issued by depositories, including those in Quincy and Tallahassee, 1861–65, Confederate Treasury Department Field Offices, District Court, and States, Florida, Collection of Confederate Records, Treasury Department, RG 365, NARA; Voucher No. 22, H. T. Titus, December 16, 1864, Citizens File, H. T. Titus, Box 1162, RG 109, NARA; Martin and Schafer, *Jacksonville's Ordeal by Fire,* 226; Schafer, *Thunder on the River,* 216, 234.

21. Boggess, *Veteran of Four Wars,* 72; "From Florida," *New York Times,* August 1, 1865, 5; Schafer, *Thunder on the River,* 266–67.

22. "From Florida," *New York Times,* August 1, 1865, 5; Edward Hopkins, July 15, 1865, and J. J. Finley, January 15, 1866, Lake City, Fla., Amnesty Oaths, 1864–66, Box 37, Civil War Amnesty and Pardon Records, 1863–67, Amnesty Records, RG 59, NARA; Faust, *Historical Times,* 260.

23. James Paine (1810–November 1882) was a Brevard County clerk and judge in the 1870s, served in the Florida House of Representatives during 1871–72, and was afterward superintendent of schools. Paine's home in St. Lucie was a boardinghouse and post office in 1878. One son was postmaster and another was the deputy collector of customs. Paine and his wife Johanna M. Paine (1822–October 28, 1895) are interred in the family graveyard presently on the entrance grounds of the St. Lucie School, 2501 Old Dixie Highway, Fort Pierce, Fla., at 27°28'52.12"N 80°20'13.69"W. The USS *Clyde* was built in 1861 at Glasgow, Scotland. Renamed the *Neptune,* it was a blockade runner until it was seized by the U.S. Navy near Mobile, Ala., on June 14, 1863. Commissioned as the USS *Clyde,* it spent the remainder of the Civil War patrolling the Florida coast. In August 1865 the steamer was decommissioned at Philadelphia. See Wise, *Lifeline of the Confederacy,* 314; 1850 South Carolina Federal Census, St. Michael and St. Phillip, Charleston, 153; 1860 Florida Federal Census, Brevard Co., 97; 1880 Florida Federal Census, Brevard Co., 272; "A Winter's Cruise in Eastern and Southern Florida," *Cazenovia (N.Y.) Republican,* September 2, 1880, 1; Shofner, *Nor Is It Over Yet,* 21, 138; Shofner, *History of Brevard County,* 1:78, 94; Hawks, *Florida Gazetteer,* 17, 131; Henshall, *Camping and Cruising in Florida,* 60–61; "Letter from Florida," *Daily Albany (N.Y.) Argus,* August 6, 1875, 2; "Early Recollections of Minnie Titus Ensey," Henry Theodore Titus Collection, North Brevard Public Library, Titusville, Fla., 2; Steamer "Indian River," 195, Master Abstracts of Enrollments, 1815–1911, vol. 31, Records Relating to Vessel Documentation, Bureau of Marine Inspection and Navigation, RG 41, NARA; Enrollment 397, Custom House Records, 1774–1955, Certificates of Enrolment, 1793–1900, Port of New York Steam Vessels, 1838–1900, November 9, 1865–April 10, 1866, http://www.latinamericanstudies.org/archive/RG-41-Vol-640.pdf.; 1850 New York Federal Census, New York City, Ward 11, 786; "A New Florida Enterprise," *Richmond Examiner,* January 8, 1866, 3.

24. "Latest Marine Intelligence," *New York Commercial Advertiser,* November 22, 1865, 4; "Letter from Florida," *Albany (N.Y.) Argus,* August 6, 1875, 2; John G. Foster to George L. Hartsuff, April 27, 1866, John Gray Foster Letterbook, Library of Congress, Manuscript Division, Washington, D.C., hereafter cited as LOC; "Early Recollections of Minnie Titus Ensey," Henry Theodore Titus Collection, North Brevard Public Library, Titusville, Fla., 2; "From Savannah, Ga.," *Boston Daily Advertiser,* December 23, 1865, 1; "Disasters," *Providence (R.I.) Evening Press,* December 28, 1865, 3; "From Savannah," *Boston Daily Advertiser,* January 8, 1866, 1; "Memoranda," *New York Commercial Advertiser,* January 19, 1866, 3.

25. "Memoranda," *New York Commercial Advertiser,* December 27, 1865, 4; "Report of Captain Greenman, of the Ill-fated Constitution," *Cincinnati Daily Enquirer,* January 3, 1866, 3; "From Savannah," *Boston Daily Advertiser,* January 8, 1866, 1; Schwartz, *A Woman Doctor's Civil War,* 244.

26. John G. Foster to George L. Hartsuff, March 6, 1866, D. M. Hammond to Lt. J. M. J. Sanno, March 1, 1866, and John T. Sprague to Capt. E. C. Woodruff, March 2, 1866, Letters Received by the Office of the Adjutant General (Main Series) 1861–70, M-619, Roll 473, RG 94, NARA. Copies of these three letters are also found in Microcopy 179, Roll 362, January 1–12, 1872, MLDS.

27. "Early Recollections of Minnie Titus Ensey," Henry Theodore Titus Collection, North Brevard Public Library, Titusville, Fla., 3, 10; Brinton, *Guide-Book of Florida,* 78–79; Olney, *Guide to Florida,* 66.

28. Wells, Provost & Co. was located at 215, 217, and 219 Front St., Wholesale Depot, New York. See D. M. Hammond to Lt. J. M. J. Sanno, February 18, 1866, Letters Received by the Office of the Adjutant General (Main Series) 1861–70, M-619, Roll 473, RG 94, NARA; Judge, *History of the Canning Industry,* 30–31; Douglas D. Dummett Collection, St. Augustine Historical Society, St. Augustine, Fla.; Schene, *Hopes, Dreams, and Promises,* 32, 79; "Early Recollections of Minnie Titus Ensey," Henry Theodore Titus Collection, North Brevard Public Library, Titusville, Fla., 3, 9; "Letter from Florida," *Auburn (N.Y.) Daily Bulletin,* February 5, 1872, 4; Shofner, *Nor Is It Over Yet,* 138; Shofner, *History of Brevard County,* 1:72, 87; *Tallahassee Floridian* quoted in "A Florida Enterprise," *Macon Telegraph,* May 8, 1866, 2; Schafer, *Thunder on the River,* 272, 274.

29. "Passengers Sailed," *New York Times,* July 29, 1866, 8; "Arrivals at the Hotels," *Savannah Daily News and Herald,* August 2, 1866; "Letter from Charleston, S.C.," *Boston Daily Advertiser,* January 15, 1866, 2.

30. Edward Stevens Hopkins was one of the major contenders who lost to William Marvin in the senatorial election. See Myron L. Mickles statement, October 16, 1866, Box 2, Letters Received, 1866, Department and District of Florida, 1865–69, U.S. Army Continental Commands 1821–1920, Pt. 1, RG 393, NARA, hereafter cited as LRDF; Myron L. Mickles to Capt. C. C. Rawn, August 31, 1866, LRDF; Schafer, *Thunder on the River,* 277–78; Brown, *Ossian Bingley Hart,* 155; Schene, *Hopes, Dreams, and Promises,* 73; Shofner, *Nor Is It Over Yet,* 37–40, 44–45, 50–51, 57.

31. Myron L. Mickles statement, October 16, 1866, Box 2, LRDF; Myron L. Mickles to Capt. C. C. Rawn, August 31, 1866, LRDF; Schene, *Hopes, Dreams, and Promises,* 73; Orloff M. Dorman Diary, October 8 [1866], vol. 5, LOC.

32. Myron L. Mickles to Capt. C. C. Rawn, August 31, 1866, LRDF; Myron L. Mickles to Col. Andrew Mahony, October 15, 1866, LRDF; Shofner, *Nor Is It Over Yet,* 96; Schene, *Hopes, Dreams, and Promises,* 74; U.S. House of Representatives, *Removal of Hon. E. M. Stanton and Others,* 92.

33. John G. Foster to Bvt. Lt. Col. George Lee, September 11, 1866, and John G. Foster to Maj. Gen. O. O. Howard, September 14, 1866, John Gray Foster Letterbook, LOC; Orloff M. Dorman Diary, October 8 [1866], vol. 5, LOC; 1860 Florida Federal Census, Division 22, St. Johns, 645.

34. John G. Foster to D. S. Walker, October 11, 1866, John Gray Foster Letterbook, LOC; Myron L. Mickles to Col. Andrew Mahony, October 15, 1866, LRDF.

35. Deed Record H-1, Madison County, Fla., 604–5, Madison County Courthouse, Madison, Fla.; *Providence Evening Press,* February 25, 1867, 3; "Col. Titus—A Noted Character," *Kansas City Journal,* August 26, 1881.

36. W. A. Work & Son v. Titus, 12 Fla., 628 (1869), in Galbraith and Meek, *Reports of Cases Argued and Adjudged in the Supreme Court of Florida,* 12:628–33; 1870 Florida Federal Census, Suburbs of Jacksonville, Duval Co., 524; H. Wilson, *Trow's New York City Directory,* 1868 (New York: John F. Trow, 1868), 1130; 1870 New York Federal Census, Brooklyn, Ward 6, 246.

37. Mary Titus purchased Lot 1, Section 3, Township 22 South, Range 35 East, in Volusia County, Fla. See Miscellaneous Records Book B, 611, 656, Volusia County, Clerk of the Circuit Court, Records Management Center, Deland, Fla., hereafter cited as VCCT; Davis, *History of Jacksonville,* 150; 1870 Florida Federal Census, Jacksonville, Duval Co., 450; Office No. 4557, Book B, 624, January 25, 1868, AABD; "Northern Farming in Florida," *New York Commercial Advertiser,* March 12, 1868, 2; Martin, *City Makers,* 90, 98.

38. Olney, *Guide to Florida,* 57; Brinton, *Guide-Book of Florida,* 78; U.S. Department of Agriculture, *Florida,* 64; "Early Recollections of Minnie Titus Ensey," Henry Theodore Titus Collection, North Brevard Public Library, Titusville, Fla., 6–9; Pierce, *Pioneer Life in Southeast Florida,* 36.

39. The forty acres that Mary Titus purchased comprised Lot 3, Section 24, Township 21 South, Range 35 East, Deed Record Book A, 341, VCCT. The post office at Sand Point was located in the Southeast Quarter of Section 29 in Township 29 South, Range South 35 East, Volusia County, Fla. See Post Office Department Reports of Site Locations, 1837–1950, Florida, Brevard, Sand Point, August 28, 1869, M-1126, Roll 88, Records of the U.S. Postal Service, RG 28, NARA; Record of Appointment of Postmasters, 1832–September 30, 1971, Volusia County, Fla., M841, Roll 21, 362, RG 28, NARA; Bradbury and Hallock, *Chronology of Florida Post Offices,* 83; 1870 Federal Census, Volusia Co., 743; "Laws of the U.S.," *Caledonian* (St. Johnsbury, Vt.), February 4, 1870, 4; "United States Mails," *Washington Evening Star,* February 1, 1868, 3; "Post-Office Bulletin," *Pomeroy's Democrat* (Chicago), June 16, 1869, 7; "Letter from Florida," *Auburn Daily Bulletin,* January 22, 1872, 1; Brinton, *Guide-Book of Florida,* 78.

40. William M. Lanehart (1841–1924) moved to Miami in 1880. He purchased ninety-seven acres in West Palm Beach three years later and was settled there until his demise. See Bradbury and Hallock, *Chronology of Florida Post Offices,* 83; Office of the Postmaster General, Immediate Office of the Postmaster General, Orders ("Journals"), 1835–1953, vol. 65, June 16, 1870, 465, RG 28, NARA; William M. Lanehart, December 12, 1870, vol. 66, http://www.latinamericanstudies.org/archive/RG-28-Vol-66.pdf; 1870 Federal Census, Volusia Co., 743; Record of County Commissioners Book 1869–81, July 18, 1870, p. 27, VCCT; Hawks, *Florida Gazetteer,* 116; "Early Recollections of Minnie Titus Ensey," Henry Theodore Titus Collection, North Brevard Public Library, Titusville, Fla., 10–11.

41. The Faber Company in 1900 became Faber-Castell, a leading international maker of pens, pencils, and art and office supplies. See "Early Recollections of Minnie Titus Ensey," Henry Theodore Titus Collection, North Brevard Public Library, Titusville, Fla., 11; *Cincinnati Commercial Tribune,* August 7, 1870, 1.

42. Barbour, *Florida for Tourists,* 34–35; "Trip to Indian River, Florida," *Hartford Daily Courant,* April 17, 1875, 2; Probate File 2104, Clerk of Courts, Archives and Record Center, Brevard County, Titusville, Fla.; "Early Recollections of Minnie Titus Ensey," Henry Theodore Titus Collection, North Brevard Public Library, Titusville, Fla., 12; Hawks, *Florida Gazetteer,* 130.

43. John Wesley Joyner moved to Ocala, Fla., in 1860 with his wife Rachel and their four children. She died after childbirth, and he remarried in March 1861 and had three more offspring. Joyner served as a private in Company K of the Florida Tenth Volunteer Infantry Regiment, CSA, during the Civil War. See *Leavenworth Bulletin,* June 16, 1870, 1; *Daily Illinois State Journal* (Springfield), June 27, 1870, 2; *Connecticut Courant* (Hartford), July 9, 1870, 2; *Jackson (Mich.) Citizen,* July 12, 1870, 6; *Burlington (Vt.) Weekly Free Press,* July 15, 1870, 4; Hawks, *Florida Gazetteer,* 96; Schene, *Hopes, Dreams, and Promises,* 79; Shofner, *History of Brevard County,* 1:88, 94; Revenue Book, Henry T. Titus, 1870, VCCT; 1860 Florida Federal Census, Marion Co., 270; 1870 Florida Federal Census, Division 17, Volusia Co., 729, 740, 743; "Early Recollections of Minnie Titus Ensey," Henry Theodore Titus Collection, North Brevard Public Library, Titusville, Fla., 10, 12.

44. 1870 Florida Federal Census, Division 17, Volusia Co., 729–50; Hawks, *Florida Gazetteer,* 95; "Early Recollections of Minnie Titus Ensey," Henry Theodore Titus Collection, North Brevard Public Library, Titusville, Fla., 7–8.

45. Hawks, *Florida Gazetteer,* 88, 93, 127–28; Schene, *Hopes, Dreams, and Promises,* 79–80.

46. SE Quarter of SE Quarter, Section 22, Township 21 South, Range 34 East, Deed Record Book A, 342, VCCT; Office No. 5588, Book S, 251, December 22, 1870, January 12, 1871, AABD; 1870 Florida Federal Census, Duval Co., Baldwin, 432, and Duval Co., Jacksonville, 454; Miscellaneous Records Book A, January 14, 1871, 29, VCCT; "Letter from Florida," *Auburn Daily Bulletin,* February 5, 1872, 4; Olney, *Guide to Florida,* 25, 28, 75.

47. Miscellaneous Records Book A, 76, BCCV; Record of County Commissioners Book 1869–81, June 5, 1871, 52, VCCT; Revenue Book, Henry T. Titus, 1871, BCCV.

48. A decade later the Atlantic Mutual Marine Insurance Company had more than $13 million in assets. See "Financial," *New York Times,* May 2, 1883, 7; "The Lost Lodona," *New York Herald,* September 5, 1871, 5; "The Loss of the Lodona," *Milwaukee Sentinel,* September 16, 1871; "Disasters on the Coast," *New York Times,* August 28, 1871, 1; "Survivors of the Vera Cruz," *Daily Inter Ocean* (Chicago), September 11, 1880, 3; "Early Recollections of Minnie Titus Ensey," Henry Theodore Titus Collection, North Brevard Public Library, Titusville, Fla., 9–10.

49. Capt. Mills Olcott Burnham (September 8, 1817–April 17, 1886), a gunsmith born in Vermont, moved to Florida in 1839. Three years later he was an early settler at Fort Pierce introducing pineapple cultivation, laboring as a commercial fisherman, and catching green sea turtles, which he sold in Charleston, S.C. Burnham tended the Cape Canaveral lighthouse from 1853 until his death in 1886. He was a Unionist during the Civil War and owned a grove a few miles west of the lighthouse near the Banana River. According to Minnie Titus, Burnham "had a large sloop called the Osceola, and would take the young people on delightful boat rides. We played and sang and the boat was large enough to have square dances." See Shofner, *History of Brevard County,* 1:48, 65–66, 70, 137; "Shipwrecks," *New York Herald,* September 2, 1871, 8; DuBois, "Two South Florida Lighthouse Keepers," 49; "Early Recollections of Minnie Titus Ensey," Henry Theodore Titus Collection, North Brevard Public Library, Titusville, Fla., 9, 16.

50. John Freeman Young (October 30, 1820–November 15, 1885), a Maine native ordained to the priesthood in 1846, served Episcopal parishes in Texas, Mississippi, Louisiana, New York, and Florida. As assistant rector at Trinity Church in New York City, he translated European hymns and carols into English, including the now popular Austrian tune "Silent Night." See Pennington, *Soldier and Servant,* 21–22; 1880 Florida Federal Census, Precinct 2, Orange Co., 414.

51. Pennington, *Soldier and Servant,* 22–23; "Early Recollections of Minnie Titus Ensey," Henry Theodore Titus Collection, North Brevard Public Library, Titusville, Fla., 8; Shofner, *History of Brevard County,* 1:196; 1870 Florida Federal Census, Division 17, Volusia Co., 743.

52. "Letters from Florida," *Auburn Daily Bulletin,* January 27, 1872, 1; John Varner, March 15, 1872, and William Lanehart, May 9, 1872, vol. 67, Postmaster General, Orders ("Journals"), 1835–1953; Record of Appointment of Postmasters, 1832–September 30, 1971, Volusia County, Fla., M841, Roll 21, 362, RG 28, NARA.

53. James Arango Armour (September 5, 1825–July 6, 1910), a native New Yorker, served as Brevard County sheriff in 1855–57 and on June 12, 1862, enlisted as a private in Company G, Florida Eighth Infantry Regiment, CSA, in Camp Ward, Fla., deserting the following month. He seized the hidden Jupiter lighthouse mechanism and turned it over to the Union forces at Key West. He was appointed assistant lighthouse keeper in 1866 and two years later was promoted to keeper, a post he held for forty years. See Miscellaneous Records Book C, 97, 449, VCCT; H. T. Titus to President Light House Board, August 10 [1872], Letters Received by the Lighthouse Service, 1829–1900, Miscellaneous, July 1872–May 1873, vol. 315, Box 111, Records of the U.S. Coast Guard, RG 26, NARA; James Armour and Family Papers, Palm Beach County Historical Society, Palm Beach, Fla.; Henshall, *Camping and Cruising in Florida,* 79; Shofner, *History of Brevard County,* 1:63; DuBois, "Two South Florida Lighthouse Keepers," 41.

54. Henry T. Titus to President, Light House Board, September 23, 1872, Letters Received by the Lighthouse Service, 1829–1900; Daniel O'Hara affidavit, ibid.

55. Pierce, *Pioneer Life in Southeast Florida,* 40–41; 1870 Florida Federal Census, Volusia Co., 742; W. S. Abbott, December 26, 1872, vol. 71, Postmaster General, Orders ("Journals"), 1835–1953; Record of Appointment of Postmasters, 1832–September 30, 1971, Volusia County, Fla., M841, Roll 21, 362, RG 28, NARA.

56. Henry Titus to A. S. Johnson, January [1873], Letters Received by the Lighthouse Service, 1829–1900; Christian, *My Lost Millions,* 13; "Disasters at Sea," *New York Tribune,* October 29, 1872, 1; Shofner, *History of Brevard County,* 1:96.

57. "Florida as an Invalid Resort," *Springfield Republican,* June 4, 1873, 6; "Notes on Florida," *St. Albans (Vt.) Daily Messenger,* April 9, 1875, 2.

58. "Early Recollections of Minnie Titus Ensey," Henry Theodore Titus Collection, North Brevard Public Library, Titusville, Fla., 7.

59. Ibid., 14–16.

60. Isaac Dunlin Parkinson (1812–May 8, 1890), born in Lincolnshire, England, was a graduate of Jesus College in Cambridge. He was arrested in 1864 by the Union army in Key West even though he claimed to be a refugee and a British citizen. Parkinson was principal of the Brookeville Academy in Brookeville, Md., from 1865 to 1870, afterward migrating to Florida. By 1880 he was residing in Jacksonville with his Canadian wife Mary. He was interred in Evergreen Cemetery in Jacksonville. See G. W. Pratt, June 6, 1872, Letters Received by the Office of the Adjutant General, 1871–80, M666, Roll 64, RG 94, NARA; 1880 Florida Federal Census, Duval Co., 625; SE Corner, Lot 1, Range 35 East, Township 22 South, on the west bank of Indian River, in Section 3 of above range and township, bounded on the south by the land of Mary Carlile, Deed Book B, 5–7, VCCT; Discontinuances and Appointments, May 27, 1873, vol. 72, Postmaster General, Orders ("Journals"), 1835–1953; Record of Appointment of Postmasters, 1832–September 30, 1971, Volusia County, Fla., M841, Roll 21, 362, RG 28, NARA; Bradbury and Hallock, *Chronology of Florida Post Offices,* 83; 1880 Florida Federal Census, Brevard Co., 276.

61. Bartholomew Einig (August 29, 1825–1880s), born in Salcherath, Germany, migrated to Ohio in 1841. He married Magdalena Schneider in Lorain, Ohio, in 1849, and they had three children. Einig was employed as an engineer, farmer, and sawmill operator before the family moved in 1869 to Orange Mills, Putnam Co., Fla. Magdalena died in 1872, and Einig moved to Titusville the following year. He had two sons with his second wife. See 1850 Ohio Federal Census, Cleveland Ward 1, Cuyahoga Co., 173; 1860 Ohio Federal Census, Amherst, Lorain Co., 336; 1870 Florida Federal Census, Orange Mills, Putnam Co., 512; 1880 Florida Federal Census, Brevard Co., 278; Fraction 2, Section 3, Township 22 S, Range 35 E, Deed Book B, 41–45, VCCT; Shofner, *History of Brevard County,* 1:88; Name Changed, October 16, 1873, vol. 72, Postmaster General, Orders ("Journals"), 1835–1953; Florida, Office of the Secretary of State, *State and County Directories 1845–1961,* 2:234, SAF; December 24, 1873, Record of Commissions, E, vol. 20, 488, Secretary of State, SAF; Brown, *Ossian Bingley Hart,* 122, 126.

62. Aristides H. Doggett (July 30, 1832–April 29, 1890) was a lieutenant and captain of Company A, Florida Third Regiment Infantry, CSA. H. W. Van Buren acquired the S.E. Quarter of S.E. Quarter, Section 22, Township 21 South, Range 34 East; see Deed Book B, 169–70, VCCT. The Titus House was on Lot 1, Section 3, Township 22 South, Range 35 East; see Deed Book B, 243–45, VCCT. See also Miscellaneous Record Book A, 197, VCCT; 1870 Georgia Federal Census, Glynn Co., 128; 1880 Florida Federal Census, Brevard Co., 276; 1910 Florida Federal Census, Titusville, Brevard Co., 11; Florida State Census of 1885, M845, Roll 2, NARA; Georgia Tax Digests, 1874–78, Effingham Co., District 11, Georgia Archives, Morrow, Ga.

63. "The Farming in Florida," *New York Sun,* May 28, 1873, 2; "The Home of the Turtles," *New York Sun,* August 6, 1874, 3; Christian, *My Lost Millions,* 21; "Trip to Indian River, Florida," *Hartford Daily Courant,* April 17, 1875, 2; "Pictures from Florida," *Scribner's Monthly* (1), November 1874, 29.

64. Record of County Commissioners Book 1869–81, September 7 and 8, 1874, 129, 132, VCCT; half acre on Indian River shore, 35 yards front, running west 70 yards, Township 22 South, Range 35 East, November 26, 1874, Deed Book B, 396–98, VCCT; Henshall, *Camping*

and Cruising in Florida, 61; 1880 Florida Federal Census, Brevard Co., 272, 277; Reiger, "Sailing in South Florida Waters," 47; Hallock, *Camp Life in Florida,* 231.

65. Thomas Sedgwick Steele (June 11, 1845–September 9, 1903) was a jeweler adept at writing, painting, and drawing. His books were illustrated with his own realist style artwork focusing on nature. See "Trip to Indian River, Florida," *Hartford Daily Courant,* April 17, 1875, 2; "New York Supreme Court," *New York Commercial Advertiser,* March 2, 1870, 1.

66. Perry E. Wager (1820–April 1886) disappeared when he was walking from his house to his plantation accompanied by his son. He fell behind after being advised to walk slowly due to ill health. Search parties never found a trace of him after a reward was offered. See Section 3, Township 22 South, Range 35 East, Deed Book B, June 28, 1875, 470–71, VCCT; 1870 New York Federal Census, Cambridge, Washington Co., 42; 1880 Florida Federal Census, Brevard Co., 277; Barbour, *Florida for Tourists,* 35–36; "A Planter's Strange Disappearance," *Troy (N.Y.) Times,* April 15, 1886, 3.

67. Florida, Office of the Secretary of State, *State and County Directories 1845–1961,* 2:236, SAF; Record of Commissions, C, vol. 18, 179, SAF; *Cedar Keys Journal* quoted in "State Officials in Volusia County," *Tallahassee Weekly Floridian,* August 10, 1875, 3.

68. Christian, *My Lost Millions,* 10.

69. Ibid., 10–12.

70. "Southern Travels," *Forest Republican* (Tionesta, Pa.), May 3, 1876, 1; Douglas, *Florida,* 217.

71. "Early Recollections of Minnie Titus Ensey," Henry Theodore Titus Collection, North Brevard Public Library, Titusville, Fla., 7, 13–14.

72. Hallock, *Camp Life in Florida,* 230; "Rambler," *Guide to Florida,* 87; U.S. House of Representatives, *Offers for Carrying the Mails,* 1076.

73. Miscellaneous Records Book C, 339, VCCT; Index Adjudicated Cases, vol. 1, Civil No. 12B, 1876, VCCT; Justice Court & Circuit Court Docket 91, No. 22, VCCT; 1880 Florida Federal Census, Duval Co., 538, 546; 1870 Florida Federal Census, Levy Co., 720; Shofner, *History of Brevard County,* 1:88.

74. Adger C. McCrorey (1825–December 23, 1889) was born in Winnsboro, S.C., and moved to Georgia with his father. He served the Confederacy as a lieutenant in Company K of the Twenty-seventh Georgia Infantry Regiment. See 1860 Georgia Federal Census, Valley, Talbot Co., 100; 1880 Florida Federal Census, Brevard Co., 277; Record of County Commissioners Book 1869–81, October 9, 1876, 218-20, VCCT; U.S. House of Representatives, Finley vs. Bisbee, 739; Shofner, *Nor Is It Over Yet,* 333.

75. Thomas Walker Lund (1831–May 9, 1898) was born in New York and moved with his widowed mother and blind older sister to Louisville, Ky., where at the age of fourteen he apprenticed as a marine engineer and machinist, followed by a steamboat career on the Mississippi River. He moved to Augusta, Ga., in the 1850s as commodore engineer of the Savannah Line steamers. After the Civil War, Lund moved to Jacksonville to captain a steamboat on the St. Johns River. By 1889 his Lund House needed a new roof and foundation, before it was destroyed by fire six years later. In October 1897 Lund was elected mayor of Titusville without opposition. He had served on the Board of Aldermen for several terms and was vice president of the Board of Trade when he was stricken at his son's home in Jacksonville by a paralysis that left his unconscious for a week before his death. See 1850 Kentucky Federal Census, Louisville, Jefferson Co., 426; "Titusville's Mayor Dead," *Titusville Indian River Advocate,* May 13, 1898, 1; "Capt. Thos. Lund Is Mourned," *Augusta Chronicle,* May 15, 1898, 5; "Was a Native of Louisville," *Louisville Courier-Journal,* May 16, 1898, 8; "Local Laconics," *Florida Star* (Titusville), July 24, 1889, 8; Part of Lot 1, Section 3, Township 22 S, Range 35 E, Deed Book C, 638–40, VCCT; 1880 Florida Federal Census, Jacksonville, Duval Co., 563; Henshall, *Camping and Cruising in Florida,* 13, 16; Shofner, *History of Brevard County,* 1:94; Pierce, *Pioneer Life in Southeast Florida,* 115; Eriksen, *Brevard County,* 105; "Early Recollections of Minnie Titus

Ensey," Henry Theodore Titus Collection, North Brevard Public Library, Titusville, Fla., 6, 17.

76. Deed Book E, 144, 515, VCCT; 1880 Florida Federal Census, Brevard Co., 278.

77. The incorporators of the St. Johns and Indian River Railroad Co. tramway were Edward Stevens Hopkins, president; Thomas W. Lund, secretary; J. C. Marcy, assistant secretary; S. J. Fox, treasurer; and W. H. Churchill, superintendent, with general offices at Titusville. See Henshall, *Camping and Cruising in Florida,* 4, 12–13, 16; Allen, *Travelers' Official Railway Guide,* 649; "Early Recollections of Minnie Titus Ensey," Henry Theodore Titus Collection, North Brevard Public Library, Titusville, Fla., 13; 1880 Florida Federal Census, Volusia Co., 386, 402; "Local Jottings," *Florida Star,* May 29, 1879, 3.

78. Henshall, *Camping and Cruising in Florida,* 12–14, 19.

79. Miscellaneous Records Book D, 63–65, VCCT; Deed Book E, 450, VCCT; 1880 Florida Federal Census, Brevard Co., 277.

80. The Volusia County area annexed to Brevard County was "a line commencing on the Atlantic coast, on township line between townships nineteen (19) and twenty (20), running west along said line to the range line between ranges thirty-three (33) and thirty-four (34); thence south along said line to township line between townships twenty-one (21) and twenty-two (22); thence west along said line to the middle of the St. Johns River; thence southerly up the middle of said stream to the township line between townships twenty-three (23) and twenty-four (24)." See *Acts and Resolutions Adopted by the Legislature of Florida,* 140, 142–43; *Brief Description of Brevard County,* 5; Shofner, *History of Brevard County,* 1:80; "Early Recollections of Minnie Titus Ensey," Henry Theodore Titus Collection, North Brevard Public Library, Titusville, Fla., 11–12; Nabors, *Countdown in History,* 21.

81. "Indian River," *Augusta Chronicle,* January 13, 1880, 1.

82. Ibid.

83. "A Winter's Cruise in Eastern and Southern Florida," *Cazenovia (N.Y.) Republican,* September 2, 1880, 1; St. John & Indian River Train & Rail Road Co. vs. Henry Titus, Bill for Relief, Chancery Docket No. 10H, Spring Term 1879, and Index Adjudicated Cases, vol. 1, VCCT.

84. "A Winter's Cruise in Eastern and Southern Florida," *Cazenovia (N.Y.) Republican,* September 2, 1880, 1.

85. 1880 Florida Federal Census, Brevard Co., 272–81; "Volusia," *Florida Mirror* (Fernandina), July 17, 1880, 1; "One Life for Seven," *New York Truth,* October 2, 1881, 1.

86. 1880 Florida Federal Census, Brevard Co., 276, and Duval Co., 588; Probate File 2104, Clerk of Courts, Archives and Record Center, Brevard County, Titusville, Fla.

87. "Fears for a Ship's Safety," *New York Times,* September 3, 1880, 8; *New York Times,* September 4, 1880, 1, 2; "The Wrecked Steam-Ship," *New York Times,* September 5, 1880, 1; "The Vera Cruz," *Macon Telegraph,* September 11, 1880, 1; "Survivors of the Vera Cruz," *Chicago Daily Inter Ocean,* September 11, 1880, 3; "Other Survivors," *New York Times,* September 11, 1880, 2; Warner, *Generals in Blue,* 508–9; "General Torbert's Remains," *New York Herald,* September 23, 1880, 10.

88. Probate File 2104, Clerk of Courts, Archives and Record Center, Brevard County, Titusville, Fla.; *Florida Star,* November 3, 1880, and January 26, 1881, 4.

89. *Florida Star,* December 8, 1880, 2, and January 26, 1881, 4.

90. "Arrivals at the Titus House," *Florida Star,* February 2 and 23, and April 13, 1881, 4; "Local Items," *Florida Star,* March 16, April 6, and July 27, 1881, 4; "Early Recollections of Minnie Titus Ensey," Henry Theodore Titus Collection, North Brevard Public Library, Titusville, Fla., 12; Brown, *Reminiscences of Gov. R. J. Walker,* 78; "Reminiscences of Gov. Robert J. Walker," *Rockford (Ill.) Weekly Gazette,* March 9, 1881, 7.

91. U.S. House of Representatives, Bisbee vs. Finley, 1–7; Shofner, *History of Brevard County,* 1:80.

92. U.S. House of Representatives, Bisbee vs. Finley, 403–5.

93. Ibid., 405, 1086, 1094; 1880 Florida Federal Census, District East of St. Johns River, Brevard Co., 2; Shofner, *History of Brevard County,* 1:80.

94. Pierce, *Pioneer Life in Southeast Florida,* 148; *Florida Dispatch* (Jacksonville), June 29, 1881, 1; Shofner, *History of Brevard County,* 1:99; *Florida Star* quoted in *Tallahassee Weekly Floridian,* August 2, 1881.

95. *Florida Dispatch,* August 3, 1881, 2.

96. "Local Items," *Florida Star,* August 10, 1881, 4; *Florida Union* (Jacksonville) quoted in *Weekly Floridian,* August 16, 1881; "Col. Titus," *Lawrence Western Home Journal,* September 1, 1881; *Calhoun (Ga.) Times,* August 27, 1881; "Personal and Otherwise," *Duluth Daily Tribune,* August 26, 1881, 2; "Elmore in Florida," *Augusta Chronicle,* June 2, 1882, 3; *Portland (Maine) Daily Press,* August 26, 1881, 1.

Epilogue

1. *Baltimore Sun,* November 7, 1882, 1; U.S. Department of Agriculture, *Florida,* 37; Shofner, *History of Brevard County,* 1:106; Pierce, *Pioneer Life in Southeast Florida,* 198.

2. Shofner, *History of Brevard County,* 1:120; Hine, *On the Indian River,* 66, 67; "The Indian-River Country, Florida," *Chambers's Journal of Popular Literature Science and Arts* 11, no. 550 (July 7, 1894): 425.

3. Pierce, *Pioneer Life in Southeast Florida,* 185; "Local Laconics," *Florida Star,* December 19, 1889, January 2 and June 19, 1890, 1; 1900 Florida Federal Census, Titusville, 14, 16; "Bits of Fact and Gossip," *Florida Star,* August 30, 1901, 1; Shofner, *History of Brevard County,* 1:123; "News from Three States," *Weekly Columbus Enquirer,* January 3, 1887, 8.

4. Joanna Combs (March 31, 1863–1943) married Carl Curtis in 1888. See 1900 New York Federal Census, Brooklyn, Ward 30, 29; 1910 New Jersey Federal Census, Paterson Ward 7, Passaic, 19.

5. "Another Version," *Florida Star,* January 17, 1889, 1; "Titus Is Said to Have Had Eventful Life," *San Diego Evening Tribune,* April 13, 1909, 4; "There Were Others," *Charlotte Observer,* July 7, 1897, 4; "Sized Up," *Charlotte Observer,* September 1, 1897, 5; "Boston Convicted," *Washington Evening Star,* December 1, 1898, 16; "Trial for Housebreaking," *Washington Evening Star,* December 21, 1898, 6; "Miscellaneous," *Washington Times,* January 4, 1899, 3.

6. "Held for Grand Jury," *Washington Evening Star,* December 19, 1899, 12; "Howell Titus Convicted," *Washington Evening Star,* February 2, 1900, 16; "Bond Forfeited," *Washington Evening Star,* February 24, 1900, 10; "Howell Titus in Custody," *Washington Evening Star,* March 5, 1900, 5; "Titus Surrenders," New Orleans *Times-Picayune,* March 5, 1900, 10; "Titus Is Said to Have Had Eventful Life," *San Diego Evening Tribune,* April 13, 1909, 4; "Titus Brought Back," *Washington Evening Star,* March 16, 1900, 10; "Attorneys Disbarred," *Washington Evening Star,* October 3, 1900, 8; "In the Criminal Court," *Washington Evening Star,* February 1, 1901, 2; "Titus Case Nolle Prossed" and "City Criminal Court," *Montgomery Advertiser,* November 13, 1901, 7; Register of Enlistments in the U.S. Army, 1798–1914, Records of the Adjutant General's Office, 1780s–1917, 234, M233, RG 94, NARA.

7. "Titus Is Said to Have Had Eventful Life," *San Diego Evening Tribune,* April 13, 1909, 4; "Brothers," *Cincinnati Enquirer,* September 2, 1902, 1; "Brothers Question Each Other's Sanity," *Philadelphia Inquirer,* September 8, 1907, 6.

8. "Titus Is Said to Have Had Eventful Life," *San Diego Evening Tribune,* April 13, 1909, 4; "Past Reveals Shady Record," *San Diego Union,* April 4, 1909, 8; "Howell Titus Seeks Damages," *Florida Star,* September 4, 1908, 1.

9. "Gets $100.00 On Bad Checks and Skips the Town," *San Diego Evening Tribune,* March 23, 1901, 5; "Titus Insane May Be Plea of Defendant," *San Diego Evening Tribune,* April 1, 1909, 5; "Titus Hearing Started: Mind Off Is Claim," *San Diego Evening Tribune,* April 8,

1909, 3; "Titus Is Said to Have Had Eventful Life," *San Diego Evening Tribune,* April 13, 1909, 4; "The Courts," *El Paso Herald,* June 10, 1910, 4; 1920 Mississippi Federal Census, Water Valley, 8; *Daytona City Directory* 1924–1925, 574; *Polk's Jacksonville and South Jacksonville City Directory* 1925, 819; 1930 Florida Federal Census, Putman County, Palatka, 11; Tenth Census of the State of Florida, 1935, Duval County, 44, S5, Roll 9, SAF.

10. Henry T. Titus, Jr., Henry T. Titus Biography File, SAF; "Local Laconics," *Florida Star,* May 22 and June 19, 1890, 1; 1900 Florida Federal Census, Titusville, 9; 1910 Florida Federal Census, Daytona City, 32; 1920 Florida Federal Census, Daytona City, 7; 1930 Florida Federal Census, Daytona Beach, 3; 1940 Florida Federal Census, Daytona Beach, 3.

11. Ellett Livingston Titus was interred on October 20, 1894, in Grave 5, Section 153, Lot 21558, Green-Wood Cemetery, Brooklyn. His aunt Helen C. Hodgskin was buried in the same lot on September 1, 1902. See "Dreadful Tragedy," *Jersey Journal,* October 18, 1894, 6; "Died Strangely in a Bath House," *New York Herald,* October 19, 1894, 5; "Funerals of the Dead Lovers," *New York Tribune,* October 22, 1894, 12.

12. Undated newspaper articles and obituary, Henry T. Titus, Jr., Henry T. Titus Biography File, SAF.

13. 1900 Florida Federal Census, Brevard County, Titusville, 166; 1910 Florida Federal Census, Volusia County, Precinct 10, 13; *R. L. Polk & Co.'s Jacksonville City Directory* 1915, 904; United States, Selective Service System, World War I Selective Service System Draft Registration Cards, 1917–18, M1509, Roll 1530907, Records of the Selective Service System (World War I) 1917–39, RG 163, NARA; 1920 California Federal Census, Los Angeles Assembly District 75, 7.

14. "Col. Titus—A Noted Character," *Kansas City Journal,* August 26, 1881.

★ BIBLIOGRAPHY ★

ARCHIVAL MATERIALS

Non-U.S. Sources
Costa Rica
   Dirección General del Archivo Nacional, Departamento Archivo Histórico, San José
Cuba
   Archivo Nacional, Havana
Great Britain
   London Metropolitan Archives; The National Archives of the UK, London
Spain
   Archivo General Militar de Madrid
   Archivo General Militar de Segovia

U.S. Archives and Records Administration
Record Group 15, Records of the Department of Veterans Affairs
   Mexican War Service Case Files
Record Group 21, U.S. Circuit Courts
   Eastern District of Louisiana, New Orleans Circuit Court; General Case Files (E-121);
      Northern District of Florida, Tallahassee; Minute Book, 1846–67; Southern District of
      Florida, Key West Division; Admiralty Docket, April 1861–April 1867; Admiralty Final
      Record Books, 1829–1911; Admiralty Order Books, April 1861–July 1863 and November
      1863–March 1865; Southern District of Georgia, Savannah Division; Minutes, 1857–69;
      Mixed Cases, 1790–1860
Record Group 24, Records of the Bureau of Naval Personnel
   Logs of Ships and Stations, 1801–1946; Logs of U.S. Naval Ships, 1801–1915
Record Group 26, Records of the United States Coast Guard
   Letters Received by the Lighthouse Service, 1829–1900
Record Group 28, Records of the U.S. Postal Service
   Office of the Postmaster General, Immediate Office of the Postmaster General, Orders ("Jour-
      nals"), 1835–1953; Post Office Department Reports of Site Locations, 1837–1950, Florida,
      Brevard, Sand Point; Record of Appointment of Postmasters, 1832–September 30, 1971
Record Group 36, Records of the U.S. Customs Service
   Passenger Lists of Vessels Arriving at New York, New York, 1820–97
Record Group 41, Bureau of Marine Inspection and Navigation
   Custom House Records, 1774–1955, Certificates of Enrolment, 1793–1900, Port of New
      York Steam Vessels, 1838–1900; Records Relating to Vessel Documentation, Master Ab-
      stracts of Enrollments, 1815–1911
*Record Group 45, Records of the Naval Records Collection of the Office of Naval Records and
Library*
   Letters Received by the Secretary of the Navy from Commanders, 1804–86; Letters
      Received by the Secretary of the Navy from Commanding Officers of Squadrons

("Squadron Letters"), 1841–86, Pacific Squadron, July 10, 1856–November 16, 1857;
    Letters Received by the Secretary of the Navy from Commanding Officers of Squad-
    rons ("Squadron Letters"), 1841–86, Home Squadron, January 1, 1857–March 19, 1858.
Record Group 48, Office of the Secretary of the Interior
    Records Concerning the Cuban Expedition, 1850–51
Record Group 49, Records of the Bureau of Land Management
    Florida, St. Augustine Land Office; Letters Received by the Surveyor General of New
    Mexico, 1854–1907
Record Group 59, Department of State
    Correspondence on the Lopez Expedition to Cuba, 1849–51; Despatches from United
    States Consuls in Havana; Despatches from United States Consuls in San Juan del
    Norte, 1851–1906; Miscellaneous Letters of the Department of State; State Department
    Territorial Papers, Kansas, 1854–61; U.S. Passport Applications, 1795–1905
Record Group 85, Records of the Immigration and Naturalization Service
    Index to New England Naturalization Petitions, 1791–1906
Record Group 94, Records of the Adjutant General's Office, 1780's–1917
    Case Files of Applications from Former Confederates for Presidential Pardons ("Amnes-
    ty Papers"), 1865–67; Compiled Service Records of Volunteer Soldiers Who Served in
    Organizations from the State of Florida during the Florida Indian Wars, 1835–58; Index
    to Compiled Service Records of Confederate Soldiers Who Served in Organizations
    from the State of Louisiana; Letters Received by the Office of the Adjutant General,
    1861–70, 1871–80; Miscellaneous Files; U.S. Military Academy Cadet Application Pa-
    pers, 1805–66; Register of Enlistments in the U.S. Army, 1798–1914; Returns from U.S.
    Military Posts, 1800–1916
Record Group 109, War Department Collection of Confederate Records
    Carded Records Showing Military Service of Soldiers Who Fought in Confederate Orga-
    nizations; Compiled Service Records of Confederate Soldiers Who Served in Organi-
    zations from the State of Florida; Confederate Papers Relating to Citizens or Business
    Firms; Citizens File, H. T. Titus
Record Group 163, Records of the Selective Service System (World War I) 1917–1939
    World War I Selective Service System Draft Registration Cards, 1917–18
Record Group 206, Records of the Solicitor of the Treasury, 1791–1934
    Letters Received, U.S. Attorneys, Clerks of Courts, and Marshals, Florida, 1846–April 1863
Record Group 365, Treasury Department Collection of Confederate Records
    Confederate Treasury Department Field Offices, District Court, and States, Florida
Record Group 393, U.S. Army Continental Commands, 1821–1920
    Letters Received, 1866, Department and District of Florida, 1865–69

GOVERNMENT DOCUMENTS

*The Acts and Resolutions Adopted by the Legislature of Florida, at Its Tenth Session, under the
    Constitution of A.D.* 1868. Tallahassee, Fla.: Floridian Office, 1879.
Boletin Oficial. San José, Costa Rica.
Great Britain. Foreign Office. North America: 1864. No. 18. *Further Papers Respecting the
    Arrest and Imprisonment of Mr. James McHugh in the United States.* London: Harrison
    and Sons, 1864.
New York State. Legislature Assembly, 72nd Session. *Journal of the Assembly of the State of New
    York.* Vol. 2. Albany, N.Y.: Weed, Parsons, 1849.
Report of the Adjutant General of the State of Kentucky, Confederate Kentucky Volunteers, War,
    1861–65. Vol. 1. Frankfort, Ky.: State Journal Company, 1915.

Report of the Governor of Arizona to the Secretary of the Interior: 1899. Washington, D.C.: United States Government Printing Office, 1899.

Strickler, Hiram J. *Commissioner to Audit, under the Laws of the Territorial Legislature of Kansas, the Claims of the Citizens of That Territory for Losses Sustained in Carrying into Effect the Laws of the Territory, or Growing out of Any Difficulties in the Territory.* 35th Congress, 2nd Session, 1859, H. Misc. Doc. 43. Washington, D.C.: James B. Steedman, Printer, 1859.

U.S. Congress. *Biographical Dictionary of the United States Congress 1774–1989.* Washington, D.C.: United States Government Printing Office, 1989.

U.S. Department of Agriculture. *Florida: It's Climate, Soil, Products and Agricultural Capabilities.* Washington, D.C.: United States Government Printing Office, 1882.

U.S. Department of State. *Register of All Officers and Agents, Civil, Military, and Naval, in the Service of the United States.* Washington, D.C.: J. & G. S. Giddeon, Printers, 1845.

U.S. House of Representatives. *Barque Georgiana and Brig Susan Loud.* March 23, 1852. 32nd Congress, 1st Session, Exec. Doc. 83.

———. *Bisbee vs. Finley:* Testimony in the Contested Election Case of Horatio Bisbee, Jr., vs. Jesse J. Finley, from the Second Congressional District of Florida. December 27, 1881. 47th Congress, 1st Session, Mis. Doc. 11.

———. *Certain Private Land Grants in Arizona Territory.* January 29, 1886. 49th Congress, 1st Session, Report 192.

———. *Finley vs. Bisbee:* Papers in the Case of Finley vs. Bisbee, Second Congressional District of Florida. November 8, 1877. 45th Congress, 1st Session, Mis. Doc. 10

———. *Kansas Claims.* 36th Congress, 2nd Session, 1861, H. Report 104, Serial 1106.

———. *Kansas Constitution.* May 11, 1858. 35th Congress, 1st Session, Report 377, Serial 966.

———. *Offers for Carrying the Mails.* 44th Congress, 2nd Session, Exec. Doc. 43, Serial 1758.

———. *Private Land Grants in Arizona.* February 24, 1882. 47th Congress, 1st Session, Report 530.

———. *Removal of Hon. E. M. Stanton and Others.* 40th Congress, 2nd Session, Exec. Doc. 57.

U.S. Senate. *Message of the President of the United States, Transmitting Reports of the Several Heads of Department Relative to the Subject of the Resolution of the Senate of the 23d May, as to Alleged Revolutionary Movements in Cuba.* June 19, 1850. 31st Congress, 1st Session, Exec. Doc. 57.

———. *Message of the President of the United States.* 1854. 33nd Congress, 1st Session, Exec. Doc. 8.

———. *Report of the Affairs in the Department of New Mexico and Statistical Report on the Sickness and Mortality in the Army of the United States.* 1860. 36th Congress, 1st Session.

U.S. War Department. *Official Records of the Union and Confederate Navies in the War of the Rebellion.* 31 vols. Washington, D.C.: United States Government Printing Office, 1894–1927.

———. *The War of the Rebellion: A Compilation of the Official Records of the Union and Confederate Armies.* 128 vols. Washington, D.C.: United States Government Printing Office, 1880–1901.

War Office, Great Britain. *A List of the Officers of the Army and Royal Marines on Full, Retired, and Half-Pay: With an Index,* 1824. London: C. Roworth, 1824.

MANUSCRIPT AND RECORD COLLECTIONS

Alabama Department of Archives and History, Montgomery, Alabama
    Confederate Pension Applications, 1880–1940
Amelia Island Museum, Fernandina Beach, Florida
    Harrison Family Papers

Arizona Historical Society, Tucson, Arizona
    Elias Brevoort Folder; Edward E. Cross Folder; Christopher C. Dodson Folder; Mickey
    Free Folder; Bernard John Dowling Irwin Papers; C. B. Marshall Folder; George D.
    Mercer Folder; Charles Debrille Poston Papers; William C. Wadsworth Folder; John
    Ward Folder
Baker Library, Harvard University, Boston, Massachusetts
    R. G. Dun and Company Credit Report Volumes
Brevard County, Clerk of Courts, Archives and Record Center, Titusville, Florida
    Probate Files
Chemung County Clerk's Office, Elmira, New York
    Tioga Deeds, Chemung County
Cuyahoga County Archive, Cleveland, Ohio
    Cuyahoga County, Ohio, Marriage Records, 1810–1973
Dolph Briscoe Center for American History, University of Texas at Austin
    A. C. Allen Papers; Lewis Miles Hobbs Washington Family Papers
Duval County Courthouse, Jacksonville, Florida
    Archibald Abstract Book
Filson Historical Society, Louisville, Kentucky
    Marshall Family Papers
Florida Department of Military Affairs, State Arsenal, St. Augustine, Florida
    Florida Militia Muster Rolls, Seminole Indian Wars
Georgia Archives, Morrow, Georgia
    Georgia Tax Digests, 1874–78
Hargrett Rare Book and Manuscript Library, University of Georgia, Athens, Georgia
    Keith M. Read Collection
Henry E. Huntington Library, San Marino, California
    F. Biertu Journal
Historical Society of Pennsylvania, Philadelphia, Pennsylvania
    Salmon P. Chase Papers
Houghton Library, Harvard University, Boston, Massachusetts
    John Anthony Quitman Papers
Jackson County Recorder of Deeds, Kansas City, Missouri
    Deed of Trust
Kansas City Public Library, Kansas City, Missouri
    Kansas City, Missouri, Statistical Facts, May 1857, Special Collections Vertical File
Kansas State Historical Society, Topeka, Kansas
    Peter T. Abell Miscellaneous Collection; William I. R. Blackman Collection; James Blood Col-
        lection; John Brown Collection; Richard Hinton Collection; Thaddeus Hyatt Collection;
        Kansas Historical Collections; Kansas Tract Books, 1854–1965; Miscellaneous Collection;
        Muster Roll of Captain Samuel Walker; James M. Pelot, M.D., Miscellaneous Collection
    Kenneth Spencer Research Library, University of Kansas, Lawrence
    Douglas County Deed Records; Josiah Miller Collection
Latin American Library, Tulane University, New Orleans, Louisiana
    Callender Fayssoux Collection
Library of Congress, Manuscript Division, Washington, D.C.
    Orloff M. Dorman Diary; John Gray Foster Letterbook
Luzerne County Historical Society, Wilkes-Barre, Pennsylvania
    Ashley Planes File; St. Stephen's Cemetery File
Madison County Courthouse, Madison, Florida
    Deed Records

Manuscripts and Folklife Archives, Western Kentucky University, Bowling Green, Kentucky
   E. S. Baker Collection
Mississippi Department of Archives and History, Jackson, Mississippi
   John A. Quitman
National Society of the Sons of the American Revolution, Louisville, Kentucky
   Membership Application 89952, Michael Louis Regan, March 28, 1963
North Brevard Public Library, Titusville, Florida
   Henry Theodore Titus Collection
Palm Beach County Historical Society, Palm Beach, Florida
   James Armour and Family Papers
Patagonia-Sonoita Creek Preserve Visitor Center, Patagonia, Arizona
   Correspondence File
Potter County Historical Society, Potter County Historical Society, Coudersport, Pennsylvania
   Col. Hugh Young File
St. Augustine Historical Society, St. Augustine, Florida
   Circuit Court Papers, St. Johns County, Florida; Douglas D. Dummett Collection
Schuyler County Clerks' Office, Watkins Glen, New York
   Deed Records
Shelby County Courthouse, Shelbyville, Kentucky
   Deed Book; Marriage Book; Will Book
Southern Historical Collection. University of North Carolina, Chapel Hill, North Carolina
   John Hunt Morgan Papers; John Thomas Wheat Papers
State Archives of Florida, Tallahassee, Florida
   Washington M. Ives Journal, 1860–62; Miscellaneous Military Expenditure Documents,
      1840–69; Payrolls for Officers, 1861–62; Record of Commissions; State and County
      Directories, 1845–61; Henry T. Titus Biography File
Sterling Memorial Library, Yale University, New Haven, Connecticut
   John White Geary Papers; Rufus and S. Willard Saxton Papers
Steuben County Clerk's Office, Bath, New York
   Miscellaneous Book A
University of Arizona Library Special Collections, Tucson
   San Rafael de la Zanja Land Grant Collection, 1880–87
Volusia County, Clerk of the Circuit Court, Records Management Center, Deland, Florida
   Chancery Docket; Deed Book B; Miscellaneous Records Book B; Record of County
      Commissioners Book, 1869–81

Diary

Máximo Blanco Diary (3rd revision), in possession of Werner Korte, San José, Costa Rica

Books, Pamphlets, City Directories, and Articles

Allen, W. F., ed. *Travelers' Official Railway Guide for the United States and Canada.* Philadelphia: National Railway, 1878.
Andreas, A. T. *History of the State of Kansas.* Chicago: A. T. Andreas, 1883.
Barbour, George M. *Florida for Tourists, Invalids, and Settlers.* New York: D. Appleton, 1884.
Bay, W. V. N. *Reminiscences of the Bench and Bar of Missouri.* St. Louis: F. H. Thomas, 1878.
Blake, William P. "Silver and Copper Mining in Arizona, with a Map," *Mining Magazine and Journal of Geology* 1, no. 1 (November 1859): 1–22.

Boggess, F. C. M. *A Veteran of Four Wars.* Arcadia, Fla.: Champion Job Rooms, 1900.

Brewerton, G. Douglas. *The War in Kansas: A Rough Trip to the Border, among New Homes and a Strange People.* New York: Derby & Jackson, 1856.

A Brief Description of Brevard County, Florida, or the Indian River Country. 4th ed. Jacksonville, Fla.: Da Costa Printing House, 1891.

Brinton, Daniel G. *A Guide-Book of Florida and the South, for Tourists, Invalids and Emigrants.* Philadelphia: George Maclelan, 1869.

Brown, George W. *Reminiscences of Gov. R. J. Walker; with the True Story of the Rescue of Kansas from Slavery.* Rockford, Ill.: n.p., 1902.

Burnett, Peter H. *Recollections and Opinions of an Old Pioneer.* New York: D. Appleton, 1880.

Calcagno, Francisco. *Diccionario Biográfico Cubano.* New York: Imprenta y Librería de N. Ponce de León, 1878.

Christian, George B. *My Lost Millions: Florida Past Present and Future.* Marion, Ohio: Marion Printing Co., 1926.

Clancy, Anne Robinson, ed. *A Yankee in a Confederate Town: The Journal of Calvin L. Robinson.* Sarasota, Fla.: Pineapple Press, 2002.

Cory, C. E. "Slavery in Kansas," *Kansas Historical Collections,* 1901–1902 7 (1902): 229–42.

Cozzens, Samuel W. *The Marvellous Country; or, Three Years in Arizona and New Mexico.* London: Sampson Low, Marston, Low, and Searle, 1875.

Cuba en la Mano: Enciclopedia Popular Ilustrada. Havana: Ucar, García y Cia, 1940.

Cullum, George W. *Biographical Register of the Officers and Graduates of the U.S. Military Academy, from 1802 to 1867.* 2 vols. New York: James Miller, 1879.

Daytona City Directory 1924–1925. Jacksonville, Fla.: R. L. Polk, 1924.

Dickison, J. J. *Confederate Military History of Florida.* Gulf Breeze, Fla.: eBooks OnDisk, 2002, reprint.

Doubleday, C. W. *Reminiscences of the "Filibuster" War in Nicaragua.* New York: G. P. Putnam's Sons, 1886.

"Executive Minutes Kept during Governor Shannon's Administration," *Kansas Historical Collections,* 1883-1885 3 (1886): 283–337.

"Executive Minutes of Governor John W. Geary," *Kansas Historical Collections,* 1886–1888 4 (1888): 520–742.

Freret, William. *Correspondence between the Treasury Department, &c., in Relation to the Cuban Expedition, and William Freret, Late Collector.* New Orleans: Alex, Levy, 1851.

Galbraith, John B., and A. R. Meek. *Reports of Cases Argued and Adjudged in the Supreme Court of Florida, at Terms Held in* 1867–8–'9. Vol. 12, pt. 2. Tallahassee: Edw. M. Cheney, State Printer, 1869.

Gihon, John H. *Geary and Kansas.* Philadelphia: Chas. C. Rhodes, 1857.

Gonzales, Ambrosio José. *Manifesto on Cuban Affairs Addressed to the People of the United States.* New Orleans: Daily Delta, 1853.

Hallock, Charles. *Camp Life in Florida: A Handbook for Sportsmen and Settlers.* New York: Forest and Stream, 1876.

Hardy, Richardson. *The History and Adventures of the Cuban Expedition.* Cincinnati: Lorenzo Straton, 1850.

Hawks, J. M. *Florida Gazetteer.* New Orleans: Bronze Pen Steam Book and Job Office, 1871.

Henshall, James A. *Camping and Cruising in Florida.* Cincinnati: Robert Clarke, 1884.

Hertslet, Edward, ed. *A Complete Collection of the Treaties and Conventions and Reciprocal Regulations at Present Subsisting between Great Britain and Foreign Powers.* 30 vols. London: Butterworth's, 1877.

Higginson, Thomas Wentworth. *Army Life in a Black Regiment.* East Lansing: Michigan State University Press, 1960.

Hine, C. Vickerstaff. *On the Indian River.* Chicago: Charles H. Sergel, 1891.

Hinton, Richard J. *The Hand-Book to Arizona: Its Resources, History, Towns, Mines, Ruins and Scenery.* San Francisco: Payot, Upham, 1878.

History of Tioga, Chemung, Tompkins, and Schuyler Counties, New York. Philadelphia: Everts & Ensign, 1879.

Hodge, Hiram C. *Arizona as It Is; or the Coming Country.* New York: Hurd and Houghton, 1877.

Ibáñez Montoya, Joaquín. *Estudio asesor para la restauración del fuerte de la Inmaculada Concepción de Río de San Juan en Nicaragua: reconocimiento técnico, histórico y militar.* 3 vols. Madrid: Organización de los Estados Americanos, 1976.

Jackson, Henry R. *The Wanderer Case: The Speech of Hon. Henry J. Jackson of Savannah, Ga.* Atlanta: Franklin Printing and Publishing, 1891.

Manning, William R. *Diplomatic Correspondence of the United States: Inter-American Affairs 1831–1860, Vol. XI—Spain.* Washington, D.C.: Carnegie Endowment for International Peace, 1939.

"Masonry in the Kansas Troubles," *Freemason's Monthly Magazine* 20, no. 6 (April 1861): 183–84.

Moore, John Bassett. *History and Digest of the International Arbitrations to Which the United States Has Been a Party.* 8 vols. Washington, D.C.: United States Government Printing Office, 1898.

———. *A Digest of International Law.* 8 vols. Washington, D.C.: United States Government Printing Office, 1906.

Morrison, Wayne E., ed. *Early History &c. Havana, New York.* Ovid, N.Y.: Morrison and Son Printers, n.d.

Mowry, Sylvester. *Arizona and Sonora: The Geography, History, and Resources of the Silver Region of North America.* 3rd ed. New York: Harper and Brothers, 1864.

Noel, Theo. *A Campaign from Santa Fe to the Mississippi: Being a History of the Old Sibley Brigade from Its First Organization to the Present Time.* Shreveport, La.: Shreveport News Printing, 1865.

Obregón Quesada, Clotilde, ed. *Diarios de Faustino Montes de Oca Gamero.* San José, Costa Rica: Editorial UCR, 2007.

O.D.D.O. [J. C. Davis]. *The History of the Late Expedition to Cuba.* New Orleans: Daily Delta, 1850.

Olney, G. W. *A Guide to Florida, "The Land of Flowers."* New York: Cushing, Bardua, 1872.

Paxton, William McClung. *Annals of Platte County, Missouri: From Its Exploration Down to June 1, 1897.* Kansas City: Hudson-Kimberly, 1897.

Phillips, William. *The Conquest of Kansas, by Missouri and Her Allies.* Boston: Phillips, Sampson, 1856.

Pierce, Charles. *Pioneer Life in Southeast Florida.* Ed. Donald W. Curl. Coral Gables, Fla.: University of Miami Press, 1970.

Polk's Jacksonville and South Jacksonville City Directory 1925. Jacksonville, Fla.: R. L. Polk, 1925.

Proceedings of the Grand Lodge of the Most Ancient and Honorable Fraternity of Free and Accepted Masons, of the State of Florida: At Its Several Grand Communications, from Its Organization, A.D. 1830, to 1859, Inclusive. New York: J. F. Brennan, 1859.

Pumpelly, Raphael. *My Reminiscences.* 2 vols. New York: Henry Holt, 1918.

"Rambler." *Guide to Florida.* New York: American News Company, 1876.

Reid, Whitelaw. *Ohio in the War: Her Statesmen, Her Generals, and Soldiers.* 2 vols. Cincinnati: Moore, Wilstach & Baldwin, 1868.

Report of the Sonora Exploring and Mining Co., Made to the Stockholders, December, 1856. Cincinnati: Railroad Record Print, 1856.

R. L. Polk & Co.'s Jacksonville City Directory 1915. Jacksonville, Fla.: R. L. Polk, 1915.

Robarts, William Hugh. *A Complete Roster of the Regular and Volunteer Troops in the War between the United States and Mexico, from 1846 to 1848.* Washington, D.C.: Brentano's, 1887.

Robinson, Sara T. L. *Kansas: Its Interior and Exterior Life.* Boston: Crosby, Nichols, 1856.

Schlesinger, Louis. "Personal Narrative of Louis Schlesinger, of Adventures in Cuba and Ceuta," *Democratic Review* 31 (September 1852): 210–24.

Schwartz, Gerald, ed. *A Woman Doctor's Civil War: Esther Hill Hawk's Diary.* Columbia: University of South Carolina Press, 1984.

Squier, Ephraim G. "San Juan de Nicaragua," *Harper's New Monthly Magazine* 10, no. 55 (December 1854): 50–61.

Stout, Peter F. *Nicaragua: Past, Present and Future.* Philadelphia: John E. Potter, 1859.

Strickler, Hiram J. *Commissioner to Audit, under the Laws of the Territorial Legislature of Kansas, the Claims of the Citizens of That Territory for Losses Sustained in Carrying into Effect the Laws of the Territory, or Growing out of Any Difficulties in the Territory,* 35th Congress, 2nd session, 1859, H. Misc. Doc. 43. Washington, D.C.: James B. Steedman, Printer, 1859.

Tomlinson, William P. *Kansas in Eighteen Fifty-eight.* New York: H. Dayton, 1859.

Twain, Mark. *Roughing It.* 2 vols. New York: Harper & Brothers, 1913.

Walker, William. *The War in Nicaragua.* Mobile, Ala.: S. H. Goetzel, 1860.

Washington, Peter G., and Columbus Alexander, eds. *The United States Postal Guide and Official Advertiser* 1, no. 4 (October 1850).

Webb's Jacksonville and Consolidated Directory on the Representative Cities of East and South Florida, 1886. Jacksonville, Fla.: Wanton S. Webb, 1886.

Williams' Cincinnati Directory, June, 1871. Cincinnati: Cincinnati Directory Office, 1871.

Wilson, H. *Trow's New York City Directory,* 1868. New York: John F. Trow, 1868.

Wilson, James Grant, and John Fiske, eds. *Appletons' Cyclopedia of American Biography.* 7 vols. New York: D. Appleton, 1887.

SECONDARY SOURCES

Abels, Jules. *Man on Fire: John Brown and the Cause of Liberty.* New York: Macmillan, 1971.

Africa, J. Simpson. *History of Huntingdon and Blair Counties, Pennsylvania.* Philadelphia: Louis H. Everts, 1883.

Ahumada y Centurión, José. *Memoria Histórico Política de la Isla de Cuba.* Havana: A. Pego, 1874.

Alberts, Don E., ed. *Rebels on the Rio Grande: The Civil War Journal of A. B. Peticolas.* Albuquerque: University of New Mexico Press, 1984.

Altshuler, Constance Wynn. *Starting with Defiance: Nineteenth Century Arizona Military Posts.* Tucson: Arizona Historical Society, 1983.

Argilagos, Francisco R. *Próceres de la Independencia de Cuba.* Havana: Imprenta "El Siglo XX," 1916.

Balaguer, Joaquín. *Literatura dominicana.* Buenos Aires: Editorial Americalee, 1950.

Barnes, Will C. *Arizona Place Names.* Tucson: University of Arizona Press, 1960.

Beezley, William H. "LandOffice Spoilsmen in 'Bleeding Kansas,'" *Great Plains Journal* 9 (Spring 1970): 67–78.

Biographical Souvenir of the States of Georgia and Florida. Chicago: F. A. Battey, 1889.

Blackmar, Frank W., ed. *Kansas: A Cyclopedia of State History, Embracing Events, Institutions, Industries, Counties, Cities, Towns, Prominent Persons, Etc.* 3 vols. Chicago: Standard, 1912.

Bolaños Geyer, Alejandro. *Campana Rota, Camalotes Tumbas y Olvido.* Masaya, Nicaragua: Privately printed, 1999.

Bradbury, Alford G., and E. Story Hallock. *A Chronology of Florida Post Offices.* [Vero Beach, Fla.]: Florida Federation of Stamp Clubs, 1962.

Brown, Canter, Jr. *Ossian Bingley Hart: Florida's Loyalist Reconstruction Governor.* Baton Rouge: Louisiana State University Press, 1997.

Brownell, Elizabeth R. *They Lived in Tubac.* Tucson: Westernlore Press, 1986.

Bubar, Donald. *Along the Early Trails of the Southwest.* Austin, Tex.: Pemberton Press, 1969.

Cabrera Geserick, Marco Antonio. "The Legacy of the Filibuster War: National Identity, Collective Memory, and Cultural Anti-Imperialism." Ph.D. diss., Arizona State University, 2013.

"Col. M. C. Taylor's Diary in López Cárdenas Expedition, 1850," *Register of the Kentucky Historical Society* 19, no. 57 (September 1921): 79–89.

Comisión de Investigación Histórica de la Campaña de 1856–1857. *Proclamas y Mensajes.* San José: Editorial Costa Rica, 2003.

Cooley, Henry S. *A Study of Slavery in New Jersey.* Baltimore, Md.: Johns Hopkins University Press, 1896.

Cordley, Richard. *A History of Lawrence, Kansas from the First Settlement to the Close of the Rebellion.* Lawrence, Kans.: Lawrence Journal Press, 1895.

Craig, James C. "Isaiah David Hart, City Founder." In *The Jacksonville Historical Society Papers,* vol. 3. Jacksonville, Fla.: Jacksonville Historical Society, 1954.

Davis, T. Frederick. *History of Jacksonville, Florida and Vicinity 1513 to 1924.* St. Augustine, Fla.: Record Company, 1925.

Davis, William Watson. *The Civil War and Reconstruction in Florida.* London: P. S. King & Son, 1913.

Day, Donald Eugene. "A Life of Wilson Shannon, Governor of Ohio, Diplomat, Territorial Governor of Kansas." Ph.D. diss., Ohio State University, 1978.

De la Cova, Antonio Rafael. *Cuban Confederate Colonel: The Life of Ambrosio José Gonzales.* Columbia: University of South Carolina Press, 2003.

———. "Filibusters and Freemasons: The Sworn Obligation," *Journal of the Early Republic* 17, no. 1 (Spring 1997): 89–114.

———. "The Kentucky Regiment That Invaded Cuba in 1850," *Register of the Kentucky Historical Society* 105, no. 4 (Autumn 2007): 571–615.

———. "Samuel J. Kookogey in Bleeding Kansas: A 'Fearless Vindicator of the Rights of the South,'" *Kansas History* 35, no. 3 (Autumn 2012): 146–63.

———. "The Taylor Administration Versus Mississippi Sovereignty: The Round Island Expedition of 1849," *Journal of Mississippi History* 62, no. 4 (Winter 2000): 1–33.

Denslow, William R. *10,000 Famous Freemasons.* 5 vols. Trenton, Mo.: Transactions of the Missouri Lodge of Research, 1961.

Douglas, Marjorie Stoneman. *Florida: The Long Frontier.* New York: Harper & Row, 1967.

Douglas, Richard L. "A History of Manufactures in the Kansas District." In *Collections of the Kansas State Historical Society,* 1909–1910, vol. 11. Topeka: State Printing Office, 1910, 81–215.

"Dr. Aristides Rodrigue: Passing through Cambria County on the Way to 'Bloody Kansas,'" *Cambria County Heritage* 26, no. 2 (Spring 2006): 1–2.

DuBois, Bessie Wilson. "Two South Florida Lighthouse Keepers," *Tequesta* 1, no. 33 (1973): 41–50.

Dufour, Charles L. *Gentle Tiger: The Gallant Life of Roberdeau Wheat.* Baton Rouge: Louisiana State University Press, 1957.

Dunn, Roy Sylvan. "The KGC in Texas, 1860–1861," *Southwestern Historical Quarterly* 70, no. 4 (April 1967): 543–73.

Dunning, Charles H. *Rock to Riches.* Phoenix: Southwest, 1959.

Eaton, W. Clement. "Frontier Life in Southern Arizona, 1858–1861," *Southwestern Historical Quarterly* 36, no. 3 (January 1933): 173–92.

Emerson, Gary. *A Link in the Great Chain: A History of the Chemung Canal.* Fleischmanns, N.Y.: Purple Mountain Press, 2004.

Eriksen, John M. *Brevard County: A History to 1955.* Tampa: Florida Historical Society Press, 1994.

Esgate, James. *Jacksonville, the Metropolis of Florida.* Jacksonville, Fla.: Wm. G. J. Perry, 1885.

Farish, Thomas Edwin. *History of Arizona.* 8 vols. San Francisco: Filmer Brothers Electrotype Company, 1915.

Faust, Patricia L., ed. *Historical Times Illustrated Encyclopedia of the Civil War.* New York: Harper & Row, 1986.

Featherstonhaugh, Thomas. "John Brown's Men: The Lives of Those Killed at Harper's Ferry," *Publications of the Southern History Association* 3, no. 4 (October 1899): 281–306.

Fleming, Walter L. "The Buford Expedition to Kansas," *American Historical Review* 6, no. 1 (October 1900): 38–48.

Florin, Lambert. "Mowry, Arizona," *Desert* 30, no. 6 (June 1967): 37.

Fontana, Bernard L., and J. Cameron Greenleaf. "Johnny Ward's Ranch: A Study in Historic Archaeology," *Kiva* 28, nos. 1–2 (October–December 1962): 1–115.

Gard, Wayne, et al. *Along the Early Trails of the Southwest.* Austin, Tex.: Pemberton Press, 1969.

Gleed, Charles S. "Samuel Walker," *Kansas Historical Collections* 1897-1900 6 (1900): 249–74.

Greene, A. C. *900 Miles on the Butterfield Trail.* Denton: University of North Texas Press, 1994.

Hall, Martin Hardwick. "The Formation of Sibley's Brigade and the March to New Mexico," *Southwestern Historical Quarterly* 61, no. 3 (January 1958): 383–405.

Hambrecht, F. T., and J. L. Koste. "Biographical Register of Physicians Who Served the Confederacy in a Medical Capacity." November 24, 2013. Unpublished database.

Hayden, Horace Edwin, ed. "The Parish Register of St. Stephen's Protestant Episcopal Church, Wilkes-Barre, Pa. 1839–1866." In *Proceedings and Collections of the Wyoming Historical and Geological Society, for the Year* 1917, vol. 15. Wilkes-Barre, Pa.: E. B. Yordy, 1917.

Hellberg, Carlos. *Historia Estadística de Cárdenas.* Repr., Cárdenas: Comité ProCalles de Cárdenas, 1957.

Holland, Keith V., Lee B. Manley, and James W. Towart. *The Maple Leaf: An Extraordinary American Civil War Shipwreck.* Jacksonville, Fla.: St. Johns Archaeological Expeditions, 1993.

Hollister, Ovando J. *Colorado Volunteers in New Mexico, 1862.* Chicago: R. R. Donnelley & Sons, 1962.

Holloway, J. N. *History of Kansas: From the First Exploration of the Mississippi Valley, to Its Admission into the Union.* Lafayette, Ind.: James, Emmons, 1868.

Hudson, Linda S. *Mistress of Manifest Destiny: A Biography of Jane McManus Storm Cazneau, 1807–1878.* Austin: Texas State Historical Association, 2001.

Hughes, Nathaniel Cheairs, Jr., and Thomas C. Ware. *Theodore O'Hara: Poet-Soldier of the Old South.* Knoxville: University of Tennessee Press, 1998.

Huxford, Folks. *Pioneers of Wiregrass Georgia.* 11 vols. Homerville, Ga.: n.p., 1951.

Ingalls, Sheffield. *History of Atchison County, Kansas.* Lawrence, Kans.: Standard, 1916.

Johannsen, Robert W. "The Lecompton Constitutional Convention: An Analysis of Its Membership," *Kansas Historical Quarterly* 23, no. 3 (Autumn 1957): 225–43.

Johnston, J. Stoddard. "Sketch of Theodore O'Hara," *Register of Kentucky State Historical Society* 11 (September 1913): 67–72.

Juárez Cano, Jorge. *Hombres del 51.* Havana: Imprenta "El Siglo XX," 1930.

Judge, Arthur Ignatius, ed. *A History of the Canning Industry.* Baltimore, Md.: Canning Trade, 1914.

Karsner, David. *John Brown Terrible "Saint."* New York: Dodd, Mead, 1934.

Keehn, David C. *Knights of the Golden Circle: Secret Empire, Southern Secession, Civil War.* Baton Rouge: Louisiana State University Press, 2013.

"La vida en San Jose a mediados del siglo XIX: Remembranzas de Chico Rohrmoser," *Revista Herencia* 23, no. 2 (2010): 25–47.

Mackie, J. D. "Dugald Dalgetty and Scottish Soldiers of Fortune," *Scottish Historical Review* 12, no. 47 (April 1915): 221–37.

Malin, James C. "Colonel Harvey and His Forty Thieves," *Mississippi Valley Historical Review* 19, no. 1 (June 1932): 57–76.

Manning, John T., and Robert H. Hudson. *North Brevard County.* Charleston, S.C.: Arcadia, 1999.

Marley, David F. *Wars of the Americas: A Chronology of Armed Conflict in the New World, 1492 to the Present.* Santa Barbara, Calif.: "BC-CLIO," 1998.

Martin, Richard A. *The City Makers.* Jacksonville. Fla.: Convention Press, 1972.

———. "River and Forest: Jacksonville's Antebellum Lumber Industry," *Northeast Florida History* 1, no. 1 (1992): 19–33.

———, with Daniel L. Schafer. *Jacksonville's Ordeal by Fire: A Civil War History.* Jacksonville, Fla.: Florida Publishing Company, 1984.

May, Robert E. *John Anthony Quitman: Old South Crusader.* Baton Rouge: Louisiana State University Press, 1985.

———. *Manifest Destiny's Underworld: Filibustering in Antebellum America.* Chapel Hill: University of North Carolina Press, 2002.

McKivigan, John R. *Forgotten Firebrand: James Redpath and the Making of Nineteenth-Century America.* Ithaca, N.Y.: Cornell University Press, 2008.

Merritt, Webster. *A Century of Medicine in Jacksonville and Duval County.* Gainesville: University of Florida Press, 1949.

Moody, Ralph. *Stagecoach West.* New York: Thomas Y. Crowell, 1967.

Morales y Morales, Vidal. *Iniciadores y primeros mártires de la revolución cubana.* 3 vols. Havana: Cultural, S.A., 1931.

Morton, Jennie C. "Theodore O'Hara," *Register of Kentucky State Historical Society* 1, no. 3 (September 1903): 49–56.

Mullis, Tony R. *Peacekeeping on the Plains: Army Operations in Bleeding Kansas.* Columbia: University of Missouri Press, 2004.

Nabors, Robert L. *Countdown in History: Titusville Centennial 1867–1967 Historical Booklet and Program.* Titusville, Fla.: n.p., 1967.

Nance, Ellwood C., ed. *The East Coast of Florida: A History 1500–1961.* 3 vols. Delray Beach, Fla.: Southern, 1962.

Nevins, Allan. *The Emergence of Lincoln.* 2 vols. New York: Scribner's, 1950.

Newman, Anna Pearl Leonard. *Stories of Early Life along Beautiful Indian River.* Stuart, Fla.: Stuart Daily News, 1953.

Nulty, William H. *Confederate Florida: The Road to Olustee.* Tuscaloosa, Ala.: University of Alabama Press, 1994.

Obregón, Rafael. *Costa Rica y la guerra contra los filibusteros.* Alajuela, Costa Rica: Museo Histórico Cultural Juan Santamaría, 1991.

Palmer, Friend. *Early Days in Detroit.* Detroit: Hunt & June, 1906.

Paxton, W. M. *The Marshall Family.* Cincinnati: Robert Clarke, 1885.

Pennington, Edgar Legare. *Soldier and Servant: John Freeman Young, Second Bishop of Florida.* Hartford, Conn.: Church Missions, 1939.

Pfanz, Donald C. *Richard S. Ewell: A Soldier's Life.* Chapel Hill: University of North Carolina Press, 1998.

Pike, Albert. "John Anthony Quitman." In *Proceedings of the Grand Lodge of Mississippi, Ancient, Free and Accepted Masons.* Jackson, Miss.: Clarion Steam Printing Establishment, 1882.

Portell Vilá, Herminio. *Historia de Cárdenas.* Havana: Talleres Gráficos "Cuba Intelectual," 1928.

———. *Narciso López y su época.* 3 vols. Havana, 1930–58.

Poston, Charles D. "Building a State in Apache Land," *Overland Monthly and Out West* 24, no. 140 (August 1894): 203–13.

Prime, Nathaniel S. *A History of Long Island.* New York: Robert Carter, 1845.

Quisenberry, Anderson C. *Lopez's Expeditions to Cuba* 1850–1851. Louisville, Ky.: John P. Morton, 1906.

Radbourne, Allan. *Mickey Free: Apache Captive, Interpreter, and Indian Scout.* Tucson: Arizona Historical Society, 2005.

———. *Salvador or Martinez? The Parentage and Origins of Mickey Free.* London: English Westerner's Society, 1972.

Rauch, Basil. *American Interest in Cuba: 1848–1855.* New York: Columbia University Press, 1948.

Recopilación Museo Histórico Cultural Juan Santamaría. *El Combate de La Trinidad.* San José: Imprenta Nacional, 1999.

Reiger, John F., ed. "Sailing in South Florida Waters in the Early 1880s," *Tequesta* 1, no. 31 (1971): 43–66.

Roberts, Virginia Culin. *With Their Own Blood: A Saga of Southwestern Pioneers.* Fort Worth: Texas Christian University Press, 1992.

Sacks, Benjamin. "The Origins of Fort Buchanan, Myth and Fact," *Arizona and the West* 7, no. 3 (Autumn 1965): 207–26.

Sanborn, Franklin Benjamin, ed. *The Life and Letters of John Brown, Liberator of Kansas, and Martyr of Virginia.* Boston: Roberts Brothers, 1891.

Schafer, Daniel L. *Thunder on the River: The Civil War in Northeast Florida.* Gainesville: University Press of Florida, 2010.

Schene, Michael G. *Hopes, Dreams, and Promises: A History of Volusia County, Florida.* Daytona Beach, Fla.: News-Journal Corporation, 1976.

Shofner, Jerrell H. *History of Brevard County.* 2 vols. Stuart, Fla.: Southeastern Printing Co., 1995.

———. *Nor Is It Over Yet: Florida in the Era of Reconstruction 1863–1877.* Gainesville: University Presses of Florida, 1974.

Smith, Clifford Neal. *Early Nineteenth-Century German Settlers in Ohio, Kentucky, and Other States.* Pt. 4A. Baltimore, Md.: Genealogical Publishing Co., 2004.

Snodgrass, Dena E. "A Remarkable Man." In *The Jacksonville Historical Society Papers,* vol. 5. Jacksonville, Fla.: Jacksonville Historical Society, 1969, 42–46.

Snyder, James D. *A Light in the Wilderness: The Story of Jupiter Inlet Lighthouse & the Southeast Florida Frontier.* Jupiter, Fla.: Pharos Books, 2006.

Speer, John. *Life of Gen. James H. Lane.* Garden City, Kans.: John Speer, printer, 1896.

Stephenson, Wendell Holmes. *Publications of the Kansas State Historical Society Embracing the Political Career of General James H. Lane, III.* Topeka: B. P. Walker, State Printer, 1930.

Stout, Joseph A., Jr. *Schemers & Dreamers: Filibustering in Mexico 1848–1921.* Fort Worth: Texas Christian University Press, 2002.

Swain, Charles H. "Report on the Mines Known as the Old Mowry Mines, 1893." Unpub. ms. Arizona Historical Society, Tucson.

Thornburg, Florence. "The Sonoita Valley," *Arizona Highways* 34, no. 9 (September 1958): 4–6.

Tilton, George H. *A History of Rehoboth Massachusetts.* Boston: Published by the author, 1918.

Titus, Leo J., Jr. *Titus: A North American Family History.* Baltimore, Md.: Gateway Press, 2004.

Treacy, Patricia. *Grand Hotels of Saint Louis.* Mount Pleasant, S.C.: Arcadia, 2005.

Van Ravenswaay, Charles. *Saint Louis: An Informal History of the City and Its People, 1764–1865.* St. Louis: Missouri Historical Society Press, 1991.

Villard, Oswald Garrison. *John Brown 1800–1859: A Biography Fifty Years After.* London: Constable, 1910.

Warner, Ezra J. *Generals in Blue: Lives of the Union Commanders.* Baton Rouge: Louisiana State University Press, 1991.

Watts, Dale E. "How Bloody Was Bleeding Kansas? Political Killings in Kansas Territory, 1854–1861," *Kansas History: A Journal of the Central Plains* 18, no. 2 (Summer 1995): 116–29.

Wehrman, Georgia. "Harshaw: Mining Camp of the Patagonias," *Journal of Arizona History* 6, no. 1 (Spring 1965): 21–36.

Weisberger, Bernard A. "The Newspaper Reporter and the Kansas Imbroglio," *Mississippi Valley Historical Review* 36, no. 4 (March 1950): 633–56.

Welles, Tom Henderson. *The Slave Ship* Wanderer. Athens: University of Georgia Press, 2009.

Whitford, Noble E. *History of the Canal System of the State of New York.* Albany, N.Y.: Brandow Printing Company, 1906.

Wilder, Daniel W. *The Annals of Kansas.* Topeka: Geo. W. Martin, Kansas Publishing House, 1875.

Wilson, Hill Peebles. *John Brown Soldier of Fortune.* Lawrence, Kans.: H. P. Wilson, 1913.

Wilson, John P. *Islands in the Desert: A History of the Uplands of Southeastern Arizona.* Albuquerque: University of New Mexico Press, 1995.

Wiltsee, Ernest A. *Gold Rush Steamers of the Pacific.* San Francisco: Grabhorn Press, 1938.

Wise, Stephen R. *Lifeline of the Confederacy: Blockade Running during the Civil War.* Columbia: University of South Carolina Press, 1988.

Zaragoza, Justo. *Las insurrecciones en Cuba.* 2 vols. Madrid: Imprenta de Miguel G. Hernández, 1872–73.

★ INDEX ★

Cramer, Samuel, 71, 83
Crane, R. S., 67–68
Crane Jr., Samuel, 67
Crane Sr., Samuel, 67–68
Creek War, 18
Crespo, José Antonio, 160
Crimean War, 109, 213, 262n7
Crockett, Davy, 21
Cross, Edward Ephraim, 157, 162, 171, 280n28
Crystal Theater, 221
Cuba, 1–2, 5, 16, 26, 28, 31, 34, 37, 40,
    94, 96–97, 100, 144, 154, 182, 185, 222,
    231n16, 238n55, 268n30, 276n90
Cuban annexation to the U.S., 31, 33, 35
Cuban flag, 22–23, 34, 37
Cureton, John M., 26, 28, 33
Curtis, Carl, 295n4
Custer, George Armstrong, 248n27
Cutler, George Albert, 62, 67
Cutter, Calvin, 66, 70, 72, 81, 249n37
Cutter's Physiology, 249n37
Cuyahoga County, Ohio, 262n8

D'Aumaile, Robert L., 169, 283n56
Daily Chronicle, 132
Daily Cleveland Herald, 77
Daily Evening Bulletin, 140, 164, 169, 283n56
Dalgetty, Dugald, 4
Dallas, Tex., 153
Dana, Amasa, 12, 229n4
Danville, Ky., 231n16
Darien, Ga., 28, 35, 42
Davenport, Dudley, 38
Davidson, Ida J., 222
Davidson, Rebecca Landis, 274n64
Davis, Charles Henry, 139–42
Davis, George P., 162
Davis, Jefferson, 83, 234n25
Davis Mountains, Tex., 155
Day, Robert, 42
Daytona Beach, Fla., 192, 215, 220–21
D'Barbour, Lucy, 220
De Brissot, Julius, 116, 269n34
De Horsey, Algernon Frederick Rous, 128,
    133–34
de la Cova, Carlina, 6
de la Cruz Rivero, Francisco Javier, 233n21
De Treville, Robert, 56
Dear, Lt., 25
Deer Range plantation, 259n2
Deerfield, Mass., 249n36

Deitzler, George Washington, 56, 245n16
Deland, Fla., 252n52
Delaware and Lehigh National Heritage
    Corridor, 230n11
Delaware River, 11–12, 146,
Democratic Party, 19, 31, 35–36, 38, 40, 64,
    160, 165, 190, 206, 215, 224, 229n4, 232n19,
    237n50, 241n78, 243n6, 251n47, 261n5
Democratic Review, 17
Denis, Charles, 212
Denver, James W., 151, 153
Department of the South, 182
De Saussure, William Ford, 54
Desha, John R., 231n16
Desha, Joseph, 231n16
Detroit, Mich., 44, 45, 68, 281n32
Devers, William, 284n62
Devine, Pvt., 106
Dibble, Charles H., 32
District of Columbia, 158, 231n16
Dixon, John M., 206–7
Doboy Sound, Ga., 35
Dodson, Christopher C., 168
Doggett, Aristides H., 188–89, 201, 292n62
Dominican Republic, 276n90
Donaldson, John "Jack," 56, 89–90, 95–96,
Donalson, Israel D., 52–56, 60–61; resigns, 92
Donalson, William F., 55, 68, 73, 81–82
Doniphan County, Kans., 54
Doniphan Tigers, 54–55
Dorchester County, Md., 258n96
Dorman, Orloff M., 188–89, 286n11
Doss, Mr., 159
Doubleday, Charles William, 104, 114–15,
    117, 127, 132, 139, 262n8
Doubtful Canyon, Ariz., 156
Dougherty, Charles, 209
Douglas, Marjory Stoneman, 8, 205
Douglas County, Kans., 50–53, 55, 82–83,
    87, 91, 93, 245n16, 246n18, 248n27
Douglas County Militia, 53, 61, 222
Douglass, James W., 159
Dozier, M. H., 62–64
Dragoon Springs, Ariz., 156
Drew, George Franklin, 206
Drolet, John, 284n62
Dry Wood Creek, Mo., 151
Du Pont, Samuel Francis, 177
Duff, Mary S., 221
DuFour, Mary Evelina, 241n78
Dummett, Douglas, 186, 214

- Jamaica

s

l

Index 321

Hopkins, F. N., 190
Hopkins, Francis Carara, 221
Hopkins, J. M., 203, 206
Hopkins, John L., 27, 32, 38, 40
Hopkins, Mary Evelina. See Mary Evelina Titus
Hopkinsville, Ky., 221
Horsehead Crossing, Tex., 154
Hotel Munger, Daytona Beach, 220
Houghton, Joab, 281n32
Houston, Thomas Truxton, 140, 276n85
Howard, Oliver O., 188
Howe, Albion Parris, 82, 255n72
Howell, Catherine Ellett, 12, 16
Howell, Ellett, 12
Hoyt, David Starr, 65–66, 69, 80, 99, 249n36
Hubby, Leander M., 263n8
Hubby, Sarah Louise, 263n8
Hudson, Ohio, 269n40
Huntington, N.Y., 236n43
Hutchinson, George W., 53
Hutchinson, William B. Randolph, 51, 53, 60, 68
Hutchinson and Co., G. W. and W., ordered abated, 53; sacked, 58, 98

Illinois, 77, 165, 245n16, 247n24
Illinois Militia, 247n24
Illinois State Gazette, 51
Illinois State Legislature, 227n1, 247n24
Indian River, Fla., 3, 7–8, 183–84, 190–91, 194, 196–97, 200–202, 204–5, 207–9, 211, 213, 217, 224; description, 185–86, 199
Indian River City, Fla., 9, 192
Indian-River Steamboat Company, 218
Indian War of 1794, 231n16
Indiana, 243n5
Indiana University, 246n18
Indians, 61, 157, 162, 170, 172–73
Internal Improvements Fund, 191, 194
Iowa, 31, 247n24
Iowa City, Iowa, 66, 252n51
Ireland, 242n86, 280n29
Irwin, Bernard John Dowling, 158, 280nn27 and 29
Isabel steamship, 26
Isaacs, Andrew J., 60
Italy, 232n19, 284n62
Ithaca, N.Y., 229n4

Jackson, Andrew, 259n2
Jackson County, Mo., 97
Jackson, revenue cutter, 38–39
Jackson, Zadock, 58
Jacksonville, Fla., 2, 5, 26–27, 30–42, 44, 47–48, 94, 170, 175, 180–86, 207–8, 211–13, 215–16, 219–21, 223–24, 236n43, 240n70, 285n6, 286n9–10, 292n60, 293n75; conflagration, 46, 177, 181, 286n9; first Union occupation, 176–78; second Union occupation, 179; third Union occupation, 180, 287n18; fourth Union occupation, 182, 235n36; Unionists in, 178, 180; under Reconstruction, 187–89, 192, 194–95, 199–201, 204, 206
Jacksonville Battalion of Cuba filibusters, 27–29, 34–35, 37–38
Jacksonville Committee of Vigilance and Safety, 43
Jacksonville Hotel, 26–29, 31–34, 37, 39
Jacksonville Naval Air Station, 240n70
Jacksonville, Tampa and Key West Railway, 218
Jacksonville University, 5
Jaffrey, N.H., 249n36
Jamaica, 276n90
James, Dr., 185
James Island, S.C., 253n56
Jefferson, Ala., 220
Jefferson, Tex., 161
Jefferson Barracks, Mo., 82
Jefferson City, Mo., 96, 101
Jefferson County, Ala., 261n6
Jekyll Island, Ga., 267n27
Jenkins, Gaius, 243n5
Jenkins, Henry, 168, 284n62
Jerez, Máximo, 262n8
Jesuits, 155, 158
Jewett, Edward S., 99
Jiménez, Dionisio, 107
Johnson, Capt., 168–69, 283n54
Johnson, Dr., 140–41
Johnson County, Kans., 148
Johnson, Andrew, 187
Johnson, Andrew J., 27
Johnson, Thomas, 196
Johnston, Albert Sydney, 231n16
Jones, A. W., 99, 246n19
Jones, Alexander, 136
Jones, John J. Ottawa, 83, 255n74

Susan Loud, brigantine, 19–20

Susquehanna River, 12

Sutton, Robert, 180

Swart, Isaac, 43

Syracuse, Mo., 166

Syracuse, N.Y., 195

Szeged, Hungary, 109

Tallahassee, Fla., 28–29, 48, 179, 191, 194, 242n86

Tallahassee Floridian, 186

Tamajo, Ercole, 213–14

Tappan, Samuel F., 51, 64, 92

Taylor, John Winthrop, 141, 276n88

Taylor House, Jacksonville, 187

Taylorsville, Ky., 233n22

Teasdale, H. R., 181

Tecumseh, Kans., 92, 95, 257n90

Telles, Félix, 161, 175, 285n4

Templeton, William Caldwell, 40–41

Tennessee, 18, 20, 32, 78, 96, 220

Tennessee Mounted Volunteers, 18

Tenth Florida Infantry Regiment, 286n10

Teurbe Tolón, Miguel, 238n55

Texas, 9–10, 16, 20, 101, 137, 152–54, 156, 165, 216, 220, 255n72, 261n6, 274n64, 276n90, 280n29, 291n50

Texas Light Artillery, Eighth Field Battery, 176

Texas Rangers, 112

Texas Republican, 158

Texas Revolution, 130

Thatcher, William M., 162

Third Georgia Battalion, 260n3

Third South Carolina (Palmetto) Battalion Light Artillery, 253n56

Thirteenth Amendment, 179

Thirty-fourth USCT, 185–86

Thirty-fifth Penn. Infantry Regt., 251n45

Thomas, George H., 153

Thomas, Ruth M., 233n22

Thomasville, Ga., 219, 221

Thompson, John, 40

Thompson, William E., 147

Tilton, Edward G., 134–35

Tioga County, N.Y., 13

Titus, Andrew, 12

Titus, Catharine Carrie Eugenia, 181, 229n3

Titus, Catherine Kate Howell, 174, 200, 207, 219

Titus, Edmund, 11

Titus, Edward Hopkins, 165, 170, 204, 215, 219, 283n46

Titus, Ellett Howell, 5, 15, 151, 172, 229n3; arrived in Jacksonville, 28; death of, 176, 285n5; grocer, 41; miner, 163, 169, 171, 284n62; railroad accident, 16; sawmill operator, 28; shipwrecked, 44

Titus, Ellett Livingston, 191, 196, 221, 296n11

Titus, Hannah, 11

Titus, Harry Wayne, 10

Titus, Helen Catherine, 181, 221, 229n3

Titus, Henry Theodore: accused of shooting Henry J. Shombre, 71; accused of betraying the Confederacy, 178; accused of treachery in Nicaragua, 140, 144; aide to William Walker, 137–38, 143, 145; alias H. H. James, 175; arrests in Kansas made by, 60, 92; arrested in N.Y.C., 175; arrives in Arizona, 157; arrives in Jacksonville, 26–27, 31–32, 39, 46–47, 170, 175, 184, 187, 190; arrives in Kansas, 50, 146; arrives in Kansas City, 147; arrives in N.Y.C., 142, 163, 169–70, 172, 174, 184, 186; arrives in Nicaragua, 108; assaulted by abolitionists, 80; attacks El Castillo, 121–31; attacks Lawrence, 57–58; avoids Confederate service, 177, 180, 183; birth, 12, 229n3; blockade runner, 7–10; brawler, 4–5, 40, 46, 63, 92, 131, 147–50, 164, 173–75, 187–89, 222; business enterprises, 1, 3, 13, 44–46, 149–50, 165, 169–70, 172–74, 183–86, 191–93, 201–2, 211, 213; called the gallant Floridian, 97; canner, 183–86, 222; cemetery plot, 218; character, 1, 3–4, 8–9, 13, 21, 23, 28–29, 40, 46–47, 55, 91, 97, 99–100, 102, 108, 116, 118, 127–38, 140–41, 143–45, 150, 162, 164–65, 173, 175, 178–79, 183, 187, 189, 197–98, 204, 209, 211, 216, 223–25; children, 2, 50, 74, 80, 165, 170, 184, 193, 196, 205, 212, 219–23, 225; civic leader, 209, 224; commissioned as colonel, 2, 64, 88–89, 98, 100; courageous, 23, 25, 72–73, 78, 216, 222; courtroom cases, 46, 150, 175, 188–90, 202, 211; death of, 216; denounces abolitionist outrages against him, 76, 82, 85–86; denounces William Walker, 142; deserted Walker camp, 140–42, 145; detained by the British navy, 134; donates land to Brevard County, 209; education, 12–14; electoral fraud in Kansas, 2–3, 148–49, 173; enumerated in census, 12, 15, 170, 172, 193, 211; escapes